P. AELIUS ARISTIDES
THE COMPLETE WORKS
VOLUME II. ORATIONS XVII-LIII

P. AELIUS ARISTIDES

THE COMPLETE WORKS

VOLUME II. ORATIONS XVII-LIII

TRANSLATED INTO ENGLISH

BY

CHARLES A. BEHR

LEIDEN - E. J. BRILL - 1981

ISBN 90 04 06384 6

Copyright 1981 by E. J. Brill, Leiden, The Netherlands

All rights reserved. No part of this book may be reproduced or translated in any form, by print, photoprint, microfilm, microfiche or any other means without written permission from the publisher

PRINTED IN THE NETHERLANDS

CONTENTS

Preface VII

XVII.	The Smyrnaean Oration (I)	1
XVIII.	A Monody for Smyrna	7
XIX.	A Letter to the Emperors Concerning Smyrna .	10
XX.	A Palinode for Smyrna	14
XXI.	The Smyrnaean Oration (II)	19
XXII.	The Eleusinian Oration	23
XXIII.	Concerning Concord	26
XXIV.	To the Rhodians: Concerning Concord	45
XXV.	The Rhodian Oration	58
XXVI.	Regarding Rome	73
XXVII.	Panegyric in Cyzicus	98
XXVIII.	Concerning a Remark in Passing	107
XXIX.	Concerning the Prohibition of Comedy	140
XXX.	Birthday Speech to Apellas	147
XXXI.	Funeral Oration for Eteoneus	154
XXXII.	Funeral Address in honor of Alexander	158
XXXIII.	To Those Who Criticize Him Because He Does Not Declaim	166
XXXIV.	Against Those Who Burlesque The Mysteries (of Oratory)	173
XXXV.	Regarding the Emperor	185
XXXVI.	The Egyptian Discourse	193
XXXVII.	Athena	223
XXXVIII.	The Sons of Asclepius	230
XXXIX.	Regarding the Well in the Temple of Asclepius	235
XL.	Heracles	239
XLI.	Dionysus	244
XLII.	An Address Regarding Asclepius	247
XLIII.	Regarding Zeus	251
XLIV.	Regarding the Aegean Sea	257
XLV.	Regarding Sarapis	261
XLVI.	The Isthmian Oration: Regarding Poseidon ...	269
XLVII.	The Sacred Tales: I	278
XLVIII.	The Sacred Tales: II	292

XLIX.	The Sacred Tales: III	308
L.	The Sacred Tales: IV	318
LI.	The Sacred Tales: V	340
LII.	The Sacred Tales: VI	353
LIII.	A Panegyric on the Water in Pergamum	354

Notes	356
Appendix	447
Index	471

PREFACE

The translation has been made from my edition of the Greek text *P. Aelii Aristidis Opera Quae Exstant Omnia,* E. J. Brill, 1976 -   . Since I have often changed the Greek text as printed by Bruno Keil in 1898, and the new edition of the Greek text is unlikely to appear before the translation, I have enumerated in an appendix on pp. 447 ff. those alterations which affect the translation.

Most of the works contained in this volume have heretofore not been rendered into a modern language. This fact and the explanatory notes will, I hope, make the writings of Aristides more accessible to the world of scholarship than they evidently have been in the past.

The notes themselves have been composed with the hope that the translation may be consulted both by educated laymen as well as scholars. Consequently the notes contain material which will be unintelligible to the former and unnecessary to the latter. Throughout the notes I have found it convenient to refer to two studies of mine concerning the historical problems of Aristides' life. *Aelius Aristides and the Sacred Tales,* Hakkert, Amsterdam, 1968, is simply cited as *Aelius Aristides* and *Studies on the Biography of Aelius Aristides* to be published in the series Aufstieg und Niedergang der römischen Welt, Bd. II 34, as *Studies on the Biography.*

XVII. THE SMYRNAEAN ORATION (I)[1]

(1) For our city speaking must be approached in a different way than for other peoples. The sights which other peoples have to offer would fall short of their claims; whereas our claims would fall short of all the sights which we can provide. But custom must be obliged, since those here demand it. Perhaps there is even an advantage to the city in this, and to the speaker nearly the least peril. For the fairer the sights, so much more understandably will he seem deficient, so that at the same instant he will be refuted and will find an excuse in the means of his refutation. On the other hand, there is additional glory for the city, in view of the quality and quantity of the things that can be shown, if it is bolstered not only by its sights, but also by discourses about its history. (2) The good fortune of our city in not recent, but dates from our ancestors, and it itself has been like a colony and mother city to itself. It is the third after the original city.[2] For just as statues and carefully written orations have undergone a second and third hand, so must then a city, which has been founded by a third hand, have attained a perfect beauty. And while remaining the same, it is both most ancient and most modern, having rejuvenated itself, as in the story of the sacred bird.[3] (3) The most ancient city was founded on the Sipylus, where they say[4] are the couches of the gods and the dances of the Curetes about the mother of Zeus. From the start it was so dear to the gods, that the poets say[5] that the gods and the heroes assembled in it when they feasted together. The Nymphs have received that city, and now it is under water, submerged in its lake, as they say.[6] (4) Afterwards a second city was settled at the foot of the Sipylus along the breakwater of the beach between the ancient and present city, which, compared to this city, has now become the ancient one.[7] These works were as if practice models for the founding of our city, done on other cheaper figures.[8] By its third step, as the poets put it,[9] the city achieved this single, harmonious form. (5) Its people, who were most ancient, were natives of the soil. And when colonists had to be admitted, it admitted also the descendants of the natives of the soil of the other continent.[10] And in a divine way it was blended with the Greeks across the sea, by giving and receiving founders: giving to the Peloponnesians the

man who bestowed on them his name and their proud title,[11] but receiving from Athens, as the story goes, the sons of Erechtheus, after the war against the Amazons and later on later settlers.[12] And from their mother city they enjoyed both a delicate life[13] and a boldness in warfare, which made it unprofitable for most men to fight with them, so that this characteristic has been called by some poets "Smyrnaean behavior".[14] One proof will suffice, a memorial to which you will also see—for they summon you here at the first moment of spring.[15] At the Dionysia,[16] a sacred trireme is carried around the market place in honor of Dionysus. (6) This is a token of how once the Chians sailed against the city, to capture it in the absence of its men, who had gone off to the temple on the mountain.[17] And when the Chians were seen by the men of the city who were descending, not only did they fail in their attempt, but they also lost their ships besides. And the Smyrnaeans then danced a war dance in honor of Dionysus and performed the Bacchic rites upon the Chians' bodies.[18] (7) And this is but a garnish for the deeds of the city, and is, as it were, a token of others which must be omitted. So it is famous among many people. One could tell of many other contests of the city, and it is a task requiring much leisure to recount those final ones always on your behalf and in alliance with you.[19] What need is there to linger over these matters? It is reasonable that those cities, whose glory lies in myths and history, revert to these subjects. But a city which triumphs at first sight and does not leave time for the investigation of its ancient history, why should I honor this from the past and not guide the spectator about it, as it were holding him by the hand and making him a witness to my words? (8) I think, if an image of some city had to appear in heaven, like the story of Ariadne's crown and of all the other images of rivers and animals which were honored by the gods, this city's image would have prevailed to appear. It seems to me by its nature to be the very model of a city, and neither to need its citizen poet[20] to woo favor for it nor any other art to praise it, but it itself recommends a love of itself among all mankind, and it itself holds the eyes in thrall without beguiling the ears. (9) It lies spread above the sea, ever displaying the flower of its beauty, as if it had not been settled gradually, but all at once arose from the earth with a magnitude unforced and unhurried. Everywhere it possesses greatness and harmony, and its magnitude adds to its beauty. And you would not say that it was many cities scattered about bit by bit, but a single city the equal of many, and a single city consistent in appearance, harmonious, its parts compatible with the whole, like the human body. (10) The adornments in it and surrounding it are similarly numerous and distinguished, and have left no others more desirable. The whole city is like an embroidered gown.[21] Proceeding from west to east, you go from temple to temple and from hill to hill, along a single avenue which is fairer than its name.[22] As you stand on the Acropolis,[23] beneath flows the sea and the suburbs ride at anchor. The city itself, interwoven with both, takes one's breath away through three spectacles most fair, nor can one find a place where he might rest his eyes. Each object attracts him, like the stones in a variegated necklace. Descending from the Acropolis, you come to the east side of the city and an avenue named for its shrines,[24] and again a temple, it too most fair, of the goddess who has been allotted the city.[25] To commemorate properly what follows is a hard task for even a man of long experience.[26] (11) Everything as far as the seacoast is resplendent with gymnasiums, market places, theaters, temple precincts, harbors, and natural and man made beauties, competing with one another. Nothing is without adornment or use. There are so many baths, that you would not know where to bathe, and there are streets of every kind, some deep in the city, others at its limits, each keeping the others from being the fairest, and springs and fountains for every house, and more than for every house, and avenues like market places, intersecting one another four times to receive the sun[27]—I am close to saying what I denied before[28]—creating many cities in their compass, each an imitation of the whole city. (12) The spring and summer breezes sound more sweetly than the nightingales and cicadas of the poets and each gusts through a different spot and makes the whole city like a grove. Is not all this superior to what any painting or sculpture can imitate? The city, as if it were adorned for an annual festival, is always beautiful with its private and public structures, a more exquisite spectacle than the tent of the Medes.[29] (13) Delight never forsakes it, nor of all the arts which come to the cities of men is there any which dwells apart. Many are native to it, many are imported. As far as education goes, you would say that it is the hearth of the continent.[30] As to all the theaters for contests and other displays, there is an indescribable abundance of them. In addition, there is the variety of manufacture and the competing produce of earth and sea. To sum up, this single city is best suited to both groups of men, all those who have preferred to live their life in ease, and all those who choose to be genuine philosophers; for they have a means of relaxation to compensate for their labors and so forestall illness. (14) An adornment before the gates, like Apollo of the Ways, at the entrance of the city, is the eponymous Meles,[31] a channel of the Nymphs from the springs to the sea, so that it is for them a flowing bath and after a brief interval receives the Nereids from Nereus.[32] The stream of the Meles rises from caves, houses, trees, as well as the midst of its bed, and so proceeds to the sea. The part by the highland springs is circular and you would best compare it to a necklace, and its subsequent course to a tidal strait. At its mouth, it is least noisy. It silently joins the sea, smoothing its waves, on the one hand carrying it away as it is driven in by the wind, on the other following its ebb and making a single surface from each water, so that you would not know where they met. (15) Indeed, children would tell you and all can see that it is everywhere full of fish, which are also quite domesticated and are companions of the men who camp upon the banks, and which dance to the flute only not on dry land, but in their place,[33] and in their drunkenness dive into the hands of the invited guests. A fairer offspring of the river and one who pertains to all cities is Homer,[34] the common foster father of the Greeks and a friend to each from boyhood as well as from tradition. Therefore I think that everyone would in justice make his maiden speech to the springs of the Meles, like the offering of a lock of hair, as he said in regard to the Sperchius,[35] and would sing of the river for Homer's sake. (16) Crossing the Meles, a region confronts you, a gift to the city from Poseidon, as it seems to me, similar and dissimilar to that told of in Thessaly. There Poseidon sundered the mountains, and from a lake made Thessaly into a level land by discharging through the fissure the river Peneus. But here he drew the sea back from the mountains and he made the beauty of the mainland correspond to that of the sea and in harmony with the city. Neither did he leave mud behind, nor yet did he quite make the ground firm. There are signs of its ancient nature if you should dig it up and if you should gaze out upon the surrounding mountains against which the sea once thrust, so too if you should cross, amid thin soil and springs, what is a littoral plain and at that the perfect one.[36] (17) And when you have proceeded a little ways, the city again is visible as if it were escorting you, and here its beauty can more closely be counted and measured. And no one is in such a hurry that he stares straight ahead at the road and does not change his view, shifting that before his eyes to his right, and what was to his left before his gaze.[37] For the city attracts him as a magnet draws bits of iron and masters him with a voluntary compulsion. It is the same with the city in regard to its environs as with its environs in regard to the city. You never have enough of gazing on the suburbs from the city, and if one should view the city from without, there is, ever more, always an absence of full satisfaction. (18) This city alone is harmed by its reputation. For no stranger, hearing about it, would succeed in completely comprehending it. I think that all men would privately resolve that as it is said that a man bitten by a viper does not wish to tell anyone other than a man who has had the same experience,[38] so too he who has seen the beauties of the city should only communicate with one who has seen them or intends to presently, but should not lightly reveal the story to others, as it were sacred rites to profane men. (19) Perhaps a poet would express it in this way and charm us thereby. The harbor is the navel of the city, and the sea its eye, no less visible to those far away on either side than to those who live next to it; and the Acropolis rises aloft through the whole city and the sea stretches along side of it like a base,[39] extending beyond the Meles to the east only as far as to pass by in a curve.[40] And one could praise other features in their turn. (20) There is that charm which is spread over everything like a rainbow, and which tunes the city like a lyre so that it harmonizes with itself and with its external adornments; and there is that pervasive splendor, like that of the bronze which Homer mentions,[41] rising unbroken to heaven. By whom could these things be described? Neither is the Meles so blessed in its child nor anyone so fortunate in his oratorical skill. (21) Indeed, this city alone requires careful investigation, not hearsay, and not an investigation so much as the continual presence and association of him who intends to observe it fairly and to carry away from here the recompense of praise. I shall add only this to my description. A little before[42] I mentioned the interior of the gulf. What remains to be said concerning the whole gulf is brief. (22) Its name is completely appropriate to this city[43] and to no other. For it is a "bosom" in its gentleness, utility, beauty, and form, but in its nature it is an open sea. Although it has the name of a single gulf,[44] it unwinds into many gulfs like folded tablets. Each promontory forms a different gulf. And there are countless harbors and resting places. You would say that it is like those many spouted bowls. So with peninsulas at brief intervals, it always provides anchorages, not a few days of sailing if one should put in at each anchorage. (23) And it is time for me to anchor my speech here. What need is there to speak about the people? For you yourself will judge them and will make them better still by prescribing for them in the best way.[45] Now I know that I seem both to you and to many of those present to have discoursed well enough. But all this will quickly prove to be too little. I myself am satisfied to be inferior to such a subject.

XVIII. A MONODY FOR SMYRNA[1]

(1) O Zeus, what am I to do? Am I to be silent when Smyrna has fallen? Have I such an adamantine nature or such self-control? But am I to weep? What mode am I to use, how can I be so bold? For if all the voices of the Greeks and the barbarians, those still upon the earth and those of every age, I say if all came together, they would be too little for this calamity, even to undertake the task, not to mention maintaining its true proportion. Ah me, I have used my eyes and ears for much too long! O time who brings all things,[2] what a city was your invention and contrivance! And you have destroyed it! (2) How different is everything from its former state! Of old, the dances of the Curetes, the nurture and birth of the gods, and the crossing of people like Pelops from here, and the Peloponnesus a colony, and Theseus the founder of the territory beneath the Sipylus, and the birth of Homer, and the contests, trophies, victories in alliance with the rulers of every race, and the descriptions of writers naming it the fairest city of all—.[3] (3) Indeed, the sights were beyond description. Immediately upon approaching there was a sheen of beauty and there was proportion, measure, and stability in its magnitude, as it were in a single harmony.[4] Its feet set firmly on the beaches, harbors, and glades; its central portion rising above the plain the same distance by which it fell short of the heights, its southern extremity gradually elevated, everywhere level and imperceptibly ending in the Acropolis, which serves as a lookout point over the sea and the city.[5] (4) There was that which cannot be expressed in words or firmly grasped by seeing it, but is somehow elusive, yet ever afforded us the desire to comprehend it, the splendor which rose over the whole city, not destroying our vision, as Sappho said,[6] but at the same time increasing, nurturing, strengthening, and delighting it, in no way like the hyacinth,[7] but a thing such as earth and sun never before revealed to mankind. (5) Just as a statue which has been carefully worked must be viewed on all sides, so you, who were formerly the fairest of cities, but now have thrown up an untimely ugliness,[8] were rich in points of observation. You caused the fairest form to appear, when you suddenly sprang into view, when one was directly opposite, when seen from the vantage of the suburbs, the straits,

the gulf, the land, the sea. This was before entering. (6) Was mankind satiated for all their intercourse and association? What other city for them came close? The springs, theaters, avenues, and streets both covered and open to the air! The beautiful and splendid market place! The streets named for gold and sacred rites, at every square each like a market place![9] The harbors longing for the embrace of their city most dear! The indescribable beauty of the gymnasiums! The grace of the temples and the precincts! Where in the earth did you sink? The monuments of the seacoast! All those dreams! (7) What springs of tears are sufficient for so great an evil? What concerts and symphonies of all the choruses will be enough to bewail the city of fair choruses, much-hymned and thrice-desired by mankind? The fall of Asia! The remaining cities! All the earth, and all the sea within and without Gadira![10] The orb of the stars! Sun who beholds all things! What a spectacle did you endure to see![11] Child's play the sack of Ilium, child's play the misfortunes of the Athenians in Sicily and the destruction of Thebes,[12] and the loss of armies, the collapse of cities, and everything which fire, war, and earthquake has thus far accomplished! You, who formerly cast all the cities into the shade with your beauty and culture, and now have cast into the shade the fall of Rhodes![13] You were fated to become a proverb for the Greeks, "Second things worse"![14] (8) A day of offerings to the dead for all members of the clan! An unlucky day in common for the Greeks! Such is the head which you have taken from our people, such is the eye which you have plucked out! Ornament of the earth! Theater of Greece! Robe of the Nymphs and Graces! I who have endured all things, in what land now am I to sing my monody? Where is my Council Chamber? Where are the assemblies and applause of young and old, who gave me everything? Once there was a city on the Sipylus, which, according to legend, sank beneath the lake.[15] O Smyrna, how distant was the overture sung for you! What sort of fortune were you heir to, least of all fitting for you? (9) Now all birds of omen[16] ought to leap into the flames—the city provides enough of that. The whole continent ought to have cut its hair in mourning[17]—for its fair lock is wholly gone. Now the rivers ought to have flowed with tears, now the merchant ships to have sailed out with black sails.[18] The Meles,[19] flowing through a waste land! The present tunes to answer the former ones! The song of the swans and the chorus of the nightingales! Such now is the tragedy in which you were fated to mourn so much![20] Indeed, if the Gorgons were alive, they would not have grieved for Medusa and for the loss of their eye, but for the eye of Asia. (10) Is there a Bosporus, or are there Cataracts, or a Tartessus, which your fame has not reached, O ill-starred city? Is there a Massalia or Borysthenes which will mark the limits of this mourning?[21] What Greek is so far away from Greece, what barbarian so untamable and unassailable by the shafts and charms of Smyrna, who did not love it by report, and who will not be pained by the report? It is said that the Heliades, grieving for their brother, finally changed into poplars and that their tears were hardened into amber.[22] Now it is time for the trees themselves to mourn you, O most gracious of cities.

Subscription: Composed in a moment at the time of the message.[23]

XIX. A LETTER TO THE EMPERORS CONCERNING SMYRNA[1]

(1) To the Emperor Caesar Marcus Aurelius Antoninus Augustus and the Emperor Caesar Lucius Aurelius Commodus Augustus, Aelius Aristides sends greetings.

In the past, O Emperors most high, I sent you pieces from oratorical contests, lectures, and such things. But now the god of fortune has given another subject. Smyrna, the ornament of Asia, the jewel of your empire, has fallen, crushed by fire and earthquake. In the name of god offer a helping hand, and one such as befits you. Smyrna, which was the most fortunate city of present day Greece through the efforts of the gods and you emperors past and present, as well as the Senate, has now suffered the greatest misfortune in our memory. Still even in these circumstances the god of fortune preserved one thing for it, almost like a token of salvation. You saw the city. You know the loss.[2] (2) Remember what you said when you viewed it on approaching, remember what you said when you entered, how you were affected, what you did. The Theoxenia was being celebrated,[3] while you rested, as it were, in the most civilized of your possessions. Was there a view which did not make you more cheerful? Which sight did you behold in silence and not praise as befits you? These are things which even after your departure you did not forget. All now lies in the dust. (3) The harbor, which you saw, has closed its eyes,[4] the beauty of the market place is gone, the adornments of the streets have disappeared, the gymnasiums together with the men and boys who used them are destroyed, some of the temples have fallen, some sunk beneath the ground. That which was the most beautiful city to behold and bore the title of "fair" among all mankind has been made the most unpleasant of spectacles, a hill of ruins and corpses. The west winds blow through a waste land. All that is left looks to you, all the rest of Asia joins them, now and always praying for good on your behalf and for your pity for Smyrna, if this empty ground is indeed Smyrna. (4) I know that I shall speak strangely, but not senselessly, I think. For even if the plot was not to your wish, it was appropriate to your good fortune which has now given you an opportunity to make use of your nature in the fairest and clearest way after the many great achievements which you formerly displayed. No longer speak to me of Lysimachus or Alexander himself, or Theseus and such myths.[5] But do you become the founders of the city, make it new again, let the whole city in every way belong to you. Whether you thought of it as a veil of empresses or as a crown of emperors or however it may be, save the city. What founders, what kings will you not cast in the shade? What bounds of magnanimity will you not surpass by causing all that the city possessed separately through the years to become part of a single foundation? (5) And I have not said these things as if I were advising you and teaching you in your ignorance—I have not been so deranged by this misfortune—, but men generally pray in this way: "Grant victory to Ajax",[6] "Now Athena love me again".[7] Then there is no reproach in writing to you in the same fashion in which we address the gods. Indeed, for these things we pray to the gods, but you we beseech as most divine rulers. It is fitting to beseech such assistance from gods and men. (6) Perhaps you desire to hear how I myself escaped. A few days before the event the god moved me and brought me to a certain estate of mine,[8] and ordered me to remain there. And while I was staying there, I learned what had happened. When I learned of it, I could not remain quiet. Nothing else was left for me, I think, other than to call on the gods and you. For this reason I did not wait for a public embassy, nor did I feel that I should take my cue from another's actions. But thinking that the matter spoke to me,[9] if to anyone at all, I appointed myself to this service, believing myself to be suitable, even if for nothing else, at least to bewail the misfortunes of the city.

(7) Others who were powerful at the courts of kings acquired gifts for their countries in times of prosperity. But if I have any influence with you, I ask and beg that the city receive this favor, not to be thrown away like a broken utensil, condemned for uselessness, but that it live again through you. I am reminded of the story of Solon. It is said[10] that when the constitution was overthrown, he took a shield and spear and sat before his house, being unable to help, I think, but showing how he felt. My contribution is even greater. For I knew that even if I could contribute nothing effectively, invoking your generosity was effective enough, so that my effort would not be in vain. (8) Indeed, all that lies without the gates does not much disturb me, since I did not support the leaders when they

went to needless expense.[11] Let whoever wishes, beg on behalf of this region. I do not object. But all that lies within the circuit of the walls, the old and new memorials of both the honor shown to you and the honor given by you, that which was a source of pride to the city both in the eyes of its citizens and visiting strangers and also provided to strangers an impulse for every achievement and a consolation for every fortune, gladly should I see that day when I shall behold this part restored. (9) Indeed, whenever I think to myself that one of the old emperors,[12] not of your house—heaven forfend!—nor would it be done by any of you—but that one of those former emperors in the middle of playing draughts, as it is told, said in passing that he did not wish the Nasamones to exist, and so the Nasamones perished, then I believe that I should reasonably expect in your case that if you purpose it and behave as you always do and only say and indicate that you wish Smyrna to exist, quickly you will show all of us what we desire. (10) I shall no longer employ alien exemples,[13] but those of you yourselves, the great care which you showed for the complete recovery of the cities in Italy.[14] You restored those cities which long ago were sick. But Smyrna, which just now was flourishing and just now collapsed, enroll again in the catalogue of cities. Formerly you adorned its temples, now preserve its whole form. (11) The city deserves to be saved not only for its appearance, but also for the goodwill which it displayed toward you Romans at all times, joining you in the war against Antiochus, joining you in that against Aristonicus, enduring sieges and fighting in no small battles, of which there were still now memorials in its gates.[15] Further when your army needed clothing and your general had been slain, they brought the general into the city and buried him within the present gates,[16] and they distributed their shirts to the soldiers, one man giving his to another.[17] (12) Such was their conduct toward you, our rulers. But how did they behave toward their fellow Greeks? It would be no small task to write about everything. But when once there were frequent earthquakes and famines about the coast of Asia in this region and some places had even been destroyed by the fissures[18] and various misfortunes afflicted the cities, they saved some of the cities, the Chians, Erythraeans, Teians, and Halicarnassians, with gifts of wheat and money and by wanting nothing in zeal. There is no city now sufficient to assist it in the way in which one city then aided other peoples. Hope in you remains. (13) Indeed, formerly it won the highest prizes for its accomplishments, land, suits of armor, and the spoils of war, with which you Romans honored it. But now it has taken from the hand of the god of fortune the prize in misery, the resolution of which rests with you. Most of all we should speak in bewilderment of the change in fortune. It is said to have obtained the temple, which has now sunk beneath the ground, with such distinction that while Asia was preferred to all other provinces in the contest, Smyrna was preferred to the cities in Asia to such an extent that the rest of Asia took only seven votes, but the city alone received four hundred.[19] Perhaps it could recover this temple through the help of Asia if you approve, but the restoration of the whole city belongs alone to you, to whom the gods have given such great resources. (14) Whenever I consider the magnitude of the misfortune, it seems to me that no word suffices, but that everything falls short. But whenever I consider your virtue, nature, and readiness for good deeds, it occurs to me to be afraid that I may seem to have said too much. I think that such is not the case. But if it is, I know that you will excuse me. A man says many things, even contrary to his nature, when he has been overtaken by misfortune, especially by the kind which he would never have expected.

XX. A PALINODE FOR SMYRNA[1]

(1) The same thing has happened to me, O men of Greece, as to those characters in tragedy who remain silent for a long time and then when occasion permits speak out either to the chorus or to anyone at all. Formerly I restrained myself after those events, which you know, took place, and neither did I undertake to console my fellow citizens nor did I do anything else except to write to our leaders[2] as much as was opportune and to consider the subsequent course of action. But now that the gods in their kindness and the Emperors, under the guidance of the will of the gods and in their own direction of human affairs, on our behalf have repulsed a fortune foreign to the city and introduced in turn the good fortune which of old was proper to it, I think that a speech by me would have been appropriate. (2) If I were permitted to go where I wish, I would be present to speak to you. But since the Savior[3] restrains me, there was left only to address you by letter. And if an example can be given for this practice, there is no need to wonder at it. But if this has been done by no one else up to the present, but it is proper for us, it is not right for you to be resentful. (3) When I had learned what had taken place—for I happened not to be present, but had left earlier, and consider by whose will![4]—I sang out some monodies, until unawares through my suffering I had composed some speeches. Not otherwise could I have endured if I had not given myself over to these. But now it is time for me to imitate Stesichorus with this palinode,[5] and not now to remain silent about the answer to my prayers after I had sung about things which I did not wish. Yet I think that I shall differ from Stesichorus to this extent. For he wrote his second poem as a retraction of his slander of Helen. But what then I lauded in grief, now I shall laud in joy, offering praise free from lamentation. (4) Our fall, O men of Greece, was in accord with the common fate of man, because of which it is impossible for men to come to their end without experience of evil. But recovery was through the city's fortune, on account of which it has never lacked a share of anything fair. One would realize this, if he considers when the event took place. How would an intelligent man not attribute to the part of good fortune the fact that the city fell at a time when it was not going to lie in

ruins after its collapse and experience something like the death of a man, as already has happened before to certain other cities, but when it was going to rise on greater foundations? (5) The god of fortune, as it seems, considered the conjunction. For the founding of the fairest city bore honor to these best of all emperors, who hold all cities beneath their sway, and for the city to be raised up by their aid and to inscribe such men as its founders changed its misfortune to success. Formerly we sang of Theseus and Alexander,[6] the one, I think, the most generous of the Greeks, the other the most admired of all kings because of his daring in war. But now we have added to their number still more glorious and greater founders, to whom every land and sea is subject both by their inheritance and by their own additional acquisitions, and who excel no less in wisdom, justice, truth, and goodness, if not more, than in prowess under arms.[7] (6) Who lives so far without the Pillars of Heracles or beyond the Caucasus so that he has not heard of their generosity and nobility? They did not stand idly by while the name of Smyrna became a myth, but they channeled a sort of effluent of their own fortune into it and caused us not to mourn the fall, but to celebrate a feast of union. (7) It is told that the sleep of Alexander was the prelude of the city's foundation.[8] But they displayed such great wakefulness that they had restored us before the messenger came to tell them what we had suffered. (8) They employed the most divine and glorious instruments, when they consoled us with their words and proved, as Hesiod once predicted,[9] how great a thing is culture joined with kingship and when they provided every resource to cure what had happened and in addition to invest us with other adornments. Nor was this enough. But as if they were engaged in the government of the city itself, they arranged for sources of money, invited the aid of men who would be ambitious through the hope of future honor, and promised the help of workmen if we wished it, but said that if we did not wish them, they would not trouble us. And if ever we had an immediate need for anything else besides, they bade us tell them so that they might gratify us. (9) Therefore not even all the money of mankind seems to me to have a value equal to this continual generosity. If it is proper to say so, it made the earthquake expedient for the city. Before this fortune befell it, it was unclear how much it was honored, nor how others ought to feel about it. But now it is possible to repeat that saying of Themistocles, if this story must be believed about him. After he had received his gifts from the Persian, he made some such remark to his sons, 'that now they were saved, when they had been lost.'[10] That man is said to have made these remarks, when he had been deprived of his country. But in addition to getting back our country, we have received at the same time money, adornments, honors, emperors as founders and advisers, and all the fairest things. (10) Should I not say that these things represent the Emperors' invincible fortune as well as the city's good fortune, providing eternal recognition for them from the circumstances of their being founders and of their other deeds, and for the city from the circumstances of its founding. They displayed such great extravagance, that they did not think that even this was enough, to have embarked on the foundation without being requested. Instead of waiting for ambassadors from us, they became ambassadors on our behalf to the Roman Senate, requesting them to pass decrees for which no one of us would have dared to ask. (11) Has not every sorrow and every individual's memory of private and public misfortune been erased by these acts, and has there not come instead high spirits and joyful praise and the desire to live with good hope for the future, now, if ever, and a sense of gratitude properly owing to the gods, the Emperors, and the chorus[11] which accepted the measures of its leaders with pleasure and was duly mindful of Smyrna? (12) Your part, O men of Greece, as fellow members of the race should also be mentioned, how you were affected in the same way as the Romans and displayed in the clearest way the goodwill which you have always had for the city. One would better understand this by considering the situation of the first and oldest Greek city, I mean Athens, during the times of its misfortune. And I do not say these things because I think that I should detract from its reputation—may I never be so patriotic—, but because I wish to console my fellow citizens and at the same time to demonstrate to those present that success is native to our city in every circumstance, and that our city has been allotted, as it were, a desirable fate. (13) When the Athenians had been deprived of their ships, and when they had been deprived of their walls and their whole empire and had reached the point where the people were forced into exile from their country—, for I shall not mention the many events in between—but when they so fared, no one except Pharsalus, Argos, and Thebes showed any gratitude, either more or less, for the Athenians' kindnesses during every age,[12] or because the city was sung of as "the bulwark" of the race.[13] But the people whom I mentioned received the exiles, opposed those who demanded them back, and layed up this store of favor with a city excelling in everything, in which the oracles said was the home of good fortune.[14] (14) Come now, let us also consider the circumstances of our own city, whether it was ever proper for any of its lovers to have been ashamed of it. Up to this time it had stood, as it were, as an example of beauty, enthralling at first sight those coming to it by land or sea; and for those who had entered it, revealing and preparing the fairest spectacles, which could neither sate the eyes nor any length of stay and to list which would be endless. (15) We have already recounted[15] the zeal which our rulers thought to display when it was fated for it to experience the other side of fortune. But what action did you, our fellow Greeks, omit to take? Was there not mourning throughout all the cities while in the common council chambers[16] men made fervent offers of assistance and expressed a desire for the city as if for their own country and asked that the national festivals be dissolved and made speeches in regard to it, as each could? You felt as if all Asia had fallen. (16) Who can say that up till then such actual help took place among the Greeks? There were markets which came from everywhere, by land and sea, for those who remained on the spot, and there was the rivalry and zeal displayed by the greatest cities on each continent, inviting the refugees and dispatching wagons and other means of conveyance, and also providing housing, a share of their council chambers, and every other means of assistance, as if for their own parents or children; and the same was done by those who were less great, but wanted nothing in their enthusiasm and their show of honor. (17) Who did not regard it as his own good fortune, who did not think that he received a favor rather than that he bestowed one, to take into his home those who were so preeminent? Who would ever finish his enumeration of the money contributed and the promises for the future made by each continent, and the many acts of kindness done according to the ability of each? And not for this reason did the city think that it should take everything without exception or as the donors wished, but in so far as it was fair for it to receive these things. (18) And why should these kindnesses be listed separately? All the races, which comprise our Asia,[17] displayed in regard to the city a common zeal in the restoration of the greatest of its ancient monuments. In respect to this city alone that ancient saying has been proved false, that when men fare badly they are forgotten by their friends.[18] So much distinction, grace, and glory was kept for it by the god of fortune even during its time of trouble. (19) But now all that pertains to a mournful tune and to unpleasing dress and whose praise originates from grief has gone away. The continent wears white; Greece assembles to see a happy plot; the city, as if in a play,[19] has changed its age and once more is rejuvenated, being both old and new, as is the tale of the phoenix which is resurrected from itself. For god did not approve of there being another phoenix instead of and after that one.[20] (20) Everything seems, as it were, to have proceeded in course. After Theseus had originally founded it, later Alexander brought it to its present state. But a third hand, that of those who are in every way triumphant, now raises it up and puts it together.[21] Because of their love for the existing city, they did not think that they should move it, but they are restoring it upon its remains. The nature of the city, which honors two founding goddesses, also desired a pair of founders.[22] (21) The harbors are getting back the embrace of their most beloved city,[23] and it in turn is adorned by them, and nothing prevents the Meles from having neighbors.[24] In spring and summer the city's gates are opened, decked with crowns of flowers.[25] The choruses of Nymphs and Muses dance in the city and about it. The breeze of the west winds will cause no pain.[26] (22) O blessed are the older men who will reach that day in which they will see Smyrna with her old beauty. Blessed the boys who will suffer no loss, but will behold their country such as it was when their parents dwelled in it. Blessed the young men who have shared in the toil and labor, and will share the sacrifice and feasting between themselves and those newly arrived, since future expectations are even better than the present good. (23) O Zeus of the City, and you goddesses who have been allotted this city,[27] and Poseidon, whose province is both earthquake and preservation, and you gods of the Emperors[28] and of the Greeks, grant that this foundation take place for us with "second attempts better and more secure",[29] with much joy and glory to the founders, and with good results for the city for all future time, and that my part too be something among the Greeks now and afterwards.

XXI. THE SMYRNAEAN ORATION (II)[1]

(1) I should have particularly wished, Excellency, that the city appear such as you left it; but if not, that I were present to deliver my speech, so that I might profit in two ways, by being with you and by duly enjoying the city now restored for us. Since it has turned out otherwise, I did not think that I ought to be debarred from everything, but that there should be some trace of our voice for you to recognize as well as for those Greeks who are there, both citizens and visitors. (2) In general it has almost become my custom to celebrate festivals while absent, since god[2] so guides me. I find my present speech very opportune. Since I was the first to write a memorial on behalf of the city to our all-excellent Emperors, delaying no more than a single night after the arrival of that unexpected report,[3] it is reasonable to feel that matters pertaining to the lauding of Smyrna are also my concern. (3) You remember that you heard me speak of ancient tales, during that first office in which you served with your father:[4] the birth of Zeus, the dances of the Curetes, the foundation of the first city on the Sipylus,[5] Pelops' crossing from here to what was formerly Apia and then was called the Peloponnesus after him,[6] he whose grandson in the third generation became the king of all Greece and overthrew the empire of the barbarians.[7] (4) In the second part of my laudation there was Theseus the founder and the name of Smyrna bestowed on this city and the Attic race and later the immigration of the Ionians, as it were, into their own land.[8] And there was the third establishment and founding by him to whom these two fairest and greatest monuments belong, this city and that by the Nile.[9] Such things you heard me say. And a certain trireme was displayed at the Dionysia and hymned at the Landings, as a token of an ancient victory in which the Smyrnaeans while celebrating the Bacchic rites defeated the Chians who were armed with weapons and ships.[10] (5) There was that whose telling was left to the eyes, and no longer were tales and stories of prose writers and poets appropriate; but even Homer himself if he were present would have believed it safer to keep silent than to speak about them. You saw a market place which was a hearth of the gods, and harbors here encircling the city, there located in the midst of the city, and the beauty of the temples and

their precincts, equally adorned by nature and art,[11] and all the adornment of the chain of anchorages,[12] and what was the greatest mark of the city, its complete concord and harmony which rendered the whole body a kind of unity, as if it had been fitted together at the start to the tune of the lyre and harp like the myth told of the Theban wall.[13] (6) Well! As for the ancient history and history not so old, but things which were still appearing yesterday and the day before, one might say, such you heard and such you saw. Yet all of the things of man, as they say, are subject to change. Even the earth is covered by the sea, and the sea becomes part of the mainland, and some cities have sunk beneath the earth, and others have vanished through inundations from the heavens and the sea. Change is a characteristic of the race of man, and many are the wonders of time. (7) And thus it befell to our city, which was so greatly superior, to slip in a way. Here it clearly appeared how great an adornment it was for Asia, I do not mean only that up to the springs of the Meander and what your proconsular lot defines, but what the Greeks originally called Asia, and they principally applied the name to one of the three continents[14]—but as to what I wished to say, when the fall of the city occurred, everything seemed to have been stripped bare, and everyone was searching, as it were, for the eye of the body. (8) It befell, I say, to the city to stumble in keeping with the common fate and nature of all mankind, but what followed was part of the good fortune which from the start has been allotted the city. For even the times offered ready assistance,[15] since then there were such men as leaders of the world, who least of all were going to stand idly by while the city lay in ruins, nay, who most of all were going to be eager not only to raise it up again, but also to exalt it to the highest degree. "All these things are now accomplished", to quote the son of the Meles.[16] (9) Indeed, who would not have marveled in admiration at the nobility of the people—for let not our whole discussion be about buildings? Neither were they terrified at the misfortune nor did they seek nor wait for any fairer consolation than that which the Emperors provided by word and by deed, so that what was an occasion for grief has become for them a kind of celebration. (10) Indeed, what follows we know only by report,[17] but you are an eyewitness and would yourself explain it to others. For the city seems not to have fared far differently from the myth which was told about its founder. You know that the poets say[18] that Pelops was cut up limb by limb, boiled in a cauldron, and taken from the cauldron was put back together anew, but that since his shoulder was missing, he received an ivory one in place of his old one. And they say that this shoulder was the work of Demeter. So too for the city. After that cauldron which burned all of it,[19] its second composition has achieved a wonderful excess of beauty, as if Poseidon had intentionally shaken it with his trident, so that he might behold it more beautiful than before. Such also is the generosity which he is said to have displayed in Thessaly by making a gorge for the Peneus so as to create Tempe.[20] (11) Formerly it was not possible even to conceive of anything better, but the city seemed to be an example of beauty.[21] Now, however, we have been shown to have held a false opinion. For then it was superior to the other cities, but now, one might almost say, to itself. And it seems to me to have had the same experience as its mother city.[22] I shall not give a mythical comparison, but one which must be believed. (12) After that city had been burned by the Persian and entirely destroyed, it expanded on every side.[23] And its ruin was advantageous to this city. It has been raised up by such a hand, so that it is everywhere more august, loftier, and better sheltered. We invoke Adrasteia.[24] Although all these visible adornments are fair, it has received besides another benefit greater than these. For its founders are those who hold all cities under their sway, and whom no one has surpassed either in kindness or in the achievement of mighty works,[25] and who alone had the power, I think, to invent something better than the old Smyrna. (13) Such then was fortune's palinode about our city. And Ionia's crown has been fairly saved, and Asia has recovered her ornament. The circumstances of the city have become an example of the unexpected: that nothing is impossible in fair sailing, nor when the ship has foundered, should we despair of something better happening. (14) Now I leave it to others to honor the Meles.[26] Yet when it is seen, it is its own greatest adornment. For it summer and winter have the same meaning, and it has never inflicted injury swollen by the rains, nor has it yielded to drought; but as if it were some kind of changeless object, it always preserves one shape, one appearance. (15) Indeed, the Meles is not erratic, nor such as to wander off its course, but it is like a sort of lover of the city, who does not dare to be farther apart from it; for it has, I think, a ceaseless love for it and guards it ceaselessly, so that it begins and ends here, stretching itself, as it were, beside the city's leg. Like those maddened by the Nymphs, I seem, through a certain power of the Nymphs themselves, to have added to my song these remarks concerning the Meles, although I did not propose to do so. Perhaps this too must be preserved for the next generation like the other portions of the speech.[27] (16) One would account it as a good omen that you have come to our cities and that your course is such[28] that you have in every detail repeated your father's office by your stay at Smyrna. The city's opportunity is great. May its good fortune in every way prevail.[29]

XXII. THE ELEUSINIAN ORATION[1]

(1) O Eleusis, of old it was more pleasant for me to sing of you! Is there an Orpheus or Thamyris, or Musaeus,[2] he who dwelled in Eleusis, who will be adequate for so great a calamity? With what harp or lyre will he bewail the common ruin, the common assembly of the earth? What is this subject you have proposed, O Zeus? As I come to speak, I grow numb, and turn back, and I am compelled to speak for this one reason, because I cannot keep silent. (2) Is there any Greek or barbarian who was so stupid or ignorant, or is there anyone who dwelled so far apart from the earth or the gods, or in sum, who was so insensitive to beauty,—except those who will perish most horribly, the perpetrators of these acts—who did not regard Eleusis as a sort of common precinct of the earth, which was of all the things pertaining to the gods the most frightening and the most joyful for mankind? Of what other place or myth were more wonderful tales told, or where did the sacred ritual cause greater fear, or the sights more compete with what one had heard?[3] (3) As for the spectacles, they have been seen in the secret apparitions[4] by numerous generations of blessed men and women. As for what is public knowledge, this is celebrated by all the poets, writers of myths, and historians: that for a time the daughter of Demeter vanished, and Demeter wandered over all the earth and sea in search of her daughter. Meanwhile she was unable to find her, but having come to Eleusis, she created a name for the place;[5] and when she had found her daughter, she created the mysteries. (4) And the two goddesses gave wheat to the city of Athens and the city in turn gave it to all the Greeks and barbarians.[6] And Celeus, Metaneira, and Triptolemus[7] are referred to in connection with these acts, and winged chariots of dragons borne over every land and sea. And the first strangers to be initiated were Heracles and the Dioscuri,[8] and the first gymnastic contest took place at Eleusis in Attica, and the prize consisted of the grain which had just now appeared, while men made trial of how strong they had grown from cultivated nourishment.[9] The Greeks brought the first fruits of their crops each year to the city of Athens as it was their mother city and the mother of the crops.[10] The Eumolpidae and the Kerykes, who trace themselves back to Poseidon and Hermes, have provided, the

one Hierophants and the other Torch-bearers.[11] And such are the things which go back to myth. (5) Later, some time after the Heraclidae had returned to the Peloponnesus, the Dorians campaigned against Athens.[12] But when they had reached Eleusis, whether we should say out of shame or fear, they departed by the same road. The unrest caused by the Dorians then colonized our part of Ionia.[13] (6) When the Persian expedition took place and not only Greece but also everything outside of the Persian Empire was faced by the greatest peril and danger, many of the temples in Greece were burned, and in addition, the summit of Greece, the city of Athens; but Eleusis was so favored, that it not only survived, one might say, unsacked, but also at the naval battle Iacchus came forth to fight as an ally, and a cloud arose from Eleusis, crested, and fell upon the ships to the accompaniment of the initiate's song.[14] Xerxes fled in terror, and the empire of the Medes perished. (7) When the Greeks engaged in a great war against one another[15] and everything was topsy-turvy, Eleusis alone in a way remained untouched. And neither the cavalry of the Boeotians, nor the invasions of the Lacedaemonians and the Peloponnesians violated its precinct; they did not behold the temple with other than proper eyes. When Sphodrias later attacked from Thespiae,[16] the appearance of the torches was sufficient to extinguish his daring. All the other truces were transgressed. In the course of the Pythian festival, the Cadmea was seized,[17] and the Argives and the Corinthians conducted the same sacred procession to the Isthmian games, when the one conquered the other by force of arms.[18] I omit mention of the battle at the Alpheus,[19] except that even here the daring and victory of those deprived of their rights was no bad sign on the part of Zeus. The truce of the Mysteries alone has preserved its name, and during the Eleusinian celebration alone was Greece's behavior sound, and this festival was most clearly a purge for madness and every unnatural misfortune. And why must I recount each single event? (8) The Philips, Alexanders, Antipaters, and the whole catalogue of later dynasts, although they caused much unrest in Greece, regarded Eleusis alone as something truly inviolate and above them. And I omit the Gauls who finally burst riotously into Greece,[20] and all such things that one might add. Always the sanctuary escaped unscathed. To the city and to Greece alone was left this monument of ancient felicity and dignity. The naval battles, land battles, laws, constitutions, pride, dialects,[21] everything, one might say, are gone. But the Mysteries have endured. (9) The other festivals are celebrated either every fourth or every other year, but only the festival of the Mysteries has prevailed to be annual. Yet what is greatest and most divine is that only this festival was contained and held in a single building,[22] and the full complement of citizens and of the precinct of Eleusis was the same.[23] (10) Who would not have rejoiced to see the statues, paintings, the general adornment, even that at the crossways,[24] not to mention the appendages of the more revered rites? But the gain from the festival lay not only in the present joy and the release and liberation from the troubles of the past, but also in men having fairer hopes about death, that they will have a better existence and will not be in the darkness and mud which await the uninitiated.[25] (11) At least up to that terrible day. But that which the god of fortune has now given us to witness and to tell of, is there an Argive dirge, is there a singer of the Egyptians or Phrygians who will fill its measure?[26] Is there an Eleusinian Aeschylus who will sing it to his chorus?[27] Are there any "fiery snares of Nauplius", as Sophocles expressed it,[28] which should be compared to this conflagration? O torches![29] By what sort of men have you been extinguished? O dread and lightless day, which took away the torch-bearing nights! O fire, what was your appearance at Eleusis, what in place of what! O mist and gloom, which now hold Greece! O Demeter, who of old found your daughter here! Now it is left for you to seek your temple. (12) And the Mysteries are approaching, O earth and gods! This month of Boedromion now requires a different kind of cry,[30] not such as when Ion ran with a battle cry to Athens.[31] O the proclamation![32] O the catalogue of the sacred days and nights! In what sort of day have you ended! Who should grieve more, the uninitiated or the initiates? The one group has been deprived of the fairest sights which they have seen, the other of what they could have seen. (13) O you who have evilly betrayed the Mysteries,[33] who have revealed what was hidden, common enemies of the gods beneath and above the earth! O you Greeks, who were children of old[34] and now are truly children, who stood idly by at the approach of so great an evil! Will you not now, dear sirs, at all events get control of yourselves?[35] Will you not even save Athens?

Subscription: The Eleusinian Oration was written almost at the exact moment in Smyrna, in Lous, the tenth month, in the proconsulship of Macrinus, the author being fifty-three years, six months of age.[36] It was delivered in Smyrna in the Council Chamber.

XXIII. CONCERNING CONCORD[1]

(1) Most orators, O men of Greece, are accustomed to select fictitious subjects and to declaim all the time, but to be as far from actually speaking as they would be if they did nothing which pertained to this; or scorning such practices, to engage in a thing no more serious than this, in disputatious conduct and the incitement of those who come to hear them, by which acts they pain their audience but neither themselves appear at all better speakers nor are able to improve others. (2) A certain distinguished and ancient sophist[2] once prided himself at the beginning of some composition on the fact that he did not intend to do any such thing, or to use refinements, but that he was going to discourse on behalf of these two themes, concord toward one another and war against the barbarians, undertaking, in my judgment, a very noble and proper topic for discussion. (3) I see that it is no longer opportune to speak on behalf of a war against the barbarians. For I think that the gods and our Emperors will be concerned with the full punishment of all wrongdoers and, to speak by the grace of the gods, I do not believe that there will be a great contest, seeing that while the whole world is firmly held, one small part now has opposed us in their folly.[3] But I shall speak, as well as I can, on the remaining point, concord toward one another. (4) I believe that from my continual work and practice in oratory something useful accrues especially for such contests. We are not always declaiming so that we may never say anything of use. But whoever has the ability and courage to say what is necessary, he is the one who proves that his declamation has not been performed in vain or without purpose. (5) I have long known that many speakers have found, as it were, a bulwark and refuge in always praising their present audience, among whomever they are speaking, and that many after they have run off from one city, speak slanderously of it to whatever other city they are in, especially if these cities have some preexisting quarrel with one another. I should not be able to offer unlimited praise, if there should not be some use in it and the audience would not depart improved as much as possible; nor, to the extent that justice requires me to be a pleasing speaker, shall I serve the city before my eyes, but would avoid to give the other cities their proper due. Nor in this

speech first of all shall I set the cities at odds, just as most bad speakers do; but I shall praise them all to the extent that each of them should be praised, and I shall begin my address on this point. (6) I believe that it is incumbent upon whoever wishes to create a common friendship for the cities with one another, not to laud some of them and slander others, but to mention them all with praise, so that, to begin with, by being pleased you may all more eagerly accept his advice, and one part of concordant behavior may already be accomplished. (7) For if you accept being praised in common and none of you regards the praise of the others as an act of dishonor toward himself, but each of you is delighted by the attributes of one another as if they were your own, first of all right from the start you shall give a demonstration of concord, and next you will gradually become accustomed also to praise one another and to have thoughts which are expedient for all of you in common. But to come to advise concord and at the same time to hesitate to praise you, seems to me to be a kind of cowardice, and even the act of one who is destroying his argument, and either has badly attempted it, or does not know in what way it is proper to deal with it.

(8) First of all let us consider the whole political union to which all of us here belong, both the larger and the smaller, and how much it is believed in the judgment of our rulers and in that of nearly all others, one might say, to excel other unions.[4] (9) No other union among all of them has either so many cities, or such kinds of very large cities. Further let us consider the sundry attractions of the region, the temperance of the seasons, the various styles of life, the general location, how it is set in the navel of the whole Empire, ringed on land and sea by many pacified nations and races who are round about it. It dwells in good order, and one could neither blame it for arrogance nor excessive servility, but treading a middle course, it has the best form of government under the sun. (10) It has achieved such distinction that although the whole region is so great, in the interior bounded by the Phasis and by the Nile, and at the beginning all this inclusively was called "Asia" by the Greeks, now this part near the sea has deprived the continent of its name and has appropriated it for itself. Thus it has succeeded in displacing all the rest of the continent. (11) Besides, the respect shown by our governors, their generosity, and their concessions on every matter have made us seem more than of equal rank with most of the subject peoples. Then how would all not likely rejoice in their pre-

sent situation and even feel about their common good as if about their own and in no way engage in faction against themselves concerning matters over which no foreign people engage in faction and not be angry because each is not in every way superior? (12) Come let me describe those cities which now vie for first place and which are the greatest source of strife, no more through their fault, as I should say, than through that of all the other people who have taken sides with these. For everyone wishes to revile the other cities as much as he can on behalf of the city to which he happens to be favorably disposed. Neither would I do this myself, nor do I believe that whoever else does this has good sense. I shall proceed in an entirely opposite direction, and I shall laud these cities as much as possible, using, as is likely, summary points of praise.

(13) I shall begin with the city which now receives us and which provides the Council Chamber for the speeches on this topic.[5] I think that I shall omit mention of how it once ruled the neighboring regions,[6] and how later these rites in which we take pride had their origin from here.[7] But as to what immediately strikes the eye, there is the Acropolis, of such magnitude, splendid from afar on every side, as it were, a sort of common summit of the province. Beneath it the rest of the city is different at each location and is variously sited and formed. You would say that many towns have merged and settled together, and that as if they had been neighbors, some people in the course of time had come to live together as their mutual borders had continually expanded. There are adornments, both ancient and new, which cover the whole city, any one of which is enough to be an adornment even for an entire city. (14) One could say many things about the other districts—whether they should be called parts or little cities. But who could pass by in silence that which is the most honored of all and ever in my mind? I mean the final segment of the city, which has been consecrated to the Savior[8] for the common good fortune of all mankind. (15) For when it was fated for the god also to cross over to this continent,[9] first he crossed over to here and made the city a starting point for his association with the whole continent. And in point of time, this colony, as it were, sent hither from Greece is second to that of those who came with Telephus from Arcadia,[10] but in point of rank and importance it is by far the first of all colonies. For here in Asia was founded the hearth of Asclepius, and here friendly beacons are raised for all mankind by the god who calls men to him and holds aloft a

true light indeed. (16) And neither membership in a chorus, nor the companionship of a voyage, nor having the same teachers is so great a circumstance, as the gain and profit in having been fellow pilgrims at the Temple of Asclepius and having been initiated in the highest of the rites under the fairest and most perfect Torch-bearer and Mystagogue,[11] and under him to whom every law of necessity yields.[12] I myself am one of those who, under the god's protection, have lived not twice, but many, various lives, and who on this account regard their disease as profitable,[13] and who in addition have won approval,[14] in place of which I would not choose all the so-called felicity of mankind. (17) One would not even say that the region here was without a harbor, but it is most correct and just to state that this is the most secure and firmest of all harbors,[15] and the one which receives the largest number of people and enjoys the greatest calm, where for all mankind the stern cables of safety have been fastened to Asclepius. (18) So who would not be accounted reasonable in assisting a city of such magnitude and quality, and in wishing it well, and in bestowing on it all the praise possible? I believe that just as this city through the power of the god[16] is a general source of good for all mankind, so also it would justly receive good will and honor from all men in common.

(19) So be it! But is the situation of Smyrna something base and ordinary, or such for which an example can be found in many places? All who have not seen it, would not even be able to imagine it properly, and those who have seen it, would say that it is the work of the gods, just as Homer said[17] that the shield of Achilles and the cities in it were the creation of Hephaestus. (20) The view from land and sea would cause much argument between those who use the harbors and those who use the roads as to which of them had the greater pleasure. The city emerges in an oblong form, with the beach as its base, and the surface of its upper side as its summit, rising gradually from the plain and glades,[18] always with an unbroken façade. Indeed, this was not only outward show, but the interior surpasses it. For all adornment which has been allotted a practical use, which provides for the body beneficial relaxation, yet affords to the soul power and ease for the exercize of its proper labors, has been formed out of the city's temples, baths, harbors, and streets, so that there is no one who would find the time to call it the greatest city, once he had been enchanted by its abundant beauty. (21) The sea, the rivers, and the suburbs are worthy of one another and

of the city, as if they had been allotted to the city not more by chance than by choice. You would say in the words of the Smyrnaean poet,[19] "Without brotherhood, without law, without hearth is he", who loves not the beauty of Smyrna more than anything else. (22) Again its greatest and most praiseworthy feature are the choruses of the Muses and Graces who always haunt the city,[20] because of whom the city customarily sends off its visitors not only made happier, but also improved. Then how is it reasonable for us who are improved in the arts and in other respects in this city, to behave worse toward it and not to be improved by its mysteries,[21] and for all men to become proficient in and to practice oratory somehow especially there, but not to bestow upon that city among the very first all that pertains to the praise and gratitude which is oratory's to give?

(23) Come let us remember, as it were, the third libation.[22] Now I mean third in number, not in rank. For let no one hunting for nuances in my expression, twist my speech around to the opposite meaning. Straightway it is possible to make this most impressive claim about it, that despite the existence of these two cities, and again the large number of things which have been said about them, there remains something different and no wit inferior to be said about this city. (24) I think that all men who live between the Pillars of Hercules and the river Phasis would rightly regard Ephesus as having a connection with them both through the accessibility of its harbors and through all its other means of reception. All men journey to it, as if to their own country, and no one is so foolish, or so flies in the face of reality, that he would not concede that the city is the common chancellery of Asia[23] and a refuge in time of need. Nor is there anyone so fond of finding fault that he would criticize the boundaries of that city.[24] It is extensive for whoever journeys into the interior; it is even extensive on the seacoast; it is everywhere capable of providing all that a city needs and of satisfying every way of life that men can live and choose to live. (25) Yet how is it reasonable for it to be of use to all men in common, but not to receive good will from all men in common, and for it to be of equal importance to all that the city flourish, but for all not equally to join in praying that the city flourish? And in Persian times for Artemis to have received such great reverence by the barbarians,[25] but when her temple itself has been erected greater than before, and the greatest and most important empire of all has

been established, for this one fact not to be sufficient to draw men into friendship with the city, the fact of the goddess's honor, both that with which she has honored the city and that which it is reasonable that she receive from mankind?

(26) Indeed two of these cities are colonies of one and the same city, Athens,[26] which no one, I think, would be ashamed to call an ornament of the whole Greek race.[27] But this city here[28] can make a boast similar to Athens itself in respect to its generation of aboriginal men and heroes. But if not, then a similar boast to these cities. For its colonists are descended from aboriginal Arcadians, so that from this cause it is reasonable for you to have recognized one another as friends and to have paid each other appropriate honors.

(27) So be it! I have stated in all brevity, as it seems to me, and not at all badly, as you have indicated, what ought to be granted in common to the member races of the province and to the cities which claim the first place. And I am very grateful to you for being so well disposed when you heard these remarks. It now remains for me to add the rest of my speech, the exhortation, if you are not only going to be charmed by my address, but also receive some practical use from it as well; and it remains for you to be willing also to hear this part with an equal resolve, so that you may not only honor my speech with immediate praise, but also by being mindful of it for all time and by applying it to the circumstances themselves.

(28) O you who are best of the Greeks in the province, if each of you were going to have to abandon those things in which he now takes pride in favor of seemly conduct and communal feeling toward other men, I myself should not advise the adorning of a neighbor's possessions at the expense of one's own. But when each of you has so many reasons for pride and there is no necessity for feeling less self-esteem if you behave virtuously toward one another, I do not see what sense there is in this dispute. Rather I should say, quite to the contrary, that kindly relations with others is the act of those who wish to preserve their honor, and proceeding to strife and contention the act of those who despise their circumstances. (29) For in concord lies the praising of others and hearing one's own virtues being praised, but in dissension the slandering of others and being slandered improperly in return, so that as much as one prefers to be praised and to enjoy his existing advantages, so much the more must he begin with fairness and conduct himself in a seemly way. But it would be the most senseless thing of all to be an-

noyed at the good of others, yet to injure one's own good, and to be angrier if someone else will be properly honored than if one will not obtain what is his due from all men voluntarily. Indeed, as soon as he will become annoyed at the good of others, it will be quite apparent that he envies them. But this is not the act of one who is superior. By no means. (30) It should also be considered that all these goods that we recounted a little before[29] and all such that one would mention, as for example the beauty of the public buildings, the magnitude of the temple precincts, the fair locations, the great wealth from land and sea, and everything which pertains to this subject, should be said to belong to fortune which gives and again takes away each of these, whenever it wishes. But the choice of concord and proper behavior toward one another is the act of those who will it so. Therefore it is reasonable that they who excel in fortune not feel as much pride as they who are superior in their behavior. (31) Indeed, it can be said that those things do not properly belong in turn to everyone, but only to those who built them and from whom we have received each particular structure, whether as contemporaries or of a later generation. But good counsel and moderate behavior belong to everyone who is willing to have it. Just as we do not judge that house best established which is built of stones which are as beautiful as possible, but which is dwelled in with the greatest harmony, so also it is fitting to believe that those cities are best inhabited which know how to think harmoniously. Everywhere faction is a terrible, disruptive thing, and like consumption.[30] For having fastened itself to the body politic it drains off, sucks out, and depletes all its strength, and does not cease until it has entirely worn it away, using the sick themselves as a means for their own destruction. (32) Indeed, it is clear that a group of three or more cities of the same nation will in all likelihood cling to that which is the finest characteristic and the firmest means of safety for every nation. For it is certainly not the case that what is expedient for all the cities in common in the nation, does not have the same significance for some of them. If they are vying for preeminence, this does not make the faction any better, but here in particular one would find even more to blame. (33) For if what no one would even admit is appropriate to ordinary people will be thought proper for themselves by those who claim to excel and will not be guarded against by them as much as possible, how does the accusation not take added force, or how are their wishes not at odds with their deeds? They wish distinction as forsooth the best men, but in this case they would clearly be in the same situation as the very worst. (34) I believe that just as everyone would most certainly think that generals should be better than their soldiers, or at least not worse, so also the cities which have the chief voice in the Council[31] should not be less intelligent than the mass of inferior cities. It is not the case that good order and discipline are fitting for soldiers, yet dishonorable for generals; but if the masses are going to maintain order, their leaders must first take the lead in this, since it is impossible for the army to be harmonious when the generals engage in disruptive faction against one another. So also we must believe that moderate behavior is most incumbent on those cities which stand in common as an adornment for the whole race. (35) It amazes me that in the event of war everyone would think it to his advantage to face danger with as many and as noble allies as possible. But when it is possible to enjoy the fruits of one's possessions without danger, if they will be shared with others, everyone will reckon this as a loss and will not consider that by as much as he thinks himself worthy of greater rank, it is the more likely that he wish that others too have favorable circumstances, since preeminence over those of no worth is without dignity, but rivalry with distinguished men is safe in two ways. For then the pride and glory of victory is a fair thing; and if there is some other result, consolation is ready at hand. (36) It also is possible to learn this from Homer. Indeed, since this poet is our most common possession,[32] it is not a bad idea to employ him too for such purposes. He praises all the heroes, one might say, and those who are the greatest enemies of one another, in the belief that the victors thus would have greater glory. And when he catalogued the cities, he praised each one in a different way, but all as much as possible, nowhere omitting whatever small honor he could give any of them. Gracious praise, they say, is easy to bear. Therefore Pindar,[33] I think, remarks that a certain god advised Heracles that he should not even deprive his enemies of this when they had done something good. (37) Thus the act of praise is something divine in nature; and it is not only opportune whenever we intend to begin a sacrifice,[34] but also in most human affairs. This expression of the herald and the priests which is spoken whenever we ask for good from the gods is a token that those who use praise as much as possible would act pleasingly to the gods. (38) Therefore when this kind of speech is proper for requesting good things, it is certainly reasonable to think that if we honor it everywhere, we should fare better and maintain a better way of life. Again if this is the situation, how should faction not be avoided for this very reason, since there is nothing which is more contrary to praise than this evil? For it by itself is opposed to the two finest things. It permits neither the speaking nor the doing of what is best, but it produces slander instead of praise and trouble instead of good fortune. So where there is praise, there is also success; but where there is faction, there is neither. (39) Indeed, the man who thinks that he should in no way detract from his neighbors seems to do this out of self-confidence, as if he would not be thought the less of thereby; but the man who counts abuse of others to his own advantage, aside from his other wickedness, also makes himself suspect as to the merit of his argument, as if he really did not have as much to say as he wished. Therefore he would not even seem to behave in this way through courage, which expression one would only employ to apply a euphemism to willfulness, but quite the contrary through fear for his own position. (40) Just as in gymnastic contests the abandonment of the customary and proper mode of fighting and the tricky use of some foreign method is not the act of those who are very confident in themselves and believe that they are able to win by means of their own resources, so also in practical affairs untimely strife and pride without propriety seem to be the act of those who are entirely inferior. Therefore faction is not only the cause of envy, but also of fear, crime, folly, and in sum of every evil and it is most of all contrary to the title which you have bestowed upon yourselves.[35] (41) Apart from this, perhaps there would be some excuse for being hostilely and contentiously disposed toward foreign races. But no one would claim that it is either intelligent or fortunate to behave with such distrust and dissension toward one another. You could prove this by the example of past events. For if the circumstances are not the same and the occasions are not similar, at least the application of good sense is in some way always constant. (42) Refer back to ancient Greece, since it happens that nearly all of you are also colonists of the Greeks there. I shall speak of nothing new, but what you all know, of the Lacedaemonians and the Athenians. While they shared the same goals and had one point of view concerning their affairs, they were envied by all the Greeks and were the cause of much great good for one another and for others who had need of them. (43) And when all men, one might say, combined against the Greeks,[36] so that the sea was filled with triremes and the land with infantry and the expectation of evil was thought an advantage because the evil was not present,[37] they were not at a loss about what to do. Although they heard that earth and sea were changed into one another and that the sun was hidden by arrows and that the rivers failed as the approaching men drank from them[38] and that whole nations and cities were expended for the reckoning of the king's dinner[39] and that in addition the god had driven away with terrible threats and menaces the emissaries who had come to Delphi,[40] they were not frightened nor were they inferior to the approaching troubles. Although no small part of Greece was sick and some speciously remained neutral, if indeed this conduct should be called "specious", and others openly took the side of the Persians, they showed how valuable a resource was concord between the leading cities. (44) For the one had a strong fleet, and the other infantry, and first of all by both these means they provided help in common to themselves and the other Greeks. And what one would find much more amazing, they did not divide the command, but as if one city had supplied both these forces, they decided to share their zeal, but to be under a single command.[41] (45) And it turned out to be no less advantageous to those who gave up the command than to those who were thought deserving of it, nor were the former held in less esteem either at the moment by the Greeks or afterwards by all mankind. Then indeed the Athenians seemed to have led the Greeks in two ways, in preparations against the enemy and in seemly conduct toward one another, when they who alone manned two thirds of all the triremes, permitted the Lacedaemonians who contributed not even a tenth, to command them, in the belief that if they should not first display concord toward one another, not even twice the number of ships would have helped the situation. (46) Since they associated with one another on these terms and shared everything and had the same definition of expediency, they freed Athens itself then held and settled by the Persians, and they liberated Greece, then borne beneath the flood and nearly all destroyed, and in infantry battles and naval battles they adorned land and sea with their victories, which were as great as they could want. They reduced the king, who equated his empire with that of Zeus, to such fear and humility that he leaped from his throne and went off in flight from land to land, while his fleet fled by a different route to northern Asia.[42] Trophies were hung from trophies, and there came into the land the altars of Zeus Giver of Freedom, and the tripods of the Greeks in common at Delphi, and the offerings, and tithes,[43] and the adornments of the cities, and every kind of growth, and other such gains. (47) And the Athenians took over the command of the Greeks in return for their timely concession then, receiving it from the Greeks themselves voluntarily in the same fashion in which they then voluntarily gave it up. On the other hand, the Lacedaemonians paid them back in turn and neither hindered them nor disputed with them about it; but in the belief that the Athenians were superior to them in naval power and overseas expeditions, they removed their own commanders and entrusted the leadership to the Athenians. Thereafter Sestus, Eion, Cyprus, Eurymedon,[44] a doubly adorned catalogue of naval and land victories, rivaling one another. All the fairest deeds, one might say, were strung together. The barbarians retreated in turn, regarding the Greeks in place of the king as their masters. (48) These things certainly were the result of their concord; they were advantages to be enjoyed in common by both parties and by all whom they commanded. But when they engaged in faction over command, and in the belief that seemly behavior was cowardice, honored willfulness as virtue,[45] and the demagogues and leaders on both sides instead of foreseeing the future and restraining and soothing the masses, goaded and brought the cities into conflict, selling all the future for a momentary pleasure, then the Spartan herald, as if dispatched by one of the gods, declared, "that day will begin great evils for the Greeks".[46] These were soon brought to pass. (49) The Lacedaemonians, who seemed to be invincible and impregnable, were captured alive with their weapons[47] and they desired the Athenians to make a truce, although in the beginning it was possible to have persuaded them to keep the peace. But as for the Athenians who were so greatly superior to them in this war and who had formerly been responsible for liberating the Greeks, when afterwards a second war broke out again, the Decelian one,[48] having made every effort, they were seen to suffer things which cannot even be spoken of without tears, until they threw down their walls with their own hands and lost all their command.[49] No one would sufficiently describe the exiles, the mutual slaughter of the Greeks, and the fortunes ruined in the general destruction. (50) The Lacedaemonians held each empire. Yet when a brief time had passed, they were exiled from the sea and trampled on the land,[50] and a third city, Thebes, surpassed both of them.[51] And for some time she flourished extraordinarily among the Greeks. But not even she was settled in the calm of moderation. Even while she rose to power, she was in the process of decline. (51) Since these cities were three in number, and some of the Greeks supported the Athenians, others the Lacedaemonians, and others showed admiration for the Thebans, but nothing was done in common nor directed with intelligence and reason, immediately there followed in quick succession the Phocian wars, the disturbances at Thermopylae,[52] and other shameful matters. The end was Philip, then leader of the Greeks, and Antipater their lord[53]—for I shall pass over Alexander—, but all those former accomplishments sank like water beneath the earth. Scarcely has a small remnant of Greece come down to you, restored by the virtue of our present rulers.[54] Then does the difference between faction and concord seem to you a small and silly thing? (52) Again if you wish to consider the Athenians alone. When they had constitutional equality, at the time of the attack of the barbarians they were superior to all men. In the Peloponnesian war, after they had endured everything else, misfortunes in Sicily, defections of their allies, Cyrus,[55] the king,[56] and all mankind as their enemy, they were only confounded by this one act, dissension, and they were not mastered by the enemy until they did not wish to be mastered by themselves. When they reached this point of fortune, that the popular party went off in exile because of the faction then, they were in the worst condition. Again when upon the return of that party they voted an amnesty, they enjoyed the best reputation and once more were almost as they were in the beginning.[57]

(53) Thus friendship and concord with one another is naturally the cause of great good for the nation, the leading cities, and each individual city in common, and on the contrary faction the cause of the most extreme evils. For it is impossible to attempt a pleasant course of action with an unpleasant disposition. But if someone believes that these examples are foolish because at present there is no war,[58] he does not realize that he is speaking nonsense. The truth of the matter is as follows, I think. (54) Whenever war is at hand, faction injures the conduct of the war; but when there is peace, it is an enemy of the blessings of peace. Its nature is always to cause harm, and the harm occurs at all times. But it is the strangest thing of all, that when you are so very grateful to our rulers because they preserve you from suffering the evils of war, still

you willingly choose an evil which is much greater than war. (55) Faction is a harder thing than war to the extent that war has a successful outcome through concord, but peace is destroyed by faction. And often it is possible to experience no difficulty in war, but there is nothing useful in peace if ever it is involved in faction. Indeed, faction ends peace, but sometimes war ends faction. So much more preferable is war than faction. Actually where there is faction, here there is also war against oneselves; but where there is proper war, the danger is both simple and easier. (56) Indeed, there are two sides to the question of war: whether it should or should not be waged. But no one has ever dared to say that it would be better if faction would take place, nor if it should take place, that it would be better for it to continue. Concerning wars some say that they should not be ended, but concerning faction no one has ever openly said that it is unnecessary for it to be stopped as quickly as possible. With good reason. (57) Wars have in the past conferred a reputation for moderation and courage upon those who have waged them and have increased their power, and indeed have allowed them a sense of security for the future. For military superiority over the enemy makes men, I think, least contemptible; and this contributes no small part to dwelling free of danger in one's country. But faction is, as it were, the sum of all things which are shameful and evil, and far from letting men be superior to others, it does not even let them be equal to themselves. Do not think that if nothing incurable now occurs,—and may it never occur, O Zeus and you other gods—. Yet we are told that not even the seed of bad fruit should be kept. (58) It should be believed that Homer also tells the truth when he says that strife begins in a very small way and increases to the greatest size. For aside from the fact that he composed the whole *Iliad* on this point and that the entire poem is an accusation against faction, he wrote indeed expressly in regard to Strife the following lines:[59] "She at first in a small way raises up her head, but then she has fixed her head in heaven and walks upon the earth". I cannot concede that strife touches heaven. For the gates of Zeus, I think, are strong enough to block the entrance of every disease. But this much I could affirm, that this of all human things least has prescribed limits.

(59) In short, I think, no prize either beneath the earth or lying in the open should be thought so great as to be worth such great madness. But if this also must be said, consider that then the

Lacedaemonians, the Athenians, and also the Thebans had a certain distinction of dealing in real affairs with one another. For the leadership of the Greeks, the power to command one's decisions, the going to those peoples by men in need,[60] the collection of tribute, and many such things were like an incentive to contention. Their course of action was not entirely, I think, admirable—who in his right mind would say so? Nevertheless their disease, one might say, in a way made sense. (60) But you gentlemen of Ionia[61] and you gentlemen, whether it pleases you to be called aborigines or Arcadians,[62] if someone would ask you for what reason do you engage in faction, act contentiously, are so restless and demented, what shall you answer, by the gods? For what leadership or for what allies, or what harbors, or triremes, or revenues, or districts shall you say you behave in this way? Or what is so great which prevails over all reason? Did not your ancestors—[63]? (61) And by Zeus, let me now be given the right of some free speech. Indeed, doctors do not cure every disease pleasurably, but it is enough if they do not cure the majority of them distastefully. Come now let us briefly mention this point if upon hearing it you give up your pride, at least a little. Those men were satisfied with whomever they had as a leader, and they were always in this condition, sometimes believing that the Athenians were their benefactors because they liberated them from the Persians, and again the Lacedaemonians because they freed them from the Athenians, and once again they gladly gave themselves to Philip and Alexander. They were so busily engaged in seeking first place! (62) But as to present affairs and the order which now exists through our good fortune, who is such a child or who so senile that he does not know that a single city, which is first and greatest, holds all the earth beneath her sway, and one house leads everything,[64] and according to law governors come to us annually,[65] and they have been entrusted with the task of carrying out everything, both great and small, however they think best? (63) Tell me then, for what reason do we trouble ourselves, and dream, and fight about a shadow, and when it is possible for us to enjoy the peace which they rightly create, why do we annoy these men who wish nothing of the kind, and desire imported trouble, as if we did not know how to use our own good? (64) Who would not misunderstand the fashion in which we now behave toward the governors? With good will and faithfully, I think. Why not? Who more so than we? But somehow in our association with them we mix willfulness with fawning. For whenever each of you thinks that he should attend them more than they desire, and fixes the time during which they must remain with him,[66] threatening not to endure it, if they should not obey, and promises them every kind of service whether they wish it or not, and commands them to make use of himself alone or most of all, yet does not believe that the "masters"[67] must do whatever the governors may decide, what is one to say of such conduct other than that it is a mixture of two dissimilar practices,[68] whose commencement was not more remarkable than the fact that you clearly do not wish to end it? Indeed, the worst sort of men initiate such conduct, but the best put an end to it. Therefore how would it not be a total disaster to wish to pay attention to the former forever, but not to pay attention to us, if only to give us our turn. (65) I find it remarkable that while you take no little pride in the temples and contests which you regard as common to you all, yet because of these very things you have entered into dissension.[69] Still whenever you fight about what you are proud of as belonging to you all in common, about what shall you agree in the future? For I think that "common" and "private" are to be distinguished in the following way and that the saying of the Wise Men[70] means this, that it is fitting that all things be held in common by those who will have as good a life as possible. For where each has separate possessions, what is expedient for each is also separate. Hence faction, battles, and disputes. For "this is not yours, but mine" begins every argument. But where men believe that possessions belong to all in common, they also have a common point of view about them.

(66) As if you meant these titles to be refutations of faction, you have called your council chambers "common", your temples and contests "common", and everything which is most important, one might say, "common". Yet how must you not be in error in one way or the other? For if you are rightly proud of these things which are held in common, how should you not be ashamed to engage in strife because of them? But if none of them are worthwhile, what reason is there to feel so proud of them? (67) If up to now this had escaped you and someone had discovered it and showed you that some of these things also pertain to other men and that they do not only belong to their possessors, but are common to all, just as words are, and that it is impossible to exclude others from taking pride in them, I think that you would all reasonably stop your dispute. But

when you have understood this, use these expressions, feel pride in the title, and then turn what is the starting point of concord into faction and misuse the praise embodied in these terms to create difficulties in your affairs, and become sick from the things which were expected to cure you, who would not say that it was the same as if certain men far from getting better from the drugs prepared to make them well, even would be killed by them? (68) Let this not be, dear sirs! No one would resent your wish to exalt your countries and to honor what you have, but I advise you to dispense with the unpleasantness connected with this. Do you wish me to say how this can be done? Take care that you give me a friendly hearing. It can be done, my good sirs, if ever you give up a little of your admiration for stones and think that you yourselves are more valuable than buildings and trust that the old saying is true,[71] that neither walls, nor concert halls, nor stoas, nor the adornments of inanimate objects are cities, but that cities are men who know how to be confident in themselves. (69) This does not mean a random contempt for your neighbors, nor the belief that everything is yours. How could it? But good sense is a small and simple thing. Those who have it in their thoughts, least take refuge in walls and harbors, have the least need of money, stoas, and all imported sources of pride, but they know that even if they camp out in the open air, they are no worse than the Babylonians drunk within their gates.[72] The following contributes most of all to their high spirits. They do not think that they are an appendage of their property, but they regard all of their possessions as second to themselves. (70) Indeed those adornments require expense, time, and menial labor, but good sense is available to all who can recognize it. And it requires no effort, but it is enough to wish to possess this good. Those who use good judgment ought to wish in every way to prevail over their enemies, but they ought to know how to yield to their friends when the occasion calls for it.[73] (71) Not every victory is good, nor divinely comes to men, but tragedy is full of people giving the following advice. One says somewhere:[74] "You will rule your friends by not prevailing over them as much as you wish". Again another states:[75] "You prevail over your friends by yielding to them". Demosthenes writing to the Athenians about concord said[76] that "yielding in such matters was judged a good and proper victory by those with good sense", meaning the way sons yield to their parents. (72) If you also wish to use this reasoning and first of all are so disposed that you become like lovers of one another, considering that not even the most handsome person ever loved himself, but someone else; and next if it also occurs to the leaders and officials of each of you to use these enchantments on you with complete freedom and in the same way that they now contrive how to say and do everything which provokes contention, so in the future to contrive how to use their arts for your friendship and concord with one another, perhaps just as any other undertaking which receives proper care, even this would be fully accomplished by you and "remain in force" to use the expression of prayer. (73) Now we are so senselessly disposed that we engage in strife and fight for the sake of that from which we do not even expect to experience any good, while we utterly disregard those things which we can enjoy if we behave in a seemly fashion, and at that when, as I indeed remember, the best of emperors, who also surpassed all in cultivation, expressly wrote to you on this subject right at the beginning of his reign and promised that he would adjudge that city to be finest and best, which voluntarily initiated the concord.[77] (74) Now whenever an earthquake or some danger befalls, we recognize that we are on the same side, pray together, and one group says that it is saved through another, so that we should be very grateful for dangers. But whenever we are on our own and do what we wish, we become our own earthquakes and we can neither remain quiet nor plan anything for the common good, but just like a balance scale when the load has been removed, we move up and down without purpose. Thus there even seems to be a kind of foppery in our conduct.[78]

(75) Shall you not stop this, dear sirs, and shall you not realize that these things to which we are devoted, even if they have some value, are nonetheless mortal and of the second rank, but that good sense is the closest thing of all to the gods, and not the least part of it is a disposition toward friendship? If in sieges it is least profitable for garrisons to be widely dispersed, do not think that in government and in our associations with one another many factions are profitable, but that here too, if anywhere, harmony is best. (76) This is the true adornment of cities, this is their greatest protection, this is their greatest glory. This is the part of those who look upwards, not at excavations and rocks, of those who have truly seen nature, not the nature of stone and wood, but that under whose sway the Universe is led, of those who have taken their share of that

part of the divine government which falls to us. Indeed, one will together with the power of friendship administers all the heavens and Universe, which itself has received the greatest glory and title of all.[79] (77) And in conjunction with this power the sun proceeds in its course ever preserving its proper place, and the phases of the moon and the motion of the stars go on, and the revolutions and the positions of each in respect to one another and their proper distances,[80] and again their harmonies are preserved, since agreement prevails among them, and there are no differences present nor do they arise, but all things have yielded to the law of nature[81] and they use one will concerning all their duties, so that if imitation of the gods is an act of men of good sense, it would be the part of men of good sense to believe that they are all a unity, as far as is possible. (78) You also have the greatest human example before your eyes, our Emperors who are best in everything and whose fairest possession, although they have many great ones, seems to be the concord and zeal which they display toward one another.[82] They who rule over all cities, both the greater and the smaller, have shared them all. Yet how is it not strange to felicitate ourselves because we are ruled by such men, but to be unwilling to imitate them as far as possible? (79) Indeed, kings would best guide human affairs by making themselves like the gods who are the lords of all, but cities would best be guided by coming as near as possible to the intention of their rulers. In as much as we are honored beyond other people both by the Emperors and by the inspectors who arrive here annually[83]—for I shall end even where I began[84]—, how is it not reasonable for us also to exercize greater care that we do not appear to do anything which would seem improper to them? Quite the contrary! For the sake of the gods themselves and our divine Emperors and for all the things which are good and are believed in, let us wish to compose ourselves, and if I can use the expression, engage in this single struggle against one another, as to who will first initiate the concord and as to who will display more and clearer acts of virtue toward the others. (80) I wish and expect this. And I should rather have made this speech than have erected for you the greatest and the largest number of buildings,—I except temples. If you are persuaded, you shall make it clear by your action that the fault was not yours, but that of these men here,[85] who have hesitated up to now to mention this subject to you. But if you are disposed in the other way—and may it not be so—, you shall give them a fair excuse. For they will seem rightly to have kept silent since they knew that they were going to improve none of you, but rather were going to offend all of you. Therefore let us engage in an honorable rivalry. Let me give you the best counsel with all good will and courage, and do you show that it is not pointless to tell you these things, but that you know how to make use of those who offer the best advice.

XXIV. TO THE RHODIANS: CONCERNING CONCORD[1]

(1) If, O men of Rhodes, my physical condition were such as I would wish and you have prayed for it to be, I should have crossed over[2] and spoken to you for many reasons. Since perhaps news of our condition has even reached you, I leave the care of my affairs to the gods,[3] through whom I have been saved during this time. But there remained for me only to send you a written speech and for the present to be with you in this fashion. (2) In all likelihood I should not be thought of as officious if I regard your city like my own country. For it is no vain reasoning for a man who seems to belong to not the meanest rank of the Greeks to believe that he ought to care for everything Greek. And you have not forgotten my private claims on you,[4] in return for which, no matter what I think I should say and do on your behalf, I should in justice be forgiven. (3) You would best learn from your ambassadors how I reacted to the misfortune of the earthquake and comported myself toward them when they came to Egypt in those times. But when the present situation, which is much more terrible, if it is possible to say so, was reported to me, that you distrust one another, have taken sides, and are involved in disturbances unsuited to you, I did not know whether I should credit it or disbelieve it. For the messengers were your fellow citizens and otherwise trustworthy men, and yet it was impossible to accept easily such accusations against you. Therefore if Terpander of Lesbos were alive,[5] I should have prayed that he come to you. But since you must be persuaded and your affairs settled in prose, I make the contest mine.

(4) First of all consider that it is possible to argue both ways on any other matter, but no one ever has disputed the fact that concord is the greatest good for cities. Each person has a different view concerning the forms of government itself and its practices; but that in every government there is no greater obstacle than faction nor anything which more injures existing conditions, this view has prevailed, as it were, unanimously. Yet how is it not strange that all men agree on this particular point, that concord is a fair thing and a means of safety, but that you show no care for concord and think that you should engage in strife, and at that unproductively, and

that the Rhodians have been unaware of things which no other Greek or barbarian should properly be in ignorance of? Indeed, it is not even consistent with human nature to admit knowledge of the means of safety, but willingly to ignore safety itself. (5) I would most willingly, I think, be criticized because my arguments were old and I had found no new ideas. For is it not strange for you to blame the speaker because his advice is well known, stale, and accepted by all, yet for you yourselves not to dare to make use of such obvious arguments, but not only to be factioulsy disposed toward one another, but also to be at odds with all your history up to now? I believe that neither an adviser nor those who employ him should give any consideration to the following, the one to how his remarks will be original, the other to how they will hear new material, but that they should prefer a speech on what will be expedient for all in common. In our bodily needs each of us has not sought to learn of some new treatment, but the best doctor is the one who knows how to make men well. No one of you will be annoyed if he is saved by the same means as someone has been before. (6) Moreover, just as I believe that I can gratify you also on this point by saying something even beyond those who before us undertook the same subject, so I should also wish that you were willing to gratify yourselves and that you not only agree during the time in which you now listen to this speech—you will be affected in this way, for I well know your cultivation and fondness for oratory[6]—but that also in the future you have a harmonious attitude toward your affairs and so give in addition actual proof of how you enjoyed the speech. (7) I think that you would all concur that just as you believe those courtroom arguments to be most truthful, to which there are the most and best known witnesses, so also in matters of advice the most trust must be shown to that which has the most and weightiest witnesses. Therefore refer back to Homer, the common adviser and patron of the Greeks, who depicted the wisest Greek of that day as praying for Nausicaa, who was still a girl, that the gods grant husband, home, and to them both concord[7]: "For there is nothing greater and better than this, than when husband and wife maintain their house with concordant thoughts. They are a great grief to their enemies and a joy to their friends. And indeed, the gods heard him". (8) Yet do not think that a single house would be properly settled in one way, but a whole city in another. Rather if concordant thought is the single means of safety for the individual home, cities must be so much more disposed in this way by as much as a cure for the dissension of a single house is lightly found, but it is not even easy to conceive of one for a city. And whether a single house fares well or badly makes little difference for the people as a whole; but when the people thrive collectively, it is likely for even private houses to fare better. If, therefore, that adviser thought that it was now opportune to pray for concord, even for those who were going to set up housekeeping, indeed it is the duty of those who have lived in a city from antiquity, and one which is so famous, to regard all else as secondary to this. (9) So be it. Let us make a threefold distinction, and having first examined a city and then a single house, let us next proceed in our argument to a single man and let us consider what is the sort of man whom one would not be ashamed to be like. Even here we would especially descry the natural good of concord. (10) For who is so foolish or ignorant of human nature that he would prefer to employ the inconstant, fickle man who never remains firm nor keeps to his resolves? For example who would wish to form a marriage alliance with such a man, or make a contract, or be his tent mate, or participate in any of mankind's joint ventures, a person who does not even know what he wishes, but is borne up and down like a tide, at war and in a state of faction with himself? Then in the eyes of all judges is not his opposite superior, who is unaffected, noble, truthful, constant in his judgments, and as concordant with himself as possible? (11) Is it not strange that when two men are postulated, the one like a city in faction, the other being as a concordant city should be, although you revile the former as incurable and favor the latter as being best, yet you do not consistently maintain what was to be expected, but in your public conduct clearly imitate the man whom one would pray never to meet? (12) Indeed, no scandal ought to be avoided as carefully by private citizens as by a city collectively. For by as much as its dignity is greater and there are more people who will be aware of its faults, it is reasonable for it to be so much the more untainted by all things shameful. But apart from this, the danger is not even the same. For although a private citizen is inconstant, he is still in no way his own murderer, but he suffers only to the extent of having a bad reputation. But a city in dissension, first of all, wins the prize of a double folly, and next is clearly affected by its own actions, and is punished in the deed itself. (13) And it seems to me that Hesiod foresaw this and divided all strife into two kinds and advised us to love the good kind, but to banish afar the other, which is not constructive.[8] With good reason. For no iron, palisade, or weapon is frightening to cities, if only they wish to use good sense. But most men through their folly give these implements strength against themselves. Other oversights cause a temporary loss and the error is not total; but turning against one another and the belief of each individual that by dissolving and tearing asunder this settlement which was made for the general safety, he is properly arranging his affairs surpasses all the folly of man. It is so excessive. (14) Indeed, I think that it would not be inopportune for me to mention Solon, especially where an examination of both laws and a constitution is involved. When he discussed his administration in his elegies,[9] he was most of all proud of the fact that he brought the people together with the rich, so that they might dwell in harmony in their city, neither side being stronger than was expedient for all in common. Yet this is not only the act of one who exhorts us to concord, but also of one who shows the way by which concord must be acquired. (15) And why should I speak of individual men? For there is no poet, no legislator, no orator who, one might say, begins with any other point or honors anything more than friendship and trust in one another. With good reason and necessarily. If those allies who have the same friends and enemies are the most trustworthy and closely bound, there is, indeed, no safety in viewing oneselves as enemies. For on what outside help can they rely who cannot rely on themselves? (16) One would realize it even by the evidence of nomenclature. This alone is called "the disease" of a city. Yet how is it not strange to take such great care against physical illnesses, which only injure some part of the body, yet not to seek the quickest release from those which publicly destroy cities, but rather to further their growth as much as possible; and to ask the gods to avert unwanted things, as famine, pestilence, and the like, but as for what causes greater harm than these and can be cured by good sense, not to wish to heal this? (17) Shall you even deny that you pray for concord? What other good shall you pray for? Or, by Zeus, shall you claim that you do so eagerly? It is strange to bother the gods, but not to wish to do what the gods themselves think is in your power. (18) Indeed, if internal diseases are the gravest for the body and require the most care, how ought not internal corruption seem to be the most extreme of misfortunes for a city? Or while we judge enemies who have entered within the walls to be more terrifying, yet shall we believe that to wage war with one another in the middle of the city is a trivial thing? (19) Indeed, I shall not even accept the statement that "internecine faction is worse than war by as much as war is worse than peace".[10] For I see that a war often occurs which is preferable to peace, but never faction which is preferable to concord. Waging war has in the past been expedient for many in respect to acquiring money, in regard to reputation, strength, and anything else which one could name. But those who have employed faction and hatred against one another have never even enjoyed their existing good. They were so far from acquiring any other additional ones. To sum up, in peace time the impulse to engage in faction is so much worse than that to engage in war, by as much as it is worse to injure oneselves rather than others. But in time of war, this same thing is worse, by as much as war is worse than peace. (20) Indeed, it is not the case that it now seems, but formerly did not seem to be the most extreme of evils. And this is proved by the fact that the ancients often gave up their liberty and chose tyranny to end an existing faction. For tyranny is more moderate than faction, first of all by as much as it is a lighter thing for one person to mistreat a city than for everyone throughout the city to do this; and next no one in his right mind has ever thought that he should liberate a city so that it might engage in faction, but some people in the past have purposely established tyrannies so that there might be no faction. And some of the legislators themselves have in the past said[11] that it is even better to legislate with the aid of a tyrant, but no one has ever thought it possible for a constitution to be formed at all or to abide through faction. (21) Indeed, in the past some cities, which have been subjected to tyrannies, have increased in size and adornment, but we could not discover any people who was not destroyed by faction. Yet how is it reasonable to have proclaimed rewards for tyrannicides, but not even to wish to obey those who put an end to faction? (22) You are proud of the fact that you are free and you praise your democracy so much that you would not even accept immortality unless someone would allow you to keep this form of government.[12] Yet how is it not unreasonable for you to pay democracy such honor, but to be unwilling to realize that you are mocking it, and if someone would make it into a monarchy, for you to be angry, yet for you willingly to abet a situation which has been proved worse than monarchy by all the arguments which I have enumerated; and for you not even to be able to calculate that if things continue in this fashion, it is quite possible that you will be in danger of being deprived of this apparent liberty? And if you do not voluntarily heed this advice, another will come who will forcibly save you, since, as a rule, rulers are neither ignorant of such behavior nor disregard it.[13] Therefore if for no other reason, then for the sake of being free and doing what you wish, abandon this present conduct so that you may not suffer anxieties which will be as great as your present audacity, and so that you may not lose your ancient source of pride. (23) There is this benefit to be gained from the past, the application of well known examples to the present. And to recount these examples to anyone else would perhaps be childish, but it is not without use to tell them to you who are pure Greek and have been raised from childhood in these traditions. (24) Consider the city of the Lacedaemonians, who are your fellow tribesmen.[14] While it engaged in faction, it was better than none of its neighbors, but even was often defeated in war, as is said. But when it settled down in good order through the arguments and laws of Lycurgus,[15] it was a leader of the Greeks, both of individual cities and collectively. (25) Again observe the situation of the Athenians. When they engaged in faction, they lacked the means to be useful either to themselves or to others; but when freed of their tyrants, they displayed concord toward one another, they liberated not only their city, but also Greece in times of the greatest crisis.[16] After they had got their empire, so long as they had unity of purpose, they held out against almost all mankind on land and sea. But when they were affected by dissension, they threw down their own walls and gave up their fleet.[17] (26) And when the people had suffered very great misfortune in their exile and had returned again, although they could have taken revenge on those who attacked them and against whom they went to battle, they preferred concord and rated the common safety of the city before their private complaints.[18] And again they entered into world affairs and in turn were the leaders of almost all the Greeks. So great an evil for cities is faction and so great a good the wish to stop it as quickly as possible. (27) If it is also necessary to mention your Argive ancestors,[19] it is said that when these were involved in internal unrest and an embassy from Athens came to them and instructed them how they had settled their own affairs, they obeyed, ended the faction, and came back together again.[20]

XXIV. TO THE RHODIANS: CONCERNING CONCORD 51

(28) Now it is fitting, O men of Rhodes, to believe that a common embassy has come to you from all these cities, urging you to reconciliation, and that we plead and speak on your behalf what we believe to be in every way best for you. (29) Indeed, it is not necessary for you to do the same as the Athenians, nor as proof of your good faith,[21] to join those who borrowed money disadvantageously for you in paying back however many talents it may be. But without cost moderation lies ready at hand if you are mindful of what I have said and if you no longer consider one or two cities, but the common history of the Greeks and all the Greek cities, whose great change in status was caused by neither columns of enemy infantry nor troops of cavalry nor anything else which seems to be terrifying, but by faction against one another, and distrust, and by a state of general disharmony and also individual unsoundness. (30) And let none of you think that because times are different all is secure. But let him bear in mind that there is a common argument against every faction, that its nature is ever to deprive people of their existing advantages. Apart from this, O men of Rhodes, the misfortune is even greater if in such times as these when there is no fear or danger and it is possible to enjoy as much felicity as one wishes, you shall intentionally abandon, as it were, the portion of the public fund[22] which has fallen to you. (31) For while Greek affairs were in a state of dissension, it was reasonable for you to share in the sickness and for some of you to choose this side and others that. But now what cause is there for faction, or what lack of opportunity for a pleasant life?[23] Is not all the earth united, is there not one emperor and common laws for all, and is there not as much freedom as one wishes, to engage in politics and to keep silent, and to travel and to remain at home? What need is there of imported evils or this wholly superfluous madness?

(32) It is not very hard to prove that faction is the most extreme of evils, but perhaps it is difficult to find how you shall be rid of it. For you do not seem to me to err so much out of ignorance of what is expedient, as much as, if it can be said, through a certain desperation and because you have willingly fallen victim to your disputes. I say, to begin with, let all anger depart, as it were from a siege, taking with it its possessions, since practical matters are not best decided by strong emotions. Next let each side dispense with its envy and greed. I speak of the envy felt by the poor for the rich, and of the greed of the rich against the poor. In sum, imitate the form

and fashion of a household. (33) What is this? There are rulers in a household, the fathers of the sons and the masters of the slaves. How do these administer their households well? Whenever the rulers do not think that they can do anything, but voluntarily give up some of their authority, and the others accept as authoritative whatever their superiors decide. But without this considerateness on each side, it is not easy to discover a household which will be preserved. (34) It seems best to me now that you apply this conduct to the public affairs of your city. Those who think that they should be superior should calculate that if they willingly destroy their inferiors, they injure their own source of pride—for the existence of inferiors is an advantage to superiors since they will be able to point out those over whom they are superior—; and those who are deficient either in property or in some other fortune should calculate that if they abuse the rich, they injure their own security much more than if they willingly tore down their walls. (35) For this is a natural law,[24] which has truly been promulgated by the gods, our superiors, that the inferior obey the superior. And if someone regards the corruption of law as a sign of liberty, he deceives himself and does the same as if all men together should envy the gods and then should not believe in them. (36) But if any of you because of his many terrible sufferings thinks that a reconciliation is intolerable until he has exacted punishment, first of all he is inconsistent. For if faction is the cause of so many and such great evils, so that someone thinks life unlivable unless he will somehow or other exact punishment for them, how is it not best to flee from it? It is the act of intelligent men not to wish to abstain from what they have found by experience gives them pleasure, but to desist as quickly as possible from what they have discovered to be so harsh, disruptive, and everywhere full of distastefulness, not regarding evil as a remedy for evil,[25] but in the belief that memory and forgetfulness are two opposite terms for two opposite matters, and that good things should be underlined by memory and bad things crossed out by forgetfulness. (37) Next, whenever your anger in every way assails you, you should take as your ally its old opponent reason and speak to yourselves as follows: "We are Rhodians, and if some Greek or barbarian argues with us over lineage, we should wish to prevail over him. Since we wish this, our country must be preserved for all in common, so that we may keep that in which we are proud. If we engage in faction, it is lost; but if we have a single purpose, it becomes both fairer and greater. Why then do we overthrow ourselves?" If each person would wish to say this to himself, he will leave no room for anger. (38) How is it not truly strange that all of you would be disposed in the same way in regard to speaking on behalf of your country, if it should be necessary, but that you do not dare to behave concordantly so as to save your country and to be able to use words of praise about it? Rather you destroy it by your actions, while you honor it in your speech, and you await the victory of Cleomenes the Laconian,[26] who chopped up his body, beginning with his feet. (39) Or, what, by the gods, do you think will happen, if each of you proclaims this goal, that you will behave with moderation only after you get rid of your enemies? Is there any alternative other than that out of so many of both sexes one man and one woman will be left, just as in the story of the survivors of the flood? And how shall you differ from the women who tore Pentheus apart,[27] when you yourselves have torn apart with your own hands the body of the city which you all share? (40) Those who have suffered what has taken place should attribute it to the times and to chance, but should believe that there is no greater gain than this.[28] Again those who have committed these wrongs should not be proud of their actions, but should undo their former deeds by voluntarily beginning the concord, in the belief that they have received sufficient pay for that act in that they are not punished.

(41) I believe that there are so many evils in faction that while in regard to any other thing one wishing to deter someone ought to say how much harm it would cause, in regard to this, quite to the contrary, it is better for one who does not intend to act contrariwise to his wishes to keep silent rather than stir up memories of what each has suffered. The arguments which one could make on behalf of the other side, concord, already are found in innumerable writers. Still it is fitting to imitate the refrains which often seem to accomplish something by repeating the same words. (42) Concord alone preserves the order of the seasons which are given by Zeus,[29] alone confirms all things, adorning the countryside with farming and granting profit from one's property along with additional possessions, while in the city it conducts affairs as one would pray for, for through it there are seasonable offers of marriage to be given and received, to whom and from whom one wishes, and the raising of children, and education according to ancestral custom, and for women there is security, and there is faith in keeping contracts, and

the reception of guests, and the worship of the gods, and processions, and choruses, and pleasures. Furthermore there are the assemblies and council chambers which Law the eldest of the gods convenes, and means of life for the poor, and the enjoyment of their possessions for the rich, and maintenance for the old and an orderly life for the young, and as the saying goes, " all things are held in common", just as the light of the sun, under whose sway we are kept safe.[30] (43) Yet how is it not senseless to give the highest praise to those officials who provide the most pleasures for you, either in thinking up ideas for spectacles, or in distributing money, or in some single way adorning the city, yet even voluntarily to abdicate these great advantages, as if you were injuring someone else and not yourself? (44) Then as if some painter had set forth pictures of both, you must gaze at each in turn: the one shapely, compact, with good complexion, charming, throughout harmonious in every detail, and come from the gods to earth; but the other the bitterest of all sights, with head flung back, livid lips, cross-eyed, puffy, ever encompassed with new shed tears, with palsied hands, carrying in concealment a sword at her breast, raised up on thin, bandy legs, with gloom and darkness surrounding her, like a net, because of which she dwells mostly in tombs instead of temples—gazing at these images, it is fitting thus to make your choice, by examining at leisure with which of the two it is better to live. (45) Indeed, it is worth everything for all mankind to work seriously for concord, but it needs not much argument to show how worthwhile it is for you beyond all the others, since you are originally Dorians from the Peloponnesus,[31] and alone to this day have remained purely Greek, and have had as your founders and kings, the Heraclidae and the Asclepiadae.[32] In addition, yours is the fairest Greek city because of all its adornment. Yet it is a terrible thing that while even strangers show a great concern for the beautiful bodies of others, you do not spare your own objects of beauty. (46) Consider what great honor comes to you from the things said by the poets in regard to you. I shall omit what the others said and mention only the testimony of Homer. How does it go?[33]: "They inhabit Rhodes, ordered in three locations, Lindus, Ielysus, and gleaming Camirus". Now I bite my tongue at the word,[34] considering how undeserving of it we are, since we now have no order. What is the rest of the testimony?[35]: "But they were settled in three divisions according to their tribe and were loved by

XXIV. TO THE RHODIANS: CONCERNING CONCORD

Zeus who is king of gods and men''. (47) Consider that although the poet has praised the Greeks in nearly every way, he has given the greatest praise of all to you. Then do you think that you would be more beloved by the gods and would more confirm the poet's remarks when you are in a state of faction and unrest and hate one another than when you govern your city with good order and concord? (48) Well! If you are beloved by the gods, do you think that you should be involved in faction and unrest and live to suit the curses of your enemies or rather on the contrary act in accordance with the prayers of men of moderation, honoring the gods, accepting one another, and thriving in every way? Since faction is both foreign to you and hateful to the gods, and concord appears to be the only means of safety, it is surely proper to accept the result as you would the calculation of a sum. (49) Indeed, it does not even make sense that your ancestors, who had formerly been divided into three parts, united because of their trust in one another and settled in one city formed from all the others,[36] while you by your divisiveness have made many cities out of one. It would be extraordinary if you were shown to have a unified and harmonious outlook when you lived in three separate settlements, while you shall wage war with one another when you live together. (50) Do you not feel a sense of shame before the Sun, who for others is a witness of what takes place, but is the founder of your race? Will not each of you regard this present day to be the first day of the island's birth when it rose from the sea as a gift to the god?[37] Will not each of you be concerned that he may appear worse than a temple robber because he is harming the god's allotment? Will he not raise up his hands in reverence and fear and ask the gods' pardon for his faults up to now? (51) Although you dwell in a city sacred to the Sun, you are as it were corrupted in darkness. Or do you believe that Odysseus and his Cephallenians will seem to be so cursed by the god[38] as you, if you shall sack his city? Indeed—if this also must be added—as long as they listened to the best counsel and were concordant, they abstained from the cows and were saved. But when they fell into dissension, they perished except for the one man who gave them the best advice.[39] (52) Look at these tripods in the Temple of Dionysus[40]—and it gives you great pleasure to gaze at them—: Do you think that these ever would have been erected if the members of each chorus fought among themselves? Or is it quite clear that even if they did not sing in opposite ways or each member something different, but all sang the same text, yet not in the same way, all that would be left for them would be to flee the stage? Indeed, no chorus out of harmony is so unpleasant a spectacle as the people of Rhodes in disagreement. (53) Well! Consider the men who ran down the pirates and adorned the docks with those beaks and great triremes which we saw before the earthquake.[41] By the gods, if they had not fought against the Etruscans[42] or the pirate vessels, but against themselves, ship against ship, would they ever have ruled the sea or have brought these adornments into the city or have left their descendants the right to be proud over these deeds? I think, their first concern would have been their survival. (54) While faction is unsafe in a single ship, in a city, and at that seagirt, is it an act of moderation for men closely united to slay one another, or being Rhodians to imitate the evils of the Lesbians and the Mytilenaeans?[43] It was much better for them to appear desirous of your good order than for you to endure to become imitators of their misfortune. (55) Yet one could say fittingly and properly even to them: "O men of Lesbos, to what extremes have you been carried? You say that your whole island is musical and that Orpheus' head is the cause of this. But are you not ashamed to be so inharmoniously disposed? And once you surpassed the Greeks with your lyre players, but in your inability to take measures on your own behalf, you are in danger of being inferior to all mankind. And formerly men came from you to other places and put an end to faction,[44] but now you are not even able in your own home to know yourselves".[45] I think that someone would be right in offering such admonitions on their behalf. (56) However, as it seems, this senseless misfortune has been their fate from the time of antiquity and often they have been shown to be in a state of disorder. But this disease in no way befits you. When we visited you, we saw you even in the assembly using not only a single dialect,[46] but if I can say it, for the most part even a single phrase. For sometimes it was enough for you to exclaim, "Well said"! and "Crown him", and such things, with the name of the speaker.[47] It was delightful to see you using a nod of your head instead of voting with your hands, so that one would have said that you alone kept an eternal truce.[48] (57) Now I learn things which are unworthy of this and differ not a little nor imperceptibly from that order. I am also distressed by the following. In speaking Greek you used to employ native words with such obvious insistence, that it was impossible, one might say,

XXIV. TO THE RHODIANS: CONCERNING CONCORD

beginning with your foreign residents[49] to find any word among you which was not Dorian. Yet in your government you will abandon your ancestral harmony which was truly in the Dorian mode[50] and will become heirs to foreign evils which are proper to anyone rather than you. (58) Let it not be so, my fine gentlemen! Consider this old saying[51]: it is impossible to do away with any fault which has been committed on the one side or the other; rather they have an end such as time brings. Yet "the hearts of good men are curable", as he who praises the Rhodians says[52], and being without fault from the start is an attribute of the gods[53], which has not come to even one of us upon the earth. But a willingness to heed the good speaker befits you. And believe that especially in this way you would gratify that marine god to whom the poet has consecrated this verse[54] and in addition that it is more profitable to be a slave than to use freedom as a means for evil, and that nonetheless there is some fear that you may even be deprived of this means.[55] (59) Most important of all, feel shame before your temples, tombs, and the name of Rhodes which up to now has been envied, and desist from this earthquake which everywhere encompasses you, and do not desire "the second round to be worse".[56] But control yourselves, so that we may take pride in you as our good comrades and you in us as having the power of persuading whatever the occasion requires.

ANONYMOUS

XXV. THE RHODIAN ORATION[1]

(1) O men of Rhodes, those who have survived, neither is it easy to forget what has happened nor in remembering to bear it with moderation. For what greater misfortune might there be than the present one, the loss of the common ornament of the race, not only for you who once boasted that you lived in Rhodes, but also for whoever at all is a Greek? (2) One would especially weep when he considered that formerly in discussing the city the greatest praise which one could offer was that while among other people stories were told and remains of a trophy were seen, and a tomb, and a spring, and the guide pointed out obscure landmarks: this is the chamber of Semele, this one of Harmonia or Leda,[2] or some such thing, only when one was with you, did he see precisely, not only hear what the city was. Everything appeared as if the city had just now finished work on it, so that the tour was not like a dirge, but was a cause of amazement and envy in all the spectators. (3) Upon sailing in, immediately you were met by so many great harbors. They jutted out into the sea with stones as breakwaters, some receiving those from Ionia, some those from Caria, and others those from Egypt, Cyprus, and Phoenicia, as if each had been made for the reception of a different city. Lying near the harbors there were many handsome docks when you ruled the sea, and they became no less great through the years, nor was one compelled to guess where they were located, but their mere sight caused astonishment. And if one should look down upon their roofs from above, he would compare them to a kind of hanging field. (4) After this could be seen triremes, with two and three banks of oars, or with seven and nine rows, some ready for sailing, others in dry dock, as it were in storage; but if one wished to launch and sail any of them, it was possible. There could be seen bronze beaks, some at the harbors, others distributed in the upper parts of the city along with many other glorious spoils of war, some taken from the Etruscans' pirate fleet, some from the campaigns of Alexander,[3] others from wherever each had been brought into the city. (5) There could be seen the precincts of the gods, temples and statues,

of such numbers, size, and beauty, that they were worthy thank offerings for all the other works, and that it was impossible to decide which of them one would admire more, for any one of them was a sufficient source of pride for another city.[4] After this, bronze statues equal to all those in the rest of Greece, and paintings of every style, various ones set up in different parts of the city, and adornments, some unique to this place, others the fairest. (6) And the Acropolis full of fields and groves, in the rest of the city nothing higher than anything else, but the construction ample and equal, so that it would seem to belong not to a city, but to a single house. The avenues uninterrupted from beginning to end, least deserving to be called lanes. The city glorious and gloriously extended in every direction. (7) But a wonder, both before and after all this, which could not satiate the eye, the circuit of the walls and the height and beauty of the interspersed towers, which were like beacons for those sailing in, so that only at Rhodes did men, landing and taking in the view, immediately grow in spirit. What was fairest of all was the fact that this circuit was not separated from the rest of the city nor was there any empty space in between, but it clung to the city and like a crown circled its head. (8) Of Rhodes alone could it be said that it had been fortified house by house and all in common. For its walls were like a courtyard fence, and they differed from the city within only to the extent of defining its borders, since everything was of equal distinction. One ancient attribute was absent, one might say, its sea battles.[5] But all the rest of the city was preserved purely pure. And you would only say that it had sensibly given up its empire, and that the former city was not an empty name, but that which it actually was.

(9) Now the beauty of the harbors has gone, the fairest of crowns has fallen, the temples are barren of statues, and the altars of sacrifices, the streets and theaters are empty of men. One who formerly did not know would not even guess where on earth or sea were the docks. The huge number of statues, indescribable in either respect[6], has been mixed in with and scattered among the rocks and the remains of decomposed bodies. Gone is the ivory and gold which was inferior to its artistry. The walls which everywhere supported the trophies of war have perished along with their adornment. As for the trophies of swords and spears, they were brought here from the enemy, but here in the time of trouble they also injured those who fell against them, so that there might be most

especially an excess of misfortune. The city has been left as dust, not leveled to the extent that stones, which stir memories of the suffering, jut up in the air. (10) The city's misfortune has far exceeded all that we have heard about in Greek history. Among the sights of other cities which I just now mentioned[7] there are exhibited at least the actual palaces of kings and some of their chambers—and even some parts of the cities are still left, and you would say that they had only grown smaller. But here is left not even enough for a guide to inhabit. And there you would see a monument and a trophy. Yet here not even a tomb has remained untouched by violence; but both without and within the city has fared the same and it itself has become a tomb for its citizens. No longer do those who are making for port still at sea behold the city, but after disembarking they must investigate what each thing was, for they see an unsightly mound instead of a city. So much does it differ from what it was and from the misfortunes of others, that you would be excused for giving vent to any expression or committing any act. (11) But even in such circumstances you must endure, in the belief that the old saying is true,[8] that what has occurred can no longer be otherwise, not even if in blaming and reviling fortune, you should resort to every expression and in every way destroy yourselves with despair. To endure these things as best one can is no small gain in such circumstances. (12) You are not lacking in misfortunes, so as to add to these. Rather you would show good sense and do what is necessary by diminishing the misfortunes which have befallen you and by making a start from whatever possible opportunity. You must know that you are still Rhodians, as many of you as are left, and that no fortune has deprived you as well of this name which is proud and honorable in the eyes of the Greeks and the barbarians, if it is clear that your spirit remains worthy. (13) Now is the time, if ever, O men of Rhodes, to save yourselves from these circumstances, to aid the race of the island, and to stand gloriously against fortune, keeping in mind the words of your fellow citizen, the helmsman, who when his ship was tempest tossed and he expected that she would sink, made that famous remark: "Know well, Poseidon, that I will lose my ship on an even keel";[9] as if he had done nothing ignoble nor humble even in the present circumstances, but had fulfilled all his duties before his terrible death, since his death and the sinking of his ship always lay in fortune's hands, but the demand for proper conduct before

XXV. THE RHODIAN ORATION

this time no longer rested with another, but one owed this to himself and must not prematurely abandon, while still alive, the only thing over which he has control. (14) Do not cast down still more your fallen city by adding humility to the time of your travail. Since your city has been smitten and has collapsed before its time, do you survivors remain firm. For it is shameful and self-accusing[10] for the city, I mean you here collectively, to appear more ignoble than a single man and not to show that even in misfortune you know who you are. (15) In this way you will also seem to have suffered these misfortunes undeservedly. I think that a victory in arms is a fair thing, and to erect a trophy after a naval engagement is glorious, and it is not right for good men to abandon their zeal for such activities, from which your ancestors once earned a reputation which was with good reason great and with just cause admirable. But when all bases for such contests have become obsolete and the present situation demands another kind of contest from you, you must undertake this. (16) And for you it is a much more glorious and fairer thing than those contests ever were, to array yourself against fortune and to triumph over it, even if for the present it has savagely sprung upon you.[11] There is no one so great that he has a perpetual claim on victory there,[12] but the largest part belongs to the god of fortune. Yet the will is master of victory here. Show that you have the proper sort of will and do not be overcome by misfortune, but now struggle against it, since before it was not possible.[13] (17) If we can properly mourn the city, even if it means joining together all the remaining days and nights of our lives, let us do this—for such is proper for Greece[14]—and as for Rhodes, which has suffered so, let us call upon it not only three times, but even ten thousand times.[15] (18) Now what oratory is so powerful, or what sophist so excellent or competent, that he would worthily mourn the present circumstances, without omitting not a small fraction of what he believes that he is telling, but simply all of it? This is even the strangest thing of all, that in bewailing what has happened and in describing it as unsurpassable we omit most of it and we believe that we are telling it, while we are not. (19) Who would worthily describe these misfortunes which were strange, unusual, and beyond any crop of evil, or who would describe the very height of the trouble which befell you? Who would still behave with moderation when he remembered that wretched noon hour, in which the evil first began and fell upon you, when the sea stood still awaiting what was to come[15a], as it were expecting some other great and deadly storm, and all the air was silent, as it were in anticipation of what shall be, and the birds and all else remained quiet for that which was to come. The city was being prepared for such a catastrophe and the whole force of the earthquake was being readied against it. The sun for the last time then shone upon his city.[16] And suddenly every terror was at hand at once. (20) The sea drew back, and all the interior of the harbors was laid bare, and the houses were thrown upwards, and the tombs broken open, and the towers collapsed upon the harbors, and the storage sheds upon the triremes, and the temples upon the altars, and the offerings upon the statues, and men upon men, and everything upon one another. In the time that it took for a man to raise anchor to sail off, when he turned around, he could no longer see the city, but everything was jumbled together, the harbors on dry land, the city in the dust, empty streets in place of the houses from avenue to avenue, death at every house, at the temples, doors, and gates. (21) The tombs cast out their contents, within the new dead lay concealed. Like votive offerings,[17] there were seen upon the tops of the walls the hands of some, the feet of others, and of others different remains. And it was impossible to guess to whom each of these remnants belonged. (22) And some in fleeing their own houses perished in those of others, others transfixed by fear perished in their own, some overtaken while running out; others left behind half alive, unable to emerge or save themselves, starved in addition to their other miseries, and profiting only to the extent of knowing that their country did not exist, they perished. Others' bodies were sundered by chance, half left within doors, half lay exposed without. And in addition other bodies fell upon them, and household implements, and stones, and whatever the earthquake carried off and tossed upon each. (23) Some waited, some were searching for their relatives, others did not know whether to mourn themselves or their families. Some bewailed their city, others were consumed in flames when the roofs and hearths crashed together. Some were overtaken in the very act of snatching away their children, others committed suicide. (24) There was a savage revel at lunch time then.[18] Those who not long before had been called bridegrooms lay dead having sung their pretty wedding song to no purpose. It was not easy to decide whether they or their brides were more unfortunate. Those who had returned from the sea found their ancestral hearth more treacherous than the sea. Those who were hastening to set sail, then for the last time put out from home, since their country sank before their return. (25) Everything happened at once: the earthquake from the sea, the cloud, the noise, the cries, the crash of the ruins, the heaving of the earth. I think that neither the cataracts south of Egypt nor the surf of the outer ocean nor fiery thunderbolts nor whatever sounds the loudest among men can be compared with that evil and din then, which arose as a combination of everything, forming an unexpected and unpleasing symphony in which Rhodes rose up in destruction. And there were thrown together corpses and altars, ceilings and dust, blood and utensils, roofs and foundations, slaves and masters, the limbs of bodies and statues, sacrifices at tombs and dinners. (26) Some did not realize that they were encamped on the bodies of their dearest friends, others sought their own remains: some their feet, some their hands, others whatever part of their body each had lost. Some even buried these together with their own families; others suffered, held fast by what had toppled upon them from every side; others were buried before they died. There was every kind of misfortune, and then first took place what no one had ever conceived of. The survivors did not know whether to pray for rescue or death. (27) What heralds or what poets will mourn these sufferings with a worthy voice? Who is capable of narrating them? What suffering more bitter, or if you wish, more prolonged in all of time befell any Greek or barbarian city? The city was overthrown and fell quicker than ever a sinking ship. The ensuing days and nights revealed those who were alive, at least who were breathing, to be wounded and those who had already died to be rotting, and without any limbs intact, but however the ruin had worked its amputations and its graftings on each.[19] (28) Unaccustomed pyres burned both night and day, in contrast to the former sacred months.[20] Instead of the excavations of the gold and silver mines, the land of the city was sufficient to dispose cleanly of the dead for months. And formerly—O god!—you held murder trials without the gates, since it was not even in keeping with your religion to pass a death sentence within the walls.[21] But now in one day the god of fortune has condemned so many men to annihilation both within the city and along with the city, and he has made the city which could not be entered by murderers a grave for each of the slain. (29) And the following myth was once told, that this island which lay hidden beneath the sea was raised by the gods as a gift to the Sun.[22] But now it has come about to tell the opposite story, that this city has sunk beneath the earth and has gone from mankind while the Sun was above the earth and when the Sun beheld in Rhodes spectacles which he should not have seen. (30) And Homer said[23] that Zeus "poured wealth" upon the island and upon Tlepolemus[24] and your ancestors. And Pindar in this tradition said[25] that Zeus set overhead "a yellow cloud and rained down gold". But now what sort of gifts did the god of fortune pour upon you, what sort of cloud did he stand over the city! How unworthy they were of those former gifts, how unworthy of you and the beauty of your city! (31) And now Carpathus, Casus,[26] and other islands can be seen to be inhabited, although they have nothing to boast of and you formerly regarded their tribute as a slight matter; so too other sandy and dubious hamlets. Yet Rhodes, O Zeus and the Sun who observes all things except Rhodes!, is nowhere. But like narrators of myths, those who inherit the tradition from us must tell posterity that there was also once a Rhodes, a city opposite Caria,[27] famous for its beauty and greatness, and they must point out the site like that of Ialysus and Camirus[28] now. (32) And you shall celebrate the contest of the Halieia,[29] and the spot where you shall celebrate it has remained safe. But this city, named after the bride of the god,[30] has taken on the appearance of a desolate strand. And of old you showed to visitors the engines of war made from the shorn hair of your women[31] and it was a wonderful thing. But now it remains to present to visitors the city itself in such an aspect, the theater and council chamber[32] with tablets half-broken and crags instead of towers, and you can show the now pitiful remnants of once famous Rhodes. (33) When the greatness of other cities is publicly discussed, you will be unable either to make a counterclaim or to keep from bursting in your silence. You shall simply know of what sort of city your are deprived, but you shall not be able to show what sort it is. And indeed for the present you can call as witnesses those Greeks who formerly knew her. But when their due fate has taken even these away, what remains except to lose your case by default, as they say, being known, O you gods of fortune, not from your naval battles, nor from your harbors and docks, nor from the adornments which were throughout your city, but because you have suffered the greatest misfortune of the Greeks. And when you remember Rhodes, it will be necessary for you not to rejoice, but to mourn. Through your present suffering alone both those men who were famous six hundred years before[33] and those without official connection with your city have been equally injured. For by adorning the city with their works[34] they were in turn adorned by memory.

(34) These sufferings, although so terrible and not admitting any consolation, as one would suppose, must be endured, especially and first of all following the counsel of necessity and so much the more in that they have gone beyond the capacity of tears. For what we cannot mourn, as it deserves, should we not give up grieving for this and let it be, and in the words of the proverb, "shut our eyes to it"?[35] (35) Further trifling misfortunes require no great outfitting, but the greater ones must also be greatly endured—I do not mean "greatly" in a simple sense, but with spirit. For just as there is also need of more outfitting for major wars, while one would conduct minor wars with less, so also all great misfortunes require on the part of the sufferers strength to face them. (36) You must forcibly oppose them and outfitted with all your courage you must engage in this contest, if you are not going to be overtaken and carried away, considering that formerly those who viewed your paintings and statues admired the art of their makers, but that now everyone will admire your resolve if even without these things you are clearly proud of yourselves. In short just as the touchstone proves gold, so misfortune judges good men. And now all this will prove what kind of men you are, the earthquake, the conflagration, everything which followed that one initial evil. (37) Yet I am doing a strange thing. Although I myself require consolation because of your misfortune, I have determined to restrain your grief. And this circumstance would also justly aid in my efforts at persuasion. For I believe that those who are sympathetic would with good reason also be regarded as trustworthy advisers by intelligent men. It is likely that those who are touched by the same things are also concerned about these matters and speak out of goodwill and confirm the possibility of their advice first of all by the fact that although they are affected in the same way, still they clearly demand endurance. (38) I believe that great disasters are not stored up for the most unimportant of mankind nor for those who have no heights from which to fall, but for those who have the capacity for this measure of misfortune. By the gods, do you think that this ruin is suited to Seriphus or Syme here or any other of the many islands

round about? Rhodes, indeed, was able to be deprived of so many and such great things. But the god of fortune has bestowed upon you both extremes. You surpassed the other famous states in virtue, power, and the adornment of your city. But when there was also need to experience the opposite, in a way in which there was no need,[36] fortune also equated these misfortunes to your former advantages. Since you had the greatest things, you lost the greatest things. (39) Just as Hesiod said[37] that the collision of heaven and earth would produce the greatest din, since this would be the greatest fall in the upper regions, so the fall of Rhodes sounded greatest upon the earth, and most men perceived it, both Greeks and barbarians, and even the rulers of the Greeks and barbarians. It was nothing other than that whole sea has been deprived of its ornament and henceforth lacks what it least should. (40) Therefore with good reason you also have most men sharing in your grief. For neither is the matter obscure because of its magnitude nor will any rejoice over you. You were the common hosts and friends of all and also the saviors of many, good guides and escort to those who sailed by your island in either direction, kinder and more glorious than the mythical Phaeacians of whom Homer wrote,[38] famous even among those at the ends of the earth. (41) So even those who have not known the city, but have heard of it from others, although they could tell of other pleasurable events in their lives, still think that they have lacked this one and not the least experience, that they have not yet seen Rhodes. And indeed one would not know who ought more to grieve, they who have not seen the city or they who were familiar with it. For the former have been deprived of the fairest spectacle; and the latter of the greatest thing which they have ever seen and their advantage equals their loss, for they are not unaware of what greatness has perished. (42) Therefore it is especially fitting for you to be desirous of handling the present circumstances with good cheer and nobility, because you have many observers and witnesses as to how you shall carry through. And it is fair and an act of the Rhodians to show to them your abundant nobility, that even if your walls fell ten times, the dignity of the city will not fall, so long as one Rhodian is left, but it will remain firm and sound, so that they may not share your grief rather than admire you, nor remember your city with mourning, but with envy toward the survivors, nor may send missions to console you, but that you may do this for them preserving the ancestral pride of the

Dorians,[39] which is now exhibited in you alone, or at least in the largest measure among the Greeks. (43) And if it were not a very strange thing for me to say, I would have told you to send embassies throughout Greece, to offer consolation to each people and to tell them not to mourn you, since it is not traditional for Rhodes and you as Rhodians to be lamented rather than to be envied. And this embassy, to my thinking, was no more dishonorable to your city than these ambassadors going about and asking various things from different people. I think that these actions are also necessary and useful—who would censure them?—the dispatch of various people to different places to make the announcement, imposing common taxes on all the Greeks as if they were your fellow citizens. And I too approve of this. However, that noble act would also contribute to this same end. Who would not admire it? Who would not help? Who would not think that he gratified himself rather than that it was a favor for you? (44) If it is not possible or feasible to send this embassy about, you ought to serve as ambassadors to yourselves in this matter, so that you may restore the third member to the two qualities which I just now mentioned[40] and may not be deficient only in that for which there is the greatest need. You were the greatest of the Greeks and you received the greatest blow. You must endure this suffering best, so that on every count the city may clearly have obtained the greatest things and may fare the same from beginning to end, and a single middle term may be included along with the extremes which are suited to you, and that what now seems to be terrible and incurable may turn out to be to your advantage. For your fame will be greater by as much as you appear superior to these sufferings. (45) The poets also say about the heroes,[41] that god has granted them to be the fortunate ones, whose lives he has mixed in content, interchanging portions of good and evil, but that he has utterly destroyed those to whom he simply has given the portion of evil; as if the continual possession of good did not belong to mankind, but mankind had two kinds of lives, the one entirely evil and the other mixed. (46) God thought you deserving, first and longest, of the portion of good. Let this, indeed, be your greatest consolation, that your preeminence lasted for a long time and each day the city fared worthily of itself, but that the misfortune was for a day, and not a whole day, but for just one hour[42], if you use good sense. (47) Do not make it last for ever nor extend the earthquake beyond the time in which it stopped. For it is strange to blame fortune and to be angry over what has taken place as being excessive, but yourselves to add misfortunes which the earthquake omitted. (48) What lay in the power of the earthquake? And what now lies in your power? It had power over houses, walls, and bodies, to cast down and destroy them. You have the power of opposing your reason to what has taken place. Do not allow this faculty to escape you or your good sense to share in the general ruin, in order that, just as once sailors putting in and sailing out viewed the city and the circuit of the walls at great distances and for a very long period of time, so now those, who can, may behold the city's pride standing firm and may see that neither the earthquake nor the conflagration nor the deprivation of your property nor the loss of your homes nor anything else has destroyed this or will ever destroy this, or has plundered it or will ever plunder it. (49) If this stands firm, Rhodes stands firm for those who see aright, since the very walls, docks, and the other adornments along with them were the possessions of men who had pride and who could reason properly about practical affairs, and these were dedicated by the resolve of those men, who for the sake of admiration and the glory due their fair achievements thought that they must endure every toil, every danger, wherefore they sailed all the navigable sea, and fought in many great and renowned contests both alone and as allies. And you must be worthy of them, considering, even if it is strange to say at first, that it is easier for you to be able to accomplish all that is necessary than for those men of that time. For now there is no need to dispatch expeditions or to go out on campaigns, or to risk dangers facing the arms of a strong people, or to leave your country and be carried at different times to different parts of the sea, subject to storms and to the enemy, the former now, the latter in the future, but you need only remain at home, enjoy the fruits of your country, and behave with moderation. For your island has not also sunk beneath the sea, so that the surviving Rhodians have no place to stand.

(50) To those of you who think that life is unendurable unless they will live in a country with the greatness and qualities of the past, I say the following—and let no one be angry at my words. There was a time when Rhodes was not yet this city, not even this island, as the poets tell it. But this was once barren sea.[43] I do not say this. But nearly all of you know that in the times before Lysander, the admiral of the Lacedaemonians, the city had certain-

ly not yet been jointly settled by you, but the name belonged only to the island,[44] while Rhodes was not yet a city nor was it inhabited by anyone, but the Rhodians of those times inhabited three ancient cities which are also listed in Homer.[45] Later when they joined together, they founded, with not entirely good omens, this one city from all their cities, and if you say that its name, glory, beauty, and whatever else you wish was great and admired, you will not be mistaken. (51) This argument of mine makes two points. First, O men of Rhodes, imagine that you are alive in those times when you did not yet possess the city, and endure your misfortune with greater moderation. Second and most important, do not now despair of the present or give up, using the example of your ancestors, who had the necessary resolve and created an existing city out of a nonexistent one, a great city out of no city, and a famous city out of one obscure at the beginning; and do not misuse for mere self-torture, "Where can we endure to live deprived of such a city", but turn it to amending what has taken place in whatever way appears possible. (52) Yet if you consider the matter correctly, the restoration of your city is much easier for you than the original foundation was for them. For they did not even have a site as a starting place, nor did they have harbors, nor statues, nor adornments, nor stones, one might say, and I think, there was much discussion and doubt first of all as to what part of the land they would inhabit. And so they created this city, and most important of all, according to no existing example, but they themselves were the discoverers and first to make public a true model, as it were, of a city. (53) Now there is no need for you to debate the total plan, and you are assisted besides by whatever old remains exist. These are many in their total number, even if very few compared to all that there were. Now there is no need for you to build moles for your harbors, or to raise anew your council chamber or theater, or to plant your groves. There are also some pictures left on the tablets, and at least a sample of the bronze work, and the great statue,[46] and this place here of ours,[47] in which we have often engaged in many contests in your presence. And if you scorn these things and judge what is left to be nothing compared to what there was originally, know well that other cities would rejoice if they had even a part of them. Indeed, you do not even require a model nor do you need to emulate some foreign city, only to make a Rhodes from Rhodes, a new city from the old one. (54) Furthermore your ancestors founded the city in times of war and unrest, when they were unable to have much peace and quiet and all the rest of Greece was turned upside down, right at the moment of naval and military expeditions, as if fortifying a garrison or camp on a campaign. (55) But in a time of much peace and a deep calm which has benefited and prospered the affairs of all mankind, when many people will not only not block you but even aid you, you should confidently expect that there will be many Greeks to assist in the restoration, as if they were making a common contribution to the race, some paying you back the kindness which they received when they were once in need, others setting to rights in your person the uncertainty of their own fortune, and others presenting their contribution to you in your present circumstances as an indication of their culture and generosity. (56) But most important of all is that you have hope in a ruler,[48] who should certainly decide apace to restore the city as much as he can, so that the fairest of his possessions may not lie upon the earth in dishonor and so that in the future the condition of Rhodes may not be crags and dust. (57) You should also consider ancient history. Truly it shows a lack of perception to contrast your misfortunes to anyone else's—for, as I said,[49] a parallel, which alone would lighten your misfortunes, is not found in the present circumstances—; yet even if no one has been deprived of such great advantages, or has fallen into such manifold evil, nonetheless there are examples of many cities, some of which have been toppled by abandonment when their possessors were uprooted, some torn down, and others burned. (58) And you should select all the most notable of these cases, bear them in mind and say to yourselves that Ilium was captured, the most powerful city in Asia in those times, but nonetheless Ilium is now inhabited, and in fact it was captured twice, as they say, once by Heracles and a second time by the Greeks in common in that famous war.[50] Some tell even of a third time later on.[51] Thebes is inhabited, although it was twice torn down and all of its men were slain.[52] And here the earthquake was not so thorough, conferring a kindness at least in this respect. (59) In these great and terrible happenings this circumstance at any rate may be endurable for you. For your city did not perish captured in war, nor was it seen to be conquered by other men, nor did anyone triumph over it, nor will anyone adorn their temples with your offerings, as you have adorned your own city with foreign spoils. But like a man who has died in the flower of his life, the city perished in its own special way, with a rather divine death. And neither has any Rhodian been led off as a prisoner of war, nor has Rhodes been demolished, but after it had flourished for as long as was possible, it has suddenly disappeared. (60) Yet it has befallen that such deaths are not without glory even in the case of individuals. Amphiaraus, who sank beneath the earth with his chariot, is now sung of as a proud hero, and the spot which received him has a magical force so as to be his precinct in the future.[53] (61) I am close to declaring that even this has contributed to the praise of the city. We can say of the city of the Lacedaemonians that it has not remained unsacked, and it is possible to suspect the future of other cities. Many dangers face those which survive, and many men have already been cast down contrary to their rank and every expectation by quite ordinary people, men who before they reached this point maintained their pride pure and above all that could be anticipated. (62) But this city has perished with a record of total invincibility, like an athlete who has ended his labors successfully, and it has confirmed its former greatness, power, and glory by its end. For having fared well, it did not next fare worse, nor ever gradually diminish until it was extinguished. But while it existed, it was the greatest, and it came to its annihilation before it lost any of its existing dignity. (63) In view of this, you should neither be excessively sorrowful at what has befallen nor yet give up your grief,[54] but you should see that just as your city has passed from the greatest good fortune to the most extreme bad fortune, so it is not unlikely that having thus fared it will rise again and for it to expect a change now to the other side of fortune, in as much as the city is more accustomed to fare well than badly. Both in the past and now it has shown many proofs that it is dear to the gods, and it has avoided the opposite as far as it was possible. (64) For all these reasons you should endure what has befallen as calmly as you can and take a strong grip on the future, and confirm the saying[55] that not houses fairly roofed, nor the well-worked stones of walls, nor avenues and docks are the city, but men who are able to handle whatever circumstances confront them, and you should not believe that there is any misfortune so strong, for which a solution cannot be found, or that you have resources so small, through which you would not overcome even the greatest misfortunes, since you know from tradition (65) that when the Athenians had been deprived of their empire and had torn down their walls with their own hands and had fallen so far from their old felicity so that they were in the power of thirty masters and the garrisons from Lacedaemonia, then seventy men,[56] having first banded together and seized Phyle, once more effected so great a change in all their affairs, so that they seized the Piraeus, got control of the harbors, saved both themselves and their fellow citizens, and having driven out the Lacedaemonian garrisons, recovered their city and their ancestral constitution. And after this, the city was again able to make decisions about itself and about the other Greeks, and to build its walls, and to recover its naval empire through the efforts of one man, an exile, Conon, who when their triremes were lost at Aegospotami, alone of all escaped.[57] (66) If Thrasybulus[58] neither despaired of the situation nor considered "What would seventy men be against the empire of the Lacedaemonians and the fortune which then mastered all of Greece?"—for all men equally bowed low before them—and if Conon did not perceive that he desired the impossible when, having nothing except his body, he decided to raise the city's walls again and restore her empire, how is it not clear that most matters are decided by resolve, pride, and enduring spirit, and not by an abundance of resources? (67) What need is there to speak of their old abandonment of the city, when they purposely gave it up along with the temples and the tombs in the land for the barbarians to burn, and of their plan at Salamis on behalf of the Greeks, and of what they achieved because of this?[59] For no Greek or barbarian is unaware of these things, and least of all you, in as much as you also far excel all men in culture. And do you now make use of these examples. (68) Others in such circumstances will remember that you were also good men and will make you and your situation an example for themselves and theirs, so that for the sake of your glory both among men of today and future generations, and most important, for the sake of your very safety, you should be emulous and win a place yourselves among those who recovered their ancient greatness from the little that was left. (69) Think that the dead, your fathers, brothers, and other kinsmen, also beseech this of you and supplicate you by their memory and by what remains of the foundations of the city, that if you wish to gratify them in any way, do not stand by while the name of Rhodes once and for all passes from mankind, but aid it and resurrect it as much as you can. But, I pray to Zeus and all the gods, may you resurrect it with more fortunate and better omens!

XXVI. REGARDING ROME[1]

(1) It is customary for those traveling by sea or by land to make whatever vows each may conceive of. Some poet once said[2] in jest that he vowed "golden-horned frankincense". But we, gentlemen, during our journey here and our sailing, made this vow, which was not uncultured, out of tune, or separated from our art, that if we should be kept safe, we would publicly address the city. (2) It was impossible to vow a speech equal to the measure of the city, but that truly again required another vow. Perhaps it is even for one greater than I to be able to carry out such a speech,[3] which will equal the great and weighty dignity of the city. Yet we promised to make an address, however we could, since others even use things which are equal to their measure for what is equal to the measure of the gods.[4] (3) But, gentlemen, who inhabit this great city, if you have any concern that my vow not prove false, aid my daring, so that right at the beginning of our praise we can even say that straight off it was possible to meet men of such quality, through whom "if ever one was formerly uncultured", to quote Euripides,[5] he immediately becomes tuneful and clever, and can even speak on subjects beyond his ability. (4) All men sing of and will sing of this city, but they detract from it more than if they were silent, in as much as in silence it can be neither magnified nor diminished from its existing state, but it remains to be known in an uncontaminated condition. Speeches, on the other hand, do the opposite of what they intend. In their praise they do not depict precisely what they admire. But if some painter in endeavoring to depict with artistry a handsome and admired body should fail, everyone would surely say that it would be better if he did not paint it at all, but either let the body itself be seen or not display an inferior imitation to them. So also the same holds true, I think, about this city. (5) Speeches detract from many of its wonders and seem to me to have the same effect as if someone wishing to report the number of an expedition, for example that of Xerxes,[6] and being full of admiration, should say that he saw ten or twenty thousand soldiers and so and so many cavalry, while not even telling a fraction of all the things which amaze him.

(6) This city is the first to have exposed the power of oratory as not entirely sufficient. Far from being able to speak properly about

it, it is not even possible to view it properly, but truly some all-seeing Argus is required, or rather the all-seeing god who holds the city.[7] For who upon viewing so many occupied hills or the urbanized pastures of the plains, or a territory so extensive brought together into the name of a single city, could accurately observe all these things? Where would be his lookout point? (7) What Homer said of snow,[8] that it poured over and covered "the high mountain peaks and the summits of the headlands and the fields of asphodel and the rich works of men; and it poured over", he says, "the harbors and the beaches of the gray sea", such this city also does. It covers the summits of the headlands,[9] it covers the land in the interior, and it even descends down to the sea, where lies the common trading center of mankind and the common market of the produce of the earth. Wherever in the city one is, nothing prevents him from being in its center all the same. (8) And it is not only poured over the surface, but indeed far beyond the simile it rises up in the air to the greatest height, so that its elevation cannot be compared to a covering of snow, but rather to the headlands themselves. And just as a man, who is far superior to all others in size and strength, is not satisfied unless he lifts others over his head, so also this city is not satisfied with having been settled on so large an expanse of land, but it lifts up and carries over its head other cities of equal measure, one upon another. Thus its name has been given to it and the situation here is nothing other than strength.[10] Therefore if someone should wish to unfold all of it and to plant and set the cities, which are now aloft in the air, upon the earth, one beside another, I think that all the now intervening space in Italy would have been filled up and that one continuous city, extending to the Ionian Sea, would have been formed. (9) Although it is so great that perhaps even now I have not sufficiently described it, but the eye is a better witness, it is not, as is seen in the case, one might say, of other cities, limited to here. Someone remarked[11] of the cities of the Athenians and the Lacedaemonians, that the size of the former was double its strength and that the size of the latter would appear to be much less than its strength—would that this ill-omened remark were absent from the example. But it could not be said of this city, which is great in every respect, that it has not acquired power consistent with such size. If one considers the whole empire, he is amazed at the city when he thinks that a fraction of the world rules over the whole of it. Yet if he regards the city itself and the boundaries of the city, he is no longer amazed that the whole world is ruled by so great a city. (10) A certain prose writer said about Asia[12] that one man "rules all as far as is the course of the sun", untruly since he excluded all Africa and Europe from the sun's rising and setting. But it has now turned out to be true that the course of the sun and your possessions are equal and that the sun's course is always in your land. No marine rocks and no Chelidonean and Cyanean islands define your empire,[13] nor the day's ride of a horse to the sea, nor do you rule within fixed boundaries, nor does another prescribe the limit of your power. But the sea is drawn as a kind of belt without distinction through the middle of the inhabited world and your empire. (11) About the sea the continents lie "vast and vastly spread",[14] ever supplying you with products from those regions. Here is brought from every land and sea all the crops of the seasons and the produce of each land, river, lake, as well as of the arts of the Greeks and barbarians, so that if someone should wish to view all these things, he must either see them by traveling over the whole world or be in this city. It cannot be otherwise than that there always be here an abundance of all that grows and is manufactured among each people. So many merchant ships arrive here, conveying every kind of goods from every people every hour and every day,[15] so that the city is like a factory common to the whole earth. (12) It is possible to see so many cargoes from India and even from Arabia Felix, if you wish, that one imagines that for the future the trees are left bare for the people there and that they must come here to beg for their own produce if they need anything. Again there can be seen clothing from Babylon and ornaments from the barbarian world beyond, which arrive in much larger quantity and more easily than if merchantmen bringing goods from Naxus or Cythnus[16] had only to put into Athens. Your farmlands are Egypt, Sicily, and all of Africa which is cultivated. (13) The arrivals and departures of the ships never stop, so that one would express admiration not only for the harbor, but even for the sea. Hesiod said about the limits of the Ocean,[17] that it is a place where everything has been channeled into one beginning and end. So everything comes together here, trade, seafaring, farming, the scourings of the mines, all the crafts that exist or have existed, all that is produced and grown. Whatever one does not see here, is not a thing which has existed or exists, so that it is not easy to decide which has the greater superiority, the city in regard to present day cities, or the empire in regard to the empires which have gone before.

(14) Indeed, I blush if after having spoken of so many and such great things, words should fail me and I shall be seen to mention either some barbarian empire or Greek power, and I shall appear to do the opposite of the Aeolian poets.[18] Whenever they wished to belittle something of their time, they compared it to what was great and famous among the ancients, in the belief that in this way they would especially expose it. But since I can in no other way show how superior are your circumstances, I shall compare them with the trivial affairs of the ancients. For you have made everything, even the greatest things, into the most trivial, through your superiority. Although I shall select the greatest things for discussion, perhaps you will laugh at these.

(15) Let us consider the Persian empire which once enjoyed much fame among the Greeks and gave to the king who held it the title "Great". I shall omit the empires before it as being of less importance. And let us regard everything in order, its size and what took place in it. We must also examine how they enjoyed their possessions and how they treated their subjects. (16) First of all, what the Atlantic Ocean now means for you, was then simply the Mediterranean for the King. Here were the borders of his empire, so that the Ionians and Aeolians lived on the limits of his territory. When that king "of everything from the rising to the setting sun"[19] once attempted to cross over to Greece, he excited admiration only for his great failure. And he proved his distinction by the fact that he could be stripped of many, great possessions. Indeed, since he was so far from ruling Greece, and Ionia formed the limit of his kingdom, he did not, in fact, fall short of your empire by the throw of a discus or the distance of a bowshot, but by a whole half of the inhabited world and the Mediterranean itself besides. (17) No, not even up to these boundaries was he always properly king, but depending on the Athenians' power or the Lacedaemonians' fortune, now he was king up to the Ionians, Aeolians, and the Mediterranean, and again no longer of the Ionians nor up to the Mediterranean, but as far as the Lydians, not seeing the sea west of the Cyanean Island,[20] indeed as if he were a king in a children's game, now remaining upcountry and again descending, needing people who will permit him to be king.[21] Agesilaus' force and before him that of Clearchus and the Ten Thousand made this clear, the

former crossing up to Phrygia as if through its own country, and the latter going beyond the Euphrates as if through a deserted region.[22] (18) They enjoyed their empire in accordance with the dictum of Oebaras,[23] who is first said to have told Cyrus angry because of his extensive traveling that it was required and necessary for him to journey everywhere in his empire whether he wanted to or not, if he were going to be king, and that he should consider the hide, how on whatever part he stepped, this flattened out and touched the ground, and when he left it, again it rose up, and once more flattened out when he walked upon it,—certain wandering kings, differing from the nomadic Scythians only in that they did not go about on wagons, but in covered carriages, through distrust and fear of remaining in the same place, truly pressing their land as a kind of hide, and in this way now controlling Babylon, then Susa, next Ecbatana, not only not knowing how to hold these places permanently, but not even caring for them as herdsmen would. (19) Such were truly the characteristics of those who, as it were, disbelieved that the empire really was theirs. They did not care for it as their own, nor did they increase the beauty and greatness of either the cities or territories. But like those who have made an incursion upon what does not belong to them, they shamefully and badly depleted their empire, seeking to rule over the weakest possible subjects. And as if they contended against one another in a murder competition, the second man always tried to surpass the one preceding like those in the pentathlon. And the contest was to slaughter as many as possible and to uproot as many homes and peoples as possible and to break as many oaths as possible. (20) This is what they enjoyed from their wonderful power and further what the law of nature has arranged as a concomitant, hatred and plotting on the part of those who were treated in this way, revolts, civil war, continual strife, and unceasing contention. (21) This indeed is what they themselves enjoyed, ruling more, as it were, under a curse than in answer to a prayer. Their subjects enjoyed all that those who are ruled by such people must. Some of this has more or less already been mentioned.[24] The beauty of a child caused fear for the parents, that of a wife caused fear for the husband. The greatest criminal need not perish, but he with the most possessions. Then more cities were destroyed and torn down than now—I am close to saying—are founded. (22) Survival was easier for an enemy than a subject. For in battle they were easily defeated, but in power they were immoderate in their crimes. And they despised their followers as slaves, and they punished free men as enemies, as a result of which policy they were forever full of hatred and hated in return. Often they were more afraid of their subjects than their enemies, since they generally used war as a means of reconciliation. (23) The reason was that they did not know how to rule nor did their subjects fulfill their duty. For it is impossible to be good subjects whenever the rulers rule badly. Empire and despotism had not yet been distinguished, but king and master were the same. Therefore with good reason they did not make much progress. For this word[25] does not go far beyond the household. Whenever it is extended to cities and nations, it is easily cast aside.

(24) Again although Alexander possessed the great empire up to the time of yours and overran the earth, truly, as they say, he was more like one who got possession of a kingdom than a king. Just as if some private citizen should acquire much good land and should die before enjoying the fruits of it, so it seems to me to have befallen him. (25) He advanced over the most territory, subdued all who opposed him, and enjoyed to the full every difficulty. Yet he was a unable to establish his empire and to put an end to his toils, but he died in the middle course of his work, so that one would say that he was successful in most battles, but was least a king, and that he was a great competitor for the kingdom, yet enjoyed nothing worthy of his plans and art, but had the same experience as if a contestant in the Olympic games overcame his opponents and then died right after his victory before he had well and fairly fitted the crown to his head. (26) What laws did he institute for each people? Or what lasting arrangements relative to finances, or to the army, or to the fleet did he make? Or with what kind of regular administration, one routinely proceeding in fixed cycles, did he direct affairs? What measures of government did he take among his subjects? He left only one deed and monument worthy of his nature, the city named after him in Egypt.[26] This he generously founded for you, so that you might possess and rule over the greatest city after your own. Therefore he overthrew the Persian rulers, but he himself almost did not rule at all. (27) When he died, the Macedonians were immediately split into innumerable parts, proving in fact that empire was beyond them. They were no longer even able to keep possession of their own country, but they sank to so low a fortune that they were forced to leave their own country, in order to rule another's,[27] more like

men who had been expelled from their homeland than men able to rule. And it was like a riddle, Macedonians not in Macedonia, but each ruling where they could, as if they were garrisons for these cities and lands rather than rulers, having become in a way uprooted kings, not through the Great King,[28] but through themselves, and if it can be said, like satraps without a king. Shall we say that such a state is more like brigandage or kingship? (28) Now, indeed, the boundaries of your empire are of an extent not to be despised, nor such that their interior can be measured. Proceeding westward from the point where the limit of the Persian empire was then fixed, the remainder of your empire is much greater than the whole of that one. Nothing escapes you, neither city, nor nation, nor harbor, nor land, unless you have condemned something as useless. The Red Sea, the cataracts of the Nile, and Lake Maeotis,[29] which former men spoke of as at the ends of the earth, are for this city like "the fence of courtyard".[30] As to the Ocean, which certain writers neither believed existed at all nor that it flowed around the earth[31] and whose name they thought that the poets had invented and put in their compositions to please their audience, you have discovered this ocean so thoroughly that not even the island in it has escaped your notice.[32] (29) Although your empire is so large and so great, it is much greater in its good order than in its circumference. The King's land is not held by Mysians or Sacae or Pisidians,[33] or others in between, some having settled the land by force, others in revolt and unable to be taken; nor is it called "the King's land", while belonging to all who can hold it; nor are satraps fighting against one another, as if they had no king; nor do some cities side with these and others with those, while to some garrisons are sent, and from others expelled. But like the enclosure of a courtyard, cleansed of every disturbance, a circle encompasses your empire. So the whole inhabited world speaks in greater harmony than a chorus, praying that this empire last for all time. So fairly is it forged together by this chorus-leader prince.[34] (30) All everywhere are equally subjects.[35] And those who have been settled in the mountains are more humble than those in the deepest valleys as far as not creating any opposition goes; the colonists and inhabitants of the rich plains are your farmers.[36] No longer is there any difference between continent and island, but like one uninterrupted land and one tribe, all obey in silence. (31) Everything is accomplished by edict and by a sign of assent more easily than one would strike the chord of a lyre. And if something must be done, it is enough to decree it and it is accomplished. The rulers who are sent to the cities and to the peoples[37] are each the rulers of those under them, but in regard to their personal position and their relations to each other are equally subjects. And, indeed, one would say that in this respect they differ from their subjects, in that they first teach the duties of a subject. So much fear is instilled in all for the great ruler and president of the whole. (32) Therefore they believe that he has more knowledge of their actions than they do of themselves, and they have more fear and respect for him than anyone would for the presence of his master who was supervising and giving orders. No one is so confident in himself that he is able to remain calm after only hearing his name. But he stands up, praises, and reverences him, and offers a double prayer, one to the gods on the emperor's behalf, the other concerning his personal affairs to the emperor himself. If they should have even some small doubt over suits and the legal privileges of their subjects, either public or private,[38] whether any are entitled to these privileges, they immediately send to him, asking what should be done, and they wait for his signal, no less than a chorus waits upon its teacher. (33) Therefore there is no need for him to wear himself out by journeying over the whole empire, nor by visiting different people at different times to confirm individual matters, whenever he enters their land. But it is very easy for him to govern the whole inhabited world by dispatching letters[39] without moving from the spot. And the letters are almost no sooner written than they arrive, as if borne by winged messengers. (34) Now I shall speak of what is particularly worthy of admiration and of amazement and of gratitude shown in word and deed. Although you hold so great an empire and rule with such authority and power, you have also proved most successful in that quality which is in every way peculiar to you. (36) For you are the only ones ever to rule over free men. And Caria has not been given to Tissaphernes nor Phrygia to Pharnabazus,[40] nor Egypt to another, nor are the people, like a household, spoken of as belonging to so-and-so, to whomever they were given to serve, although not even that man was free. But like those in individual cities, you govern throughout the whole inhabited world as if in a single city and you appoint governors as it were by election[41] for the protection and care of their subjects, not to be their masters. Therefore governor is succeeded by governor whenever his term has expired; and it is improbable that he would even meet his successor—so far would he be from raising a dispute as if the land were his own. (37) Cases under judicial review, like an appeal from one's demesmen to the courts,[42] take place with no less fear in regard to the verdict on the part of those who have handled the cases than on the part of those who institute the appeals,[43] so that one would say that people now are governed by those sent out to them in so far as it pleases them. (38) How is this form of government not beyond every democracy? There it is not possible after the verdict is given in the city to go elsewhere or to other judges, but one must be satisfied with the decision,[44] unless it is some small city which needs outside judges. But among you now a convicted defendant or even a prosecutor, who has not won his case, can take exception to the verdict and the undeserved loss.[45] Another great judge remains, whom no aspect of justice ever escapes. (39) And here there is a great and fair equality between weak and powerful, obscure and famous, poor and rich and noble. And Hesiod's words come to pass:[46] "For easily he makes one strong and easily he crushes the strong", this great judge and governor, however justice guides him, like a breeze blowing on a ship, which does not, indeed, favor and escort the rich man more and the poor man less, but equally assists him to whomever it may come.

(40) I shall now also recount Greek affairs, since I have reached this point in my speech, although I am ashamed and afraid that I may seem to deal in trifles. However, as I just now said,[47] I shall not recount them as if I were comparing equal things. But since there are no other examples, I am compelled to use those which exist. Again it is also silly to show with a sense of amazement that it is impossible to find any other accomplishments equal to yours or even near to them, but that everything has been cast in the shade by these, yet to wait to make comparisons until we can mention accomplishments of the same importance. In fact, I do not think that such a course should be followed, because the accomplishments would not be similarly remarkable, even if we could speak of certain similar matters. (41) Indeed, I am not unaware that these accomplishments will appear even inferior to those which I have just now investigated, both in the scope of empire and in the weight of affairs. But to excel the barbarians in wealth and power, while surpassing the Greeks in knowledge and moderation, seems to me

to be an important matter, perfect in regard to virtue, and an oratorical theme more glorious than any other. (42) Therefore I shall discuss how they conducted themselves and how great was their sphere of influence. And if they obviously have been unable to maintain even a much smaller sphere, it is clear that the vote will be cast in your favor. (43) The Athenians and the Lacedaemonians undertook every action for the sake of their empire and rule. And the extent of their power was to sail the sea, rule the Cyclades, hold possessions in Thrace, Thermopylae, the Hellespont, and Coryphasium.[48] Such was their power. And their experience was the same as if someone in his desire to obtain mastery over a body, should get hold of some nails and hair instead of the whole body, and having these should think that he has what he wished.[49] So even they, in their desire for empire, enjoyed the fruit of little islands, headlands by the sea, harbors, and such things, and their energies were expended in the region of the sea, dreaming more of empire than being able to possess it. (44) Nonetheless although, as it were in the cycle of a lot, each was leader of the Greeks at times, they did not even maintain their place for one generation, one might say. And not even then did they hold it blamelessly, but in the struggle for empire, as the proverb has it, they won "a Cadmean victory"[50] over one another, as if the one side thought that the other side should not alone be continually hated, but that it too should have a share. (45) A single commander of the Lacedaemonians[51] treated the Greeks in such a way that being free of the Lacedaemonians the Greeks gladly sought other rulers for themselves. But when they had handed themselves over to the Athenians, after not much time had passed, they repented. For they could not bear either the immoderate tribute or those who robbed them with this for an excuse, and they were dragged off every year to submit an account of their affairs at Athens, while colonists were sent to their land and ships gathering taxes besides the tribute, if ever other needs should arise. (46) In addition they were unable to have free citadels and they were subject to the Athenians' popular leaders, no matter whether benevolent or not, and they were often compelled to go on unnecessary expeditions during sacred feasts and festivals, and to put it simply, they got no great use out of the Athenians' protection for which it was worthwhile to endure these things. (47) Therefore many of them grew angry at the Athenians and again went back to the Lacedaemonians in the same way that they formerly left them for the Athenians, and again they were deceived. For when the Lacedaemonians declared that they would wage war against the Athenians on behalf of the freedom of the Greeks and thereby won over many of them, after they had torn down the Athenians' walls[52] and had got control of affairs and secured full power of action, they so outdid the Athenians that they established tyrannies in all the Greek cities, which they euphemistically called "decarchies".[53] (48) And having destroyed the single rule of the Athenians, they introduced in its place many of their own which did not mistreat their subjects from a central administration at Athens or Sparta, but each one was perpetually established and, as it were, interwoven in its own country. Therefore if at the commencement of the war the Lacedaemonians had declared to the Greeks that they would fight the Athenians so that they might more often afflict the Greeks with greater injuries than the Athenians did and might show that the treatment of the Greeks by the Athenians was real freedom, they would not have better kept their promise. (49) And they were immediately defeated by one exile,[54] and were abandoned by the Thebans, hated by the Corinthians. The sea was filled with their expelled "Regulators",[55] since they were unregulated and when installed did not hold their cities in keeping with their title. (50) And when through their crimes and the hatred thereby felt toward them by the Greeks, the Thebans grew strong and conquered them, as soon as the Lacedaemonians were removed, no one again could endure the Thebans after their success in a single battle.[56] But it was clearly more advantageous for the Cadmea[57] still to be held rather than for the Thebans to have conquered the Lacedaemonians. They were so hated. (51) And I have certainly not prepared this account as a common indictment of the Greeks, like that extraordinary man who wrote *The Three-headed Monster*[58]—may that never be necessary!—, but in the desire to show that before you the knowledge of how to govern did not yet exist. For if it existed, it would have been found among the Greeks, who certainly far excelled all other races in knowledge. But this too is your invention and it was introduced along with the rest. Indeed, what has been said of the Athenians is very likely to be true if it should be said of all the Greeks, since they were better than anything in opposing the unjust,[59] conquering Persians and Lydians,[60] not being awestruck by wealth,[61] and enduring toils; but they were as yet uneducated in the art of government, and when they attempted it, they failed. (52) First of all they sent to the cities garrisons, who were always no less numerous than the individual native population and than those to whom they were sent.[62] They also created a suspicion in the minds of those not yet guarded by garrisons, that they conducted all their affairs through force and violence. In consequence they did not hold the cities securely and they were hated as well, and they reaped the evils of empire instead of its good, having no solid advantage over the others, but a strong reputation for taking advantage. (53) There is more. Being always scattered and separated, they became weaker at home and unable to preserve their own country because they sought to possess the countries of others. At that time neither could they surpass in the number of those whom they sent out the people whom they desired to rule, nor did they leave for themselves equal strength behind. But they were too few without, too few at home; and the extension of their empire became an embarrassment for them, since in the end they had no means by which they could retain it, so that they aimed their efforts contrary to their needs. And the achievement of their ambitions caused them difficulty and was like a curse. Failure was less burdensome and embodied fewer dangers. Instead of rulers they resembled nothing other than people uprooted and scattered abroad and those who toil for the sake of toiling. In the end the sum of their work was immediately, if quietly, undone, and as the poets put it, all again fell back to where things were at the start.[63] (54) Further it was neither expedient for them that their subjects be strong because of the danger of plots nor again weak on account of foreign wars and so that there might be some use from the alliance. They were disposed toward them as if it were a game, advancing them with one hand and drawing them back with the other,[64] not knowing what to do with them, but as if they wished them both to exist and not to exist; indeed, managing and guiding them, but to what purpose they could not say. (55) The most ridiculous and strangest thing of all was that they compelled their remaining allies to fight against those who were in revolt, although these allies intended to do the same, as if they were trying to persuade the rebels to fight against themselves, and they did not consider that they were leading against the rebels people belonging to the same party, and it was certainly not to their advantage to show the remaining allies that they could be harmed if these allies seriously aided the others. Therefore even here they brought about the opposite of what they desired and was expedient. (56) While they wished to win over the rebels, they even caused those who would have remained faithful to revolt. For they showed them that by remaining loyal they would serve the Athenians' interest against one another; but if they all revolted in common, they would be safe and free. For in the end no people would be left by whom they would be captured. Therefore the Athenians caused themselves more harm than their faithless allies, in as much as the allies individually deserted, but the Athenians by their course of action introduced the idea of a common revolt. (57) Thus then there was not yet an orderly procedure of government, nor did they consciously pursue this. Although their possessions were minute, for example border lands and allotments, they could not even preserve these through their inexperience and inability in government, since they neither led their cities with generosity nor were able to hold them firmly, being at the same time oppressive and weak. Finally they were stripped like Aesop's daw[65] and fought alone against all the others.

(58) However, that which formerly had escaped all mankind, one might say, has been reserved for you alone to discover and fulfill. And no wonder! For just as the science of other things arises when there is material for it, so when the greatest empire and a surpassing power was formed, then in its wake its science was also composed and introduced, and both, indeed, were strengthened by one another. Experience necessarily arose through the greatness of the empire, and again the empire both justly and reasonably increased through the knowledge of how to govern. (59) But the following is by far most worthy of consideration and admiration in your government, the magnanimity of your conception, since there is nothing at all like it.[66] For you have divided into two parts all the men in your empire—with this expression I have indicated the whole inhabited world—and everywhere you have made citizens all those who are the more accomplished, noble, and powerful people, even if they retain their native affinities,[67] while the remainder you have made subjects and the governed. (60) And neither does the sea nor a great expanse of intervening land keep one from being a citizen, nor here are Asia and Europe distinguished. But all lies open to all men. No one is a foreigner who deserves to hold office or to be trusted, but there has been established a common democracy of the world, under one man, the best ruler and director, and all

men assemble here as it were at a common meeting place, each to obtain his due. (61) What a city is to its boundaries and its territories, so this city is to the whole inhabited world, as if it had been designated its common town. You would say that all the *perioeci* or all the people settled in different places *deme* by *deme* assemble at this one acropolis.[68] (62) It has never refused anyone. But just as the earth's ground supports all men, so it too receives men from every land, just as the sea receives the rivers. It also has this in common with the sea. The sea does not become greater through the discharge of the rivers, as it would if it were fated that the rivers contain within themselves the greatness which flows into the sea[69]—here nothing of the addition is evident because of its greatness. But like those who put things in the folds of their robes, so the city holds everything concealed, being and appearing equal despite arrivals and departures. (63) And at the prompting of my speech, let that remark be made in passing. As we have said, you are great and have laid out your city in great dimensions.[70] And in your pride you have not made it admired by giving no one else a share of it, but you have sought a citizen body worthy of it, and you have caused the word "Roman" to belong not to a city, but to be the name of a sort of common race, and this not one out of all the races, but a balance to all the remaining ones. You do not now divide the races into Greeks and barbarians, nor have you made your distinction a foolish one in the eyes of mankind, since you present a city more populous than the whole Greek race, one might say. But you have divided people into Romans and non-Romans. So far have you extended the use of the city's name. (64) Since people have been divided in this way, many in each city are citizens of yours no less than of their fellow natives, and some of them have not even seen this city. There is no need of garrisons holding acropolises, but the most important and powerful people in each place guard their countries for you. And you hold their cities in a double way, from here and individually through them. (65) Yet no envy walks in your empire. For you yourselves were the first not to begrudge anything, since you made everything available to all in common and granted those who are capable not to be subjects rather than rulers in turn. There is not even a residue of hatred on the part of those left out. Since the government is universal and like that of a single city, the governors with good reason rule not foreigners, but, as it were, their own people. In addition under this government all of the masses have a sense of security against the powerful among them, provided by your wrath and vengeance which will immediately fall upon the powerful if they dare some lawless change. (66) Thus with good reason the present circumstances are satisfactory and expedient for both poor and rich, and there is no better way to live. And there has arisen a single harmonious government which has embraced all men; and that which formerly seemed impossible to happen has been combined under you, the great and real power of empire and of generosity. And of those who have been rulers, you alone have come to possess true power.[71] (67) Thus the cities are free of garrisons; cohorts and cavalry troops[72] are sufficient to guard whole provinces, and not even many of these are quartered throughout the cities of each race, but few when account is taken of the other inhabitants, and they are scattered in the countryside, so that many provinces do not know where their garrison is. If some city through its excessive greatness has lost the power of exercizing self-control, you have not even begrudged these people officials to oversee and protect them.[73] All men pay taxes to you with greater pleasure than some people would collect them from others. With good reason! (68) It is unsafe to be rulers for those who lack ability, but as they say, the second course is for them to be ruled by their superiors. Now to be ruled by you has been shown to be the first course. Therefore all men cling tightly to you and would no more think of defecting from you than a ship's passengers from the helmsman. Just as bats in caves cling closely to one another and to the rocks,[74] so all men depend on you and are fearfully concerned that someone may fall from this chain, and it is more the case that they are afraid of being abandoned by you than that they would abandon you themselves. (69) In place of the disputes over empire and preeminence, through which all former wars broke out, some of these people enjoy a most pleasant calm like a silently flowing stream, gladly done with their toils and troubles, repenting their vain shadowboxing. Others of them do not even recognize or remember the empire which they once held. Indeed, like the tale of the Pamphylian, or if it was not his, of Plato,[75] the cities, as it were already lying on their funeral pyre through strife and disorder against one another, have received all at once a leader and have forthwith been resurrected. But how they reached this state, they cannot say, nor do they know anything except to marvel at their present circumstances. They have had the same experience as those who have awakened and in place of the dreams which they have just now had, forthwith observe these things and are involved in them.[76] (70) It is no longer even believed that wars ever took place, but most men hear of them like idle myths. Even if somewhere on the borders clashes should occur, as is likely to happen in an immeasurably great empire, through the madness of the Dacians, or the ill fortune of the Moors, or the wretchedness of the people of the Red Sea,[77] who are not equal to making use of the advantages of the age, indeed these wars and the discussions about them have quickly passed away like myths. (71) Such great peace do you have, even if war is native to you! [Those who were yesterday shoemakers and carpenters are not today infantry and cavalrymen, nor as on the stage is one transformed into a soldier who was just now a farmer. Nor as in a poor home where the same people do the cooking and keep house and make the beds, have you also mixed your occupations. Nor did you wait for those who are involved in other tasks to become soldiers out of need. Nor have you given your enemies the privilege of assembling your forces].[78]

(72) I have discussed the decision which you have reached in regard to the whole of your empire and its governance and how you have established it.[79] Now it is time to speak of your fighting force and of military affairs, again of how you have conceived it and the organization which you have given to it. Your knowledge of this matter was also remarkable and entirely without example. (73) The Egyptians also proceeded to the point of isolating their fighting force,[80] and they seemed to have made a most wise discovery, in that those who fought in defense of the land were settled by them separately and apart from the others, just as they also seemed in many other respects beyond other men, as they say, "wise Egyptians". Although you reached the same decision, you did not act in the same way. But you made you division so much better and wiser, since in the Egyptian arrangement there was no equality of citizenship between the two groups, but the soldiers who alone toiled continually were in a position inferior to those who did not fight—perhaps they were not at all satisfied with this—, yet since with you everyone has equal rights, the fighting force can be settled apart. Thus the daring shown by the soldiers of the Greeks, Egyptians, and whomever one would name is less than that of your soldiery. (74) And although all men are so very inferior to you in force of arms, they are still further behind in their conception of an

army. You believed for people from the city to perform military service and suffer hardships was not to enjoy fruits worthy of your empire and the present felicity, but you did not trust foreigners. Yet there was need of soldiers before the moment of necessity. What did you do? You discovered your own army, without imposing upon your citizens. Your policy in regard to your whole empire enabled you to do this and the fact that you classify no one as a foreigner in respect to any service which he is capable of performing and which needs to be done. (75) What was the manner of conscripting your army? You traveled to all your subject lands and searched for those from there who would perform this service. And when you found them, at the same time you severed their ties with their own country and you gave them your city in return,[81] so that in the future they were ashamed to declare their former origins. Having made them citizens, you also made them soldiers, with the result that the people from your city do not perform military service and those who do perform military service are none the less citizens, having been dissociated from their original city at the time of joining the army, and from the same day having become citizens and protectors of your city. (76) And thus all men obey and no city is angry. You have recruited only so many soldiers from each people as will neither be a burden for those who supply them nor by themselves will be sufficient to make up the complement of a single army of their own. Therefore all the cities display goodwill toward the soldiers who have been sent out to them, as if they were their partners, but individually each city has no force made up of its own people, nor do the soldiers sent out look elsewhere than to you, since they have been carefully assigned with this end alone in view.[82] (77) Indeed, after you had levied the most suitable men from each region, your next innovation was of no small advantage. You did not think that it was necessary for those who were selected, as being in the best condition and physically superior, for the national festivals and crown contests to go into training for these,[83] but for those who were going to be contestants in the most important and real actions and victors too in as many victories as they chance to have on behalf of such an empire, for these, I say, once they had been selected as the best and especially as the most suitable of all to assemble at the very moment and not long before to go into training for these actions, so that immediately upon taking their place in the line they might be superior. (78) You "purified" these and "selected" them in the common sense of the word,[84] not apart from the privileges which I have mentioned,[85] nor in such a way that they would still envy the others who remained in the city, since originally they did not enjoy the same rank as the others, but so that they would receive as their share of honor participation in the right of citizenship. And when you made this innovation and treated them in this way, you brought them to the ends of your empire, and here stationed them at intervals and gave each people the task of guarding different regions. (79) You also have new plans and ideas in the matter of walls. This should now be mentioned. It could not be said that this city is unfortified in the stubborn manner of the Lacedaemonians nor again walled in the ostentatious fashion of Babylon, or whatever other city before or afterwards has been fortified with more grandeur. But you have shown this fortification to be child's play and truly the work of a woman.[86] (80) You believed that it was base and inconsistent with your other conceptions to put walls about the city itself,[87] as it were concealing it or fleeing your subjects, as if some master should show himself in fear of his own slaves. However, you did not neglect walls, but you put these about your empire, not your city. And you erected them as far off as possible, glorious and worthy of you, worth seeing by those within the circuit, but the journey to them, if one should wish to see them, starting from the city, is a matter of months and years.[88] (81) For beyond the outermost circle of the inhabited world, indeed like a second line of defense in the fortification of a city, you have drawn another circle, which is more flexible and more easily guarded, and here you have put up your defensive walls and have built border cities, filling each in a different place with inhabitants, and supplying them with useful crafts and providing them with other adornments. (82) Just as a trench encircles an army camp, all this can be called the circuit and perimeter of the walls, so that the circumference of this perimeter is not calculated at ten parasangs,[89] nor twenty, nor a little more, nor as much as you would say right off, but by all that is enclosed by the inhabited portion of Ethiopia and the Phasis on the one side and the Euphrates inland, and to the west that final great island.[90] (83) These walls have not been built of bitumen or baked brick, nor do they stand gleaming with stucco—but there are also these usual kind of walls in each place, and many of them indeed, closely and carefully fitted with stones, as Homer[91] said of the house wall, and they are immense in size and gleam with more brilliance than bronze. (84) This circuit, which is much greater and grander than those walls, is on every side in every way unbreakable and indissoluble, shining far beyond all circuits—nor was ever any so compacted—, men[92] who hold out their shields in protection of those walls, not believing in flight, joined to one another with all the instruments of war in that harmony which Homer attributes to the Myrmidons,[93] then comparing them to the wall which I mentioned.[94] So closely do their helmets join to one another that an arrow could not pass between. Their shields raised over their heads would hold elevated walks[95] so much more stabile than those fashioned in the city, that it is possible for even the cavalry to ride upon them; and then you will truly say in the words of Euripides[96] that you see a "bronze-shod plain". And their breastplates so closely cling to one another that even if you should station an unarmed man in the middle, he is protected by the armaments at each side. And their spears falling like rain form a steady stream. In such harmony then have been enclosed the circle of their tactical revolutions and the circle on the borders of the whole world.[97] (85) Of old Darius together with Artaphernes and Datis was able to capture a single city on a single island by netting it.[98] But if it can be so expressed, you have netted the whole inhabited world and in this way you keep it safe by means of those who both are partners in it and are foreigners,[99] men whom, as I said,[100] you selected from all mankind and led forth, having given them hope that they would not regret being brave men. For who at any time held the highest command would not inevitably be a patrician, and the second in command from the next class,[101] and so on for the other ranks, but a man would hold the rank which he merited since in this profession not titles but deeds judge good men. And you gave clear examples of this to all, so that all these men regard idleness as a misfortune and believe that action is the means to attaining their desires, and are of one mind against the enemy, but engage in a lifelong struggle against one another for promotions, and alone of mankind pray that they may find the enemy. (86) Therefore whenever one considers the training and formation of the army, he will believe, to use Homer's expression,[102] that even were there "ten times as many" opponents, they would have been quickly routed and left a man less than the Romans.[103] But whenever he regards its staffing and drafting, he will be reminded of the story of the Egyptian. When Cambyses was plundering the land and sacking the temples in it, this man stood upon the walls of Thebes and stretched forth to him a clod of earth and a cup of water from the Nile, meaning that so long as he cannot carry off and plunder Egypt itself and the river Nile, he has not yet captured the wealth of the Egyptians, but that while these remain, the people will quickly possess as much again and wealth will never fail Egypt.[104] It is possible to believe this about your army and to say that, so long as no one can uproot the land itself from its foundations and leave it empty and so long as the inhabited world must remain in its place, it is impossible for your military drafts to fail you, but coming from every land which is inhabited they must be as large as you wish. (87) And in the matter of tactics, you have shown all mankind to be children. For you have not only prescribed to your soldiers and commanders to practice this against the enemy, but first of all against themselves. Therefore every day they live in the line and no one ever leaves the post assigned to him; but as if in some sort of eternal chorus each man knows and keeps his place, and for this reason the subordinate does not envy his superior, but is in full command over those whom he himself outranks. (88) It is annoying that formerly others have said of the Lacedaemonians[105] that save for a few men "their army consists of officers over officers". For it was fitting for this to have been reserved for and first said of you. But that gentleman produced it prematurely. Still the Lacedaemonian army is likely to consist of such numbers that it is not improbable for all men to be officers. But when in such great numbers of drafts and races, whose names it is not even easy to discover, you begin with one man, whose authority is all pervasive and who oversees everything, nations, cities, legions, the generals themselves, and end with one man who commands four or two men[106]—for we have omitted everything in between—, and when just as the spinning of thread ever proceeds from a larger to smaller number of strands, so in this way one is ever ranked after another right up to the end, how have you not gone beyond all human organization? (89) It occurs to me to quote the following Homeric verse, after altering the end a little:[107] "Such indeed is Olympian Zeus' empire within". For whenever one man commands so many, while those who are servants and legates for him are far inferior to him, but far superior to those over whom they have charge, whenever they accomplish everything quietly without disturbance and confusion, whenever there is no envy, whenever everything everywhere is full of justice and respect,[108] whenever the fruits of virtue are lost to no one, how is this verse not most suitable?

(90) Even in your city itself you seem to me to have established a form of government such as no one else of mankind has done.[109] Formerly there seemed to be three forms of government among mankind, two with two names apiece, according to how each was considered in regard to the character of the possessor, tyranny and oligarchy, and kingship and aristocracy. The third was named democracy, whether it was conducted well or badly. States have made a selection from among these forms, however each people chose or fate prevailed. Yet your government is not at all the same, but it is like a mixture of all the constitutions without the inferior side of each. And so such a form of constitution has proved best. Therefore whenever one considers the power of the people and how easily they attain all their wishes and requests, he will believe that it is a democracy and lacks nothing except the people's errors. But whenever he considers the Senate deliberating and holding office, he will believe that there is no more perfect aristocracy than this. But when he has considered the overseer and president of all these,[110] from whose hands the people receive the fulfillment of its wishes and the upper-classes receive their offices and power, he sees in this man the possessor of the most perfect monarchy, free of the evils of the tyrant and greater than the dignity of the king. (91) And it is not unreasonable for you alone to have made this distinction and to have seen the matter so clearly both in respect to your government outside the city and within it itself. For you alone are natural rulers, one might say. The others who held power before you and became in turn the masters and slaves of one another and were the illegitimate heirs of empire[111] passed in succession, changing their place, as it were on a rotating sphere,[112] and the Macedonians were slaves of the Persians, the Persians of the Medes, the Medes of the Assyrians.[113] But all men have known you as rulers for as long as they have known you. Since you were free from the beginning and, as it were, were born directly to be rulers, you have well prepared all that pertains to this and have discovered a form of government which no one had before, and have imposed unvarying law and order on all men.

(92) What long ago occurred to me and often has disconcerted me by being at my lips, but until now has always been put off by the course of my speech, if I say this now, perhaps I would not be out of

place. It has been said how much you surpass all men in the expanse of your whole empire as well as in your authority and in your conception of government.[114] Now I think that one would not be wrong in saying that all former men, even those who ruled the largest portions of the earth, ruled over, as it were, only the naked bodies of their people, but you have filled your whole empire with cities and adornments. (93) When were there so many cities on land or throughout the sea, or when have they been so thoroughly adorned? Who then ever made such a journey, numbering the cities by the days of his trip, or sometimes passing through two or three cities on the same day, as it were through avenues? Therefore those former men are not only greatly inferior in the total extent of their empires, but also where they ruled the same lands as you, each people did not enjoy equal and similar conditions under their rule, but to the tribe which then existed there can be counterpoised the city which now exists among them. And one would say that those men had been kings, as it were, of deserts and garrisons, but that you alone are rulers of cities. (94) Now all of the Greek cities flourish under you, and the offerings in them, the arts, and all their adornments bring honor to you, as an adornment in a suburb.[115] The seacoasts and the interiors have been filled with cities, some founded, others increased under you and by you. (95) Ionia,[116] much fought over, freed of its garrisons and satraps, is set forth for all as a model of beauty, having now surpassed herself to the extent that she formerly seemed to exceed the other races in grace and adornment. The proud and great city of Alexander in Egypt has become an ornament of your empire, like a necklace or bracelet of a rich woman among many other possessions.[117] (96) You continually care for the Greeks as if they were your foster fathers,[118] protecting them and, as it were, resurrecting them, giving freedom and self-rule to the best of them,[119] who were of old rulers, while guiding the others with moderation and with great consideration and care, and educating the barbarians gently or harshly depending on the nature of each people, as it is likely for you to be no worse than the trainers of horses, since you are the rulers of men, but rather for you to have examined their natures and to lead them accordingly.[120] (97) And the whole inhabited world, as it were attending a national festival, has laid aside its old dress, the carrying of weapons,[121] and has turned, with full authority to do so, to adornments and all kinds of pleasures. And all the other sources of contention have died out in the cities, but this single rivalry holds all of them, how each will appear as fair and charming as possible.[122] Everything is full of gymnasiums, fountains, gateways, temples, handicrafts, and schools. And it can be said in medical terms that the inhabited world was, as it were, ill at the start and has now recovered. (98) Never does the flow of gifts from you to these cities stop, nor can it be discovered who has received the greater share, because your generosity is equal toward all. (99) Indeed, the cities shine with radiance and grace, and the whole earth has been adorned like a pleasure garden. Gone beyond land and sea is the smoke rising from the fields and the signal fires of friend and foe, as if a breeze had fanned them away. There has been introduced instead every kind of charming spectacle and a boundless number of games. Therefore the celebration of national festivals, like a sacred and inextinguishable fire, never ceases, but passes at different times to different people, yet always is somewhere. For now all men deserve this. Therefore those outside your empire, if there are any, alone should be pitied since they are deprived of such advantages. (100) Indeed, you best have proved that well-known saying, that the earth is the mother of all and the universal country of all. Now it is possible for both Greek and barbarian, with his possessions or without them, to travel easily wherever he wishes, quite as if he were going from one country of his to another. And he is frightened neither by the Cilician Gates,[123] nor by the sandy, narrow passage through Arabia to Egypt, nor by impassable mountains, nor by boundless, huge rivers, nor by inhospitable barbarian races. But it is enough for his safety that he is a Roman, or rather one of those under you. (101) And what was said by Homer,[124] "The earth was common to all", you have made a reality, by surveying the whole inhabited world, by bridging the rivers in various ways, by cutting carriage roads through the mountains, by filling desert places with post stations, and by civilizing everything with your way of life and good order. Therefore I conceive of life before your time as the life thought to exist before Triptolemus,[125] harsh, rustic, and little different from living on a mountain; yet if not entirely so, still that while Athens initiated our present, cultivated existence, this has been confirmed by you "with second attempts better", as they say.[126] (102) And now, indeed, there is no need to write a description of the world, nor to enumerate the laws of each people, but you have become universal geographers for all men by opening up all the gates of the inhabited world and by giving to all who wish it the power to be observers of everything and by assigning universal laws for all men and by stopping practices which formerly were pleasant to read about, but were intolerable if one should actually consider them[127] and by making marriage legal between all peoples[128] and by organizing the whole inhabited world like a single household. (103) Indeed, the poets[129] say that before the rule of Zeus everything was filled with faction, uproar, and disorder, but that when Zeus came to rule, everything was put in order and the Titans were banished to the deepest corners of the earth, driven there by him and the gods who aided him. So too, in view of the situation before you and under you, one would suppose that before your empire everything was in confusion, topsy-turvy, and completely disorganized, but that when you took charge, the confusion and faction ceased and there entered in universal order and a glorious light[130] in life and government and the laws came to the fore and the altars of the gods were believed in. (104) Formerly as it were emasculating their fathers, men ravaged the earth. And they did not swallow their children,[131] but in the strife of faction they slew those of one another and their own even at the temples. But now total security, universal and clear to all, has been given to the earth itself and those who inhabit it. And men seem to me to have found many means for being completely free from suffering evil and for being well governed. And it seems that the gods, watching from above, in their benevolence join with you in making your empire successful and that they confirm your possession of it. (105) Zeus, because you well care for the inhabited world, "his well made work", as they say.[132] Hera, because of the marriages which take place under law. Athena and Hephaestus, since the arts are honored. Dionysus and Demeter, because their fruits are not injured. Poseidon, since his sea is cleansed of fighting and he has exchanged merchant vessels for warships. Indeed, the chorus of Apollo, Artemis, and the Muses never ceases to behold its servants in the theaters. Hermes is not without his share of contests and embassies nor Aphrodite of her seed and grace.—When were the times more suitable or when did the cities have a greater portion?[133] The grace of Asclepius and the Egyptian gods now has experienced the most extensive increase among mankind.[134] Nor has Ares been dishonored by you, nor is there fear that he may throw everything into confusion because he was neglected as in the banquet of the Lapiths.[135] But on the banks of the rivers without your empire he dances an endless dance, keeping his weapons clean of blood.[136] Indeed, the Sun, who watches over all things, has seen under you no act of violence or of injustice nor things of the sort which were frequent in former times, so that with good reason he watches over your empire with the greatest pleasure. (106) Homer was not unaware that your empire would exist, but he foresaw it and proclaimed it in verse.[137] So too it seems to me that if Hesiod were as perfect a poet as Homer and endowed with the same power of divination, he would not as now describe the generations of man by beginning with the golden race. Or at any rate when he had made this beginning, in his discussion of the final race of iron, he would not say that their destruction would occur,[138] "When they were born with gray temples". But he would say that the iron race would perish on the earth when your leadership and empire were established, and then he would grant Justice and Reverence to return to mankind, and he would have pitied those born before you. (107) So then your precious institutions ever abide, truly introduced by you and ever more confirmed. Indeed, the present ruler,[139] like a great contestant, clearly excels his predecessors by as much as—and it is not easy to describe—he himself excels other men. And one would say that whatever decision he might render is truly justice and law. And one would add that the following surpasses all the rest. What is this? Clearly that he has treated as equals his partners in the administration of the empire, whom he regards as kinsmen, and that he has more of them than any of his predecessors.[140]

(108) The original contest, to make our speech equal to the magnitude of your empire, is beyond the capability of any man and requires a time nearly as long as the duration of the empire. This would be all eternity. Therefore, like the poets of the dithyrambs and paeans,[141] it is best to add a prayer and so to conclude our speech. (109) Let all the gods and the sons of the gods[142] be invoked, and let them grant that this empire and this city bloom forever and not cease until "the anvils stand above the sea"[143] and "the trees cease blooming in spring",[144] and that the great emperor and his sons[145] be kept safe and obtain good for all mankind. My act of daring has been completed. Whether successfully or not, you can now decide.

XXVII. PANEGYRIC IN CYZICUS[1]

(1) All men, I believe, would have sufficient reason for speaking in the present circumstance. For this city, if any other Greek city, deserves our regard, and the accomplishment, for which it celebrates the festival, is the greatest which mankind has seen and these are the best and most perfect times that ever were. But my reason is particularly clear and is a part of the custom of our life. (2) Asclepius orders me to speak,[2] so that I can neither argue the considerations of physical weakness with the Savior himself nor fear the greatness of the subject and the difficulty of success. As Pindar said,[3] "When god has shown the beginning", there is no obstacle. Above all, we do not make trial of him now for the first time, but even before in many great undertakings we learned from our own circumstances, not those of others, what abundant powers he possesses for creating an easy way[4] in matters which seem to be absolutely hopeless, not to mention those which were difficult, but not necessarily desperate. (3) I have become so confident in another's care, that in a certain way I am extemporizing,[5] if not completely orally, still in writing. For I did not know beforehand what I should say until the time when I had to speak. And he who has commanded me is greater than any preparation. (4) There is a difference, I think, between great affairs and great seas. For by as much as the seas are greater, they cause more fear.[6] But in some ways great affairs are also helpful. For it is possible, as it were, to find safe anchorage in many places, so that unless someone should be completely unfortunate, he will avoid the appearance of total failure.

(5) I think that even the Hyperboreans[7] by this time have heard of the oracle which pertains to Cyzicus and of the witness of the city's felicity, who is an interpreter of oracles for the other cities, but also a founder for this city.[8] For he founded the other cities through the founders whom he dispatched everywhere. But he himself was the direct founder of this city. Therefore how is not Cyzicus fortunate when it had such a beginning and can refer back to both such a founder and witness? (6) In view of its location and total nature, one would immediately realize that the god had given it a suitable title.[9] Such is its situation on both land and sea. For it is located before Asia, beginning from an island and ending in a continent,[10]

on the one side having the Euxine sea as a protective barrier, and on the other side the Hellespont, being a kind of link between the two seas, or rather between every sea upon which men sail. Sailors never cease sailing by it, around it, and into its ports. Some, with a fair breeze behind them, are conveyed out to sea through the city's islands, while others run up and down the waterways leading to the city. (7) Yet if the poets decided to call the city of Corinth "fortunate"[11] because it is located on the Isthmus and receives those journeying in either direction, certainly this city has a clear right to the title. For located in the midst of the sea, it brings all mankind together, escorting some from the inner to the outer sea, and others from without to within,[12] as if it were a kind of navel stone at the point between Gadira and the Phasis.[13] (8) Other islands too, I think, have happened to be located within the boundless sea, and Homer in praising Crete said[14] that it was located "in the midst of the wine-dark sea". But the situation of this city is more glorious. For it has not occupied the midst of a single sea. But it can be said that it not only possesses a great sea, but also a manifold sea, to the north above a sort of spring and origin for every navigable sea,[15] and again to the west the longest and most charming strait.[16] And this third sea between both these in nature and position has, one might say, completed its full complement.[17] (9) Such is its situation on the sea. Again that on land is consistent and in keeping with this. For the whole region is great, vast, of such size that one would think that it should be called a continent. It has many natures, far different from one another, and all inclining to what is best. For here the mountains are more cultivated than the plains of other people, and the plains are sufficient not only for a city, but for nations, and the rivers, lakes, marshes, and glades are in a way things that would rejoice the blessed. (10) Therefore if one should wish to settle the whole region, there would be many cities about the lakes, many on the beaches by the sea, yet not a few in the interior. And it would be possible that many cities, at least all that did not happen to be contiguous, would not even know about each other. And such is the city's situation on land and such on sea; they vie with one another and are not found in many examples. (11) Indeed, you would call the city itself an island, a peninsula, or whatever term there is between peninsula and continent. Because it is not easily crossed at the neck and it does not start from a narrow point, but extends along the continent for a great distance and is joined to it at both causeways,[18] it has surpassed the example of Tyre and whatever other city or island is nearly part of a continent. (12) Indeed, Thucydides praises Sicily[19] because it is at least twenty stades distant from the continent. But this city is so far from the continent that it is possible even to forget that it is not an island; and that if someone should remove the embankments and the bridges, one would swim to it from the continent. So both the whole island and the city are no less distinguished in their nature than the greatest islands, Crete and Sicily. (13) As to the beauty of the public buildings and all of the construction in and greatness of the city, no one is so unskilled in speech, so that he would be unable to praise these, nor so competent a speaker, so that he would easily describe them. I shall omit all the rest and shall select the edifice which I ought most particularly to mention. (14) It seems to me that this token best proves who the founder was[20] and that the city is the work of one of the gods. It is like a city sacred to all the gods, just as the so-called "gods' Assembly".[21] For as if it had been set aside and allotted among all the gods, it has now been all parceled out, and the temples have divided it up, as if the gods were competing against one another on behalf of the safety of the city. There are sacrifices, parades, processions, and divine services under established codes, and this is a far cry from not using kinship for the best ends.[22] Indeed, the other faculties of the city are consistent with this. For the city has so much that one should not be ashamed to say that it was "the backer" of the temples elsewhere and of other public adornments.[23] (15) It possesses resources which are so glorious and which are shared with all. And neither does Italy scorn its possessions nor Egypt so far off, nor the Tyrrhenian Sea nor "the haunts of the Syrians and Cilicians", as some poet would say.[24] Nor is there any nation, one might say, either mainland or insular, which has not been adorned by this city. Why should one speak of the Ionians and Aeolians and the islands and cities near at hand? Although they grant a large head start, good runners easily catch up.[25] So too, although you have provided all mankind with what they needed, you also catch up, appearing suddenly at the end.

(16) I have come to the tempest itself.[26] How should I say all that I wish? But I should say as much as, when said, would satisfy my obligation. I am close to declaring that you have shown all men who have attempted similar works to be like children, by having erected a work so great that it would have seemed to be an act of madness to

have conceived it and beyond the power of man to accomplish it. (17) One would be uncertain as to whether most of the island[27] has been transferred here or remains in its place. But I think that all would agree that this would be the offering of no other city or quarry than your own. For their nature would not suffice. Formerly sailors used to judge their position by the peaks of the islands, 'Here is Cyzicus', 'This is Proconnesus', and whatever other island one beheld. But now the temple is equal to the mountains, and you alone have no need for beacons, signal fires, and towers for those putting into port. But the temple fills every vista, and at the same time reveals the city and the magnanimity of its inhabitants. And although it is so great, its beauty exceeds its size. (18) If Homer and Hesiod[28] had happened to be alive, I think that they would have readily transferred to here the tale about the Trojan wall and would have told how Poseidon and Apollo jointly designed and fashioned this work for the city, the former by providing rock from the depths of the sea and at the same time making it possible for it to be brought here, and the latter through his desire to adorn his city with such a great addition, as it is likely that a founder would do. (19) You would say that each of the stones was meant to be the whole temple,[29] and the temple the whole precinct, and again that the temple's precinct was big enough to be a city. (20) If you wish to consider the comfort and luxury which it provides, it is possible to view this very great temple like three storied houses or like three decked ships,[30] many times greater than other temples, and itself of a threefold nature. For part of the spectacle is subterranean,[31] part on an upper story, and part in between in the usual position. There are walks which traverse it all about, underground and hanging,[32] as it were made not as an additional adornment, but actually to be walks. (21) There is no need to praise these things in speech, but they can be left to the geometricians and technical experts, at least to as many of these as are fully trained and capable of measuring so great a work, since I fear that not even all of these may be able to attain to accuracy in this matter. If someone should forego speaking about the temple itself, it is enough to express admiration for the engineering equipment and the transport, whose invention was prompted by the requirements of the temple, since they formerly did not exist among mankind.

(22) You should also be congratulated for your good fortune. For while you have inscribed upon it the name of the best emperor up to

that time,[33] your work has been completed in these times,[34] whose lot again has been the fairest of the fair and for which most justly would so great a thank offering be erected to the gods, since it is not easy to find a greater. (23) It is a long tale and by no means easily concluded, to speak of how these emperors[35] have exhibited the largest number of forebearers who were emperors of any of their predecessors, and what was the original condition of their family on both sides, and how they were educated and under whom[36], and of the abundance of all of their cultivation. But we shall spend our time, as far as possible, on that which seems to me particularly fitting for the present assembly to hear and which is an object of praise most peculiar to them and is the most remarkable of all the distinguished acts which have been recorded, and which has compassed all nobility and culture, and about which no private citizen can remain silent, and at which every city and race of mankind has been struck with admiration. (24) It is these who have exalted the proverb to the highest degree and through the greatest deeds have defined it, that the possessions of friends are indeed held in common, not because they shared a herd of horses, or pots and pans, or some acres of land, or by the greatest amount of sharing which was formerly attained, but because they reached such a peak of magnanimity that they included the whole earth and sea in this proverb and nothing existing escaped them unshared, truly, to quote Homer,[37] making "the earth to be in common", theirs to rule and for all to use: an act for which formerly one might pray as far as justice was concerned, yet for which there was never much expectation. But such a definition of felicity seemed truly like a prayer. (25) Generals in times of danger have already taken other generals as their partners, and cities have joined one another in emergencies, and kings have made pacts of friendship and treaties with kings, and at that for the most part when they were compelled by need. And to this extent we know that sharing has occurred. But now for the first time an emperor has voluntarily taken another emperor as his partner in the whole empire, and alone in all the ages has not sought additional rule rather than an additional ruler on terms of complete equality. (26) By sharing his empire, he did not diminish it as far as he was concerned, but by this very act he enlarged his empire and that of him who was to be his fellow ruler. Alexander astonished men because he did not accept a partnership with Darius, and perhaps he did well since he was not going to divide Asia with an equal.[38] Still I think that even if there had been someone much better than Darius, not even so would he have agreed to rule over all the others in company with another. But they have made their rule a token of the most perfect justice, as if they undertook the direction of the affairs of mankind for this purpose, so that they might share in being teachers of virtue to all men. (27) Such conduct is beyond any marching around the Caucasus, beyond the capture of the Indians and the Caspian Gates[39], beyond every human action. This conduct excels in what is finest and in natural propriety. Neither if they added to their possessions a land beyond the Atlantic Ocean, if there is any, nor if on discovering that all the regions within their domains, which were uninhabitable because of their excessive cold or heat, had been made temperate by the gods, they made them an addition to their empire, each somehow privately for himself, would they seem to me to have so greatly surpassed all men in virtue to the extent that they now have by sharing their possessions and valuing one another more than all their property. (28) Admirable is he who does not desire to be emperor, unless his brother should approve! Admirable is he who does not agree to being emperor, except with his brother! These men, who have repaid one another with equal gifts, alone similar to one another to the greatest degree, alone most different from all men, partners in the greatest enterprise, yet without other equal partners! (29) The king of the Persians seemed to have had an extraordinary possession, the men called the King's Eye and the King's Ear.[40] And perhaps this had some use, but mostly, it seems to me, it was humbug, so that he might seem to see and hear twice as much as other men. (30) But they have made a most fair and wise discovery, exceedingly so. For both became the ears and eyes of one another, and they doubled a natural function, and by sharing everything they made the protection of their empire not another's care, but truly their own. And in no way has the advantage of monarchy been any more corrupted, but it is a marvelous monarchy, since a single resolve is established in two bodies and two souls, like some harmony which uses all the strings. (31) What music would be better than this? What symphony dearer to Apollo and the Muses? What harmony more universal for the human race? Amphion and Zethus proceeded to the point of walling Thebes —and here some people criticize the music of one of them.[41] But they have shared their music and sing in harmony on behalf of all the cities and of all mankind, inheriting the tune from their father, I suppose, and their ancestors, yet making it in every way still more glorious, as if their ancestors had indeed been children in the art of singing. (32) This conception of theirs also seems to me in keeping with their form of government. For this city[42] alone has changed the old custom. All other men, both Greeks and barbarians, who to a small degree have touched on power, have had this one policy, that no one share in their fortune, but that all be kept apart as far as possible. But these[43] alone of all people have set out their advantages to be shared like prizes by the best people. And it makes no difference whether one lives in Europe, Asia, or Africa,[44] nor is there any restrictive boundary, whether the Tanais, or Lake Maeotis,[45] or the island Atlantis,[46] or whatever place one would mention. But all men and all races are connected with the city, and all have the right to exercize due authority. They knew that their ancestors had established for all worthy men the right to share in common in these particulars. So too they themselves, who to the greatest degree surpass all men in virtue, shared their empire over everything. (33) And the most charming feature of their conception is that just as formerly the Roman people furnished a pair of annual rulers to those at home and those abroad, so now it is possible to name our perpetual rulers both by one patronymic and in concert.[47] Thus they have framed a policy which is consistent with their whole form of government and have acted above and beyond every expectation. (34) Indeed, Homer said somewhere in praising kings[48]: "Great is the anger of Zeus-nurtured kings". Yet they have not made the strength of their anger or the immoderation of their wrath as signs of their empire, but they have displayed the best sort of generosity and magnanimity, and in fact have made clear that their nurture was divine. (35) Their reason is, indeed, divine and truly has a model from above and looks toward that government, if I must speak summarily, since they say that it is friendship and sharing which holds together the gods themselves and the whole Universe and heaven,[49] and because of these everything moves securely in its course for eternity, while in the houses and the ways of the gods there neither is nor arises envy and hostility.[50] (36) Some men by adding palisades and walls increase their empires with some small and truly mortal possessions. But these men by having presented to all mankind examples of virtue, justice, and friendship, so glorious and marvelous to behold, have truly possessed their victory from the hands of the gods. These men have been adorned with the crown of the immortals. It is reasonable for these men to be regarded in every way as dear to the gods, as they are to one another, and as benefactors of mankind. (37) Those who are skilled in writing draw on tablets hung above their heads exaggerated letters which are written as large and fair as possible for boys to imitate as far as they can.[51] So too these men have revealed what is fairest for mankind by the greatest example, so that each man could imitate it as far as he could and use the emperors as teachers for his own concerns. (38) Could this be surpassed by the monuments of Sesostris,[52] which in his journeys he erected on both continents, or rather could they seem even to come close to this? Has any man both won so great a victory and one so profitable for the conquered? Fear reconciles subjects to other rulers, but on behalf of these men there are prayers and universal gratitude[53] from all people, and these take place publicly not only for show, but from the purest feelings of the heart. (39) I am even reminded of the relationship of the two Savior gods,[54] who encompass the whole earth and save in common and work together, sending to one another and bestowing benefits in common and sharing the gratitude which they receive from mankind. In the eyes of those two gods who more is likely to win approval than these men or whose safety is likely to be of greater account, since they have become, as it were, prophets and a representation of the resolve of those gods, by forming the fairest kind of friendship for the benefit of the whole human race?

(40) We should be grateful to the gods, but we should congratulate the emperors and join in prayer for them. We should felicitate ourselves for living in this age, but in addition to felicitation, we should properly enjoy this empire. These adornments of construction are fair and exercize a remarkable persuasion over the masses.[55] But what is perfect and truly the gift of some god occurs whenever both adornments are in harmony, that in the soul and that of construction. (41) For just as we praise the harmony in the latter and the fact that each element preserves its proper relationship, so it is also fitting to think that a well lived life takes place whenever harmony and order prevail throughout. This adornment is truly proper to cities. This preserves both individual man and city. This need not be bought at the cost of money, or the expenditure of time, nor must you set up engineering equipment and be con-

cerned with public works.⁵⁶ But each man need only persuade himself to choose the better course. (42) And do not be surprised that although I have nothing to censure, I think that I should offer some advice. And do not think that advice is the act of only those who come to speak in criticism. But it is also the business of those who bestow praise. This is clear from that old and well-known proverb about runners. For no one, one might say, urges on those of them who are in last place and who have been completely left behind, but those who he sees are near to victory. I think that generals also do not expend their exhortations on those soldiers to whom it makes no difference whether much or nothing is said, but on those to whom it is going to be most useful. (43) So too we now say to you nothing clever or wise, but more or less the very things which you do and in which you have been raised, that is respect for your rulers, honor for the laws, and the practice of concord, which is, indeed, a matter always to be approved, but is particularly in keeping with the present times. (44) Now you must regard all cities as sisters to one another, now you must entirely do away with faction, disturbance, strife, and pettiness over vanities, in the belief that these are the diseases of wild beasts and should be left to them, but that true peace, guileless friendship, justice, and sharing in every way, if it is possible, should be regarded as the greatest gain. In your visits to one another's cities you must realize, as the old saying has it, "that you are strangers",⁵⁷ but in your reception of strangers you must not exercize your full rights in the knowledge that sometimes even defeat is more decorous and more valuable than victory.⁵⁸ (45) These practices were best from the start and are appropriate to the present times and directly of themselves have a natural advantage, and make a remarkably great difference in regard to the honor which is shown by the emperors. For in no way would you more gratify them than by such conduct nor would you more attain your desires from them than if you would show yourselves such as they would most wish. (46) Yet, as I said,⁵⁹ my advice is more or less no different from your actions. But just as I praised the temple after looking at it and through no invention of my own, so now too I have neither invented nor said anything unusual. But I have praised what I saw your conduct to be, and at that for the sake of the good omen,⁶⁰ so that nothing which ought to be present might be wanting in my speech. This is the extent of our, as it were, extemporaneous contribution to you for the national festival, and perhaps it is enough.

XXVIII. CONCERNING A REMARK IN PASSING[1]

(1) Some people are clever at admonishing others, while exempting themselves. And if they did this using a direct approach, it would be helpful. For one either would have been persuaded to their way of thinking or would have settled the matter by persuading them. But now by bringing in others to serve up their advice, they truly compel one to fight with shadows.[2] And yet their opening remarks are devilishly round about: 'How well I am disposed to him', 'That I am one of his friends', and so forth. It is more than enough to make one sick. (2) And recently someone using the same cover bade one of my friends to tell me that I improperly made a remark in passing in a speech in praise of the goddess.[3] 'For it was not reasonable for anyone to speak about himself and his own affairs, especially in the presence of those who were perfectly acquainted with them. But everyone was completely aware of the excellence of our speeches—for he added this—and that if anyone had achieved anything, we had achieved this'. He attempted to ingratiate himself in many such ways so that we might admit the charge. But come now, let us answer him, since even our "host of yesterday" has this privilege.[4]

(3) At what point should we begin to undertake his reeducation, a man so proud and of such advanced learning that he so easily undertakes even the admonition of others? In my eagerness I think that I shall treat what should be last first. I shall present him as a witness against himself, that he is a malicious slanderer. And let the man take the stand, whether he is here or not. For I do not know what his name is—I do not even know him at all![5] Let him answer, as if he were present. (4) The question is as follows: "My dear sir, you are generous in permitting the composition of speeches. But tell us this much: While permitting their composition, yet do you not grant to anyone to understand these very things which he is composing? And how charming that would be, a writer, but without understanding of his writing! Is it possible for one to have an understanding of things, but to have no thoughts on that which he understands? Indeed, this is a riddle, and perhaps would be more than a riddle. Do not the philosophers say that one must also speak about matters on which he has thoughts, unless even here you claim

something else? (5) Consider how by having granted the first single point, you have conceded the whole argument. For if, according to you yourself, the composition of speeches is a fair act, and it is impossible to compose anything well without understanding it, but certainly one must also have thoughts on that which he understands and also speak about that on which he has thoughts, then you have granted that one must also speak about his work". (6) "Yes, by Zeus, but the remarks were made before an audience well aware of the facts". Then what would you have done? Would you not have denounced me, if you had caught me lying, since you have accused me of improprieties in matters to which you say all men are my witnesses? And as it seems, if ever I take the role[6] of Demosthenes, Miltiades, Themistocles, or my namesake, then according to you I am a much better judge than you of what kind of speeches are suitable for each. Yet you are much better able to know the kind of speeches which it is suitable for me to write about myself and my own affairs? And how should I be using good sense if I granted that you know better? (7) Indeed, I must guess at their character, but, I think, I clearly know my own. And now whether I should speak about Athena herself, I should be a better judge than you according to your reasoning. But you are a better judge than I as to what should be said concerning my speech to Athena? And you say that others understand these matters, but do you not grant me this understanding? (8) And do you censure us, but shall I not have the right to censure those such as you, and at that to admonish you? And have you, although a member of the audience, taken the guise of an orator, but do you think that the orator should remain quiet in respect to his own affairs, and speak on behalf of others, but in his own behalf be silent? (9) Then what would you have done if after careful selection you had made a gift to us of that place "where is the richest plain in dear Calydon",[7] or of that 'about which the Chalcidians and Eretrians once disputed',[8] or of "the region between Corinth and Sicyon", as the oracle said,[9] when having attended only as an act of friendship itself and having had the finest enjoyment, since our work would be of the finest quality—unless this also offends you—, next you did not even grant us as payment as much as to pardon us even if we did make a foolish remark. (10) Do you not know that even if you should combine the Nomes of Egypt[10] and add the land of Babylon and give them to me as payment for this speech—for now I shall also

XXVIII. CONCERNING A REMARK IN PASSING   109

annoy you—, you will never come near to its worth? But what is in fact our proper fee? Friendship, goodwill, intelligence, memory, a moderate degree of honor shown towards the speech, and respect for its writer.

(11) Since you are afraid that my actions may seem to be close to willfulness or humbug, come let me reassure you. Listen and consider how I feel about these matters. And if you catch me lying, in the words of Sophocles,[11] "Say that I know nothing----", and strike out "in respect to divination". I believe that a man is not sound, whose pride exceeds his means[12] or who even postures to astound the masses whether in words or deeds; but that this man is that humbug, trickster, or whatever such term you wish. But whoever realizing the extent of his ability is proud to this degree and to that of his true worth, and neither seeks nor hunts for anything more, this man precisely fulfills the definition of freedom. (12) Just as in matters of money, we call him a humbug, a fool, and a man of unsound character, who, I think, cloaks himself in an ostentation beyond his resources, and wandering about creates a senseless flurry, and has made a point to deceive those who meet him, and again the man who thinks that he should appear more humble than his resources, and who voluntarily restricts himself, and is more ready to deny than admit his wealth, is certainly not described as liberal—and if you should call him stingy, greedy, and avaricious, you would be more correct—, such, I think, is the case with speeches and everything else, one might say, in nature. (13) Each claim is judged according to its true worth. And, it seems to me, "this is the truly simple, not the complex man",[13] who knows how to be either more or less proud of his actions, who praises his own and his neighbors' actions, if they please him, who also criticizes his own and his neighbors' actions, if he finds anything to blame in them, since he never prefers anything to that which seems to be true. (14) Consider the matter also in the following way—for perhaps you have not yet met me,[14] since you would have known how much in my own work I criticize. How do you think I feel about the parts which I cross out and change? I say that there is no greater inequality among mankind than for all men to be equally proud of their actions. But the divine inscription, "Know thyself",[15] seems to me clearly to give this order and command, to wit, not simply "Say that you are nothing", but "Neither exaggerate nor underrate your ability". The second inscription supports and

confirms that this is the intention of the first. For, I think, "Nothing in excess"[16] pertains to this subject. (15) Apollo, since he is a seer and a poet, and in both capacities an exponent of the truth, commands that real worth be honored. And if you are wise and not an enemy of the gods, you will consider it everywhere. How will you consider it? By means of all of one's abilities.[17] And you will not forever be dishonoring it, but you will always make use of these criteria in every case, and so you will make your decision by applying you judgment to the following question, 'What kind of man is each of us and what is his real worth'. (16) For the same claims have real worth for some and none for others. For example when Thersites says,[18] "Whomever I or another Achaean bound and led off", it is ridiculous, I think. "You bound? Will you not be satisfied if some other Achaean does not bind you? Will you not realize that your babbling will cost your back a beating?" But when Achilles, I think, tells his tale:[19] "With my ships I destroyed twelve cities of men, and on foot, I say, eleven in fertile Troy. And from all these I took much good treasure, and I brought and gave all of it to Agamemnon", none of the Achaeans will still be indignant. (17) Why? Because his words agree with his deeds. "I took twenty-three cities", he says. Well? Did he actually take them all himself? We cannot deny it. But he did not take some at sea, and others on foot, or so many of the one and so many of the other. The audience also knows that he did. Then everything is true. "I also was most zealous for the common good of all", he says. Until you prove that he was not most zealous, he is not talking nonsense. For these reasons the same man, Odysseus, whipped Thersites, but went as a supplicant to Achilles.[20] (18) Hear the nature and the number of the examples which have escaped you, so that you may know that pride in one's actions is in every way an old custom and a Greek one too, and that without this pride there would be accomplished among mankind neither a memorable deed nor a significant word, nor anything else. It is likely that I shall make remarks in some way similar to those of yesterday. For my answer more or less involves the same idea. (19) You remember all the things which Homer himself clearly said on his own behalf, while telling the tattletales to go hang,[21] so that I leave them out of consideration. Yet those verses more or less directly say that Homer votes himself to be the greatest poet. As far as you are concerned, Homer has been left out of consideration. But observe also the pride of Hesiod, if you have not noticed it before. (20) At the beginning of *The Theogony,* in his hymn to the Muses, he says right off,[22] "Who once taught Hesiod fair song". And he was such a wretched and brazen fellow that he did not even wait at least to complete the introduction for the goddesses. But while saying that the Muses "hymn Zeus"[23] and "Leto and Iapetus, and crooked-counseling Cronus",[24] he did not restrain himself, but almost in the midst of the names of the gods, he said, "Who once taught Hesiod fair song", as if, unless this would also seem to be an accomplishment of the Muses, having made Hesiod a poet as well as singing of the gods, they would lose a part of their glory. And he not only said that he received the art of "song" from them, but he also added that it was "fair." Yes, by Zeus, you would say, and without danger, since he assigned his work to the Muses. (21) Then did we not also assign to the Muses and the goddess those remarks which we were carried away into making? Indeed, we said, if you remember, that we had related directly from memory certain of the expressions which the goddess had revealed to us,[25] unless you object. Since you force the issue, learn how much better our behavior is than Hesiod's. For he inserted this verse, praise of himself, one might say, in the course of composing a hymn to the goddesses. But we made a small, extemporaneous remark in passing about ourselves after we had completely finished an uninterrupted speech to the goddess. (22) And Hesiod did not stop after he had simply said that he had received the art of song from the Muses nor after the earlier addition of how it was "fair". But he was such a humbug and so ambitious, that he said that he also received a scepter from them.[26] What does he mean by this? More than a lazy reader would think. Refer to Homer. What does he say about the scepter?[27] "Now the sons of the Achaeans who give judgment carry it in their hands". And I, says Hesiod, as far as concerns the Muses, am one of these. (23) What does he say in this excess of self-praise?[28] That "he plucked something marvelous", as if he had not taken an ordinary sprig, but that out of many scepters Hesiod had the most admirable one. And he did not even stop here in his wantonness. As if he were purposefully making you burst with anger, he added:[29] "And they inspired me with song". (24) And here he ended the verse, yet not all the praise. But again he also added "divine",[30] and what was better still, like those sophists who are everywhere extravagant, "so that I might make famous what will be and what was before".[31]

What does this mean? He said[32] that the Muses hymned "What will be and what was before", and that it was their nature to do so. And I, he says, hymn the same things as the Muses. If it seems best to you to strike out these verses of Hesiod, we shall also accept your censure. But you shall certainly first prove that you are the equal of the verses.[33]

(25) Come now let us return to the men whom they discuss.[34] Does not Homer seem to you to have described Achilles, as clear as man can, aside from other monologues, once in these lines?[35] "But I sit by the ships, a vain burden to the earth, although I am such as is no one of the bronze-clad Achaeans". (26) Yes, by Zeus, but Achilles is a hot-headed youth. Yet what does Odysseus, who is a middle-aged man, say, and at that to this very person?[36] "O Achilles, son of Peleus", if you think that you are superior in some other respect, I concede it. "But I would surpass you in intelligence". And he has also added, "much". For the construction is not such as it is made out by the incompetent elementary school teachers who ruin it. They separate "much" from what precedes and attribute it to what follows and what it precedes, because it is at the beginning of the verse. (27) But these people seem to me not at all to understand literature. For there is a sharp antithesis. Odysseus says in the former line,[37] "In arms you are superior and not a little better than I am". Next:[38] "But I would surpass you much in intelligence". See how the antithesis is arranged. "In arms" there, here becomes "in intelligence". In place of "not a little" was put "much", as if in varying the expressions he had spoken as follows: "You are much superior to me in warfare, but in these matters I am not a little superior to you". (28) I shall convince you still more forcibly, if you wish. For Homer does not at all use such additions in respect to age, at least as far as I can remember at present. But he often uses them for judgments of merit. For example what do I mean? In speaking of Zeus and Poseidon, he says,[39] "But Zeus was the older", and only this, and he does not add, "much". Yet it is clear that Zeus was "much" older, even though Homer has not added that word to this and other passages about him. For Homer is always singing of Zeus as "the father of men and gods".[40] Therefore how is Zeus not by far the oldest of all? In another place Homer says:[41] "But the hero Protesilaus was both older and braver". He says only so much, that he was "older". But how much "older", he does not say. But

XXVIII. CONCERNING A REMARK IN PASSING   113

whenever he makes a judgment, he adds "much", "by far", or some such expression:[42] "Again Ajax, son of Telamon, was by far the bravest of men while Achilles sulked in rage". Then in what way? "For he was much better". (29) This habit of his own he also transferred to Odysseus, in the belief that it was also proper for him to have said that I am much superior to you in intelligence. And, I think, Odysseus added this with confidence. For he knew that Achilles too did not pretend to that in which he lacked ability and that he was no humbug. For the verses which I just now cited,[43] in which Achilles spoke freely, consistently agreed with the remarks of Odysseus since Achilles also made this distinction when he said:[44] "But in council there are also others who are better". Since Odysseus was assured of his approval and was well aware that Achilles would not hear the truth with displeasure, but that it was the part of the same person to speak the truth and to be willing to hear it spoken, he said, 'In those respects you are much superior to me, and in these I am so much again superior to you.' (30) The following is better still. Nestor is no longer even a middle-aged man, but so very ancient and ripe that in his time,[45] "Two generations of mortal men had perished, who before were born and raised with him. But he ruled over the third". He will seem in your judgment to behave so childishly that there is nothing more talkative or willful than he. For after once having praised himself, he did not stop, but he is everywhere the same. (31) First of all in the course of reconciling the kings, he says[46] that he used to associate with men unlike those of the present time, but who were by far the best of all, through them praising himself, so that he did not even conceal his pride, but openly declared,[47] "And they understood my counsels and obeyed my words", being, he says, men of such quality. (32) Still more striking is the following:[48] "And with these I associated, having come from Pylus, far off from a distant land. For they themselves summoned me". Two additional points are made: that they were the ones who invited him and had need of him, and that he came from "far off from a distant land", as if he were so very famous and admired. (33) If you shall say that the verse,[49] "And I fought by myself" is prudent and moderate, I too agree, and I have never praised mad men. But the verses under discussion also reflect the same good sense, and somehow both are true and accord with my argument. For in a field in which Nestor was inferior to those men,[50] he said, "And I fought by myself". But in a field in which he was superior both to those men and to the men to whom he was talking, he says that he was judged best by those men and he thinks that these men should yield to him, and he is precisely of the same mind as Odysseus who says to Achilles that he is inferior to Achilles in warfare, but a better judge of what is necessary, just as Achilles also formerly agreed in regard to himself. It is nothing but a case where on this issue the three of them, the young man, the middle-aged man, and the old man appear to be of one mind, that one should be proud of oneself and speak in accordance with the real worth of one's abilities. (34) When the old man himself delivers an exhortation to the Achaeans to accept Hector's challenge, he talks of nothing but his own praise. Here he speaks as if he had been the best warrior, and he is in no way tolerable, beginning with:[51] "Would that I were so young as when they fought at the swift-flowing Celadon". Yet what follows is the limit of humbug. For it was not even enough for him to declare that he slew his opponent, but as if he were writing a hymn of victory for himself, he says:[52] "He was the greatest and mightiest man I slew; for he lay huge sprawling here and there". In the course of speaking he also makes it clear that he had slain many other great and noble men. (35) Yet, dear sir, take care that he may not purposelessly put on this humbug, but may intentionally speak to arouse the Achaeans. And the poet who has written all this attests that he hit the mark and made an impression upon them. For he adds this verse after Nestor's speech:[53] "Thus the old man abused them. But nine in all arose to meet the challenge". (36) And Nestor does not only behave in this way in his public discourses, but also in his private conversations he will appear to you to be a humbug.[54] When Patroclus had been sent to him by Achilles to inquire about whom he was leading out of battle, although Patroclus was in such a hurry that he did not even wish to rest through fear that Achilles might blame him, nonetheless Nestor intentionally ordered him to sit down and to listen to his speech. And again after more or less the same opening, when he had lamented and called upon his former youth, he recounted to the end a long story, whose other particulars are even difficult to remember, but the following is the most insolent of his verses and nothing at all like my own remarks, which I recently made in passing:[55] "But all offered prayers to Zeus among the gods and to Nestor among men". (37) I omit the sort of answer which our clever man even gave Agamemnon,[56] when the latter was busily reviewing the battle lines. But the following is the best of all. When Achilles was holding the funeral games for Patroclus and various men were winning victories in different events, Nestor himself was unable to enter any contest, but, as the saying goes,[57] "being no longer anything" in this respect because of old age, he talked about his former victories, as it were being active in this manner. And he said to the Achaeans, not in these very words, but dressing up his speech in a way, that as for each of you, one has won or will win in the foot race, and another perhaps in wrestling, and another in another sport. But[58] "in boxing I defeated Clytomedes, son of Oenops, and in wrestling Ancaeus of Pleuron, who met my challenge, and in the foot race I outdistanced Iphiclus, although he was a good man, and in spear throwing I surpassed Phyleus and Polydorus". 'To such an extent am I superior to the present victors, even if I have yielded to old age'. (38) Again if you wish, how much haughtiness is there in the Phocian boxer![59] "Let him come near, whoever will bear away the two-handled cup. But I say that no one will lead away the mule". "For so I declare, and it will be brought to pass. I shall tear his skin straight through, and I shall crush his bones. But let them be present who will care for him", he says, "to bear his body forth after he has been overcome by my hands". Did he make threats, but not carry them out? It was nothing but a case where he predicted what he was going to do. (39) I think, in his conduct he was not an insolent braggart, but somehow lived up to his claims. Indeed, as if in his defense, that he said these things to the others neither out of hatred nor hostile willfulness, but was only indicating what he knew to be true of himself, Homer says that he struck as he predicted, but that when he saw that the blow was severe, he was one of those who cared for Euryalus. Homer says:[60] "But great-hearted Epeus grasped him and raised him up with the hand" with which he had also knocked him down. (40) Odysseus among the Phaeacians also is not reserved in this respect. But in the course of the games of the Phaeacians, having become angered at the youth Euryalus, he omits no self-praise, saying with what charm the grace and beauty of oratory have surpassed physical beauty, whatever that is worth. Or does he not seem to you to say the following in respect to himself?[61] "But god crowns his form with words. In delight they gaze upon him. But he speaks with assurance and with a gracious reverence. He is much distinguished in their gatherings. They behold him as a god going through the city". Indeed, that his words pertain to himself is clear from a second remark to the opposite effect. For he says:[62] "So you have a very handsome appearance". For of the two qualities, the one he grants to him, the other to himself. (41) And he did not make these remarks out of willfulness, O you aid to learning and "great glory of the Achaeans",[63] nor purposelessly, surrendering himself to anger, but out of a desire to admonish that youth, who had been raised in luxury and had missed the truth by a great deal. And he helped him, as it seems. For the youth repented not long afterwards and called him "father"[64] instead of those earlier expressions, and was reconciled with him. (42) Again when Odysseus speaks about his prowess in athletic contests, he states directly, like Nestor in *The Iliad,* how superior he is, enumerating each particular:[65] "I am not entirely bad in as many as are the contests among men. I know well how to handle the polished bow, and shooting in the presence of a throng of the enemy, I should first hit my man, even if many comrades should stand nearby and should take aim at the men". "I[66] throw the spear as far as no other man shoots an arrow". (43) He said these things while the Phaeacians looked on, before even telling them what his name was. But when he was asked for this at the banquet, he said:[67] "I am Odysseus, son of Laertes, who through my guile am a care to all men, and my fame rises up to heaven". For he knew well that the Phaeacians would not show the same attention to what he had to say if they believed that he was one of the masses, as when they realized beforehand that now the best of the Greeks was talking to them. He was not shy in praising himself, since he was not even shy in helping others by his advice. (44) Thus self-pride is displayed by the poets themselves and by the men about whom they speak and whom they especially praise for their own part. But if someone should ask you whether you revile those who tell lies about themselves or those who tell about themselves at all, if you shall say the former, prove that we lied; but if you find fault with those who tell about themselves in any way at all, if ever one utters a syllable, consider how you will handle what follows. For what you would call shameful in a man, you could not deny is far from being proper for the gods. But what you would say is improper for any god, is hardly likely to be proper for the best of the gods. (45) Why then has Homer described Zeus as making so many remarks of this sort about himself, and frightening and terrifying the other gods as if they were small children? There is this verse in the assembly of the gods, when he threatens them in common:[68] "Next you shall know by how far I am the mightiest of all the gods", whoever disobeys his commands. And after this:[69] "But come, make trial of me, O gods, so that you all may know the truth of what I say. Hang a golden rope from heaven, and all you gods and goddesses, fasten yourselves to it. But you would not pull down Zeus, the highest counselor, from heaven to the plain, not even if you should toil much. But whenever I in my eagerness should wish to pull it up, I should pull it up along with the earth and the sea itself". "So[70] superior am I to gods and men". And he said these things in fact in the presence of the gods who knew them well. For not then for the first time did they learn that Zeus was superior to them. Who would easily single out all the other such remarks which he made offhand either to Hera in his anger or for any other reason? (46) And take care that you do not at this point become clever with me and with a laugh say, 'What great claim could Zeus not make?' For this is not what is disputed. But if no one, who excels in anything and to any extent, has the right to speak about himself and feel pride, but it is enough if there are people who realize the truth, then Zeus least of all has the right to speak about himself. For he is the mightiest of all, and all men know this, and in turn he himself realizes that all men know it. (47) Then choose the reason for which you are maliciously slandering me: because you claim that I have no right to make these statements, which one would make who knows more about himself than his audience does; or because you absolutely forbid any free speech at all. (48) Indeed, you would not say that such conduct brings shame to me, but is not shameful for Homer, who attributes it to Zeus. In all likelihood Zeus expounds to the gods what is true, so that he may keep the Universe safe, and so Homer has described this as proper conduct. And Apollo himself displays the same behavior in his oracles, and no longer are his words given through the medium of a poet, but as it has been ordained for him:[71] "I know the number of the sands and the measure of the sea, and I understand the mute, and I hear him who does not speak". For who has a greater duty to tell the truth about himself than he who declares and speaks the truth about all things? (49) Thus all men who are dear to the gods and who excel their fellows are not ashamed to speak the truth, but they believe that beggars are great liars out of poverty and because of their need have created this word, "humbug",[72] which you loathe, and that humbug is entirely opposite to the direction in which the truthful man proceeds. (50) It is not insult which is simply prohibited under the law, but slander. Just as in speaking to another an insult is not terrible but slander is, so if someone praises himself, he would not justly be blamed, so long as he does not tell lies. Thus the truthful man will neither slander another unjustly nor avoid praising himself when necessary.

(51) I think that even you have read Sappho, where boasting to some of those women who seem to be fortunate she says that the Muses have made her truly rich and enviable, and that even after her death she would not be forgotten.[73] And you also have read where the Laconian poet says in respect to himself and his chorus,[74] "Either the Muse or the shrill Siren cried out". (52) Yet did I make any such remark in passing about myself or my speech? Did I compare it with the songs of the Sirens? Or is it a more willful act to request comparison of a book with other books, or to have said that one's voice was like the voice of the Muses? (53) Add that, although the poet begged the Muse in the beginning, that he might be made active by her inspiration, he next, as if in ecstasy, says that the chorus by itself has made this song its source of inspiration. And if he said this without the encouragement of the Muse, my action has nothing in common with that with which he is charged, for I abdicated my claim to what was good in my speech in favor of the goddess. But if the Muse, having been invoked and now at hand, put these thoughts in his mind, the Muses, as it seems, also approve of their devotees speaking freely of such things. (54) In another place,[75] priding himself over the number of people among whom he is famous, he lists nations of such a number and nature that even now the wretched elementary school teachers are seeking in what place on earth they are located. But, as it seems, it is more to their advantage to go off on long journey than to concern themselves fruitlessly with "the Shadow-Feet".[76] Elsewhere he becomes so strongly inspired by god that you would say that in this case he is not "inspired"[77] in the meaning of the expression, but here forsooth speaks like a *deus ex machina*[78]: "Tell me this, O you tribes of mortal men". By the gods, what will you yourself claim to be?

(55) Come now, consider this too, if you are able:[79] "Those with acquired learning, turbulent in their garrulity, like crows, speak meaningless things against the divine bird of Zeus." Here does not

XXVIII. CONCERNING A REMARK IN PASSING 119

the poet, whoever he is, call the other poets crows, and himself an eagle compared to them? Does he not say that he is as superior to the other poets, as an eagle is to crows? (56) Again he wrote as follows against one of his audience when he had seen him nodding in sleep and unaware of whose recitation he attended:[80] "A tawny lion I lie behind the brazen foxes". For you certainly shall not say that under my persuasion Pindar inserted these things into his poetry. (57) Listen to some more:[81] "A golden foundation has been laid for sacred songs. Come now let us build as a wall a manifold, vocal adornment of words". Heracles! These things are not even faultless, but nonetheless he is also proud of them as if they were no less valuable than nectar, and he says that this adornment of words,[82] "will make Thebes, although it is famous already, still more famous throughout the ways of gods and men". As if it were not enough if it were famous only among mankind, but the gods also would more honor the city of Thebes in the future because of him. (58) Another passage is still more striking:[83] "By Olympian Zeus, I beseech you, O golden seer-famed Pytho, in company with the Graces and Aphrodite, to receive me in the holy time,[84] a reverend prophet of the Pierians". Do you see that even in the course of praying he did not restrain himself, but here too made proud boasts? Yet what would he have been like if he had achieved his prayers, who right at the beginning of his prayer is so proud of himself, when speaking of himself? (59) Although I could mention countless other men who were not even of much worth and were emboldened to be proud of themselves, I intentionally omit them in the fear that I may develop the opposite argument, that to praise oneself in this way is the act of bad men. But you certainly know of the moderation of Simonides. If you do not, still others know that this is one of his virtues, almost the best known in respect to his poetry and to his life itself. (60) This man too will seem to you to behave childishly, and as they say, "on the threshold of old age"[85] to taste the sweets of humbug. He dared to claim:[86] "I say that no one is the equal of Simonides in the strength of his memory". For certainly no other person says this about Simonides, but he has written it of himself. So that he might not seem to say this while he was still young and boyish, he adds:[87] "The eighty year old son of Leoprepes". As if he were clearly saying that I am proud of myself for this, and I proclaim it, being eighty years of age. Therefore I am not behaving childishly, but I have spoken the truth. (61) What is most important of all is that both Simonides and Pindar clearly will have written hymns of victory for themselves without concealment just as for anyone else. For the earth did not yet bear you, but free men still had the privilege of doing such things. (62) On these grounds you would also censure the athletes who receive hymns of victory from the poets. For in a certain way they praise themselves by calling upon the services of the poets and paying them, and finally when they have received the hymn of victory, by singing of themselves to the accompaniment of a flute and chorus. (63) As it seems, you would also accuse of humbug those who erect trophies. Indeed, it too can be said to them, 'Gentlemen, what more do you wish? It is enough to have been victorious.' But what does that additional clause[88] mean as far as you are concerned? "The Athenians from the spoils of the Thebans", or "from the Persians", or "the Lacedaemonians from the spoils of so-and-so?" Or whatever the inscription is, must it be erased? Then you shall also think that the following is a kind of humbug:[89] "The Athenians fighting for the Greeks at Marathon slew ninety thousand Medes". And:[90] "And all who died at Byzantium, men swift in war, saving a land rich in fish". And all those epigrams, which are fairer, I think, than your speeches. (64) And still more:[91] "From the time that the sea separated Europe from Asia, and fierce Ares harries the cities of men, no man on earth did a fairer deed at the same time on land and sea. For these having slain many in the land of Medes, captured at sea one hundred ships of the Phonecians, full of men; and Asia groaned loudly, smitten by them with both hands in the might of war". And earlier:[92] "The sons of the Athenians having subdued the nations of the Boeotians and Chalcidians", the epigram says, I think, and many other things as well. (65) Yes, by Zeus, but these are Attic epigrams and somewhat passionate. But it is clear to everyone that in our style of oratory we too belong to no other people. Yet examine the Dorian and the Lacedaemonian epigrams, if you wish:[93] "Here four thousand from the Peloponnesus once fought with three million". Then is this not much humbug and clear willfulness besides? Being four thousand in number, they say, we opposed three million of the enemy. (66) Again others say:[94] "We lie here, having saved with our lives all Greece from slavery when it stood at the razor's edge. But we bound many pains in the hearts of the Persians, memories of the harsh naval battle. Salamis holds our bones. But our country, Corinth, has erected this monument in return for our good deeds". Therefore it is time for you to mock these men as babbling corpses who do not know how to keep still. (67) And next some Simonidean man will answer you:[95] "Dear sir, though still alive, you are more dead than those beneath the ground". Come now examine this too:[96] "For the Muse does not give me in needy fashion to taste only what is at hand, but she goes on her way reaping everything". Does the poet not seem to you clearly to say this in praise of himself, as if he were fertile and productive in lyric verse? What then, when he says:[97] "Do not stop it, once the sweet-sounding many-stringed flute has begun its most charming songs?"

(68) Yes, by Zeus, but only poets had such pride. Then consider the orators too, whom alone you claim to admire, since you are by nature very like them. But first I wish to examine those who are between the poets and the orators. (69) "Here[98] is presented the inquiry of Herodotus of Halicarnassus, so that neither what mankind has done may vanish through time, nor the great and wonderful deeds, some done by the Greeks, others even by the barbarians, may be without renown". Well then, my dear Herodotus, do you think that it should rest with you and your writings, whether the memory of all the deeds of the Greeks and the barbarians is preserved or lost? I do, says Herodotus, unless you are quite asleep. (70) And it seems to me that Herodotus' action slightly irritated the other of the pair.[99] Not knowing what to do, he exaggerated the war. And since he wished to say, I think, that he was the most important historian, he gave his vote to his war. And the sum of his effort was as I say. But he approached the matter with great cunning and disparaged the wars which you would think are more important. This meant nothing other than that he was showing to Herodotus, the Hellanicuses and the Hecataeuses[100] and all this group that first of all I am superior to you in judgment. I selected what was best and wrote about it. But most of your material was childishness. (71) You would also find that there is pride in Thucydides throughout his whole history. First of all for the most part his speakers share in this characteristic both when they speak as cities and as individuals. Who does not know the character of his Pericles, if you have even heard of the name of Pericles? He does not make remarks in passing in a small gathering and thus with complete freedom, which you recently deprived us of. But when he himself together with all the people had become involved in such

circumstances, in which you would have advised him to make a supplicating petition, when the land was being destroyed by war, when those in the city were perishing through the plague, when all attacked him and were angry at him as if he alone were the cause of their troubles, then he came forward and spoke somewhat as follows:[101] 'I expected these things, O men of Athens, and you do wrong in that you are angry. For I am,' he says, 'in every way the best man among you', as if he were some Homeric Zeus.[102] (72) And one would be less amazed at his other arguments. But, O Zeus and you other gods! That a man who was an orator and a general, who was speaking in the assembly and was suspected by the people, perhaps even for this oratorical ability, did not guard against this or conceal it as inimical to him! That when he ought to have made excuses and said what any other man would have, 'And do not think, O men of Athens, that by means of my oratorical ability either at the start I persuaded you or now think that you should be confident about the present circumstances—,' instead of such subtlety and concealment, he said that along with his other accomplishments he was superior in this respect, because he was also the best speaker among them, and that right at the beginning of his speech! For I seem more or less to remember his words. Was this your work, Thucydides, or was it Pericles'? (73) Again another speaks through the same poet:[103] "And it is proper for me to hold office, O men of Athens. For I must begin at this point since I was attacked", he says—and we might add, 'by no one like you but'—"by Nicias". Indeed, I do not think that he would have endured, even under compulsion, to have mentioned your name. (74) Does not Hermocrates speaking in Syracuse seem to you to be a thorough braggart? He says in praise of himself and the Syracusans:[104] "Show the Athenians that men here are not from Ionia or the Hellespont", when he orders them,[105] "to meet the invaders" outside of Sicily. And these remarks are rather moderate. But consider this extravagance:[106] "To attack the enemy not only with pride, but also with proud scorn". But you have deprived him of the expression "with pride". And he thinks that they should proudly scorn danger, but you think that there should be no pride at all, beginning with yourself, as it seems to me.

(75) Come now, learn of "the artistry" of another man, like that of "the Trojan Horse".[107] For I think that, if you have read nothing else of the works of Demosthenes, at any rate you have read

XXVIII. CONCERNING A REMARK IN PASSING 123

this famous speech on behalf of the proclamation of the crown. We find here in Demosthenes, whose name alone you admire, as it seems:[108] "I have been persuaded concerning myself—perhaps I am unperceptive—, but still I have been persuaded—" do you see how he provokes you by twice saying "I have been persuaded"—"that no one who draws up decrees would draw up a better one than I"—but I remarked in passing only about what I had written and what I was presenting at the moment, and at that because I was confident in the revelation of the gods.[109] But he adds—"and that no one who serves in the government or acts as ambassador would serve and act more zealously and justly. For this reason I involved myself in all affairs". (76) When Philip's letter has been read, he says:[110] "Philip was driven to these straits"—by whom? Not by the Athenian people but—"by my policy, Aeschines. Philip himself said this, although formerly he had hurled many bold speeches at the city". It goes somehow in this way, for I do not remember the words exactly. (77) But the following, at the end of the speech, is still more striking than this and somehow of a Periclean cast:[111] "If there had been one man in each of the Greek cities of the sort that I was among you in the position which I took, or rather if Thessaly had only one man who held the same views as I did and Arcadia had only one, none of the Greeks, either without Thermopylae or within, would have experienced the present troubles, but all would have been free and autonomous and would have lived in their countries with complete security, safety, and felicity, full of gratitude to you and the other Athenians through my efforts for these many benefits". (78) And perhaps then some people were annoyed when Demosthenes said this, small and ill-starred men, and they called him a humbug. Yet the future showed that nothing was exaggerated in the speech, but that the birth of one such man was a sufficient crop even for the whole of Greece. Therefore there is no dispute with him over preeminence, not even among those to whom he spoke extolling himself. Why then do you believe that it is enough for me if my speech is made without any sense of pride? (79) And answer me this by the gods. If you had been born at the same time as he, then would you have also criticized this in Demosthenes, or would you have exonerated him? For if you had also blamed him for this, then you are far gone as a malicious slanderer. But if you had exonerated him, then you are slandering me for the same thing. But I think that the epigram which we now read in the Ceramicus is not far from the way which Demosthenes felt.[112]

(80) I have done enough, now that I have mentioned the orators. For you would assign us too to this part of the chorus.[113] However for the sake of the truth, I wish to make my argument complete in every respect, so that even you may realize that what sort of man you are to admonish me, when the proverb says, "Herd your own goats". (81) Consider also another defense, that of a philosopher, who was so far from boasting that he even went around refuting the sophists for their vain confidence.[114] He speaks menacingly to the Athenians, that 'if they kill him, they will not find another like him'.[115] And 'he refers his claim to a trustworthy witness, the god in Delphi'.[116] And he says:[117] "I think that you have had no greater good in this city than my service to the god". (82) Some such things are in *The Apology* of Socrates. And he was also convicted for this reason, you would say. And those who condemned him repented, their descendants would say. Yes, by Zeus, but Socrates himself did not make this speech. Granted. But if he did not make it at all, and another of equal status made these remarks as being appropriate to him, it amounts to the same thing. (83) I say that Socrates was boastful throughout his life, even if this has escaped many people. Or what do you think his great irony is? I believe that he spoke to people as if they were children, actually mocking them and behaving toward them as if they were simpletons. When he did not really admire those whom he claimed to admire, nor again thought that he himself was really worthless, but still clearly uses these expressions, is anything left other than that he thought that other people were worthless compared to himself? One would say that such is the case.

(84) And I leave out Socrates, if you wish. But consider Iphicrates, a man not between an orator and a general, but one who had succeeded in both fields. Then have you ever gone through his *Defense of the Bribe*?[118] Yet if you wish, regard the speech as the work of Lysias.[119] Or regard it as that of Iphicrates, if you prefer. There is nothing so apparent in the whole argument as his pride, which in fact makes the speech superior to most of Lysias. (85) Among other remarks to the Athenians alien to your spirit, he says:[120] "If you had seven generals such as I, Lacedaemon would be uninhabited". And mentioning Harmodius and Aristogeiton,[121] whom the Athenians regarded as the first of all their benefactors, he

says[122] that if he had lived in their times, "he would have made them his associates or would have been invited by them to participate in their deed". And he says:[123] "You think, O men of Athens, that these decrees and this monument which you have bestowed upon me is something noble. But there has been erected for me a monument in the Peloponnesus which reaches to heaven and bears witness to my virtue". He is so uninhibited in his speech that[124] he compares himself with both the generals of his fellow citizens and the enemy. Yet, by the gods, if Iphicrates then when he was about to make his defense, had sat you by his side as his adviser, would you have advised him to make this kind of defense or to fall upon his knees and supplicate the judges? (86) In his defense about the bribe, he clearly speaks rather freely. But when his life was placed in danger by the prosecution of Aristophon, did he change? But even there he maintained his character. For when he asked Aristophon, as they say,[125] "if you were in charge of the fleet would you have betrayed it or not", and after Aristophon denied this he said: "You would not have betrayed it, although you are Aristophon, but Iphicrates betrayed it?" (87) When I have mentioned one more remark of his, I shall turn to another point. For it is said[126] that when he was deploying his forces in Egypt, and the battle was about to take place, he said to those present, that he was satisfied with everything else, but that the most important thing was missing. When someone asked him what he meant, "that", he said, "the enemy do not know the name of Iphicrates", which he said served him as the greatest antidote against the dangers in Greece. (88) I also hear that Epaminondas' *Defense* to the Thebans is even beyond that of Iphicrates.[127] And why should one be amazed at this? But recently a comrade—so he sits very near me as an incubant[128]—taught me the following epigram of a painter:[129] "Even if unbelievable things are heard, I make the following declaration. I say that what are clearly the boundaries of this art have been discovered by our hand. An unsurpassable limit has been set. Yet nothing has come into being for mortals which is blameless". By Zeus, did you think that some artist should exaggerate so much about himself and speak with such freedom, when it even accorded with his art "to accomplish his work in silence"?[130] Yet it appeared remarkable and terrible to you for a man numbered among few men—for at present I say nothing else about my speeches—even to make a little remark in passing? (89) Listen to the epigram of another painter, a humbug, as you would say, but no more proud than he should be, as professional critics indicate. What does he say? "Heraclea[131] is my country. Zeuxis my name. If any man says that he has reached the limits of our art, when he has proved it, let him take first place". "But I think", he says, "that we are not second". And neither did that man reject this epigram as being bold nor did any of his companions advise him to erase it when he had written it. (90) "But once more such a deed he did and he dared",[132] that wanton, to inscribe the following. When he had completed the picture of Helen, he inscribed in addition upon it these verses of Homer:[133] "No blame comes to the Trojans and the well-greaved Achaeans for having long suffered woes for such a woman". As if it were the same thing for him to have made a painting of Helen and for Zeus to have begot Helen herself.

(91) And for your sake, I dismiss the painters. But I have read a passage where some comic poet uses wonderfully solemn phrases. Yet if someone asked the comic poets, of what they are so very proud, they would say, I think, because they arouse laughter, as one of them even admitted, although no one asked him.[134] But still they also demand that a distinction be made between the jokes of urbane men and those of the masses. (92) And one of them,[135] boasting at the beginning of his play, like a prophet, makes this proclamation: "Every spectator must awake, wiping from his lids the drivel of ephemeral poets". As if on that day he were going to make all of them wise and serious. But when he produced *The Chirons*, again he added scornfully at the end:[136] "We scarcely finished this in two years". But he says that, "he challenges all the other poets to imitate it in a life time", clearly because no one would succeed in doing so. (93) Another one of them says,[137] "With the wrath of Heracles, he attacks the greatest men". And again further on, he adds an expression consistent with this:[138] "Having found such a protecting purifier of this land". Then is it not terrible, O earth and gods, for Aristophanes to attempt to compare his jokes to the deeds of Heracles, while in your judgment for the poets of serious works, as even Aristophanes himself would grant, it seems to be a criminal act to claim the right of comparing their own writings with their own writings? (94) And Aristophanes, in praise of one of his comedies, elsewhere says:[139] "He makes many libations one after another and swears by Dionysus that no one has ever heard better comic verses than these". But you did not even permit me to praise

without an oath, and only extemporaneously at that, my speech which was written for the goddess and with the aid of the goddess. (95) And I omit mention of the others. But so that you may catch yourself right in the act of being a criminal, a slanderer, and a busybody, consider who it was who so praised his speech that right in it he spoke about himself, like a comic poet discussing his play. On the one hand, in the beginning, in the introduction,[140] he promises that he will speak worthily of "the subject and the time spent by him on the speech", and further adds worthily of "all of his life". And on the other hand, at the end,[141] he challenges, as it were, everyone to compete with him and vie with him, as if no one would even come near his ability. (96) Yet what shall you say? Did he have more right to be proud of his work? Or did he have the privilege of being prouder than he ought to have been, but I not even as much as I deserve? And did he have the privilege to write down in his very speech what he thought about it, but I not even only to make a remark in passing outside the speech? (97) And one would see that the directors of contests and the spectators permit the comic and tragic poets and the relatives of these contestants[142] to step forward to discuss themselves a little.[143] And often they remove their masks in the middle of the art form which they are playing and make proud speeches. But you have not even allowed us to share in this much respite, although you are a nobody and ought to be satisfied even if you were present at the proceedings in the capacity of a slave.

(98) What shall you say, by the gods, if someone should ask your opinion? 'By Zeus, these practices are annoying and vulgar.' If the people find them so, why are they not annoyed? But if you find them so, why do you take refuge with the people? For these people appear more or less to be one man, and a jealous man at that, but if he is not, then certainly a man without taste. (99) Indeed, if you yourself praised the speech, then what was said satisfied you. Certainly you did not think that you should share in the enjoyment of my work, while you regarded it as your misfortune to see that I was also pleased? But if the beauty of the speech escaped you, we said these things with good reason. (100) In what way did you feel about the actual remarks which I made in passing? If you were also annoyed by them, they were made for this purpose, so that you might be troubled. For you certainly shall not regard it as a loss when I am pleased with my own work, while I shall not regard it as

a gain if ever you are pained on this account? But if you accepted what was said, how do you now find fault with that with which you then agreed? Or which verdict do you denounce whenever you are so disposed? Either way you no less clearly denounce yourself. (101) Such remarks, it will be found, are judged not simply on the basis of the men who made them and their true worth, but also with a view to the occasions when they were made as well as to whatever the cause might be. For example if someone chooses such statements out of pride and scorn, or because he is intentionally dishonoring the general populace and regards them as worthless, or as I just now said,[144] because of some "slave", such as those men whom I have seen, with raised eyebrows walking about as if they were the owners of those who meet them and artificially forming their life style in such a way that they immediately astound those who come in contact with them, such men, I think, it is just to rebuke and to believe that they are the offspring of the Gorgon's head[145] and have not made the best use of the oratory which they exhibit. (102) But as for the man who has preferred the rest of his life to be so moderate and ordinary, that he is especially recognized from this very characteristic and that this is a token of him—unless even now unawares I spoke boastfully and must excuse myself—, yet who whenever god moves him, then says something about himself, whatever it is, and who spoke during the contest and at a time when it was reasonable for him to mention nothing beside oratory, and then stopped, why should anyone criticize such behavior in this man? But tell me, by Zeus, had you so very little to do that you dismissed that dream[146] and picked up, as birds will, small, worthless bits, so that you might depart with material to slander, as if you had made some lucky find? (103) Then say that I too acted out of generosity, so that you might not be entirely disheartened, but might have a reason to wish to live. For you had an oracle from the Pythian, as it seems, that you are doomed whenever you praise everything. Therefore you owe me a reward. And if you find fault with this, you do so with justice. Or do you also carefully examine the Pythia herself and the expounders of the oracles and peer at their postures and expressions, whenever they speak spontaneously? And if they will seem to speak too boldly to you, do you later criticize them, O wretched man, far from the gods? All such conduct is suited to the occasion. (104) I shall remind you also of Xenophon,[147] who in speaking about Cyrus the

XXVIII. CONCERNING A REMARK IN PASSING 129

Great remarks that at all other times he was composed, orderly, and very least a humbug, yet whenever he engaged in battle and became somewhat heated, his speech was not mild nor was he reserved, but he extolled both himself and his soldiers. With good reason. For, dear sir, if ever you have removed the goad from one's soul, you have taken away his means of courage. (105) And examine me too in this way, and add a still more important fact. If I was not about to contend at a future time, but if I had already entered the contest, if because of an actual need, if under the power of the god, if while my speech seethed in passion, if when first I was inspired and next stirred the people with the same goad, then I made these remarks in passing as an admonition and as a means of assisting the whole audience, as to what we approve in our *Introductory Hymns*[148] and where we say their deficiencies lie, if you find the circumstances present which I mention, have the courage to say:[149] "Not without the presence of a god does he rage in this way", but Athena is at hand, to whom is consecrated the noblest part of moderation. (106) You have read that passage of Homer where he speaks about contestants:[150] "But he raged as when spear-shaking Ares, or destructive fire rages on the mountains, in the thickets of the deep forest. And there was foam about his lips". And you know the rest,—so that I may even oblige you.[151] 'Yes, by Zeus, but this man was a barbarian[152] and unable to control himself.' (107) But what are we to say of that other man, the most handsome of the Achaeans? Will you not remember how Homer again arms him after the renunciation of the wrath?[153] "But in their midst divine Achilles armed himself. And there was a gnashing of his teeth. His eyes shone like the gleam of fire. But unbearable grief entered his heart. Raging at the Trojans, he donned the gifts of the god". Do you see that he has attributed all these things at the same time to that man, the gnashing of the teeth, the fire in the eyes, the anger against the enemy, the grief over his misfortune, the adornment of himself before his fellow soldiers? (108) The dancers of Enyo and Enyalius[154] stand in this fashion, unable to keep their passions steady, and still much less keeping their hands steady. But their lips and every part of their body are moved in a strange way, and they are possessed by a certain wonderful mixture of grief, anger, desire, and reason. And if ever they speak, they say some such things in the course of their work:[155] "Come closer" and:[156] "The sons of wretched men confront my might". (109) But as for the dancers of

Hermes and the Muses, in whose hands Zeus, the king of the gods, ordained that there be the beauty and the daring of winged words, shall you think that they should display their accomplishments with their eyes lowered to the earth like the Erembi,[157] differing in no way from pack asses, half awake and half asleep? Or shall you think that they should appear no less dull than those possessed by the Corybants[158] or by some other hot tempered spirit, but rather that their movements should be in keeping with their song? (110) You do not find fault with the helmet and the shield of Diomedes which emitted fire, as Homer says,[159] but you even express admiration for them and make that a token of their greatness. Yet do you not share your compassionate understanding with those from whose very head the goddess[160] emits fire? And what battle shall you claim is proceeded by so much heat as proceeds true and living oratory? Perhaps, as Darius said,[161] "fire has ordered the whole Universe", an expression not more proper to a king than to a philosopher. But this is the one fount of oratory, the truly sacred and divine fire from the hearth of Zeus, under whose influence the initiate, brought before the public, can have, in fact, no rest. (111) Then you demand that he should watch you and your expressions, as if he were a child, fearful that he might utter a syllable which will displease you. You are placing limits not on a torrent, but on the river Nile, and at that a river which has proportion along with its magnitude.[162] Do you not realize that that man has fashioned creations which move by themselves like the implements of Hephaestus?[163] I think that somewhere[164] even the arrows of Apollo gave out a sound on their own initiative, when they had joined in his anger. (112) So[165] too in contests involving speeches inspired by the gods, many such parts of the speeches, which have a rhythm of their own, are, as it were, carried off course, and then the speech sounds in a way which is inevitable and consistent with its rapid course, like a missile carried along with a whizzing noise. (113) I am afraid that I am talking to one who is deaf. And in a certain way I am betraying the mystery by revealing the sacred rites to one who is uninitiated.[166] But still like a kind of secret tale in a religious myth, it will be told to those who can understand it, but no more to you. (114) I say that whenever the light of god has come over the speaker and in the words of the proverb, "there is lightning through the Chariot",[167] such chariots as those which the poets have given to the Muses,[168] and it has possessed his soul like a

XXVIII. CONCERNING A REMARK IN PASSING

drink which has come from the springs of Apollo, then straightway it fills him with strength and warmth and good spirits, and lifts up his eyes and causes his hair to rise;[169] and a man in such a state—call him dancer or bacchant as you wish—looks to no other thing, either present or absent, than to the words themselves and to their stewards, like people who look toward those who offer anything else to them, especially whenever it is thrust forth from above. (115) "And he has emitted", it is said,[170] "a certain word which unspoken" was unbearable—for the right moment bears many things which someone not privy to such contests would not imagine. And it is impossible, if one has relaxed his mind and paid attention to the audience, to preserve the stimulus proper to his speech. But the heat, like some drug, alone escorts and guides the speech as if it were a ship, and it has no room for that which is contrary to it. Whenever it leaves, the words ebb away and a numbing chill prevails, and it is necessary that such an orator plunge downwards, grown cold through dullness, like an eagle lowering its wings.

(116) I can also tell you a kind of sacred tale, which I heard at night not long ago from one of the gods,[171] concerning the nature of divine madness. The tale was somehow as follows:[172] "It is necessary", he said, "for your mind to be moved first of all away from the common and ordinary, but when it has been moved and has become scornful, for it to associate with god and to excel. And neither", said my teacher, "is remarkable. For he excels who has scorned the general populace and has conversed with god". (117) Here are your notes of "the sacred night", as the poets call it,[173] which have come through "the horn",[174] but are truly more radiant than any ivory. Therefore even if we could name no one in any genre who was proud of himself, and such an experience was unnecessary in oratory, but god now led us to this madness, we would not count this privilege as our misfortune. You are criticizing that which is the token of the orator. (118) Or by the gods, shall the best audience be not the one which is very sedate, but that which knows how to be moved and which directly confronts what is said, while the best orator is not he who is the warmest and first understands his powers, but he who is the servant of his audience and needs to learn from them the nature and quality of his speech? (119) Consider also this. I claim that it often becomes necessary for the completely ingenuous and generous man to make remarks in

passing on account of his speech itself, but that if he does not, it is necessary that certain features, which are too good to go unrecognized, escape the notice of the people. What do I mean? There are kinds of beauty in oratory, and just as in poetry, there are also certain styles, some of which are far separated, others closely related to one another; and it is not easy to acquire all of them, but each writer has taken for himself one style and become distinguished for this. But if you wish, except Homer, best of poets, from the discussion. (120) Whenever someone attempts to proceed through all these kinds of beauty and to use all the oratorical mixtures, and first of all to present a character suitable to the occasion, and next to preserve a balance: where there is need of precision, here adding charm, and where there is need of elaboration, here adding brevity, and adding clarity to redundance, and grace where there is gravity, and where there is the use of imagination, here adding that of arrangement, and where there is boldness, here adding caution, and to top it all, an easy and fluent delivery—and permit me to understand these matters better than you and your like—, at this point the whole audience grows dizzy and does not know what to do, but as if they were encircled in a battle line, they are bewildered, and each offers praise according to his natural endowments or faculties, one for the precision in the vocabulary, and another for the charming delicacy of the thought. But the orator bursts with anger for this reason. (121) What do you say? You do not see the contest, not even in the smallest degree. But, as they say, "although I play each flute separately" and at the same time use all the harmonies, you sit gazing at the movement of one of my fingers, as if when every technique was being displayed at the same time on a lyre or a harp, you would seem to hear only the sound of a single chord. (122) The orator teaches you for no other reason, but because he preserves a divine trace in himself and takes thought for you and others, but most especially for the nature of oratory so that its seed may be understood and preserved as far as possible. This is the reason, O you who understand my affairs, but are ignorant of your own, which lately moved me. (123) You change the law and reverse the order which nature has ordained not only for mankind, but also for the other animals. This is to obey one's superior. And you believe that the motion of the eagle can be the same as that of the daw, although even when it is still approaching from afar off its valor is clear to those who can see and hear it as it splits the air, as

XXVIII. CONCERNING A REMARK IN PASSING 133

when sailors split the sea with their oars.[175] (124) You demand the swiftness of a stallion and the appearance of an ass's head, circumstances which are not compatible. You have not read the following verses:[176] "His mane flies about his shoulders. Confident in his beauty his legs bear him swiftly to the haunts and pasture of the horses". But for an ass it is a sufficient cause for exaltation to be free of the burden which as his daily chore he carries about for his master while gathering more blows than he takes steps. (125) But I have been digressing, carried along by my speech as by a river's current. I shall return to the matter at hand, that you think that you should change the law of nature, which commands us to endure the excesses of the stronger and to live in accordance with our leaders. (126) It is shameful for a general to look to his soldiers, but a good thing for armies to look to their generals, just as, I think, it is a good thing for dancers to look to their leader, for sailors to their helmsman, for the people to their ruler, and for the audience to the orator.[177] If you have changed yourself from a member of the audience into a kind of orator for us, it is time for you to take over the lecture platform. But if being a small-minded man you take up some trivial criticism and spend your time on this, I have nothing nice to say to you. However, I wish to examine more thoroughly the reason for my action, which I mentioned a little before,[178] since even you would agree that most actions are adjudged on the basis of their reason.

(127) If I behaved in this proud fashion for this purpose, so that I might lure away young boys or trick their unlucky fathers and encourage them to pay me fees,[179] and if I did not only behave in this way recently, but if at any and all times, in thrall to some such desire, I have said or done anything, either small or great, then take me and do what you wish. I make no excuse. But if I was so disposed as the nature of the speech affected[180] me and led me on, and I heard my words as if they were another's, or rather on this account was wholly at a disadvantage and kept myself in check, since I was unable to revel in and enjoy my pleasure freely, as I should not have been ashamed to leap in the air if it had been another's book, why do you omit to show your admiration for my self-control, but rather find fault with a behavior which has nothing to do with me? (128) I shall go still further. Let none of this have been mentioned. Can you say, by the gods, that I did this without any need, but that I indulged in these fripperies without a real purpose according to

the custom and pomposity of the sophist and for the sake of mere show? Do not all men know how far I am from this? Is not our practice entirely otherwise? Do you all not see that my speeches have attained, as far as possible, to the utmost honesty? Do you all not see that all my intentions concerning them have done the same? What motions of the hands or grimace of the lips have I been accustomed to use intentionally beyond the limits of moderation? (129) What mournful form of dress, like those speakers who have ere now covered their heads with their clothes? Perhaps it was their estimate of their true worth.[181] But it is not my estimate of mine. Yet although I need more protection than most men require, still I avoided this cover.[182] But did I ever engage in any other kind of artificial behavior? Do I do a double dance like certain others?[183] Have I aught to do with any alien wickedness? Have I so much leisure? But I am satisfied if ever I can get through my delivery of the actual speech and what necessarily pertains to it, and I do not add imported trouble for myself. (130) I made these remarks when I had been fired by my speech. Therefore if one must abstain as much as possible from such drivel, as you say, while such behavior arises from the rapid course of the speech,[184] what use is there in impossible advice? As if when someone at sea was snatched away by the wind, you should tell him to remain calm and firm, saying to him from the beach: "Do you see, I sit quietly". And you seem to me, in the words of the proverb, "to blame the behavior of the man who has been bitten by a viper",[185] although you yourself have never been bitten. "Philoctetes, the son of Poeas",[186] would not have put up with listening to this from you. (131) But perhaps you thought that I was one of these sophists who are rightly admonished by tattletales[187]—indeed I once saw a sophist in the middle of speaking led aside by a tattletale; so the tattletale thought that he was a better judge of both what that man ought to say and for how long, and the sophist himself agreed. But do not mix everything up together, so that you may not also make yourself ridiculous. (132) Even when we were physically stricken, we did not come to ignoble supplication of the doctors.[188] But although, to speak by the grace of the gods, we possessed the friendship of the finest doctors, we took refuge in the temple of Asclepius,[189] in the belief that if it was fated for us to be saved, it was better to be saved through his agency, and that if it was not possible, it was time to die. (133) My fellow pilgrims[190] could also speak about my

XXVIII. CONCERNING A REMARK IN PASSING 135

nature. When I was a boy if my teacher[191] asked a question about something which I knew, and if another answered first, I would no longer speak, so that I might not seem to repeat the other person's answer. The situation now in the temple of Asclepius in similar. For the truth will be told to you all. Each can think the better or worse of it, as he chooses. For again toward my fellow pilgrims there, my behavior was and is such that I am annoyed at whoever does not make way for me, but I should be ashamed not to give up the place to one who had made way. (134) If you come here to govern us, persuade these people that this office is more proper to you than to us. But if you concede the rule to another, remember these verses of Homer:[192] "Comrade, sit you in silence and obey my speech", and :[193] "So let it be, O great-hearted Trojans, as I say", and:[194] "But Patroclus alone sat opposite him in silence". Do not act the general in the presence of the general. For this is shameful for both you and the general.

(135) When I have added some small points, I shall conclude. And I have intentionally drawn out these arguments, not because even any one of them is not sufficient, but so that you might know the number of refutations which convict you as a fool and that although there are many things which you have neither seen nor heard, yet you have entered on this discussion, like a man in every way profane.[195] Then although you are an initiate, do you presume to examine the initiating priest? And the newly inducted initiate is of a lower standing than the old initiate. But do you who now for the first time join the ranks of the initiates, presume to judge the initiates' teacher? (136) You seem to me to repeat the old story about Momus and Aphrodite. For they say that while she was sitting fully adorned, Momus was bursting because he could find nothing to criticize. But finally he left her alone and made fun of her slipper, so that it came to pass that neither was Aphrodite slandered nor spoke Momus a word of praise. And although you expressed admiration for the stage, you criticized the scenery at the sides; and neglecting my speech, you carefully observed my remarks in passing. So far are you from what is lawful. (137) Now listen to what Solon has to say, so that you may know that even he, the most famous of the lawgivers, made remarks in passing. Yet he has so far surpassed me in daring and willfulness—for these words fit him according to your charge—that while I driveled outside the text of my book, and at that when I was carried away by the speech, Solon in-

tentionally has written his book about himself and his government, as we wrote about Athena. And in it among other things is the following:[196] "For what I said, with the help of the gods I accomplished, and I did other things not in vain". (138) Do you see how willfully he speaks and not in accord with your advice? And these verses are in *The Tetrameters*. But the following are in *The Iambics*[197]: "In the justice of time, black Earth, the mother most great of the Olympian gods, would bear witness that these acts were best. Her boundary stones, fixed in many places, I removed. Formerly she was a slave, now she is free. I brought back to Athens, their country founded by the gods, many who had been sold, some unjustly, others justly, and some who were in exile through debts contracted by necessity, no longer speaking the Attic tongue, as it would be with those wandering about in many places. But those here who endured an unseemly slavery in fear of the ways of their masters, I made free men. I did these things forcefully by bringing into harmony force and justice, and I concluded them as I promised. I wrote codes equally for the bad and the good, applying a straight forward justice for each man. But if another had taken the goad, as I have done, an evil minded and greedy man, he would not have restrained the people". (139) Assume that Solon also speaks on our behalf. 'But if another had introduced this goad into his speech, he would not have introduced so much moderation.' But you shall refute me whenever you yourself possess the same power of oratory—but, I think, this will not be very easy for you—and then appear to exercize a greater control over your pride in yourself. But if you are a beggar and without means for daily nourishment and with your ambition fixed on two or three obols, and then you criticize the king who wrote:[198] "Nor let the expenditure of gold and silver be an obstacle", on the grounds that these remarks are only scornful and bombastic words, you shall be equally deficient in money and brains. (140) What does Solon say next:[199] "For if I had wished to do what then was pleasing to the opposite faction, and again what their opponents planned, this city would have been widowed of many men. Therefore I displayed valor on every side, and I turned like a wolf among a pack of dogs". Do you see that even Solon shows off and is prouder of himself than suits you? (141) He believed, I think, that this laudation which he wrote for himself was of use to other men as an example. For this reason "he who keeps his hand within his cloak"[200] raises up his

XXVIII. CONCERNING A REMARK IN PASSING

voice and praises his own achievements justly. For he thought, I believe, that he should keep his hand within his cloak, but not his head bowed down. (142) Come now, let me comfort you also through another of the most famous writers, since you are more cowardly than you should be, not to mention more brazen. What this man has said exceeds Solon's remarks. Consider:[201] "No one of the poets here has yet worthily hymned or will hymn the region above the heavens. But the situation is as follows". Did you notice how he puffed up all the envious by writing freely about his nature and as it was reasonable for one who is confirming the argument at hand to do, to wit, how the inspiration of the gods causes one to scorn the general populace? Or do these remarks seem to you to be the same as common vulgarities? (143) When he has concluded his speech about love, what praise of himself did he later leave out, or was there any fair compliment which he did not bestow upon himself? First of all he said that he had correctly investigated the truth,[202] 'by knowing how to compose certain arguments and how to divide others properly.' Next[203] that 'he had arranged his speech in an orderly fashion.' But most important of all, he is proud of its magnificent style, so that he even directly attacked his opponent[204] and said—unless you are so very much a child that you believe that these are the words of Phaedrus and that Plato does not speak in the person of Phaedrus:[205] "I have long been admiring your speech, how much better you have made it than the former one, so that I fear that Lysias may appear to me to have a mean style if he ever wishes to produce another speech to compete with this one". (144) Again what shall you say of the following remarks?[206] "Alas, according to you how much more technically skilled in oratory are the Nymphs, the daughters of the Achelous, and Pan, the son of Hermes, than Lysias, the son of Cephalus!" Does it not seem to you that that man has made these remarks, which are full of praise, in regard to himself, unless indeed "you have the ears of Midas", whose epigram he made fun of,[207] when he likened it to "the speech of Phaedrus' comrade"? And these remarks about himself are of necessity in keeping with all the virtues.[208] (145) For, I think, it is the part of an intelligent and moderate man to recognize his true worth, and the part of a just man to pay himself and others their proper due, and the part of a brave man not to be afraid to speak the truth. Again the man who rebukes such conduct is likely to be subject to the imputation of all the opposite traits, as long as he does not prove that the words are foreign to the speaker and attract a reputation which is greater than the truth allows. (146) Although I could offer many other arguments, I omit them. But since I mentioned Solon and his remarks about his government, come consider what this man[209] also says in the very *Laws* which he legislated:[210] 'It belongs more to the lawgiver to know these things than to all the poets put together.' Does he not seem to you directly to proclaim himself as the first and wisest of all the poets? This most necessarily is the case. For when he is the one who claims to be a lawgiver, and is also the one who claims that the poets must yield to the lawgiver, and all of them at that, how is the conclusion not what I said? (147) Have you considered through all these points how great a difference there is between you and Plato in these matters? Therefore either denounce all the best men of the Greeks or try to be milder toward us in the future. My dear sir, you are afraid about my actions, but you do not consider your own; and you think that you should speak freely to me because of your good will, but you do not allow me to speak freely to these men[211] because of my good will; and you provide yourself with free speech out of cowardice, but you do not think that I should employ an upright and just free speech out of pride. (148) I still wish to mention one or two generals. For I think that the nature of that then famous Epaminondas brought no less help to the city of Thebes than you shall claim to have provided for your own people. For besides his *Defense*, which I just now mentioned,[212] there is also another example, an epigram of his in the Peloponnesus,[213] which reveals his character. And by the gods, if someone should erase it, would you not be angry? I should be very much so, and, I think, also others who are like me, but perhaps not those who are like you. What is this epigram, of which all speak? "By our counsels Sparta was shorn of her glory, and holy Messana receives back her sons after much time". Emend this too, if you wish, by the same arguments, "that all men are aware of these things, and that you should not utter a syllable". (149) They also tell of a certain remark of Chabrias, which he made, I think, after the battle of Naxus,[214] but even if it was before the battle, it is no worse. But the man hinted at himself. For he said that "an army of deer was more terrifying when a lion commanded than an army of lions when a deer commanded".

(150) Thus it has been demonstrated to you through the agency of all the poets, orators, generals, and whoever else was of any im-

portance among the Greeks, that pride is a necessary possession and, as it were, naturally present in superior men, and that Demosthenes' statement is true:[215] "For whatever are the pursuits of men, such must also be their pride". (151) Yet it is extraordinary if in other pursuits there is a sense of pride in keeping with the true worth of their circumstances, but if this is not much more the case with those pursuits concerned with the mind itself and oratory. For pride is nothing other than, as it were, a fount and starting point for oratory, as one sees who has the time to consider the matter. (152) Such an attitude seems to me to be simply a token and, as it were, an image of the whole Greek character.[216] For one can be sure that the arts and practical sciences and all such things are not inferior among the barbarians. However, strength of character and a feeling of pride combined with an inoffensive freedom[217] were ancient and peculiar virtues of the Greeks.

(153) Since you are so well endowed to act as an educator, I wonder that you do not notice these men who purchase their praise for money not only in oratorical displays, but also in the theaters.[218] Yet what else do they seem to you to do than to praise themselves? And at that, improperly, and in the least suitable way, and besides there is the diminution of their possessions, a kind of additional folly. (154) I am cleverer than they, if in no other respect, still in this one, as it seems. For I think that I should praise myself gratis and for what I know of myself. These men[219] know that I do not do this often, so that I am not producing proof of insensitivity rather than of a kind of wisdom. Even you agree that I am not lying. (155) I shall ask you one final question. By the gods, if you should be praying for children and one of the gods should tell you that you would have them, but that they would be like this man, meaning me, in both pride and eloquence, would you not accept? You would come running, I think. Do you find fault with things in us which if you should obtain, you would think that you had achieved your prayers? And did you criticize us for things for which you would give thanks to the gods? And you did not even respect the Persian and Lacedaemonian order of justice,[220] nor did you grant a small reward for a great achievement or a lesser honor for a greater desert. (156) If we have made a reasonable enough defense as far as you are concerned, so much for that. But if not, consider what you shall do. Neither you nor anyone else will ever guide us. For our patron is satisfactory.[221]

XXIX. CONCERNING THE PROHIBITION OF COMEDY[1]

(1) The fact that his speech is pleasing to the audience is no small advantage, O men of Smyrna, for one who is going to be persuasive. Most men far from easily sharing the view point of those who wish to admonish them, do not even put up with them at all. However, all matters, which of themselves invite serious consideration, do not require an adviser, but in every case nature takes the easier course. Yet there is left to the adviser those matters which men must pursue or avoid after they have been instructed by argument. Therefore if someone does not wish to listen, for his own part he destroys the use of advice. (2) Moreover, it is to be expected that certain other people will behave in a boorish fashion. But, in my judgment, it is a most extraordinary thing for you, who seem so superior in intelligence and education, first of all not to be entirely well disposed to hearing arguments and then, if someone offers the best advice, not to take it and be grateful besides. (3) If I were going to propose some laborious task or business, perhaps first of all there would have been need of strenuous debate, and then I would have tried to teach you how that which will be expedient in every way is preferable to the pleasure of the moment. But now I am so far from making any unpleasant proposal, that I have come to advise this very course, that you neither speak nor hear anything unpleasant. So far am I from doing or advising anything which is unpleasant.

(4) I shall begin at a point where you would best follow me and with my own practice.[2] I say that it is fitting to celebrate a feast for Dionysus, and by Zeus, for Aphrodite, and all the other gods, with libations, sacrifices, paeans, the wearing of crowns, and with the omission of no act of piety. But one practice which is included in these, reasonably pleasant to the masses, but most painful of all to reasonable men, this I ask you to remove, I mean the defamation and these daytime revels, and by Zeus, those at the night festivals as well, and I ask that there be neither poets nor actors of these works, and no jokes which were better not made. (5) Such is the situation. It is not pleasant to listen to slander unwillingly, but to endure it willingly is a training ground for malicious conduct. This

XXIX. CONCERNING THE PROHIBITION OF COMEDY

is one of the principal contributors to wickedness, and no one would make a greater accusation against either a private citizen or a city than that it delights in evil. For it is necessary for one who is in thrall to this desire to be infected by that which seems to be the extreme human fault, envy, which is without excuse, and to cause this envy to grow within his soul. There is proof. No one is pleased by the slandering of those whom he loves and for whom he wishes well. (6) It can be said of assault, personal injury, and such acts, that they were involuntary. But the case of malice is so far different that first of all it is named after evil,[3] as if it admitted no excuse, and second it is the name of no act, but of a nature which wishes well to no one. Just as it is most infected by evil beginning with its name, so slander[4] is in the greatest part infected by it, beginning with their assonance. Thus both words are qualities of evil and bad men. (7) We must always choose, I believe, to think and say what is best. But how is it not reasonable to desire that in the sacred festival and in the feasts there is only auspicious language, that every mind is most civil, that all men are most friendly toward one another, as if the gods were judging this friendship and concord,[5] and to believe that the feasts are almost, one might say, symbols of friendship, and that there is no sacrifice so glorious nor libations so gratifying, that the gods would not be more pleased if we should display the very best attitude possible? (8) Indeed, what greater token would there be of reverence for the gods than neither to say nor to hear any dissonant expression before them? Or would we hesitate to make many remarks in the presence of a revered friend, even if we could insult someone with justice, yet having chosen the gods as both audience and patrons, shall some of us lightly speak and others lightly hear matter which we would not even claim is good, but which we in fact mock because it is shameful? (9) So that you may know that I am saying nothing novel, but that there long has been agreement on this matter both in law and general custom, consider the opening words of the heralds, who command the national assemblies to use auspicious language, and consider also the priests and those who begin the sacrifices for us whenever we make offerings, and further how concerned we ourselves are about auspicious language at the occasion of our prayers. (10) Yet what sense is there in believing that auspicious language is the finest of all things and most proper to sacred rites, while those who wish are free to slander? And in being so decorous when we sacrifice, while using the pretext of the very gods to whom we make the sacrifices, we hear and speak the most shameful things? And in believing that the gods are annoyed by slander, while at the same time we make them patrons of our slander of one another? (11) Indeed, if we regard this practice as dear to the gods, we contradict ourselves in avoiding the same whenever we approach the gods. But if we believe that it is hateful to them and yet we delight in it, how is our conduct pious? Or how do we honor the gods through means which we should avoid for the sake of the gods? (12) It seems to me remarkable if we regard the sounds of the birds as being most fraught with omens for us, whether we are in a lonely spot or wherever we should be, while we shall not take care to keep our own voices from being unpleasant, even in the theaters. And on approaching the Altar of Omen,[6] we should wish to hear the most auspicious remarks. So strong do we believe is the power of this goddess. Yet we shall allow to the feasts expressions which in no way should be endured. (13) And we order our children to use good language, and we teach them both at school and in their homes that it is not proper to say what it is shameful to do.[7] Yet when we have gathered together our children, wives, and every age group, we offer prizes for slander and we make it profitable for those who have trained with the best success. (14) We sing, in the middle of the sacred rites, of acts because of which it is not permitted that the doer or sufferer enter within places purified with lustral water.[8] And we regard it as an act of impiety to make an improper sacrifice, but we attribute to piety the honoring of the gods by improper means. And in all other actions we honor decorum, but we lightly view all the postures of the choruses, and lightly accept all their remarks. And if ever one of the members of the chorus is out of key, we expel him. But we regard it as our gain if ever the whole chorus sings with such a lack of cultivation. (15) And if ever we are slandered in this way by others, we are angry. But if ever we do this to ourselves, we regard it as a true feast. So strange is our behavior toward the gods and toward ourselves, quite the opposite of what it should be.

(16) Yet some men dare to say that it is a good thing to have the right to slander in the theater, for those who have lived evilly are refuted and the rest behave with moderation through their fear of being satirized. I should regard drunkenness as of great value if it were able to educate men. But it may not be easy for drunkards to moderate the behavior of others, and before they have enchanted

themselves with song, to sing to other men to make them live good lives. (17) For who of you does not know that first of all such education is not within the capacity of the masses, no more than legislation and making proposals in the assembly? Or shall we believe that "not every man can sail to Corinth",[9] while every man will understand the journey throughout the whole of life and with what pursuits it must be made and while everyone will sit at these tillers and convey the youth here and there as it pleases him? (18) And we hold selections of athletes,[10] so that the bad among them may depart in shame, at the same time even suffering physical punishment. Yet shall we so ineptly select our guides and teachers of the most serious matters from every workshop and every occupation?[11] In that case we ourselves shall seem to need teachers. (19) And we do not employ all men as doorkeepers, but those who are the most trustworthy, so that no shame may befall our house. Yet shall we hand over our children, wives, all the classes of the city,[12] and, in sum it can be said, our dignity to anyone who wishes to deal with it? And shall we have confidence in drunkards whom we condemned when they were sober? (20) Indeed, the Dionysia, if you wish, or the Sacred Marriage[13] and the Night Festivals,[14] if you prefer them, are not the occasions for educators, but for jesters. Therefore how is it reasonable at the time when we give the children a holiday from their real teachers, to put in charge of them men who have no claim to be teachers and who impose themselves, and to be unable to learn from the place itself that the pretense is senseless? (21) A teacher ought not to go to the theaters and make his admonitions there. Theaters are dedicated to pleasure and enjoyment. But there are indeed places called after his name, where he ought to practice his philosophy, and in these places, I think, he should not joke and freely slander in this fashion, but should teach his pupils as befits free men, and he should instruct them, in addition to other things, also to guard against indecorum. (22) Indeed, if they satirized wanton men and left the others alone, perhaps it would make some sense. But now the practice begins speciously, but has no pretty end. For many men are undeservedly slandered, while some whose conduct escapes no one, still avoid public ridicule. Why? Because they do not follow the behavior of teachers, censors, or men who wish to improve others—for they would first have improved themselves. But their criticism is conditioned by their hatred or by their desire to please other men, depending on whether they have asked for money and not received it, or have fallen in love with someone and not persuaded him; and again they are silent for the opposite reason, with the result that they do not make a public display of those who live shamefully. (23) Consider the matter in the following way. Who most likely buys off slander? Would you not say those who are conscious of having committed such acts? But who likely cares least of all about these matters? Is it not those who are confident in themselves and their manner of life? Clearly. Therefore the opposite of what they promised occurs. The wanton and the shameful are immune to their regard, and those are satirized who least should be. (24) Come now, let us assume that both are indiscriminately slandered, for you would not say that no one of good character will ever be slandered. Those who have been indifferent to reputation and completely corrupted by shameful desires are certainly in no way injured, but they would even count it a gain since they delight in popularity. But as for those who are brought on the stage undeservedly, how do they not very much fail to win the prizes which are owed to moderation? (25) Therefore satire should not be used to improve the youth. But if for no other reason, satire should be stopped, so that it may be possible for the youth freely to practice better habits. We can certainly requite bad men in other ways. But what reason shall we give when we afflict good men with such injuries? How is it proper that men, against whom it is not even plausible that a court action could be obtained, should be handed over without examination to whoever wishes to deprive them of their rights? (26) If some one of you replied that it will seem preferable to most good men to give up their money in order not to be slandered, and so much more so, by as much as they are more bashful, how is it not clear in every way that comedy is unpleasant and that it is better for it to be once and for all prohibited by you, since for good men it will mean one of two things, either they will not pay and be slandered, or they will buy off defamation with their money and will be fined so as not to be slandered? But as for those who care nothing about being slandered, what is it that they will suffer? (27) It is wholly impossible for a city publicly not to enjoy the reputation of its private citizens. Often everyone has seemed to have the same character as those who are satirized. Consider this also in reference to your ancestors, the Athenians, who are honored by nearly all their other forms of writing, one might say. But comedy alone traduced them and provided opportunities for those who still now wish to defame them. For they seemed to be refuted by themselves. (28) And, O earth and gods, I forbear to say how much difference there is between the present counterfeit form of comedy and all of the admonition and education which was contained in what was called the parabasis. But in the words of the proverb[15] one could "suffer from a worthy piece of wood", if it should so befall him. But where there is so much wickedness of speech, so much wantonness in song, and further shameful postures, and where no comedy would satisfactorily deal with the evils attendant on those things, what kind of pleasure is there? (29) And shall you endure these things as if they were good? What is more shameful than these things? Shall you endure them as if they were expedient to hear or to witness? Indeed, they are tokens of corruption. For whenever a man or a woman becomes accustomed to being slandered and to put up with the most shameful abuse, the mind easily becomes slack, and everyone is taught to be bad, even if he was not before. Shall you endure it as if it were one of those matters where "Dionysus does not care"?[16] It seems to me that the proverb pertains not least to such stupidities. (30) Well then! Shall you endure these things as if they made a remarkable contribution to the account of one's reputation? Whenever women, little boys, anyone at all will chant these things in the baths, on the streets, in every market place, in their homes?[17] And will it be permitted to satirize only citizens? Is it not terrible if you shall know enough to spare strangers, but shall not dare to spare yourselves? Shall you be so unlike the Lacedaemonians, so that while they kept all their affairs secret,[18] you shall even grant those who wish to accuse you undeservedly to do so? (31) By Zeus, shall we also attack strangers? We shall be very well regarded and often visited by all men. Certainly fathers will cheerfully bring their sons and older brothers their younger brothers to study here where such things are sung. Will you not stop pillorying yourselves? (32) Yes, by Zeus, but jesting is urbane. Then is it not so much more beyond the capacity of the masses, unless of course it should be thought that there are many urbane men? It would please me to ask those who delight in abuse whether they are jesting or serious. If they are jesting, why do they pretend to admonish us? But if they are serious, again it is worthwhile to inquire of them whether their abuse is true or false. If it is true, why do they not make use of the laws? But they are silent when they ought to speak, and they speak when they ought to be silent. But if they are telling lies, they ought to be satisfied if they suffer no harm, and not be indignant, if they will not be permitted to slander.

(33) I think that I would be right in offering this advice to all men, but not least of all to you. For by as much as you seem superior in education and generosity, it is so much the more shameful for you clearly to pursue what is not fitting.

XXX. BIRTHDAY SPEECH TO APELLAS[1]

[Preface.[2] Apellas happened to be one whose family belonged to the Roman Senate, a patrician, of the race of Quadratus. However, Apellas was still a boy, being about fourteen years of age, a pupil of the orator, a person well endowed mentally and moreover physically, as the orator himself says.[3] Apellas was intending in the near future to hold a contest in honor of Asclepius. For this purpose the orator delivers a kind of birthday speech. The speech is composed of many ideas which succeed one another without interruption. It also embodies cleverness and subtlety, and there is an extraordinary handling of these qualities. Furthermore marvelous is the astounding method of introducing ideas, which is both peculiar to the subject and shifts imperceptibly. In general, a kind of arrangement, which is unified from many parts, pervades the speech like a soul. Furthermore there is a vehement use of figures of speech, and a harmony in the succession of these, the preceding one being integrated into that following, and there is precise clarity of diction, and there is a fluent archaism which at the same time avoids baseness of style and bad taste. And in addition there is precision in composition, a charm befitting a festive gathering, and an oratorical beauty which guides the composition with moderation. And marvelous too is the smooth gracefulness, which is the hallmark of Aristides.]

(1) From first to last all the prayers have been suitably offered that were proper to the gods of birth and family, and before and after these, to the Savior and Guide of life[4] and whatever else you might call him. Now, while all men contribute all their zeal, there has been accomplished, as much as can be, the rites, through which one would celebrate this day, honoring the law which has been passed for these occasions. Therefore it can be judged in no small way how happily the city's glory has increased not only privately but also publicly, as if now indeed it fully perceived how much it surpasses the remaining cities in felicity,[5] since it could add to all its privileges, by which it was adjudged to be the first city, also the birth of this boy. (2) Indeed, each of those other cities—I mean those which are of any account and have a great name—virtually

make him a citizen of theirs and call him by this title when they address him as their patron. In fact, like mothers claiming a child—as now can be seen—, they grant that he belongs to his natural, allotted mother, but do not deprive themselves of being called his mother.[6] (3) When this city beholds those others forcibly transgressing nature in their desire, it redoubles its love, so that, indeed, this strife alone, according to Hesiod,[7] can be called good, and victorious without dispute is that city, in which these sacrifices and this speech now take place. (4) While this city presents the speech to you, O dearest boy, and not only this speech, but also those given every day, the god,[8] who has saved me from the most extreme dangers, has presented me to the city. And what you receive from me, you have from the gift of the city to whom I was bestowed, so that at the same time you can call the city your mother and say that you have been legitimately educated[9] in it as well. This fact, I think, redounds in no small way both to your glory and to that of the city. (5) To your glory, since you did not choose to cultivate a foreign hearth, dishonoring your country as if it were insufficient to train men in virtue and to educate a noble spirit. But your country can certainly be proud of this fact no less than anything, that it not only had the good fortune to bear you, but also that now that you are growing up it has still retained you by its side, and that in the study of oratory and philosophy, along with its other excellences, it has been judged to hold first place in company with those other cities or even before them. (6) As to contingent rewards, there is good hope of quickly obtaining some of them from you.[10] But others have already been got from your family. Indeed, this is no small reciprocal advantage, I think, to both of you,[11] I mean the fact that you[12] were not only born in this city while being able to enumerate ancestors from other places,[13] but also that your family tree beginning in the past at a point where it could not even have been discovered through the length of time, had it not been so glorious, has proceeded up to you, and through you awaits the fulfillment of the future. (7) For beginning with Quadratus[14]—the name, I think, even unspoken, is equally clear to all—it is possible, counting the generations down to this boy, to see that "the offshoot of this land", as some poet would say,[15] is legitimate and pure, and indeed that its flowers are spreading and that it will flower more, as if its bloom were always beginning and never ceasing, so long as the earth, which nurtures this fruit, remains immortal. (8) And it oc-

XXX. BIRTHDAY SPEECH TO APELLAS

curs to me also to consider this advantage of your family, which I just now thought of. For others too perhaps share the benefit of being able to say that the founders of their families were genuine citizens. But in contrast to all the rest, the family which originated from Quadratus, apart from other things, enjoys an opposite advantage. (9) The others can be proud of the fact that their founders were citizens, and this for them is a very great source of pride, as indeed it should be. But when Quadratus had been summoned by the god[16] to restore this city which had deteriorated through age, he created everything which now exists, so that in the future the other families could claim that they belong to the city, but the city that it belongs to this family. Yet these are "not my words",[17] but the city itself admits it and has shouted it out in the council chambers, in the theaters, in the assemblies, and in whatever place you would mention, since every place was adorned by that man. (10) This being the case, I think that it would be right for me to omit all of the glorious accomplishments of his glorious offspring and sons, and "the sons of his sons",[18] to use a poetic expression,[19] once they had held Roman office.[20] If they were small accomplishments, one would have mentioned them and in the course of the argument praised whatever it might be. But since they are great, and indeed unsurpassed, so that, when mentioned, it is difficult properly to recount the accomplishments of one of these men without a kind of glorious good fortune in speaking,[21] why should one both keep to the matter at hand, which itself is not small, if it is not even greater than those old accomplishments, and whose successful presentation requires divine help,[22] and run further risks in the matter of the whole family in addition to what has been proposed? But it would be best to dismiss the intervening ancestors[23] of this boy, who is in every way most noble, and to mention briefly those who are in a sense still before our eyes, and these only in so far as it pertains to the present speech. The very name of the boy suggests this,[24] so that of itself it equally supplies a beginning for his family and my speech.

(11) What should we say of Fronto, the father of this boy, who was, indeed, noble, a gentleman, and one who pursued every virtue that nature demanded of a man described by these names.[25] The audience would anticipate whatever one would say, since, I think, it was not long ago that that man departed for the lot which is better and dearer to the gods, unless one would make everything clear by

briefly addressing his son in Homeric fashion:[26] "You are of good blood, dear child". (12) The father of his father, the bearer of the same name as he, that other Apellas—for, I think, a little before[27] my argument struck up this beginning—what sort of man do we find him? I would not mention any of his other famous qualities, his courage, his magnanimity, nor all of the provinces which he governed, nor all of the honors which he enjoyed from the emperors. None of these things. For we should pray that at some time we can say the same about this present Apellas, and we should indeed be of good hope that he will not only be better than his father, but also than his grandfather, and, I shall add, than his other ancestors,[28] the other gods and the Healer[29] approving. (13) But I think that it is timely now to mention what I already observe they both have in common like their name. Indeed, now that this argument is begun, through an excess of joy I am unable to conclude what is appropriate to it and to make the transition to a new point. (14) But, O Lord Asclepius—a little before I summoned you in my prayers,[30] and may you now assist in every way and especially in my present remarks—, O Lord, this speech was your accomplishment and the contrivance of your grace. Formerly you held that other Apellas so dear, that neither did you neglect him in his rest and sleep, nor did you abandon him in his waking hours and toil. But day and night wholly counted the same as far as concerned "saving the man from the midst of fire", as they say. Yet whom would he not snatch even "from burning fire",[31] if he wished, since he would even save by means of fire, should he wish to?[32] (15) But now, as it seems, as far as we can tell, you are raising another servant[33] for yourself in his place, so that he inherits at the same time his grandfather's name and the honor which you have bestowed upon that man. Yet I think that you would rival your father[34] and I Homer in this respect. For a tree shoots up by your altars which is better in every way than the one at Delus, and I can say that it is actually your tree, and not only compare it to Apollo's, as Homer did.[35] (16) How is he not the tree trunk of the Savior himself, indeed reared in "the pure gardens of the Graces",[36] from the time that he came forth from the blessed womb. This can indeed be clearly gathered not only from the roots of his family which have been already mentioned, but also from the characteristics which take flower in him at this time of his life, both from those pertaining to the soul and from those pertaining to the body, if one chooses to divide them in this way. (17) The gentleness of his soul, inclining to old age, outstrips the flower of his youth. However, his gentleness does not appear like the enfeebled sort, such as the trials of life have created in many men. But it shares his youth and is mixed with a proper sense of pride. Let one observe it from the glance of his eyes, if anyone has not learned of it in actual practice, as the saying goes. For neither do his eyes stare intently nor are they like those held in a kind of sleep through humility. But a gentle dignity quietly raises his gaze. (18) Handsomeness, which has been assigned to boys as a gift from the gods as if through some agreement on their part, in him is in no way naked in the manner of the painters, but clothed in much respect, it has been infused in all parts of his body. No other has smiled with so much charm, nor so charmingly stayed with a blush a laugh now rising. Still he is not deficient in temper, by which one would judge masculine nature, nor yet when provoked has this temper been carried to that other wild and animal nature. He himself has provided proof of both these characteristics, now showing clearly in his face the turmoil of his soul, now steadily persuading it to relax and making it calm. (19) In work and at play who would uproot "Persuasion from his lips",[37] not only when he speaks, but even when he is silent? For no one would command such obedience by speaking as he by indicating his wishes in silence. Nor would Nestor, although an old man, seem still to speak like "honey",[38] if he were compared to this boy. In sum, "his serious endeavors are not without charm", but everything, even if it is difficult, must be "accomplished festively",[39] and his pleasures, in turn, are not free of seriousness. (20) If we are rightly enjoined by Plato's argument—and we must think that the situation is such, so that in their play children should[40] "learn gradually all of the studies that it is necessary to have learned gradually, for example by playing or doing something similar, the carpenter to measure or to calculate, and the warrior to ride a horse, and that we should try through the medium of play to turn the pleasures and desires of children to where, if they proceed, they must have a result"—if it must be said that Plato is correct in his argument—for somehow I happened to have quoted this from memory, neither subtracting nor adding anything—, what boy would there be for us from the Spartan band of children who has so abandoned the racing of horses and the training of dogs? He is so far from being disposed in an unhealthy way to anything worse than befits the involvement of his present and future life, I mean competitions. For there were the boys' contests at the palaestra and the school debates.[41] (21) But proceeding on his course, in his play he foretells the future, indeed by practicing for the position in life which fortune has given him, and he already sits as a judge.[42] His nature was not at all unaware of the road which passes through play to one's true fortune, and he would not be censured as having judged unjustly, as they say[43] that Cyrus was censured by his teacher of justice, since he is even wiser than Cyrus in the art of being a judge, although he learned it from no one. (22) Such is the pure nature, molded of undefiled "wax" according to Plato,[44] having a composition between the moist and soft and the hard and stony. But what would you say, whenever he refers his nature to god, the ruler of the Universe, and to the god to whose care he has been given by his very descent,[45] he who is his good forefathers' good and fitting heir, descendant, son, and all that one might call him? (23) O those men are thrice and many times blessed, who have reaped in you the only immortality which has been given to the human race,[46] and along with their memory have left you an inheritance more glorious than the treasures above and below the earth, their reputation,[47] upon which the god himself now safely embarks you, appearing and demanding of Apellas as much as he himself wished and the former rank of the family required. (24) For such, such another day will soon follow this day which itself is blessed and pleasing to the gods, when two commencements join within a single year. For the present one, the anniversary of your birth, is the greatest, introducing the year fortunate from beginning to end, and there is again another commencement[48] which will immediately follow this, and that in one and the same year, granting to you auspiciously your ancestral and hereditary fillet.[49] (25) And the god seems to me, in anticipation,[50] to grant to you an honor, which is not at all customary for boys,[51] in the contests of the Sacred Games of Asclepius, which descends to you from your father, as has often been said, and from those in the generations before your father, so that you have fulfilled all that was allowed, and at the same time it remains, when in the future you pass from boyhood to manhood, as indeed is ordained by imperial law, for you to be granted honors from the Emperor,[52] which he often bestows on such great young men when they are grown up. (26) Indeed, as we can see, Asclepius is not far removed from the

XXX. BIRTHDAY SPEECH TO APELLAS

art of prophecy, since he is the son of Apollo. O those are good hopes! So are the present hopes, whose fulfillment we shall soon behold! I seem to feel a kind of lightness, just as Diomedes, as described by Homer,[53] had his limbs made light and his sight made clear by Athena, and I cannot restrain myself for joy. (27) The past years of your life are fair and perhaps suitable to adorn you and to make clear all of your character. Yet this present year seems to me to be much fairer than those others, only to be surpassed by those which will follow it, but in other respects already surpassing those which came before. In this year we, your relations, kinsmen, teachers, companions, and all of your dear family, we shall behold you presenting a fairer appearance by wearing the sacred purple mantle of the Savior, befitting the summer of the year in the summer of your age,[54] wholly "like the autumn star",[55] and just as radiant as it. Indeed, in this way the president of the games suits the one who chose him.

(28) These things are your responsibility, O Lord—for so it is better to bring my speech back to its beginning with another prayer—, these things are your responsibility. Come then, take the helm yourself for us, as indeed you now hold it,[56] and save this house, and grant to this boy those honors from the great Emperor[57] which his ancestors enjoyed from the Emperor's ancestors. Grant to the Emperor himself and to the family of the Emperor to rule forever, as indeed is their portion from Zeus, and allow this family,[58] those who are the sons of its sons,[59] to live their allotted time in felicity, and preserve the succession of the race for the city and for yourself.

(Subscription[60]: Birthday Speech. It was suggested one day before it was read, during the Cathedra[61] in Pergamum, Aristides being twenty-nine years of age).[62]

XXXI. FUNERAL ORATION FOR ETEONEUS[1]

(1) This speech is by no means a happy one, nor such as we had hoped, but it is necessary to console the city and the family of Eteoneus and in addition ourselves. I think that even if mourning had not yet become a custom of mankind, it would now have rightly been instituted on account of him. For at what would one not weep? The age at which he departed? Or his courage which was unhappily buried? Or his good behavior whose model one would not easily find? Or the hopes of which he himself is deprived, as well as his family, friends, the cities, and all that belongs to the present province of Asia? (2) Is there a Simonides who will mourn these things? Is there a Pindar? And what song will he invent or what appropriate word? Is there a chorus which will speak worthily of such suffering? Did Dyseris of Thessaly feel so much grief over her dead Antiochus,[2] as much as the mother of this boy now has? (3) Indeed, it will not be enough to mourn in silence or only crying out his name, but some praise will also be added to our mourning. For why shall we be afraid that in our speech we may tell lies about one whose family first of all is so great in the city and in Asia, so that no one would even dispute its position? For all of its members, one might say, are individually preeminent. Indeed, his mother's family rivals that of his father's. As to his parents themselves, his father is the most distinguished of men, and his mother the best conducted of women, but in the care of her sons, even greater than a woman. (4) His upbringing and his nature were worthy of his birth. His mother was his nurse and guardian. His body and soul befitted each other. In appearance, he was most handsome, most tall, and most perfect of those of his age and one who afforded the eye of the beholder with the greatest pleasure. But in character, he was most orderly and gentlemanly, notable for his magnanimity and simplicity, so that it was hard to decide whether he was boy, youth, or ancient. For he had the unfinished quality of a boy, the flower of a youth, and the wisdom of an ancient. (5) In his intelligence could be admired the absence of boldness, audacity, and willfulness, but the presence of a sharp wit in a calm disposition. Again in his moderate behavior, the absence of sluggishness, supineness, and torpor, but like the time of well blended spring, the

combination of equal keenness and gentleness and the fact that moderate behavior and charm did not impede one another. (6) He clung to his mother like a babe at the breast. He loved his brother like a son. He clung to his studies, as if he could not live otherwise. He instantly understood what he heard. Directly on seeing a man, he would recognize his character and whether he should embrace him or avoid him. (7) Believing the truth of the Homeric verse[3] that "a multiplicity of rule is not good," and that many teachers contributed rather to ignorance, he chose out of all the teacher whom he chose—for it is not too seemly for me to mention this—and he was so attached to him that although he did everything that the most studious and the most devoted should do, he never thought that he came near to being worthy. (8) He rejoiced to attend his teacher's lectures, as if this time of life alone was worth living for him. Should anything prevent his attendance, he was pained, but never complained. He was so intent on listening to the declamations,[4] that he had no time for offering praise. But just as the parched drink in silence,[5] so it was enough for him to accept what was said and to indicate by his posture, nod, and smile the pleasure which he had in the declamations. You would always find him either studying a book or writing declamations or delighting his mother with his stories or lectures, and doing everything in every way with a graceful movement which it were best to have imitated in a painting. (9) The daily and nightly amusements of those who have reached this age were like unreal stories to him. The only woman with whom he dined was his mother, the only boy, his brother. His friends were those who had the same preferences and attended the same lectures. "But he was eminent amongst all".[6] (10) One would have said that he was "an image of Reverence",[7] who was satisfied with mostly being silent, but if he should say anything, had to "burn with embarrassment". Nor otherwise would you have heard his voice, but he must either blush and speak, or speak and blush. Thus he passed his life without witnessing, hearing, and experiencing all the things which are most shameful. But he saw only oratory and education, and even in his death, died in these studies, while intoning a panegyric and other declamations. (11) O most handsome of boys in every way, you did not attain your proper age, yet appeared too dignified and old for the age which you had. The choruses of your companions desire you, your elders desire you, your city which had the greatest hopes of you and which recently you delighted for the first and last time desires you. What sort of days and nights are left to your mother, who formerly was famous as one with a "handsome son",[8] but now has been proven an unhappy parent! (12) The orbs of those eyes closed for all time! The head formerly most fair, now in the dust! The hands unseen! The feet! What a master did you bear, yet you have given way! You who are more pitiful than a bridegroom just now consumed on his funeral pyre and more deserving of festive garlands than of mourning, what an untimely scene you have caused in the time of your youth, since before it was appropriate to sing your wedding hymn, it befell to sing you a dirge! A most handsome figure! A voice being perfected for all the Greeks in common! You have gone in the preface of your life, having given so much delight as much as to cause the greater pain. It occurs to me to add that verse of Pindar,[9] "the stars, the rivers, the waves of the sea" invoke your untimely death. (13) The second calamity! You have fallen such a youth after such a temple![10] This addition![11] Such was our aftershock! The god of fortune tragically inspired! He just now foreshadowed council chambers, orations, emulation, and joy, and quickly concluded the drama far from these things. The common misfortune of the gods of oratory and of those beneath the earth![12] (14) How am I to answer the honorary decrees?[13] Or am I to give this answer, that Eteoneus has gone to the gods? Cleverest of boys, such a work do I send you, such a speech do you now enjoy! But as it were truly in some tragedy, in the midst of my lamentations, I seem to hear the voice of some god on the theatrical machine,[14] who changes my mourning into words of praise by speaking as follows. (15) 'Cease, mortals. The boy, or rather the man is not to be mourned, nor ought he to be pitied for the journey which he has made. But if any other man, his mortal state stands well. For neither Cocytus nor Acheron[15] have taken him, nor will the tomb, which received him, conceal him. But he will go about for all future time, a famous and ageless hero,[16] enthroned beside Cyzicus,[17] honored by his ancestral god Apollo,[18] like Amyclas,[19] Narcissus, Hyacinthus, and whoever else possessed besides a handsome appearance a virtue greater than man's estate. (16) Therefore he must be given other honors and escorted[20] in a different way, since he is too great for tears and has departed from home not without divine fate. Indeed, death is set forth as the common boundary for all. But to close our life with a good reputation and the thought that we are worthy of the fairest prizes cannot be found fault with by man or god.[21] This does not come to all, but was given to very few of mankind. (17) Every human life is brief and not worth much in the reckoning. But if any of you tally the lives of Arganthonius, Tithonus, and Nestor of Pylus, whose span equalled three generations,[22] when you have added together the years of all of them, you shall find that they are too tiny a portion of total time even to say it. We should not love life and measure felicity by this, whether someone has had as much of life's cares as possible, and whether someone has enjoyed a long old age, such as men are accustomed to enjoy. But we should believe that he has fared the best, who has consumed in the best things that portion of life given to him, and as a poet has ended his play while people still desire to see and hear it. (18) So he goes on his journey, blessed and to be envied by all, by both those younger and older. For he has enjoyed that part of life, for which alone to be born is desirable, without suffering evil, without experience of trouble, with a good reputation, nurtured in oratory, studies, and praise, going from his beloved mother, his companion, to the ancient mother. But if someone thinks that he has not sufficiently enjoyed his reputation, now we should supply what is missing by honoring him as a hero, since praise can now be safely bestowed'.[23] (19) We should think that we hear these words from the gods and we should believe that if we were so disposed, we would come closer to the truth and we would do what is pleasing to him. It would be proper to sing of him even in the drinking songs, like Harmodius,[24] and to say, "You did not die", but if anyone else, you dwell in the midst of those who knew you, both citizens and foreigners. You have lived your life as it were a sacred rite and have died being far too good for man's estate. You were an adornment for your friends, family, and city. You held first place in the virtue to be expected of your years.[25] This is our gift to you, but the rest will be the concern of the whole city.[26]

XXXII. FUNERAL ADDRESS IN HONOR OF ALEXANDER[1]

(1) Aristides sends greetings to the Council and People of Cotiaeum.

It was understandable that people came to you from all of Greece to commiserate in such misfortune and to extol a man so very much the first of the Greeks. Therefore when I write and number myself among those who feel what has happened as a personal loss, I think that I would not be acting out of turn. (2) For as far as I am concerned that man lacked none of those designations which mankind regard as fair and honorable, and which bring joy to the young and are venerable to the old. Since I was nurtured and educated under him and afterwards eagerly shared with him in everything which fortune offered, I was able to call him foster father,[2] teacher, father, comrade, everything. But the greatest bond between us was that we could be equally proud of one another. I felt self-esteem to have had him as a teacher and he counted my career as part of his own glory. (3) While it was possible to write to him, I did this, and we engaged in a not unlearned study of oratory in our correspondence. But since it is no longer possible to communicate with him, and he has not even received in those hands most dear to me what I happened to have recently sent him, it remained to write to you and let the hearth of the city take his place. For thus I thought that I would have doubly honored Alexander, by duly remembering him and by making you my friends because of him. And I thought that in two ways I would do what was acceptable to you, by publicly showing confidence in you and by remembering a man whom you valued most highly, and, I think, not only you, but also all who in any way belong to the Greek race. (4) It happens that in memory I conceive of all of his excellent qualities, but I am unable to recount them in writing, for they all come crowding together. To tell them individually is impossible, and it seems to me not at all appropriate even to try. But if I should speak of them in part, I am afraid that it may have been better for me to be silent.

(5) He has reversed the first and principal category of praise. For he was so far from being distinguished through his membership in

his race, for example taking refuge in a nation or a city, that while your race is certainly the oldest of races[3] and again among the whole race of the Phrygians your city is the oldest, as they say, he has caused both the city and the entire race to take pride in him, and for all of you it is no little boast to the Greeks to be his fellow citizens. (6) He is said to have had the best teachers, but clearly he has surpassed them all, as if they were children. In the course of his life, he became connected with all of those who were most famous. He was a student of the ancient writers, and he was the teacher or the colleague of those who came after these. And others will say what sort of students he produced, but of those with whom he shared the task of education, there was no one greater than he.

(7) Indeed, some in their desire for the important things, neglect the minor points. But he began with the smallest points and proceeded to the greatest, just as they say[4] that "it is fitting first to be initiated in the Lesser Mysteries". Others pursued at length vestiges and principles,[5] or rather they even consumed their life in these. But some did not at all see why it was worthwhile to discover these things, and others did not succeed, as it seems. But he pursued these matters from the beginning in a methodical way, and neglected nothing anywhere which was worthy of any study whatsoever. And he became for the Greeks like their common chancellery. For one could learn from him whatever one desired relating to education, just like drawing water from a spring. (8) But his greatest accomplishment and the one most worthy of note was that which I also once in a discussion mentioned to him. For although, as I say, he had gone through all studies, and through every one more carefully than those who were concerned with each specifically, he did not ascribe to himself that most fearsome of titles,[6] but was content with his old title;[7] and he did not deprive other teachers of their classes, but he was always seen to work with each and to help them develop as far as possible. (9) And others become greater through their arts. But he for his own part made his art itself greater. For in many ways he has exalted it, so that it has taken its grandeur from him. It is enough for others to excel those in their own fields, but he was clearly first in simply all his art. For of the others who have been classified in this part of education, some seemed successful in criticism, but were ineffective speakers; some had achieved the ability to speak, but were not very learned; some were trained in encyclopedic knowledge, but by this

very fact were blinded to the more important things and forsook that which is best. But he, a unique man,[8] encompassed all. (10) Indeed, although he was so eloquent, yet he did not retire to compose histories and such kinds of writing, but chose to serve the ancient Greeks.[9] How is this not like his generous liberality toward his students, through which he has filled them with learning from the start, and supplied all whom he saw wanting in means with recommendations and salaried positions? Clearly this unique man has instructed and sent off the most disciples, and has been like a founder for the Greeks in the strict meaning of the term.[10] It is even possible to compare his conduct with mother cities. For he has settled different men in different parts of the earth for their own benefit and for the benefit of those who use them. (11) He alone has shown in fact that Hesiod lied[11] when he wrote that "bard hates bard". For he was, as it were, the common father of his colleagues, and all had more hope in him than each did in himself. He alone did not belittle the non-professional, and among the clever he earned the highest admiration. And he alone has been proved first in the multitude and in the high quality of his witnesses. (12) For the students of oratory it was a matter of pride to have studied with him. And other famous and well-known men ranked the knowledge of their having employed him like anything else which gave them distinction. Therefore he was welcome to all, and when he was not engaged in the public display of his art, he would be either with the mighty[12] or in the Palace itself. (13) Indeed, his lectures to the royal family[13] were made according to a kind of itinerary, as it were. For when he had become preeminent throughout the Greek world and had afforded countless proofs of himself, he came to the Court and to the hearing of the Emperor.[14] Therefore one Prince took him from the other and regarded him like any other royal ornament. (14) It is no small task to recount how much moderation and decorum he displayed after he had acquired such great authority and power that he had the position of foster father,[15] not only teacher of the boys. But he behaved in the same way as in his former lectures. (15) For he is said never to have caused any trouble for anyone at all in his lectures, but always to have been the cause of some good both for the pupils themselves and for their servants. For that most of them have been manumitted and have obtained other honors, Alexander was in every way the cause, especially, I think, by turning the boys of each of them into such

XXXII. FUNERAL ADDRESS IN HONOR OF ALEXANDER

good students, that their attendants, who had access to his classes with these boys, were highly regarded by those who had appointed them. Secondly he himself openly asked for such favors in place of the usual ones for which others asked. It was also the same in his service to the royal family. For he never caused anyone grief, but passed his life in doing good for kinsmen, friends, country, and various cities. (16) Although he did countless kindnesses for countless people, he never asked anyone for payment for his kindness. However, he was not ashamed to be paid for his art.[16] For he thought that it profited young men to dare to be lavish for the sake of learning, that is, those who had the means. Indeed, he did not trouble those who lacked means, but we know that he even gave them money of his own besides. (17) Nor was he so very useful through his art and teaching, but inferior to others in civic affairs and government. You would know it most of all, and from some of you I hear how he restored for you nearly the whole city anew. So his activity was not limited to words. (18) But worth more than buildings was the moderation and justice which guided everything which he thought that he should say and do, and the fact that he never went beyond the bounds of need, but provided you with sensible ambitions. Moreover, he was not good in this way without expense to himself, but your greatest adornments are a sign to you of his generosity. (19) I believe that even if he had never spent anything on you, he would most likely be regarded as a benefactor because of the other things which he said and did on your behalf. Again if he had neither said nor done anything else, but had contributed so much of his own, he most likely would be famous among the first of men. (20) Indeed, if he had been of no use to you publicly, either financially or in other respects, his position among the Greeks most likely would give you a sense of pride. For his glory is shared by the city. It is a great thing for a city and a nation to give to the world a unique man of the first rank,[17] but you, beyond others, have enjoyed his fortune. (21) For no one ever so employed his country's name. But just as other men are known by their fathers' names or by other things,[18] so he is directly named together with his city. Indeed, in the books which he corrected, there has been left this token. For after 'Alexander' was added his native city, so that as often as someone remembers him, you are famous and your city has become a kind of mother city for ancient Greece.[19] (22) In return for these services, justly do you adorn his tomb and honor the man in every way as an ancestor and founder and decree to him all the honors which you have given to those who first founded your city. When I heard these things, they consoled me a little, as much as could be done in my grief, and because of them I was particularly impelled to write in admiration of your resolve. (23) For it would be disgraceful if when the Amphipolitans thought that they should sacrifice to Brasidas as a hero and founder[20] because he freed them from the Athenians, you did not intend to honor like a founder, a universal one, indeed, for all the Greeks, as I say, this man, who commended you to all the Greeks and was never the cause of any trouble for anyone, but passed his life in helping all men in word and deed, beginning with you, his country. (24) Indeed, if the Smyrnaeans are proud of having given Homer to the world, and the Parians because of Archilochus, and the Boeotians because of Hesiod, and the Ceans because of Simonides, and the Himerians because of Stesichorus, and the Thebans because of Pindar, and the Mytilenaeans because of Sappho and Alcaeus, and other people because of various other authors—for I now omit Athens—, indeed, it is likely that you are very proud of the man who adorned and explicated all of these. (25) For, I think, if some god had granted these authors resurrection while he was still alive, they would assemble all his colleagues and demand that these colleagues learn from him what should be thought and said about themselves. I have laughed at those who parade their knowledge of Plato and philosophize only about him. He, in my opinion, was more acceptable to Plato than anyone else. He also much surpassed the others with his poets, prose writers,[21] and all the other flowers "which", they say, "the seasons engender".[22] (26) Indeed, this is likely to escape neither you nor posterity, that the writings which he left are good and better than those of all his countrymen, but nonetheless were small pale images of his education and mind. So much did he surpass them in his lectures, that a remark of Plato himself occurs to me,[23] that "writings seem trifling compared to the actual discourses of wise men". Therefore let no one ever think that he will see the whole Alexander from these writings, although the treatise on Homer[24] suffices in many ways to be an adornment for him in this respect. (27) His work on Aesop[25] seems to me to have been something witty and clever, but trifling compared to the learning of Alexander. Indeed, how small a part of the work of Alexander is the wisdom of Aesop!

XXXII. FUNERAL ADDRESS IN HONOR OF ALEXANDER 163

To such an extent has the earth brought forth for you a second crop which is better than the first.[26] (28) It is also wonderful that to him alone the god of fortune has clearly given everything in a consistent and even measure. His body was the most handsome, the strongest, the healthiest, and most majestic. Nor, in my judgment, was anyone so attractive and handsome as he in the depths of old age. His soul was the gentlest and shared in everything which was naturally good. His education was superlative. His reputation in proportion to his worth. And private citizens and royalty alike honored him, in keeping with their respective ranks. His private wealth ever increased. There was work and relaxation, and the longest limits of life. It was the combination of every kind of prayer, one might say, and just deserts were observed in conjunction with good fortune. Yet for the same man to have possessed it all seemed, until him, an impossibility. But that unique man[27] clearly has attained to all or at least to most of these advantages. (29) One would understand this from the examination of only one facet of his life, his association with the royal family, and from a comparison with that of Aristotle with Philip and Alexander. For the latter's association was not wholly blameless in the eyes of the Greeks, but he seemed to associate with the opponents and enemies of his whole race. But Alexander's association was glorious and productive. For he did not associate with the foes and enemies of the Greeks, but with their benefactors, nor with injurious consequences for his whole race. But besides causing no harm, he even helped, if ever possible, whoever of the Greeks was in need, and publicly he represented the interests of all. (30) Again as to the association of Plato with Dionysius,[28] that Dionysius in fact who was well observed later in Corinth[29]—but I omit this—, but what I wished to say about their relationship was that it is possible to call it noble, but not fortunate. But Alexander did two things. He always wished for what was best and he obtained it. It is not easy to find by which race the man was more honored, by the Romans or by the Greeks. He made himself so very valuable to our rulers. (31) Among what men is it likely that no account has been taken of him, both in the past and now? Who dwell so far away at the ends of the earth? Who are so insensitive to what is beautiful? Who will not weep when the report suddenly arrives? For even if his death was in season,[30] still it is not seasonable for the Greeks to have been deprived of such a man. (32) Indeed, all poetry, all prose has lost its bloom, everything has failed without its expounder and patron. His art is widowed, of necessity its scope has been meanly contracted in the eyes of most people. What Aristophanes says about Aeschylus,[31] "that there was darkness when he died", ought to be said now about this man in regard to education. (33) Fairest adornment, most eminent of the Greeks, you who were admired throughout your life! Desired by those who have met you, to meet you was desired by the rest. Blessed even in your end, as we hear, since you were not wasted by disease nor afflicted with pain, but after having spent the day in your usual fashion, as if summoned by the god of fortune, you gave up your soul over your book and ended your life in keeping with your name.[32] And just as those who have done anything meticulously, you went through the whole course of your life to the end and did your work to the limit of your power. (34) If the words of Pindar,[33] Plato,[34] and all of the workshop of Alexander[35] are true, and some sort of discussions occur among those in Hades, now indeed it is likely that the choruses of the poets stand around him, beginning with Homer, stretching out their right hands, so too the choruses of the historians, and of the prose writers, and of everyone else, each inviting him and asking him to dwell with him, and all honoring him with fillets[36] and wreaths, and without judging him or having him dispute against another,[37] but with an immediate acclamation. I think that not for many years will a person descend able to contend against him, but that the throne is his forever,[38] as the best herald and expounder of the Greeks.

(35) Let none of you rebuke me, if in the midst of writing to you, I uttered these remarks,[39] since the reason for this letter was the wish to hear and speak about him. Moreover, it is no fault to feel remorse for the man, even if he did depart at so great an age. For we ought not to cling to the most recent, but to the most important things. Secondly the loss is also the greater, by as much as it is a greater and rarer piece of luck to have seen a man at this point of old age acting thus in all things, and through all preserving his state of health, memory, understanding, cheerfulness, and the rest. (36) For it was much more reasonable, while he was still alive, to be troubled that he might at some time depart and to look upon him while it was possible like any other precious thing, rather than to calculate his age when he is dead. But there is no fear that any of you may censure this, who, I hear, do and say everything for him. But I shall turn again to you in my speech, and the rest will be brief.

(37) I say that you justly honor him in all your other measures, but that you also would act most rightly and in accordance with all of your plans if you remembered his family. If you regarded his wife as someone sacred and the allotment of some god of good fortune, if it is proper to say it. If you regarded his kinsmen as his fairest monuments. As to his sons, if you treated the elder ones with all respect, and if you raised the youngest one with as much zeal as possible and publicly acted as his guardian. (38) Not the least misfortune has befallen him. For although his father educated most of the Greeks and also survived to educate the sons of his pupils, he did not live to teach his own son. But the child of the universal teacher of the Greeks needs another teacher. Do you also remedy this misfortune and all the difficulties inherent in what has happened, protecting him as it were like a father, and to sum up, regarding the hearth of Alexander as your public hearth. (39) I had to make this exhortation. For as I said in the beginning of the letter,[40] or whatever you wish to call this work, he and I were very close. Indeed, I got a rich harvest back from the friendship which I felt toward him, which was that I was the friend of one who was no less a friend. But apart from other acts, he showed this in what he did when I was sick in Rome, since he was everything which meant survival for me. And he was, after the gods, most responsible for my having got home safely.[41] (40) Indeed, what would one say of his later actions? But I was also pained by a request of his, for countless times both in his own person and by letter afterwards, he asked me to dedicate to you some of my compositions and other works, and he promised that they would occupy the first place.[42] But since I still wished to revise them, I was unable to comply. Thus Alexander neither catalogued our books nor did he know the majority of them. But as to the verdict which he always rendered about our speeches, I do not know whether it was beyond envy, but it was more than extravagant. All of which makes me remember him, and to regard what has happened as no small misfortune, and besides to think that I am not being officious in now writing to you. (41) I could wish that I had a stronger constitution, among other reasons, so that you might be able to make some use of me, since I feel that those with ties to him also have ties to me.

XXXIII. TO THOSE WHO CRITICIZE HIM BECAUSE HE DOES NOT DECLAIM[1]

(1) I have not missed both opportunities.[2] While the reception and greeting of one come from abroad is a graceful act, especially when the circumstances of his trip fulfilled our prayers, it would also be something to send one off with a song. But you have afforded us the latter opportunity and we have accepted it since it coincided with our preparations.[3] Pindar says,[4] "When god has shown the beginning, the course is direct" in taking up the matter at hand. (2) And now may our patron, Asclepius,[5] and Zeus,[6] who controls the Universe, grant in every way to you to sail with a fair wind and in good circumstances, and that it be reported that "your second attempt was better".[7] Again may they grant to us to compete in our contest with a fair wind and to surpass all the Greeks "with a foaming oar",[8] as far as it is possible. And so much for this. I shall turn to a second introduction in the manner of Stesichorus.[9] (3) I know that in some way I must fight against a shadow. For those against whom my words will be addressed are not here, so that it happens that my speech would almost be, as it were, in vain; but on the other hand it is quite apparent that it is fair and proper for it to be made. For in this very action it is obvious that our conduct is not to blame either now or at any other time, to speak by the grace of the gods, but rather their customary sloth in all matters. Yet let us consider the charge as if it were a kind of affidavit or suit. (4) They say that I do wrong because I do not declaim frequently. For everything would be mine and under my spell. And they all regularly add, "if he wished" and "if ever he wishes". This is their charge. (5) Therefore if you seek to hear some pleasant speech, as whenever I happen to address a national festival, you are very much mistaken. But if you shall endure to hear me speak the truth, I think that I shall appear not entirely blameworthy. Indeed, neither is there a national festival now, nor are so many foreigners present, before whom you would be angry to be refuted—for I am speaking to these men as if they were present—, but I shall speak freely before fewer people than "at the Lenaeum".[10] (6) I discussed these matters with you before, when the plague was raging and the god[11] ordered me to come forward.[12] But what I shall say now is

also of the same purport, so that you may know that while even in the most dangerous times I did not think that I should be slothful, there are others who care little for oratory.

(7) Formerly I did not know what was meant by "thieves accuse",[13] but now I think that I understand. For whenever those who have a duty to attend declamations and lectures have ignored this and then complain that there are no speakers, how are they not accounting their faults to others, as if when the sun was brightly blazing some people should shut their eyes and say that nothing is visible? But, I believe, these are the actions of people who deceive themselves, but think that they deceive others. Yet if you wish, hear how it is reasonable and necessary to consider these matters. (8) I believe that the arts and professions are the concern of their practitioners to the point of their practicing them, and that beyond this it is no longer their concern; but that every art has a twofold employment, that of the practitioner of the work and that of the user. Whenever someone is derelict in his own task, he is responsible to this extent. For the wish of the user is thwarted. Yet whenever one does his job as best he can, but the user stands aloof, the worker who performs his job is not, I think, responsible, but those who do not use his art. (9) What is the duty of the good doctor? To have in readiness his drugs, his operative technique, and his knowledge. Yet it is no longer part of his art to order people to use these skills, but the sick must come or send for him. But if ever the doctor solicits those who need to be saved, or, by Zeus, the helmsman those who need to sail, or the judge claimants, or the general soldiers, or the orator an audience, everything would be topsy-turvy. (10) For not to mention matters so serious and of such importance, it is not customary even in the trades for the craftsman to approach those who need him, so as to solicit employment. But those who need to build a house, solicit the carpenters, not the carpenters them. The farmer will go to the doors of the smith, whenever he needs a hoe or some other such implement; and in turn the smith will go to him, whenever he needs wheat. Have you ever yet seen a barber approach someone and say, "Let me cut your hair, dear sir, or pare your nails, or shave you, for this is my art"? But, I think, whether someone wears a purple cloak or is however dignified, he will go to the barber or will summon him, whenever he requires any of his services. And what need is there to make a long list of the arts? For we shall find that it is so with nearly

everything, as one might say. (11) Next shall they who would not think that they ought to be prouder than anyone else, and, I believe, not even as proud as other men, but who even make an art of serving the people, shall they wait for those who will need them and not be humbled beyond their rank, but they who profess the best and most liberal faculty, through which all acts are examined and tested, be they small, great, good, or otherwise, shall they not, if in nothing else, imitate those men, and shall they not believe that their duty is the study and practice of oratory, and shall they not regard the employment of those men or themselves as the task of others? (12) And as it seems, if the shoemaker and the weaver give up their jobs and go about collecting customers, not only will they not perform their tasks, but they will even ruin their arts. But if the orator gives up oratory and collects an audience, will he use the best judgment in regard to his profession? He will not, but, as I should say, in this way he will even most of all squander his resources. (13) Indeed, if it is everywhere shameful and illegal to abandon one's position, the orator in this way would especially abandon his position,[14] if in cultivating an audience, he should cheapen, as far as he was concerned, the dignity of his art. (14) Consider if it seems to be good and reasonable to you for those who desire to marry to sit by the doorways of their girls, cultivating them or their parents or some other member of the family, but for those who claim to be lovers of oratory to neglect cultivating the orator himself and trying somehow or other to persuade him to accept them into his company, and then to criticize him and say that it is he who is unwilling. By the gods, was it Calchas or Mopsus who divined the meaning of this for you?[15] For you yourself never attempted to do so. (15) Indeed, it cannot even be said that while those who pursue other sciences or arts are well aware of the provisions which must be made about them, those engaged in oratory alone or most of all will be ignorant of this. But this is the finest, greatest, and truest claim that can be made on behalf of oratory: that nothing prevents those who do anything else from knowing their art while still being ignorant of the provisions which should be made about it; but that oratory aside from its other power, also confers the knowledge of how it must be employed.[16] With good reason. For it is not very likely that those whose duty it is to judge others are ignorant about themselves.

(16) Come now, given these premises, consider my own position. And if you find that I am slothful or regard anything at all more important than the practice of oratory, I mean either now or in the past, or rather that I am at all deficient in the utmost zeal and enthusiasm for these matters, criticize me and blame me as you wish. But if perhaps you find that I am not even wanting in the jibe, "that I am indeed in a way all talk",[17] and if I have never done anything else except what pertains to the gods, and our work has been done and accomplished, to speak by their grace, as carefully as we could, but has not been overdone,—if this should clearly be the case, cover your heads in shame for two reasons: since you neither dare to employ me and in addition since you imitate those women, who they say,[18] whenever they do not do what they intended, attribute their mistakes and faults to their husbands. (17) Examine and consider the matter from the beginning, like an accounting, as briefly as possible. For the god[19] granted to me, while still a young man, to employ the best teachers[20] and for their first words to me to be that I would surely excel. (18) Beginning at that point to this day I have lived by devoting my time to studies and oratory, except when I was prevented by the requirements of health or by periods bringing misfortunes which were too great for the life which I had chosen. Still we survived even in these circumstances, clinging to our raft like a kind of Odysseus,[21] since we did not sail alone,[22] but under the protection of the greatest and most humane helmsman,[23] who has ever kept our boats from sinking. (19) Alone of all the Greeks whom we know, we did not engage in oratory for wealth, reputation, honor, marriage, power, or any acquisition. But since we were its true lover, we were fittingly honored by oratory. (20) To[24] some the company of boys is sweet, to some to bathe as much as possible, to some to drink to satiety, some are excited by horses and dogs. And by Zeus, oratory has been forsaken by some intent on play and by others with different interests. But for me oratory means everything, signifies everything. For I have made it children, parents, work, relaxation, and all else. And for this purpose I invoke Aphrodite.[25] This is my play, this is my work. In this I rejoice, this I admire, its doors I haunt.[26] And although I could still say much else besides, I forbear, so that I may not appear boorish. (21) Indeed, my views on reputation are to accept and cherish it when it comes—for I would otherwise wholly be a fool—, but not to work for it beyond oratory itself and the uprightness of

my life consonant with this. If in view of this one should wish to express admiration, let him, but if not, I bid him farewell. (22) I made the most public appearances that I know of. And do not consider this from the past, if you wish, but from these present times themselves. For in what national festival or in what assembly have we neglected to honor our city[27] publicly? And at that not through a want of reputation. For to speak by the grace of the gods, our reputation has become so great that there is no need to engage in contests to acquire one, but it is prudent to keep silent in order to preserve the one which we have. (23) Indeed, for those who were eager to study with me privately, I not only made myself available when I engaged in oratorical contests,[28] but also more or less acted as an instructor in the ways in which I thought that they would be improved.

(24) Well then! Our conduct has been such as or similar to this. But consider your conduct, in turn, compared to ours, O you desperate lovers, who are so exceptionally fond of me and are convinced that I am the best of the Greeks, and shout this out in the gymnasiums and throughout the market place,[29] but behave the same way as—I shall say nothing overly biting, be brave—the sons of famous men. For it is enough for them to have such fathers, but for the most part they themselves are playboys. And it is enough for you that I am present and speak, but you thought that attendance on and participation in my lectures should be entirely left to foreigners. (25) Instead of going to lectures, most of you spend your time at the swimming pools. And then you are amazed if you miss some of the speakers. But, I think, you do not wish to tell yourselves the truth, that it is impossible for jewelry lovers, bath addicts, and admirers of the unworthy to understand oratorical lectures. But you attribute your faults to me, and you malign me with your praise, by saying, "Would that he wished" and some such things, clearly as if I were now asleep. (26) Yet, as Homer says,[30] each argument has an answer, and "whatever you say, such you should expect to hear in turn". It is the most extreme misfortune for one who claims to be an orator and who is unjustly accused, not to employ his own instruments.[31] (27) While the gods are kind, I should vehemently deny that I am afraid of oratorical contests. But I am afraid of my terrible opponents. Am I to say who? These men, anointed with oil, who carry about palm-leaf fans,[32] and who, by Zeus, do not invite people to the lectures of the orators, just as I

even once saw happen in my own case at this "Meropian Cos"[33] and in Cnidus.[34] But do you know what? They praise the swimming pools and the verse "Come hither and stay your ship",[35] and such are their recommendations and representations to those who put into port. (28) Whenever the orator enters from one side to contend, and from the other side comes your leafy[36] flaneur with such promises, with good reason, I think, the latter wins the victory, and neither old nor young readily wish to behave with moderation. This is what trips up speakers, this like a cloud or moonless night darkens all the beauty of education. (29) Besides, the cursed sophists persuade you that even Homer's greatest quality was that he was the son of the Meles.[37] Then everyone eagerly hastens to Homer's father to philosophize there.[38] And from their actions you cannot conceive this, if indeed they tell the truth, that Homer was not satisfied to dwell by the banks of his father and to swim with his brothers the fishes, as is their story, but that he lived so squalid a life that it is clear that often he was glad if he had enough of the necessities. He allowed baths which were improvised and were "for the assistance of sick bodies", as Plato says.[39] But he did not permit further luxuries.[40] (30) It is this indescribable corruption which has implanted in all men the greatest indifference to all things. For every man fearing that he may die prematurely, destroys himself in expectation. He accounts as an advantage all that is most shameful, but otherwise regards as a loss and bother all that is good, as if he would not go to the dead maimed both in body and mind, since there will be no place there for him.[41] (31) But, I think, it was quite the opposite when such corruption[42] impends. Enjoy the finest things of life while it is possible, so that if we should belong to the part which is saved, we may be saved in the finest things, in studies and in oratory, and so that we may not adjust to a swinish way,[43] and wallow in it night after night and day after day. But if we are not saved, so that one may count as a gain whatever he has done before death. (32) Or by the gods, is there profit in bathing in your lifetime, which at any rate even awaits you when you are dead, but only disagreeableness in the enjoyment of oratory in your lifetime with yourself as speaker or in attendance on another, which you are necessarily barred from after death? And is the companionship of a whore the height of felicity, but the companionship of the first of the Greeks, even for a little while, a kind of curse? And must the stomach be gratified from which most diseases emanate, but must all that pertains to oratory otherwise be regarded as unsubstantial drivel, O my good men, who educate the world before yourselves? (33) But just as you think that I should wish to speak, so exhort yourselves to make me wish to speak. But if not, each of us shall perform our own tasks. For I shall not give up speaking even so, so long as the god[44] is propitious, but you shall always be ignorant.

(34) Call these remarks, if you wish, a defense, or if you wish, a well intentioned censure, or even a combination of the two. But still they were truthful and expedient for all to hear. "Then either you must stop this behavior", says Demosthenes,[45] or not so lightly tell lies about Hippolytus and Bellerophon.[46]

XXXIV. AGAINST THOSE WHO BURLESQUE THE MYSTERIES (OF ORATORY)[1]

(1) They are charming people who make their audiences responsible for their oratorical skills—so that I may begin politely—and who say that they transgress the bounds of order and rectitude for this purpose, so that they can please as many as possible. Yet if they use this excuse in asking for compassion, why do they think that they should be praised? For praise and compassion are separate entities; and when they do not even praise themselves, it is scarcely likely that they would be praised by others. Again if their behavior raises no difficulties, but is correct, what need is there to fix the responsibility on the masses and to take refuge in this excuse? Should they not prove that their behavior is correct? (2) But, I think, they are a clever group and "they strike a double blow",[2] so that if they escape detection, they may win their case in this way; but if you apprehend them, they may have a refuge and may say that they were not ignorant of the better course, but they erred for the sake of others. This is the first and greatest condemnation which through their excessive cleverness they pass against themselves. (3) For I would certainly hope that I might be famous among all other men, but still that my reputation might begin at home and that I first persuade myself of it, and that I might not suffer the fate of the dog in the fable,[3] and that while I am gathering the good opinion of others, I might not destroy that which I ought to have about myself, and that I might not first be convinced to my despite that I am bad, before confirming my reputation with other men as an important speaker. But they seem to me to be so far from making a defense, whenever they offer these arguments, that they bring two charges against themselves instead of one: first that they follow such wanton behavior in their oratory; and second that they do so for this purpose, as if they were going to be judged better speakers thereby. (4) Indeed, whenever they seek to lead us astray as if we would immediately believe in their fabrications and would not recognize the truth, again they reveal this as another and third evidence of their folly: that they do not think that they are caught in the act. (5) But, as I believe, the truth of the matter is as follows. No one willingly abandons what is best. Some others perhaps will

agree with them, but not Plato and Pindar, wise in many other respects, and not least in the following regard. The one says,[4] "No one willingly has found his own evil". And again having started with the tale of Eriphyle, he remarks,[5] "Alas, how the ignorant cares of short-lived men are deceived". And the other throughout his works defines and proves that faults are involuntary and that no one is willingly bad.[6] (6) Nor let us be convinced by them that although they possess better skills, they willingly give these up in exchange for those that are worse. If they had gold, they would not exchange it for lead, not even if all mankind would applaud them. Nor would they exchange wheat for millet, nor wine for lees and stale lees at that, nor, I think, a rich cloak for a rush mat, nor again when they could smell of myrrh, to smell of hides. (7) These are the arguments of men who apply euphemisms to their badness and misfortune and who, I think, do not wish to say what is just and true, that they neither know the right way nor can go upon it, but who claim that they do this in the course of gratifying their audience. As if actors who were thrown off the stage and were unable to conclude their play in a normal fashion, should say that this was done in the course of gratifying the spectators, and that they were hissed and clucked off by those very spectators in return for this kindness. One would say, 'Is that really why you also are hissed off by your audience?' But let us not discuss this yet. (8) What prevents beggars clad in rags also from saying that they have at home other very valuable clothes, but that they assume this appearance before strangers? Did not the same poet, whom I mentioned a little before,[7] say that "good men turn the fair part outside"? (9) Therefore if they talk about their speeches as if they were of the better sort, what need is there to blame the masses because they desire these speeches? But if they admit that they have been at fault, they are doing the opposite of what they should. For it was much more reasonable for them to consider how they might speak in a better way for the sake of their future audiences and students, than for them to conceal their existing good qualities and display inferior ones, and at that intentionally procured. (10) We do not go to processions in our worst dress. But even if there should be nothing at home, we should borrow something, so that we would clearly have the best possible clothes, vessels, horses, and all else which the procession requires. (11) Therefore whenever they say that they have imported and procured these qualities and willingly transgress the bounds of their old style, we should ask them whether that style was worse or better. For if it was better, are they not insane, if they have abandoned their own, more valuable style and pursue one which is both worse and not properly theirs? But if they will say that it was worse, they cannot claim that they willingly abandon their better qualities, which they never possessed or saw. For this is no defense of their errors, but an admission that they would have been even worse speakers, if they had not been prevented from doing so. (12) It would please me to ask them, should it gratify their audience to view them maimed either, by Zeus, in the eyes, or the hand, or even in some other part of the body, whether they will readily provide this service, or whether they would give up no part of their body for another's pleasure, while counting as no loss the corruption of the best part of their soul. (13) Whenever I hear them using these arguments, I do not reject the notion that cripples will dare to say that they have come to this fortune not unwillingly, but willingly gave up their legs, so that they might make the most pleasant possible impression upon the beholder. I do not know who is so madly in love, but let us assume, if you wish, that all men are. But who is so unfortunate as to choose misfortune willingly? Or who maims himself to please another? (14) For while we see that acts of kindness are practiced for the reason that there is an expectation of a future return of kindness thereby, yet everyone would very much hesitate to mistreat himself in order to gratify someone. Indeed, it would be great folly to regard as bad those friends who do not wish to requite a kindness, but to act so immoderately as to treat oneself in the worst way before one's employers have done him a kindness, and to deprive oneself of his best possessions before it is clear what kind of thanks he will get for his zeal. (15) They would not offer the example of Zopyrus and the Cephallenian,[8] the former of whom cut off his nose and ears and entered Babylon,[9] and the latter of whom disfigured himself with blows and "slipped into Troy with its wide streets",[10] when the former was eager to take Babylon, and the latter Troy. (16) First of all the prizes are not equal, concerning an enemy and titillating someone's ears. Secondly the very opposite conclusion emerges from these examples. For if those men knew how to exercize so much endurance, that they did not even spare their bodies, but underwent the most extreme pain and hardship so as not to abandon any of their original plans, while these although they could maintain their subject without trouble and difficulty, prefer effeminacy, how would not any suffering on the latter's part be just? For I think that these men because of their wantonness[11] and injury to oratory would with good reason suffer at the hands of others what those men did to themselves. Indeed, would they emulate those men so as not to abandon their position,[12] when now they do everything in their abandonment of it—so that I may not say, let everything be done to them? (17) Further, Odysseus and Zopyrus endured this perhaps because they had no other way of taking the enemy. But what will these men claim? That they cannot guide and persuade mankind with the best and most upright arguments? The statement is not only false, it is shameful. But that while persuasion is possible in that way, they prefer it in this way? Then they attribute to themselves very shameful conduct. But let us repeat their contention. (18) 'It is not possible to persuade mankind in a fashion other than this one.' Let us grant this for the sake of argument, if you approve. If the better way and persuasion are separate entities, why should the better way be rejected, since, even if we do not persuade, our actions are better than their way? But if persuasion and the better way are united, if that way is the better way, it is possible to persuade in that way; but if it is possible only to persuade in their way, then their way is the better way. Why then do they make this distinction and separate what is best from the faults which they commit for the sake of other people? For they seem to me to behave in a thoroughly drunken fashion[13] in respect to oratory whenever they take refuge in these arguments.

(19) Indeed, that they do not tell the truth or anything like the truth, but that one who intends to persuade and in short to control people must choose and go upon, as far as he can, the best and firmest path and that which is wholly incorruptible and blameless, can be proved both by a long and by a very brief argument. I say "brief", because it is so very clear, but somewhat "long", because one could prove it with countless witnesses and examples. (20) First, if you wish, let us consider the contestants in warfare, whether they would be kept safer and better rout and defeat their opponents, if they used strong, sound, and firm weapons, or carried a sword made of tin, a breastplate made of bark, and again a fig-wood spear, and a helmet and shield of like construction? (21) I think that precision in the making of armaments and the fact that

they are initially manufactured from the best material and as well as possible and their ability to last through the battle are important both to the safety, reputation, victory, and all that one would assign to this category of those who own and employ those weapons. But when they have been broken, smashed, or damaged in some other way, or even right from the start are weak and rotten, those who employ them leave their bodies to chance, and not even very valiant men are able to know what to do in this situation. Homer also attests to this. For according to him, those heroes, whose spear points have been broken, are unwilling to stand firm, and much more so, whenever they completely break their spear shafts. But they leave the battle and go off to get stronger shafts.[14] (22) Again, if you wish, do they fight better when they keep their positions, stand firm, respect one another as much as possible, and obey their orders, or when they have scorned all of these things, and have fallen prey to the apparent pleasure of the moment, and at the first trumpet blast have thrown away their shields, and have judged their duty, their post, and their good order as if they were some sort of silliness and nonsense? Homer does not even allow those who are properly intent upon fighting to say anything which is shameful. And I find it remarkable, if it is shameful for warriors to say what is not good, yet it is not worse for speakers to say what is shameful. (23) Come now, let us consider those in the crown contests,[15] as for example Dorieus of Rhodes and Glaucus of Carystus, and Milo and Poulydamas, and all those to whom bronze statues have been erected. Did those in charge of the contest for Olympian Zeus crown them for their mincing, drunken behavior and their twistings and turnings like dancing girls, or because they displayed a marvelous self-control and strength of both body and soul, qualities which provide the greatest and soundest pleasures both to their possessors and to those who have recognized them? (24) By Zeus, are not the best and most remarkable horses, and the ones most pleasing to the beholder, those which have finished their run as strongly and as powerfully as possible, and without diverging from the course, and in every way maintaining the virtue and nature proper to them? In respect to its own usefulness there is an identity between the best and the most pleasant. (25) Indeed, physical beauty has this character, and whether you mention Ganymede, Pelops, or anyone, along with his allotted fortune he attracts the beholder. And with very good reason. For beauty must have its charm, I think, and from this charm must love ensue. For one must desire whatever charms him. Therefore it is denied[16] that "there is any love of the shameful", while the poets say[17] that the gods also love the beautiful. (26) Thus the beauty of oratory along with all of nature also has this power, the enchantment of the audience, so that inferior speeches need not be used for persuasion, but the attempt must be made to speak as well as possible, so that we may persuade as many as possible. For just as the best enchantments are the most seductive,[18] so the best speeches are the most persuasive. (27) But to believe that there is anything good or charming in these corruptions is the same as if we should claim in respect to physical beauty that the consumptives,[19] the dropsical, and those spotted with white and scaly leprosy have the most pleasant appearance possible and have many admirers—although, to begin with, no one would even want to meet them—, while we should be persuaded that those who, along with their excellent health, also have been honored with a handsome appearance are inferior to the former group. But in that case "the springs of the rivers would flow backwards".[20] (28) Not to mention physical beauty, in modeling and sculpture by what is the spectator most overcome? Is it not by the fairest and most magnificent statues, the ones which have achieved the limits of perfection in these matters? The Olympian Zeus, the Athena at Athens—I mean the ivory one, and also, if you wish, the bronze one, and by Zeus, if you wish, the Lemnian Athena[21]—, all these statues embody the unsurpassable skill of the craftsman and offer unsurpassable pleasure to the spectator. (29) You would also say the same, I think, about the paintings of Apelles[22] and whomever else you might wish to admire. The line, preserved in due proportion, has preserved the whole. (30) Well then! What sort and what kind of temples do we most delight to behold, do we most admire, and do we leave with the greatest regret? Is it not those which are the largest and most dignified, and at the same time have achieved the greatest harmony? (31) What kind of ship is desirable and provides the greatest joy and pleasure to the passengers? That which is rotted, broken, and rides low because of the bilge? Or quite the contrary, the one which is as perfect and sound as possible, and has long been readied to run upon the waves? (32) Then while in other matters each object which preserves its proportion in this way attracts and persuades as many people as possible, yet in oratory itself[23]—what shall we say, by the gods? (33) Indeed, if oratory was discovered for some other purpose, not for persuasion, perhaps there would be something to dispute. But when it is very clear that this is the single goal of the whole state of the faculty of reason and oratory,[24] one of these alternatives certainly must be true: either proportion[25] is improper and insufficient, or what is best and mastery over one's audience is identical. Therefore it is unnecessary to corrupt oratory to gain mastery over the audience. But just as it is the nature of siege engines to capture cities, even if none of the enemy knows the material and means of their construction, so a well composed speech performs its task, even if it has the most uncultivated audience. (34) I find it remarkable if in the case of wine, wheat, olive oil, honey, meat, cakes, milk, ointments, water, wood, and stones, no one would claim that those which were corrupted were more pleasant than those which were uncorrupted, but would say that speeches, which were in as pure and unalloyed state as possible, were less pleasant than those which were corrupted—no one would claim this. The words themselves[26] declare that this is not said to astound by its unexpectedness, but that it cannot be otherwise. (35) Who is the best epic poet?[27] Yet who pleases and delights the greatest number of men? Or did he also foresee this concerning himself? For when he speaks to the Delian girls at the end of his hymn, he says,[28] if someone should ask you: "O maidens, whom do you find the sweetest poet that comes here and in whom do you most delight? Do you all well answer with praise: He is a blind man, and he lives in rocky Chius". (36) Again who are the most distinguished in tragedy, and one might say, win by all the votes? I think, the best are Sophocles, Aeschylus, and Euripides. For let me not say who is the best of these, but only that these are beyond all the others. (37) Which of the orators up to our day is the most famous, the most admired, and has the greatest reputation among the masses?[29] The one who most excelled in the beauty of his oratory. All men, who have the greatest reputation for their work, bear witness for me.

(38) Yes by Zeus, someone would say. But the masses have followed the opinion and the initial verdict of a few experts. I do not disagree. But still it is quite clear that both among the few and among the masses the better part must enjoy distinction, and so much the more by as much as it is more perfect. (39) Further if the influence of the best experts is so great that they are the ones

who even make the reputation of others from their own judgments, how is not expertise strong in every way? Or why should one omit the cultivation of the best experts and seek to please the masses who depend upon the best experts and not upon themselves? For in that way we shall be judged and admired by both, but in this way almost by neither since the judgment of the masses is without authority. (40) But what do I think? That the masses follow the best men and immediately by themselves admire what is finest through a sort of divine fate. For it would be highly ridiculous if they know of the expert speakers by means of other experts but themselves are ignorant of these speakers, and if they judge in turn that the judges of these speakers are superior to themselves, but will not admire those who at the beginning give the finest oratorical displays, although the latter possess along with technical knowledge the real faculty of persuasion. There is no one who will deny that this is true. (41) Yet if it were impossible to persuade both groups, it would be preferable, I believe, for those who think that they should belong to the better class of speakers to persuade the best part. But when it is possible either from the start to master both these and those or by means of those also to win over these, the best style of speaking triumphs on every count. (42) We also have the poets as witnesses to this, who say that the best and soundest orators are most admired and felicitated among the masses.[30] And what need is there to list the old poets or orators? Whoever caused greater excitement in the assemblies—and may god kindly guide my speech—than we here? Or who more, to speak by the grace of the gods—for let this phrase preface all these candid remarks[31]—touched both groups, I mean both the cultivated and those whom we call the masses, who, indeed, although under the compulsion of no law, render their verdicts under oath? I omit other instances. Consider only what you are now exclaiming after these remarks. (43) Did we ever say anything to gratify our audiences? Not a syllable. Yet many and sundry were our remarks. For alone[32] of those who have ever taken up oratory, we boast—and this is the most moderate way to put it—that we have combined into a single faculty and that we display in their fullness all of the skills that exist or are believed to exist in oratory. Such is my way. And I would say that I do nothing to please and that I fail to please in nothing, for which with good reason I please in the proper way. (44) Then when I have observed in actual practice and in my own speeches that the best style of

XXXIV. AGAINST THOSE WHO BURLESQUE THE MYSTERIES   181

speaking is not left without its reward, am I to concede to these fools to tell lies against the masses when they say that they behave ignorantly for their sakes? Not while I know myself.

(45) Again if some who claim that they have chosen a style of speaking beyond the capacity of the masses do not succeed with them, but are extinguished before anyone observed their light, this is nothing against the more dignified or in short better sort of speeches. For they suffer this through their lack of the most important requirements since they have provided neither sufficient thought nor ornament in their speeches. But if they were perfect in their music, they would have the same ability which Orpheus is said to have had. They would persuade all men. Now the myth in an exaggerated fashion attributes to him the power to attract wood and stone, but they are like wood and stone in their inability to move anyone. (46) But we did not propose to investigate all the different kinds of their mistakes in oratory, nor if some other speakers also are failures, but the fact that evil has never triumphed over virtue. And we would not be ashamed to make this claim in every case. (47) Indeed, I once actually caught one of those who grovels before the masses causing an effect opposite to what he intended. For to gratify his audience, he sang, modulating his voice,[33] while he added the same final clause at the end of each sentence, as if in a song. But his darling audience was so amazed and enraptured by the song that when it reached the phrase, it itself with a laugh supplied it, not in responsion like an echo, but ahead of time. And the chorus leader[34] made quite a pretty picture by being later than his chorus. But they also added something else "to bring about this indecent comic dance",[35] so that the symphony between the sophist and his comrades, who had made him distraught, was pitiful. Such are the prizes which are won from the gods of oratory[36] by those who prefer the best forms of speech and such by those who injure oratory. (48) Next they behave in the same way as if some hermaphrodite or eunuch should not blame his physical disability or fate but should claim that he had become like this through providence. But, dear sir, you are neither telling the truth nor behaving at all with moderation if you claim that you willingly prefer this condition. (49) And now in these arguments I am in danger of being kinder to them than they are to themselves. For I represent them as unwilling and as suffering this through a kind of misfortune. But they claim that they intentionally use these embellishments. But the law orders

that willing transgressors pay twice the fine of those who have unwillingly caused injury. (50) But I seem not at all to be able to conceive of what they mean. For they seem to me to say that they are not unwillingly remiss, and again that they are not willingly, but unwillingly remiss. For whenever they refer to the audience and say that the reason lies with them, they seem to me to say that they err, as it were, unwillingly. But whenever they say that they know that their speeches are not good, but that they choose a way of speaking which will charm their audience, they seem to me to confess that they err willingly, just as those in the tragedies do when they say that they know that what they are about to do is wrong, but that they cannot control themselves.[37] Such are their riddles. (51) Yet in fact Cratinus says[38] that "he who gratifies his friends in shameful pleasures is himself a wicked man". But if they regard the masses as friends, they are no different from the masses. Therefore if they have the same pleasures, they gratify themselves no less than the masses. Again if they do not think of them as friends, why do they gratify them? For whether they gratify the masses because the masses love them or because they love the masses, they cannot avoid the shameful imputation. But they also speak in riddles on this point. For they say that the masses love them. Yet they themselves are clearly the lovers of the masses, since they behave wantonly in order to please the masses. (52) Indeed, if they care nothing about the masses, for what reason will they say they gratify them? But if they care for them, would they be better men if they educated them and showed them the true road of oratory, or if they themselves inherited their wickedness? (53) As if someone should claim to be a doctor,[39] and although he ought to give the best advice to the sick, should himself serve their desires and should limit his art to gratification. You will condemn your patients, and you yourself will be condemned before sound minded judges. Indeed, even nature has so ordained[40] that the general lead the soldiers, not follow them, and so the chorus leader the chorus, the helmsman the sailors, the charioteer the team, and the doctor those who seek his services. Then when it is possible for you yourselves to behave in a better fashion and to improve your audience, you behave in a worse fashion and choose to render them still worse than they are. (54) Indeed, true leadership is to succeed by speaking according to one's nature and preference, but divergence from one's style in order to appear to say something is to be led rather than to lead.

XXXIV. AGAINST THOSE WHO BURLESQUE THE MYSTERIES

Therefore if you cannot speak better than this, you are doubly unfortunate, both in what you do say and in what you are unable to say. But if, while it is possible to persuade your audience in the other way, you choose this way, how are you not mad? Or where is the beauty in your speeches, when you have reached such decisions about oratory? (55) Again consider this well-known argument. The orator, the philosopher, and all those involved in liberal education should not, I think, please the masses in the same fashion as these servile fellows, dancers, pantomimes,[41] and tricksters. They certainly are to be excused if they do and say anything, but how will it be proper for us to imitate their evils? (56) For when the same conduct does not seem proper to a free woman and to a whore, and still less does the same conduct seem proper to men and to women, we certainly shall not say that the same conduct is proper to men and to whores. Whenever you rank yourselves among the female entertainers and you befoul in public the rites of the Muses, should you in all justice argue about your honor, or be buried alive in the Persian manner?[42] (57) Let us also consider this, that the people do not love and admire with their whole heart these spectacles, to which one would say they have become particularly addicted. For who is there who does not think that he is better than every dancer? Or who would permit the pantomime to speak off stage? But they are titillated for the moment. Yet as soon as they have left, they deride these people, or rather even during the performance itself their pleasure is, as it were, one of derision. Nothing silly, I think, is more valuable than what is serious.[43] So the ridiculous would be far from ever taking precedence over the serious. (58) But when we even set a high premium on a good reputation for our future memory, where should one rank these men whose reputation dies each day and on the spot? (59) Yes by Zeus, but Heracles also danced among the Lydians.[44] But the same writers also tell the following tale about Heracles, that he murdered his wife and sons when he was in a condition which is not proper to mention.[45] What sensible person would believe this? But still if you are thoroughly convinced, answer me, by Heracles himself, if for this reason you too would gladly be corrupted. You shall say no. (60) I cannot say whether Heracles danced among the Lydians. But if he did, still it was for a single day, and out of playfulness, and at the same time perhaps in mockery of the Lydians, and I should add as a fourth argument, that he became no worse a man in the circumstances of his dancing, but he remained who he was. I also know of certain Laconian dances and other dances used in the tragedies, called "emmelia", I believe. For dancing itself is not shameful,[46] but what is shameful must everywhere be avoided. But not among the Lydians, nor for a single time, nor in mockery, nor while you are internally sound, but before all mankind, every day, you do a burlesque, which, not to mention Heracles, it was not even proper to praise in Omphale. (61) To which speakers is the style even suitable? Those concerned with civil and judicial orations? But they would suffer the opposite of the Thessalian Caeneus,[47] by changing from men into women. But to those concerned with philosophy? You would make a charming picture, you slippery fellow, exhorting men to moderation, courage, and self-control in this song of yours,[48] while you yourself lacked the self-control to abide in the position assigned by oratory.[49] As if Sardanapallus,[50] while weaving with his shuttle, sang exhortations to battle. But is the fashion suited to governors? To our Emperors?[51] To rulers at all? It is not even suited to a single age group. For is it suited to younger men? But they will seem to behave like whores, if they accept this. To grown men? But they will seem to belie their name. To older men? But the shame is most inopportune. Women are left, and those the most wanton, with whom these men should be compared. Yet they emulate them, but they are far inferior. (62) "I find it remarkable if death is set as the penalty for those who debase the coinage", to quote Demosthenes,[52] while we shall grant to those, who make counterfeit and falsely coined speeches, free speech or even this to begin with, the right to speak at all. If ever someone stumbles over a word, he is immediately a fool. But if ever he corrupts good order with his whole course of action, will he not remove himself from all national festivals?[53] (63) Indeed, my advice is not only on behalf of oratory, but also on behalf of all decorum and good order, and on whether one should abide by the laws or do whatever he wishes for the sake of a momentary pleasure. If my arguments prevail, law and order prevail, by which not only the cities, but also the whole earth and heaven itself is held together and preserved. But the forgeries of these men are inimical to all divine and human things.

(Subscription: Against Those Who Burlesque The Mysteries. At the games of the Provincial Assembly of Asia in Smyrna.[54] It was admired beyond all the others.[55])

ANONYMOUS

XXXV. REGARDING THE EMPEROR[1]

(1) But it seems to me to be a good thing in a feast[2] and sacred festival to mention and say something about our divine and generous Emperor. For there is no fear that having chosen to praise him, we might lack things to say. Rather the qualities of the Emperor are such that no one could speak worthily about them. Yet urged on by his goodness and generosity in other matters, I have even become confident in speaking about him. (2) Therefore I omit all the other excuses, which are customarily offered or claimed by speakers in their introductions, some alleging the magnitude of the accomplishments,[3] and others the small time spent on the speech. Without invoking the Muses, as certain poets do, or any other external aid, I shall turn right to the praise of the Emperor, not out of willfulness or contempt for the task, but since I see that those who use soft words and make excuses at the start in a certain way themselves despise the subjects of their speeches. For when they say these things, they seem to me to indicate nothing other than this—in their speaking extemporaneously—that if they had planned and prepared for a longer time, they would have provided a speech equal to the magnitude of the deeds. But when they grant this, they claim for themselves the ability to speak on the greatest matters, and they bestow on themselves this excessive praise. (3) I see that no length of time is sufficient nor is any speech worthy of the Emperor, nor will anyone be able to praise him sufficiently. Still one must not be faint hearted, but must try to speak to the limit of his ability.[4] (4) For whenever we sacrifice to the gods, we do not do this, I think, regarding it as a true return, but we repay them, as much as we can, with this act of gratitude. Therefore, even those who intend to praise the Emperor should not hesitate, but confidently undertake his praise. Perhaps our remarks about him will be wanting, but we will not want for things to say.[5]

(5) The following single statement is the first and greatest thing which can be said about him, that even before his rule was established he was worthy of the Empire. For some have possessed their empire through others or inherited it from their predecessors,[6] the

former by putting the claims of force before those of justice and the latter by preserving, as it were,[7] the sequence and succession of some family. In this way they possessed their kingdom. But for one who neither by his edict nor at his request, but at the request of all men that he rule them,[8] gave himself to those who requested and summoned him, this prize was long due to this man even for his virtue. (6) Many disputed with those other men for their empire, no one with him. Yet whether they believe that they should yield to their fear of him or to respect for one who is greater, or as I said,[9] to his best and most just resolve, how is it not clear from all these things who should have been emperor? (7) Moreover, it is possible to judge by those who ruled before him,[10] how superior he was to them right at the start in these very circumstances. For they entered upon the scene with wars and much slaughter, and they slew many in battle,[11] and for many others they were the cause of incurable misfortunes, so that many subject cities were made deserts, much territory was uprooted, and very many lives were expended, so that all did not take place lawfully for them nor could they even say this of themselves. (8) But he took over things so lawfully and well that neither in the course of becoming emperor nor at the beginning of his rule did he require any murder. Nor, as in a time of change and the settling of affairs, did anyone experience any difficulty, nor was anything done of the many necessary acts which usually happen in such circumstances. No men, no cities, no nation suffered anything incurable or terrible. But the gods so cared for him, so that he would lawfully and piously take over affairs, that they assigned to others the deeds of madness and folly,[12] but reserved for him those of justice, generosity, and the other acts of piety.[13] (9) Indeed, when he held the Empire, he did nothing grim, nor did he imitate or emulate any such acts. Nor did he act at all like other emperors before him, who, in fear of some of those in power, accused them of treason and punished some with exile and others with death. Nor did his character change. But he is so far from all such acts and so removed from wishing to cause slaughter and death, that even some of those who plot against him and are clearly guilty, still survive and live through his generosity. (10) And this is not only an indication of his gentleness, his lawful conduct toward all men and a disposition free of envy toward some of those of rank and power, but also of his utter fearlessness, his impassiveness in the face of circumstances, and of his slowness to wrath and anger,[14] and of his firm and unshakable attitude toward all men. (11) With good reason. For when a man has learned and been trained in what is proper, and has not neglected or remained ignorant of any form of culture, but has adorned his soul with every kind of virtue, it was to be expected for him to be free of every fault. (12) When the Emperor had had this education and had shared in all the finest things, of which some were his by nature and others were acquired by education,[15] not in an average way and not like some other men, but each to the fullest, he was of great use to the Empire even before he ascended to its rule. (13) For he alone or among few emperors had an exceptional quality. What do I mean? Those emperors before ascending the throne handled their own affairs and only began to care for the Empire when they came to rule. But he was so consecrated to the Empire that first of all when he held the rank which he happened to hold[16] and the future was unclear, and he saw that much of the Empire was neither well nor lawfully administered, but that much willfulness, crime, and wantonness had arisen, he did not allow it to increase or go further; but as if he were healing the rotten and diseased portions of a great and unhealthy body, or as it were restraining the fierce and disobedient nature of a wild and violent stallion,[17] sometimes carried off by it, but often restraining and impeding its continuous, senseless, and violent impulses, he acted and planned in a way expedient for it. (14) Such was he before he became Emperor. But when Providence, which administers and orders the Universe, sat this most just and lawful of emperors upon the Imperial throne, what would one say is the first and greatest advantage which we enjoy from his providence and good fortune? When everything was in a state of upheaval and was shifting, one might say, to another land,[18] and the Empire was tempest tossed, as it were, in a great storm or earthquake, and next like a ship about to sink was carried to the ends of the earth, to where some who had been rulers and emperors had formerly wandered,[19] and then as if in a labyrinth, fell upon many harsh difficulties and finally despaired, blocked from the road back and unable to return, when he saw this, he did not, like an inexperienced helmsman, allow the Empire to be carried away and run risks as it chanced to happen, but as if he were the most experienced of emperors and excelled in understanding, first of all he restrained it and stopped it from its headlong rush there and next he guided and brought it to anchor.[20] (15) And now it is anchored most securely, as a ship calmly settled after a great storm. Thus he guides and administers the Empire in the fashion which is proper to one who honors piety and justice, and also moderation, self-control, intelligence, and every other virtue. For he began, as is fitting, with piety, but proceeded even through all the other parts of virtue. For who has produced so many and such proofs of justice, generosity, and every other virtue, as this Emperor did?

(16) And first of all let us consider his justice in respect to money. For when the budget ordained for the government became excessive and more tribute was added, and not even this was enough, but the treasuries everywhere were empty, and fear about the future kept growing, he asked and sought no increase, nor did he become wicked because of money, but he remitted and lightened the burden, being in these matters not only the most just, but also the most generous of emperors. And such he was in respect to money. (17) But who would worthily praise his justice and generosity in respect to lawsuits? For what Rhadamanthys or what Aeacus[21] kept himself so just a judge in every case? Or rather, justice is not always and in every way generous, but he has a precise knowledge of justice, as if he himself were its legislator and discoverer.[22] Although he does not deviate from justice, still he confirms his generosity through this, so that his most perfect justice is equivalent to the most pure generosity. (18) The reason for this is that he does not get his concept of justice from looking to other interpreters. But from his knowledge of what is truly fine and good, derived from his education, with his additional experience in the law, so that he is unaware of nothing written concerning it, he renders his decisions in all matters. (19) Indeed, no one has departed from him without obtaining justice. Nor has anyone found fault with his decisions, neither the prosecutor when defeated nor the defendant when convicted, but both parties depart satisfied and with an obeisance,[23] and the loser and the winner give the same opinion of his verdict[24]. And if ever someone happens to be punished, they do not regard their suffering and punishment as terrible, but count it as their gain that they did not suffer more besides. For he does not think of the punishment of wrongdoers as an act of hatred, but of education, especially, if it is in any way possible, of them, but if not, of those who will hear of it. (20) Again if it is a fair and fitting thing for an emperor to be a lover of Greece,[25] this man deserves praise. For our Emperor is so much a lover of

XXXV. REGARDING THE EMPEROR

Greece[26] and has so much of this fine quality that when Greek culture had been neglected and scorned and had been stripped of its honors, and everything Greek had been thrust aside and was disregarded, our Emperor was not negligent, but added other honors to those already existing. And so much for justice. (21) What generosity is greater and more apparent than this, by which, at a time when all subjects cowered and were enslaved by fear, and many informers[27] went through all the cities and spied on men's conversations, and freedom of thought and expression were impossible, and moderate and just free speech had been removed, and every man trembled at his shadow, then he released them from this terror and liberated all men's souls, and returned to them a perfect and complete freedom. (22) The following is the greatest proof of our Emperor's generosity and is beyond every example. Although our Emperor is so young and vigorous,[28] he has surpassed all emperors in gentleness and seemly behavior, so that it is a little thing to call him, for example, "Father"[29] and "Shepherd of the people", and all the expressions which the poets have used in their praise of rulers. (23) For what kind of seemly behavior has been neglected by him? Is not his sort of generosity most available to every subject and to those who appear before him for any reason? The kindly gentleness of his appearance and the moderation of his speech and the lack of difficulty in approaching him, rather his accessibility, as it were, within a purified place, to those who even to a small degree have a good conscience, how is this not beyond all gentleness and generosity? (24) For he does not believe that by keeping himself remote and inaccessible he will get the reputation of a great and marvelous emperor and such as no other has ever been, but that he would especially confirm his title as such an emperor if he would offer his own goodwill and generosity in common to all who are in need, in the belief that the true emperor should be like the ruler of the Universe[30] in respect to his generosity and providence toward all his subjects, and that before his rule he should not display a good and moderate nature, but after he has been designated emperor, then become harsh and violent toward his subjects. Such is not the character of a seemly rule, but is the clearest proof of uncouthness and stupidity. (25) Such was the general of the Lacedaemonians, who led the Greeks against the barbarians, I mean Pausanias,[31] the son of Cleombrotus, who while he was at home, was able to behave with moderation, but when he had sailed to the Hellespont, was unmindful of his home, was unmindful of himself, and was like anyone rather than a man of Sparta, being harsh and violent toward his allies, and wanton and criminal in his way of life, and tyrannical in his behavior. (26) But he showed that both as private citizen and as Emperor it was possible for one to remain continually the same, by presenting himself to be such a man before his rule that he was justly thought worthy of it, and by having the same attitude and character in his rule, not changing or emulating wantonness, but choosing the moderate life, hating crime and lawlessness, and showing himself as an example of moderation, so that those who were up to then wanton and criminal changed their conduct when they saw his moderation and gave up their desire for money and were disposed to a more moderate behavior. (27) Indeed, we know that our Emperor is subject to none of the pleasures which rule mankind.[32] For he was so far apart from them right from the beginning that if any form of self-control is praised among mankind, that which is told of him alone seems credible. For who exercises such control over his stomach, over sexual appetites, over the other pleasures? For as I just now said,[33] he did not possess half a measure of virtue, unlike certain other emperors, who although they seemed suitable in respect to courage and generosity, were clearly most wanton in their pleasures and desires; as for example Homer in his praise of Agamemnon, the general of the Achaeans, says,[34] "Both a good king and a mighty warrior". (28) But this same king in Homer has clearly been smitten by Chryseis, and has clearly been a lover of Briseis, who belonged to Achilles, and through this desire has clearly been the cause of many great evils for the Achaeans. Achilles, the son of Thetis and Peleus, was so wanton and small-minded in respect to pleasure, that when Briseis left him and spent some time with Agamemnon, he immediately was so affected that he wept, "gazing out at the wine-dark sea",[35] calling for his mother, like a little boy who had suffered this at the hands of a playmate. When she came, he told her the reason for his tears and ordered her to ask Zeus to become an ally of the Trojans and cause the greatest harm to the Greeks. But afterwards, although he saw on each occasion many of the Achaeans falling beneath the hands of the Trojans and Hector, and although some of his comrades and friends were dying, he showed no interest or pity. (29) Those kings were very deficient in virtue, but our Emperor is "both a good king and a mighty warrior".[36] For how is he not truly brave, moderate, and self-controlled, who has so scorned pleasures that he is subject to none of them? For often even some bad men have captured walls which seemed impregnable.[37] Yet I see even many very good men mastered by pleasure. But what man is so brave that he would so easily be able to endure a life of simplicity and an inexpensive style of living? (30) Indeed, many have been brave against the enemy, but have been ruled by their own soldiers. But he so easily controlled them and kept them in order that when the soldiers were receiving many unlimited donatives, and were harsh and menacing if they should not receive this much and still more, not only did he not feed their desires, but he defined their duty and improved the soldiers in respect to physical labor and training, and he no longer allowed them to be intent on receiving donatives, but made them familiar with war maneuvers, nor did he allow them to live in luxury and pleasure, but caused them to have no time for such desires. By this act he aided the poverty of his subjects,[38] cared for the good order of the soldiers, and made the public revenues more secure. There would be no greater evidence than this of both courage and good counsel. (31) Indeed, with reason one would offer the following as evidence of his cleverness and wisdom. For to use force and compulsion to make men content is to have brought them to this state through fear and not through great sagacity. But as for persuading men to be moderate, who were insatiably disposed toward money and gifts, he could not have easily done this, I think, unless he had surpassed all men in wisdom and eloquence. (32) He has given many other proofs of intelligence in his rule, but the best and most worthy is our Emperor's good counsel and good sense in respect to war.[39] For although he saw that those who seemed to be clever and skilled in warfare thought that victory must come through battle and not through good counsel, he did not imitate or emulate them, in the belief that he should use arms against equals—for it was a fine thing to conquer such men through courage—, but that good counsel should be used against the barbarians. (33) For he knows, I think, that he who led tens of thousands of troops against the Greeks,[40] and whom neither earth nor sea was large enough to contain, was defeated by the plan of a single man.[41] For when victory is possible through good counsel,[42] what need is there here of danger? Further even bad men often achieve victory in battle, but the ability to conquer through intelligence and wisdom is characteristic of those alone who know how to use good counsel. (34) Indeed, those who wished to prove their courage on every occasion and on every pretense, in success prospered; but in defeat they involved themselves and their friends in the greatest disasters. But those who understand the necessities and make their plans accordingly, in prosperity succeed no less in their desires; but in failure are not harmed at all.[43] Our Emperor understands this and thinks that he should not imitate the foolish and reckless kind of men, but that he is secure against the barbarians through good counsel. (35) Indeed, not even in battle and arms could the enemy find fault with him,[44] but he showed them that he is able not only to conquer them by his intelligence and his other cultivation, but also by courage. For when the Germans,[45] who are the most numerous and most murderous people under the sun, after many, various attempts, now make obeisance to their lord, in recognition of the superiority of obedience and of peace to war; and when the Carpi, who formerly were most feared and dangerous to their neighbors, having been utterly annihilated by him, now no longer exist and this name of the race is alone left;[46] and when all that dwells beyond the Euphrates and the Tigris to the east, after having been shaken by war,[47] has been trained and taught to recognize its masters; (36) and when every continent enjoys peace,[48] and earth and sea crown their protector, and Greeks and barbarians now are in harmony; and when the Empire like a ship or a wall has been repaired and fortified and safely has reaped its fruits, what courage is not less than this? Or what better and more profitable state would there be than this? (37) Cannot everyone go with complete freedom where he wishes? Are not all harbors everywhere in use? Are not the mountains as secure for the traveler as the cities for their inhabitants? Does not beauty fill all the plains? Is not fear gone from everywhere? For what river fords cannot be crossed? What straits are closed? Now the national festivals are more charming and the feasts are dearer to the gods. Now too the flame of Demeter is brighter and more sacred.[49]

(38) O light of human felicity! Now all mankind seems to have found true felicity. O you who have surpassed all emperors, the wise in wisdom, the courageous in courage, in piety those who excelled in this, and in good fortune those who were most fortunate![50] In return for this we could not properly thank you either with our praise or with any other honor.

(39) But you, O noble son of noble parents,[51] may you follow in the footsteps of your father. For let this be said, since it is the greatest prayer possible in a brief compass.[52]

XXXVI. THE EGYPTIAN DISCOURSE[1]

(1) Since I only briefly and superficially answered your recent questions about the Nile and at the same time my visitors interrupted me, I wished to resume the discussion and to pay back the whole answer like any other debt. But even these arguments will be as brief as possible. For although I traveled up to the land of Ethiopia and investigated Egypt itself four times in all[2] and left nothing unexamined, not the pyramids, the Labyrinth,[3] no temple, no canals, but I got the measurements of some from books where possible, and where they were not readily available, I measured them myself with the assistance of the priests and prophets of each place, I was unable to preserve this data for you, since the notes which I had ordered my slaves to make were lost.[4] But I could at any rate acquit myself[5] of this one small question, the means of the Nile's rising and the cause of this phenomenon being contrary to other rivers in the matter of the seasons of the year. (2) You remember that at the time I immediately answered that there was a danger that no one could give any clear information about the Nile, but that idle nonsense was talked both by those who make confident assertions in respect to their opinions and by others who are in no way convinced, but pretend to be in order to impose upon the masses, so that they may seem to know something about matters which are unclear. So now I shall not tell you the cause through which this happens, but that it does not happen through the reasons which each of them alleges.

(3) I must mention certain arguments, which Herodotus[6] also controverts and refutes: first that the Etesian winds do not cause the flooding by blocking the river's flow. For if the cause lay with the Etesian winds, it is surely quite clear that this would not take place when they did not blow, which is far from the case. Further if the Etesian winds, by blowing in a southerly direction, forced back the Nile's current, certainly the winds which blow in a northerly direction should also have this same effect on the rivers on the other side,[7] I mean the Tanais and the Phasis,[8] and all those which come after them. Often many southerly and southwesterly winds have blown for a long time, both in summer and winter, and none of these rivers has undergone this phenomenon, and certainly none of

the major ones. (4) Again if they will claim that the continuity of the Etesian winds forces back the Nile, I omit the fact that the winds which I have mentioned also frequently have lasted for no less time. But the Nile certainly does not flood in the middle of the Etesian winds nor whenever they are on the point of ceasing—assuming that we attribute the increase to time—, but when they are beginning and often before they begin, so that the cause would not be the frequency of the winds, since the Nile is set in motion before they blow. (5) But the Etesian winds do not even blow entirely on the mouth of the Nile, but toward its eastern bank. For the majority of them are in fact west winds; these range from west to east. Then the Nile cannot be impeded through the Etesian winds. And if they are the reason, why does not the same thing also happen to all the rivers which flow in the same direction as the Nile? (6) Besides, the matter of the Etesian winds becomes entirely ridiculous. For if we shall accept this argument, we should also believe that winds blowing from the east stay the course of the Po and of all the rivers which join the Ionian Sea from the same direction, and that when the west winds blow, the Rhine flows inland and does not discharge into the outer ocean, and that when the northern winds blow, the rivers in the south flood, and the same for the rivers in the north when the southern winds blow. And thus we shall everywhere attribute to all rivers a phenomenon for which we seek a cause as to why it occurs in one river alone. And how is it not extraordinary, or rather simply absent-minded to seek why the Nile is special, yet to prove that all rivers are liable to the same phenomenon from the same cause? Indeed, if no other river undergoes the same phenomenon, the argument is false. But if all rivers do, why should it be said that the Nile alone does? For either the investigation does not need to be made, or this is not the cause. (7) But the following is also clear, that the Nile is not at all one of the smallest rivers, nor is it so tractable beyond all the others, that its mouths alone are blocked and changed because of the winds. For when not even the smallest river mouths are entirely blocked off, but continue to discharge, how is it likely that the very Nile, which is able to flood all Egypt, does this by being subject to the winds? And we see that sea beaches and all the shoals, far from being so flooded by great and indeed frequent winds, are in no way displaced, at least enough to say so.[9] But the waves wash against the beach and ebb, and the shoals remain unmoved. Yet water on a plane surface is more easily moved than that

XXXVI. THE EGYPTIAN DISCOURSE

flowing downward is turned back. (8) Moreover, it cannot be said that the Etesian winds fall on these regions with their strongest force. But whether we should grant that they are west winds, north winds, or whatever, obviously they strike with more force and violence those regions which are nearer and close to them. But when none of these regions are subject to this same phenomenon, how is it likely that the Nile alone is subject, which in addition to being most distant from the origin of the Etesian winds, also has a much stronger current? (9) Further the argument is simply shameless. For the Nile does not fail to discharge into the sea for this reason, that they think that the Etesian winds should provide the cause. But if you go to the mouths themselves, since the Nile will everywhere clearly have an appreciable flow when the Etesian winds are appreciable, this argument must no longer be used by those who know even a little about the Nile, in as much as it is very strange to ignore what is at hand and to dispute about what is far away and to subject the known to the unknown, but not to confirm the latter by the former, if ever it is possible. All of its mouths discharge, whether the sophists say so or not—and this is determined by sight, not by argument. And the extent of the discharge is not small, or like the range of many other river mouths, but the distance which is likely to be reached by the mouths of the greatest river of all. And again, the extent of the discharge is much greater in summer than in winter. (10) I heard the following from a man, in the words of Demosthenes,[10] "incapable of deceit", from our comrade Dion,[11] skilled both in practical matters and in literature. He said that he sailed to Egypt in summer time and that although land was not yet visible, but was so far away that there were no signs of it, the sailors drew up pure and potable water from a great depth, whether out of necessity or otherwise in their desire to put on a show for the passengers,[12] and that the Nile flowed to such an extent away from land and over the sea itself. Yet if its mouths were blocked by the Etesian winds there, how was it likely for those who were putting in in the midst of the Etesian winds and in the middle of the sea to draw up Nile water? (11) Indeed, whenever the earth is sufficiently moistened, the Egyptians also discharge their reservoirs back into the sea. Then how would their water flow out, if the Etesian winds blocked it? Since it is certainly impossible for opposing winds to impede the river at its mouth, where its flow is natural and it is at its strongest, while the winds block the water in no way, whenever its discharge is required, where it has been collected into reservoirs and is stagnant.

(12) But this argument, as in the case of special pleas, is thrust aside by the fact that all can see the river's flow and, as I said,[13] that it is much stronger in summer, as it would be because of flooding, that in winter. For if a statement had to be made which was purposely the opposite of reality, a better one could not be found. (13) But we must examine another man[14] and his argument, who says:[15] "These are the maiden-fair streams of the Nile, which in place of a divine shower irrigates Egypt's plain and fields, at the melting of the white snow". How then, O most clever Euripides, does the Nile irrigate Egypt's fields at the melting of the white snow? Where does the snow melt? In Scythia? And what has this to do with the Nile? Or in Ethiopia? Or still further away? But this is sillier than that. For the Nile certainly rises from the warmest regions of the earth, ever proceeding to a place which is less warm, however, one might say, still the warmest region which we know,[16] and here it becomes known to us. How can snow fall in a place with such a nature, especially enough snow to raise up the Nile? For where they still say that it is impossible to live because of the heat, what sort of snow is likely to exist, by means of which so great a current takes its rise? (14) For this is the same as if someone should persistently assert that the craters at Etna are the source of ice or should attempt to say that snow is a warming agent and fire a cooling one. For whenever one assumes that there is snow in the very land of heat, how is it not the same as if we should say that we know that the Nile arose among the Odrysians or Bisaltians,[17] and not from a region which we cannot even discuss, except that, on the one hand, in the course of sailing up stream you come to ever warmer regions, until it is impossible to endure it.....?[18] (15) And, as it seems, those Egyptians, who have not traveled abroad, have not even seen snow, nor can they understand what it is when another tells them about it—we ourselves could not make it clear to them, as if we were describing some other unusual phenomenon. But this was comprehensible to them in the same way as all those words which simply require interpretation for those Egyptians who know no Greek. Yet have those living at the start of the southern region more snow than heat? And would there be a greater deception on the stage than this, whether Euripides or Aeschylus[19] himself composed it? (16) The first region of Egypt differs more, one might

XXXVI. THE EGYPTIAN DISCOURSE

say, in comparison with its final region than any other nation in comparison with Egypt itself. So much does the northern region excel in heat. Then how is it likely to say that there exists at the beginning of the southern region what simply does not happen and what no one has ever heard of at our end of Egypt and in the region by the Egyptian Sea, such an abundance of ice and snow that the volume of its water is greater than that of the proper water of the river? (17) And we know that the southern winds are the warmest of all winds, and that when the sun itself is in the southern sky it scorches the interior. But are we not ashamed to assume that the regions there have an unlimited supply of that which is characteristic of the most extreme frosts and winters and of our season whenever it is most wintery, whether we ourselves advance this argument and are shameless liars, or whether we trust others who advance it and are easy dupes? But I am close to saying that this is the only thing which cannot even be imported into the country, as if it were a natural enemy. (18) Indeed, we all know that snow is much sought after during the summer.[20] Nonetheless you would find everything but this in the great city of Alexander. Yet one might especially call it, in the words of Euripides,[21] "the fringe of Egypt". Next what they cannot even import through the law of summer, does this cause the Nile to flood so greatly in the time of summer? Least of all, I think. And in response to Euripides and Aeschylus, perhaps these arguments are not only sufficient but more than sufficient, since the refutation is so clear and ready at hand and simply proves the impossibility as in the matter of the river's discharge.[22]

(19) Let us turn to an opinion held by many people and to the clever men who have invented it.[23] They say that it rains in the southern regions whenever the Etesian winds occur and that the rain clouds are driven from us down to there and burst, and that the Nile flooded by the rain with good reason is greater in summer than in winter. Therefore it is necessary for you to understand all that happens in the flooding. (20) Whenever it is time, the Nile descends from Upper Egypt.[24] But it does not descend with a noticeable increment, nor so that the added water is recognizable to the eye. But beginning with an increase of a few inches, it rises to such an extent that in nearly four months, it reaches the measure of the well-known fourteen or fifteen cubits at Memphis,[25] and in the process always keeping its increment undetected and indicating it in

this one way by its successive flooding of the earth. (21) For what purpose do I say this? Because they state that just as our rivers increase from rain in winter, so the Nile increases from rain in summer. If this were true, first of all it would be necessary for it to appear suddenly descending in flood. For just as when a stream of water is borne along the earth or a solid surface, so water in flood[26] from the rains runs upon the surface of the old water. Then why does this same phenomenon not also happen in the case of the Nile? (22) For we certainly should not refer to other rivers and form our judgments on the basis of the same phenomena, while at the same time not having the same indications in both cases.[27] For if it happened in this way only once, there was some point in the argument. But if it always rises in this way, what would they say? (23) First and most importantly, this phenomenon, which I mention, is an indication that the Nile does not flood from the rains because it is not borne along madly and violently and in a chance fashion, but as the Egyptians in fact express it, as if it were performing any other "work".[28] And its "work" ever proceeds in an orderly fashion. Next whenever the rains cease, it is, of course, natural for the huge volume of water of the other rivers to recede quickly. (24) How shall we say that the volume of the Nile's water lasts for so long a time if it originates from such a cause? For in our very comparison in another way we make the Nile dissimilar and we combine the two greatest paradoxes: having assumed that it is dissimilar to the other rivers, we try to show that it is similar; and again now assuming that it is similar, we prove that its nature is dissimilar. (25) For if its total flood was reached in three or four, or even twice as many days and this period was not a fraction of the whole time of its rise, perhaps some clever argument would have been discovered. But what argument is there from rain to account for its daily increase lasting more or less into the fourth month? (26) Indeed, our rivers are not even continually swollen in winter. But it rains, they increase. It stops, they recede. In winter itself they are constantly becoming greater and smaller by turns because of the rains. If the Nile were increased by rain, it too should not preserve a constant increase, nor in its increment ever proceed from the smallest and first stage to the fullest and largest stage, until it has reached its crest, but it should have in turn an uneven and shifting growth and recession, so that there would not be this expression, a rising of the Nile, but there would be many risings, and again in each summer many diminutions, as usually happens because of rain. (27) Further just as the other rivers do not have a constant volume in winter, so also in summer they sometimes increase beyond their natural state, whenever it rains. If then what happens to these rivers, also happened to the Nile in one way or the other,[29] the Nile would also sometimes increase in winter, just as these rivers do in summer. Therefore these rivers would equally increase at times in winter and at times in summer, and the Nile would too, save that each would show more of an increase or decrease depending on whether it was winter or summer.[30] But if the Nile is never said to have increased in winter and it is possible to see our rivers increasing in summer, whenever the rainy season prevails, some other cause for the rise must be sought, if a cause must be sought at all, since the argument which attributes the cause to rain is not suitable. (28) Not only is the Nile's increase orderly, but it also recedes in an orderly fashion, and it returns to its original state in almost no less time than the time from its rising to cresting. Yet rivers which are increased by rainfall never are subject to this phenomenon, nor do they exhibit any order in either the phenomenon of increase or decrease. With good reason, when there is no order in the rains themselves. (29) Then its single rise within the year, whereas the other rivers rise as it chances on each occasion, and the absence of recession until it crests and again its recession when it crests, and the placidity of its current afterwards forbid the belief that the cause lies with rain. (30) If it is necessary to mention this point too, when you pass the cataracts, you find sand on both sides of the Nile. The Libyan part[31] even consists entirely of barren sand dunes, so that if it rained, it was in any case unlikely for streams of water to occur, since the sand would absorb the rain. All the other great deserts which we know are subject to this phenomenon. Indeed, as to the desert at the beginning of the Arabian-Egyptian border, there will never be so much rain that it will emit a stream into the Nile's water. The Libyan desert also clearly forms a sheer drop to the side away from the river,[32] besides there being differences in two respects from our river areas, in the abundance of this sand beyond all the other deserts which we know and in the fact that the river bed is so elevated, that if the rain water even got beyond the barrier, it was a miracle. (31) And in fact they say that it rains at Meroe.[33] And if this were the cause of the rise, it would certainly not escape the notice of those who are its observers[34] and neighbors, nor would they seek from where the Nile descends, but it would be plain that its increase took place from here. It is not so, nor can the Ethiopians name the source, since they are even unable to say that they have rain. Indeed, I heard both these things from them.[35] Then how does the Nile rise because of rain? (32) Further in Lower Egypt there is often noticeable rain—in Upper Egypt often only a drop now and again over the years, but in the region by the sea rain is normally heavy—and even this rain does not cause any apparent increase in the Nile. Yet how is it likely that the rains in Egypt, however great, do not disturb the Nile, but their water is subject to the same phenomenon as that discharged into the sea, to be expended without a trace,[36] yet that the river has its growth in secret regions of the world, as it seems, as if the Nile were playing tricks or were afraid that it might appear to increase for this reason? But if this is ridiculous, such are the arguments of those who attribute the cause to rain. (33) I also wish to tell you a small story about rain clouds.[37] For when I was making my second trip up the Nile to the pinnacle of Egypt,[38] we were met in the region of Thebes,[39] in the nome called Hermounthi, by an exile from the Lower City,[40] named Draucus, and were introduced by a friend and companion of ours,[41] who was sailing with us, when he saw him there. But when it happened that Draucus was freed from exile and came to the sea, he often visited us and we treated him as a friend, as was likely. (34) And once in this circumstance, at evening, we were taking a stroll in the great avenue by the porticoes,[42] and the Etesian winds were noticeable. We gazed at the clouds, and one of those present said, "These are the winds of the Nile". For he more or less called them this. And Draucus laughed. When I asked him what he meant by this, "Do you not know", he said, "that I spent three successive years at the ends of Egypt"? "I know", I said. "But what of it"? "Because in all that time, although I looked everywhere, I could not see a cloud there in summer, but the sky, like a painting, never changed. Yet I believe", he said, "that I saw what was there. But I did not see a cloud. And you", he said, "think that these are driven from here and bursting in the south cause the inundation of the Nile". (35) At the time when I heard this, I thought it remarkable and of interest, and now I have related it to you in this report so that you may know that they are far from the truth who use this argument or believe in it and that you may simply know that the Nile, alone of rivers, is likely never to remain constant, but that it continually flows with an even, or if you wish, an uneven increase and decrease, in some way very much like the days and the nights, and the phases of the moon. (36) For when it begins to crest, it advances always making one addition to another, adding to its increase until it has reached its maximum growth; and when its waters are all collected, like the orb of the moon, it reverses itself and again begins to decline, as if it were sounding a refrain, the other way. And in turn the next flood cycle follows, but often a little of the former, as much as not to escape notice, has also remained.[43] The river is neither the same during its rise—for it is always increasing until it reaches its full crest—nor again during its recession—for it is always abating until it pays back its debt. (37) Thus the situation of the Nile seems to be more divine and special than suits the case of other rivers and streams. And if we seek the causes of this, let us also seek the causes of the phenomena which I mentioned:[44] Why it has been ordained that one day slightly exceed the next, until the maximum sum is reached, and next the days grow shorter, until they reach the shortest day, at the start one day being shorter than another, and next after the equinox even shorter than the night. The night, increasing in turn, is subject to this same phenomenon, advancing and receding in growth and diminution, until in the terms of the geometricians,[45] it reaches the point from where it began its course, perpetually subject to the same phenomenon as the day, but in reverse. (38) For if someone will say that this phenomenon is particularly clear and assign the cause to the orbit of the sun, still he will not demonstrate the reason for any of the following, except in make-believe: the very order of the orbit, or the fact that from the start these phenomena were so limited by the laws of nature.[46] For example, if you wish, the change of season being defined by three month periods, the total time given to night and day, and the boundaries fixed for the god[47] on the north and south, beyond which he cannot pass. (39) Yet there is some use in the example. For we observe that the sun has a double motion, as one might say, about all of its limits, from which it is possible to calculate the length and brevity of any given time. But when it is agreed about the Nile that even now its source and southern limit have not been discovered, how is it possible to seek its cause or to say where it arises? But perhaps it is difficult to discover causes not only in this case, as I said,[48] but also in other phenomena. (40) After I have offered four general proofs that neither rain clouds nor the Etesian winds cause the stream to rise, I shall conclude my discussion on this heading. The first is that often the river rises even before the Etesian winds occur. The second that it rises when they have not occurred at all. The third and fourth, which are consistent with this, that the river is not at its maximum whenever the strongest Etesian winds descend and stir up the most clouds, and in turn that it is not at its minimum, whenever the breezes are light, although it is likely for all these phenomena to be other than they are now, if the Etesian winds controlled the current, either by blocking it at the river's mouth or by causing the inundation through rain.

(41) So that we may not entirely dishonor Herodotus' opinion, as if it were not at all worthy of refutation, come let us consider what his view is on this matter. He says,[49] as we recall, that the sun driven off course by the storms here goes to the southern parts of Libya and evaporates the Nile's water, and by evaporation causes the Nile to be smaller in winter than in summer. Yet this argument does not tell how the Nile increases, but invents a cause for its diminution. For all men agree that it is purest in winter. But if this is so, it would increase in summer, when it is both greater and more turbid. Then the question still remains, as long as no one shows the reason for the current's rise. For the Nile's winter stream appears to be the proper and original one. (42) Apart from this if the variation in the sun's winter course was so great so as to cause summer in the land there, whenever it is winter here; and again winter, whenever it is summer among us, perhaps it would be possible to accept the argument. But now no one disputes that the regions there are not a little warmer than our own in winter. However, according to those very people[50] there is also no reason why the sun should not have less strength in winter than in summer. For we shall certainly not say that in summer the sun is strong in the northern regions, yet withdraws from Egypt and Libya. But it is even much hotter there, especially, I think, in Ethiopia, and next, as is likely, in Egypt, especially in the most southern districts, and next the heat continues to decrease proportionately, since there is no reason why in Scythia and the Pontus the summer should not be much colder than is ours, although the sun then is journeying over the northern part of the Universe. (43) Yet if the seasons of the year were reversed in these places, when the sun went south and

caused winter here, it would be summer in Egypt and the province of the Nile, and equally when the sun returned north, the northern regions would be hotter, which appears far from being the case. With good reason. For the sun, I think, moves in a northerly direction; however, it does not completely move to the north. (44) Then when it is clear that the Nile increases in summer, it is obvious that it is impossible for it to be evaporated in winter. For if the sun were the cause, it would still more restrain the rise in summer, since the sun is then at its strongest, and there particularly, so that the argument is refuted by itself. If then it caused evaporation, now it would still less allow the Nile's inundation. But if it does not cause evaporation in the winter, the Nile is not greater in the summer for this reason. (45) The claims that the sun is driven off course by storms and that the Nile is evaporated by the sun seem to me to be of the same sort. Storms do not drive the sun off course, O best of historians— for storms do not even reach the region of the sun, but the sun withdraws according to its own orbit and nature, and causes the winds to be still colder and more violent—nor does the Nile contract its stream, evaporated by the sun as the river Xanthus was by Hephaestus.[51]

(46) Although Herodotus has said the most glorious and fairest things about Egypt and the Nile, he is likely to have told the truth about few of them. I do not mean as if he exaggerated everything, since he omitted some points which are more important than those which he mentioned, which there is now no need to discuss.[52] But I mean what he has said contrary to the facts. For one example[53] that after four days journey beyond Heliopolis, Egypt again becomes broad, while it is actually ever more narrowly confined into an angle in such a way that the Nile now passes into it through a juncture of the mountains on both sides. And these are the cataracts, the descent of the river through the mountains, as it were the pinnacle of the whole of Egypt,[54] so that while you are still sailing up to the anchorage at Elephantine you would conjecture that the river's course has been blocked. For far from Egypt still being broad, you would now say that the Nile's course becomes narrow and flows beneath solid rock. You would notice, even before coming to Elephantine, I know not how many *schoenoi*[55] before, that the mountains have so closed together that there is nothing between them except the current itself, and the breadth of Egypt is the same as that of the river. (47) Or if ever someone sets about refuting his other

remarks, how great a task would it be to discuss them all! Indeed, he also says[56] that he learned about the so-called "springs of the Nile" from the Saite clerk, that there are two mountains between Syene and Elephantine, and springs flow from the midst of these mountains, and half of the stream flows toward Ethiopia and southward, and the other half toward Egypt and northward. Yet Elephantine, to which he claims to have sailed,[57] lies almost beneath the very Cataracts of the Nile, at a distance of about seven stades.[58] For I sailed there myself and I was "a more careful observer than necessary", as they say. (48) But if it is necessary, in the manner of Herodotus himself, to digress, for the sake of entertainment and without need, and to sidetrack my discourse's plan, this is what happened. When I went down country to the Altars,[59] where the Ethiopians have a garrison, I drew far away from the river bank,[60] and then crossing to the anchorage which is the first beyond the Cataracts, I went over to Philae. This is an island between Egypt and Ethiopia, no larger than the city which is on it. The Nile flows around it and it is located exactly in the river's center. When I returned, I took the same route back from Philae. And now I expected that I would see the Cataracts, and I asked the guides about them, but they did not know. (49) Thus when I was back at Syene, which the Nile separates from Elephantine, although I was in poor condition through ill health,[61] I asked the garrison commander[62] to give me a light boat and to send me back to see the Cataracts and to send with me those who would compel the men on the Cataracts' island[63]—these sailors are familiar with the current—to show us the Cataracts and whatever their naval spectacle might be. For I learned of it from those here. But the garrison commander said that it was a very difficult thing to do and expressed amazement at my intention and said that he himself was not so brave. Yet he did not absolutely refuse me. But when he did not convince me in his efforts at dissuasion, he sent me out on this trip, since he was otherwise friendly and wished to please me.[64] (50) I sailed up stream. And from the edge of the island, which rises in the midst of the Cataracts and provides a clear view of them everywhere, I watched those people shooting the rapids, as they were accustomed to do. And in addition, I too desired to board a skiff and try the sailing, not only through the same places where I saw them carried down—this was to the east of the island—, but beginning from here to sail around the whole scene, and at the

XXXVI. THE EGYPTIAN DISCOURSE

other side of the island to put out into the current for the cities.[65] My remarks are not hearsay, but I know from accurate observation that Elephantine is north of the Cataracts, and that there is nothing between Syene and Elephantine except the course of the river, and that each of these cities is located near the river bank. (51) If Herodotus ever came to Elephantine, as he said,[66] is it possible that first of all in his investigation of the ancient springs of the Nile he gave hearsay information about what he actually saw, and next that the information was so false that after he had admitted that he heard the truth from no one, nevertheless he wrote, "I heard the following from the clerk", and at that a clerk in the Saite nome in regard to matters at Elephantine?[67] Or after he had mentioned the story, if he could not keep silent about anything which he had heard, would he have used against the argument other refutations than these which I have now mentioned?[68] (52) Now he says[69] that the clerk seems to him to be joking. But he omitted the arguments through which it was likely to refute the clerk. That first of all the clerk began to describe the springs to him at a place from which proceeds only a tiny fraction of the whole course—for the Nile is still known after an upstream voyage of many months beyond this spot. And next that it is impossible, where the flow of the river is not normal, but it forces its descent and breaks over the rocks, here for half the current to be carried upstream, like birds carried aloft. For this would not be in the words of the proverb "rivers' springs going backward",[70] but it would be a tale of rivers' springs going up mountains. But since he neither went to Elephantine nor had any clear information on these matters, he used a story which has charm to those who believe it and a reference source for those who distrust it. (53) Next after this has been said, he remarks that if this is true, he thinks that there are eddies here and a regurgitation of the river. And why should he talk of regurgitation and eddies when he has ignored the fact that neither does the Nile originate here—but the region south of this point is much greater than that toward the sea—nor would the water be able to pass south over the Cataracts, unless indeed one should assume that the water is carried, in the words of Aeschylus, "shot from" the air,[71] nor is there a mountain between Syene and Elephantine, but rather Syene and Elephantine are between the mountains. (54) However, his statement is not a complete lie, but those springs actually exist between Syene and Elephantine[72]—two great rocks rise in the middle of the river's course and the Egyptians say that between them are springs. But these do not contribute water to the whole river, but to the part in Lower Egypt, and they are not old. Indeed, the Egyptians said that their depths could not be plumbed by anyone who tried[73] and that it was not expedient to try. This dissuaded me, although I was in fact engaged in doing it. For the matter was not so important. These springs have a natural flow. And I am persuaded of the existence of the springs here not only by the story, but also by the facts themselves. From this point the river becomes much greater in breadth, and in every way, one might say, and as it proceeds it is navigable by larger boats, and not only larger but also much larger. Yet rivers are subject to the opposite phenomenon. As they proceed, they become smaller whenever there is no subsidiary water supply. (55) If it is also necessary to go deeper into this argument, I shall tell you briefly what I heard from an Ethiopian, who was one of the chief men there.[74] For the Prefect happened to be absent when we visited the region, but there was a deputy, who spoke to me through interpreters. And I shall omit all that is irrelevant to the present discussion. But he said that it was a voyage of four, and, I think, he even mentioned six months, from here to Meroe, which is the largest city in Ethiopia and where the palace of the Ethiopians is located;[75] and that many cataracts followed, one after another, all told almost thirty-six, beyond Pselchis[76] up to Meroe; and that all this was the known course of the river. (56) But beyond Meroe, I do not remember the distance, he said that the stream was not single, but that there were two streams, one of which had an earth-like color, and the other a color close to air;[77] but when these combined and joined, this Nile of ours was born. But he said that neither he nor any other Ethiopian knew entirely what lay to the south, except that there were black men—blacker than themselves and their neighbors— ever beyond them; but that he could not refer the river back to any ultimate source from which and through which, in respect to springs, it flowed. (57) Yet how is it not strange and extraordinary that the Ethiopians admit that they cannot tell of the springs of the Nile, but that although this inquiry is always being undertaken and the solution has even now not yet been found, we are concerned with the cause of the Nile's rising and, as they say, "ignorant of the first principles, we inquire after the second ones"?[78] And I have not discussed this so that I might tastelessly censure

XXXVI. THE EGYPTIAN DISCOURSE

Herodotus. For I am not otherwise one of those who have endeavored to do such things,[79] but I do not even applaud those who do this. And I feel grateful to Herodotus for the very love of Egypt which he first inspired in us. And "in other respects", as those who speak freely say,[80] "the man is a friend". But the truth has not yet been told in this matter.

(58) I shall go further in my refutation, so that my argument, as it were concluded with a summation, may be confirmed by this. For the increase begins at the summer solstice or a little later. Then the sun stands directly overhead on the Ethiopian side of Egypt and on the Egyptian side of Libya.[81] And this is clear from two most important indications, neither of which occurs in any other land that we inhabit. For of the two little cities, which I just now mentioned,[82] on the edge of Egypt—for I say that Philae, which is above the Cataracts, lies between Egypt and Ethiopia—, in Elephantine everything is alight, temples, men, and monuments, and nothing casts a shadow at noon when the sun completes its greatest journey;[83] and in Syene on the same day and hour, the orb of the sun appears directly centered in the Sacred Well, like a lid, equidistant from the lip of the well on all sides.[84] (60) Yet this is an indication of two things: of the fact that the sun is not closer to Libya in the winter than in the summer, since of the two sides of Egypt, Elephantine has been built in Libya.[85] For all the districts have intersected here, Egypt, Arabia, Libya, and Ethiopia, some from this side, some from the other making their juncture. Secondly if indeed one should grant him that the sun approaches Libya and evaporates the water, this very argument is against him. For if through its approach, it evaporated the river in winter, it is clear that it would surely carry it all away in summer when it stood overhead. (61) For it cannot be said that the sun is in any other way closer to the earth than whenever it is directly aloft, since one could easily learn that the sun never actually approaches Libya or any other part of the earth. For it surely does not visit certain parts of the earth, some in summer and others in winter, but rather the earth in turn is subject to its orbit. But the sun is always equally distant from all the earth, and wherever it stands overhead at noon, it brings the greatest heat. (62) Clearly it does not block, or stay, or carry away the river at that time, or even diminish its size, but it observes it increasing and always making additions to its current, no differently than all other rivers,[86] for which you show no admiration. Yet what

208   XXXVI. THE EGYPTIAN DISCOURSE

time shall we say is left for the Nile to be evaporated by heat, if it is seen to rise at the very height of the sun? (63) Then the sun, turning back from the solstice, 'goes to the Ethiopians'—with this expression I speak somehow like Herodotus[87]—, in such a way that the sun ever goes to the more southerly regions with this same configuration. But this is the river's course, so that the sun would abstract no small part of the water and would gradually dry up the river, while it clearly does the opposite of this, if it is necessary to say so. Or rather, I think, it is clear that the sun is not the agent, but on the contrary the Nile, whether it should be called agent or subject. For when it should gradually cease in accordance with the motion of the sun, it begins to increase and gradually increases its very growth; and the sun and the river have the same beginning and the same peak, the one in its heat and the other in its flood.

(64) "But come now change the subject and sing the adornment"[88] of the philosopher and scholar Ephorus,[89] with which the man adorned himself and his book. Yet I fear that in attempting a refutation I may be more foolish than he who claims the discovery. For if the Nile did not bring down its increase from far away south of the Cataracts and from still farther south of the places known to us, perhaps one would accept the notion that water from the Libyan and Arabian mountains seeps underground and inundates Egypt which lies in between and is porous, which is what he says giving the sun's heat as the cause. (65) But now those who have never even heard the name of Ephorus know that the Nile descends in flood from the south for many days sailing and that it is extraordinarily high at the Cataracts themselves and between Syene and Elephantine, where the district which would have been called "Hermes" by the Greeks[90] marks the beginning of the region of Egypt, and that it passes through with a remarkable noise and it floods at a depth of thirty cubits,[91] moderately speaking. (66) How can it be this water from the mountains which enclose Egypt on either side, so far north of the river's rise, which causes the river's rise? And does the same water seep beneath the soil and inundate Egypt, and at the same time is it clearly borne in such volume upon the surface of the old water south of the pinnacle of Egypt?[92] Unless Ephorus will say this and make this addition to his clever theory, that just as the water flows down from higher to porous ground, so it again turns back from the porous ground to the high ground[93] and starting at the sea, the river turns and is borne again south to

the Cataracts and Meroe, like someone running a long distance race uphill. But he would not even persuade his fellow citizens with these arguments, I think.[94] And I forbear to make this point, strong as it is, although they say that thefts should be investigated until one shows the thief with the stolen goods in his hands. (67) But there is another point of his which is silly. For first of all there is his belief that either this Arabian or Libyan mountain region is full of water. What springs are there here or there? How is there as much as a suspicion of water in these places, which indeed are drier and sparer than anything which one could imagine? In the Arabian region there is the famous porphyry quarry.[95] Just as other quarries it is worked by convicts. But as they say, no one guards these convicts.[96] But those miners who stay, stay out of fear of being burned alive, the punishment any escaped convict must suffer if he is captured. And nonetheless some even prefer this punishment to being burned perpetually. For this is in truth to be burned alive. So the land everywhere is sandy and thirsts. (68) Why do not all rivers simply increase in summer on this reasoning? For if the sun drives the water into the porous part of the earth and the earth becomes full and finally is inundated through its own agency, why are rivers not at their largest when the heat is greatest, since all rivers individually are in porous parts of their earth? But instead of being largest then, then they are smallest. (69) Indeed, near other rivers are other mountains, which are not only not smaller than these, but, in addition to being manifestly larger, are further much moister, as is clear from the trees which grow upon them and the water which flows to their surface. Then how are not irreconcilables combined, if water will be driven to the depths of the earth and then will be raised in flood by the same cause? And as it seems, the same sun squeezes water from the Arabian and Libyan mountain and thrusts it underground, but in Egypt stands by inactively while this same water is raised in flood. (70) How does the land become flooded from beneath the ground, O summit of wisdom? Indeed, it is so fissured and cracked directly after the vernal equinox that it is almost all chasms and crevices, and not even pack animals can travel safely across it. "Then how" he says, "are the lakes far from the Nile filled if the Nile rises because of rain or melted snow"? (71) But if this is quite impossible, it does not any more help Ephorus' argument. For it is possible for the river to rise because of neither rain nor snow and still for the cause not to be moisture seep-ing into it underground. (72) However, my view is the complete opposite of his, that this argument is not at all an impediment to the inundation from the south, but entirely refutes on the spot[97] flooding as ridiculous. For in the absence of the other impediments, it is likely for the river to be increased by snow and rain and then to descend, and that when it descends, for the earth to be filled and to swell, and to emit moisture obliquely underground. Not from heat or because it is dried out—for it is ridiculous that when the selfsame earth lacks necessary water, it then sends its excess amount elsewhere—, but on the contrary it provides unseen channels, which are on the spot, for its surplus water. But if the porosity of the land enclosed by mountains supplied the cause, in any case the lakes far apart from the river would certainly not be filled. And Ephorus himself is a witness to this. For in trying to avoid refutation, he says that actually this phenomenon cannot take place in any other land because elsewhere the soil is neither porous nor alluvial as in Egypt, but original and as he called it "naturally compacted". Let us grant that this is true, at least up to a point. But it is no more than that. (73) Those lakes, which are near the river and in Egypt itself, obviously do not originate with themselves, but all depend on the river; and there are channels which lead to them whether Ephorus admits it or not, so that it is not at all unreasonable for them to share in whatever is the cause of the river's rise. (74) Lake Moeris and the lakes in the marshes in the north and Maria, which was formerly to the south of the Pharus[98] and is now behind Alexandria, of old were and still are gulfs of the Nile and share in its rising whenever part of its stream enters them through the channels. But on the other hand Lake Serbonis[99] is clearly outside these mountains. For it is located beyond Pelusium and one of the two mountains which enclose Egypt as you go toward Ostracine, which is right in the middle of the unsown district of Arabia. I do not need to say whether an effluent of the Nile even reaches this lake from the southern regions. But it is clear from what I have stated that the lake eludes Ephorus' boundaries. (75) Therefore his argument falters on one or the other of these two points. For if he accepts this statement, which shows that the lake is outside of the porous land, and does not refute it, why did he not also show that this same phenomenon occurs in every land, if the cause lies with heat alone? But if he thinks that this same phenomenon should not be sought elsewhere because the nature of the land is not the same, the lake still remains outside these mountains. Therefore how does it increase? Before considering the first proposition, how the Nile increases, the second proposition must be investigated, how the lake increases according to this argument. (76) Indeed, it is easy to recognize that in using this excuse, he does not otherwise even tell the truth. For in fact in the whole world, many other lands also have been created by rivers, and by this same argument it is very necessary for them to be porous and loose textured. And I forbear to speak of the other lands, but, O Zeus, one of them was directly before the gates of his country and before his eyes. (77) For there is much evidence that the plain at Larissa was anciently a sea.[100] And regard as irrelevant that the Hermus is a fraction of the size of the Nile. But the argument that this river also ought to increase in summer for the same reason is self-evident. For mountains are seen to surround the land, and the river flows through a land which is thin and which it originally created. Then why does it not only not increase in summer, but is even much smaller than many rivers, which are not nearly so great as it in winter? Often it does not even as much as flow. And one could mention countless other such phenomena. Yet he closes his discussion against those with whom he disagrees, by giving a single example. He nowhere even produces a name of a river or a land, so that its case can be judged, and still he thinks that he should win the argument. (78) "For Egypt is loose textured and easily transmits streams of water".[101] But I forbear to say that no other land is so rich, although this fact alone is a sufficient refutation. But what shall we say about this land outside of Mount Casius, which I just now mentioned?[102] For this land is obviously also not the creation of the river, but nonetheless shares in its circumstances. Moreover, you would not say that it has been deposited by another river, for the whole region aside from the lake is arid. (79) Indeed, the proponents of this theory do not even try to persuade us of it in regard to all of Egypt. But in fact they make an exception of the whole great region to the south of the pinnacle of the Delta,[103] on the grounds that it is original soil, and not simply so and in the ordinary sense of the term, but so exceptionally original that it was even the first land in Asia to produce human beings,[104] so that I say no more. Then if the river's rise happened to occur in the Delta alone, there was good reason to accept this theory in a single instance. But if the river's rise occurs in the whole of Egypt and first is as extensive in the south as is the river's current, how is it relevant that the Nile brings in or creates new land? (80) Further the nature of Ethiopia is not the same as that of Egypt. The former is somewhat sandy, dry, and grainy, and the latter is so deep and firm that it is not easy to find its equal. But the same phenomenon occurs in both places. How is it possible to allege the same causes for two places so widely different? For if Egypt's nature was the cause, then, as it seems, Ethiopia's was not, where the earliest movement of the Nile began. But if Ethiopia's nature was the cause, why should it be said that Egypt is porous and is enclosed by mountains? For the cause does not lie in Egypt, nor, as it seems, is this the cause. (81) Indeed, in the region south of the Cataracts, about Pselchis, the part to the west slopes so much that the low level of the land is not nearly as high as the river bed.[105] For there are sandy hills which form a barrier between the river and all the land below, and these end on a much lower ground level to the west. Therefore if the earth's moisture was the water, it could not flow into the river, but would stream forth to either side of the river. (82) I also heard that in Syrian Palestine, in Scythopolis,[106] near the region which produces the famous dates and date juice, there is a lake which gives "an indication", whenever the Nile rises. For this was the expression of my hosts,[107] but they said this in as much as the level of the lake increases. If this land also lies between Libya and Arabia, or is more porous than all other land, let us grant that Ephorus speaks the truth, although he is a liar in so far as he says that the phenomenon should not be sought elsewhere, for it would not be the same. (83) But if there are many lands which are more porous than this one, even if not far more, still to some extent more porous, and nevertheless they are not subject to this phenomenon, you must seek some other cause for the river's rise,[108] since it is clearly impossible to allege either the loose textured quality or the porosity of the earth, but these characteristics least of all. For if the inundation took place on the spot, neither would an increase in the level of the lakes outside the river take place nor would the river itself reach such a high crest that it so notably floods the whole region between these mountains that those who sail upon it at night sometimes take their course from the stars. For this is the same as if someone should persuade you that a plain nine gallon vat is filled by a plain half gallon jar, the whole of the one from the whole of the other. (84) But, I think, when the river descends with its great volume

XXXVI. THE EGYPTIAN DISCOURSE 213

and the earth is unable to contain it all, the water proceeds until it is absorbed, making its own channel. For this reason outside springs receive added sources of water from the river[109] and a perception of the river's rise extends to neighboring nations, and empty regions absorb the water, as when a bath chamber is filled.

(85) Let such be the tenor of our arguments against the wisdom and the novel view[110] of Ephorus, because he claims that he alone has touched upon the truth. But I was charmed by the fresh-water sea beyond Libya which flows into the Nile on account of the Etesian winds, and its crocodiles, and the Massalian tales in place of those of Sybaris.[111] For if you do not realize, most delightful Euthymenes—if Ephorus' report of your opinion is true—that you do not solve the difficulty, but raise another greater and stranger than the original one, will not some wit truly say that your mind is beyond the Pillars and Gadira if in fleeing the river you do not perceive that you are falling into the ocean, as they say that the Thracian woman once told Thales?[112] Why shall we express astonishment and seek a cause, if one alone out of all the other rivers rises in the summer, while not being much more astonished if out of all the seas, one alone is fresh-water? (86) Indeed, even if rivers flow in the same way, still they are separate and each flows individually, except those which combine in their course. But the whole sea is obviously intermixed and its nature is continuous. And if someone will separate this nature in his argument, it is left to wonder how he will treat his other arguments. But this matter must also be discussed in detail, as it seems. (87) There are four effluents of the outside ocean.[113] One of these stretches from the west through Gadira and adjacent Libya to the Phasis, and this gulf is the Mediterranean, which with the addition of Lake Maeotis and the river Tanais to its north splits the earth in two, and by means of the encircling ocean makes each segment an island, unless you wish to say that the Phasis, like in truth the Tanais, is the boundary of the two continents.[114] Such is the situation of this gulf of the sea. Another effluent is filled from the south, called the Red Sea, which makes Libya, Egypt, and the adjacent part of Arabia a peninsula,[115] open to the inner and outer sea[116] by means of an isthmus with the breadth of a three days' journey. The third gulf above these is the Persian Gulf, which makes a peninsula of Arabia Felix and all that is within the land of Persia, as you turn into it after the Red Sea. The fourth sea flows from the north and the region of the

Caspian Gates to our lands, and is called the Caspian, or if you wish, the Hyrcanian Sea.[117] (88) What is the relevance of this? I do not pointlessly tell "a tale of Alcinous".[118] Because first of all these are the regions of the sea and this is their number and no Greek or barbarian knows of any other sea besides these, certainly no one does who lives within these gulfs and the encompassing ocean. But all the other water which spreads out with its gulfs is called lakes, marshes, shoals, and such names. For as to that which some now call a sea in Syrian Phoenicia, the Dead one, we shall immediately explain how it got its name. (89) It has befallen, I think, that all these seas are of the same nature as one another and their source; and there is no one who has made an exception of any of them as being fresh-water, but they have called them equally "sea". And the nature of its water is clearly peculiar and proper to the sea alone, so that people even call by the name of "sea" all wells which incline to saltiness. And the water of the lake which I just now mentioned in Syria,[119] by having a salt content, has given it the name of "the sea" among people. (90) And the sea which flows around Libya is not fresh-water and potable, while that by Gadira itself through intermingling with the Mediterranean is like it. For first of all it should no more be salty through the Mediterranean than fresh-water through the Libyan sea, since it also intermingles with that, and at that wholesale, not through a strait. (91) Next it is also clear from the evidence of those who still now sail out that the story is fictitious. For the number of those who even now sail beyond the Pillars is certainly no less than in those times. And not once or twice after long intervals, but daily without interruption merchant ships and traders are borne through each sea, as if it were a continuous whole, since the entire coastal region has been opened to them and they sail in security through the present government.[120] We had intended such a trip, but we were forestalled by disease.[121] And neither can the fishermen at Gadira nor those who cross over to the great island opposite Spain[122] be heard to say that the outside sea is fresh-water. Yet at appropriate times various regiments cross over there and return,[123] and countless officials and private citizens cross over on every occasion. (92) It makes no sense that the whole follow the part, but that the nature of the part be the same as is that of the whole. The entire outside sea, whose western limit has not even been discovered, is not an effluent of the Mediterranean, but this gulf of ours flows in from the outside sea

XXXVI. THE EGYPTIAN DISCOURSE

and brings its nature from far off. (93) Indeed, those of the Carthaginians who have sailed beyond Gadira and who have founded cities in the deserted parts of Libya have not brought this tale home, nor written about it, nor dedicated such an inscription in their temple,[124] although they have written many other strange things. And it was certainly unlikely for them either to be ignorant of this or if they knew it, to conceal it, and at that intentionally, being as it were proud of their observations, all of which were less than to be able to say that they saw a fresh-water sea. (94) Further I wonder how this man ever traveled so far from the known world, and what were his means, and what was the reason for his journey. Indeed, it is unlikely that he sailed out alone; yet it is unlikely that if he returned with many companions he alone embellished this tale, or even only wrote it in a book, as if that were enough, or told it only to friends, but it was likely for him to announce and proclaim it publicly, I mean by his dedicating an inscription, just as the leaders of the Carthaginians dedicated writings on these matters in one of their public temples. (95) Indeed, if these things were true, what Greek would be unaware of them afterwards? For all could have sailed to Massalia[125] and learned of them and been freed of this one difficulty through the Massalians. But neither do the Massalians tell these stories, nor is this Massalian as reliable as he is a charming writer, but he is rather old-fashioned and fabulous. (96) Indeed, he should not be trusted because he inserted crocodiles and hippopotami into his tale, but here in the best way his fiction and his dressing up of it is apprehended. For he did not see crocodiles and hippopotami and then report them. But so that his other stories might seem true, he added the crocodiles and the hippopotami and took refuge in the known and drew credence for his fiction by the addition of another fiction made to look like the truth. But I think that it is better to leave such tales and fables to nurses to tell their children whenever it is bed time, a fresh-water sea, and hippopotami, and the sea flowing into the river, and all such sleeping potions.

(97) A motley account of others is reported.[126] For part of it needs no seer,[127] and part of it not even a seer would persuade you of. It is clear that the springs of the Nile are in the warmest regions, since it begins in the south. But this account says that these springs are heated in summer and attract to themselves the neighboring moisture, and that when much water is collected, they are filled,

and this is the cause of the river's rise. (98) I do not say that it would be likely that all rivers in warm regions are subject to this same phenomenon. But how is it not strange to state that the springs are in the warmest region, yet not to think that their neighboring water should be in another such region? Since they are in similar regions, ought they not to be subject to the same phenomenon? Why is it more likely that the springs of the Nile attract the other water to themselves than that the other water itself need an infusion from the Nile? But if all waters will be more in need of water,[128] first all waters will be lower in summer than in winter, and next will be unable to provide mutual assistance, being separated by the heat, and each being isolated, so that their level should even more decrease and not rise. (99) Indeed, let one grant and not dispute the truth of the springs attracting the neighboring moisture to themselves because of dryness. But what sense does it make to concede that the springs not only acquire enough water to fill out the old water, but also have such a surplus so as to send the Nile up to the sea, so much greater than other rivers and what is more, than itself? Further how shall we say that the springs are evaporated, if they daily show such an increase and for so long a period of time? Either they are expended and would be unable at the same time to emit the Nile's stream, or if they have such an abundance of water, how do they attract through dryness? For if they attracted water at the beginning, it was likely for them to be filled up and for their level to rise. Yet if the sun caused evaporation, they would be unable to crest, through this same cause, since the water which is collected is always evaporating, like the jar of the poets,[129] so that as time goes on, the springs should be lower instead of becoming continually greater.

(100) Each says some different nonsense. But every last one of them seems to me to have sought to state a reason and to be so far from telling the truth that the majority of them, conscious of their lies, even argue against their respective premises, and next, as if shooting in the dark,[130] each misses in a different way. But I do not believe that it is so wise to care about the unknown or that someone behaves with ill grace if he ignores these matters, for I regard it as the act of an intelligent man not lightly to believe assertions about the unknown. (101) But if I must make a general statement in conclusion, I say to those who lie about the agency of the Etesian winds[131] that in winter the north winds are much greater and more

violent and they gather together and stir up all the clouds and when they have stirred them up, they naturally drive them south even at that time. And anything can be said rather than that the Nile ever rose in winter. Yet why would it rise more in summer than in winter if the initial cause came from the winds? (102) To all of them in turn I say that they all are refuted by one another as novices in their arguments. For whenever some say that the river's rise occurs because of winds, and others because of rain,[132] and others because of snow,[133] and some say that the sun in winter evaporates the river,[134] and others say that the sun in summer drives the water off,[135] and others give whatever cause each wishes, and all conjecture, and no one knows, not only are they obviously refuted in their individual arguments, but also all in common collide with one another, because they have not discovered the truth, but each wished to state a reason. (103) And now, while seeming to disagree with all of them, I am in danger of using all of them as my witnesses. For the arguments by which each of them refutes the others, are of use to me against all of them. Therefore while I confirm all of their good ideas, I remove all of the nonsense that they introduce, as it were in their struggle, so that I am not only in agreement with each of them individually and all of them in common in their better arguments but also in the majority of cases. For each of them, while supporting his own view, disagrees with all the rest. But if we have devised no fewer arguments[136] than those which they formerly used, perhaps we are not deserving of blame.

(104) Indeed not even Homer is credible when he says:[137] "Back to the Aegyptus, the Zeus-fallen river". For just as one would and should attribute all things to Zeus, I would also grant that the Nile is "Zeus-fallen" and his creation, since we also call him "father of men and gods", and Homer uses this very expression.[138] Although Zeus is the father of the gods, still he is not the father of all the gods according to the poets themselves. And obviously one would not force the argument that for this reason Poseidon also is the son of Zeus and Hera his daughter, and that Homer thought so. For Homer himself shows that this was not his belief. (105) Indeed, if Zeus is "the father of men and gods", he would also be the father of rivers and of whatever arises in this Universe,[139] and he is properly called the father of the Nile no less than of the Trojan Xanthus.[140] On these terms, as I said,[141] I should admit that the Nile was the creation and child of Zeus. (106) But If Homer or any other will

speak about the Nile as about the Scamander or Simous or Granicus,[142] he should excuse us if we should say that he knows more about affairs in Troy than in Egypt. Indeed, in his epic Homer expressly said of the Pharus that it was a day's sailing from Egypt;[143] and as if this were not enough, but as it were confirming his poetic license,[144] he added;[145] "When a shrill wind blows behind it", meaning the sailing ship. (107) Yet the Pharus is about seven stades from the mainland,[146] and it is, as it were, between Libya and Egypt. I cannot believe that a ship covers only so much distance in a day, especially if "a shrill wind blows behind". Yet some of those who lightly defend other difficulties in Homer[147] say that the Pharus, as it seems, then was far away from Egypt, but now the river has shortened the distance by its continual alluvial deposits. And therefore such is the present situation, and Homer has correctly described those matters, they say. (108) But Homer himself clearly contradicts these apologists. How? Because he also knows of Menelaus' and Helen's voyage to Egypt. Canobus is the name of Menelaus' helmsman, as indeed the historian Hecataeus and common tradition report.[148] And when he died, he left his name to this place. (109) I tell this story, as the Greeks report it, since in Canobus itself I heard from a priest, who was not of the lowest rank, that the land was so named countless years before Menelaus put in there. And he did not clearly express this name, so that I could transcribe it into the Greek alphabet, but it was, as it were, similar and close to our form, yet Egyptian and rather difficult to write. In our language, he said that it meant "Golden Ground",[149] since it is an Egyptian custom to apply such names to their lands, as for example Elephantine, and again Diospolis and indeed Heliopolis. So too, he said, that name meant "Golden Ground" for a Greek. (110) But I omit this point. Yet it is likely that the Egyptians are more accurately informed on their own affairs than Homer of Smyrna and Hecataeus of Miletus, not only for the reason that one would say that it was simply probable and natural, but also—and this alone can be said of the Egyptians—because on account of their antiquity and the fact that their land suffered no deluge,[150] they are also themselves trustworthy witnesses and informants of manifestations among other peoples, and they preserve, like other valuables, records of everything on monuments in their temples. Nonetheless I also pass over this strong argument. (111) But let it be the helmsman of Menelaus, as our historians tell it, who when he died, gave his name to the place. If we must believe this account, Canobus is one hundred and twenty stades distant from the Pharus. Yet a ship running all day with a wind at its stern—and I shall add "shrill"—will cover not one hundred and twenty stades more or less, but perhaps rather one thousand two hundred stades.[151] And we have often covered this distance during fair sailing, later dividing up the total distance by the days of the journey. (112) But the poets, I think, more than anything know and follow the technique of composing stories, of enumerating the names of rivers and cities, and of using such embellishments. But they are not satisfactory witnesses about matters needing such careful examination. Pindar, who seems to keep to the truth in his reports most of all the poets, is immediately refuted in this way, not from afar, but from this very spot. For he says,[152] "Egyptian Mendes by the cliff of the sea". (113) Yet neither is there any cliff there nor does the sea sound nearby, but it lies in a great spreading plain where is located the whole nome of Mendes and its city, which they call Thmouis, so that it is not even possible to view it all, either from one end to the other or even from the middle to the side. But since he was filled with Cithaeron and Helicon and the Phician Peak,[153] he judged its geography by what he was familiar with and spoke with great freedom, although he had neither seen the place nor heard anything clear about it. But he wrote as he felt, in accordance with the poet's ancient and traditional license.[154] And why is it remarkable if poets who are so far away can say nothing positive on a matter which not even the natives themselves, and Egyptians at that, know anything?

(114) But the situation of the Nile is in every way in danger, as I said a little before,[155] of being special and entirely different from other rivers. Why, if you wish, is it the only river not to emit breezes?[156] Yet if it rose because of snow or rain, it would not be the only river not to provide breezes, but it even would provide the most and greatest ones, in as much as it is the greatest river. For when even the bare earth after being soaked emits breezes, what shall we say would be the effect on the Nile, if it rose to such a crest because of rain, or, by Zeus, because of melted snow, as is the reason given by others?[157] (115) What would you say about the order and harmony of its rise? In Syene and Elephantine it rises twenty-eight cubits, and again at Coptus, the Indian and Arabian trading center, twenty-one cubits, and then it loses another seven of

these and has the well-known fourteen cubits at Memphis, which the Greeks use as the mean for their calculations,[158] and north in the marshes it descends to seven cubits, and next, I heard, to two. Then does the Danube, or the Phasis, or the Strymon use this contrivance? Are these not contrivances of the Nile alone, which devises them against the nature of the land? (116) What river, of which we know, provides water which is not subject to aging, yet in such great volume?[159] For it neither spoils kept here nor sent abroad. But whenever the merchant ships, which go from Egypt to Italy, sail from there, the remainder of the water which they stored is fresh, and the water which they took on board afterwards becomes spoiled, as is likely in a long voyage, before the original water, which was taken on when they started out. And the Egyptians alone of the peoples whom we know fill jars with water as others do with wine and keep them at home for three, four, and even more years, and make much of their age as we do of wine's. Or will one say that the reason for this is also that the river rises because of rain? (117) And why has not the same phenomenon befallen all rivers? For all rivers are rained upon, and we do not need to conjecture that they are rained upon, but we ourselves are present during the rains and live, one might say, upon their banks.[160] And some of these rivers have been increased by the addition of rain water to the sparse amount of their original water; still not even because they are superior in this,[161] do they provide the same usefulness. But the Nile also rises in summer, yet is at its normal capacity in winter and at that time its water is best.[162] (118) How superior do you think this water is in sweetness? More than you could say. Yet what is the cause of this? Again what would one say is the cause of the fact that in some way the stream, which is channeled off from it, is always in danger of being equal in volume to the whole river proper? (119) What is not marvelous in that river? Or is not the whole river a collection of wonders? No other water aids it, even the rocks are splitting with dryness and the mountains are almost bursting into flame. Yet flowing in the midst of these difficulties, its volume of water surpasses every lake and every gulf, not only during the time of its rise, but even at all other times. It is like a single spring for the whole land.[163] And no city, or house, or region is untouched by its use and power, but it has the same value for inland cities and those on the borders of the country, as for those people who dwell upon its banks, or rather for those who actually sail in "mid-channel".[164] (120) Whenever according to the law of nature[165] the Nile must crest, then among other indescribable things those sands and fissures in the earth are like glades and marshes in that they form no obstacle for it. But indeed just as the planets whose orbits are retrograde to the Universe, it rises contrary to the seasons and the nature of the land. Yet who, even if he saw it, would not judge it an incredible thing that the river sufficed for the fissures and filled the cracks, or rather even before this, that it got through the southern desert? But it "works" its course,[166] as it were struggling against all its obstacles. (121) And first of all it sinks below the surface and fills the fissures and crevices, like underwater divers, diverting the first part of its inundation underground. Next it stands above these fissures and above the land, and continually advances, to be measured by the greatest dimensions. But if one had known its hidden work, he would have marveled at it more than at what he saw. (122) For I think that many of the rivers which are now ranked first would not have sufficed to fill the fissures underground, but would have plunged in and been buried here, just as they say that the Euphrates disappears in its course.[167] But now it is like our amazement at the sight of the tops of the pyramids, while we do not know that they have a subterranean counterpart equally as large—I repeat what I heard from the priests.[168] Indeed, all of Egypt marks the boundaries of the Nile at its crest, and we compare it to the adjacent sea.[169] It descends in such great volume. But how it reached this state and where it began its rise has escaped inquiry. (123) The fact that this land alone of all, like an animal, is affected in two ways by the river, so that sometimes it is terrestrial and forms its own habitat, and again it lives in the water, to what should we attribute this, if not to the great wisdom and providence of the god,[170] who, in a land where rain is least likely, has brought in the Nile as a kind of imitator of himself and to be like rain for the people here,[171] and again has withdrawn it in a season when it was going to be most opportune for mankind and it was going to provide for the land a crop not only not less than sufficient but even remarkable in its abundance? This I conceive is the only cause why the Nile flows through Egypt and the regions there, and indeed is greatest in summer. (124) I see that we also enjoy cures from the Savior gods,[172] one of whom has the same name as the Nile.[173] And we all know the ultimate purpose and the principal cause, that they wish to save us and make us healthy. But who has ever been able to fathom the very notion and cause behind what they tell us on each occasion? For they have cured us through means which seem to be the very opposite of what you would expect and which one would especially avoid.[174] So much for this aside, which was not planned or intended at the start, but was carried along to here by the argument, as it were by a river's current. (125) The Nile is the fairest no less than the greatest of rivers, far superior in its usefulness, the pleasure of seeing it, and in everything. And it passes through the best and fairest land, and its air is the fairest air and the purest to behold. Although the whole land is full of water, its south is the driest of all regions. Not even the Greeks before our time were unaware that the land is untouched by earthquake, plague, and deluges from heaven because of the Nile.[175] Since the Egyptians have also observed this, I think, they hold things connected with the Nile in greater veneration, so that I once heard from another of those who seem to know about the subject[176] that most of the Egyptians' customary feasts and sacrifices pertain to the Nile.

SPEECHES PRESCRIBED BY ORACLE[1]

XXXVII. ATHENA[2]

(1) Let our dream be a reality. Do you, O Mistress Athena, grant us other fortune and favor, and assist our present speech, and duly bring to pass what appeared in the dream, as it was clearly revealed at night. Now this speech to you will be a mixture of prayer and hymn, so that these visions may actually appear and be confirmed.

(2) All the fairest deeds concern and emanate from Athena. Among the most noteworthy is the birth of the goddess, principally because she is in truth the only child of the only creator and king of the Universe.[3] For he had nothing equal to himself from which he might create her. But in solitary retirement, he himself sired and gave birth to the goddess, so that she alone is with certainty a legitimate child of her father,[4] since she was born from a parentage which was equal and like unto itself. (3) Still greater than this is the fact that he also brought her forth from the fairest part of his body, from his head, since nothing fairer could come forth from his head, nor was there a better place from which Athena could arise. But both circumstances were fitting. When she was born from Zeus alone and from his head, she added a fourth wonder, no less marvelous than the others, the appearance which the goddess is said to have had at the fissure of his head. For she arose directly in full armor, like the sun rising with its rays, since she was arrayed within by her father. (4) Therefore it is not meet that she ever leave her father, but she is always by his side and lives with him, as if she had grown together with him, and she is his inspiration and solitary associate, mindful of her birth and making fitting payment for his labor pains. (5) She seems to me to be the oldest of the gods or one of the very few who were the first at that time. For otherwise Zeus would not have made his division of the world, if he had not sat Athena by his side as assessor and adviser. And she alone eternally bears the aegis.[5] In Homer's description of battle, she alone is arrayed with the weapons of her father.[6] As if on the magicians' stage,[7] Zeus and the goddess at the same time use the same weapons. (6) She is so revered by her father, and she has shared

in everything, and she alone has received first honors, so that Homer, one of the poets who would be said especially to have found favor with the goddess, in mentioning her aegis and the god who attempted to wound her,[8] calls it:[9] "dread, which not even Zeus' thunderbolt masters". A safe remark since what pertains to Athena is more valuable to Zeus than his lightning and thunderbolts. Again Pindar says,[10] that she sits at her father's right hand and receives his commands for the gods. (7) For she is greater than a messenger. Rather it is she who gives different orders to different messengers, first receiving them from her father, being like an interpreter and proposer of action for the gods, whenever there is need of this. Since she was born on the peak of Olympus and from the head of Zeus, she holds the citadels of all the cities, having truly taken them by storm.[11] And thus Folly does not walk upon the heads of all the men[12] who are dear to the gods, but Athena rises aloft and there sets her foot, preserving the token of her birth.

(8) So great is the power of the goddess in heaven and on earth. But as to how valuable she is, has been, and will be to gods and men, "the sons of the gods" could better say,[13] all who are the dancers of Athena.[14] But we must also try somehow or other to discuss this, employing the evidence of the poets to some extent, and allowing our speech enough license, so that it is nearly equal in every way to the dream. (9) It is said that when the Giants drew up their battle line in Phlegra,[15] the goddess slew Enceladus and their other leaders, but the rest of the gods had little work to do, since the goddess also slew all of the other Giants who were the best, particularly punishing them because they were her natural enemies. For they were of an opposite race to hers. They grew from the bowels of the earth and from a source most mindless, but she from what was purest in the sky. She opposed her natural adornment and her fire against the snakes which were part of their nature and against all the other attributes which they brought from the earth, until she incinerated and destroyed the race. This deed of hers is celebrated as having been accomplished on behalf of the gods and all divine nature. Yet I at least do not find it pleasing to speak of the battle of the Titans and those who were called the Olympian gods.[16] (10) But it is easier to conceive than to recount in words all of the benefits which she has stored up to her credit in respect to mankind. The greatest benefit of all, which permeates every being and extends through all times and places, is that mankind has never

erred under Athena's guidance, nor again will they ever do anything useful without Athena. (11) But if these matters must be mentioned in detail and the myths must not be neglected, let us attribute to her olive oil, a health giving drug,[17] which appeared through her agency, and clothing, which is an adornment of the body and also likewise a health giving drug. (12) But she has aided both sexes of mankind by giving women the tradition of wool working and by bestowing on men the use of weapons, and again she has cared for both seasons, war and peace, through weapons and law. Again she has dealt in two ways with each of these seasons. (13) First of all it is she who persuaded men to give up their solitary mountain life and to assemble and dwell together in the compass of a single, common settlement. And the cities are the gift of Athena, for which reason all men also call her "Poliuchus".[18] They have justly set aside their acropolises for her as a token of her birth and at the same time just as they set aside precincts and lands for their emperors and governors, so they have set aside the most important places for the goddess who has governed the Universe. I say that this truly is one universal benefit of the goddess for our daily life, government and laws. But a second is the arts of the forge and those which require no fire, which she divided and divides among individual men. For she alone is the guide of all wisdom. (14) Indeed, in regard to war, she discovered and created the two chief formations. For the infantry and the cavalry belong to the discoveries of Athena. There is double evidence of each. As to hoplite arms, the first to shelter under the shield were the Egyptians among the Asiatics,[19] but those named after the goddess among the Europeans.[20] Among the Egyptians, there is also a nome sacred to Athena,[21] to which this story is ascribed. It is also the same in the matter of horsemanship. For it is said that Erichthonius, the foster child of the goddess,[22] was the first man to yoke a chariot of horses. Again that Bellerophon received the bridle for his horse from Athena. Triptolemus[23] was younger than Erichthonius. His seed may have come from Demeter. Yet his chariot came from Athena, so that all such things must be regarded as the gift of Athena to mankind, as in war the troop of infantry and the division of cavalry. (15) I think that I shall add what just now escaped me, that seamanship also was a gift of Athena. Let this have a double place in my argument. For in respect to warfare, if one should make this division, he will show that the goddess has cared for land and naval operations. And the one naval art pertains equally to both kinds of vessels,[24] that of peace to merchant ships and commerce through these, and that of war to triremes, like the racing and the war chariot.[25] For the goddess is ambidextrous and so are her gifts. (16) But I seem to raise up a swarm of ideas, and the goddess sends them to me in pairs. For when I considered that both trade and naval warfare were gifts of Athena, a certain Buzyges occurred to me, one of those from the Acropolis,[26] and the fact that the farmer would have had no plough, nor when he had the plough, could he have yoked his oxen, "if gray-eyed Athena had not given him the wisdom",[27] through which the plough and ship was constructed, and horses and oxen were yoked.

(17) She is both most generous and most powerful. What greater sign of her power can be mentioned than that she is triumphant everywhere. For Victory is not entitled to the name Athena, but Athena is always entitled to the name Victory. The tale of Orestes attests her generosity. When he fled from Argos to Athens and was indicted at Athens by the Eumenides and the jurors' votes were equally split, she added her own vote and saved him.[28] And still now she saves all men, if ever the votes are equally split. For from that time it was decided to add to the split votes the acquitting vote of Athena. (18) Since Athena must ever be a virgin and neither god nor man must touch her in the way of Aphrodite Pandemus, even here marvelous attributes were acquired for her by her father. She has the honor of one with fine children. For she guided Leto, who wandered over every land and sea, to the fated place, where alone Leto could give birth.[29] And when she was giving birth, Athena acted as midwife and received the children and crowned Apollo as the healer of the Greeks. Therefore Artemis is in charge of lying in for other women, but this goddess was in charge of lying in for Artemis at her birth. And it seems that Athena taught her both her art and her way of life. For she alone besides Athena is a virgin. If Apollo and Artemis are extraordinary beauties, one could give Athena of Providence as the reason.[30] (19) Yet if it is even likely for the gods to be grateful on their own behalf, how is it not likely for us to be grateful on behalf of the gods, because she provided more benefactors for us? Hunting and the chase are the recreation of Apollo and Artemis, but they are also connected with the goddess. For one thing because they are a part of the art of war, or rather an image—and they say that war is Athena's concern—, and

for another because she even found the means so that those who gave their names to these arts would exist.[31] (20) In this way, in great part, she would also be connected with Asclepius.[32] The most ancient Athenians even erected an altar to Athena of Health. But if their verdict is correct, what greater evidence could be found to attest the connection between Asclepius and Athena? She also shares in Poseidon's activities, both in his capacity as god of Horses and god of the sea, for she was the first to invent the bridle and she constructed the first ship. (21) But the partnership of the goddess with Hermes is clear to everyone who invokes the Hermes of Oratory, of Merchandise, and Sale. She is even like a producer for the Hermes of Contests. Homer even directly makes her a goddess of contests, for he judges the contests through her agency.[33] When she had discovered flute playing, lyre playing, and harp playing, she gave the one to one of the Muses, another to Hermes, and the last to Apollo. (22) Thus she has a place everywhere, so that Ares is a child compared to her in his own activities. Apollo has set her before his oracles,[34] and ordered that she receive the first sacrifice. Hephaestus is compelled by love of her to practice his art, but falls short in natural talent. The Graces stand about her. The Dioscuri do their war dance under her inspiration. Iacchus and the goddesses of Eleusis perform dances in honor of the goddess. Poseidon has yielded in defeat.[35] But the height of superiority is that her plant has been designated to be a token of victory,[36] as if it were not only her right to be victorious, but also to crown the victors. (23) And the poets have attributed to her all the most desperate tasks, whenever they wish to make them practicable and possible: Odysseuses swimming in the middle of deserted seas, and old men becoming young, and ugly men handsome, and slaying suitors of many nations with mean and ridiculous assistance, a youth and two herdsmen, and other things still stranger than this.[37] (24) For they say that Bellerophon was carried on the winged Pegasus, holding on to the gift of Athena,[38] and that besides other accomplishments, he overcame the Chimaera by keeping out of range of its weapon. Perseus with his own wings was carried to the land of the Gorgons under the escort of Athena; and he was not overcome by the spectacle,[39] and when he had cut off the Gorgon's head, he brought it back, and turned into stone those who had unjustly ordered him on the mission, as well as most of their people,[40] and he himself escaped in the end unscathed, using Athena's presence as an antidote for everything. (25) Consistent with this and yet still greater are the circumstances of Heracles. For Athena clearly is the one who enrolled him as a god among the gods, since in fact, when he was a mortal, she guided him in all of his labors. And she brought him alive to the house of Hades and got him out alive after he had captured Cerberus and contrary to expectations had gone so far that he even freed one of his friends[41] as well, who was prematurely lodging there, and brought him out with himself. As often as he had to raise his bow against those divinities who opposed him,[42] he had courage through the presence of Athena, so that from these actions it seems to me that nothing other is signified than Athena's declaration of her opinion to the gods that they should decree Heracles a god. But the gods accepted this, as if Zeus himself had proposed it. It was clearly her providence that cared for the birth of Apollo and Artemis and the deification of Heracles. And Apollo, conscious of these things, for others is himself the god of the Entrance, but has made Athena to serve in this capacity for him.[43] (26) But to whom of all gods and men is the goddess not useful? Or who is a safer partner? Or what fire cannot be escaped,[44] when she does not follow but leads you? She alone of all the gods and of all the goddesses as well has no epithet taken from the word "victory", but is synonymous with victory.[45] She alone is called Worker and Providence, epithets which she has taken from her preservation of all the laws of nature.[46] Prophets and priests invoke her as the goddess of Purifications and the Warder off of evil, an overseer of the most perfect purificatory rites. With good reason. (27) For if the myths must be concluded and the activities of the goddess publicly proclaimed, she is the one who wards off our truly universal enemies and sets in order the private war in each of us,[47] since she rids us of our persistent and congenital foes, by which homes and cities are overthrown before the sound of a trumpet, one would say, and she gives each of us a true and proper victory, which is far different from the Cadmean victory[48] and is truly Olympian. Through her agency, folly, wantonness, cowardice, disorder, faction, crime, scorn of the gods, and all such conduct that one could name is banished, and there enters in its place intelligence, moderation, courage, concord, good order, success, and honor of the gods and from the gods. In sum, through Athena's efforts all is an "Assembly of the gods".[49] Thus she is closest to Zeus and both of them always hold the same opinion about everything. (28) And here it is best for me to stop. For my speech has returned to its beginning,[50] or rather it has reached the final point. If because of her activities one should say that she was more or less the faculty of Zeus,[51] he would not err. Therefore why should one be trivial and narrate all of her individual deeds,[52] when it can be said that the deeds of Zeus are shared between Zeus and Athena? (29) But "O thou before the royal palace", as sang the chorus of Aeschylus,[53] the heavenly palace of your father and the greatest palace in our land, grant, as you revealed to me at night, honor from both our emperors,[54] and grant me to be best in wisdom and oratory. May whoever opposes me repent. May I prevail to the extent that I wish. But in myself, while being the first,[55] may the better part prevail.

(Subscription: Aristides' *To Athena*. In Baris.[56] In the proconsulship of Severus,[57] being thirty-five years and one month old.)

XXXVIII. THE SONS OF ASCLEPIUS[1]

(1) "Hearken, friends, a divine dream came to me in sleep",[2] said the dream itself. For I dreamed that I made this the opening of my speech while I beheld the dream before me as if it were a reality.[3] Now let the dream be a reality and the sacred rite[4] be as was predicted. But the sense of the dream was to praise Podalirius. At first Podalirius, but afterwards I was drawn to Machaon. (2) But while I hesitated as to which I should praise, in the end I decided to praise both. For it was no longer proper to omit either of them since I had a notion of both of them, and whichever was the one from the dream, he would certainly be represented if both were praised, and I would merit his favor and the favor of both of them. (3) Well then! Since the god has proposed this subject,[5] should we be more afraid or more confident? We ought to be afraid that we may give an inferior oratorical display in the presence of so great a judge. But our hopes are better. For it is probable that he will also concern himself with our speech. He would not have proposed it if the result of the speech were not going to be satisfactory to him. (4) Besides, it is remarkably appropriate to invoke him to assist our speech. For if the poets invoke Apollo and the Muses to recite whatever they themselves decide upon[5a], certainly our invocation is better whenever we ask the very one who proposed the subject to be our Leader of the Muses along with his father. But, O you who have often been invoked for many things,[6] and I can also say, who have given us advice in other matters and in oratory itself,[7] even now guide our speech, however you wish.

(5) We need not seek too far for the beginning of our praise. The speech and the youths have the same father.[8] No Greek ever heard or told of four such generations. Like the *Thesmothetai,* they are noble born through four ancestors,[9] or rather as no *Thesmothetai* or any other race of mankind are. For they are the fourth generation from Zeus[10] and their whole line of succession is lofty. (6) For Apollo was born of Zeus himself, and Asclepius of Apollo, and they of Asclepius, and they acquired their noble breeding through a whole line of the finest natures. Achilles is the fourth generation from Zeus through Peleus and Aeacus, and Minos and Rhadamanthys are the sons of Zeus, and Theseus of Poseidon, and neither group

are the only sons of either of these two gods, but they share the honor with many gods and heroes, and are inferior to some and equal to others. (7) But the sons of Asclepius alone are without rivals both in the number and excellence of their ancestors since they are superior to those descended from Zeus and Apollo, as many of these as are heroes, of course, by the addition of Asclepius to their ancestry. When they were born, their father raised them in the gardens of Health.[11] And when their youth ensued, he did not have them taught the art of medicine, but taught them himself. For it was no longer necessary for them to go to the school of Chiron[12] since they had an instructor at home, to whom Chiron in keeping with his name was much inferior.[13] (8) So they were born, educated, and trained. And while there was peace among the Achaeans, they were a much more illustrious adornment of Thessaly[14] than its lakes, plains, and rivers. And they aided the Greeks there by participating in their government in a manner appropriate to those people and by setting to rights the personal misfortunes of each of them. And there was no sickness wherever Machaon or Podalirius appeared. (9) But when the Greeks were thrown into turmoil through the injustice of the Trojans, they neither thought that they should buy for themselves the right to stay at home, nor did they go into hiding like certain others.[15] But when they realized that it was an occasion for them and when they foresaw the fortunes of war, they voluntarily became the protectors of the health of all the Greeks. (10) When they came to Troy, they were doubly useful to the Achaeans, and they not only acted as their doctors, but also assisted them in the fighting, and they are said to have often routed the enemy.[16] The capture of Troy entirely depended on them, both for other reasons and because of the disease of Philoctetes. For Odysseus and the sons of Atreus had prematurely decided that this disease was incurable, and they unjustly abandoned Philoctetes on Lemnus. But the sons of Asclepius healed this disease which had grown for ten years. And Philoctetes was effective for the Achaeans and the shafts of Heracles were useful for Philoctetes[17] through their art.[18] (11) When Troy was captured, foreseeing that later Greeks would emigrate to Asia and at the same time desiring that as many as possible enjoy their benefits, they pacified Teuthrania[19] for the reception of their father. But as the Coans tell it, they sailed to Meropian Cos, a habitation of the Meropes,[20] which Heracles still earlier on his return from

Troy charged with injustice and sacked, and they settled it and gave it customs appropriate to the nature of the land, in imitation, as it seems, of what is said about their ancestor. (12) For the poets say that Apollo earlier stopped the motion of Delus and fixed its place in the sea when at first he was being born in it. And when the sons of Asclepius set foot upon the land of the Meropes and judged it to be the fairest island of all that were of equal size, they cured it and made it accessible for all Greeks and barbarians, although it formerly was dangerous and suspect, and they caused the island to possess good fortune. (13) I even think that although the Rhodians have long had many things to be proud of, among the first is the rule of the sons of Asclepius, when they themselves selected and chose the sons of Asclepius as their rulers, and made them the successors of the sons of Heracles. The sons of Asclepius also held the region of Caria, and Cnidus, which is sacred to Aphrodite. For whatever was the possession of the one[21] or both of them, let it now be shared between them. Cyrnus[22] also had some advantage from them. (14) But this is a long subject. They gave an additional gift by begetting sons as their co-workers and as the inheritors of their science, as it were the sum of their benefits to the Greeks—I shall add even to all men—, so that their aid and kindness might never fail the human race, but that both through their ancestors and descendants they might be immortal saviors of nature, living forever among mankind and being with all men as with those of their own time. (15) They smashed the reputations of the doctors in Egypt. They made their own benefits a token of their race. For they settled neither in Thessaly nor in the suburbs of Cos, but they filled every place with their medicine, just as Triptolemus did with wheat through his sowing.[23] For everything has come from them and by their actions. And just as they say that in her flight through the Thessalian plain Medea scattered her drugs and caused all Thessaly to be rich in drugs, so their science and generosity was scattered to the farthest limits, and adorned and still adorns, and besides saved and still saves—and let the third tense[24] be added to these two—all the cities of the Greeks and many regions of the barbarians as well. (16) But if one man alone of these, Hippocrates, had been the inheritor of their art, while the whole intervening line were not doctors, the crop would have been sufficient[25] for the land and men would have been grateful to them for their sowing. But now just as the family of the sons of Asclepius has been made a race, preserving its art through its descendants, so divine fortune guided the procreation of Machaon and Podalirius. (17) One would understand this by comparing them to the sons of Heracles in respect to their general usefulness and their private fortune. First of all, at the start, the sons of Heracles were scattered, and there was not one group of them, nor, one might say, even one tribe. For they were not of equal rank, so that they were like strangers to one another. Next the best of them are said not to have been without misfortune and to have not entirely preserved their father's art. For they did not acquire their glory by their benefits to all mankind, but by their personal power. (18) But the sons of Asclepius, beginning with Machaon and Podalirius, were a universal means of safety and security for all men, and they preserved their ancestor's art, as any other token of their family. In addition their fortune also was worthy of their chosen life. For they neither were driven into exile nor came as suppliants to any city, but they passed their lives free of misfortune, always cherishing one brotherhood and being of one mind and fortune. (19) I shall return to where I digressed,[26] to the founders of the family and to those who were the first to take the name of the sons of Asclepius. While they lived among mankind, they aided the cities through their campaigns, through their visits, through their procreation of children who were worthy of them, and in sum, through all their civic ability, and they removed not only the diseases of the body, but also cured the sicknesses of the cities,[27] or rather they did not even permit them to arise at all, saving their subjects from both by making their rule consonant with their art. (20) But since they were too great to remain among us, through the aid of their father and their ancestors they put off their flesh and came to another law, not like Menelaus and "golden-haired Rhadamanthys",[28] to the Elysian Fields and the islands beyond our world. But they became immortal and now journey throughout the earth, and they differ from their original nature only in so far as they still preserve their youth. (21) And many have already seen them in Epidaurus and have recognized them manifestly moving about, and many in many other places. And let the greatest thing which can be said about them be that while Amphiaraus and Trophonius give oracles and are seen in Boeotia and Amphilochus in Aetolia, they like stars dart everywhere over the earth, the joint attendants and precursors of their father. Wherever Asclepius has access, to these too the very gates are flung open, everywhere on the earth, and in everything their partnership with their father is preserved, in temples, sacrifices, paeans, processions, and in the acts which they perform. (22) O blessed in your earlier ancestors on both sides, and fortunate in your descendants, and also in yourselves and your sisters, since you share the company of Iaso, Panacea, Aegle, and Hygieia,[29] who is the equal of all, O sons truly named for your mother Epione![30] Your seats are not without one another nor do you dwell apart. (23) O you yourselves the fairest chorus for your father, O you who have brought upon the stage many choruses from mankind,[31] O makers of the chorus, by far the best of all, and in addition makers of sacrifice[32] and presiders over the jars of wine and all thank offerings! Other sacrifices and feasts have been established by law, one might say, but those inspired by you and your workshop are each day most numerous and equal to all the others, yet they come purely from the heart and convey the joy of our feelings. The traces of your presence are most numerous and most conspicuous. Just as a shadow follows man, so a light always follows you wherever you may go. (24) O you who have a lot equal to that of the Dioscuri and are the same age as they, although of a different generation,[33] you who have already stopped many tempests and have kindled many gleaming beacons on the islands and on each continent, you have this speech from us, composed directly after our sleep and dream. But do you in your gentleness and generosity, having disposed us to better hopes, stop our sickness, and may you give us health enough for the body to obey the wishes of the soul, and in sum, the means for a comfortable life.[34]

XXXIX. REGARDING THE WELL IN THE TEMPLE OF ASCLEPIUS[1]

(1) What could you say about the Sacred Well? Or is it clear that you will find fault with the power of speech as not entirely sufficient nor at times capable of satisfactorily depicting what an object really is? Indeed, no speech would depict the nature of its beauty and the pleasure which it gives, but we are better able to drink this water, bathe in it, and with pleasure gaze upon it than we are capable of saying anything about it. Just so the lovers of handsome youths, who are smitten by the power of their beauty and know the nature of what they love. But if someone asks them, they could not speak about their beloved when absent, and yet, I think, they would point out their features when present. (2) We have also undergone the same experience in the matter of this Well, and very many of us are its lovers, or rather nearly all of us. Yet we cannot describe its nature. But if ever anyone takes one of us aside and questions him, we should think that we ought to take him in charge and bring him to the Well, and we should point out its features. But this will not be sufficient. When he has tasted and tried it, he will think that he has tasted Homer's lotus, and he will wish to remain and only with difficulty will he be willing to depart from the Well. (3) But we must not "in the manner of thirsty men", as they say, "drink in silence",[2] but we must adorn it somewhat with speech, and address both the savior god,[3] whose work and creation this also is, and the Nymphs,[4] who hold it, who share in the work, who favor us with the right to use the favor of the god, and who join in serving us.

(4) Where should I begin? Just as whenever we drink from it, having placed the cup to our lips, we do not cease until we have drunk down all together all that we have poured in, so too will our speech make all of its remarks together? But in lieu of "applying the cup to our lips",[5] let that be our beginning, the fact that it is in the fairest spot of the whole world. For certainly the fairest spot of all in the world is the one which the god chose above all other places as being most healthful and pure and which he has made the most notable of all by his benefits. (5) Different gods have been indigenous to different places from the beginning—and these places too, I think, should seem honored in the very fact that gods were

allotted them—, but this place is more honored because when the god came here from Epidaurus itself,[6] he fell greatly in love with the spot, as is clear in that when he selected it and preferred it to the others, he remained here for the future. But what a god, and the gentlest and most generous of gods, has judged as superior, how can we, and at that his servants,[7] say other than that it is the best? (6) Thus it can be said that it is in the fairest spot of the world. Further it is in the fairest part of the region of the temple which is in the open air and is easily accessible. For it is set in the center of the center of the shrine. If you wish, its water flows from a plane tree—for like some other token, this has also grown beside the Well; or if you wish, and this is better and holier still, it flows from the very foundations on which the temple is erected. Therefore everyone believes and trusts that it flows from a place which is both healthy and the supplier of health, since it rises from the temple and the feet of the Savior. For water would flow from no healthier or purer spot than that which flows from here. (7) Since it appears in such a place and rises from such a source, it is the fairest water, as is likely. First of all, it is most delicate, very close to air; second, in consequence of this, it is most light and gentle; and third, it is most sweet and potable, originating in itself, and if you drink it, you would not want wine besides. Homer said[8] that the Titaresius flowed upon the Peneus, like a man swimming, because of the lightness of the water. But it seems to me, if you should cause another water to break in upon the Well, the Well water will rise to the surface, but the other water will sink as divers do, and head to the depths from the surface—unless this too can be said that it seems to me that through its lightness it would have raised up the water which was poured in on it. A scale shows that we are not bragging. Yet what would that branch of the Styx[9] say, whenever it was weighed and found heavier? (8) Added to this is the fact that this stream is neither a branch of the Styx nor has any other terrifying quality, but you would call it a branch of health or nectar or some such thing. (9) It also gives evidence of this. Time does not affect it; but when the water is drawn up and is without the Well, it behaves the same as whatever is left in the Well. It remains unspoiled and uncorrupted. (10) Again this Well's supply of water is greater, one might say, than that of any other well. Those who draw the water must be untiring and stay alert, so that the new rising water does not get ahead of them. When men draw upon it

XXXIX. REGARDING THE WELL IN THE TEMPLE OF ASCLEPIUS

and empty it, this Well alone of all always has an equal measure in store, just the opposite to the pierced jar.[10] For the jar is never filled, but the Well's water always stands near its lip. (11) Since it is a servant and co-worker of the most generous of gods, it is most ready to serve and is always full. And the god has no leisure to do other than to save mankind, and the Well in imitation of its master always fills the wants of those who need it, and is like some creature or gift of Asclepius, just as Homer depicted the instruments and machines of Hephaestus which move according to his wishes.[11] (12) Since I have reached this point, what water of those among mankind could be compared with this as far as usefulness is concerned? For it is not only to drink, but the same is also a most pleasant and most safe bath. Nor again is it subject to the same phenomena as other waters, but its changes are contrary to the seasons of the year,[12] since it is at its coldest in summer, but becomes as mild as possible in winter and remedies and soothes the difficulties of whatever season is at hand, being such as the sacred spring of Asclepius should be. (13) These waters are good and sweet for the user and for the observer of others, watching in summer when they stand close around the lip of the Well, like a swarm of bees, or flies around milk,[13] at dawn seeking to forestall the heat in lieu of any other drink which prevents and stops thirst, or whenever someone, while the ice is frozen fast, extends and washes his hands and becomes warmer and more comfortable than before. (14) But the god also uses it in other ways like any other co-worker, and the Well has often assisted many people in obtaining from the god what they desired. For just as the sons[14] of doctors and magicians have been trained to serve them and while they aid them astound spectators and customers, so this Well is the discovery and possession of the great magician who does everything for the safety of mankind. It aids him in everything and for many men is like a drug. (15) For many by bathing in it have recovered their sight, and many by drinking it have been cured of chest trouble and have regained the breath of life. It has cured one man's feet and another part of the body for someone else. Once someone drank it and spoke after being mute, just as those who have drunk the forbidden waters and have become prophetic. For some merely drawing up the water has been like a means of safety. And thus to the sick it is an antidote and a cure, and for those in health who reside nearby it makes the employment of all other waters subject to blame.

(16) For after this water, all other waters become for those who try them, as if someone should drink some soured wine after one with a fine bouquet. But this water alone is both for the sick and the healthy, individually and together, equally most pleasant and most useful. And you would not compare milk with it, nor would you still desire wine, but it is as Pindar described nectar[15] "originating in itself", potable, satisfactorily blended by a kind of divine mixture, so that if there should be two cups, one containing some other water and the fairest wine, and the other this water, you would hesitate over which to take. (17) Furthermore the other sacred waters are not for the use of most men, for example that in Delus, or whatever other similar water there is elsewhere. But this water is sacred because it saves those who use it, not because no one touches it. And it is satisfactory both for purifications at the temple,[16] and for men to drink and bathe in, and to be cheered in their hearts at its sight.

(18) I would not compare with this water, which is in every way sacred, either the Cydnus, or the Eurymedon, or the Choaspes which the King carried about with him and drank from,[17] or the Peneus upon each of whose banks the earth has put forth the fairest garlands, or the Nile, each half of whose stream some say is supplied on each side by a separate bottomless spring,[18] or whatever other water you will name. But I should say that it is superior among waters by as much as the god, its patron, is superior among gods. One thing is left to add, that in rendering this judgment we would also be acting piously. "For the god was the first to give this verdict about it", as they say.[19]

XL. HERACLES[1]

(1) But, O dearest Heracles, it is the most pleasant sort of labor to praise you. In every way you are much hymned. For there are many who sing your deeds in prose, and the poets have hymned you much in every fashion, but most important there is the daily praise of all men which ever arises at every occasion that befalls.[2] (2) And it is no wonder that he has so far surpassed human nature, whose father is the first of beings and whose mother was preferred from among all women by his father.[3] So concerned was his father in the matter of his procreation that they say that he slept with her for three days and nights in a row, since he wished to infuse into his offspring the largest and purest possible amount of his nature. His wish was for the sake of the Universe, so that human affairs might be properly ordered, and the earth and the sea might be made productive. And thus Heracles was born as a co-worker of his father and as prefect of the region beneath the lunar sphere, and prodigies immediately followed. (3) For when snakes had come up to his swaddling clothes, he slew them with an ordinary movement of his hand. While he was still a child, in place of other children's games, he also freed the Thebans from the tribute which they had always paid to the Orchomenians. (4) Beginning at home, he purified Greece, and then even the whole human race, visiting all men in turn, both those on the islands and on each continent, and omitting no good deed, but subduing the wild beasts,[4] by whose multitude and hugeness much of the countryside was injured, and destroying the tyrants in a fashion appropriate to each of them,[5] and moderating the behavior of the cities both by laws and by force of arms, and utterly annihilating, both in Greece and in barbarian lands, robbers on land and sea, and all men who relied on their physical strength to do wrong against weaker men. (5) For he regarded as his enemy all things which were hostile to nature.[6] And alone of those who came upon the earth he gave laws universally to everything, not only to human beings but also to the wild beasts, one might say, since he even found a means of expelling the birds who were destroying much of Arcadia,[7] as if it were not only his duty to liberate the earth and sea, but also the air. And all the lands that were oppressed by rivers and lakes, he made dry. Again as to

all that needed to be cleansed by water, by diverting rivers into them, he made them not only bearable to behold, but also productive. (6) And thus he subdued earth, sea, rivers, lakes, air, rocks, men and cities by blending law with force of arms,[8] so that there was nothing more glorious nor of more profitable use than his reign. For because of his unbreakable strength nothing which was undertaken eluded him. Yet in the greatness of his justice everything took place for the advantage of the human race. (7) Therefore the poets have composed stories about Prometheuses unchained by him, as if Heracles even had the power to unchain all that Zeus had fettered, and the tale of how he relieved Atlas by substituting for him and holding up the heavens himself, and of how he brought Cerberus up from Hades and Theseus, one of the Erechthids, along with him, and of how he wounded Pluto and Hera, and of how he subdued the Giants when he aided the gods. (8) This, I think, is an extravagant way of saying that Heracles has searched through every land and every sea and has gone to every boundary and every limit and has neglected nothing beneath the earth nor as far as the heavens, but was so very useful to all, that even the gods needed Heracles to set their affairs to rights.[9] (9) I think that he even was the first to mark the boundary between the Atlantic and the Mediterranean, wooing all this region for the Greeks as being fit to settle and that this is the meaning of the Pillars, which we still now call "of Heracles". (10) Not only would one realize that his nature was greater than man's by following the tales of the Greeks, but we also know how great a god the Egyptians regard Heracles to be[10] and that the Tyrians worship him as the first of the gods.[11] Yet if all men thus honor him in the belief that he is the same person, what greater proof could one mention of his power? But if some believe him to be one of the oldest of the gods, while we have thought our Heracles to be worthy of the same honor as theirs is, as being that one's equal, even in this way he is shown to be greater than a mere human being. This is also made clear by the oracles of the god.[12] (11) For when Heracles, purified in the manner told,[13] left the human race, Apollo immediately proclaimed the establishment of temples to Heracles and that sacrifices be made to him as to a god, and at that he revealed it to Athens which was the oldest Greek city, and, as it were, a guide for all men in the matter of piety toward the gods and in all other serious activities. Further it also had many other ties of friendship with

Heracles, including the fact that he was the first foreigner to be initiated, while he was among men.[14] And the manifestation of the Athenians' zeal was so great and his position was adjudged as so very much superior[15] that they even changed all the shrines built in honor of Theseus throughout the demes and made them shrines in honor of Heracles instead of Theseus in the belief that Theseus was the best of their citizens,[16] but that Heracles was beyond human nature. (12) But why should one speak of ancient history. For the activity of the god is still now manifest. On the one hand, as we hear, he does marvelous deeds at Gadira[17] and is believed to be second to none of all the gods. And on the other hand, in Messene in Sicily he frees men from all diseases,[18] and those who have escaped danger on the sea attribute the benefaction equally to Poseidon and Heracles. One could list many other places sacred to the god, and other manifestations of his power. (13) But what need is there to speak of things which are far away? The Praetorium[19] seems to us to be a temple of Heracles. And in this he has often been seen playing with balls of Herculean proportions. These are round stones of no small weight. The noise which they create is audible and they are moved by him from one side of the building to the other. His other manifestations are also marvelous, so that although it is a public building, the Praetorium has become like a shrine because of these things which have happened in respect to the god. (14) What would you say about the much used invocation in comedy as well as in tragedy,[20] and in every speech, since still now everybody, one might say, cries out "O Heracles",[21] "on every occasion of need", to quote Sophocles.[22] Would you not say that this is the greatest reminder and proof of his justice and power and that he was the champion of human nature and guided all men toward the best? Therefore even those of his day invoked him for everything and the expression still has remained in force from that old custom. (15) Of his titles *Kallinikos*[23] and *Alexikakos,*[24] the one was given to him alone of the gods, and the other to him among the first. The Coans, as I remember,[25] also believe in Heracles the Averter. And they have erected, because of an oracle, a statue of Heracles with the celestial sphere raised upon his back, as if he even had the power to bring the heavens into harmony. (16) Not only could one say all this about the god, some of whose deeds took place while he lived among mankind, and others of which he still now clearly performs by himself, but also the race of his sons should be held in the highest regard, whom he created to be the universal saviors of Greece and inheritors of his way of life.[26] Of them some remained in the Peloponnesus and set it in order, and others raised Italy and Sicily to such great glory.[27] Another group crossed over to Asia and settled and administered[28] the Doric cities here. (17) But the city of the Lacedaemonians even seems to be an image of Heracles, "to compare small things with great".[29] And with very good reason. For the Leonidases and Leotychidases and Archidamuses and Agesilauses and Agises,[30] and Lycurgus who gave them their laws before these, all of them are of the stream of Heracles, and they accustomed the Lacedaemonians, although few in number, to be the equal of many and to champion without reward all those in need and for one Spartan general to have more effect than an army of other men.[31] Thus both through himself and his descendants he contrived, as it were, springs of virtue for the Greeks, and he brought it about that the one group was trained for the noblest deeds and that the other had a means of safety in future. (18) Not only would one be able to mention Heracles in connection with deeds and contests, but he also holds a considerable place in the joys of life.[32] This is made clear by his statues[33] which depict him drinking. (19) He received a marvelous lot in life from the hands of all the gods. Zeus brought him to the light. Athena received him, acted as his guardian, and guided him in his labors. Aphrodite and Dionysus[34] welcomed him and gave him relief commensurate with his toils. His connection with Hera and marriage with Hebe are old tales. For so much strength, as it seems, was given to him, that although all the gods are forever untiring, Heracles especially appears to have the flower of youth.[35] Indeed, there are now statues shared between Hermes and Heracles.[36] So close is their comradeship. (20) Both in the midst of the mountains and in the cities you would see Heracles by the side of the Mother of the gods[36a], and again in the company of the Dioscuri. And the most charming baths are named after Heracles. Besides, even the springs of river water are called after the god. Such preeminence has he been allotted among the Nymphs. (21) But if the dream of the Thasian or Macedonian stranger is correct,[37] who once said that he dreamed that he sang a paean written by me which had the refrain, "O Paean Heracles Asclepius", if these things are true and proper, this union too, which appeared in a dream, would be a fine thing, the *Kallinikos* and the Savior. Thus in labors, in pleasure, in care of the

XL. HERACLES

body, and in every circumstance the god is of importance. (22) Heracles is remembered and honored by all men, and I also have a particular friendship with him, which arose from a certain divine voice. It seemed to come from the Metroon.[38] It exhorted me to endure the present circumstances,[39] since Heracles also endured his, although he was the son of Zeus. This is our speech to you, O dear Heracles, sung like any other lyric in accordance with the vision of my dream, when I dreamed that I recited a praise of Heracles in the portico of Apollo.[40]

(Subscription: *Heracles*. 48 years and 8 months.)[41]

XLI. DIONYSUS[1]

(1) Let Asclepius himself, who caused the dream to appear, guide us. Let Dionysus himself, in whose honor we must dance,[2] guide us, and again Apollo, Leader of the Muses, the father of the former and brother of the latter, as is the tale. (2) Let us leave to Orpheus, and to Musaeus, and to the ancient lawgivers[3] the complete hymns and speeches about Dionysus. But let us address the god with a suitable address as if to prove that we are not of the uninitiated.[4] Indeed, length and brevity, and everything in nature is dear to him. And somehow the matter of the dream also comes to pass, that we must be artful in oratory.

(3) Zeus had intercourse with Semele. And when Semele conceived, Zeus, in the wish to be both Dionysus' father and mother, brought Semele on a conveyance of fire from earth to Olympus, and himself took up his offspring, sewed him in his thigh and carried him for ten months, living from the start in Nysa to the south of Ethiopia. And when it was time, he summoned the Nymphs and undid the stitches. And so Dionysus was born, related to his father in two ways. Thus Zeus exceptionally honored him beyond all gods and men. For neither did he stand in this double relationship with anyone else nor did any other. (4) The god is both male and female, as they say, because for him his father shared in each nature in respect to him.[5] I have heard from some even another story on this subject, that Zeus is Dionysus.[6] (5) And what more could you say than this? But he also resembles his nature in his appearance. For he is wholly, as it were, a twin to himself. He is numbered among both the young men and girls.[7] And again, as it were, numbered among the males, he is both beardless and the Briseus,[8] and, indeed, warlike and peaceful beyond all the gods. (6) They also give him Pan as his dancer, who is "the most perfect of the gods", as Pindar hymns[9] and the priests throughout Egypt have learned.[10] Indeed, they even say that he was the only god to reconcile Hera and her son when he brought the unwilling Hephaestus up to heaven, and at that having placed him on the back of an ass. (7) And it is clear that there is a riddle in the tale, but the point of the riddle is also clear, that the power of the god is great and invincible and that he could give wings even to asses, not

only to horses,[11] just as the Laconian poet[12] even attributed to him the power of milking lions. And nothing will be so firmly bound, not by disease, not by wrath, or by any fortune, which Dionysus will not be able to set free.[13] But the sick man will be easier and the one-time enemy will be a drinking companion, and the old man will grow young and drink[14] at the urging of the god. (8) Again the Sileni, who dance about him, bear witness to this. And the fennel stalks, with which he is furnished in place of the spear, and the fawn skin in place of the lion skin, and the cup in place of the hollow shield[15] bear witness to the ease of his power, as if fighting and drinking were the same for Dionysus. And there is not much between the contest and the victory song. But they tell how he subdued the Indians and the Etruscans, hinting, it seems to me, by the Etruscans, the western world, and by the others the eastern part of the earth, as if he ruled it all. (9) Bacchae proceed him in place of cavalry and bowmen, consistent with the dress which we just now hymned,[16] and at the same time they confirm that women's armies along with those of men were also part of the way of Dionysus, and that it was no more Dionysiac to make men effeminate than to put women in the ranks of men. So great is he, manifold, and all embracing. This is also clear from the following. (10) For in partnership with Aphrodite he opens the theaters[17] and becomes the leader of drinking parties and religious revels. In union with Ares he is a god of war,[18] and together with Athena and Hephaestus, a god of the arts which require fire.[19] The Heralds and Eumolpidae[20] have given him a share in the temple of the goddesses of Eleusis, as an overseer of the crops and nurture for mankind.[21] And it seems to me fitting to add that his was the only sacred apparition to appear in the time of the Persian danger.[22] Thus although he is generous in every way, he inclines to favor the Greeks. (11) When he is blended with the Nymphs, he has done and does a great variety of dances among men, and seizes their insides more completely than Eurycles,[23] and makes one a dancer "even if one knew no music before".[24] But he skips and plays, and wishes to sing,[25] and at that from the dinner couch and chair. (12) Thus it is the nature of the god to accomplish all things. But Love, that marvelous tyrant of men,[26] having drawn on the springs of Dionysus, goes over every land with Dionysus as his leader, and neither are his seats, works, or couches separate. (13) He oversees the limits of night and day. In the night he himself is torchbearer and guide of our vision, but the day he leaves to others. Still not even so is he idle, but he passes the time always active and in motion. Although he is the oldest of the gods, he himself is also the youngest one.[27] He is the friend of whatever is the present hour and moment.[28] And, as for me, farewell to him, who is called Iacchus and these many other names! For now, as it were, the cup of friendship is full.[29]

XLII. AN ADDRESS REGARDING ASCLEPIUS[1]

(1) O you who have often for many reasons been summoned by us, night and day, publicly and privately, O Lord Asclepius, how glad and eager we were when you granted us, as it were, from a great sea[2] of despair to reach a calm harbor and to address the common hearth of mankind, in which no one, indeed, under the sun is uninitiated[3]—and we can affirm that no Greek to this day has enjoyed more advantages! For even if I am quite accustomed to saying this, I must not hesitate any the more. (2) We have not omitted these daily addresses of ours[4] and we have not given up our custom, but we even maintain it for this very reason because it has been our custom from the start. Of course, I am concerned to express my gratitude and show my respect by means of sacrifice and incense, whether this takes place in keeping with Hesiod's advice[5] or even with greater enthusiasm than my means allow. But the expression of gratitude through oratory appears particularly proper for me. (3) For if in general the study of oratory means for man the point and, as it were, the sum of life, and of speeches those concerning the gods are the most necessary and just, and our career in oratory clearly is a gift of the god himself, there is no fairer means of showing gratitude to the god, I think, than through oratory, nor would we have a better use to which to put our oratory. And let us speak, starting from the beginning. I know that these matters are well-known and much discussed. How could they not be? But they are so much more deserving to be mentioned by us by as much as we would be better worshippers by giving additional examples and by being redundant than by omitting what no one at all thinks should be kept silent.

(4) Great and many are the powers of Asclepius, or rather he possesses all powers, beyond the scope of human life. And not purposelessly did those here establish the Temple of Zeus Asclepius.[6] But if my teacher is clear and this is more than all likely—the fashion and means of his teaching have been told in *The Sacred Tales*[7]—, it is he who guides and directs the Universe, savior of the Whole and guardian of what is immortal, or if you should prefer an expression of tragedy, "the overseer of the helm",[8] who preserves both eternal being and that which comes into being. But if we

believe him to be the son of Apollo and the second generation from Zeus, again we also combine them in their names.[9] Indeed, they sometimes declare that even Zeus himself was born, and again they make him the father and creator of being. But as Plato says,[10] "let this be and be said, however it pleases the gods themselves". Let us return to where we digressed. (5) Since the god possesses all power, he has chosen to benefit mankind in every way, giving each man what is his due. He has bestowed upon all men the greatest and most universal benefaction, the rendering of the human race immortal by the means of succession,[11] by creating through the medium of health marriage, the begetting of children, and the means and resources for nurture. He has distributed individual gifts "with a view to the man",[12] for example the arts, employments, and various ways of life, with health as a kind of universal drug[13] for all labors and actions. He has established public medical offices and has assigned himself the task of practicing his art night and day to cheer whoever needs him or will need him. (6) Different men sing and will always sing of different things. So I wish to mention matters which pertain to me. Some say that they have been resurrected when they were dead, and their stories are accepted, of course, and it is an old practice of the god. We have received this benefit not only once, but it is not even easy to say how often.[14] To some he has given added years of life from his predictions. We belong to this group.[15] For this is the least offensive way to express it.[16] (7) But some, I mean both men and women, even attribute to the providence of the god the existence of the limbs of their body, when their natural limbs had been destroyed; others list other things, some in oral accounts, some in the declarations of their votive offerings. For us it is not only a part of the body, but it is the whole body which he has formed and put together and given as a gift, just as Prometheus of old is said to have fashioned man. He has freed many of many pains, sufferings, and difficulties, both those of day and night—one could not say how many. But he himself best knows our tempests[17] in this respect, and he himself has also clearly stopped them. (8) Indeed, there is very much of the marvelous in the unambiguous dreams[18] of the god, for example[19] one man drinks chalk, another hemlock, and another undresses and bathes in cold water while not at all needing a means of warmth, as one would expect. He has also honored us in this fashion, by stopping catarrhs and colds with baths in rivers and the

XLII. AN ADDRESS REGARDING ASCLEPIUS   249

sea, by curing our difficulty in reclining in bed[20] with long walks, by adding indescribable purges to continual fasting, and by commanding me to speak and write when I found it difficult to breathe, so that if people cured in this way can boast about it, we too are not without our share of boasting. (9) Indeed, some men tell stories about their endurance and all the different things which they withstood under the god's leadership, while others found, as it were, an easy means to their needs. We, indeed, have shown endurance in most things in many and in various ways. Yet some cures have been very easy and pleasurable, so that those who lead delicate lives would be of no account if you should wish to compare them. And although I could enumerate other cities of Asia and Europe, how shall I not regard beyond luxury the good will of all men who praise my lectures here and concurrently delight in them as if it were their own achievement? What would you say of the uproars in the council chambers[21] and the unparalleled enthusiasm? And the conviction, even before I said anything, that I was superior, is this not a kind of divine grace which embodies the first part of the easy means to one's needs?[22] I should say so, since it is pleasant to recall the better things.[23] (10) I have heard some people say that the god has appeared and stretched forth his hand to them when they sailed and were in trouble, and others will tell of their successes in various enterprises by following the instructions of the god. And we are no more an audience in these matters than able to speak from experience on this subject. Everything of this nature, that can be mentioned, is also found in *The Sacred Tales*. (11) But it is even said that the god revealed boxing tricks to a certain boxer of our day in his sleep, which if he used, he must of necessity have defeated one of his very famous opponents.[24] But the god has revealed to us means of study, lyric poetry, subjects for speeches, and in addition to this, the actual ideas[25] and the style, like those who teach boys to write.[26] Since I have put, as it were, the finishing touch to the god's benefits, I shall close my speech on this point.

(12) For I have received, O Lord Asclepius, as I have said, many, various gifts from you and your generosity, but the greatest, the one deserving the most gratitude, and nearly, one might say, the most wholesome is oratory.[27] You have changed what happened to Pindar.[28] For Pan danced out his paean, as the story goes. But if it is proper to express it, I say that I am the actor of your compositions. For you yourself have exhorted me to oratory and have guid-

ed my training. (13) And this was not enough for you. But you also were concerned with what was likely to come next, that your work would be famous. And there is no city, no private citizen, no official, who after even a brief association with us did not salute us and praise us as extensively as possible, and it was not, I think, the effect of my oratory, but the effect of you, my master. (14) But the greatest thing in this respect is putting me on such friendly terms with the divine Emperors,[29] and aside from contact with them by mail, by making me a speaker before them and one prized as no one ever had been, and at that equally by the Emperors and by the Princesses,[30] and by the whole Imperial chorus.[31] Odysseus received from Athena the power to give an oratorical display in the house of Alcinous and before the Phaeacians[32]—this was certainly a great thing and very timely; and my affair[33] too was accomplished in this way. And there was a sign which summoned me, when you showed in fact that you brought me before the public for many reasons, so that we might be seen engaged in oratory and that the most perfect men might hear with their own ears our superior work. (15) Privately in our heart we are not unmindful of this and of many other things, and in our lectures to our audiences we shall not cease to be as grateful as possible, so long as we have any memory and good sense. I would say that I have also received this favor from you, the fact that you who are best in everything are present with us and approve of our speeches.

XLIII. REGARDING ZEUS[1]

(1) We bring these gifts to you, O Zeus, king and savior, in accordance with our vow. But do you accept them, and just as you kindly saved me, do you also receive this thank offering and aid my speech and escort it to the greatest possible limits attainable by the speech of man, so that we may not be completely ridiculous and that we may not entirely fail. (2) Yet now that I am engaged in the speech, I do not know what to do. But I seem now to understand quite well that I was in great danger and lost my self-control because of the sea, when I made such a vow, which is not easy to fulfill, and attempting which perhaps inspires no confidence in my moderation, since I promised that I would deliver a hymn to Zeus, and at that in prose. (3) Indeed, then the sea was great and it made me do and say everything. Still—for no vow must be neglected, as they say,[2] but any kind of payment is better than absolute neglect—let us try in some way or other to fulfill our religious obligation to the god. It will be his care whether our work surpasses the mark or falls short of it. (4) And in fact complete neglect will bring a reputation for slothful conduct, which is improper in one's relations with the gods, whereas the nature of the very subject will condone lack of success. For we shall not seem to be willingly negligent, but to be inferior out of necessity. One might say, if it must be, it is better to be thought ridiculous than culpable by the gods. (5) Since we made the vow and it cannot be altered, like athletes who enroll in a competition, we must not withdraw, but come to grips with and make trial of the contest. (6) Well then! O Muses, children of Zeus—for I see no better time for one to summon you than now—, whether you sing your divine song on Olympus in company with Apollo, Leader of the Muses, while you hymn him who is the father of you and of the Universe,[3] or Pieria is your favored haunt, or you dance in Boeotian Helicon[4] the story of all the blessings of the deeds and gifts of Zeus, come, you who know all things,[5] where are we to begin? What shall we dare to say about Zeus? Grant my speech to become inspired by its subject as well as by what is appropriate in regard to him, and do not abandon me in the midst of heaven and earth.

(7) Zeus created everything, and all that exists is the work of Zeus, rivers, earth, sea, heaven, and all that is in between these, and all that is above these and all that is beneath, and gods and men, and all that has a soul, and all that is visible and all that is only conceivable. (8) But first he created himself, since he was not raised in the fragrant caves of Crete,[6] nor did Cronus intend to swallow him, nor did he swallow a stone in his place, nor was Zeus in danger, nor will he ever be in danger, nor is there anything older than Zeus, no more than sons would be older than their fathers and creations older than their creators. But he is the first and oldest and founder of the Universe, born of himself. (9) It cannot be said when he was born, but he existed from the beginning and will always exist, father to himself[7] and one too great to be born from another. And just as he gave birth to Athena from his head and required no marriage to create her, so still earlier he created himself from himself, and required nothing of any second person for his existence, but quite to the contrary all things began to exist from him. And we cannot speak of time.[8] For then time did not even exist, because there was nothing else at all. For no creation is older than the creator. Thus Zeus is the beginning of all things and all things come from Zeus. (10) Since he was greater than time and had no one to resist him, both he and the Universe existed at the same moment. So swiftly did he create everything. He created it in the following way. If we are mistaken in anything, let us invoke the Zeus Who-is-Gracious.[9] (11) He began with the foundation and created the earth so that all his works might sit firm upon it, and he rooted down its depths with infinite roots and solidified it with rocks in place of bolts, nay also with the very matter whose nature is to be soldified,[10] and he raised up the mountains as a protective barrier against rain and waves and inserted plains between as a basis for the mountains and the earth, fastening the one by the other. (12) As much in his creation as was next in weight, he then added, setting the sea in the very midst of the earth. As with neighbors, he created a means of friendship and partnership and he inserted the rivers which were going to flow from the earth to the sea and in turn flow up into the earth through other invisible courses from the sea[11] and join each element with the other. And he interwove them in such a way that each was in the midst of the other, the one element always being in the middle of the other through the agency of islands, straits, and peninsulas, and he made both elements, the

earth and the sea, secure through each other, just as he strengthened the earth through its two forms.[12] (13) He set the air above both, as a means of respiration for the earth and sea, and he set above that fire, which men call ether,[13] and he held the Universe together with this fourth element. And here he introduced as the best feature of his craftsmanship his adornment of the whole heaven with stars, as of the sea with islands,[14] his illumination of it through them, and his sending of the effluent of their fire down to earth. And he accomplished all of this not in the time which we now have taken to describe it, but faster than the very thought of the creation is possible. (14) In the course of his creation and fashioning, he made a proper division of each thing and gave out lots in which to dwell, creating animals which suited each region, and giving them appropriate homes and places to live when they were begotten: to the gods to dwell in heaven, as it were the acropolis of the Universe—which, in fact, is the fairest and purest of dwelling places, because not even old age enters into it;[15] but to men to dwell upon the earth. He gave the sea to the tribes of the sea, and the air to winged creatures, since each would most succeed to their proper due if they found places to live in keeping with their nature and faculties and if they received kindred dwelling places: the earthborn and terrestrial tribe the earth, the more aquatic the sea, the lighter and drier the air, and again the intellectual and fiery tribe, which has been placed over all of these others, the ether and the heavens. (15) Thus as it were making a city, when he had built it, he next introduced men. After he had separated matter and had prepared the Universe, he filled it with different kinds of life, creating them all in turn with a view to their harmony and with the care that there be no omission to prevent everything from being perfect and suited to each other, as he was the very creator and founder of the Universe, holding the ends of being and of power.[16] Therefore each one of all of the tribes of the gods has an effluent from the power of Zeus, the father of all things, and indeed like Homer's cord,[17] all are attached to him and fastened from him, a linkage much fairer than if it were golden or whatever other kind one would conceive of. (16) First of all he begot Love and Necessity, these two powers which are most unifying and most strong,[18] so that they might hold the Universe together for him. And he thought that the mortal race should not be wholly of one and the same lot as the gods, nor yet did he refuse to be the father of mankind as he was of the gods. But as in the manufacture of myrrh, there was left from the same race as that of the gods to be the seed of man all that was, as it were, the sediment and had remained on the bottom, having neither equal value nor power, not uncontaminated and free from evil, as was that former race, yet still more honorable than any other mortal race, since it shared in reason and was not entirely separated from the divine lot, but occupied, as it were, the final segment of a channel or stream. (17) Thus he gave preeminence, rule, and leadership to the gods, but the second rank, much later, he gave to mankind. All the creatures of the air and sea, which lie between, and all the remaining creatures of the earth, he put under the control of both gods and men, just as those on campaigns place their best troops in the front rank and their second best in the rear, and again their "bad troops", as the expression goes,[19] "in between". (18) And he gave the four regions to the gods, so that nothing anywhere might be without gods, but that they might everywhere attend upon all things which are and all things which are coming into being, having divided up among themselves, like prefects and satraps, first as their homeland the region of heaven and then that in the air and in the sea and on the earth. (19) He caused that man most of all share in their providence, since everywhere he preserved the proper due of the races and thought that their rank should not be unprofitable. Mankind, in recognition of this and in their great debt of thanks for his great kindness, when later they gathered together and began to found cities,[20] selected the acropolises for Zeus,[21] with a view to the example of the Universe, because he himself dwelled at the limits of the Universe and at the same time they willingly abandoned to Zeus their most advantageous positions, as if he were the only tyrant who knew how to rule. (20) And in a second way here also he showed to us that our kinship with the race of the gods is expedient to us as subjects.[22] For violence does not touch the gods.[23] Therefore they need no laws. Again man alone of all other animals has made use of law, so that he might not be destroyed through murder and so that theft and violence might not occur, but that justice might take precedence over violence. Zeus framed this law when he sent Reverence and Justice[24] to mankind, along with the other gods, to care for mankind and to keep safe their life. (21) Our birth is originally from Zeus, as is also that of the Universe, and so too is the preservation of our life, and our arts and laws, and the fact that although our race is mortal for the individual, it is immortal through succession.[25] And our pondering on these very matters is a gift of Zeus. (22) But Homer was far from being properly inspired when in the assembly of the gods he depicted Zeus as forbidding the gods to care for mankind.[26] Zeus did not forbid this, nor will he ever forbid this, as long as he respects himself. For it is not fitting for him to change nor to hold a different point of view either through forgetfulness or repentance of that which he originally held when he created the gods to care for mankind and mankind to be worshippers and servants of the gods, an arrangement which was going to be especially fitting and expedient for both. (23) Zeus is the cause and creator of all that is and through him all that is in heaven and upon the earth comes into being, just as his very name also intimates, being used not far from the sense of cause whenever we speak of *"Dia"*.[27] For we call him Zeus since he is the cause of the life and being of each thing;[28] and again in so far as we name anyone as a cause, in this usage of language we have made him synonymous with the word for cause by calling him *"Dia"*, since all things come and have come into being because of him. (24) And the ceaseless motion of the sun above and beneath the earth represents the proclamation of Zeus which he made to the sun concerning the illumination of the whole Universe, and the course of the moon and the dances of all the stars[29] are the arrangements of Zeus. And just as the ocean, which flows about the earth, arose from Zeus in the beginning, so it also abides and preserves its limits. And each year the seasons in turn pass over the whole earth. And the whole of time is divided into day and night, and the length of each is suitable to the moment, and it provides more or less rest and toil, as is proper. And the union of sky and rain is the work of Zeus. (25) And Apollo gives as oracles to mankind "the unerring wish of Zeus".[30] And Asclepius heals, assisting Zeus.[31] And Athena of Crafts has been allotted this position by the will of Zeus. And Hera of Marriages and Artemis, both she of Childbirth and the Huntress, benefit mankind in keeping with the will of the great benefactor of all. And the Pans who dwell in the mountains and the Nymphs who watch over the streams hold their allotment with the blessing of Zeus. Obedient to Zeus, Poseidon and the Dioscuri save those at sea. And the Muses have invented and taught the art of music, since Zeus willed that the Muses and music exist both for the sake of the gods and mankind. (26) Nay more, everything everywhere is full of Zeus,[32] and he is present everywhere at every deed as the teacher is with his pupil and the chariot fighter with his driver. And the benefits of all the gods are the work of Zeus, and all the gods care for mankind keeping to the position assigned by him, as it were, in an army by the general of all. (27) With good reason he understands whatever Fate bestows.[33] For it is he who grants this, and inescapable fate is whatever is bestowed on each by Zeus, whose creation is all being. The mountain peaks do not escape him, nor the sources of the rivers, nor the cities, nor the sand beneath the sea, nor the stars. Before his great eyes, which alone have seen the truth, stands neither night nor sleep. (28) And the fairest and most important of rivers is itself "Zeus-fallen",[34] as it imitates its father, and as if he had made it prefect of Egypt,[35] it comes itself in place of the rain of Zeus and floods the land.[36] (29) Zeus is the father of all, rivers, heaven, earth, gods, mankind, animals, and plants. And through him we see and have all that we have. He is the benefactor, overseer, and patron of all. He is the president, governor, and steward of all being and of all things coming into being. He is the giver of all things, he is the creator of all things. (30) When he grants victory in the assemblies and in trials, he is called Zeus of the Assembly, but in battle, of the Rout. When he gives aid in disease and on every occasion, he is Zeus the Savior, he is Zeus of Freedom, he is Zeus of Gentleness, with good reason since he is also the Father. He is Zeus the King, City Protector, Descender, Of Rain, Of Heaven, Of the Summit, and all the other great and appropriate epithets, which he himself has discovered. He holds the beginning and the end and the measure and the lot of all things.[37] He is equally powerful everywhere over all.[38] He alone could speak properly about himself "as a god with a greater portion".[39] For Pindar[40] has expressed this better than anything else said about Zeus by anyone. (31) With him must we begin and with him must we end,[41] invoking him as guide and helper in every word and every deed, as is likely, being the ruler of all things, himself alone founder and perfecter of the Universe.

XLIV. REGARDING THE AEGEAN SEA[1]

(1) No one, either poet or prose writer, has ever fully sung of the sea. But Homer speaks of "a violet colored sea"[2] and "a wine colored sea"[3] and "a purple sea"[4] and whatever other such expressions anyone else has used. But often they also slander the sea by calling it "salty"[5] and "deep roaring",[6] and similar things. (2) At the present time we shall not make a speech about the greatness of the whole sea and all of its usefulness for mankind and for what great reasons god created it. But we shall pay back our debt to the Aegean[7] and we shall praise it in our hymn. First of all because it has been allotted the best location, since one would also first praise the location of a city.[8]

(3) For it is, indeed, set in the middle of the whole inhabited world and of the sea, to the north leaving the Hellespont, Propontis, and Pontus, and to the south the rest of the sea, separating Asia from Europe at the point where they first divide after the Hellespont. (4) It has the most distinguished and civilized races on each of its banks, on this side Ionia and the Aeolian land, and on the other side Greece, so that only this sea could be said to be in the midst of all of Greece, if one should classify the Greeks who are on either continent as a single race. (5) Yet if the banks of rivers are famous because they have trees and meadows,[9] certainly the shores of the Aegean have a right to be famous, since they have been adorned by such races, and among them at that by the Greeks who live nearby. Indeed, a superiority of the Aegean, one located particularly in these regions, would also be a climate which is both most temperate and most pleasant in every season. (6) The point is clear on both the following arguments. For those who claim that Attica has the best climate and again those who claim this of Ionia obviously agree that the best weather simply is situated about this region.[10] In as much as the sea extends by both shores, it is in possession of whichever of the two shores one decides is superior. Again, if, as is the case in other disputes, there should be need of mutual concession and the taking of a middle position, as I said, this is what the Aegean represents. Therefore this sea has been allotted the finest climate of all.

(7) Such, indeed, is its location and in such a region of the Universe. But its nature is also marvelous. For the magnitude of the sea is first of all considerable and extended on every side if one should measure it accurately everywhere from beginning to end. And a great number of days will be consumed in your circumnavigation of it. (8) Indeed, it is not barren nor by opening an endless vista does it cause depression and despair. But the Aegean is made up of many seas and many gulfs, and in each place there is a different kind of sea. You might stop your journey even in the midst of the sea and find land, cities, and countryside, as it were, little seagirt continents. And you yourself would have various options in arranging your voyage. And again you might return before crossing the whole sea and equally accomplish your aim. (9) For there is no need, as on Homer's sea,[11] to pass through a deserted region to reach an inhabited place, so that the journey is pleasing to none of the gods because of the isolation. But here, indeed, "the choruses of the Nereids unfold the fairest steps",[12] because this is the most inhabited and flourishing region of the sea. And one can sail as much as he wishes, and again travel on land as often as he does not wish to circumnavigate the islands. But he can cross over to another shore, put in, and set sail from that island.[13] For this sea alone is no less inhabited than the earth itself, and it has cities which are only as distant from one another as the intervening countryside would separate the cities on the mainland. (10) Therefore, on the one hand, it is most frightening because of the sudden changes of the sea and the immensity of the total voyage, and again it is most gentle because of its resting places.[14] Although it is most rapidly stirred up, it also provides the most safety, preserving its divine nature. For it must be fearsome because of its strength, yet a means of safety because of its gentleness. (11) Of all seas it sounds most sweetly around its gifts and creatures, just as the poets say that the Pans and Satyrs sound in the mountains and by the trees when they delight in the spring of the year. And this is because the Aegean also has the most musical of the gods as its citizens and inhabitants, Apollo and Artemis, whom Zeus, the father of all, caused to be born in this place, as if it were the fairest in the world, so that they might be perfect in the art of music. And he led Leto through three other islands[15] to Delus in the very midst of the Aegean, having made Athena the guide for her journey. (12) It is clear to everyone that the sea is naturally musical, since right at the start it

raised up a chorus of islands, like any other chorus.[16] And they have divided up the sea, many close to one another, and to sailors and passengers appear as a more sacred sight than any dithyrambic chorus. And they are a consolation in danger and a wonderful means of relaxation for a journey going according to plan. (13) For all told, the islands lie without and within one another, just as when in summer time and before the coming of the west winds, many fishing boats take to the sea. And once you have entered the sea, before and aft, starboard and port, everywhere the same, your view ends in an island, so that at first you are in doubt what course you should take through them. The function of rescue ships is also performed by these islands for those caught in storms, and, as it were, they stretch out a helping hand to arrivals and invite them to put in. Such are the contrivances of the Aegean, which has mingled together land and sea, just as dappled deer and leopard skins intermingle color and spots. (14) So the whole sea here is radiantly alight, and meadows full of flowers on the two mainlands and whatever else one might think of are inferior to this beauty and adornment. With good reason. For everything which is on the mainland is also here on the lands in the midst of the sea. But the two continents do not possess its beauty. As heaven is adorned with stars, so too is the Aegean sea adorned with islands. (15) Therefore even one who had no need for a voyage would sail with good reason for this very purpose, to be carried across the Aegean. So this is the fairest of seas and of all things upon the earth. Therefore beauty is even a particular token of the Aegean, and it begins at that point where, one might say, the islands begin when you pass over the barren sea. (16) The Aegean alone cannot be called "unharvested". For it is neither empty nor without fruit, but it is exceptionally rich in wine. It is productive in wheat and all "which the seasons engender".[17] It is rich in fish and game, such as Homer said[18] the sea of happy men should be. And it provides all needs, all pleasures and spectacles, since it is full of harbors, full of temples, full of flutes, and paeans, and springs and rivers, and is the foster father of Dionysus,[19] and equally pleasing to the Dioscuri and to the Nymphs.[20] It offers every kind of happy life to its inhabitants and to merchants, being profitable and safe to whomever it is kindly disposed. (17) Just as both the beginning and end of a handsome body are seemly, so too it may be that both the beginning and end of this sea alone are pleasing. For it begins with its first chain of islands at the south and ends in the straits of the Hellespont, about which it flows and makes a peninsula worth seeing. Therefore, as the expression goes, its beauty extends "from head to foot".[21] But it is impossible to describe the number and the beauty of its effluents and gulfs. (18) Although men are most afraid of the Aegean, all also most desire to cross it a second time. In fact, men cross it for the most pleasant reasons. Contests, mysteries, and the beauties of Greece fill it with travelers. And it is the Aegean sea which gathers together and provides what is everywhere exquisite and noble, serving up the fairest of the most pleasant spectacles to the most glorious gods. Let this be our song to you, O dear savior Aegean, sung in our form of music.[22] But do you, if you are pleased, ever preserve me myself and my sailing companions.

XLV. REGARDING SARAPIS[1]

(1) Fortunate, indeed, is the race of poets[2] and in every way it has been freed of difficulty. For not only are they privileged to employ on each occasion whatever sort of subject they wish, although it is untrue and sometimes unconvincing and without substance at all if one should wish to view it properly, but also they write it up with whatever thoughts and conceptions they choose; and if one should remove what precedes and follows some of these thoughts and conceptions, they are in themselves unintelligible. But when they have all been recited together, we understand them and we accept them, as if we were satisfied because we have understood them. In some cases the poets have declared the beginning of their thoughts and conceptions and omitted the rest, as if they condemned them. Although they had stripped some thoughts of their beginnings or removed the central portion from others, they believed it to be satisfactory, behaving, as it were, like tyrants toward them. (2) There is nothing which they do not dare or which presents difficulties for them. But they raise up their gods on machines,[3] and embark their gods on voyages to sail with whomever they wish them to.[4] And they depict them not only as sitting beside human beings, if ever the occasion arises, but even drinking with them[5] and holding lamps and giving them light.[6] (3) And thus indeed they are so grand, in Homer's own expression, "with easy lives",[7] whenever they compose hymns and paeans to the gods. In two strophies or periods they have completed everything. And when they have said "seagirt Delus",[8] or "Zeus who delights in thunder",[9] or "the loud roaring sea",[10] and then have told in passing how Heracles came to the Hyperboreans[11] and how Iamus was an ancient seer,[12] or how Heracles slew Antaeus,[13] or when they have added Minos, or Rhadamanthys, or the Phasis or the Danube, or have declared that they are "the creatures of the Muses" and "invincible in their wisdom",[14] they believe their hymn to be sufficient, and no ordinary person seeks any more from them. (4) So very sacred do we regard them and we honor them so much that we ourselves have conceded to them to write hymns and to address the gods, as if they were truly the prophets of the gods. Nay, we believe that there is no need to use for the gods that form of speech to which

belongs the correct way of outlining what is proper, the handling of it with complete circumspection, and the accomplishment of it with all precision, to the limits set as possible for man.[15] But we employ prose for all other contests, and we praise national festivals, and narrate heroic deeds and wars, and write tales, and contend in the courts, and prose comes to mind for all of our actions, one might say. Yet we do not at all think that we should use it for the gods themselves, who have given it to us. In drawing up our codes we have defined in prose how sacred rites and the performance of sacrifices should be conducted. Yet we do not believe that we ought to compose hymns in this manner. (5) Then do poets have need of the gods, while we—? But this is not fitting to express. Indeed, it is attested by the poets themselves that "all men need the gods".[16] Therefore it is also reasonable for all men to honor them with the means which each possesses. (6) But are poets alone dear to the gods and do the gods receive their gifts with the greatest pleasure? Why then have we not also made poets alone priests of the gods? (7) Is it, by Zeus, that all the prophets of the gods, who can predict the future, indicate metrically what must be done? Yet, by Zeus, most oracles are not given metrically by the prophetess herself in Delphi, by the priestesses in Dodona, by Trophonius, and by the dreams from Asclepius and Sarapis. (8) Indeed, it is more natural for man to use prose, just as, I think, it is more natural to walk than to be carried in a conveyance.[17] For the meters did not first come into existence, and next prose and dialogue were discovered.[18] Nor when poets came into being did they set out the words which men must use. But when the words and prose already existed, there was later introduced for the sake of grace and charm poetry, which produces these things. Therefore if we honor nature, we would honor the very ordinance and intention of the gods. And if the earlier and older is better even according to the poets themselves,[19] we would show more honor to the gods, who have arranged all these things, by addressing them in this mode of address, just as we are not ashamed to address ourselves without meter. (9) I have said this not in dishonor of the race of poets nor acting to deprive them of their rank, but as a proof from the actual concessions of the poets that we would also justly believe in, as it were, this kind of offering in addition to the existing modes. And if what is natural in whatever circumstance you name is more gratifying to the gods, we would in all likelihood gratify them more by honoring them in this way than in that, and the gods would honor us more if we would place the highest value on the same things that they do. Indeed, while the word measure[20] bestows an honorable name upon the poets, in actual usage it is much more our affair.[21] (10) For there it only measures the hexameter or the trimeter, as to whether they fill out the meter. But here is measures the whole speech, and truly passes all through it, and it begins right with the word.[22] For it allows neither excess nor falling short of true worth, but it demands a proper usage for each word. Next it prohibits the insertion of unnecessary material to fill out the measure, which would, in fact, be absurd. Next as far as concerns periods, it requires sufficiency, the hardest kind of all measures, I think. And after all, it considers what I said[23], whether the whole work is harmonious and whether it has fulfilled the goal which was set for it. (11) Just as the measures which we use in the market place, I think, are what they are called, yet we should strenuously deny that the attainment of true measure lies with the merchants because they possess quarts and pints—but these are particular measures, or rather, one might say, the names of a measure, but as to the whole measure, for which there is often need of these measures[24] and to which everything should be referred in respect to every matter and which is truly all worthy and pertains to virtue, we should say that this measure has another meaning and quality—, so even here the poets possess, I think, these individual measures, but the whole measure is not theirs. (12) And certainly we must not hesitate because of an honorable word,[25] as if poets alone knew the measure of words. For it is possible to attain measure without such measures and the contrary, just as it is possible for a doctor without weights and measures to calculate a necessary dosage and again for one who uses these to err through inexperience in a matter for which there is need of measures. (13) But I am not unaware, as I said,[26] that it is much easier to accomplish these things through the agency of song than in prose and that such contests have been left to poets alone. With good reason. For they have many advantages and have full authority to do whatever they wish. But we are not permitted to speak of "opening the jar of hymns"[27] or of "the Muses' chariot"[28] or of "the unguent-bearing merchant ship"[29] or of "cloud griffins",[30] or of any other such thing. We cannot be brazen and insert an argument outside the subject, but one must truly abide by the measure and be mindful of himself in everything, as it were keeping to his post in a campaign.[31] Still we must try to accomplish our address, especially in fulfillment of our vow since we were saved[32] and at the same time since a discussion and lecture on measure is not now appropriate. (14) Well then! Everyone calls upon you as a helper on every occasion,[33] Sarapis. Graciously grant me the power to recite my speech—nothing at all is impossible for you. And give me whatever beginning you prefer. And just as you have granted me my first request, so may you also heed my second one.[34] For through your agency and because of you everywhere everything comes to us which we would most wish to have.

(15) Let it be left to the Egyptian priests and writers to say and to know who, indeed, the god is and what is his nature. But our praise would be sufficient for the present if we should tell of the number and nature of the benefits he is shown to have given to mankind. And at the same time through these very acts it will also be possible to consider his nature. For if ever we declare his powers and gifts, we have more or less stated his identity and nature. For he is not different from what he appears to be and is shown to be by his deeds. (16) What are the deeds of Sarapis? This, too, seems to me to require an answer beyond the power of man. Homer said[35] that although he had ten tongues and ten mouths, he would not be able to recount the number of ships that followed the Achaeans, unless the Muses should tell him and direct his speech. But as for me, even if I possessed the mouths of all men and the sum of human vocal power, it would certainly be impossible for me to recount the deeds of the greatest of the gods and his gifts which are ever being given to mankind, unless some gods would truly direct my speech. And let the gods be invoked again, and let us tell of the deeds of the god, for he himself wishes it and grants us the power to tell of them. The deeds of Sarapis are those by which the life of mankind is saved and administered.[36] But, as they say,[37] "we must begin at the beginning". (17) The following three things are the subject of speculation in regard to every man and comprise all of life: the soul, the body, and all externals pertaining to the needs of these. This god is in charge of all these things. At the beginning he brings us to the light and to his kingdom. And when we have come into being, he is concerned that we shall have every means. He adorns our soul with wisdom, which alone reveals mankind's kinship with the gods and through which we differ from other mortal beings, which has given to men a conception of the gods themselves and has discovered

sacrifices, rites, and all means of honoring the gods, and further has taught and established the laws and government and all contrivances and all the arts, and has given the means of distinguishing between falsehood and truth, and, one might say, has created life.[38] (18) He preserves the soul, as I said,[39] by purifying it with wisdom, and the body by giving to it health, without which it is impossible either to make use of the goods of the soul or to enjoy any other good fortune.[40] He has such great power and honor among gods and men, that he does not even depart from the house of the gods,[41] at least not before the stars would depart from heaven and heaven itself would depart from its place. Whatever men he forsakes are more pitied in their lifetime than when they have died.[42] Alone he is honored equally by kings and by private citizens, equally by wise men and by foolish men, by great men and by lesser men, by successful men and by unsuccessful men, since he gives to the former the use of their existing felicity and for the latter by himself alone makes up for all their other troubles. Again Sarapis bestows the possession of money,[43] which after health is most sought by mankind,[44] and he gives this without wars, fighting, and danger. (19) Thus he passes through every aspect of our lives and no place has been left untouched by this god. He examines everything and is a benefactor in every way, beginning with the soul and ending in external wealth.[45] (20) And he has made life for us, as it were, a harmony and has bound it together through his gifts, by making us love wisdom through the agency of health and by causing health to be more pleasurable in conjunction with wealth, and by connecting and making firm the extremes by means of the middle term, as it were with a peg,[46] the goods of the soul and the profit of possessions by means of health. How then should he not be proclaimed at all the national festivals and every day, as the guardian and savior of all mankind, a self-sufficient god? (21) Indeed, since he comprises for mankind all the measures of life and is the steward of the life to be lived, for this reason he would rightly be believed to have embraced everything and, as it were, to steer the course of our whole life.[47] The citizens of the great city in Egypt[48] even invoke him as "the one, the Zeus",[49] because he has no deficiency through his abundant power, but he has passed through everything and has filled the Universe. (22) The powers and honors of the other gods are divided, and men invoke different ones for different reasons. But he, as it were the chorus leader[50] of all things, holds their beginnings and their ends.⁵¹ He alone is ready to help when one has need of anything. Therefore in regard to other gods men do not proceed in the same way, but different men honor different gods; yet in him alone all men believe as in their own gods. (23) Since he possesses the powers of all of them, some men worship him in place of all the gods, and others also believe in him as being a special universal god for the whole world, in addition to those gods in whom they believe in any given circumstance. Although one god, not only does he possess all the powers on the earth singly unlike other gods who are each assigned to different places, and otherwise than in the allotment of Homer⁵² he has not drawn a portion, as Homer said that Zeus, Poseidon, and Pluto divided up their lots, but this god is also great on the sea—both merchant ships and warships are steered under his protection—and in the air and in the clouds. (24) Homer said⁵³ that the earth and Olympus was left as common territory for the gods. But he clearly is exceptional, being the holder of the lot of the earth and again in other matters being the partner of each god in his particular sphere. Although one himself he is all things. Although one he has the same power as all the gods. He assists in all actions and provides all means on every occasion and in every place, possessing, as the poets would say, the keys of earth and sea.⁵⁴ Indeed, even after the necessary termination of life he still remains as ruler for mankind.⁵⁵ (25) And our fate is to go at his side⁵⁶ from him to him, as is the saying "from home to home".⁵⁷ It is he who assigns places for each man in accordance with the worth of their life on earth, and he is the judge of the after life, in the day time traversing the region above the earth, and at night rendering decisions,⁵⁸ which are unseen by the living, being both a savior and a guide of the dead, who brings us into the light and again receives us, who embraces all of us everywhere. (26) When mindful of Sarapis, if any of the gods, man is filled at the same time with joy and fear.⁵⁹ For he is both the most generous and the most terrifying of the gods, and he inspires a profitable fear in mankind, so that they neither wrong one another nor suffer wrong at one another's hands. Yet he is more readily turned to pity, and he especially confirms Homer's statement⁶⁰ about all the gods, that they can be turned and pleaded with. So many turns does he make to save whoever is in need. (27) And mankind exceptionally makes this god alone a full partner in their sacrifices, summoning him to the feast and making him both their chief guest and host,⁶¹ so that while different gods contribute to different banquets,[62] he is the universal contributor to all banquets and has the rank of mess president for those who assemble at times for his sake. Just as Homer said[63] that Athena both participated in the libation and brought each prayer to pass, so he is a participant in the libations and is the one who receives the libations, and he goes as a guest to the revel and issues the invitations to the revelers, who under his guidance perform a dance secure from the consequences of evil[64] and who bring home along with their crowns high spirits and respond with a return invitation.[65] (28) Partnership with him in other dealings is also the same, an association between equals. For example merchants and ship captains not only bring him tithes, but also let him share equally in the profits, as they would with a fellow merchant and partner in all the intervening work.[66] To such an extent is he involved in human affairs. (29) It is he who is truly the steward of the winds much more than the islander of whom Homer wrote. He has the power "to stop and to stir up whichever wind he wishes".[67] It is he who has caused potable water to rise in the middle of the sea.[68] It is he who has resurrected the dead. It is he who has revealed the much sought after light of the sun[69] to observers,[70] whose sacred chests contain an infinite number of sacred books. (30) The market places are full, as they say,[71] and the harbors, and the plazas of the cities with those who recount his individual acts. But if I shall try to tell them, an endless influx of days will find the catalogue equally incomplete. For his deeds have not stopped, nor is their number what it was in the past, but every day and every night new ones are added. And just as it is impossible to say in the daily progress of eternity what part has been expended of the total sum—the same amount of time always being left—, so in the case of the god's deeds it cannot be said whether those which we have received or those which lie in the future make up the larger number. They are so numerous. (31) If, indeed, someone should attempt to enumerate these, he will pursue an elusive quarry,[72] like those who chase behind river currents, and he will do the same as if he should think that he would live for all eternity. For he will need all of it. But on every occasion different people will shout out different acts, some what took place in their own person, some what they saw taking place in the persons of other people. And let it be proclaimed by us with the voice of all men, as in the declaration of a truce. There is no fear at all that we are lying. (32) Our initial premise,[73] that the deeds of Sarapis are those by which the human race is guided and that we never elude his power, but that his providence is shown in life as well as in death is proved in every way. He is in charge of the birth and nurture of all creatures, and many of the sacred animals, just like men, live according to his prescription.[74] It is he who brings the Nile in summer, it is he who recalls it in winter.[75] It is he who holds and adorns forty-two temples throughout Egypt[76] as well as all of the temples in world. He is guardian of what is manifest and what is secret, he is leader of men and gods. And now he turns our speech to himself, and it is time to conclude with an address to him.

(33) O you who possess the fairest of all the cities within your sight,[77] which celebrates a yearly festival for you,[78] O universal light for all mankind, you who were recently manifested to us when, at the time that the vast sea rose from all sides and rushed in upon us and nothing was visible except the destruction which was approaching and had well-nigh arrived, you stretched out your hand, revealed the hidden heavens, and granted us to behold the earth and to make port, so much beyond our expectation that we were unconvinced even when we set foot on shore. (34) For this I am very grateful to you, O much honored god. And now do you not abandon me, but make my recovery complete and graciously accept this hymn composed as it is in such circumstances, a thank offering for those former deeds and a prayer and also a supplication for the future, that it may be happier and better than the present.[79]

XLVI. THE ISTHMIAN ORATION: REGARDING POSEIDON[1]

(1) After I was kept from the national festival at Olympia,[2] since unfortunately I was physically unable to participate in the proceedings with you and I was in extreme danger from the illness which I had then contracted, and now that I have found favor[3] with Zeus the Savior and Poseidon the Securer, brother of Zeus, and have reached, as it were, a kind of harbor, I mean my present state of health, safety, and opportunity to stay with you, (2) and besides since some story has been circulated to this effect, that certain people desired my presence, and at that the most distinguished people, not so much on my account, I think, nor on account of my speeches,[4] but in a display of their nobility, of their zeal in such matters, and of the honor and goodwill which they feel toward all their seniors whose lives are spent in this discipline and by whom often before they recall they have been delighted and charmed in the festivals shared by all the Greeks: in view of all these reasons I decided that I must not hesitate to appear before you, but at the same time on the same occasion I must make a double payment to the two brothers, both the older, more ancient, and in a fashion the usual kind of payment[5] and that which now is about to take place.[6] (3) For I decided that possibly it is not even pious, when I am mindful of the divine everywhere and when most of my lectures, more or less, are concerned with this, for me to seem to have overlooked an oratorical contribution to this god alone and for no speech of mine to be named either after the god or this place where we now are, but for so important a matter to have been neglected. For this reason I decided that perhaps it would be well to propitiate and placate the god on my behalf, to pardon the past if I have made any omissions in this respect, and graciously and in a kindly spirit to accept this present offering, and to grant me other goods and the ability to make this a proper speech, and if it turns out otherwise than proper, to consider my capability and not the magnitude of the subject, since it is beyond the limits of language and even the attempt to discuss this matter is the same as if one should wish "to count the pitchers of water in the ocean".[7] (4) However, since this god is accustomed to make even the greatest and boundless seas

traversable, and sometimes even with fair winds for those toward whom he happens to be well disposed, let our speech about him now be put to sea and let it be made fast to the god himself, like a stern cable,[8] as one might say.

(5) All that has been said by those who first undertook these philosophic discussions[9] when they felt that they should refer their arguments about this god back to the nature of the Universe, as if all the moist element in the Universe were either the greatest part of the whole or even this whole itself, I mean the so-called moist essence—just as is also attested by the arguments of the poets, that this element is the source of the gods, and when it is somewhere said,[10] "Ocean, source of the gods", they are calling it under another name the nourishment and means of life for all things that are divine and of a lower order, (6) and just as it is attested that for this reason this element again under another name, that of the water Styx, is the greatest oath of the gods[11]—, and the earliest men believed the springs, rivers, and even streams to be the first and greatest gods—, and finally just as it is attested that everything which shares in generation comes from here and at its destruction returns again to there and that this is the meaning of Homer's curse when he cursed everything to return to water, to quote the verse,[12] "But may you all become water and earth"—and all the other things of this sort that have been said and discovered by wise men and wise poets, let us either entirely omit them, or discuss them only so far, at least for the present. (7) But now it would in a way be fitting to mention what is universally recognized and well-known to all men and before the eyes of all. Not even this story is unattested, but it too has the poets as witnesses to its tale. (8) For it is agreed that Cronus had three sons from Rhea, their mother, Poseidon, Zeus, and the third whose name we hear after these.[13] And they divided up the lot of their father, apportioning the Universe with the most just division, on the following terms: that Zeus receive the heavens and the ether and what was in this, and that this be the source of his power; that Poseidon receive the sea; and that the third brother receive the region beneath the earth. (9) Now let us consider among ourselves which of them ruled with greater generosity and more for the common welfare, he who shared none of his domain with anyone, or he who shared it, but not until death, or he who admits all men while they are alive, and grants them to live with him, associate with him, and to be members of his com-

munity, and to cultivate the finest of lots, the sea, and all of the goods of the sea, which have been found in it and through it, and who gives himself in every way to the human race. (10) Indeed, as long as he remained only on the earth, how did man differ from the trees growing in the soil? Before this god unlocked the sea and next opened it wide, what beauty did man have? Or what was there to see or hear? Man did not even know of the earth itself where he remained, except for what lay before him,[14] not to mention its limits, or the other continent, or the land directly opposite him. But those former men, who are called blessed, lived like wild beasts in holes, crevices, and trees. What was more wretched than they who neither knew nor saw anything, nor possessed anything except enough for each day just like mindless animals? (11) But when this god told them to visit him with confidence and to ply the sea, and showed them the way how, and removed the fear from their soul, which they felt for the sea, as it were for a terrible and frightening beast in the constant expectation that both they and the whole earth would be carried off by the winds, then it is not easy to express in words the multitude of goods which came to the earth from the sea: both these elements were united—Poseidon's greatest accomplishment —and they joined in friendship and commerce. Yet formerly this was not so, but the earth and sea were enemies of one another. (12) Now they were settled together by this god, and here he built cities for mankind which we now call islands, so that even in the sea there was no desire for land, nor was there any difference from being on land. And he brought forth everything which exists,[15] on the one hand animals of all sorts, and on the other plants, some for the use of mankind and others even for their delight and pleasure. Indeed, he also set a much more bountiful table than the land and he discovered countless means for relaxation. (13) And, to put it simply, he endowed man with wings, and man almost used, as it were, feathers[16] in crossing the sea. And he arranged for man to be carried with the winds and did not even begrudge him this, far from begrudging him anything else, and it is not said of him, unlike his eldest brother,[17] that he admitted Perseus alone into his kingdom, and at that at a small distance from the earth and sea, and later Bellerophon, who came from here,[18] with no fair result.[19] But this god admits everyone who so desires, man, woman, and even children. (14) And some he even caused to appear from the sea, like Apollo and Artemis. And with good reason Zeus would be grateful to him for this, because he did not stand idly by either while Leto was forever driven about because of the favors which she received, or while Zeus' offspring were almost left uncared for. This god also brought forth the beauteous Aphrodite from himself, from the sea, as it were, from his head, in imitation of Zeus,[20] since Zeus is first not only in respect to human things, but also in respect to things divine, as attests the tale told on Trojan Ida.[21] (15) Since we have mentioned Leto, it has occurred to me how many other love affairs he has helped his brother prosecute. For there is that of Io, the daughter of Inachus, and of the beautiful Europa, and perhaps elsewhere various others, whose names are still now spoken of by mankind. But as to the handsome boy with his beautiful mother, he adopted the former, and he made both the boy and his mother partners in his empire. (16) But this tale awaits us when its proper time comes.[22] Now, before one another, we have discussed the nature and greatness of Poseidon's deeds, and the high value to be placed upon his empire. Next perhaps it would be best to discuss the nature and the high value of the honors which he has received among mankind. For all the most noted and famous parts of the earth have been consecrated to Poseidon. (17) At the entrance of the Black sea, where the narrowest part of the sea spreads itself into a great sea, here is named the Dark Rock[23] and the Gates of the Sea, which formerly different men at different times thought could be closed.[24] And where the sea descends from there to us,[25] there is the headland Leucates,[26] which is named like that at Actium,[27] although it is not a mere rock as this is, but a great land mass jutting forth into the sea and forming a long promontory to the sea in a semi-circular form, very much like a sickle so that this name is also given to the promontory[28] and a certain tale or story is told about it, how here the deed done to Cronus was accomplished by his sons.[29] (18) But when you have passed the Propontis and the Hellespont and have sailed through the islands called the Cyclades, in the sea next to the Aegean[30] there is Euboea and its headlands and the harbor at Geraestus and a temple of the god which Homer also mentions in the return of the Achaeans and the sailing from Ilium.[31] At the entrance to the Ionian sea, the headland at Taenarus[32] and the embarkation point from there belong to the god. (19) Homer has also described him going off to Aegae and Helice to feast[33] and both him and his horses running on the top of the waves, not even touching the sea,[34] like his brother going to the milk-eaters[35]—and he suggested a double means of conveyance for mankind,[36] a chariot on land, but a ship on sea—and here are found his temples, and precincts, and his "incense filled altar", as Homer himself said.[37]

(20) For all told, if I must not involve my speech with inessentials, every shore, every harbor, every part of the earth and sea is a shrine, an offering, an image, a precinct, and a temple of Poseidon. However nothing is so dear, beloved, and honored by him as this isthmus and this region here. And I call this Poseidon's chancellery,[38] palace, court—just as Homer spoke of "the court of Zeus"[39]—, and the headquarters of his kingdom. (21) I base my judgment, among other reasons, on the fact that he centered the whole sea on every side around this point after he had set gates on either side of it and had spread the land which is called the isthmus equally to the east and west of it, and at the same time had closed it off so that the seas might not join, not with a great expanse of land, but, as it were, with a narrow pipe, and had legislated and had ordained for the seas, that each[40] preserve its own boundaries, (22) and again had spread them all open and had given to each a somewhat wide expanse in the distance, so that—and this is the strangest and at the same time most pleasant of all the spectacles on the earth—people on each side sail in and sail out at the same instant with favorable breezes and men put out to sea and into port with the same winds in this land and sea alone of all, and everything from everywhere comes here both by land and sea, and this is the reason why the land even from earliest times was praised as "rich" by the poets,[41] both because of the multitude of the advantages which are at hand and the felicity which is embodied in it. (23) For it is, as it were, a kind of market place, and at that common to all the Greeks, and a national festival, not like this present one which the Greek race celebrates here every two years,[42] but one which is celebrated every year and daily. If just as men enjoy the official status of being public friends with foreign cities, so too did cities enter into this relationship with one another, the city would have this title[43] and honor everywhere. (24) For it receives all cities and sends them off again and is a common refuge for all, like a kind of route and passage for all mankind, no matter where one would travel, and it is a common city for all the Greeks,[44] indeed, as it were, a kind of metropolis and mother in this respect. For among other reasons, there is no place where one would rest as on a

mother's lap with more pleasure or enjoyment. Such is the relaxation, refuge, and safety for all who come to it. (25) But so great is the abundance of beauty, desire, and love, which clings to it, that it chains all men with pleasure and all men are equally inflamed by it, while it possesses in itself 'love, desire, friendly converse, and allurement so as to steal away the mind[45]' even of those who are proud of themselves, and it has whatever else there is in addition to these, everything that is called the charms of the goddess, so that it is clearly the city of Aphrodite. And it even occurs to me to name it "the cestus",[46] whatever this object is through which the goddess chains all men to herself, and to say that it is, as it were, the pendant and necklace of all of Greece,[47] and a precinct of the Nymphs, since all the Naiads dwell here, and a chamber of the Seasons[48] where they forever sit and from which they come forth when they have opened the gates—whether you wish to call them the gates of Zeus or Poseidon.[49] But if the cities ever happened to contend about their beauty, as the goddesses are said once to have done among themselves, this city would have Aphrodite's role.[50] And what would one say about the appearance of the city? Not even the eyes of all men are sufficient to take it in. (26) What more evidence would one offer of its greatness than that it has been extended to all the seas and has been settled beside and along them, not just the one but not the other, but all of them equally. (27) Indeed, the city was of old a starting point for good order,[51] and even now[52] administers justice for the Greeks. Indeed, you would see it everywhere full of wealth and an abundance of goods, as much as is likely, since the earth on every side and the sea on every side flood it with these, as if it dwelled in the midst of its goods and was washed all around by them, like a merchant ship. (28) While traveling about the city, you would find wisdom and you would learn and hear it from its inanimate objects. So numerous are the treasures of paintings all about it, wherever one would simply look, throughout the streets themselves and the porticoes. And further the gymnasiums and schools are instruction and stories.[53] (29) Why should I mention Sisyphus, or "Corinthus the son of Zeus",[54] or Bellerophon the son of Poseidon, or any other of the heroes and demigods? Or again those who afterwards invented weights, scales, measures,[55] and the justice inherent in these, and the story of how this city built the first ship, not only the trireme,[56] but even the Argo itself, I would say? Indeed, the leader of its expedition clearly

XLVI. THE ISTHMIAN ORATION: REGARDING POSEIDON 275

put in and anchored the Argo here because he put out from here.[57] Or again the deeds on land, the so-called wings of Pegasus, whether you will speak of him as a horse or as a bird, and he who first dared to ride him, the flying knight?[58] (30) But these are old and fabulous stories. Indeed, as to all its deeds in peace and war, which are still even now remembered, are they not more glorious than those of any Greek city, are they not more notable than any other's on land and sea? Whose deeds and actions are more distinguished? (31) But the present is not a time of war, so that it is not appropriate to raise the memory of such things when the Greeks are celebrating a national festival and act in concord in this the best and most famous national festival—which assembles every two years and meets twice as often as the others[59] and draws up, surpasses, and again overtakes the rest, just as in a chariot race, if it were somehow possible for those who are mere human beings to witness the course of Poseidon's chariot[60]—and when men assemble at the common wine bowl, and at the same time make libations and sacrifices and launch the festival pilgrimages for Poseidon, Amphitrite, Palaemon, and Leucothea. Now it would be well for us to hymn these things and to discuss them and speak about them.

(32) In a way these are our remarks and hymn to Poseidon himself, and they are not bad, as it seems to me—and I see that such too is your feeling—and yes, by Zeus, this holds true for our hymn to the city as well, given in the briefest possible compass, one would say.[61] But I see that it remains for us to speak about the two gods, the child and his mother, whether this part of the speech should be called a tale or a myth.[62] (33) I fear this part, and I am very frightened and uncertain how I should handle it in your presence: whether we should be persuaded of the sufferings of the gods, as most men, including Homer, are, for example the chaining of Ares, and the hired service of Apollo, and the casting of Hephaestus into the sea,[63] and so also the sufferings and flight of Ino, or that we should say that this is neither a holy nor a pious story, especially when one is speaking about the gods, but that we must banish this tale not only from the Isthmus and the Peloponnesus, but also from all of Greece. And if it should be necessary, we must even go to both seas and purify ourselves of the story of Athamas, whoever he was, and his madness, whether real or falsely told by those most villainous men who composed for us each of these particulars. (34) But Ino neither existed nor did she ever

become what most men say she became.[64] Or if she existed and did become thus, still she had nothing to do with what takes place here. But Leucothea was a goddess right from the start and did not begin to be one at the point where most men think. But if she had "a voice", as he said who wrote this,[65] still she was not "mortal". But Homer has also depicted the gods as if they were men, speaking directly to and talking to men, Athena, Hermes, and Poseidon himself. (35) Perhaps it would be well for us and pleasing to the gods to speak of and hear in this assembly the following version. Poseidon loved Leucothea and in his love kept her by his side—just as he loved Tyro, the daughter of Salmoneus, and Amymone,[66] and all the other pretty girls—and he hid her, in truth, beneath the waves. But her journey here from there,[67] if we should in fact accept this, was not the act of a person in flight, but of one who was going to the sea as if it were to her wedding chamber. Nor did she snatch up and carry off the child, who in fact was born to her from another's couch,[68] but he was made a ward of Poseidon and was a source of joy for him and a gift to him. (36) The truth itself, and the tales still now told, and the mysteries performed concerning them, as would be done for gods,[69] make clear that such is the case. For there is no evil among the gods, nor could it ever arise[70]—for it has been banished to the terrestrial region—, nor are there sufferings and misfortunes among them. Such would hardly be the beginning of immortality for anyone. For evil comes from evil. But the acts of the gods are good. It is in no way fitting that they be otherwise. (37) But if a human being was not fortunate, how would he become a god—tell me that? But if he was dear to the gods, he would never have been unfortunate. And if she had not been such from the beginning, she would not have been such afterwards—for if the gods are able to free man from evil, and even forbidding the approach of evil is in their power, and indeed if they can give good in place of evil, and most important of all if they can grant the lot of immortality and that one would immediately be born with this, then Leucothea was a goddess right from the beginning and misfortune did not bring her to this state, but the fact that she was such right from her birth also prevented her from being at all involved in any misfortune—nor then would she have been a goddess with the gods nor would she have possessed as much power as we hear she did.[71] (38) Now since we must trust Homer's story, there is likely to be embodied in her person a kind of supreme rule over the kingdom of the sea and for Poseidon himself to have no power, except with her consent. For let this be said since he could not even take vengeance on the murderer of his son,[72] although he held the murderer in his very hands, as one would say, but he made vain noises, and his stirring up everything and all that he did when he snatched his trident were nothing against the shield of this goddess, whether it should be called poetically "a veil",[73] or by some other term. But there was preservation and safety in the midst of danger, and it is clear that these events did not occur forcibly or unwelcomely, but that Poseidon yields to her in everything and permits her to do whatever she wishes. (39) Happily has my speech reached this point, especially because rather happily for us from it Leucothea has clearly appeared to be a sort of lover of wisdom, not only full of compassion and an admirer of the Greeks. For she saved Odysseus who was the wisest and best of the Greeks, and it is clear that she saves each and all who have a passion for wisdom and wish to be "good speakers, sharp witted, and wise",[74] as is also said of Odysseus. (40) Let so much be said about her, and this is pleasing, I think, even to Poseidon himself. But it is good also to mention Palaemon and to speak his name and take his oath,[75] and to participate in his rites and celebrations[76]—such attraction does the boy possess—and to see in the paintings[77] the bloom, the beauty, and the flower of the boy, as he is borne upon a dolphin,[78] or even upon the very waves of the sea, or even in his mother's arms. For these sights are the sweetest of sights to see and hear. And it is also good to behold here the presence of the Sea[79] and of the Calm and the boy smiling upon Poseidon who receives him in his robe. (41) But it is not good to add any other scenes to these, such as those terrifying and impious paintings in some places,[80] which cause me to wonder how the first spectators tolerated them and did not angrily attack the artists and craftsmen, and how they still even now tolerate them in the midst of their temples. But perhaps it is not my task to criticize such things.

(42) It remains for each of us to go to our respective duties[81] after a prayer to Poseidon, Amphitrite, Leucothea, Palaemon, the Nereids, and all the gods and goddesses of the sea, to grant safety and preservation on land and sea to the great Emperor,[82] to his whole family, and to the Greek race, and to us to thrive in oratory and in other respects as well.

XLVII. THE SACRED TALES: I[1]

Winter 170/171 A.D.

(1) It seems to me that I shall speak like Homer's Helen. For she says that she would not tell all "the toils of stout-hearted Odysseus".[2] But she takes, I think, some one deed of his and narrates it to Telemachus and Menelaus. And I myself would not tell all the achievements[3] of the Savior,[4] which I have enjoyed to this very day. Nor at this point shall I add that Homeric phrase, "not if I had ten tongues, ten mouths".[5] For this were too little. Not even if I should surpass all human strength, speech, and wisdom, could I ever do justice to them. (2) I have never been persuaded by any of my friends, whoever have asked or encouraged me to speak or write about these things, and so I have avoided the impossible. For it seemed to me to be the same as if after swimming through the whole sea under water,[6] I should be compelled to produce records of the total number of the waves which I encountered, and how I found the sea at each of them, and what it was that saved me. (3) For each of our days, as well as our nights, has a story, if someone, who was present at them,[7] wished either to record the events or to narrate the providence of the god, wherein he revealed somethings openly in his own presence[8] and others by the sending of dreams,[9] as far as it was possible to obtain sleep. But this was rare, due to the tempests of my body.[10] (4) In view of this, I decided to submit to the god, truly as to a doctor,[11] and to do in silence whatever he wishes.

January 4 to February 15, 166 A.D.

But now I wish to indicate to you the condition of my abdomen. I shall reckon each matter day by day.[12] (5) It was the month of Poseideon,[13] and what a winter it was! During those nights my stomach was upset and I had extraordinary insomnia, so that I could not digest the smallest morsel. Not the least cause was the continuous succession of stormy weather, which it was said even the tiling did not sustain. Indeed, I perspired all this time,[14] except when I bathed.

January 4, 5&6

(6) On the twelfth of the month, *the god instructed me not to bathe*, and the same on the next day, and on the day after that. I passed these three days in a row, both night and day, wholly without perspiring, so that I did not even need to wear an undershirt,[15] and never before did I feel more comfortable. I passed the time in walk-

ing about the house and in games, as these were holidays. For the Vigil of the god[16] followed upon the preceding holiday in honor of Poseidon.

(7) After this, there was a dream which contained a notion[17] of bathing, although this was far from certain. *I dreamed that I had been in some way befouled.* Nevertheless I decided that I would bathe; that if I had actually experienced this befouling, there was need of water. And immediately thereafter I was not especially comfortable in the bath and when I came out, I seemed to feel full and my breath was like that of a man gasping for air, so that I stopped as soon as I began to eat. After this at night, stomach trouble, which reached such a pitch, that it scarcely ceased a little before noon. (8) But there was a dream vision somewhat as follows: *I was in the warm bath. Bending forward I saw that the lower part of my stomach was in a rather strange state. I determined to persist in not bathing. But someone said that the trouble which had appeared was not in the bathing itself and that it was not reasonable to guard against bathing as the cause.*

January 7 Night&Day

I bathed at evening and at dawn I had pains in my abdomen, and the pain spread over the right side and down to the groin.

January 8

(9) On the seventeenth no bathing after a dream, and on the eighteenth no bathing. On the nineteenth, *I dreamed that some Parthians had got me in their power, and one of them approached me and made as if to brand me. Next he inserted a finger right in my throat and poured in something, according to some native custom, and named it 'heartburn.' Later I recounted these things as they had appeared in the dream.*[18] And the audience marveled and said that the cause of my being thirsty, yet unable to drink, was this, that my food turned sour. Then vomiting was indicated and the Parthian ordered that today I abstain from bathing and produce one servant as a witness of this. No bathing, and vomiting, and comfort.

January 9, 10&11

(10) On the twentieth, *I dreamed that I was at the propylaea of the Temple of Asclepius,*[19] *and a certain one of my friends met me, embraced me, and greeted me warmly, since he had not seen me for a long time. I said to him that I had been nauseated; and as the conversation continued, I recalled how many things had been disturbed around the Temple. And we went in while we were speaking.* (11) *When we were by the statues of Good Fortune and the Good God,*[20] *we stopped but were still conversing. And seeing one of the temple servants, I asked him where the priest was. He replied, "Behind the Temple".* For it was about the time of the Sacred Lamps,[21] and the temple warden[22] was bringing the keys. And at this time the Temple happened to have been closed. Still in such a way, so that although closed, a kind of entrance re-

January 12

mained and the interior was visible. I went up to the doors and saw, instead of the old statue, another with downcast eyes. As I marveled and inquired where the old statue was, someone brought it to me, and I seemed not wholly to recognize it, but still I worshipped it eagerly. (12) *Afterwards, while walking about, we met the priest and I began the following conversation with him: "I also had dreams in Smyrna that I had spoken with you about the Temple, and believing the matter too great for me, I kept silent. And now recently I have had dreams concerning these very matters". And at the same time, I intended to speak about putting the statue in its old place. While I was walking about, a slipper fell off one of my feet, and the priest picked it up and brought it to me. And I was pleased by the honor. Wishing, as it were, to requite and honor him, I received it with a bow.* (13) *At this time, a bull menaced me right by the god's Ears.*[23] *I was afraid and tried somehow to protect myself. Yet he did nothing else but contuse my right knee. Theodotus*[24] *took a lancet and cleansed it. Therefore I intended to say to him, "that you yourself made it a wound".* (14) This was what appeared and here my fear ceased. And there was a small sore, like a carbuncle,[25] beneath my right knee, and it seemed to be good for the upper part of the digestive tract.

January 13

(15) On the twenty-first, *I dreamed that I had the clothes of a priest and that I saw the priest himself present. I also dreamed that when I saw one of my friends limping from the region of his seat, I said to him that rest would cure this.* Vomiting was also ordered through many tokens, and this was the fifth day in a row without bathing. (16) It is worthwhile also to tell of collateral dreams.[26] *I dreamed that as in my accustomed declamations, I was practicing some Demosthenes*[27] *and spoke to the Athenians as if I were he: "You ask through the herald, 'Who wishes to speak?' But I would rather ask you, Who wishes to act?"*[28] *Or is the rest but a comedy?" I spoke in reference to* The Telemessians *of Aristophanes, since there someone contended with words but not in deed.*[29]

January 14

(17) On the twenty-second, *I dreamed that, as it were, in Smyrna, I went at evening to the Temple of Asclepius, which is in the district of the Gymnasium.*[30] *I went with Zeno.*[31] *And the Temple was larger and covered as much of the portico as was paved. At the same time, I was also thinking about this temple as if it were a vestibule. While I prayed and called upon the god, Zeno said, "Nothing is more gentle". Also, speaking of the god, he named him a refuge and such things. I examined, as it were, in this vestibule, a statue of me. At one time I saw it as if it were of me, and again it seemed to be a great and fair statue of Asclepius. Then I recounted to Zeno himself these things which appeared to me in my dream. And the part about the statue seemed to be very honorable. Again I saw the statue as if it were in the long portico of the Gymnasium.*

(18) Concerning a bathing establishment, I dreamed the following: *First, as if in the middle of rubbing myself down, I entered a private bath. Then I said, as if I had entered unawares, "During days of not bathing!" Next it seemed to me that Phoebus[32] was present and encouraged me, so that I entered the water without hesitation.*

(19) Again I dreamed that by the statue of Asclepius himself a certain young athlete, still beardless, was talking about bathing establishments, praising the great ones and assuming that such were the pleasures of life.[33] *I showed him the sea and asked him if it were also better to bathe there or in a small space. "In a small space", he said. After this, I showed him a certain lake and asked him if it were also better in so great a lake or a small space. Here also he agreed that bathing in a small space was preferable. "Then", I said, "the greater is not everywhere preferable, but even a small thing has a certain charm". And at the same time, I thought to myself that if I were declaiming somewhere it also would be well to say that the pleasures of other men are in danger of being the pleasures of pigs, but that mine would be purely that of a man, as I study and delight in oratory. (20) The youth seemed to say these things about the bath by the Ephesian Gates. Finally it seemed to me fitting to try. When else to be bold, if not now? Thus I decided upon the noon hour as then it is safest move about.*[34] *(21) When the hour came, I accused Bassus*[35] *of procrastinating. "You see", I said, "how the shadow is passing by?", indicating the shadow of the columns. We went, and when we arrived, standing at the pool of cold water without,*[36] *I tried the water. Unexpectedly it seemed to me not to be very cold, but bluish and pleasant in appearance. And I said, "Fine!", since I recognized the beneficial quality of the water. When I went in, again I found other water in the warmer bathhouse which was milder. And I entered the warm bath and at the same moment I was undressing. I also bathed with much pleasure.*

On the twenty-third, vomiting in the evening, and this according to a dream. — January 15

(22) On the twenty-fourth, *I dreamed that I was at the warm springs.*[37] *Some men with daggers and otherwise behaving suspiciously happened to be nearby. Finally some of them approached me, as if desiring some legal defense, for they said that they were accused by certain men. When I had been surrounded, I was greatly disturbed, neither trusting them nor wishing to show that I was distrustful. Then I went along some path, and next there was a very long vault, where I was terribly afraid that they might attack me. But when to my relief I got through, I appeared to be in the city of Smyrna, in the market place, and I considered how the people might be assembled as quickly as possible*[38] *and I might show them what really happened. And afterwards, I* — January 16

myself took a torch, and all those in the market place bore torches, and they recited this verse of Euripides:[39] "O Sun, on swift horses, turning thy flame". For I dreamed that I arrived at the rising of the sun. I also dreamed that later I recounted these things, as they appeared in the dream, to the Governor Quadratus,[40] and that he said, "Do so". And the torch was raised. No bathing.

January 17

(23) On the twenty-fifth, *I dreamed that with my teacher Alexander,*[41] *I approached the Emperor, who sat upon a dais. When Alexander, since he was a long time friend and acquaintance, first saluted him and was saluted by him and his retinue, I approached. When I too saluted him and stood there, the Emperor wondered why I too did not come forward and kiss him. And I said that I was a worshipper of Asclepius.*[42] *For I was content to say so much about myself. "In addition to other things", I said, "the god has also instructed me not to kiss in this fashion". And he replied, "I am content ". I was silent. And he said, "Asclepius is better than all to worship".*

January 18

(24) On the twenty-sixth, *there appeared the Temple of Apollo, which is on Mount Milyas.*[43] *Certain buildings seemed to have been added and the name of the place to be Elephantine from Elephantine in Egypt.*[44] *I was pleased, both because of the buildings themselves and because of the similarity of the one place to the other.* (25) *And the priest of the god was the priest of Isis in Smyrna,*[45] *and I was staying with him. And I thought to myself that we had long been fast friends. And I happened before to have bought something from him. Then having something left over, I wished to make a trade.* (26) *After this, I dreamed that someone said, "Kuphi*[46] *with wine". I immediately took it as a medicine and considered whether it was necessary to apply it on my face or internally. And when someone said that it would burn wherever it was applied, I thought that it would be above all suitable to be a drug for a cold. And somehow after this, I said to the priest that it was clear from what I had read that there would be no need to eat. Thereupon I intended to pass the day in fasting.* I fasted.

January 19
January 20

On the following day, there was no bathing again.

(27) On the twenty-eighth, *I dreamed that after my food had not digested properly, I consulted Zosimus*[47]*, my foster father, about bathing and asked if it were necessary to bathe more. But he did not agree. After this, I bathed and then had stomach trouble, and I said to Zosimus, "Was it necessary to have fasted"? And he said, "It was necessary".* Again I fasted.

January 21

(28) And on the following day, I vomited again at evening. *There was a dream that a bone was troubling me and there was need to expel it. There was also a notion of drawing blood from the ankles.*[48] And I did so, and there was a very slight discharge.

(29) On the first of Lenaeon,[49] *I dreamed that I was anointed in the Hadrianeion,*[50] *but did not bathe. When I came out, I said to one of my friends that I did not bathe, but that I anointed myself. But he said, "I too have only anointed myself".* There had been no bathing for six days. — January 24

(30) On the second, *I dreamed that I was in the Temple of Asclepius at dawn, having come straight from some journey, and was glad because it had been opened early. I dreamed also that the boys sang the old song, which begins:*[51]
    "I celebrate Zeus, the highest of all",
and were in the following part of the song:
    "By far, by far the essence of life for me
    Is to sing of the gods and in joy
    To soothe my heart under such a teacher".
Therefore I marveled that the song appeared spontaneously. (31) *Again as if my birthday were approaching,*[52] *I sent servants to the Temple conveying certain offerings, and I also wrote down inscriptions on that which they conveyed. And I used artifice for the sake of a good omen, so that I might succeed in all that is needed in speaking.* — January 25

(32) On the third, *the lamps*[53] *appeared to be brought into the Temple by the porter in accordance with a vow on my behalf, and it was necessary to vomit.* I vomited. — January 26

(33) On the fifth, *I dreamed that I prayed to the gods, some things in common to those to whom I am wont to pray, and again privately to Zeus and Ares and the gods who hold Syria.*[54] *And the habitations there appeared nearly the same as those at home. And after this, there was a procession to the Emperor. I took part in the procession to the Emperor, who was then in Syria. And it turned out well.* — January 28

(34) On the seventh, *I dreamed that I saw, in some dressing room of a bath, the orator Charidemus,*[55] *from Phoenicia, shining and just bathed, and I said to him, with my greeting, that he bathed too early, and at the same time I also undressed myself.* I bathed. — January 30

(35) And again on the tenth of the month, *Antoninus, the son of Pythodorus,*[56] *seemed to me to discourse on the praises of the Nymphs. I too said that there were no more charming goddesses, and that a proper person could assuredly enjoy them, even if he did not bathe much, but moderately. I dreamed that I said these things and also some praise of Hygieia.*[57] — February 2

(36) On the twelfth, *I dreamed that Antoninus, the elder Emperor,*[58] *and the king of our enemies made a treaty of peace and friendship with one another. Vologases' retinue talked not a little as they advanced, and they seemed to speak Greek. Next they both came to me in their royal trappings. And An-* — February 4

toninus was well in his prime, and the other somewhat imposing to look upon. He sat not far from me, and on the other side, upon a throne, Antoninus. (37) The Mede seemed to me to have some experience in medical affairs. Greeting me, he said, "When are you going to give a reading to us"? And I was pleased by his remark and said, "Whenever you two bid me". And they prepared to listen, but I went off to select some of my writings. (38) And I decided to compose a brief prologue for them, and it went somehow so—in my dream I recalled the whole composition, but this alone I have preserved: "Somebody who wished to indicate his pleasure, when some good thing happened to him, said, 'that he was more than doubled with joy;' and somebody else, 'that he seemed to be in the Isles of the Blest.[59]' Such are also my feelings through the good fortune of the present day". And at the same time, I considered whether it was fitting to share the speech between them, or to give the greater portion to our Emperor, and next deal with that for the other party. I spoke somewhat as follows: "Therefore", I said, "if I had not been trained in divine visions, I think that I would not easily endure this spectacle. So wonderful does it seem to me and greater than man's estate". I said "divine visions", meaning especially Asclepius and Sarapis. So much for that. (39) Meanwhile I judged it proper to select one of my writings. Next I decided to bring in the casket and permit them to take whatever they wished. For this otherwise had a certain charm, and at the same time it particularly astounded them. I also dreamed that I recounted later word for word to Pelops[60] how these dreams appeared.

(40) Later I thought that there was brought to me, when I had bathed, first, as it were, cold water, then, as it were, milk. I was in doubt and said to Zosimus that I was neither thirsty nor hungry. "Why then should one eat?" And after this fasting was sanctioned, for the priest seemed to drain my lips.[61] This was a day of fasting.

February 5&6
The following of not bathing; the day after that of not bathing and vomiting.

February 7
(41) On the fifteenth, *I dreamed that the Governor[62] sent me a letter and addressed me so: "Greetings to Aristides the Priest"*. And this too was a day of not bathing.

February 8
On the following day, *it was necessary to overturn some casks*. Next no bathing.

February 10
(42) On the eighteenth, *Metrodorus,[63] the poet, seemed to me to be in a contest of poets in Smyrna, which was taking place almost on that very day. Before he entered, he spoke to me about certain things and at the same time ate leek leaves and an egg with bread, and left a portion of the egg. I, however, said to him, "Contend only after you have paused a little"*.[64] There was also

a discussion about the Temple in Pergamum and the Well, how it is to approach it oneself and to drink from it, how to see another person drink from it, how to see it itself.[65] I dreamed that I discussed these things in this way and that I happened to have heard that if I should be in the god's hands, there would be hope. (43) And somehow at the same time I stood, as it were, at home, on the porch. Since my foot was numb, I went into the main house. And one of those from the Temple of Olympian Zeus[66] came in. I recounted to him how I had dreams from the god, and ordered him to serve me. But he too said that he had had a dream, that he took a ham hock and when he had prepared it in the way which I am accustomed to employ, he put it to sleep in the *Temple of Asclepius.*[67] (44) After this, I dreamed, as it were in Pergamum, that I sent a large sized crown to the god, the sort which men particularly bring to Asclepius. And I ordered the man who took it—his name was Agathion[68]—to bring back another to me from the temple warden.[69] But when he brought it, I set it by my side while I happened to be lying to the right. (45) After this, I thought that I was somewhere or other. But getting up, I sought my nurse.[70] She was living opposite me. And someone answered that certain obstacles had arisen for her, before in fact I saw my nurse herself approaching and my foster sister, Callityche,[71] following behind. My nurse bore, I first conjectured, as it were, apples. Next they were three boiled and peeled eggs, as if I were going to eat. When she brought them, she said, "Such are the things from the country". And I marveled and said that the eggs came by the will of god. "For the god bade", I said, "that today I use an egg, and greens, and set by my side a crown from the god". I did these things. The crown was from the Temple of Zeus Asclepius.[72] No bathing was also indicated through many tokens.

(46) On the nineteenth, *I dreamed that I was staying in the Palace, and that the care and honor, which the Emperors*[73] *showed to me in all their activities, was marvelous and unsurpassable. For I alone was granted everything, and no one else had even a small part of these honors. And in this way I passed my time within and shared their lodgings, and no other of those fearsome fellows*[74] *was present. Later they took me along on a tour. They went off to inspect some drainage ditch, which they happened to be putting about the city, to prevent the inundation of the river from causing harm.*[75] I also saw the excavation of this ditch taking place. (47) They behaved marvelously to me during the trip. For many times I was between the two of them, and whenever I wished to go to one side so that the elder stood in the middle, the younger himself did this. But I remained always in the same place. He also seemed to me to have the age of a boy. (48) And this happened many times. And when, as it were, a ladder must be placed at some steep point, first the younger one

February 11

assisted me up, and I cried out, for I was grateful. Next above at the end of the ladder, the elder Emperor assisted me. And when he asked, "How did he help?", I said, "In all and everything". (49) *And after this, desiring to leave, I remarked, "I thank you", I said, "O Emperors, for all the care and honor which you have paid me". But they said in reply, "We thank the gods to have known such a man. For we also believe him to be an equally capable orator". And after this, the elder Emperor began to say that it was an attribute of the same man to be morally good and a good speaker. The younger continued with the saying of someone that 'words follow character.*[76]*' And I said that "I wished that this were so. For it would profit me in speaking, if indeed in other things I am so regarded by you and if at the same time I would have two goods instead of one". I answered them somewhat in this manner. But there were countless other things which happened and which were said, greater than I could tell or hope.*

Next after this, having fallen asleep again,[77] *I dreamed that an acquaintance, named Diophanes,*[78] *spoke to me of these exceedingly great honors, as if he were present and witnessed them. And one of my younger companions was also present and marveled when he heard that I was so distinguished among all men.*

(50) *After this, I appeared to be in some bath. And first of all it occurred to me what I had done,*[79] *that I had bathed before I saw the Emperors. For I seemed to have met them yesterday. Next when I massaged myself and began to perspire, I said, "Let us go in". So I bathed and vomited at evening, for I took note of the dumping of the excavation.*

February 12

(51) *Nevertheless I still was considering making a journey to Pergamum because of former dreams. Now it was clearly indicated that I stay here. On the one hand, I started at evening, changed my mind, and said that it was impossible to reach Hadrianutherae.*[80] *And on the other hand, I dreamed that someone came from Hadrianutherae, bringing some work of Menander,*[81] *and he said that the mud was unmanageable and the marsh was also impossible to get through.* (52) *Again I thought that it rained and that someone came to me and said that one of my adversaries in a lawsuit was at Hadrianutherae and that I had to go down there to handle the matter. And I said, "What's the use, since the god has declared that I stay?" Again I thought that I told this to certain people and that I thus apprehended everything, in that when I was rather angry about staying, the god, wishing to change my mind, so that I might stay with more pleasure, gave me a way out.*[82] *There were also in the dream tokens for not bathing. And afterwards at evening, there was rain and a hard storm.*

XLVII. THE SACRED TALES: I 287

(53) On the next day, there was no bathing and there was vomiting of food. And when I vomited, my condition was such that I was glad if I could suffice for the day following.   February 13

(54) On the day following, fasting was enjoined, but enjoined in this way. *I dreamed that I was in Smyrna, fully distrusting everything which was plain and visible, because I was not aware that I had made the journey. Figs were offered to me. Next the prophet Corus[83] was present and showed that there was a quick acting poison in them. After this, I was full of suspicion and eagerly vomited, and at the same time considered what if I should not have vomited completely? Next someone said that there was also some poison in some other figs. I was still more distressed and angry because I did not hear it sooner.* (55) After these things were seen, I suspected that fasting was indicated, but if not, still I preferred it. But I asked the god to show more clearly which he meant, fasting or vomiting.   February 14

I slept again and *I thought that I was in the Temple at Pergamum and that the middle of the day had passed and I was fasting. And Theodotus[84] came to me with some friends, and having entered, he sat down beside me while I was lying thus upon a couch.* (56) *I said to him that I was fasting. But he indicated that he knew, and said that "after all the things which these men are doing, I have put off performing a phlebotomy on you. For the aggravation comes from the kidneys and fasting", he said, "is sort of a bastard outlet, which goes through the chest, for the inflammation". And while he said this, two sparks appeared before me. And in wonder I looked at Theodotus and felt it an omen of his words, and I asked him what these were. He said that they were from this inflammation, and he indicated what was troubling me.* Then I awoke, and I found that it was that very hour, in which I thought that Theodotus spoke to me, and friends had actually now come to visit me.

(57) These dreams appeared to me while the doctor[85] had arrived and had prepared himself to help, as much as he knew how. But when he heard the dreams, being a sensible man, he also yielded to the god. And we recognized the true and proper doctor for us, and we did what he commanded.

My night was wholly endurable and everything was without pain.   February 15

(58) *Later in the form of the temple warden, Asclepiacus,[86] he gave me goose fat and told me to inquire of the god, "for whom they make assembly in the Mysian plain".[87] For he said that I would learn from that god whatever I wanted. And the god declared that nothing would be difficult.*   c. December 166 A.D.

Winter
171 A.D.

(59) What should one say of the matter of not bathing? I have not bathed for five consecutive years and some months besides, unless, of course, in winter time, he ordered me to use the sea or rivers or wells. The purgation of my upper intestinal tract has taken place in the same way for nearly two years and two months in succession, together with enemas and phlebotomies, as many as no one has ever counted, and at that with little nourishment and that forced. (60) But despite all the fastings, both those still before these things and those which came afterwards, we spent the whole period, nearly to this winter, paradoxically in writing and speaking and correcting that which had been written. And mostly we worked on until at least midnight. Next on each following day, having performed our usual routine, we took some little food. And when fasting followed upon vomiting, this work and study was my consolation. So that whenever I consider Socrates, who passed the day in the Lyceum after the symposium,[88] I think that I should owe no less thanks to the god for such endurance and strength.

October to
January
148 A.D.

(61) So much for my abdomen. But like the matter of the abdomen, many years before, occurred that of the tumor.[89] For the god predicted for a long time that I should beware of dropsy, and he gave me various drugs and Egyptian slippers,[90] which the priests are accustomed to use. And it seemed best to him to divert the discharge downwards. (62) And a tumor grew from no apparent cause, at first as it might be for anyone else, and next it increased to an extraordinary size, and my groin was distended, and everything was swollen and terrible pains ensued, and a fever for some days. At this point, the doctors cried out all sorts of things, some said surgery, some said cauterization by drug, or that an infection would arise and I must surely die. (63) But the god gave a contrary opinion and told me to endure and foster the growth. And clearly there was no choice between listening to the doctors or to the god. But the growth increased even more, and there was much dismay. Some of my friends marveled at my endurance, others criticized me because I acted too much on account of dreams, and some even blamed me for being cowardly, since I neither permitted surgery nor again suffered any cauterizing drugs. But the god remained firm throughout and ordered me to bear up with the present circumstances. *He said that this was wholly for my safety, for the source of this discharge was located above, and these gardeners did not know where they ought to turn the channels.* (64) Wonderful things kept hap-

pening. There were approximately four months of this kind of life. But during these, my head and upper intestinal tract were as comfortable as one could pray for. There was also, as it were, a national assembly in the house. For my friends, who were the foremost of the Greeks of that time, were always coming to see me and were present for my speeches. For I declaimed right from my bed.

(65) We were ordered to do many strange things. Of what I remember, there was a race, which it was necessary to run unshod in winter time. And again horse back riding, a most difficult matter. And I also remember some such thing. When the harbor[91] was stormy from a southwest wind and the boats were being tossed about, I had to sail across to the opposite side, and having eaten honey and acorns, to vomit, and so the purge was complete. All these things were done while the inflamed tumor was at its worst and was spreading right up to my navel. (66) Finally the Savior indicated on the same night the same thing to me and to my foster father—for Zosimus was then alive—, so that I sent to him to tell him what the god had said, but he himself came to see me to tell me what he had heard from the god. There was a certain drug, whose particulars I do not remember, except that it contained salt. When we applied this, most of the growth quickly disappeared, and at dawn my friends were present, happy and incredulous. (67) From here on, the doctors stopped their criticisms, expressed extraordinary admiration for the providence of the god in each particular, and said that it was some other greater disease, which he secretly cured. But they considered how the loose skin[92] might be restored to normal. Now it seemed to them that there was full need of surgery, for it would not otherwise be restored to its original state. And they thought that I should grant this, for what concerned the god had been wholly accomplished. (68) He did not even allow them this. But there was a remarkably great lesion and all my skin seemed to change. And he commanded me to smear on an egg and so cured me. And he brought everything back together, so that after a few days had passed, no one was able to find on which thigh the tumor had been, but they were both unscarred in every respect.[93]

(69) It was this Zosimus, to whom a great gift was given by the god later on.[94] It was thus. We were going through Mysia to Pergamum, but because of a dream which stopped me on the road, I waited for several days, while the dream continually recurred. Meanwhile he ran back to some farm of ours[95] for some reason, and

late summer 148 A.D.

290   XLVII. THE SACRED TALES: I

soon after fell sick. The condition of my stomach, palate, all my head, and entire body began to be such, that I was in an extreme state, and I was prevented from taking nourishment. And whatever I took, straightway turned sour, and I could not breathe, and my strength was gone. (70) We were approximately 120 stades[96] apart. It happened that when we learned how each of us was, we were much more troubled by what we heard than by our own circumstances.

(71) *When the god appeared, I grasped his head with each hand in turn, and having grasped him, I entreated him to save Zosimus for me. The god refused. Again having grasped him in the same way, I entreated him to assent. Again he refused. For the third time I grasped him and tried to persuade him to assent. He neither refused nor assented, but held his head steady, and told me certain phrases, which it is proper to say in such circumstances since they are efficacious.* And while I remember these, I do not think that I should reveal them purposelessly. *But he said that when these were recited, it would suffice. One of them was: Keep him!*[97] (72) What happened to him after this? First of all Zosimus recovered beyond expectation from that disease, having been purged with barley gruel and lentils, as the god foretold to me on his behalf, and next he lived four months besides. So we met one another and feasted together, since the god also helped me much, continuously and strangely. (73) One example of this is the following. When I was faint and wholly at a loss, I wrote a poem about the marriage of Coronis[98] and the birth of the god, and I stretched the strophe to great lengths. And thus I wrote the verses peacefully and in solitary reflection, and I was entirely oblivious of all difficulties. And I was enjoined to take enemas, so that the doctor[99] did not have the courage to apply them, when he saw the thinness and weakness of my body. But he believed that he would, as it were, kill me. I persuaded him with difficulty and immediately recovered. He gave me, as nourishment, wild greens, which provided me with some means of digestion and strength.

November 148 A.D.

(74) So this happened. But Zosimus was felicitated by all, and he himself did not know what to do, being both thankful to the god for his providence and to me for my service. And I think that he would have lived even longer, were it not because of a brave act of his. (75) For when he learned that one of my most useful servants was sick, he went off in winter time 40 stades[100] to visit him and to help however he could. For he was also skilled in medicine. Having

fallen from his carriage into much snow and ice, and having suffered many terrible things, both coming and going, he fell most seriously ill a second time, so that at first he did not even have the heart to reveal to me any of the things which had happened to him. And when I learned of it, I did not go to him, since I was angry because I had not persuaded him. (76) For during the previous night, I had the following dream vision: *The temple warden Asclepiacus seemed to say to me, "Zosimus must regain his strength while it is possible"*. After this dream, I did not allow him to move about, when the message about the servant came. But he disobeyed me and went, and because of this he died. (77) So his additional life was due to the grace of the god, who truly kept him for me,[101] and he died because he had moved about contrary to my dreams. And thus ended what in the beginning was indicated by the god, when I grasped his head and supplicated him.

(78) He saved countless times, beyond expectation, my old nurse, named Philumene, than whom nothing was dearer to me.[102] Once when she was in bed, he restored her by sending me from Pergamum *and foretelling that I would make my nurse easier. And at the same time, I found a letter lying before my feet in the Temple of Zeus Asclepius, and made it an omen.*[103] *I discovered every particular written in it, all but explicitly.* So I departed in great joy, and I found my nurse with strength enough only to recognize me approaching. But when she recognized me, she cried out and got up very soon thereafter.

<small>January 148 A.D.</small>

XLVIII. THE SACRED TALES: II[1]

170/171 A.D.

(1) Come let us also recall earlier events, if we are able.[2] In the beginning it did not occur to me to write about any of these, because I did not believe that I would survive. Next my body was also in such a state that it did not give me leisure for these things. Again as time passed, it seemed to be an impossibility to remember each thing and to tell it precisely. So I thought that it was better to keep completely silent than to spoil such great deeds. And for these reasons I made many excuses both to the god and to my friends, who from time to time asked me to speak and write about these things. (2) Now so many years afterwards, dream visions compel us to bring these things somehow to light. Still I can say this much that straight from the beginning the god ordered me to write down my dreams.[3] And this was the first of his commands. I made a copy of my dreams, dictating them, whenever I was unable to write myself. However I did not add in what circumstances of mine each took place nor what resulted after them. But I was satisfied, as it were, to fulfill my duty to the god, because of the weakness, as I said, of my body, and at the same time I never would have expected that the god would be so providential. I invoke him and Adrasteia![4] (3) Moreover, as if annoyed by the fact that I did not start to write down all things from the beginning, I also neglected the rest, some willingly, and some unwillingly. But I found other ways of thanking the god, and yet I believe that at least three hundred thousand lines are in my copy book.[5] But it is neither very easy to go over them nor to fit them into their proper chronology. Besides, some have also been scattered through various losses and confusion at home during these times. (4) The only thing left is to speak in summary fashion, as I remember different things from different sources, however the god will lead and stimulate me. We call on him even in this, as in all things. But he is surely to be called on in all things, if any of the gods.[6]

October 144 A.D.

(5) When I was brought from Italy,[7] after I had contracted many varied ailments from constant sickness and the stormy weather which I experienced while departing through Thrace and Macedonia—for I had left home while I was still sick—, the doctors were wholly at a loss not only as to how to help, but even to

recognize what the whole thing was.[8] (6) But the hardest and most difficult thing of all was that my breathing was blocked. With much effort and disbelief, scarcely would I draw a rasping and shallow breath, and a constant constriction in my throat followed and I had fits of shivering,[9] and there was need for more covering than I could bear. Besides, other things, which are impossible to describe, troubled me. (7) It seemed best to use the warm springs,[10] if ever I could be a little more comfortable or somehow better tolerate the climate. For it was winter time, and they were not far from the city.

Here first the Savior began to make his revelations.[11] *He ordered me to go forth unshod. And I cried out in my dream, as if in a waking state*[12] *and after I had accomplished the orders of the dream: "Great is Asclepius! The order is accomplished". I seemed to cry out these things, while I went forth.*

c. December 144 A.D.

After this an invitation and a journey from Smyrna to Pergamum with good fortune.[13] (8) To narrate what came next is not within the power of man. Still I must try, as I have proposed to do,[14] to recount some of these things in a cursory way. But if someone will wish to know precisely what has befallen us from the god, it is time for him to seek out the parchment books and the dreams themselves.[15] For he will find cures of all kinds and some discourses and full scale orations and various visions, and all of the prophecies and oracles about every kind of matter, some in prose, some in verse, and all deserving of a gratitude to the god greater than one might expect.[16] (9) Now let us begin at some place or other, since when we entered the Temple on the first night, the god appeared to my foster father[17] in the form of Salvius, one of the consulars.[18] But then we did not yet know who Salvius was, but he happened to be applying to the god at that time.[19] My foster father said that in this form he spoke to him, I believe, concerning my speeches and among other things designated them by the name[20] "The Sacred Tales". So much for this. (10) After this, he gave to me myself medicines, of which the first was, as I remember, the sap of the balsam, and he said that it was a gift of the Pergamene Telesphorus.[21] I had to use it while bathing and going from the warm water to the cold. Next there was soap mixed with raisins and with other things, and after that countless thousands of medicines. But perforce passing all these by, I wish to recall strange happenings.

summer 145 A.D.

(11) Where should one begin, when there are so many different things and at the same time when all are not remembered, only the

January 149 A.D.

gratitude because of them?[22] He sent me to Chius,[23] saying that he sent me for a purgation. We went off on the road to Smyrna, although it was distasteful and we believed that we were without a protector and that we truly sailed alone,[24] once we were outside the Temple. (12) Why should one mention the way that everyone in Smyrna was astounded when they saw my unhoped for appearance? When we arrived at Clazomenae, it seemed fated to cross straight to Phocaea.[25] For when we were near the islands Drymussa and Pele, a breeze from the southeast arose, and as we went further, the southeast wind became sharp, and finally a portentous gale broke out. And the ship rose at the prow and dipped at the stern and nearly sank. Next it was awash everywhere. Then it turned out to the open sea. The seamen sweated and shouted, and the passengers screamed. For some friends were also sailing with me. But I was content to say only, "O Asclepius!" After we had faced many kinds of danger and finally near the very landing were turned and driven back countless times and had caused much anguish to the spectators, scarcely and hardly were we saved. (13) When night came, *the god ordered me to perform my purgation, and showed me from what. And it produced no less an effect than a purge by hellebore would, as those who had experience in this said, since everything was stirred up by the tempest.*[26] *And he made everything clear, that it was fated for me to suffer shipwreck, and for that reason these things happened, and now it would be also necessary for my safety and in order to fulfill my destiny completely, to embark in a skiff and to arrange it in the harbor, so that the skiff overturn and sink, but that I myself be picked up by someone and brought to land. For thus my fate would be fulfilled.* Of course, we did this quite gladly. (14) And the contrivance of the shipwreck, which occurred with real danger, seemed wonderful to all. Wherein we also knew that it was even he who saved us from the sea. An additional benefaction was the purgation.

January 27
149 A.D.

(15) After this, he kept me in Phocaea and sent me marvelous signs, not only pertaining to my body, but also many, many other ones.[27] And we heard pretty much in advance about the winds which would occur, so that whenever our host Rufus[28] heard our dreams—in other respects he was the first of the Phocaeans, and himself in a way also not ignorant of Asclepius—, he was greatly amazed to hear these things from us indoors, which he had left without, when he entered. (16) Once at the god's command, there was need of milk. But there was none, for it was approximate-

ly the fourth of the month of Dystrus,[29] according to our usage in Asia. But it seemed necessary to search for it. And Rufus went out to a corner of his estate and found a sheep, who had given birth that very night. And he brought and provided the milk.

(17) Finally the god remitted our sailing to Chius with other signs and prophecies, and after all these *I thought that the ship had been smashed to pieces and was no more.* There is a region called Genais, not far from Phocaea. He diverted us here for some days, at the warm springs, and then brought us back to Smyrna.

(18) When we arrived at Smyrna, he appeared to me in some such form. *He was at the same time Asclepius, and Apollo, both the Clarian and he who is called the Callitecnus*[30] *in Pergamum and whose is the first of the three temples.*[31] *Standing before my bed in this form, when he had extended his fingers and calculated the time, he said, "You have ten years from me and three from Sarapis", and at the same time the three and the ten appeared by the position of the fingers as seventeen.*[32] *He said that "this was not a dream, but a waking state",*[33] *and that I would also know it. And at the same time he commanded that I go down to the river, which flows before the city,*[34] *and bathe. He said that a young boy would lead the way. And he pointed out the boy.* This is a summary of the divine manifestation, and I would place a high premium on being able to recount exactly each particular of it. (19) It was the middle of winter and the north wind was stormy and it was icy cold, and the pebbles were fixed to one another by the frost so that they seemed like a continuous sheet of ice, and the water was such as is likely in such weather. (20) When the divine manifestation was announced, friends escorted us and various doctors, some of them acquaintances, and others who came either out of concern or even for the purposes of investigation. There was also another great crowd, for some distribution[35] happened to be taking place outside the gates. And everything was visible from the bridge. There was a certain Heracleon,[36] a doctor, a companion of ours, who confessed to me on the day after that he had gone having persuaded himself that if I should fare as well as possible, I should be afflicted with *opisthotonos*[37] or some other such thing. (21) When we reached the river, there was no need for anyone to encourage us. But being still full of warmth from the vision of the god, I cast off my clothes, and not wanting a massage, flung myself where the river was deepest. Then as in a pool of very gentle and tempered water, I passed my time swimming all about and splashing myself all over. When I

came out, all my skin had a rosy hue and there was a lightness throughout my body. There was also much shouting from those present and those coming up, shouting that celebrated phrase, "Great is Asclepius!"[38] (22) Who could tell what came next. During all the rest of the day and night till bed time, I preserved the condition which I had after the bath, nor did I feel any part of my body to be drier or moister. None of the warmth abated, none was added, nor again was the warmth such as one would have from a human contrivance, but it was a certain continuous body heat, producing the same effect throughout the whole of my body and during the whole time.[39] (23) My mental state was also nearly the same. For there was neither, as it were, conspicuous pleasure, nor would you say that it was like a human joy. But there was a certain inexplicable contentment, which regarded everything as less than the present moment, so that even when I saw other things, I seemed not to see them. Thus I was wholly with the god.

(24) But as to what follows it is your task, O Lord, to make clear and to reveal, by saying what and by turning where, we would do what is gratifying to you and would best continue our tale. Since I have mentioned the river and the terrible winter and the bath, am I next to speak of other things of the same category and am I to compile, as it were, a catalogue of wintry, divine, and very strange baths? Or dividing up my tale, shall I narrate some intermediate events? Or is it best to pass over all the intermediate things and give the conclusion of my first tale,[40] how the oracle about the years held and how everything turned out? (25) For the god also gave me many other signs when he snatched me from the dangers which ever beset me and which were frequent every night and day, different ones confronting me at different times, sometimes the same ones recurring, and whenever one was quit of them, others taking their place. And antidotes for each of these things came from the god, and he consoled me in various ways by word and deed.

end of March 146 A.D.

This one thing, I remember, was also done by him once.[41] (26) *He said that it was fated that I die in two days and that this was inevitable. And at the same time, he gave me tokens about certain events on the following day, and the state of the weather, and where the constellation of the Charioteer would appear, and he gave me other tokens of his truthfulness. (27) But he said that it was necessary to do the following. First having got into a wagon, to go to the river which flows through the city,[42] and when I was at the place where it is outside the city, to make sacrifices "at the trench"—for so he called them. It was necessary to dig a trench and to make sacrifices in it to whomever of the gods it was necessary. Next upon turning back to take some small coins,*[43] *to cross the river and cast them away. And he ordered some other things, I think, in addition to this. After this to go to the Temple and make a full sacrifice*[44] *to Asclepius, and to have sacred bowls set up, and to distribute the sacred portions of the sacrifice to all my fellow pilgrims.*[45] *Also it was necessary to cut off some part of my body for the sake of the well-being of the whole. But since this was difficult, he remitted it for me. Instead of this, he ordered me to remove the ring which I wore and to dedicate it to Telesphorus—for this had the same effect, as if I should give up my finger*[46]—*and to inscribe on the band of the ring, "O son of Cronus". And if I did this, I would be saved.* (28) After this it is impossible to imagine our condition and into what kind of harmony the god again brought us. For we engaged in all this, almost as if in an initiation, since there was great hope together with fear.

But in conformity to this, being to the same purpose and taking place later on, was the cause of my drinking wormwood.[47] (29) It is obvious that it would be in every way more awesome and clearer to narrate the simple visions themselves, but in most things it is necessary to use the plan which I have instituted and to discuss summarily the main points, as they occur in the tale.[48] (30) The other temple warden was Philadelphus.[49] On the same night this man had a dream vision which I too had, but somehow a little different. Philadelphus dreamed—for so much can I remember—that there was a multitude of men in the Sacred Theater,[50] who wore white garments[51] and were assembled before the god,[52] and that standing among them, I made a public address and hymned the god, and that among many other things, I told how many another time he averted my fate and recently when he found the wormwood and commanded me to drink it diluted with vinegar, so that I might not be disgusted by it. And he reported a certain sacred ladder, I believe, and the presence and certain wonderful powers of the god. (31) Philadelphus dreamed these things. But the following happened to me. *I dreamed that I stood at the propylaea of the Temple.*[53] *Many others were also gathered together, as whenever there is a purificatory ceremony at the Temple.*[54] *And they wore white garments, and the rest was of an appropriate form. Here among other things which I cried out to the god, I called him "the arbiter of fate", since he assigned men their fates.*[55] *This word took its origin from my own circumstances. And after this there was the wormwood, made clear in some way. But it was made as clear as possible, just as countless*

winter
146 A.D.

other things also clearly contained the presence of the god. (32) For there was a seeming, as it were, to touch him and to perceive that he himself had come, and to be between sleep and waking, and to wish to look up and to be in anguish that he might depart too soon, and to strain the ears and to hear some things as in a dream, some as in a waking state. Hair stood straight, and there were tears with joy, and the pride of one's heart was inoffensive.[56] *And what man could describe these things in words? If any man has been initiated, he knows and understands.* (34) After these things had been seen, when it was dawn, I summoned the doctor Theodotus.[57] And when he came, I recounted my dreams to him. He marveled at how divine they were, but was at a loss as to what he should do, because it was winter time and he feared the excessive weakness of my body. For I had lain indoors for many successive months. (35) We thought that it was not a bad idea to send also for the temple warden Asclepiacus.[58] At that time I was living in his house,[59] and besides I was accustomed to share many of my dreams with him. The temple warden came. And we did not get the chance to begin the conversation, but he began to report to us. "Just now", he said, "I have come from my partner"—meaning Philadelphus. "He himself summoned me. For he saw at night a marvelous vision, which concerns you". And thus Asclepiacus recounted what Philadelphus saw. When he was summoned by us, Philadelphus himself recounted it again. Since the dreams agreed, we used the curative, and I drank as much as no one before, and again on the next day, as the god gave the same signs. Why should one need to describe the ease in drinking it, or how much it helped? (36) To return to my argument—the subject was fate—, how he arranged mine in the face of the many dangers which beset me[60]—, many other oracles were revealed with such help in dreams which occurred before and afterwards in the same way as these two.[61]

summer
165 A.D.

(37) But come now, let us finish the first story, and add how the oracle concerning the years turned out.[62] For they understand, as many as know even a little of our situation, that during all this time he was my Savior and gave me one day after another, or rather even now is my Savior. But when the time of the prediction elapsed, the following took place. I shall go back a little. (38) I happened to be in the suburbs[63] at the height of summer. A plague[64] infected nearly all my neighbors. First two or three of my servants grew sick, then one after another. Then all were in bed, both the younger and the older. I was last to be attacked. Doctors came from the city and

we used their attendants as servants. Even certain of the doctors who cared for me acted as servants. The livestock too became sick. And if anyone tried to move, he immediately lay dead before the front door. So in view of the circumstances it was no longer possible to enjoy fair sailing. Everything was filled with despair, and wailing, and groans, and every kind of difficulty. There was also terrible sickness in the city. (39) Meanwhile I persisted in my concern for the safety of the others, no less than for my own. Then the disease increased and I was attacked by the terrible burning of a bilious mixture, which troubled me continuously day and night, and I was prevented from taking nourishment and my strength failed. And the doctors gave up and finally despaired entirely, and it was announced that I would die immediately. However even here you could use that Homeric phrase,[65] "Still his mind was firm". Thus I was conscious of myself as if I were another person, and I perceived my body ever slipping away, until I was near death. (40) During these circumstances I happened to have turned to the inside of my bed.[66] *I seemed, as it were in a dream*—it was then the end[67]—*I seemed even to be at the conclusion of the play and to put aside my buskins, and to be going to take my father's shoes.* And while I was about this, Asclepius, the Savior, turned me suddenly to the outside. *(41) Then not much later, Athena appeared with her aegis and the beauty and magnitude and the whole form of the Athena of Phidias in Athens.*[68] *There was also a scent from the aegis as sweet as could be, and it was like wax, and it too was marvelous in beauty and magnitude. She appeared to me alone, standing before me, even from where I would behold her as well as possible.* I also pointed her out to those present—they were two of my friends and my foster sister[69]—and I cried out and I named her Athena, saying that she stood before me and spoke to me, and I pointed out the aegis. They did not know what they should do, but were at a loss, and were afraid that I had become delirious, until they saw that my strength was being restored and heard the words which I had heard from the goddess. And I remember the following: (42) *She reminded me of* The Odyssey[70] *and said that these were not idle tales, but that this could be judged even by the present circumstances. It was necessary to persevere.*[71] *I myself was indeed both Odysseus and Telemachus, and she must help me.*[72] And I heard other things of this sort. Thus the goddess appeared and consoled me, and saved me, while I was in my sick bed and nothing was wanting for my death. (43) And it immediately occurred to me to have an enema of Attic honey, and there was a purge of my bile. And after this came drugs and nourishment. First, I think, goose liver after much refusal of all food. Then some sausage. Then I was brought to the city in a long,[73] covered carriage. And thus little by little, with trouble and difficulty, I recovered. (44) The fever, however, did not completely leave me until the most valued of my foster children died.[74] He died, as I later learned, on the same day as my disease ended. Thus I had my life up to this time as a bounty from the gods, and after this, I was given a new life through the gods, and as it were, this kind of exchange occurred. (45) And thus took place the prediction concerning the years, and my later sickness, which agreed with this, and the divine manifestations pertaining to these things.

summer
145 A.D.

Perhaps it would be fitting to speak about the baths, which he had us use,[75] since even in the beginning, together with his prediction, he commanded bathing in the river.[76] (46) I had catarrhs and difficulty with my palate, and everything was full of frost and fire,[77] and among many other various difficulties, my stomach trouble was at its peak, and I was confined to the house in summer time. And these things happened in Pergamum, in the house of the temple warden Asclepiacus. (47) *First he commanded that I have blood drawn from my elbow, and he added, as far as I remember, "sixty pints".* This was to show that there would be need of not a few phlebotomies, but that appeared from later dreams. For the temple wardens, being of such years, and all who were worshippers of the god[78] and who held office in the Temple,[79] agreed that they never knew of anyone at all who had been operated on so much, except Ischuron,[80] and that his case was among the strange ones, but even so that ours surpassed it, without the other strange things which were added to the phlebotomies, such as even then immediately happened. (48) For one, I think, or two days later, *he commanded me again to draw blood from my forehead.* And he commanded the same also of one of the Roman Senators, who was consulting him, and indicated that it also had been enjoined upon Aristides. His name was Sedatius,[81] the best of men, and he himself recounted these things to me. In the middle of these phlebotomies, *he ordered me to bathe in the Caicus.*[82] *And it was necessary to journey there and bathe, after I had taken off my woolen wrappings.*[83] *He said that I would see a horse bathing and the temple warden Asclepiacus standing on the bank.* These things were predicted and these things happened. (49) While still approaching the river, I saw a horse bathing. While I bathed, the temple warden was present and standing on the bank, saw me. The comfort and relaxation which ensued was very easy for a god to understand, but not at all easy for a man to conceive of or write about.

(50) Moreover another bath in Smyrna was ordered when winter began.[84] *It was necessary to travel to the warm springs*[85] *and not to use the warm water, but the river which flows by.* And the whole day was damp and cold, and the water was so low that it could be forded. And this was the first miracle. It was late afternoon, and the bath took place, and there was a strong northwind.

c. December 144 A.D.

(51) These things again in Pergamum, in winter, and while my body was remarkably weak, so that for a long time I did not at all leave the room where I lay.[86] *He ordered me to wash in the river which flows through the city*[87]—but it was rising high from the rains—*and he predicted that there would be three baths.* When they learned of this command, the most serious of my friends assembled, both to escort me and through their concern about what would happen, and at the same time because they desired to see these events instead of hearing another's report. And indeed the day was stormy. (52) First it rained on us during the journey, and this was the first of the baths. For in our wish to find pure water and that which had not been contaminated by the city, we went further up along the road to Hippon. When we reached the river bank, none of my friends had the heart to encourage me, although the temple warden himself was present and some of the philosophers,[88] noble men. But nonetheless it was clear that they were all troubled and in anguish. I cast off my garments and having called upon the god, dove into the middle of the river. (53) Within it rocks churned and timber was carried along, and waves rose as if from the winds. And none of the river bed was visible, but there was a loud roaring sound. Here rocks, instead of leaves, whirled about, but the water was freer of debris than any crystal stream, and I dallied for as long as possible. When I emerged on the bank, a warmth passed through my whole body. And much steam rose up, and all my skin had a reddish hue, and we sang the paean.[89] And when we went back, it rained again, and thus ended the third of the baths.[90]

winter 145/ 146 A.D.

(54) Another bath took place in Elaea here.[91] *He sent me to wash in the sea, and he foretold that the ship Asclepius was lying at anchor in the mouth of the harbor, into which I had to throw myself, and some cries of the sailors, and other things, all of which I do not remember in sequence, but*

winter 145/ 146 A.D.

which agreed with what happened in broad daylight. When we went down to Elaea, we were outside at the harbor, and immediately the ship with name *Asclepius* was found, and the sailors immediately cried out to the god, when they saw what was taking place. The northwind was sharp, so that when I emerged, I needed covering. (55) Again on the following night, *he ordered me to use the sea in the same way, but when I emerged from the water, to stand before the wind and thus to cure my body.*

And I know that such things have been prescribed for many people.[92] But first of all, in itself, this activity of the god is rather wonderful, since he often and frequently revealed his power and providence,[93] and secondly if someone would consider our general condition. (56) And yet who could comprehend in what state we were then? Those, who were present at each event, know how I was both externally and internally, and besides for how many days and nights the flow from my head and the turmoil in my chest continued, and how my breath encountered the flow above and was caught in my throat and caused an inflammation, and that my expectation of death was always so great that I did not even have the courage to call for a servant, but believed that I would call in vain, for it would all be over with first. (57) In addition to this, there were various symptoms in my teeth and ears, and a tension everywhere in my arteries, the inability to retain any nourishment, yet even so the inability to vomit. For whatever small morsel would touch my throat or palate, closed the passage, and then it was impossible to retrieve it. There was the fiery pain, which penetrated to my brain, and all kinds of attacks, and the impossibility of reclining at night, but I had to raise myself, and persevere bent forward, with my head on my knees. (58) But with this and, I believe, countless other such things, there followed of necessity being wrapt in wool and other coverings, and being strictly confined, with everything shut up, so that day was equal to night, and the nights were sleepless instead of the days. "What mortal man might tell all these things"?[94] "For neither five nor six years"[95] are sufficient, but the narration perhaps needs no less time than that, in which the events took place. (59) If someone should take these things into account and consider with how many and what sort of sufferings and with what necessary result for these he bore me to the sea and rivers and wells, and commanded me to contend with the winter, he will say that all is truly beyond miracles, and he will see more clearly the power and the providence of the god, and will rejoice with me for the honor which I had, and would not be more grieved because of my sickness.

(60) Perhaps someone would desire to hear the origin of such great troubles.[96] It is beyond or like the story told to Alcinous,[97] but I shall try somehow to speak cursorily. I set out for Rome in the middle of winter, although I was sick right at the start after the waters[98] and a cold. I paid no heed to my present ailments, but trusted to the training of my body and to my general good luck. When I had got as far as the Hellespont, my ears troubled me greatly, and in other respects my condition was not normal. And feeling a little easier, I went on. (61) After this,[99] there was rain, frost, ice and all the winds. The Hebrus just now had been chopped up, so that it was viable by boat, but if it had not been, it was all solid ice. The fields swampy as far as the eye could see. There was a dearth of inns, and more rain came in through their roofs than from the sky without. And in all this, there was my haste and speed contrary to the season and the strength of my body. For not even the military couriers passed us, to say no more, and the majority of my servants traveled leisurely. I myself sought out the guides if there was any need, and this itself was no easy matter. For it was necessary to drag the men, who fled like barbarians,[100] sometimes by persuasion, sometimes even by force. (62) From all these things the disease increased. And I was very worried about my teeth falling out, so that I was always holding up my hands as if to catch them. I was absolutely prevented from taking nourishment, except only milk. Then first I noticed the shortness of breath in my chest, and I was attacked by strong fevers and other indescribable ailments. And I lay at Edessa by the cataract,[101] and scarcely on the one hundredth day after I started from home,[102] I arrived at Rome.

And shortly thereafter[103] my intestines swelled, I trembled with cold, shivering ran through all my body, and my breathing was blocked.[104] (63) And the doctors produced purges, and I was purged for two days by drinking *elaterium*,[105] until finally there was a bloody discharge. And fevers attacked me, and everything was despaired of, and there was not any hope even for my survival. And finally the doctors made an incision, beginning from my chest all the way down to the bladder. And when the cupping instruments were applied, my breathing was completely stopped, and a pain, numbing and impossible to bear, passed through me and

January 144 A.D.

spring 144 A.D.

everything was smeared with blood, and I was violently purged. And I felt as if my intestines were cold and hanging out, and the difficulty in my respiration was intensified. (64) And I did not know what to do, for in the midst of taking food and of talking, there was a blockage, and I thought that I must choke. And my other physical debilities were consonant with these things. Antidotes and various other drugs were given in vain.

autumn
144 A.D.

It seemed fitting to be taken home, if I could somehow endure.[106] It was impossible by land, for my body would not bear the shaking. We attempted sailing. Some of the pack animals, which we had brought, had died in the bad weather, and we sold the survivors. (65) And a sort of *Odyssey* took place. Right at the start in the Tyrrhenian Sea, there was a squall, darkness, a southwester. And the sea was uncontrollably rough, and the steersman let go of the rudders, and the captain and the sailors poured ashes on their heads, and bewailed themselves and the ship. The sea rushed in full fury over the prow and stern, and I was deluged by wind and waves, and these things happened day and night. (66) It was nearly midnight when we were borne to the Peloric promontory of Sicily. Then we wandered and ran in the strait, sometimes forwards, sometimes backwards. We crossed the Adriatic in two nights and a day, escorted noiselessly by the current. When it was necessary to put in at Cephallenia, again the waves grew high and the wind was not favorable, but we wandered up and down. My body was troubled in various ways and broke down.

September
22 144 A.D.

(67) You could not put in words what happened again in the Achaean straits,[107] right at the equinox, when the good sailors put out from Patrae, although I was unwilling and opposed it from the first, in all of which my chest and the rest of my body were still more injured.[108] (68) What took place in the Aegean sea was nearly the same and occurred through the incapacity of the steersman and the sailors, who decided to sail in unfavorable winds and did not wish to listen to me. Again there were fourteen stormy days and nights, and we were carried through the whole sea, and during these days there was not a little fasting.

October
144 A.D.

And with difficulty we put in at Miletus.[109] And I was unable to stand, and my ears had become quite deaf, and there was nothing which did not trouble me. And proceeding by short stages, thus we arrived at Smyrna, beyond all expectation.

XLVIII. THE SACRED TALES: II   305

(69) And it was already winter, and my palatal region was in very bad condition, and the rest as well.[110] And doctors and gymnastic trainers[111] assembled. And neither could they help nor did they recognize the variety of my disease.[112] But so much did they agree on, that I be brought to the warm springs,[113] since I was not even able to bear the climate in the city. What came after this, I narrated a little before.[114] (70) From such great origins, to speak briefly and obscurely, my disease formed and grew, ever progressing as time went on.

And when a year and some months had passed, we came to the Cathedra in Pergamum.[115]

(71) Now let us return to the divine baths, whence we digressed.[116] Let the pains, the diseases, and all the dangers be forgot. I was lying,[117] in accordance with a certain dream vision, between the doors and the latticed gates of the Temple, and the god gave me the following verse as an oracle: *"In the evening they flourished by the grassy springs"*. Then I anointed myself in the open air, in the enclosure of the Temple, and bathed in the Sacred Well, and there was no one who believed what he saw. (72) And I almost god rid of all my disease, save that when the god gave me signs and changed my regimen, I myself was ready to act in this way, but "the evil counsel of my comrades prevailed",[118] who pretending to wisdom and seeming to have a certain cleverness in these matters, explained my dreams rather unnaturally and said that the god expressly indicated that it was necessary to keep to the same things. And I yielded, although unwilling and suspicious, and believing that I myself knew better, but in order that I might not seem to be one who trusts only in himself. By experience I learned well that I was right.[119] (73) But whatever errors my advisers[120] made, let them be put aside. Yet even these things seem to belong to that which has strong reference to the god. For whenever the god prescribed and clearly stated them, the same regimen and the same things brought to my body and to my spirit salvation and strength and comfort and ease and high spirits, and every good thing. But when some other person advised me and missed the intention of the god, they brought everything opposite to this. How is this not the greatest sign of the god's power?

Come let us again recall his commands.[121] (74) It was the vernal equinox, when men daub themselves with mud in honor of the god.[122] It was impossible for me, if he should not give a sign, to stir

November 144 A.D.

c. summer 145 A.D.

before March 22 146 A.D.

March 22 146 A.D.

myself. Therefore I hesitated. The day, as I remember, was also very warm. Not many days later, there arose a storm and the northwind stirred up all the heavens, and a line of black clouds gathered together, and again anew winter weather. In these circumstances, *he commanded me to smear on mud by the Sacred Well and to bathe there.* Even then I afforded a spectacle. So great was the coldness of the mud and air, that I regarded myself lucky to run up to the Well. And the Well water sufficed me instead of other warmth. And these things are the first part of the miracle.

(75) On the following night, *he commanded me again to smear on the mud in the same way and to run in a circle about the Temples three times.* And the strength of the northwind was indescribable, and the icy cold had increased. Thus you would not have found heavy clothing to be suitable covering, but the wind passed through and struck my side like a spear. (76) Some of my comrades, as if wishing to console me, although I did not want this, decided to face the danger and imitate me. I smeared myself with mud and ran around the Temples, and permitted the northwind to card me well and fair, and finally going to the Well, I bathed. Of them, one immediately turned back, one was seized with convulsions, and having been taken quickly to a bathhouse, was warmed with much difficulty. But after this, we passed the day like one in spring.

winter 146/147 A.D.

(77) Again in winter time,[123] with ice and the coldest wind, *he ordered me to take some mud, pour it on myself, and sit in the courtyard of the Sacred Gymnasium,*[124] *calling on Zeus, the highest and best of gods.*[125] This also happened before many spectators.

winter 146/147 A.D.

(78) There was an affair which caused no less wonder than what has been said. For when there was continual frost for forty days and more, and even some of the harbors were frozen, and all the Elaean littoral from Pergamum on down, then *he commanded me to put on a small linen tunic and nothing else, but to persevere in this, and going from my bed, to wash at the spring without.*[126] (79) It was hard work to reach the water. Everything was frozen solid, and the water flow immediately congealed, and was, as it were, sort of a pipe of ice, and whatever warm water you might pour on, froze on the spot. Nevertheless we approached the spring, and the linen sufficed. And all the others were much colder. And nearly all of my regimen was done around the Temple.

(80) Akin to these things was my continually going unshod in winter[127] and my incubations throughout the whole Temple in the

open air and wherever it might be, and not least frequently on the temple road, under the Sacred Lamp of the goddess.[128] I also wore my shirt without an undershirt, I know not for how many days. And again it would be impossible to tell how often he commanded me to use the rivers or the springs, or even the sea, either before or after this, sometimes at Elaea, sometimes at Smyrna, and in what circumstances each of these things took place.

(81) But when recently he sent me to Ephesus to speak, during the journey on the third day, we were much rained upon.[129] For he himself stopped us on the second day, and the rain happened to start right then. However, what appeared in my dreams pertained more or less not only to that day, but also to the following day, and I foretold these things to those who were with me. But they, on the contrary, decided to continue, especially when they noted how zealously men behaved toward us. For when some people, who were going to Pergamum for the festivals,[130] saw us, they hastened back to Ephesus. (82) And so much for this. But after I had been rained upon and was in anguish, not many days later when I had arrived at Ephesus, *he ordered a cold bath* and I bathed in the gymnasium at Coressus.[131] The spectators wondered no less at the bath than at my words. But the god was the cause of both.

August 170 A.D.

XLIX. THE SACRED TALES: III[1]

spring
146 A.D.

(1) I happened to be staying in Aliani[2] since the god had sent me. Then I also had many frequent difficulties. I could neither take nourishment nor retain that which I had tasted, but it immediately effected a blockage and there was much burning and it tore at my throat and cut off my breathing, and fiery spasms arose to my head. My attempts to vomit had no result, but even a drop caused a tempest, because the stuff was held within and choked me. I would hardly be free of it with much trouble and utter exhaustion, nor bloodlessly, but the whole passage was torn anew and returned to normal only so that another wound might form. My exhaustion and the general weakness of my body and its deterioration were consistent with these circumstances. (2) And none of my friends and acquaintances was present, but each was off in a different place, except that one happened to be using the warm springs then, *of whom I formerly dreamed that when I lay alone on the road, after the horse which I rode had stumbled, he said to me that this too was fated, that I be left alone.* (3) This had taken place in Pergamum, a little before my departure. Then when I was in hard straits in Aliani, I remember that I had the following dream. *I dreamed that I was carried alone on a raft in the Egyptian Sea. I was at the very edge[3] near land. In my distress, my foster father Zosimus appeared to me on land, with a horse. And I somehow disembarked and gladly took the horse.* So much for this. (4) *I also dreamed that passing through Alexandria, I saw a children's school. They were reading out and singing the following verses, responding to one another most sweetly:*

"He has saved many from manifest death,
While they even stood at the inflexible gates
Of Hades".[4]

These are our verses, almost the first which we wrote for the god. I marveled at how they had come to Egypt, and I was exceedingly pleased that I happened to have found my own compositions being sung.

(5) This is a summary of the dreams.[5] As soon as day broke, I mounted my horse, for I happened to have one at hand. And I, whom one would not think sufficient for this first journey[6], raced the horse and felt more comfortable while it was still running, and much of the heaviness of my upper parts left me, and a certain strength was collected, as much as could be in such circumstances, and again I

had hope. At night I even heard the voice of someone saying: *"You have been cured"*, and this when I was in the most extreme difficulty. (6) Because of the abundance of stories and troubles, I must omit in what way I got back safely to Pergamum, and under what sort of regimen I lived after that.

I went on another journey to the warm springs in the height of summer,[7] and *it was foretold to me to return immediately, once I had bathed and had chopped up some cassia and smeared it about my neck*. Again I accomplished what was a total of two hundred and forty stades round trip,[8] while it was remarkably stifling, and I endured the thirst more easily than someone going home from the baths. *Again he sent me, after commanding me to drink cold water.* And I drank it all. (7) And so much for now about these things.

summer 148 A.D.

As to what happened in Lebedus:[9] I was sent from the incubation which I was performing in the Temple of the Saviors,[10] even at his command, although I was so weak that I could not even endure in bed at home. (8) And the doctor Satyrus, a sophist,[11] as was said, of no mean rank, was at this time in Pergamum. This man visited me while I was lying in bed, and felt my chest and abdomen. When during the course of the conversation, he heard how many purges of blood I had had, he ordered me to stop them and not to undermine my body. "But I", he said, "shall give you a very light and simple plaster, which you should put on your stomach and abdomen, and you will see how much it will help". (9) He advised these things. And as regards my blood, I said that I did not have the authority to do one thing or the other, but that while the god commanded the letting of my blood, I would obey whether willing or not, or rather never unwillingly. Still I did not ignore Satyrus' prescription, but took and kept it. It was no cornucopia.[12]

September 147 A.D.

(10) When I was taken to Lebedus,[13] and very unexpectedly and scarcely survived, I counted this much at least as a gain. But I needed constant help, and used the warm springs with difficulty and sparingly. I decided to put Satyrus' drug on my stomach and chest,[14] as Satyrus had prescribed. I thought indeed that I was not departing much from the cure which came from the god. (11) Right off the first application did not please me, but it seemed to be too cold. Nevertheless I decided to persevere and to entrust myself to the drug, to see if truly at least with time it might accomplish something. And so I developed a terrible chest cold, and a constant and strong cough ensued, and I was in difficulty. *And the*

October 147 A.D.

god showed that it was consumption.[15] And on the following day, there was a tension in the muscles of my temples and the whole of my face,[16] and my jaws were locked together, and then, if ever, there was confusion.

(12) When this tension relaxed a little, it occurred to me to consult the god in Colophon[17] both concerning my present troubles and general weakness. Colophon is not far from Lebedus,[18] and the Sacred Night happened to be near. Since it seemed best to do this, I sent Zosimus. When night came, Zosimus received the following oracle, which pertained to me:

"Asclepius will cure and heal your disease
In honor of the famous city of Telephus,[19]
Not far from the streams of the Caicus".

(13) The following happened to me on the same night, to recollect it in summary fashion. *I dreamed that I was at the ancestral hearth.*[20] *On the wall where the statues of the gods are were the following inscriptions: "Such and such, saved from death, give thank offerings to all the gods". And there appeared to be the traces of sacrifices.* And this vision inaugurated for me continuous sacrifices, and not only because I considered the dream, but I was receiving such great benefits from the gods and was also so inclined. We left Lebedus in high spirits when it seemed best to the god, and I enjoyed a remarkable comfort.

late January 148 A.D.

(14) As to what he said about the consumption,[21] the god confirmed it later by signs to the temple warden, as Asclepiacus himself recounted to me, having heard before nothing from me. For he said that he heard the god say that he had got rid of my consumption and catarrh, and even cured my stomach.

February 148 A.D.

(15) He also revealed, approximately at the same time,[22] very wonderful things in the person of Neritus, one of my foster fathers. For I believe that he dreamed that the god, together with Telesphorus, said to him, in regard to me, that it was necessary to remove my bones and put in tendons, for the existing ones had failed. Then he was in great fear and anguish, when he heard these things about me, but the god said, in consolation and instruction, that it was not necessary to knock the bones out directly and cut out the existing tendons, but that there needed to be, as it were, a certain change of those existing. Thus there was need of a great and strange correction. And he gave a cure to Neritus, to tell me: unsalted olive oil three times a day. And thereafter I did so, and when I tried it, it proved helpful.

(16) These other things happened to me at the ancestral hearth, in the height of winter and my disease. I was reclining at lunch, and strong and terrible pains occurred in my head, and there was a tension in the muscles of my face, and my lips were locked together, and I was in great difficulty. Constricted, as I was, I rushed into my bedroom, and lay down in some fashion, and a great and strong fever arose. I was unable to breathe, and my mother and nurse and the other servants started to wail, and Zosimus was also highly agitated. And somehow I nodded to the majority to leave, and made ready for what would happen. (17) And after this, when the sun set, or even still later, a convulsion was added to the fever, neither describable nor such as one might conceive. But my body was drawn in every direction. My knees were borne upwards to my head, and dashed against it. It was impossible to control my hands, but they beat against my neck and face. My chest was thrust forward, and my back drawn backward like a sail billowing in the wind. No part of my body was still, nor did it change a little from its natural condition, but mostly there were convulsions and the unspeakable racking pain[23] which did not let me be silent, and ever more ended in screams. (18) These things continued even up to midnight or later, and abated not a bit. Then it lost some of its force, however it did not wholly stop. I was laid upon and wrapt all about in warm wool, and every kind of fomentation was used, and scarcely thus I survived. And before it was daytime, someone ran to summon the doctor.[24] He came, either on the following day or even a day later. (19) And at noon, I think, I again had an attack, and not much later I had a bowel movement of black bile.[25] And while I was sitting on the night stool, there came over me a terrible looseness in my bowels and perspiring and faintness. And the doctor became highly agitated and decided that I should be fed. But this was not, it seems, the trouble. (20) Night arose, as in a pitching, rolling sea, and I slept only enough to dream. *I received a command to go to the hearth of my foster fathers and make obeisance to the statue of Zeus, by which I was brought up. And there were certain utterances, I think, and the kind of supplication was defined.* There was not a little snow, and everything was thoroughly impassable. And the small house was more than a stade[26] from the main house. I mounted a horse, went, and made obeisance, and even before I got back, everything had returned to normal.

c. February 148 A.D.

August
148 A.D.

(21) Immediately after he cured my difficulty in breathing,[27] he healed in the following way the trouble about my neck and the tension in my ears and the *opisthotonus*,[28] which was now fully developed. *He said that there was a royal ointment. It was necessary to get it from his wife. And somehow after this, a servant of the palace, clad in white and girdled, appeared at Telesphorus' Temple and statue, and escorted by a herald, went out by the doors where the statue of Artemis*[29] *is, and bore the remainder of the ointment to the Emperor.* This more or less was the dream, to recollect it unclearly. (22) When I entered the Temple and was walking about in the direction of the statue of Telesphorus, the temple warden Asclepiacus came up to me. And while he happened to stand by the statue, I told him the vision which I had, and I asked him, "What might the ointment be, or who should use it?" But when he had listened and marveled, as he was accustomed to do, he said, "The search is not far nor need there be much traveling, but I shall bring it to you right from here. For it lies by the feet of Hygieia,[30] since Tyche[31] herself just now put it there, as soon as the Temple was opened". Tyche was a noble lady. And going to the Temple of Hygieia, he brought the ointment. And I anointed myself, where I happened to stand. The ointment also had a wonderful smell, and its power was immediately manifest. For faster than I have said it, the tension relaxed. (23) Later after asking the temple warden, I learned that the mixture was compounded of three ingredients, of fig sap, with which I anointed myself, of myrrh of nard, and of another expensive myrrh, named, I believe, after its leaf.[32] Thus I made a preparation of it and used it in the future, and all those symptoms abated. But at night, *Telesphorus also appeared dancing about my neck,*[33] *and a light shone on the opposite wall, as if from the sun.*

(24) About this time, I had the following dream, either when I had begun the practice of vomiting at evening, or the vomiting had not yet even taken place. *On arising from bed, I had to eat nuts, dried figs, date nut, and some bread in addition to these things.* Afterwards I used these things beside the ointment, and they helped me very much.

(25) He also gave me a drug for my stomach, abdomen, and this general region, which, I think, was plastered above these places. He gave it by providing the following vision: *I dreamed that the doctor Asclepiacus*[34] *visited me and upon examining me, made a poultice of a drug called by the name dittany, and at the same time prescribed that I use it for thirty days.* I used it, and on the thirtieth night, again *I dreamed that Asclepiacus came and removed the poultice.*

(26) Later he added something, which he compounded of four ingredients, of which I remember two, pitch from wine and sheep's wool grease. We shall add the other two, if ever the collection of dreams[35] turns up. (27) And concerning the drinking of the antidote, I remember the following. I happened to be eating only one meal[36] and to have omitted to eat for much of the day. *But he ordered me to dine and after rising from the table to drink this drug.* And this continued for five days, although I knew that the doctors ordered the opposite: whenever one intended to drink the drug, not to dine; and up to this time, this had been my wont. (28) *Again he ordered me to consume this same drug with bread,* and I consumed it at the Sacred Tripod,[37] and made this in a way a means for my health.

(29) There is, I believe, a certain mixture of Philo.[38] Formerly I was not even able to smell this. But when the god indicated that I should use it, and at the same time the hour when it should be done, I not only drank it with pleasure, but after I drank it, I was immediately more comfortable and easier.

(30) It would be possible to tell countless other things, pertaining to drugs, some of which he compounded himself, some public and known, which he prescribed as a cure for my body, however things stood on each occasion. When I had frequent catarrhs and my palate was very sore, and my uvula was swollen,[39] and my veins did not cease being stretched taut, *I thought that I read an excellent book, the particulars of which—for I shall say the same thing again*[40]*—I would not be able to tell. How could I so much later, especially since my record removed the need to memorize them?* (31) *But at the end of the book, there was, indeed, the following—it was said, as it were, concerning some athlete: "When the god had considered all these things and saw that the flow was abundant, he commanded him to drink water and to abstain from wine, if he desired at all to be victorious. 'If you too imitate this,' he said, 'it is possible for you to win the crown of victory or to share in it' ". Here it ended. Next the title of the discourse was subjoined as "The Crown Lover" or "The Crown Desirer".*
(32) I also cannot say for how long I endured water drinking, but it was easy and pleasant, although before I always found water somehow disagreeable and disgusting.

When this duty also had been performed, he took me off water, and *assigned me a measure of wine. The word was "a demiroyal".* It is quite clear that he meant a half cup.[41] I used this, and it sufficed, as formerly twice the amount did not. Sometimes there was even some wine left over, since I was sparing through fear that it might be harmful. Nor did I add this residue to the next day, but I had to be content anew with the measure.

When he had also made this experiment, he permitted me to drink as much as I wished, *and made some sort of joke, to the effect that they are foolish men who are rich in material goods and do not dare to use them freely.* (33) And this book which I mentioned seemed to be Antisthenes' On Use.[42] *It pertained to wine, and there were certain tokens of Dionysus*[43] *as well.* I became so accustomed to it that, although the god granted it, I deviated but slightly in the measure of my drinking. And in some way, I longed for the stewardship of those times.

(34) For a long time[44] I abstained from all living things, except chicken, and all greens, except wild ones and lettuce. Indeed, I even abstained from all sweetmeats. *Once he commanded me to use only one food,* and I used chicken, I, for whom even this order was difficult.[45] And we endured some of these things without bathing and with phlebotomies and enemas, and some, as each circumstance might be. (35) For six years[46] I have also abstained from all fish. I do not know how long from pork. Again when he allowed it, I used both. Then, in turn, I was kept from some things, and used some, according to each particular circumstance. Indeed, he has kept me completely from fish sauce, for *he said that it was not safe for my head, and least of all for my teeth.* (36) He gave me remedies for my teeth. First there was: *Burn the tooth of a lion, and grinding it up, use it as a dentifrice.* Second: *Clean your teeth with that famous ointment, sap of silphium.*[47] After this, *pepper, which he added for warmth.* After all these things, *came Indian nard, this also as a dentifrice.*[48] (37) And these are dreams which have recently appeared.

I have been kept from beef in this way.[49] *I dreamed that an oracle had fallen to Zosimus,*[50] *"that he would live as long as the cow in the field lived".*[51] *And then I said to him: "Do you know what the oracle means? It commands you to abstain from beef".* Zosimus was said, in addition to the cold from which he died, to have been harmed also by touching some beef from a sacrifice. There was, as is likely, much nicety and care about not even secretly touching it with the tip of my finger.

(38) And later,[52] when Albus[53] was Governor of Asia, there were many frequent earthquakes, and Mytilene, on the one hand, was nearly all leveled and, on the other hand, in many other cities there were many shocks, and some villages were wholly destroyed. The Ephesians and the Smyrnaeans ran to one another in great agitation. The series of earthquakes and terrors was extraordinary. And

on the one hand, they sent emissaries to Clarus, and the Oracle[54] was fought about, and on the other, holding the olive branch of supplication, they made processions about the altars and the market places and the circuit of the cities, no one daring to stay at home. And finally they gave up supplicating. (39) In these circumstances, the god commanded me, who was then living in Smyrna, or rather in the suburbs of the city, to sacrifice publicly an ox to Zeus the Savior.[55] While I hesitated being both suspicious and fearful of that former prophecy, some notion occurred also to me, that I was not going to sacrifice a cow, and that it was not even necessary to taste it.[56] I also had the following dream, which was most clear and by which emboldened, I sacrificed. *For I thought that while I stood by the very altar of Zeus in the market place and was asking him to give me a sign if it were better to sacrifice, a shining star darted through the market place and sanctioned the sacrifice.* So I boldly sacrificed. (40) As to what happened next, who wishes to believe, let him believe, and who does not, to him I say farewell! For all those earthquakes stopped, and after that day there was no longer any trouble, through the providence and power of the gods, and by our necessary ministration.

The following is no less marvelous than this, if not even more. (41) On about the sixth or seventh day before the earthquakes began, he ordered me to send to the old hearth, which is at the Temple of Olympian Zeus, and to make sacrifices and to establish altars on the crest of the hill of Atys.[57] (42) And these things were just finished, when the earthquake came and so ravaged all the other land in between that not an inn was left standing, except some small ruin. But it did not proceed up the Atys, nor to our Laneion estate at the south of the Atys, except only to perceive it, and ravaged nothing beyond. (43) And I became so bold that, almost in the midst of the earthquakes, as I was returning from the warm springs[58] to the city in accordance with my dreams and saw men in supplication and distraught, I intended to say that there was no need to be afraid, for no harm would befall. For under these conditions, I would not have been summoned to the city. Then I stopped, so that I might not seem to be some demagogue, but I asserted to those who were with me, how "I had obtained safe conduct", using these very words.

(44) I have finished concerning the earthquakes, and how we first sacrificed an ox during them. Once when the god gave a sign, during the Cathedra in Pergamum,[59] we sought a goose egg. And it

145 A.D. to 147 A.D.

was found nowhere in the market place. But there was a certain Milates from the Acropolis,[60] and those engaged in the search finally came to him both by chance and by report. And Milates said to them that he had the egg, but that he was keeping it for a remedy, for so the god had foretold to him. "Indeed, this is our purpose", the searchers said, and he, making obeisance, gave them the egg. How I used it, when I got it, I do not know because of the multitude of years which have passed.

winter 144/145 A.D.

(45) Nearly the same as this, still at the beginning of my sickness,[61] was the command of Isis, which concerned geese themselves. I was staying at the warm springs, and the goddess ordered me to sacrifice two geese to her. I went to the city, having first sent ahead men to look for them, and having told them to meet me at the Temple of Isis with the geese. On that day there were no other geese for sale, except for only two. When my people approached and tried to buy them, the man who raised the geese said that he was not able to sell them, for it was foretold to him by Isis to keep them for Aristides, and that he would surely come and sacrifice them. When he learned the whole story, he was dumbstruck and making obeisance, gave the geese to them. And I learned these things at the sacrifice itself. (46) *There was also a light from Isis and other things which cannot be told and which pertained to my salvation. Sarapis also appeared on the same night, both he himself and Asclepius.*[62] *They were marvelous in their beauty and magnitude, and in some way like one another.*

winter 149 A.D.

(47) When Zosimus' misfortune occurred—for I pass by those things which the god predicted and said in consolation when it was going to happen—, but when it happened and I was miserable with grief,[63] *it seemed to me that Sarapis, in the form of his seated statues, took some sort of lancet, and made an incision around my face, going somehow under the gum itself in the root of the lips,*[64] *as it were, removing and purging refuse and changing it to its proper state.*

So even later, *I had a vision from the gods of the Underworld,*[65] *that if I gave up my strong grief for the dead, it would be to my advantage.*

c. April 25 149 A.D.

(48) But that which appeared later,[66] contained something much more frightening than these things, *in which there were ladders, which delimited the region above and beneath the earth, and the power of the god on each side, and there were other things, which caused a wonderful feeling of terror, and cannot perhaps be told to all, with the result that I gladly beheld the tokens.*[67] *The summary point was about the power of the god, that both*

without conveyance and without bodies Sarapis is able to carry men wherever he wishes. Such was the initiation,⁶⁸ and not easily recognized, I arose.

And in addition to these things, a certain sacrifice was indicated, which is due to Zeus and is publicly announced, but here was offered, as if it belonged to Sarapis. But it was also offered to Zeus, and I can say even on the Sacred Days, which the city of Alexandria celebrates for the god,⁶⁹ for he himself gave many signs, many times, on each single day, and while the day of the feast was still approaching.

(49) But if it is necessary to recount something even more frightening, I had sacrificed to Isis and Sarapis in the Temple of Isis, I mean the one which is in Smyrna. As I went out the propylaea, two of the sacred geese rushed up, and going before me, they led me so exactly in the way in which I intended to go, that it became quite apparent to me.⁷⁰ And I comprehended the situation and I said to my friends and those who were accompanying me, "Look, even these accompany me in the chorus of my friends". And at the same time I spoke about the terrible majesty of the god,⁷¹ and how great was his power "both in oracles and omens",⁷² and that many times already an answer had come to my prayers. "And now", I said, "he has sent us these as guides in a way for our journey". (50) We discussed such things, and at the same time observed what they would do. When we had gone, I do not know how far from the Temple, I, showing off to my friends, made sport of the geese and said, "You have sufficiently done your duty, sirs. Go!" I had not finished speaking, when they turned and went.

L. THE SACRED TALES: IV[1]

c. December 22 152 A.D.

(1) At the beginning of the tenth year of my illness,[2] a vision came and said the following: *"Sick with the same disease, at the start of the tenth year, by the will of Asclepius, I went to the places where the disease began, and was rid of it"*. Such was what was said, and it seemed to have been written. Then too we were staying at the Temple of Olympian Zeus.[3] It was winter, a little after the solstice, but the air was mild. When this oracle was given, I was, as is likely, joyful and wonderfully eager to depart. (2) The Aesepus and the warm springs near it[4] are a two days journey from the region of the Temple. And there my body first slipped away through a cold in winter time,[5] when I had been soaked by a strong rain after many baths, and at evening had gone off to an estate and a farm house of mine, which was near, one might say. Moreover, contrary to the season and my condition, in consequence of which I returned,[6] I had done more than I should, and in addition to these things there was a difficult trip to Italy a few days later. These things took place nine years before.

Then we set out, in high spirits, as on a pilgrimage. The weather was marvelous, and the road inviting. (3) Poemanenos[7] is a place in Mysia, and in it is a sacred and famous temple of Asclepius. Here we completed about one hundred and sixty stades, and nearly sixty of these at night, as we started when the day was advanced. And about this place we also met with some mud from earlier rains, which was not easy to cross. The journey was made by torch light. (4) Here I was completely consecrated, as it were, and possessed.[8] And I composed many lyrics to the Savior himself, while I was sitting in the carriage, and many to the Aesepus, the Nymphs, and Artemis Thermaea, who keeps the warm springs, to free me from all my troubles and to return me to my original state.

(5) When I reached Poemanenos, the god gave me oracles and kept me there for some days,[9] and he purged my upper intestinal tract and that nearly once and for all.[10] And a farmer, who did not know me, except by reputation, had a dream. He dreamed that someone said to him that Aristides had vomited up the head of a viper. Having seen this vision, he told one of my people and he told me. So much for this.

(6) When the god sent me to the Aesepus, he ordered me to abstain from the baths there, but he prescribed my other regimen every day. And here there were purifications at the river by libation, and purgations at home through vomiting. And when three or four days had passed, *there was a voice in a dream saying that it was over and it was necessary to return.* (7) It was all not only like an initiation into a mystery, since the rituals were so divine and strange,[11] but there was also coincidentally something marvelous and unaccustomed. For at the same time there was gladness, and joy, and a contentment of spirit and body,[12] and again, as it were, an incredulity that it will ever be possible to see the day when one will see himself free from such great troubles, and in addition, a fear that some one of the usual things will again befall and harm one's hopes about the whole. Thus was my state of mind, and my return took place with such happiness and at the same time anguish.

(8) Since the gods so granted, from this time, the change in my whole body and regimen became clear, and it was easier to bear the climate and to travel, on the whole no less than those who were extremely healthy. And I dispensed with excessive covering,[13] and the indescribable catarrhs, and pains in my head, and the tension in my arteries and tendons ceased.[14] My eating habits became in some way more regular, and we engaged in full scale rhetorical contests at home and in public. And under the guidance of the god, with good fame and fortune, we toured the cities.[15]

(9) And years later that plague occurred,[16] from which the Savior and Lady Athena manifestly saved me. And for some six months after this, my condition was wonderful. Then I became very constipated,[17] and other things troubled me, all of which the god settled, and if I may say so by his grace, he still settles them by daily regimens and predictions.

summer 165 A.D.

(10) Then on my return from the Aesepus,[18] I heard propitious remarks from both children and others, right while I was approaching, and in their play, they cried out, "Hail to the Master"! And my nurse immediately got up and met me, and regained her strength,[19] and there took place what is likely in such circumstances.

c. January 153 A.D.

(11) *Then the god commanded—since this must be done in place of being buried—to sprinkle some white earth*[20] *on myself, in the manner of the wrestling ground, for security and so that in some way the burial also might be fulfilled. Also to bathe in cold water, that is, to bathe in snow.* So snow

covered everything, the ground, the trees, and the springs. Clearly we also gladly obeyed in this.

(12) Such happened in my journey to the Aesepus and my return again from there. The governor of Asia then was a very distinguished man, Severus, from Upper Phrygia,[21] during whose time wonderful things, of special importance to me, were done by the god. Concerning these it would probably be best to speak next. (13) First, as I said, it was my intention to recount immediately his benefactions in this matter. Then it seemed best to go back to former times and to preface, as far as possible, the other honors from the god, first as many as there were in regard to my speeches, and then those which pertained to legal actions in each governorship.[22] Then whenever the past events are settled with,[23] the limits of the first part of the speech will be fixed, to which it will be necessary to connect the rest.

(14) During approximately the first year of my sickness,[24] I gave up the study of oratory, since I was in such great physical discomfort. And at the same time I had become despondent.

While I rested[25] in Pergamum because of a divine summons and my supplication, I received from the god a command and exhortation not to abandon oratory. (15) It is impossible to say through the length of time whatever dream came first, or the nature of each on the whole. But those which occurred at the very beginning were exhortatory dreams. *It befits you to speak in the manner of Socrates, Demosthenes, and Thucydides.*[26] *And one of the distinguished personages, who were older than I, was pointed out, in order that I would be especially moved to speak. And the god commanded me to go to the Temple Stoa, which is at the Theater,*[27] *and to offer to him the very first fruits of these improvised and competitive orations.* And so it happened. (16) There was a very magnificent spectacle in the city, either a bull hunt,[28] I think, or some such thing. All those from the Temple had rushed down, and the city was engaged in these things. We had been left alone in the Temple, two of the more distinguished worshippers, I and a Nicaean, a man of praetorian rank, called Sedatius, but originally Theophilus.[29] We were sitting in the Temple of Hygieia, where the statue of Telesphorus is, and we were asking one another, as we were accustomed, whether the god had prescribed anything new. For in a way certain of our diseases were also similar. (17) I said that I did not know what I should do, for the prescription was like an order to fly, the practice of oratory, for one who could not breathe, and this here—I meant the Stoa—and I recounted the dream to him. And when he heard it, he said, "What will you do, and how do you feel about it?" "What else", I said, "than I shall do whatever I can? Arrange on my clothes, stand so, make a note of the problem to myself, begin some little thing, and then I shall stop. And so my obligation has been fulfilled". "Not at all", he said, "not so. But you have me here as a listener. Then contend with all zeal. Strength will be the god's concern. How do you know whether your dream does not pertain to more than this?" And at the same time he told me a marvelous deed of the god, how he commanded some sick man to contend in this way, and by causing him to perspire through the exercize, brought an end to the whole disease. It seemed necessary to do this. (18) And while we were talking and taking counsel, Maximus, the African,[30] entered in the third place, a worshipper of the ancients, and in a fashion zealous about oratory. It was he who proposed the problem. And the problem was as follows, for I remember it, since it was the first which I received: "While Alexander", he said, "is in India, Demosthenes advises that it is time to act".[31] I immediately accepted the omen of Demosthenes speaking again and of the subject, which was about empire. And pausing a little, I contended, and my new strength was such as is of the god's divising, and the year seemed not to have been passed in silence, but in training.

(19) This was the beginning of the practice of oratory for us, and so we returned to it. There were also many other dreams which pertained to the same, and the following was particularly encouraging. Rhosander was a philosopher[32] and especially diligent in the service of the god. *This man seemed to me to come from a gentleman who was a distinguished philosopher and who had just now held a seminar, and to stand before my bed, as it were, inspired and very serious. Next he spoke about the great improvement of my speeches. He remembered Plato and Demosthenes, in whatever way he remembered each.* Finally he added, "For us you have surpassed Demosthenes in dignity, so that not even the very philosophers can scorn you". This remark[33] kindled all my later ambition. This made me feel that everything, which I might do in oratory, was less than I should do. (20) Moreover, the god himself set his seal to this when I was awake. For right after that night which brought the dream at dawn itself,[34] I began practicing, still at the beginning, as I said.[35] And those present, having learned nothing of the dream before, but hearing my words then for the first time, especially approved of their dignity, and because of this they gave me much applause.

(21) Later I had the following dream, which pertained to Rhosander. *I dreamed that during some lecture on the grounds of the Temple of Olympian Zeus, either I thought to myself, or someone speaking to me, indicated that Rhosander*[36] *can signify the god. And he gave a demonstration of this through some diagram, in the manner of the geometricians, by writing in equal proportion upon the earth two successive names, the one, "Rhosander", the other, "Theodotus". And somehow in writing this was "Theodōtēs".*[37] *But this was clear, that the doctor Theodotus signified the god.*[38] Therefore "Rhosander" also has the equivalent meaning, since "Rhosander" and "Theodotus" are equal. Such did he reveal concerning the name "Rhosander".

(22) It was often my experience that when I received my problems and stood ready for the contest, I was in difficulty and scarcely recovered from the failure of my breath; but as I proceeded in my introduction, I held my breath more easily and was able to breathe; and as my speech proceeded further, I was filled with strength and lightness and strung my words together so well that the audience scarcely followed them. And in my estimation, at least, greater things were seen than heard.

(23) Others also had dreams about me, which pertained to the same end. On the one hand, Euarestus of Crete,[39] one of those who studied philosophy, came from Egypt in search of information about the god. He was an acquaintance and companion of mine during my stay in Egypt.[40] And he said that the god commanded him to exhort me to take up oratory, since it befitted me more than anything. On the other hand, Hermocrates of Rhodes,[41] the lyric poet, had this dream, as Hermocrates himself said to me—I had given up speaking, I think, for one or two days: "Then Aristides will be angry, and not wishing to speak, will say that he has pains in the stomach". (24) Thus, on the one hand, because of encouragement on every side this practice became continual; and on the other hand, in many ways the god solidified and increased my strength. For he told me which of the ancients it was proper to study, I mean poets as well as the others, and he even fixed the period for which I was to use certain of them. And after that day they all appeared to me almost as comrades through the god's introduction.

(25) Indeed the greatest and most valuable part of my training was my access to and communion with these dreams. *For I heard many things which excelled in purity of style and were gloriously beyond my models,*[42] *and I dreamed that I myself said many things better than my wont,*

and things of which I had never thought. As many of these as I remembered, I put in the copies of my dreams, among which is the speech given *In Defense of Running,* when he commanded me to practice running, and there are many other things. And there is scattered in our books a speech in praise of *Athena* and *Dionysus,*[43] and of others, according to the circumstance. (26) Many problems[44] also came up, and it was shown how it was necessary to handle them in general, apart from phrases which were carefully remembered.[45] There was also the technique of unseen preparation,[46] which led to improvement. For I had to arise fully stimulated and prepared to speak, from the night before, just like the athlete who works out at dawn. Once even the following command came, *to weave a speech through mere thought, just as we do through phrases, and it was clear to me that the god was introducing thoughtfulness.* Therefore as to the state of our oratory, to speak by his grace, even if for the most part it was not especially despicable before, we ourselves were aware and it was recognized by those acquainted with the facts, that it was continually developing. (27) And once that famous Pardalas,[47] who, I would say, was the greatest expert of the Greeks of our time in the science of oratory, dared to say and affirm to me that he believed that I had become ill through some divine good fortune,[48] so that by my association with the god, I might make this improvement.[49] But it lies outside my plan and intention to tell of the many other things, which either he was accustomed to say in praise of our speeches, or the best and most distinguished of the other elderly men of those times.

(28) But I wish to speak of a dream. *I dreamed that I was at the estate where I was raised. Rufinus*[50] *was present, to whose generosity are due the great offerings at Pergamum and the Temple with the many cult statues.*[51] *Then after other warm greetings he said aloud, "If so and so, the 'Declamator', were alive, where would he be now"?* For he used this expression,[52] meaning *"the chorus leader of our age".*[53] *And I comprehended what he meant and said to Bassus,*[54] *"Here! Do you see what the god says about me, that is Rufinus?"*

(29) But the god also ordered me to compose speeches, not only to contend extemporaneously, and besides sometimes to learn them word for word. And the matter afforded me much difficulty, for neither was I at all able to conceive of any of the things which were to follow, nor could I trust his purpose. Indeed, in these circumstances—how could I have so much ease?—first I had to be

saved.⁵⁵ Yet, as it seems, these were contrivances of his for the present moment, but at the same time he had better plans than salvation alone. Therefore he saved me by means worth more than the act of being saved.

170/171 A.D. (30) And once I happened to have a toothache,⁵⁶ and I was unable to open my mouth, and I was in terrible difficulty. *But he commanded me to summon a gathering of my friends and to read to them one of the speeches which I had written.* Then I had in hand the third of my speeches to him.⁵⁷ I read this through, and before I had completed all of it, I was rid of the pain.

July 13
144 A.D. (31) He also urged me to the composition of lyric poetry.⁵⁸ I began composing in Rome on account of Apollo. *For I had a dream which declared that it was necessary to write a paean to the god, together with its beginning. And it was something like this:*

"*I shall praise Paean, king of the lyre*".⁵⁹

I was at a loss as to what I should do, for I had no previous experience in these matters. I thought that it was absolutely impossible. Nevertheless I tried. And with a firm hold on the beginning, as it were the first step of the ladder, I finished the song in two strophes, and I added, I think, a third, which the grammarians, I believe, call an epode.⁶⁰ And just when the song was completed, someone announced to me that it was the feast of Apollo, the Apollonia,⁶¹ in which the Romans have chariot racing for the god.

c. September
30 144 A.D. (32) So much for this. And when we were carried back from Greece,⁶² during stormy weather, by some divine good fortune, first we got safely to Delus, then to Miletus, both places sacred to Apollo. The following is also worthy to attribute to Delian Apollo, the Savior, since we have come to this point in our tale. (33) For when I disembarked at Delus, I was angry at the helmsman who was crazy and sailed against the winds, and acted as if he were on dry land.⁶³ Immediately I swore that I would not set sail for two days. "But if he wanted to, let him sail", I said, "by himself"⁶⁴. (34) And when I had sacrificed to the god and spent as much time as I could at the Temple, I went to my room and instructed the servants, that if someone came from the ship, they should tell him to go away,⁶⁵ and I rested in the harbor of Delus. But the sailors came, "heavy with wine",⁶⁶ at about the beginning of night, and stood by the door and knocked, and told me to come out and set sail, for it was an excellent time to depart. When the slaves answered that they were talking nonsense and that I would not move for any

reason, they departed in anger, as if they were being greatly inconvenienced. (35) Cock crow was near, when an extraordinary hurricane broke out, and the sea was stirred up by a fierce whirlwind, and everything was deluged, and some of the small ships in the harbor were cast up on land, and others collided and were crushed. The merchant ship, which was carrying us, had its cables broken, and was tossed up and down, and with much shouting and confusion on the part of the sailors was scarcely saved. And besides there was a great and violent rain storm, and the confusion on the island was the same as on a ship. (36) At dawn, my friends, whom I happened to have taken along on the voyage at my own expense, came in haste, calling me "Benefactor and Savior", and congratulating me for the providence of the gods. The sailors also came, grateful, and marveling at the nature of the impending evils from which they had been saved. So great was the gain and profit of my song,[67] just as they say it befell to Simonides to be saved alone by the Dioscuri for the hymns which he had written to them,[68] except that then not only we, but also our friends were saved with us. (37) Let it be, however one wishes, whether this was the reward and thanks for the paean and through this salvation occurred, or this in any case would have happened so, but the god, in his providence, gave a sign for everything which was going to take place, on the one hand, that dangers would befall on the sea and salvation from these, and on the other hand, that he himself would be the healer[69] of my body's troubles, as well as the first of his sons,[70] who knows how to stop all things of which men are sick.

(38) Tale follows tale,[71] and let us say again that along with other things, Asclepius, the Savior, also commanded us to spend time on songs and lyric verse, and to relax and maintain a chorus of boys.[72] There would be no end of saying in how many other ways we benefited from this advice in contentment and self-sufficiency. But the children sang my songs; and whenever I happened to choke, if my throat were suddenly constricted, or my stomach became disordered, or whenever I had some other troublesome attack, the doctor Theodotus,[73] being in attendance and remembering my dreams, used to order the boys to sing some of my lyric verse. And while they were singing, there arose unnoticed a feeling of comfort, and sometimes everything which pained me went completely away.

145 A.D. to 146 A.D.

(39) And this was a very great gain, and the honor which I received was still greater than this, for my lyric verse also found favor with the god. He ordered me to compose not only for him, but also indicated others, as Pan, Hecate, the Achelous, and whatever else it might be. There also came a dream from Athena, *which contained a hymn to the goddess, and the following beginning,*

"*Young men come to Pergamum*".

And another from Dionysus, where the refrain was,

"*Hail King, ivy crowned*".

While this was sung in my sleep, a marvelous sound also flowed about my ears. And I had to bend my right knee, and to supplicate and call the god "the Deliverer".[74] And these things are in the copies of my songs.

(40) And another dream came from Zeus himself, but I cannot remember which of these was first or second, and another again from Dionysus, *which said to address the god, as "curly haired".*

Hermes was also seen with his dog skin cap, and he was marvelously handsome and extraordinarily mobile. And while I was singing of him and feeling pleased that I had easily said the proper things, I awoke.

(41) *Concerning the goddesses of Smyrna,*[75] *I also thought that I heard, I believe, from my foster father*[76] *that I happened not rightly to have neglected them, for it was fitting to take the trouble to write a hymn also for these.*

But most things were written for Apollo and Asclepius through the inspiration of my dreams, and many of these more or less from what I recollected of my dreams,[77] as whenever I was riding in a carriage, or even was walking.

(42) And a Macedonian man, one of my fellow pilgrims, had a dream[78]—as Theodotus reported to me, for he himself was not an acquaintance of mine—, which pertained directly to me. He dreamed that he sang a paean of mine, in which there was the invocation, 'Hail Paean, Heracles Asclepius'. And so I offered the paean in common to both gods.

August
147 A.D.

(43) And I also gave public choral performances,[79] ten in all, some of boys and some of men. And the following took place, when I was going to bring on the first chorus. Rufinus,[80] whom I mentioned a little before, was in the Temple. Seeing him, I said, "You have come at the right moment, if you also have some spare time. For I am going to give a choral performance for the god, and it is clear that you will hear it for our sake". "But it is not necessary", he said, "for me to be invited by you, but I have been already invited by the god. Judge", he said, "even by the hour. For formerly

I never arrived so early, but I was accustomed to come much later. But I have been invited", he said, "for this reason and fortunately at that, and we shall stand by your side", meaning himself and Sedatius,[81] who was our fellow pilgrim then. (44) And this took place at my first staging of the chorus. Again after the completion of the tenth performance, in which I happened to have omitted some song, because it was written entirely impromptu, with little thought,[82] and, as they say, "almost only for itself",[83] *a dream came, which demanded this too,* and we also offered it. (45) When these things were accomplished, it seemed fitting to dedicate a silver tripod, as a thank offering to the god, and at the same time as a memorial of the choral performances which we gave. And I prepared the following elegiac couplet:

"The poet, judge, and backer too,
Has dedicated to you, O King, this monument of his choral performance".

Then after this there were two other verses, one of which contained my name, and the other that these things occurred under the patronage of the god. But the god's version prevailed. For on the day, I believe, on which it was necessary to make the dedication, or a little before it, around dawn, or even still sooner, a divinely inspired inscription came to me, which ran as follows:

"Not unknown to the Greeks, Aristides dedicated this,
The glorious charioteer of everlasting words".

And I dreamed that I had this inscribed and that I was going to make the dedication, as it were, to Zeus. I immediately held fast to the inscription, as I rejoiced in my sleep and while I was still waking. And I practiced it and studied it, that it might not slip my mind. And so I mastered it.[84] (46) After this, when we took counsel in common about the dedication, it seemed best to us, the priest and the temple wardens, to dedicate it in the Temple of Zeus Asclepius,[85] for there was no fairer place than this. And so the prophecy of the dream turned out. And the tripod is under the right hand of the god, and it has three golden statues, one on each foot, of Asclepius, of Hygieia, and of Telesphorus. And the inscription is inscribed, and it has been added that it is from a dream. I also dedicated to Olympian Zeus the inscription and another dedication, so that the oracle was in every way fulfilled. (47) After the inscription, I became much more eager, and it seemed in every way to be fitting to keep on with oratory, as our name would live even among future men, since the god happened to have called our speeches "everlasting".

(48) And so took place the matter of the choral performances. A little later, I do not know how much, I had the following vision. *I dreamed that I was at the hearth of the Temple of the Ancestral Olympian Zeus. When there was a public assembly at forenoon, the sacred herald stood right by the base of the god's statue and called out my name with all of its adjuncts,*[86] *as if I were being publicly crowned, as when in the assemblies we are crowned with a golden crown, and he added, "because of his speeches". He confirmed this by another addition, saying besides, "For he is invincible in oratory". (49) When this was proclaimed, I crossed over to the garden of Asclepius, which lies before my ancestral home. And here I found, on the right of the Temple, a common tomb for me and Alexander,*[87] *the son of Philip, which was separated by a partition in the middle. And he lay on one side, and I would lie on the other. Standing there and bending forward, I enjoyed the wonderfully sweet smell of incense, and some of this belonged to his tomb, and some was set aside for me as well. I rejoiced and conjectured that we both had reached the top of our professions, he in military and I in oratorical power. And in addition, it also occurred to me, that this man was very important in Pella, and that those here would be proud of me. I thought that I heard and saw such things, and that I spoke to myself and calculated some of these things by the statue of Zeus, and some in the Temple of Asclepius before my house.* (50) As to what comes next, if it is fitting, let it be said and written, and if not, may you be fully concerned, Lord Asclepius, to prompt me to describe it without causing any disagreeableness. *First the cult statue appeared to have three heads*[88] *and to shine about with fire, except for the heads. Next we worshippers stood by it, just as when the paean is sung, I almost among the first. At this point, the god, in the posture in which he is represented in his statues, signaled our departure. All the others were going out, and I was turning to go out, and the god, with his hand, indicated for me to stay. And I was delighted by the honor and the extent to which I was preferred to the others, and I shouted out, "The One", meaning the god. But he said, "It is you".*[89] (51) For me this remark, Lord Asclepius, was greater than life itself, and every disease was less than this, every grace was less than this. This made me able and willing to live. And now that we have said these things, may we have no less honor than before from the god.

(52) Once I heard the following tale, which pertained to oratory and divine communion.[90] *He said that it was fitting that my mind be changed from its present condition, and having been changed, associate with god, and by its association be superior to man's estate, and that neither was remarkable, either by associating with god, to be superior, or being superior, to associate with god.*

(53) And the name Theodorus[91] was given to me in the following manner. *I thought that I had been addressed, as it were, by someone in Smyrna, who heartily congratulated me, "Hail Theodorus". And, I think, "Asiarch"*[92] *was added to his salutation. I accepted the title, since everything of mine was a gift of the god.* (54) After this, another dream occurred as follows. It was Epagathus,[93] one of my foster fathers, who first raised me. He was a very good man, and was most clearly in communion with the gods, and related from memory whole oracles from his dreams. They came to pass almost one might say, on the same day. Such a man was Epagathus. The dream was as follows. *This man seemed to me, either when I asked him, or even moved by himself, to tell me that he had the following dream. "The Mother of the gods*[94] *will care about Theodorus". And I, understanding, said, "It is likely that the Mother of the gods holds the same opinion concerning me as Asclepius does. For first from that source I received the name 'Theodorus' ".*

(55) The god also gave me a demonstration of his nature, partly by sight, partly also by word.[95] It was as follows. The morning star had risen, when the dream occurred. *I dreamed that I was walking on a certain road through my estate, and was gazing at the star which had just now appeared, for my path was towards the east. Pyrallianus,*[96] *from the Temple, a man who was a comrade of ours and one highly trained in Plato's dialogues, was present.* (56) *Jesting and bantering with him, as it were on a leisurely walk, I said, "Can you tell me by the gods—we are entirely alone—why you Platonists put on this mummery and shock men?"* This remark of mine was in reference to Plato's dialogues about nature and being. *And he ordered me to pay attention and walk behind him. Then he led and I followed. And having gone a little ways, he held up his hand and showed me a certain place in heaven. And at the same time as he showed it, he said, "This, as far as you are concerned, is what Plato calls the soul of the Universe".*[97] *I looked up and I saw Asclepius of Pergamum established in heaven. And just after this, I woke up, and I perceived that it was the very hour, in which I dreamed that I saw these things.*[98]

(57) Furthermore I remember the following other dreams.[99] *I dreamed that I saw Plato himself standing in my room, directly across from my bed and me. He happened to be working on his letter to Dionysius,*[100] *and was very angry. He glanced at me and said, "How suited do I appear to you for letter writing? No worse than Celer?"—meaning the Imperial Secretary.*[101] *And I said, "Hush! Great as you are to be thinking about what kind of man you are!"*[102] *And not much later, he disappeared, and I was held in meditation. But someone present said, "This man who spoke with you just now as*

January 148 A.D.

Plato is your Hermes*", —meaning him to whom has been allotted my nativity.*[103] *"But"*, he said, *"he has been made to look like Plato".*

c. autumn
147 A.D.

(58) I had this dream in Smyrna, but another somewhat before this in Pergamum.[104] *Whoever it was who gave the reason, gave the planet Jupiter as the reason for these dreams and the manifest care of the gods. For he said that it split the mid-degree of the midst of heaven, when I was born.* And moreover the astrologers say that Leo was then in the midst of heaven and Jupiter was beneath Leo and in quartile dexter aspect to Mercury, both planets oriental.[105]

(59) It came about that I beheld nearly all the other ancients who were most famous in literature, both prose writers and poets alike. The affair of Lysias is also worthy of telling. I was sick with a very grave tertian fever, and *I saw the orator Lysias, a not ungracious youth.* The day of the attack came, and the fever did not occur, but at this time the disease was ended.[106]

(60) *And once I thought that the poet Sophocles came to my house. When he came, he stood before the room where I happened to be living. And while he stood there in silence, his lips of their own accord sounded as sweetly as possible. His whole appearance was that of a handsome old man.* (61) *I was glad to see him, and rising, I welcomed him, and asked: "Where is your brother?" And he said, "Have I any brother?" "It is Aeschylus"*, I said, and at the same time I went out with him. And when we appeared to be at the front door, one of the very distinguished sophists of our time slipped and lay to the left a little apart from the door.

(62) We saw others of different appearance and form, dignified and familiar, on various occasions. The following also contributed to my high spirits. *When, in my dream, I was giving an oratorical display and was winning much approval, and someone of my audience said in praise, "Just as so and so", whom he admired most of the ancients, I dreamed that my teacher,*[107] *who was present, grew fidgety and said, "Will you not also add such and such?" And he intended next to mention others, since no one man should be compared to me.*

September
153 A.D. to
September
154 A.D.

(63) And I had determined, when I had said these things, to bring my speech on this subject to an end,[108] but another wonderful thing has occurred to me, if any other, worthy of no little thanks to the god. When the orator Quadratus[109] entered upon the governorship of Asia, I thought that it was opportune for me to address him especially since I had certain troubles from former times, which will be told immediately.[110] And I wrote to him, and made it clear who I was, and what was my profession. (64) On the day in which he

was going to receive my letter—for we learned this later from reports, but it was also possible to reach this conclusion right away by calculating the days—, *it seemed to me that he who is still the present priest of Asclepius[111] and this man's grandfather, in whose time, as we have learned, the god performed many great operations[112]—and he is still the most distinguished of all up to the present[113]—, these men seemed to me to enter the residence of Quadratus, and to be closeted with him, the one sitting by his side, and the elder sitting at the head of his very bed.*[114] (65) *They recommended me to Quadratus with great zeal, and among other kind remarks, they told how the elder priest was taken with my speeches, and these also had to be praised to Quadratus. "Concerning the speeches"—, he said, somehow stressing this word and pausing deliberately, since he especially intended to interest him in what was going to be said next. But while he was still going to praise my speeches extravagantly, Quadratus interrupted him and said, "Will you quote the proverb, 'One must marry such a woman or not marry at all'?"*[115] *Some such things were said on either side.* (66) *After this, I dreamed that they departed, and that I went out with them. And when we reached the postern gate, where the turn off to the Temple is, they went straight to the Temple, but taking my leave, I shook their hands and thanked them, because they honored me in every way and were much concerned with my affairs.* (67) As to how the letter won immediate approval, since it was read by the governor himself to everybody, and everyone fought to get it, and what he replied to it, and what he did in conclusion when he left office, if one recounted this, he would seem to be boasting, because of the excessive praise which was involved; and in another way, it would be a kind of pettiness to linger over these things, after the honors given by the gods. But in this way, indeed, took place that which pertained to the present subject.

(68) And these things happened in former times. But when I had reached this part of the speech, and I intended to turn to the other benefactions of the god and to write in order those which occurred under other governors and other circumstances, in the midst of composing, I had a dream, which pertained somehow again to these things.[116] (69) It was as follows: *I thought that I was giving an oratorical display and spoke among certain people, and in the midst of the speech with which I contended, I called on the god in this way: "Lord Asclepius, if in fact I excel in oratory and excel much, grant me health and cause the envious to burst". I happened to have seen these things in the dream, and when it was day, I took up some book and read it. In it I found what I had said. In wonder, I said to Zosimus,*[117] *"Behold, what I dreamed that I*

170/171 A.D.

said, I find written in the book". Thus even these new things have been added to the old. If we have understood the god's intent, he himself would know best.

(70) As to the practice of oratory, how he brought us to it in the beginning, and what was his verdict about our career, and all the oracles which he gave pertaining to this, and how he added "Theodorus" to my old name, and what sort of things he revealed concerning his nature, and as much as there is of this character, not nearly all has been said, but as much as was ringing in my ears, and from which it is possible to conjecture about the rest.

January
153 A.D.

(71) I shall return to where a little before,[118] I said that I would stop and abandon my tale, so that I may tell of how he clearly gave me other signs and performed other deeds, and was in every way my protector.[119] Severus[120] ruled as governor of Asia, I think, a year before our comrade.[121] He was a man proud in his ways, and he would not concede to anyone whatever he had decided and approved. While I was staying at the Aesepus[122] and again at the Temple of Zeus,[123] he did the following. (72) In those times there was sent to the governors from each city each year the names of the ten leading men. The governor had to examine these and appoint one, whomever he approved, from each group, as police commissioner.[124] From a town in Mysia,[125] whose name I have no need to say, the names, which had been selected, reached him. (73) As yet knowing nothing certain of my affairs, except that he had heard that I had possessions in this place, and, I suppose, that my other rank was not undistinguished, he ignored and dishonored all the names which had been sent, and chose me to hold office, and considered neither that it had been Smyrna's right to submit my name long before the others had hopes of being a city, nor that our circumstances were wholly different.[126] And he sent a letter to the officials of the city, but did not address it to them, but to me. They came and gave it to me. The letter ordered me "to take charge of the peace". (74) I was in great difficulty. For it was possible neither to appeal the case, since there was no open legal adversary, but it was the governor himself who had proposed the name and confirmed it, nor to find with whom one might contend,[127] or against whom, and how one might arrange the matter. But this alone seemed best to us and the officials when we took counsel together, to make an appeal, as it were, against the officials themselves who gave me the letter. (75) Evening came, and I

asked the god what all this meant, and what should be done. And I received the verse from Delphi:

"*These things will be a care to me and the white maidens*".[128]

How was this fulfilled? Not many days later, letters[129] came to me from Italy, from the Imperial family, the Emperor himself and his son,[130] which praised me in other ways and confirmed to me immunity because of my oratorical career, provided that I happened to be practicing it.[131] I also received, together with the Imperial letters, letters from Heliodorus, who had been Prefect of Egypt,[132] one for me myself and another on my behalf to the governor. They were very splendid and ennobling, and had been written much before this need, but arrived then opportunely. (76) I immediately referred "the white maidens" to the letters. Although heartened by the oracle and by this chance occurrence, I was unable to move since the god restrained me,[133] but I sent a letter to the governor, and made clear the nature of this whole affair of mine, and that those who told him my name seemed in every way to say nothing more than the name. I made clear who they were who exempted me,[134] and the letters which had newly arrived. At the same time, together with my own letter, I also sent these, both the ones of recommendation and of exemption.

(77) While the matter was still pending, all sorts of orders kept coming from the notaries, as many as seemed to be friendly toward me, and at the same time to see correctly the necessities. For they pointed out the great power of the man, and that he was one of the Imperial judges,[135] and especially his tenacity and strength of purpose, and that for no reason would he change whatever he had once approved. And they begged me not to offend him in vain. I also intentionally wrote to them rather long and audacious letters, since I knew well that these would fall into Severus' hands, for I heard that they were rather close to him. But the principal argument, which I also wrote to him, was that they requested impossible things.

(78) After this,[136] Severus went down from the Upper Districts to Ephesus,[137] to hold the assizes. When he had read my letters, he commanded me to appear there. But I sent others. When the appointed day arrived, and my name was called, the city attorneys[138] approached. And before they even spoke, Severus said: "I have long known of Aristides, and I marvel at his reputation, and I agree that he holds the first place in oratory, and these things have also been written to me by my friends in Rome. I ask him", he said, "to

February 153 A.D.

share in my administration. But I also confirm to him the rights of immunity, and they remain in force". He said these things publicly. He inscribed them in the minutes. (79) When the judgment turned out thus, those whom I had sent for the suit, on the one hand, believed that they had accomplished something and that they returned not completely without results, as it seems, since the city attorneys offered congratulations for this honor and the others made much of the fact that Severus said that he did these things in the measure of a request and that he confirmed the immunity for all future time for me, and at that when I was absent. And, on the other hand, they did not know how it was proper to make the appeal, when a man was not imposing the office by right of judicial authority, but, as it were, asking a favor and beginning thereby a sort of friendship. But having acquiesced in the present circumstances, they returned to me and recounted the whole affair.

Meanwhile the day fixed for the appeal also passed. (80) We were still worse off than before, for I was not satisfied to have received empty honors. Again I solicited the god, and asked and inquired how one should handle this matter. And he gave to me a very wonderful dream, the particulars of which I would not be able to tell, but the sum of it, as it were, was as follows. (81) *I dreamed that I spoke to the clerk of the governor about these things. He had come to me. When he had heard everything, he promised that he would undo and change the verdict, and he ordered me to pay about five hundred drachmas.* (82) When I had had the dream, in one way I became happier, because there appeared to be some kind of promise in it, and there was no outright refusal. But in another way, it seemed to me to incline to the same thing as a refusal. For how would someone buy off so great a matter for five hundred drachmas, and at that from a man so incorruptible, that one might sooner stay the flow of the rivers than bribe him, a man again so clever in affairs, and who would least of all be deceived? The promise seemed to be a refusal, for it lacked any possibility. (83) I was troubled by these things.

Meanwhile the god called me again to Pergamum, and Rufinus[139] happened to be in town. It was his care to honor us as much as he was able. Meeting him, I recounted what had been done and I asked him to help. I said that even Severus himself had fully agreed that my immunity was legal. But the written verdict was not enough. For it would be possible for every other governor to command some different thing of me, with this same clause, and so the immunity would be undone through the addition of "it remains in force".[140] I wanted not a specious phrase, but the thing itself. For such was my physical condition.[141] (84) I seemed to Rufinus to speak justly, and he gave me a letter to Severus, which he had written in his own tongue[142] as zealously as possible, and in which after a review of other matters, with some recommendations and some advice, he hinted concerning the future, what would happen if he would not willingly exempt me.

(85) To conclude,[143] we arrived at Smyrna, at the Dionysia,[144] and Severus was present for the festival. There was a certain one of those called legates[145] who was in other respects remarkably close to him and was almost like his secretary. For he had authority over all correspondence. And then since we met him first, for he was in charge of the assize district at Smyrna,[146] we showed the letter to him. (86) And I told him everything, as much as it was necessary to say in an oral presentation, so that he might know and inform the governor exactly. And when I saw that he accepted my arguments and was swayed to my rights, I remembered the voice in the dream, how the secretary promised that he would aid me. And I recounted the dream itself to him and I asked him to obey the god, for I said that this man was the man who promised, meaning him. He was pleased by the speech, brought us to the governor, and joined us in giving him the letter. (87) And while he was still reading it, it was clear that he tried various shifts and in many parts of the letter stopped and turned back. Now Pardalas,[147] who was our comrade and a close friend of his from childhood, had written many laudatory things to him about my oratorical career, and when he also received this letter and went over both, "No one", he said, "is investigating oratory, but it is one thing to be first of the Greeks and supreme in oratory"—for so he called me,—" and another to be engaged in this and have pupils". And pausing a little, he said, "Go to the Council and persuade the citizens".[148] And at the same time he encouraged and advised me someday to accept young men as pupils. And I answered only that I had no need of a request, but the god had sent me for this very purpose, so that I must obey.

(88) Such was the beginning and state of the affair, and my first appearance after the judgment which was given at Ephesus. When the matter was still pending,[149] a second difficulty took place which was as follows. Before I came to the Council and there was any discussion about these things, the Council, at the suggestion of two

March 3
153 A.D.

July
153 A.D.

or three men, proposed me as a prytanis—the election for them was held at that time.[150] And the affair had taken a strange turn. For instead of persuading them of that for which the governor had sent me, I was compelled again to appeal from them to the governor's court, and there were now two suits instead of one, and the judge was the same as in the beginning.

August
153 A.D.

(89) And we went to Pergamum.[151] To be brief, none of us knew when the suit would be called. For the day had not been announced. But a dream, which came at dawn, declared this much:

"Citizens of Cadmus, it is necessary to say timely things".[152]

It was immediately clear that it would be necessary to contend, and so I prepared myself. And not much later someone came and reported that my name was now being called. (90) While I was going down from the Temple to the city, when there was a delay and my name was called again, they said that Severus remarked very courteously that I would come and that there was no need to be impatient. And after this, when he saw me drawing near, he immediately sent his lictors to make my approach easy—for I had earlier requested this of him. (91) And when I came forward, I received all due respect from him and from the ranks of the assessors, as well as from the pleaders who stood by, and from all the others who were present, and there was more of the air of an oratorical display than of a lawsuit. For their goodwill was wonderful, and then they signified their eagerness for my speech both by their hands and voices, and they behaved entirely like an audience at a lecture. (92) Five measures of the water clock[153] were used up, and I spoke rather freely[154] and insinuated how one would behave while making this speech in the presence of the Emperor. Then after one of the attorneys from the city[155] appeared briefly and deferentially against us, finally Severus, out of respect for the Council and in the belief that it would make no difference to me and that this was the best judgment, sent me again to the Council with an honorable letter. (93) And it befell to me not only to have my immunity confirmed, but with such great honor and pomp, that I seemed to share this privilege with no one else. He did not even mention to me the other office[156] to which he himself nominated me, nor did we to him, but he wrote of his own accord to the officials[157] and ordered them to appoint another instead of me.

(94) Thus the god's prediction was fulfilled. And when I calculated what had been spent, both as fees for the notaries and as

travel money for my servants, if I sent any somewhere because of these matters, the five hundred drachmas somehow just about tallied.[158]

Again something similar happened nearly a year before these things,[159] when Pollio was governor of Asia.[160] (95) I had just now gone to the Council Chamber, after a long rest, as I said,[161] since the god was encouraging me in oratory. All were in hopes that I would now also teach the young. The wretched sophists were dying with fear, not all, but those who had the sense to be distressed.[162] (96) I was chosen tax collector.[163] The matter came to the legate. He confirmed the election, in my absence, in the courts in Philadelphia. After this, the legate's judgment was read in the Council. And an appeal was made by us to Rome,[164] and letters were sent—what they said can be imagined—to Pollio himself and to the legate. (97) But the god gave the following sign. *I dreamed that my steward Alcimus,*[165] *whom I had sent for this purpose, returned and brought me Demosthenes' oration* On the Crown, *which was not as now, but otherwise and differently composed. And again there were promises, that the famous Glabrio*[166] *would lend a hand in setting everything to rights.*[167] He happened then, I think, to be in town. I also received oracles from Sarapis and Isis. *They said that "the matter would be accomplished, and you will make friends with your enemies".* (98) And such, in summary, were the oracles and dreams. Those, whom I had sent, came to Philadelphia, and, as they said, it was a holiday when they presented my letters. But Pollio read them, and—when there was an opportunity and it was made clear by those present at the salutation what Festus, the former governor, had once decided about us[168]—recognizing the simplicity of the legate, he ordered him to come immediately, hold court and correct his judgment. The legate did this and convened his court for this single purpose and gave another letter to the Council. (99) When this was dispatched, the President,[169] who had opposed me with the utmost vigor and had read out the opposite decree before, being disturbed and frightened, sent to the governor's staff[170] to inquire about the letter. But they gave no answer. He came to me and begged my pardon. And I went to the Council, was exempted from the service, and obtained immunity. First then, and afterwards, the President became a very dear friend, and the legate himself a very dear friend.

July 152 A.D.

338   L. THE SACRED TALES: IV

September 23 147 A.D.

(100) Come now, as if we were ever ascending a ladder, let us recall another of the things before this.[171] Festus,[172] whom I mentioned a little before,[173] was governor. When the year began[174] and the first assembly was being held, men came from the People to summon me, since I had come[175] after a long time; and at the same time they announced that they intended to sacrifice publicly on my behalf, which they had also done many times before. (101) When I had entered the Assembly and the People shouted their customary approval, those, who had prepared themselves, went to work, applauding and offering me the common priesthood of Asia,[176] and they won over the People without any difficulty. And at the same time, the officials stood about me, each from a different place praising me and shouting out and vying with the people in their request. But I had had from my dreams clear and manifest signs, in which I was thoroughly confident. (102) Having asked the right to speak, I was so persuasive that the People gave up this demand, but they unanimously voted me with great pleasure the priesthood of Asclepius. The temple at the outer harbor was then still under construction.[177] And I know that I found approval with my reply. For I said that it was impossible for me to do anything, either important or trifling, without the god, and therefore it was not possible to think even of serving as a priest, until I had inquired about this from the god himself. They marveled and yielded. When this took place, my speeches were much esteemed and provoked excitement, and I thought that I no longer need be troubled. But the god—surely you do not think that the matter ended here?—had "a concealed dagger".[178]

January 1 148 A.D.

(103) And it happened after this,[179] that the delegates of Smyrna[180] went to Upper Phrygia[181] and intended to nominate me in the Provincial Assembly, but that I got wind of it in advance and sent my foster father Zosimus.[182] And I was elected in the third or fourth place.[183]

After this, there was an appeal, a summons of the governor, and a summons of the Savior to Pergamum.

August 148 A.D.

During this time I was staying at the estate where I usually live,[184] since he had sent me there. (104) On the day after I had started out, a man, who was bringing the governor's letter, met me. And when I had read the letter, I said, "But I have been summoned first by the god, and you rouse a running man".[185] What need is there to be long? I was exempted from all troubles. I did not take my turn as high priest of Asia, but I have never stopped being a worshipper in the precinct of the temples in the shrine of Asclepius.[186] So the governor was disposed toward us, but no more, I think, than he, who is truly and forever governor.[187]

(105) Similar to this was that which happened first of all these things.[188] Laneion, which I also mentioned in the tales above,[189] is an estate not far from the Temple of Zeus. After my people had purchased this estate for me, during my stay in Egypt,[190] certain Mysians, first saying and next even doing many different things, tried to appropriate it. When they despaired, not to slander myself,[191] they gathered together as many servants and hired men as they could, and attacked, armed with every weapon. Then some of them from a distance tossed and cast stones and clods, and some joined in hand to hand combat, some took possession of the house and treated the contents, as if they belonged to them. Everything was full of confusion and wounds.

August 146 A.D.

(106) When these things had been reported in Pergamum, my physical condition was such that I could scarcely breathe. The assizes were being held, but I was at a loss as to what I should do. However, the god found me admittance to the governor and provided an opportunity. And the last of my dreams was *the Emperor Hadrian in the court of the Temple,*[192] *honoring me, who had just now become acquainted with him, and offering great hopes.* The following happened right after this vision. (107) I went to the Temple, as best I could. And while I was still lingering there, the governor Julianus[193] arrived and with him Rufinus.[194] Recognizing the opportunity, I told my troubles to Rufinus, and approached Julianus, who turned around, somehow in the very place, which I saw in the dream. And I said as much as I had the opportunity to, and Rufinus was not wanting in zeal. But the governor became so possessed, that he immediately embraced me, as if he were an old, close friend. And taking me by the hand, he told me to have courage and to attend to the god, but that these things would be his concern. And finally, he declared, "They will not scorn us". (108) He arrived at the court, and when he had called the suit and not many words had been spoken, he grew angry over what had happened and even threw into jail one of those who had participated in the attack. And he adjudged the estate to us, and we entered into it under court order. Armed men, slingers, all those things yielded to the god.

LI. THE SACRED TALES: V[1]

August
165 A.D.

(1) In summer time,[2] my stomach was upset, and I was thirsty night and day, and perspired unspeakably, and my body was weak, and scarcely would two or three men drag me from my bed, when I desired to get up. And while I was in Smyrna during this time, *the god indicated a journey to me.* And I had to leave immediately. And we went out on the road to Pergamum. (2) While the carriages were being got together, noon arrived and a clear, burning heat arose. We decided to stay in the suburbs and so pàss the very peak of the heat. We started out for Myrina, and the pack animals preceded us here. But since the weather was stifling, and at the same time the place was delightful and we had certain business matters besides, we wasted a great part of the day, so that at sunset we only reached an inn before the Hermus. (3) And I was at a loss at to what to do. Since on entering I did not endure the disagreeableness of the rooms, and my servants were not present because I had sent them ahead, it seemed fitting to push on. And now that I had crossed the river,[3] the night was clear, and a light and cool breeze struck me, and somehow my body recovered and my will power was imbued by a certain energy and contentment, and I found the weather pleasant, and at the same time contrasted how different the present circumstances were from the day past.

(4) In the depths of evening, I came to Larissa, and I was happy to find that I had not caught up with the carriages and that the conditions of the inn were no better than those before, but that it remained necessary to hold to the road and persevere. And it was midnight or still a little later, and we reached Cyme, and everything was closed, which was satisfactory as far as I was concerned. (5) Exhorting my attendants, who were escorting me from my estate, to endure also the remaining distance, since everything would not be closed to them, and saying that it was very brief and it was not a little better not to seem to go astray from my plan, I went out of the gates, and the cold was damper, so that I required some means of warmth.

And reaching Myrina, at about cock crow, I saw my people before one of the inns, still packed up for the journey, because, as they said, they did not find anything open. (6) There was a small couch at the entrance of the inn. We passed the time moving this all over. For no matter where it was put, it was everywhere uncomfortable. There was no profit in knocking on the doors, either of friends or of any one at all. For no one answered. It was late when finally we found means of getting into the house of an acquaintance, but through the evil genius of the doorkeepers the fire went out and there was no other, either small or great. We entered in darkness, and were led by the hand, neither seeing nor being seen. (7) While the fire was being brought and after it had been brought, I intended to anoint myself and to drink, and then the morning star arose and there shone forth the light of day. I thought it best not to be soft and sleep, when it was day, but to pile work on work,[4] and to walk to the Temple of Apollo, to Gryneion, as it was my custom to sacrifice to the god, both when I went and when I returned.

(8) When I reached Gryneion, having sacrificed to Apollo and spent my time as usual, I came to Elaea and rested. And when I reached Pergamum on the following day, my intention was, as can be imagined, to delay there, but a dream came, whether right at that evening or a day or two later, *and ordered me to press on and not to do otherwise. "For they are in pursuit"*. And with this, the window shutters, which were very well closed, both inside and out, opened in a gust of wind, which had never happened before, and the doors creaked. When I awoke, I no longer lingered, but telling the servants to follow, I got in my carriage and drove the length of the journey. (9) And the northwind pressed hard, stirring up everything. During this time, my throat troubled me, for it was pressed by a persistent lesion[5] and was torn by everything which came in contact with it. Then although much sand was blown in my face by the wind and clouds of dust fell thickly from all sides, it happened that I was no more anxious than I was confident, partly, as it were, through a certain desperation and obstinance—for there was no escape—and partly since I was enduring contrary to all likelihood. The doctors before ordered gargling and prescribed very careful covering and such things. (10) On the second or third day, I passed by my ancestral home and reached the Temple of Olympian Zeus. And I sacrificed, before I ended my journey, just as it was even foretold to me right at the start in Smyrna, *to go straight to the land of Zeus*. And after this, my way of life was manifestly more comfortable.

late summer
166 A.D.

(11) After a little under a year and a month,[6] the Cyzicenes celebrated the Sacred Month[7] of the Temple. My sleep was troubled, and I could scarcely digest anything, although resting for a great part of the following day, but not sleeping. (12) Then when the dream came, it had long been day and I had got only as much sleep as to dream what I dreamed. It was as follows. *The doctor Porphyrio*[8] *seemed to me to come to the Cyzicenes and to say nearly the same things as Athena said to the Phaeacians,*[9] *extolling me and soliciting their attendance at my speech. They were persuaded. And at the same time there was a theater and I was in the theater. And there were some other things which pertained to this.* (13) I got up and told the servants to pack and to leave immediately. I rode out not much before noon. Since I was waiting for the servants, I proceeded rather leisurely, and some of the day was consumed in this. And in late afternoon, I reached the warm springs,[10] and the whole place was packed with a noisy multitude, so that it was impossible to find shelter, but I had to ride past. And by this time few followed me. (14) I proceeded forty stades[11] to some village, and as nothing there attracted me, I decided to make use of the night. I had determined to ride to Cyzicus itself, but my attendants— there were about two left—were exhausted, so that I was compelled to stop at the lake[12] one hundred and twenty stades[13] from the city. I had completed three hundred and twenty stades.[14] (15) I entered my room and found myself possessed of a small couch and a clean mattress, and I was glad for them, since I had nothing with me. I passed the night, sitting mostly on the couch, just as I was from the journey, thirsty and full of dust, in the clothes which I wore sitting in the carriage. When the stars were turning toward day, I got up and waiting for no one, I finished the trip.

(16) And my consolation for the journey was in giving my attention to the speech which I had to present to the Cyzicenes[15] in accordance with the prophecy of the dream, so that I even composed it in this way, always recalling the ideas which I had conceived during the trip. Those who were present, and those who heard about it from these, would know the enthusiasm which was shown toward my speech, not only when it was presented in the Council Chamber, but also later at the festival. But it is not so pleasant for me to linger over such things.

autumn
166 A.D.

(17) But when he commanded me to return,[16] by praising the water at Laneion,[17] almost as if sounding a refrain,[18] we returned somehow in nearly the same way both in the time of departure,

because then too we left on the same day as the command, and in the fact that the journey was uninterrupted. For without stopping or eating, I reached, a little before midnight, some farm of mine,[19] four hundred stades in all,[20] and on the next day from there Laneion. (18) And thus took place my first journey to Cyzicus and my stay there.

When winter came,[21] he led me again on the road to Smyrna, and the first day was very mild. On the following night, when I descended to the plain,[22] among other dreams which restrained me, *I dreamed that I was studying* The Clouds *of Aristophanes.*[23] And at dawn there were clouds and it rained not much later, so that some congratulated me because I had not gone on, and others marveled at the precision of the prophecy. (19) When I had remained here for some days, it was reported to me that the daughter of my foster sister[24] was ill and in a dangerous condition. I sent a doctor to her. But I myself, as soon as it was possible, held to the journey. And as I proceeded, the weather changed a little, as if it were going to rain and storm. And there was fear that we might be caught, especially when things were impassable. Nevertheless the weather held except for the last two stades[25] to the Temple of Apollo.[26] Then a deep mist descended and it drizzled a little, and by the time that we went into the Temple, it was raining heavily. Therefore we made it a holiday. Since my dreams also held me here, I remained.

December 166 A.D.

In addition to those which restrained me, I also had the following dream.[27] (20) *I dreamed that having immolated a sacrificial animal, I inspected what was called, I think, "the God and Deliverer".*[28] *And when one of the seers arrived, I asked what "Deliverer" meant, whether it delivered something once and for all, or made it smaller instead of greater, and was a sign of delay.*[29] *He seemed like one who did not at all have a very firm conviction as far as "once and for all" was concerned, but he laid the responsibility on the climate, stars, and such things.*[30]

December 27 166 A.D.

And at this time, it was announced that the girl had died. (21) It immediately seemed on hearing it that it was an act of god that I did not happen to be present at the misfortune, but had gone on ahead.[31] It became still clearer from later oracles that all this did not take place without some divine agency.

(22) For two nights after I descended from the mountain,[32] the following was seen—I had stayed for several days since the god continued to restrain me. *Telesphorus*[33] *was a muleteer. This man seemed to me, starting from there,*[34] *to come back and to report oracles which had been*

December 29 166 A.D.

given for Philumene, for this was the girl's name. He said that they had been given to Alcimus, the father of the girl. And he had a letter, either sealed or not, which he said that Alcimus, after he had heard about[35] *her at night, noted and copied down; and it was of marvelous length and power, and pertained to me, so that I wondered how he even noted it down.* (23) *But the sum was that all of Philumene's trouble had been inscribed on her very body and on her insides, as it were on the entrails of sacrificial animals. There also appeared rather a lot of the intestine,*[36] *and somehow at the same time I saw it. The upper parts were healthy and in good condition, but what was diseased was on the extreme lower end; and it was all exhibited by one who stood by, whoever he was. And indeed I asked him, "What causes my sluggishness and difficulty?"*[37] *He exhibited that place.* (24) *The oracles were somewhat as follows. My name had been inscribed in this way: "Aelius Aristides". And there was, more or less at intervals, different nominal devices. "Sosimenes"*[38] *had been added and other such names, which heralded safety and declared that Philumene had given a soul for a soul and a body for a body, hers for mine. And the other oracles which pertained to the same were in the dream, all written in certain books, all of which Alcimus wrote and Telesphorus seemed to carry back home.*[39] *There was also in it advice of the doctor Porphyrio,*[40] *as it were to her mother, particularly to bathe, but if not, at least to take nourishment.* (25) *The brother of this girl was that Hermias, who, when the goddess*[41] *also appeared to me, died in the great plague*[42] *and nearly, one might say, instead of me. For he died, as I later learned, on the same day as I was freed of a fever, and at that one of very long duration. Both were the children of my foster sister Callityche. And so much for this.*

December 29 to January 2 167 A.D.

(26) *I stayed five days at the foot of the mountain,*[43] *and used the regimen which he had prescribed, but when he moved me on the sixth, I went to Pergamum.*

January 3 167 A.D.

And these were the days following that which the Romans celebrate as the first of the year.[44] *The winter was so violent, that I could not easily endure it, even when I stayed at home.* (27) *And a most divine thing happened on the journey—for in the words of Homer it was clear that some one of the gods guided me, whoever the god was.*[45] *A very cold northwind was pressing from behind, and it drove along thick black clouds. On the right everything was covered with snow, on the left it was raining. And this was during the whole day's travel. Through the whole sky, one zone, as it were, extended right over the road and led to the Temple, and provided both shelter and light.*[46] (28) *And drawing far apart from* the others, I went toward the Temple with one attendant, having covered no less than three hundred stades.[47] It was the time after the Sacred Lamps.[48] While I waited for those who had been left behind, and an inn was being got ready, I spent my time, just as I was from the road, walking about the temples and going up and down about the sacred precinct. In the late evening, I found my servants and I washed here by lantern light; and after having eaten very little food, I rested. (29) Indeed, what followed clearly took place with the god's help, the eagerness of the people, the assemblies to hear me speak, and the fear that we might leave too quickly.

These same things also happened later,[49] when we reached Smyrna. Or rather before I even entered the city, people came to meet me as in the oracle which I had received,[50] and the most distinguished young men offered themselves as students. And a certain kind of lecturing had been arranged, and the summons[51] was exactly fulfilled in every detail. (30) About this time, a certain little Egyptian[52] burst into the city and corrupted some of the Councilors, and even led some ordinary people to believe that he would take part in civic affairs and with his money exercize his wonderfully great ambition.[53] He broke into the theater somehow, and great shame held the city. I did not know of these things, except that I heard about them afterwards, in as much as my social life was limited to friends at home. Just now he was intending to go to the Odeon by the harbor and hold a lecture there, either by public decree or in some other way. (31) But I had a dream. *I dreamed that I saw the sun rising from the market place, and had on my lips, "Aristides will declaim today in the Council Chamber at ten o'clock"*. While saying and hearing these things, I woke up, so that I wondered whether it was a dream or had really happened. (32) I summoned the most important of my friends and told them the command. And then the notice[54] was posted, and the hour of the dream drew near, and we were directly present in accordance with it. Nevertheless despite my sudden entrance and the fact that many people were taken unawares, the Council was so packed that it was impossible to see anything except men's heads, and there was not even room to shove your hand between the people. (33) Indeed, the shouting and good will, or rather, if it is fitting to tell the truth, the frenzy was so great from all sides that no one was seen to sit either during the introduction or when I arose to contend, but they stood from the first

167 A.D.

word, felt the emotions of anguish, joy, and fear, assented to what was said, cried out things which were never heard before, and every man counted it his gain, if he should bestow some very great compliment on me. (34) When we left the Council Chamber and were engaged in bathing, then someone reported to me that that fellow three days before also had put up a public notice for this day and had collected at the Odeon seventeen people in all. And moreover from that day he began to exercize moderation. More I shall not say, nor would I have mentioned these things, if I had not wished to show how clearly my dream came to pass and that the god also had a care for these things. And at the same time, it was consistent with the original tale of how he raised me up and restored me to Smyrna.

167 A.D. (35) Not much later,[55] he brought me to Ephesus, *by predicting crowns,*[56] *as if for an athlete, and by preparing me so that I awoke shouting, "Ephesus".* However, it is not seemly for me to tell the things which were done there, but there are many who will recount them to those who desire to know.

(36) But it is necessary to try to make clear all of my oratorical career that pertains to the god and, as far as I can, to omit nothing of it. For it would be strange if both I and others would recount whatever cure he gave to my body even at home, but would pass by in silence those things which at the same time raised up my body, strengthened my soul, and increased the glory of my oratory. (37) I have well persuaded myself and many men that no human accomplishments ever puffed me up, and that I was not elated when I worsted either few or many, and that I do not believe that I should be proud of such things any more than I should be ashamed of my pride.

January 170 A.D. (38) But the continual activity of the god is marvelous,[57] as for example in the matter of that great oratorical display, which took place later in Smyrna. *For he commanded me to go to the Council Chamber, but to go when I had eaten.* And I did this. There was a certain "custodian"[58] of the Council Chamber, a man remarkably thick-skinned.[59] When this man saw my people approaching, he requested that they grant to him first, in his customary way, to lecture to his students, and caused a delay until noon. (39) Then I entered, and having gone in, I exploited at length the theme against the sophists,[60] and regarded this as the sweetest of all days because of the speech. For I myself was filled, as it were, with a feeling of ease,[61] and I gladly made use of it, and the audience vied not to fall behind what was said.[62] Whatever you might conceive or declare, you will say less than what happened then. (40) When I had finished, I got up to leave, for I believed that even this much was more than any contest required. They did not endure it, but as if with one voice, they all ordered me to stay and to receive problems and, indeed, to contend a second time. And meanwhile I refused, especially because of the lateness of the hour. When their request became more violent, I considered the dream and that the god had also foretold these things, not to enter without eating, so that I might avoid fatigue. (41) I undertook the contest, and as it advanced, I was unable to contain myself, but I confessed the prediction of the god and that I came prepared. They marveled at all of these things. When I had fully contended to the limit of my strength, I left, a little before sunset. And I again contended on the following day in the same circumstances, since during those times the god led me in this way.

(42) Come now, let me tell of a recent trip to Cyzicus,[63] which took place on the same month and almost on the same days, four years later, when the Olympic games[64] were approaching. It was not much different from the former trip. For on the first day I fasted, and the water was bad.[65] And at the same time it became clear through the multitude of mosquitoes that I would have to forego sleep. And on the following day, after having eaten a little gruel, I traveled at early dawn. And on my return, I stopped at the warm springs, since it rained, and this too was foretold. But when I came back, I concluded the fasting, which had been imposed until the following day. (43) Indeed, the circumstances of my stay in the city took place nearly as had been foretold. For the following appeared in my dream. I myself had asked the god to give a sign, since there were lawsuits[66] and my friends begged me to come. (44) *I dreamed that I was looking for an opportunity of approaching the Emperor, and that while he was sacrificing I happened to be lying down. When the gasping cock came near my hands, I grabbed it and regarded it as an omen, and as I held it in my hands, I began my salutation.*[67] In all of this I was inspired by the Homeric passage where Odysseus, having filled his cup, addresses and speaks to Achilles.[68] But the words were somewhat as follows: "*For the good of the Emperor, for the good also of both Emperors,*[69] *as even for all of us*". (45) *He was amazed; and when he had tested my speech, he said that he valued it at any price, and added,* "Would that there were also an audience of about fifty present at this speech".[70] And I said in reply, "If you

late summer 170 A.D.

wish, Emperor, there will also be an audience and'', I said, "so that you may well be amazed, these things which you now say have been foretold to me by Asclepius". And I was prepared to show him what had been written down.[71] After this, he turned away somewhere, and I considered that that occasion of the oratorical display was meant to be like this. Thereupon I dreamed that I was walking toward Cyzicus. This was what prompted me.

(46) When I reached the city, there was much excitement on the part of the governor's staff[72] as well as on the part of the others. Nevertheless I did not make a public appearance, although they expected me daily and did marvelous things. But I consorted at home with the most distinguished personages and the prophecy of the dream was nearly fulfilled, for the gathering numbered about fifty men.

autumn 170 A.D.

(47) But when my stay grew long,[73] although I was pleased both by the place and the present circumstances, among other dreams which uprooted me, there was one which made it quite clear that *the upper part of the Hellespont was not suitable for a stay.* Therefore we returned. For the national sacrifice of Olympian Zeus[74] was drawing near, and there were additional indications from all sides that *I must be present and sacrifice.* (48) It also happened, during this time, that my physical condition was the most comfortable and at its brightest since I first was sick. For as long as we were in Cyzicus and afterwards, when we returned, for six whole months in a row, I was at my strongest, and I arose at dawn, and I took long walks many times during the day, and I was as close as possible to my old nature. And nothing of my accustomed oratorical practice was neglected, so that all congratulated me, both privately and publicly.

autumn 170 A.D.

In so far as even in this time I happened to fall ill for some days, the god cured me most miraculously and in his usual way.[75] (49) For there was an autumnal northwind, and I was unable to move, so that I shrunk from even getting up. But he ordered it. Perhaps it is better to narrate the dream itself, for it is still ringing in my ears and there in no need to omit it. *Two doctors came and at the doorway, among other things, discussed, I believe, a cold bath. One asked the question, and the other answered. "What does Hippocrates say?", he said. "What else than to run ten stades[76] to the sea, and then jump in?"*[77] *I dreamed that these things had appeared in my dream.*[78] (50) After this, the doctors themselves, in fact, came in, and I marveled at the precision of the dream, and said to them, "Just now I dreamed that I saw you and just now you have come. Indeed, which one of you", I said, "was the one who inquired and which one, the one who answered, I cannot say. But the answer was as follows: 'That Hippocrates ordered one who intended to take a cold bath, to run ten stades' ". At the same time I changed in my own interest the phrase "to the sea", as if I were making clear the descent to the river. And so I said, "to run ten stades, by running parallel to the river". I thought of this because of being in the interior. It seemed to be clear and to be necessary to do this. (51) Then somehow after this, I thought that I was reclining, as it were, for lunch. Remembering that it was first necessary to bathe with cold water according to the prediction, I got up and ordered the others. When one of the doctors asked about the time of the bath, I said that I must be moved at eleven o'clock, for it would take place at twelve.[79] I added that it is troublesome either to bathe or eat earlier than is suitable,[80] for it is not conducive to the very thing which seems to be the useful part of it,[81] to have an easier digestion, for insomnia comes from it. (52) "Why then", said the doctor, "did you not declaim for us in the meantime?" "Because, by Zeus", I said, "it is more important for me to revise some things which I have written. For I must also converse with posterity". And at the same time I indicated that I was pressing myself, lest something happen first. And he augured many years for me. And I said, "I would wish to live many years, if I should be engaged in oratory". (53) Such was the dream.

A river flowed by the estate where I was staying,[82] but the descent to it was rather rough and steep, and at the same time less than ten stades. Furthermore it was not possible to run by running parallel to the river, but only obliquely and in the direction of the bank. Then, however, the river proceeded to flow by another estate, where there was a fair and picturesque spot for wading.[83] I contrived the following. (54) I ordered that the distance of the one estate from the other be measured by a rope, and that a marker be left at each stade. When the whole distance appeared as sixteen stades,[84] I left the last ten stades for the race, but I proceeded over the first six[85] in a carriage. Then I alighted and ran, and I scarcely dragged my feet, and at the same time a raging northwind drove my clothes back,[86] and caused a remarkable amount of perspiration. Therefore when there was no end of it, I allowed it to chill me as much as it wished. (55) When I reached the bank, I gladly threw myself into the water. And when I emerged and stood up, since I was covered with sand, I bathed again for a second time in the middle of the stream. Among other things I also was able to rub myself down on the opposite bank, under a fair sun and with a gentle wind. I went to the neighboring estate, and stayed long enough to consider some of the things which had happened, and I returned before even taking the time to drink, and enjoyed a marvelous warmth and a wholly different constitution.

And after this, everything was easy until the middle of winter.[87] He cured what happened in winter with various kinds and sorts of regimens.

(56) I calculated how much time I had been away from Smyrna, and this when honorary decrees[88] had come, and that I was already middle-aged, and in addition the many former times when it was possible, if one was healthy, to tour the cities, and that there was a danger that I might be deprived even of my existing reputation through long idleness. I considered these things, as it is likely that a man would, but I knew well that everything was foolishness in comparison to obeying the god. No longer was I troubled by my solitude, but I counted it more profitable.

When I was in this state, I had the following dream vision. (57) *I dreamed that I had just come to Athens, and that I was living behind the Acropolis in the house of the doctor Theodotus,*[89] *and that it was the first house on the east side. The back chamber of the Temple of Athena was visible from it,*[90] *and the house was very much below the Acropolis. A procession in honor of Eros happened to be taking place outside the gates, and Theodotus and certain others, who had been assigned thereto, were busy about these things. But I stayed inside at this time. And one of my comrades, Lucius,*[91] *happened to be present and others who were interested in oratory. And Lucius, as he was accustomed, urged me to maintain my studies in oratory and to admit young men as students,* (58) *and what is more, a certain boy. And Lucius made other complimentary remarks about me to him, and praised me somehow in the following fashion. "This man", he said, "is Plato and Thucydides, and Plato and so and so". And thus he listed many men, while always joining someone with Plato, as if I had the powers of all these men.*[92] *And I looked at the boy and said, "I think it right that you trust Lucius in everything except this".* (59) *And it seemed to me that Lucius praised the facility of my answer, but that he did not happily bear my retirement. Again when the boy in reply spoke skillfully to me, as if he were declaiming, I interrupted him and jestingly said, "But if you are able to speak in this way, I should be amazed if you would need me as a teacher".*

(60) *After this, I dreamed that I went out of the house with some young acquaintance, and that I noticed and approved the thinness of the air. But when there were many sudden changes, and at the same time the southwind also blew*

up, and sometimes it was stormy, sometimes very hot, I said approvingly[93] that the air here is thin, but that at home is more stable.

(61) After this, we went to where the Lyceum[94] is and next there was a certain temple, no less great and fair than the Hecatompedus.[95] And one had to go up some steps to reach the temple. Some men stood round about, it seemed to me, like those who hold out olive boughs.[96] When I ascended, a small boy offered me three eggs. And I had an uneasy feeling—for I passed by without taking them—that it was necessary to take them for the sake of the omen.[97] After I had turned around and taken them, I went up. And when I arrived at the temple, I gave the eggs to one of the officials of the sacred precinct, who stood by a certain pillar. But he intended to add one from his own store. (62) When I reached the entrance, I saw that it was a temple of Plato, the philosopher, and that a great and fair image of him was erected there, and a statue of someone was erected on his right. A very beautiful woman sat upon the threshold and spoke about Plato and the statue. Some others also took part in the discussion, and at the same time spoke about it as if it were ancient. And I said, "It is not possible to say that it is ancient. For the form of the workmanship is shown to be rather recent, and there was not much regard of Plato in Plato's own life time, but", I said, "his reputation grew later". (63) Yet when someone said that there ought to be three temples of Plato, "Why not", I said extravagantly, "eighty of Demosthenes, and of Homer at any rate, I think?". And, having said this, I added, "But perhaps it is proper to consecrate temples to the gods, but to honor famous men with the offering of books,[98] since", I said, "our most valuable possessions are what we say. For statues and images are the monuments of bodies, but books of words".

(64) When I had said and heard these things, I returned. And when I saw my foster brother approaching,[99] I recalled how much time had passed since we were formerly together at Athens. After I had turned toward the Acropolis, so that I might go home, a flash of lightning darted by from the right and skimmed the edge of my hair in such a way, that I wondered that it had not been set on fire.[100] I was anxious, but I took the sign more as an auspicious one, for the youth who was with me said that it portended glory for me, especially since it was on the right. (65) It seemed to me that the majority of the buildings had certain ladders attached, and that I had to go up and down these, so that I grew somewhat annoyed at this. Nevertheless somehow I got inside.

And meanwhile those who were making the procession in honor of Eros had returned, and the interpreter,[101] having learned of the sign, also said that it was auspicious and that my sacrifices had turned out correctly.[102] (66) It seemed to me that there had been a dream before that I had made sacrifices to Zeus and Artemis and some other gods.

And after all these things, I dreamed that I called Eudoxus[103] *to copy them down, because they were rather long and I wished to preserve them exactly for myself.* (67) These dreams, in addition to many others, were revealed to me both about my later glory and the necessity of not moving about.[104]

LII. THE SACRED TALES: VI[1]

(1) Thus the god directed us in many things, giving signs as to what should be done, and finding us obedient, if ever any other man was obedient to the god. In the second year after I left the Aesepus,[2] and in the twelfth from the time that I was first sick, many marvelous visions came to me, which led me to Epidaurus,[3] sacred to the god. And one, which was among the first, was the following. (2) *Someone, encouraging me to be brave, told a story of Musonius.*[4] *"When that man"*, *he said, "wished to raise up someone who was sick and had given up, he spoke somewhat in the following way, censuring him: 'Why do you stay? Where do you look? Or until god himself stands by you and makes an utterance? Strike out the dead part of your soul, and you will know god' ".* (3) Such things he said that Musonius said. And in addition to these things, there were voices, *"Save yourself for the city of Athens"*,[5] which meant for the Greeks. And there were great predictions about things in Italy.[6].........

after April 155 A.D.

LIII. A PANEGYRIC ON THE WATER IN PERGAMUM[1]

(1) Homer said of the meeting of the torrents:[2] "And their noise the shepherd heard far off in the mountains". And he states that the shepherd shuddered and drove his flock into a cave.[3] Although I am now so far away from you, when I heard of the eruption of the water and the great adornment added to the city, I could not keep still through my delight, but I said what I said, and I felt a kind of physical exaltation,[4] and my joy was complete. (2) Two days before I heard the report—for perhaps I should tell you, for you will hear this with pleasure on account of the revelation of the god and at the same time because of its auspiciousness—I had a dream vision, which showed me the city as it were twice its normal size, through the accession of certain territory, which had been procured adjacent to it, and of public monuments, which had been added, somehow rather similar to those at the Temple of Zeus Philius.[5] Therefore I rejoiced in the dream; and when I got up, I took it as a good omen both for the city and myself. (3) Two days later, a message came from a man who is a friend of mine, which reported that all of Asia joins you in celebrating your thoroughly good fortune. For the water is the most abundant and fairest of all that any city ever received. I not only regarded it as a spring day, but as it is likely to regard the day of Zeus of Good Tidings[6] and Asclepius the Savior, who bestows his honors in every way. And I congratulated the city for its acquisition and myself since I was thought worthy to hear of it in advance, clearly because my ties with the city are less than no man's.[7] (4) After this, I considered that rejoicing is common to all, men, children, and women, since it is seeing which provides the pleasure; but that the adornment of the Nymphs' gift with a speech perhaps would be the task of one of those who passed their time with the Healer and who were ordered to spend their lives in oratory. I remembered that the poets somehow are always bringing together the Nymphs and the Muses, and again that they call Hermes a chorus leader of the Nymphs[8] and Apollo also a chorus leader of the Muses. This same god is called by you the Callitecnus[9] because of his fatherhood. In every way it appeared fitting and not untimely to blend the grace of the Muses with that of the Nymphs. For then I would do what befitted all the gods whom I mentioned.

(5) From the beginning, as it seems, the fairest gifts were given to the city by both gods and men. On the one hand, the oldest of the divinities, the Cabiri,[10] are said to have originated here as well as their rites and mysteries which are believed to possess so much power that during unseasonable storms.................

NOTES TO XVII

1. The speech was delivered in honor of the arrival of the governor of Asia (*cf.* Turzewitsch in Wilamowitz SB Berl. Akad. 28, p. 352) at the assizes in Smyrna at the celebration of the Dionysia, c. March 3 (perhaps alluded to in § 6). Perversely some scholars still claim that the Emperor Marcus Aurelius was the recipient, but this theory is disproved notably by XXI 7, which concerns this man's son. The speech comes from the most active and best period of Aristides' career, from the time of the *Panathenaicus,* to which it shows some affinity, (*e.g. cf.* § 13 and also *ibid.* the use of ἐξοικεῖ). I have conjecturally dated it to 157 A.D. and identified the recipient as P. Cluvius Maximus Paullinus (*Aelius Aristides,* pp. 91-92). Aristides echoed its themes twenty-two years later in oration XXI, when on the same occasion this proconsul's son entered the city as governor.

This charming little speech, despite its rhetorical allusiveness, gives about the best description of ancient Smyrna which we possess. It takes the governor on a tour (in § 21 it is even called a περίοδος), beginning with the two hills in the heart of the city and the "golden way" connecting them § 10, apparently northward to the "sacred way", then to the Metroon § 10-11, then outside the northern end of the city to the river Meles § 14, and finally over the road which led north along the gulf § 16-22. Probably the very route which the proconsul would take.

The sections of the speech are:
A. § 1 Proem
B. § 2-7 History. Population
C. § 8-22 Geography. Sights
D. § 23 Peroration.

2. For the three cities, alleged foundations of Tantalus or Pelops, Theseus, and Alexander the Great, *cf.* § 3-5 and XXI 3-4, 10.

3. The phoenix; *cf.* XX 19.

4. *Iliad* XXIV 615.

5. Pindar *Olymp.* I 37.

6. At Naulochon, at the northern extremity of the Gulf of Smyrna. It was destroyed by the Lydian king Alyattes *c.* 588 B.C.

7. A fictitious foundation. In XX 20 Aristides reports only a Smyrna of Theseus and Alexander.

8. *Cf.* Plato *Politicus* 286 A.

9. Pindar *Pyth.* III 43. For the foundation by Alexander the Great, *cf.* Pausanias VII 5, 1-3. Strabo XIV 37 (646) more correctly credits the third city to Antigonus and Lysimachus, the latter of whom established the final form of the city *c.* 290 B.C.

10. *i.e.* the Athenians, *cf. e.g.* I 25-34, 328.

11. Pelops, the son of Tantalus; *cf.* XXI 3.

12. *i.e.* the Athenians under Theseus. For the later settlers, *cf.* XXI 4.

13. *Cf.* Thucydides I 6, 3.

14. *Cf.* Pindar frgs. 219-220 Turyn (= 204, 264 Schroeder).

15. The date of the assizes at Smyrna, *cf.* L 85. Since it is *c.* March 3, the expression is hyperbolic, *cf.* Lucian *Podagr.* 43.

16. Also called the Anthesteria; *cf.* XXI 4, XXIX 4, 20, XLI 10, L 85; for the trireme, in which Polemo, Aristides' teacher, and his descendants had the right to ride, *cf.* Philostratus *Vitae Sophistarum* I 25 (530-531 Olearius); M. P. Nilsson, *Griechische Feste,* pp. 267-271; A. W. Pickard-Cambridge, *Dramatic Festivals of Athens,* pp. 1-22; Behr, *Aelius Aristides,* p. 83.

17. One would assume that "the temple" (which word is restored by emendation) is that of Dionysus Briseus, which is thought to lie just outside the walls on the mountain between Mt. Pagus and Deirman Tepe, south of the stadium; *cf.* C. J. Cadoux, *Ancient Smyrna,* pp. 16, 102, 208.

18. *i.e.* they were torn to pieces. Perhaps a real event during the war between Ptolemy III and Seleucus II in 244 B.C.; *cf.* C. J. Cadoux, *Ancient Smyrna,* pp. 114-115. But a somewhat similar story is told in Herodotus I 150 of a successful attack by the Colophonians well before 700 B.C.

19. An allusion to Smyrna's aid to Rome against Antiochus and Aristonicus; *cf.* XIX 11 and notes 14-16 there.

20. Homer; *cf.* § 15.

21. Actually a "shirt".

22. The χρυσῆ ὁδός, mentioned only by Aristides; *cf.* XVIII 6. The geography is unclear, but I believe that Aristides refers to the height of Deirman Tepe, called the κορυφή by Pausanias VII 5, 9, which lay near the sea and on which was a temple of Zeus Acraeus; and to the east, connected by the "golden way", lay ὁ Πάγος (*cf.* Pausanias VII 5, 2), the acropolis of Smyrna, on which was built the temple of the Nemeseis (in the south of the city, *cf.* XVIII 3). Strabo XIV 646 writes of the straight alignment of the streets, and Aristides himself describes Smyrna as an oblong rectangle, πλαίσιον, with its βάσις on the sea, *cf.* XVII 19, XXIII 20. I presume that the other great avenue, the ἱερὰ ὁδός (XVIII 6), ran parallel in an east-west direction from the Μητρῷον at Tepejik to the "eastern gate". Two other main arteries connected these streets so as to form four intersections (§ 11, XVIII 6). This synopsis seems to conform to Bürchner's view in R.E. III A *s.v.* Smyrna 757-758. However, C. J. Cadoux, *Ancient Smyrna,* p. 176, believes that "Golden Street" connected ὁ Πάγος with the Metroon and ran in a curve from near Tepejik through "the eastern gate" round south-westwards through the city to the Ephesian gate. But I am doubtful whether Aristides could say that the Metroon lay east of the Πάγος. Cadoux does not locate the "Sacred Way".

23. ὁ Πάγος, it would seem; *cf.* n. 22. Other writers do not speak of «an acropolis» of Smyrna.

24. "The sacred way", *cf.* XVIII 6.

25. The Μητρῷον, *cf.* n. 22. In CIG 3387 Magna Mater is also called τῇ [ἀρχηγέτι]δι, but elsewhere in Aristides the Nemeseis (*cf.* n. 22) have this title, *cf.* XX 20, 23; see note 22 to oration XX. The text may be more seriously corrupt than I have suggested.

26. Literally "a middle-aged man".

27. *Cf.* XVIII 6 and n. 22.

28. § 9.

29. An allusion to Xerxes' opulent tent; *cf.* Herodotus IX 82.

30. Aristides echoes himself in I 401.

31. "Eponymous" since it gave its name to the Nymphs of the region and to the gulf; *cf.* XXI 15. The Meles is now plausibly identified with the Halka-Bunar.

32. The Mediterranean.

33. *Cf.* Aesop 24 Chambry, Herodotus I 141.

34. *Cf.* XXI 8; XXXIII 29; Pausanias VII 5, 12. In Smyrna itself there was a Homereium, *cf.* Strabo XIV 646.

35. *Iliad* XXIII 148.

36. On the road to Naulochon.

37. *i.e.* at Naulochon the coastline begins to curve westward, so that by turning left one can look across the gulf toward Smyrna.

38. *Cf.* XXVIII 130; Plato *Symposium* 217 E.

39. *Cf.* XVIII 3; XXIII 20 and n. 22.

40. *i.e.* the Meles marked the effective limit of the base as well as of the southern side of the gulf.
41. *Iliad* II 457.
42. §§ 14, 19.
43. Κόλπος means either "gulf" or "bosom". This gulf is soft and gentle like a "bosom". For κατ' ἐπωνυμίαν, *cf.* III 599; XXXII 33.
44. The *Sinus Hermius*.
45. The governor will pronounce his verdicts during the trials at the assizes.

NOTES TO XVIII

1. Written shortly after January 177 A.D., when Aristides at his Laneion estate received the news of Smyrna's destruction. For the date of this earthquake, which is generally given as 178 A.D., *cf.* Behr, *Aelius Aristides,* p. 112 n. 68. The speech, composed in short rhythmical cola, offers a characteristic example of "Asianism". The sections are:
A. § 1 Destruction of Smyrna
B. § 2-6 Former state
C. § 7-10 Threnody
This work has been closely imitated by Libanius in his LXth and LXIst orations.
2. Perhaps a quotation. For the idea, *cf.* XX 15, but also Aeschylus *Persians* 262.
3. This is a pastiche of allusions to oration XVII: § 3 (Curetes, birth of gods); § 4-5 (Pelops, Theseus, Sipylus; *cf.* XXI 3); § 15 (Homer); § 7 (contests; *cf.* XIX 11, 13). Strabo XIV 646, for one, named Smyrna "the fairest of all cities". In his grief, Aristides breaks off the argument. Consequently there is nothing to answer the μέν at the start of the sentence.
4. *Cf.* XVII 17. Στάσεις may be a play on στάσιμον.
5. *Cf.* XVII 19 and n. 22 to XVII.
6. Frg. 196 Lobel-Page *Poetarum Lesbiorum Fragmenta*. Possibly frg. 31 vs. 11 Lobel-Page is meant.
7. Homer *Odyssey* VII 231.
8. *Cf.* XXXI 12, whence the suggested supplement in the Greek text (= "have thrown up").
9. *Cf.* n. 22 to XVII.
10. *i.e.* the literary western limit of the inhabited world.
11. *Cf.* XLV 33, Aristides' earliest preserved speech, where it is said of the Sun-Sarapis τὴν καλλίστην ὧν ἐφορᾷς κατέχων πόλιν.
12. In 413 B.C. and 335 B.C. respectively.
13. Rhodes was devastated by an earthquake in 142 A.D., and Aristides, then in Egypt, delivered a speech, which is now lost, on this catastrophe (*cf.* Behr, *Aelius Aristides,* p. 16). The spurious oration XXV, preserved among Aristides' works, also refers to this event. Later in 149 A.D., in oration XXIV, Aristides also concerned himself with civil disorders which subsequently arose in Rhodes; see note 14 for a possible allusion.
14. He inverts a favorite proverb of his, "second attempts are better", as in XXIV 59; for the proper form, *cf.* XX 23 and XXVI 101.
15. *Cf.* XVII 3.
16. If the text is sound, the meaning is obscure. There is an expression εἰς πῦρ ἅλλεσθαι, "to leap into the fire" (Xenophon *Memorab.* I 3, 9) for foolhardy daring. Aristides may be playing with this. He may simply mean that the birds, having presaged the burning of the city, should punish themselves in sorrow by plunging into the conflagration.

17. *Cf.* Lysias II 60.

18. A sign of death, from the Theseus legend. The ships, which transported the Athenian youths and maidens who were to be victims of the Minotaur, carried black sail.

19. See note 31 to XVII.

20. The swan (*cf. e.g.* Aeschylus *Agamemnon* 1444 and Plato *Phaedo* 84 E) and at times the nightingale (from the legend of Tereus, Procne, and Philomela) were standard symbols of sorrow in tragedy.

21. Outposts of the Greco-Roman world. The Bosporus (here obviously the Cimmerian Bosporus) is the strait between the Black Sea and the Sea of Azov; the Cataracts are in Egypt; Tartessus in Spain near Gibraltar; Massalia modern Marseilles (not really an outpost, but an early Greek colony); Borysthenes on the Black Sea in southern Russia and one of the most remote Greek colonies.

22. The daughters of the Sun and sisters of Phaethon.

23. The few surviving subscriptions are enormously valuable in reconstructing Aristides' life. Ultimately they depend on Aristides' own notes, but they seem to have come down to us in the form given to them by Aristides' earliest editor; *cf.* the introduction to *Aelii Aristidis Opera Quae Exstant Omnia*, p. LXX.

NOTES TO XIX

1. After the earthquake (see note 1 to XVIII), Aristides claimed that he waited only one day before writing to the emperors (XXI 2). His efforts on Smyrna's behalf were recognized at least by Philostratus *Vitae Sophistarum* 582 Olearius. This forceful appeal falls into the following sections:

A. § 1 Appeal for help
B. § 2-5 The emperors' connection with Smyrna
C. § 6-8 Aristides' conduct
D. § 9-10 The power of the emperors
E. § 11-12 Smyrna's former generosity
F. § 13-14 An appeal to help it in its misfortune.

2. After the suppression of the rebellion of Avidius Cassius, the imperial family on tour in the east stopped at Smyrna in early autumn 176 A.D. Here Aristides spoke before them, *cf.* XLII 14; Philostratus *Vitae Sophistarum* 582-583 Olearius. On this incident, *cf.* Behr, *Aelius Aristides*, pp. 111, 143-144.

3. A feast of Apollo, but here it probably was held in honor of the "divine emperors".

4. For the imagery, *cf. Anthologia Palatina* X 15, 1.

5. Real and mythical founders of the city; *cf.* notes 2 and 9 to XVII.

6. Homer *Iliad* VII 203.

7. Homer *Iliad* V 117.

8. *Cf.* XX 3. The estate is probably Aristides' favorite, Laneion, which lay near Hadrianutherae, north of Pergamum in Mysia; *cf.* Behr, *Aelius Aristides*, p. 6. The god is Asclepius.

9. *i.e.* "concerned me". A strong metaphor licensed perhaps by III 589 and Demosthenes XLIII 59. There may, however, be a lacuna in the Greek.

10. *Cf. e.g.* Aristotle *Ath. Pol.* 14, 2.

11. An obscure reference, doubtless motivated by some personal pique. Aristides kept a house in the suburbs; *cf.* Behr, *Aelius Aristides*, p. 7.

12. Domitian, who ordered the extinction of the Nasamones, an African tribe near Mt. Atlas in 85/86 A.D.; *cf.* Cassius Dio LXVII 4, 6. However, the story is

somewhat exaggerated since Aristides' contemporary Pausanias I 33, 5 speaks of them as still existing.

13. For the expression, cf. Isocrates V 113 and IX 77.

14. Cf. SHA vita Marci 11, 3 in reference to the supplying of grain in times of famine.

15. Antiochus III, king of Syria, was defeated in 190 B.C. by the brothers Scipio. Aristonicus, a pretender to the Pergamene throne, which had been willed to Rome by its last legitimate king, was defeated by Perpenna in 130 B.C.

16. P. Licinius Crassus, who intercepted by a contingent of Thracians at the beginning of the war against Aristonicus, to avoid the shame of falling into Aristonicus' hands, provoked his jailer into killing him; cf. e.g. Valerius Maximus III, cap. II, 12.

17. Cf. Tacitus Annales IV 56. This event occurred at the end of the first Mithridatic war when Sulla was wintering with his army in Asia in 85/84 B.C. Aristides has mistakenly attributed this incident to the war against Aristonicus.

18. These earthquakes may possibly have occurred in 165 A.D.; cf. Behr, Studies on the Biography § 8, where I have emended Eusebius Historia Ecclesiastica IV 13, so that a rescript quoted there refers to earthquakes in Marcus' 19th trib. pot. and not his 15th (161 A.D.) as the manuscripts read. It seems improbable that the earthquake which devastated Cyzicus in 161 A.D. is meant. On famines in 166 A.D., cf. Behr, Aelius Aristides, p. 97.

19. The temple was dedicated to Tiberius, Livia, and the Roman Senate. For the incident which arose in 23 A.D. and was finally adjudicated in 26 A.D., cf. Tacitus Annales IV 15, 3; 37; 55-56; Cassius Dio LIX 28, 1. Asia alone was involved, and Aristides rhetorically exaggerates by claiming that it was preferred to other provinces.

NOTES TO XX

1. By 178 A.D. the reconstruction of Smyrna was well under way. It would appear that the Provincial Assembly met here this year (cf. the play on the word κοινόν in § 15; see also Behr, Aelius Aristides, pp. 112-113; and for the cycle of the Assembly meetings Studies on the Biography § 7, The Electoral Procedure in τὸ κοινὸν τῆς 'Ασίας). This oration has been sent to the Assembly by Aristides from Laneion to celebrate the work in progress (§ 21-23 show that the reconstruction was not yet finished). The speech treats the following themes:
A. § 1-3 End of grief
B. § 4-11 The fortune of the city and its new founders
C. § 12-19 Help of other Greeks and the good fortune of the city
D. §20-23 The restoration.

2. i.e. the Emperors; for προστάται, cf. XXI 8; otherwise used of city officials in XIX 8.

3. Asclepius.

4. Asclepius; cf. XIX 6.

5. Stesichorus, having slandered the mythical Helen, the cause of the Trojan war, in a poem, allegedly lost his sight through her divine agency. Thereupon he wrote a retraction, "a palinode" and was able to see again; cf. Plato Phaedrus 234 A and Page Poetae Melici Graeci 192.

6. XIX 4.

7. An allusion to the conclusion in 175 A.D. of the wars against the Germans and Sarmatians.

8. Cf. Pausanias VII 5, 1-3 and note 9 to XVII.

9. *Theogony* 81 ff.

10. *Cf.* Plutarch *Themistocles* 29; *Reg. et Imp. Apophth.* 185 F.

11. *i.e.* the Roman Senate; *cf.* XIX 1. The restoration in the Greek text of a metaphorical "chorus" (*cf.* its employment for the imperial court in XLII 14) is perhaps justified by τῶν κορυφαίων ("chorus leaders").

12. After Athens' defeat in the Peloponnesian war (404 B.C.) the rule of the Thirty was established by Sparta. These drove the party of "the people" into exile. "The people" under Thrasybulus, using Boeotia (Thebes) as a base, expelled the Thirty in 403 B.C. During Sparta's hegemony (404-394 B.C.) Argos and Thebes were its chief opponents. The role of Pharsalos (a town in Thessaly) seems not to be mentioned elsewhere.

13. Pindar fragment 76 Schroeder, 92 Turyn; *cf.* I 401.

14. The source of this particular oracle is unknown; *cf.* the list cited in I 399-401.

15. § 8, 10.

16. τοῖς κοινοῖς συνεδρίοις, as well as κοινοῦ πτώματος just below, seems to be an allusion to the meeting of τὸ κοινὸν τῆς 'Ασίας; see note 1.

17. The province as opposed to Asia in a wider geographical sense; *cf.* XXI 7.

18. From Sophocles, *cf.* Nauck, FTG² 667; also I 60.

19. For such rejuvenation at the hands of Medea, *cf.* Aeschylus Διονύσου Τροφοί (cited in the Hypothesis to Euripides' *Medea* and a scholium to Aristophanes' *Equites* 1321, where, indeed, Demos himself is rejuvenated). Keil in his edition suggests the boiling of Pelops (*cf.* XXI 10); yet Pelops was resurrected but not made younger thereby.

20. *Cf.* XVII 2.

21. This account disagrees with the version in XVII 3, XVIII 2, and XXI 3-4, where Theseus is presented as the founder of "the second" Smyrna and Alexander of "the third" one.

22. *i.e.* Marcus and Commodus are compared to the Nemeseis, whose appearance in a dream was said to have caused Alexander to found Smyrna. Their temple was located on Mt. Pagos, the site of the incident; *cf.* Pausanias VII 5, 2-3 (with the note of J. G. Frazer *Pausanias's Description of Greece* vol. IV, p. 125), *ibid.* I 33, 7; IX 35, 6; Dio Chrysostom XL 14; *Anthologia Palatina* XII 193; Aristides below § 23; XLVII 35; L 41. In XVII 10 the Magna Mater is named as the city's guardian deity; see note 25 to XVII.

23. *Cf.* XVIII 6.

24. Apparently the harbors (*cf.* perhaps XXI 4), but possibly the citizens of Smyrna (*cf.* XVII 15).

25. *Cf.* Pindar fragment 75.15 Schroeder, 91.15 Turyn; also Aristides XLVI 25.

26. An allusion to XIX 3.

27. The Nemeseis; see note 22.

28. Presumably the gods of the Romans; *cf.* XXXVII 29.

29. *Cf.* note 14 to XVIII.

NOTES TO XXI

1. In March, 179 A.D., when the rebuilding of Smyrna was essentially completed (*cf. e.g.* § 8, but when Marcus still seems to be ruling with Commodus, *e.g.* § 2, 8, 9), the son and former legate of the recipient of oration XVII, possibly P. Cluvius Maximus Paullinus (*cf.* Behr, *Aelius Aristides,* p. 92 n. 1a), entered Smyrna as governor in his own right for the assizes. From his estate in Mysia, Laneion,

Aristides sent him this oration, which copies in a loose way, as if Aristides were writing from memory without consulting the original, the themes of XVII. We note in particular the handling of the topics in § 3-4, which have been treated in XVII, but not precisely in the form in which it is implied. The themes of the speech are as follows:

A. § 1-2 Excuse for absence
B. § 3-5 The occasion of the former speech
C. § 6-9 Destruction and restoration of Smyrna
D. § 10-13 New beauty greater
E. § 14-15 The Meles
F. § 16 Peroration.

2. Asclepius; cf. XIX 6.
3. Cf. subscription to XVIII; XIX 6.
4. As *legatus proconsulis*. It was common practice for proconsuls to appoint their sons as one of their three legates.
5. Cf. XVII 3. Neither Tantalus nor Pelops are named there as founders, although Pelops is in XXI 10.
6. Cf. XVII 5.
7. Agamemnon.
8. Cf. XVII 5.
9. Cf. XVII 4: Alexander the Great; the city by the Nile is Alexandria.
10. XVII 5-6. The Κατάπλοοι, which is not mentioned in the earlier account, could be either the place where the sacred boat was landed or, more probably, a part of the festival.
11. Cf. XVII 10.
12. Cf. XVII 22.
13. Amphion's playing caused the stones of the wall to move by themselves into place. The story was told in Euripides' *Antiope*, a play to which Aristides several times alludes; e.g. c.f. II 394.
14. Cf. XXIII 10.
15. A bold metaphor, for which, in emending a corrupt text, I may be responsible. I would compare for the use of καιρός, Pindar *Pyth*. IV 286. Aristides also plays upon the phrase χεῖρα ὀρέγειν, "to lend a helping hand" (cf. XIX 1). For the construction τε γάρ, see Paul *Romans* 7.7 (Liddell-Scott-Jones s.v. τε C. 10. c.).
16. Homer (for the Meles as his father, cf. XVII 15 and note 34 to XVII) *Iliad* II 330.
17. Aristides is writing from his Laneion estate in Mysia. He had not returned to Smyrna during its reconstruction and, indeed, never seems to have gone back there before his death near the year 180 A.D.
18. Pindar *Olymp*. I 26-27.
19. The phrase is from Herodotus VIII 32.
20. Cf. XVII 16.
21. Cf. XVII 8 (XX 14).
22. Athens; cf. § 4; XVII 5. Theseus founded "the second" Smyrna.
23. After 479 B.C.; cf. e.g. I 191.
24. Goddess of envy. The phrase is much like our "touch wood".
25. Cf. Herodotus I 207. 7.
26. For the Meles, see note 31 to XVII; XVII 14-15, 19.
27. If the text is sound, Aristides seems to be playing on the meaning of μοῖρα, as "the part" of oration XVII in which the Meles was mentioned and as "an inheritance", which as the other subjects of XVII must be left to the next generation (literally "the sons") to which the present proconsul belonged (cf. XX 22). The father was the recipient of XVII and this was part of the son's legacy. However, I

should not conceal the fact that the passage has been interpreted in other ways. Keil, in his edition, thought that the subject of the Meles was to be left to one of a number of youths who were to deliver a speech of greeting to the emperor (*sic*). Boulanger, *Aelius Aristide,* p. 390 n. 1, suggested that it meant that the theme was so trivial that it should be left to the handling of boys.

28. Aristides plays upon the notion of the *cursus honorum,* in which the son is repeating the offices formerly held by his father, and upon the idea of the progress of the proconsul to the various sites of the assizes in the province. Also he alludes to the tour of the city which the father made, *cf.* XVII 21.

29. *Cf.* § 8.

NOTES TO XXII

1. According to the subscription the speech was delivered in Smyrna in the Council Chamber between June 23-25, 171 A.D. (see Behr, *Studies on the Biography,* §1), after news had reached Smyrna of the looting and burning of the temple complex. The destruction is thought, with some probability, to have been connected with an incursion of the Costoboci, a Sarmatian tribe, whom Pausanias X 34.5 reports overran Greece after 162 A.D. (*cf.* Magie, *Roman Rule in Asia Minor,* p. 1535 n. 13), although he only names Elatea in northern Greece as one of the objects of their attack. Notice of Marcus Aurelius' contribution to the reconstruction of Eleusis may be contained in a scholium of Sopater to Aristides' *Panathenaicus,* vol. 3, p. 308, 35 ff. Ddf.

It cannot be affirmed with absolute certainty that Aristides himself was an initiate (*cf.* Behr, *Aelius Aristides,* pp. 110, 150-151, 157). However, Wilamowitz's objection in *Der Glaube der Hellenen* II, p. 470, rests on his own misunderstanding of XXII 9 (see note 23). I suspect that Aristides was initiated, although it is unclear whether he was only a μύστης or achieved the higher grade of ἐπόπτης. He had ample opportunity to be initiated when he was resident in Athens as a student under Herodes. Initiation carried a social cachet, which would have appealed to him at that time. Finally it is difficult to see why Aristides otherwise would have been so strongly moved by the news to exert himself with such alacrity. His early association with the Mysteries and later the relationship which we know that the Mysteries shared with the cult of Asclepius would explain his interest. For a useful account of all that pertains to these Mysteries, *cf.* P. Foucart, *Les Mystères d'Éleusis* (1914, reprinted 1975).

The speech amplifies and reworks themes already found in oration I. Moreover, it is in a traditional form which anticipates the later oration XVIII. In outline it is as follows:

A. § 1-2 Mourning
B. § 3-8 History
C. § 9-10 Celebration of the Mysteries
D. § 11-13 Destruction.

2. Famous bards of mythology. Thamyris of Thrace was blinded by the Muses for claiming that he was a better singer. Musaeus in some versions was regarded as one of the Eumolpidae, the family which provided the hereditary Hierophants of the Mysteries, and was himself in office when Heracles was initiated.

3. Aristides neatly sums up the three categories of the rites, δρώμενα, λεγόμενα, δεικνύμενα; *cf.* Foucart, *Les Mystères,* pp. 356, 418.

4. To reveal these secrets was an act of impiety, *e.g. cf.* Lysias VI 51 . Even when prosecution no longer threatened, it was thought to provoke divine retribution, *cf.* Horace *Odes* III 2, 26 ff.; also Aristides I 330, 341; Foucart, *Les Mystères,* pp. 358 ff.

364   NOTES TO XXII

5. Ἔλευσις means "advent".
6. *Cf.* e.g. I 34; for crops I 18, 23, 24, 25, 31, 32, 34, 37, 49, 113, 336, 339, 342, 354, 358, 386; wheat I 38, 45, 50, 74, 339.
7. Celeus, king of Eleusis, husband of Metaneira and father of Triptolemus, entertained Demeter during her stay. Triptolemus became Demeter's agent in the distribution of wheat throughout the world; *cf.* I 36.
8. *Cf.* I 50, 374.
9. *Cf.* I 362, the Eleusinia.
10. *Cf.* I 37, 358, 399.
11. These are the two major priestly families of Eleusis. The senior, the Eumolpidae, traced themselves back to Eumolpus, the son of Poseidon. The junior, the Kerykes, to Hermes and Aglauros, a daughter of Cecrops. (However, the Eumolpidae claimed that Keryx was a younger brother of Eumolpus; *cf.* Foucart, *Les Mystères*, p. 156). The offices of Hierophant and Torch-bearer were for life.
12. *Cf.* I 87; *c.* 1100 B.C.
13. *Cf.* I 55. An opposite view is found in Thucydides I 12, 4.
14. Iacchus, the son of Zeus and Demeter, a central figure in the Mysteries, whose statue was carried from Athens to Eleusis at the beginning of the festival. On him, *cf.* Foucart, *Les Mystères*, pp. 110 ff. For the event in question in 479 B.C., *cf.* I 168, III 320; Herodotus VIII 65; Plutarch *Themistocles* 15.
15. The Peloponnesian War, 431-404 B.C.
16. 378 B.C., a Lacedaemonian general; *cf.* Xenophon *Hellenica* V 4. 21-22.
17. 382 B.C.; *cf.* I 293. Xenophon *Hellenica* V. 2. 29 reports that the Lacedaemonians seized the Cadmea during a celebration of the Thesmophoria.
18. 390 B.C., the Corinthians under the Spartan king Agesilaus. Two games were in consequence celebrated; *cf.* Xenophon *Hellenica* IV 5. 1-2.
19. 364 B.C., during the Olympic games the Eleans, who were being kept from the games, defeated the Arcadians; *cf.* Xenophon *Hellenica* VII 4. 29 ff.
20. 278 B.C., under the chieftain Brennus, who was stopped before Delphi; *cf.* Justin XXIV 4-8. And oracle produced by Apollo in reference to his protection of his shrine was cited by Aristides L 75 (*cf.* Cicero *De Divinatione* I 81; scholium in Aristophanes' *Nubes* 144).
21. For φωναί, *cf.* I 326-327.
22. The Τελεστήριον, *cf.* Plutarch *Pericles* 13. 4; called ὁ μυστικὸς σηκός by Strabo IX 395. It is estimated that it could hold 3000 people, *cf.* Foucart, *Les Mystères*, p. 351.
23. *Cf.* I 373. For the claim that practically all Athenian citizens were initiated, *cf.* Lucian *Demonax* 11. Τὸ Ἐλευσίνιον is not to be confused with Eleusinion temple, which was located in Athens, apparently south-east of the Agora. There was also an Eleusinion in Eleusis, *e.g. cf.* Tod, *A Selection of Greek Historical Inscriptions* (2nd ed.). vol. I, no. 74, line 29; Lysias VI 4 (by implication). Presumably the Eleusinion at Eleusis refers to the whole walled precinct, in which was located the Telesterion, just as at Pergamum the whole precinct was called τὸ Ἀσκληπιεῖον; *cf.* Foucart, *Les Mystères*, p. 348.
24. Profane sights permitted to those not initiated; *cf.* also XXVIII 142.
25. *Cf.* Plato *Phaedo* 69 C; also XXXIII 30-31.
26. The Argive dirge refers to the Linus song, yearly sung by the women of Argos, *cf.* Conon 19 (Jacoby *FGrHist.* Vol. I, p. 195). The Egyptian singers mourn the dead Apis; the Phrygians, worshippers of Cybele, the dead Attis.
27. Aeschylus was born in the deme of Eleusis.
28. Frg. 402 N².
29. Torchlight parades were part of the festival. *Cf* e.g. Aristophanes *Frogs* 340 ff.

30. The Mysteries were celebrated between Boedromion 13-22, "cum longae redit hora nocti/crescere et somnos cupiens quietos/libra Phoebeos tenet aequa currus", Seneca *Hercules Furens* 842 ff. In the months preceding the Mysteries, the σπονδοφόροι announced them throughout the Greek world, so that hostilities might cease and the initiates might prepare to attend; *cf.* Aeschines II 133.

31. Ion aided the Athenians in their war against Eumolpus, king of Eleusis, and became their king.

32. Made at the Eleusinion of Athens on the 15th of Boedromion, barring from participation all "not pure in hands and understanding in voice"; *cf.* Foucart, *Les Mystères,* p. 311.

33. Literally by burlesquing them, as Alcibiades had done. This phrase forms the title of oration XXXIV.

34. *Cf.* Plato *Timaeus* 22 B.

35. *Cf.* XXIV 59; the Greeks in their insouciance still behave like children.

36. Because of Aristides' time of birth the date must fall between June 23-June 25, 171, A.D. (cf. Behr, *Studies on the Biography* § 1). The procosul of Asia, 170/171 A.D., is M. Nonius Macrinus, cos. 154 A.D.

NOTES TO XXIII

1. Inspired perhaps by a dream (*cf.* XLVII 59, Behr *Aelius Aristides,* pp. 103 ff.), Aristides journeyed from his Mysian estates to Pergamum and addressed the Κοινόν (the general assembly of the cities of the province) of Asia, which was convened in Pergamum, perhaps for the celebration of the *nuncupatio votorum* (vows for the new year) on January 3, 167 A.D. (for the cycle of the meetings of the assembly, *cf.* Behr *Aelius Aristides,* pp. 63 ff. and *Studies on the Biography* § 7). The speech, which treats a subject which was raised several months before in oration XXVII, is directed toward curbing the discord caused by the struggles of the leading cities of Asia (notably the three metropolises, Ephesus, Smyrna, and Pergamum) to outdo one another in their ambition for titles and other empty symbols of rank (for the temples and contests honoring Rome, the outward signs of these distinctions, *cf.* § 65; and see now Merkelbach, *Der Rangstreit der Städte Asiens,* Zeitschrift für Papyrologie und Epigraphik 32, 1978, pp. 287-296). This amazing rivalry had become notorious (*cf.* Dio Chrysostom XXXIV 48, 51; Cassius Dio LII 37. 10; Philostratus *Vitae Sophistarum* 539-540 Olearius; D. Magie, *Roman Rule in Asia Minor,* pp. 1496, 1500-1501; Behr, *Aelius Aristides,* p. 105). The rivalry (an all too human quality, symptomatic of the peace and security which Asia enjoyed at that time, *cf.* § 3, 53-54, 63) reached such proportions that it had to be curbed by the emperor himself; *cf.* XXIII 73; SIG[3] 849 = Abbott and Johnson, *Municipal Documents,* no. 100. The latter example (dated between 140-144 A.D.) is most instructive. Ephesus had received the right to call itself "the first and greatest metropolis of Asia" (*cf.* Magie, *Roman Rule in Asia Minor,* p. 1496). Smyrna, which did not then enjoy so exalted a distinction, in a decree concerning Ephesus omitted this title, and the Ephesians wrote to Pius to complain. In his reply, Pius pointed out that Smyrna's conduct may have been inadvertent and in any case the situation would improve if in future Ephesus in their own communications gave Smyrna its proper title.

The speech, which is expertly written (we may note here the careful avoidance of hiatus), is divided as follows:

A. § 1-7 Proem. Better than frivolous or disruptive themes is that of concord.
B. § 8-26 Praise of province. Three chief cities
C. § 27-40 Exhortation. Advantages of concord. Disadvantages of faction

D. § 41-52 Examples from history
E. § 53-58 Faction worse than war
F. § 59-64 No reality or power exists here
G. § 65-79 Advantages of holding things in common
H. § 80 Peroration.

2. Isocrates *Panegyricus* 15 ff. On the latent criticism implied in the use of τις .....σοφιστῶν ἐσεμνύνατο (despite Aristides' admiration for Isocrates himself, as in the careful avoidance of hiatus), *cf.* Behr, *Studies on the Biography*, §4, example no. 23.

3. The Parthian war was concluded in 165 A.D. The beginning of the invasion of Italy by the Marcomanni in 167 A.D., from the perspective of the security which Asia enjoyed, might well seem trivial; for the peace, *cf.* also § 53-54, 63.

4. Either the province or more likely the Κοινόν, which represented the province, is compared to that of other provinces in the Empire. On these assemblies, *cf.* J. Deininger, *Die Provinziallandtage der römischen Kaiserzeit* (1965).

5. Pergamum. On the description of this city, *cf.* the series *Die Altertümer von Pergamum* of the German Archeological Institute.

6. The kingdom of Pergamum was in effect founded by Eumenes in 263 B.C. and lasted until 133 B.C. when it was willed to Rome by Attalus III.

7. Pergamum had the first temple (of Rome and Augustus) of the imperial cult, about which the rites of the Κοινόν centered, in 19 B.C.; *cf.* Magie, *Roman Rule in Asia Minor,* pp. 447, 1293, n. 52. Later similar temples were granted to the other major cities of the province.

8. Asclepius.

9. The temple of Pergamum was founded *c.* 350 B.C., the first in Asia, from the parent temple at Epidaurus; *cf.* Behr, *Aelius Aristides,* pp. 26-27.

10. In myth Telephus, an emigré, succeeded the native Teuthras as king of Mysia.

11. These are offices of the Eleusinian mysteries, with which the cult of Asclepius seems to have had some connection (*cf.* Behr, *Aelius Aristides,* p. 149 n. 9), but Aristides probably uses these terms on his own initiative to emphasize his feeling of the holiness of this cult.

12. *Cf.* § 77, XXXVI 120.

13. *Cf.* XLII 6, L 27; Behr, *Aelius Aristides,* p. 46 n. 20.

14. of Asclepius; *cf.* XLII 15.

15. Pergamum was inland and had no harbors. For the metaphor, *cf.* XLII 1 and XLVII 2.

16. Asclepius.

17. *Iliad* XVIII 478, 490.

18. *Cf.* note 22 to XVII. Κορυφή elsewhere refers to Deirman Tepe (Pausanias VII 5, 9), but the acropolis (Mt. Pagus) is meant; *cf.* XVII 19, XVIII 3.

19. Homer (*cf.* XVII 8, 15) *Iliad* IX 63.

20. *Cf.* XVII 13.

21. of oratory; *cf.* Behr, *Aelius Aristides,* p. 45 n. 18; p. 107 n. 42; *Studies on the Biography,* § 4.

22. Traditionally three libations were offered at the end of a banquet (*cf.* Xenophon *Cyropaedia* II 3. 1), the third usually to Zeus Soter.

23. It was, indeed, the seat of the governor and his offices.

24. For a recent review of the excavations at Ephesus, *cf.* RE supp. 12 (1970), Anhang *s.v.* Ephesos. It is typical of Aristides' self-centered attitude that although he had visited and lectured at Ephesus on more than one occasion, the city clearly meant nothing to him and so he does not describe it.

25. *Cf.* Strabo XIV 640 on Herostratus.

26. Smyrna and Ephesus.
27. *Cf.* XXI 13. He imitates Herodotus V 28.
28. Pergamum, spoken of as if it were an ancient Teuthranian city (*cf.* XXXVIII 11), founded by aboriginal Mysians.
29. § 13-26.
30. The metaphor is the stronger since Aristides seems to have suffered from this disease, *cf.* Behr, *Aelius Aristides,* pp. 162, 165 n. 10.
31. In the Κοινόν it would appear that there was weighted voting. *Digesta* XXVII 1. 6. 2 gives a triple ranking of Asian cities (metropoleis, sites of the assizes, and other cities) and we know from Strabo XIV 664-665 that such weighted voting was practiced in the Lycian federation, where the largest cities had three votes, the medium sized two, and the others one.
32. A play on κοινόν.
33. *Pythian* IX 98 Turyn. Heracles is not named in Pindar, but Georg Kaibel in Keil's edition thought that his name might have occurred in a fuller scholium to Pindar now lost. The existing scholia attribute the saying to Nereus. The slip is probably Aristides', as in II 95.
34. An allusion to εὐφημεῖτε.
35. Τὸ Κοινόν.
36. During Xerxes' invasion in 480 B.C.
37. *Cf.* I 126.
38. *Cf.* I 120-122.
39. Herodotus VII 118-120.
40. *Cf.* especially Herodotus VII 140, 148 f., 169; also Aristides I 117, which refers to the oracle in Herodotus VII 140.
41. *Cf.* I 137-149.
42. *Cf.* Herodotus VIII 130. 1.
43. *Cf.* Herodotus VIII 27. 5 and IX 81 and Aristides I 190. The offerings at Delphi were paid for by a tithe of the booty taken from the Persians.
44. Between 479-468 B.C.
45. *Cf.* Thucydides III 82.
46. In 431 B.C. *Cf.* Thucydides II 12. 3.
47. At Sphacteria in 425 B.C.
48. In 413 B.C.
49. In 404 B.C.
50. Their primacy lasted between 404-394 B.C.; cf. I 283.
51. Thebes' primacy began after she defeated Sparta at Leuctra in 371 B.C. After the battle of Mantinea in 362 B.C. she lost her preeminence.
52. In 352 B.C. the Phocians, who achieved considerable power after the decline of Thebes, their southern neighbors, drove off an invasion of Philip of Macedon. In 339 B.C., when Phocis began to decay, Philip successfully entered Greece through Thermopylae and won his decisive victory over Thebes at Chaeronea in 338 B.C.
53. At the news of Alexander the Great's death in 323 B.C. Greece revolted against Macedonia. The rebellion was suppressed by Antipater, one of Alexander's leading generals, and the Athenian democratic constitution ruthlessly altered.
54. The Romans.
55. In 407 B.C. This Cyrus was the son of King Darius II and the younger brother of Artaxerxes II.
56. Artaxerxes II on the throne between 405-359 B.C.
57. In 403 B.C.
58. See note 3.
59. *Iliad* IV 442-443.

60. The text may be more corrupt than indicated, but ἐκείνους seems to refer to the Lacedaemonians, Athenians, and Thebans, with an especial reference to the notorious Athenian courts where the allies had often to appear for trial; cf. Pseudo-Xenophon, *Ath. Pol.* I 16 ff., Isocrates V 63.
61. The Smyrnaeans and Ephesians.
62. The Pergamenes, cf. § 15, 26.
63. An aposiopesis. The thought, too unflattering to be expressed, is that they were satisfied to be followers.
64. Aristides shared in the official Roman view that the emperors from Nerva through Marcus and Verus formed one dynasty; cf. Behr, *Studies on the Biography* § 10.
65. At this time chosen by lot from former holders of the consulship fourteen to seventeen years after that office. They held office for one year, from September to September it would seem; cf. Behr, *Aelius Aristides,* pp. 131 ff.
66. During his year of office the governor toured the province and stopped at the major cities to hold assizes; cf. Behr, *Aelius Aristides,* p. 133.
67. Aristides is ironic. The cities "command" and think of themselves as "masters", not subjects; cf. § 59.
68. *i.e.* willfulness and fawning.
69. Many of these temples honoring variously Rome, Augustus, and other members of the imperial family as well as the Roman Senate (cf. J. Deininger, *Die Provinziallandtage,* pp. 37 f.) formed in the larger cities, which sometimes had more than one temple, the center around which was constructed the cult of the Κοινόν (the provincial assembly) as well as its games (Τὰ κοινά); cf. Behr, *Studies on the Biography* § 7.
70. Κοινὰ τὰ φίλων; cf. XXVII 24.
71. *Cf.* Alcaeus 35. 10 D. = 112 Lobel-Page.
72. *Cf.* Herodotus I 191. 6 ἐν εὐπαθείῃσι.
73. *Cf.* XXVII 44.
74. *Tragicorum Graecorum Fragmenta* Anon. 40 N.[2].
75. Sophocles *Ajax* 1353.
76. *Epistle* 3. 45.
77. Either Hadrian (cf. XXVII 22) or Antoninus Pius, for one of whose rescripts on this subject, SIG[3] 849, cf. note 1. Keil in his edition, followed by Chr. Habicht, *Die Inschriften des Asklepieions* (1969), p. 33, badly suggested Marcus. But in § 78 Marcus and Verus are referred to as still reigning.
78. *Cf.* § 60-64.
79. A play on κόσμος = Universe and beauty; cf. XXVII 35.
80. This is somewhat reminiscent of Xenophon *Memorabilia* IV 7. 5; cf. also Aristides XXIV 42, XXVII 35.
81. *Cf.* XXXVI 120.
82. Marcus and Verus; cf. XXVII 23-39.
83. The governors of the province; cf. note 65.
84. § 8, 11; cf. § 62.
85. The other speakers; cf. § 1, 4, 5, 61, and Dio Chrysostom XXXVIII 51.

NOTES TO XXIV

1. The speech was written in Smyrna shortly before September 149 A.D., it would seem; cf. Behr, *Aelius Aristides,* pp. 73-74. Its purpose was to put an end to a class struggle which broke out in Rhodes, perhaps in connection with public loans taken to repair the damages of the terrible earthquake of 142 A.D. (cf. especially

§ 29, 32, 40; on Rhodian finacial matters, *cf.* also Dio Chrysostom XXXI 46). It is the closest that Aristides ever approaches to dealing with social problems which we know from Dio Chrysostom were beginning to become serious in Asia at this time.

The speech is divided into the following sections.
A. § 1-3 Proem. Aristides' past help
B. § 4-21 Concord an indisputable good: traditional evidence
C. § 22 Faction injurious to Rhodes' freedom
D. § 23-27 Examples from history
E. § 28-40 Appeal for settlement of present dispute
F. § 41-44 Praise of concord
G. § 45-57 Rhodes' glorious tradition opposes faction
H. § 58-59 Peroration

2. From Smyrna.

3. Not only Asclepius, but also Sarapis, Isis, and Zeus, whom Aristides is known to have invoked at this time.

4. Aristides' help after the earthquake of 142 A.D., when he spoke on behalf of the Rhodians during his stay in Egypt; *cf.* Behr, *Aelius Aristides*, pp. 15-16.

5. Semi-legendary, *c.* 675 B.C. He was summoned to Sparta by a Delphic oracle and his singing put an end to faction there; *cf.* § 55.

6. If the text, as slightly emended, is correct, Aristides pays himself a compliment. The Rhodians will agree (not be factious) with Aristides' arguments.

7. *Odyssey* VI 182-185. In the last line the *Odyssey* reads αὐτοί instead of αὐτοῦ and means "they know it best themselves". Aristides seems to have made the change.

8. *Works and Days* 11-24.

9. Frg. 5 Diehl.

10. Herodotus VIII 3, 1.

11. Plato *Laws* 710 D-E.

12. *Cf.* § 58. Rhodes' nominal "liberty"—mostly freedom from direct imperial supervision of her affairs and from minor Roman officials—was at least twice revoked in the empire, once by Claudius in 44 A.D., who restored it himself in 53 A.D. (*cf.* Magie, *Roman Rule in Asia Minor,* p. 1406 n. 24) and again by Vespasian and later restored by Titus between 79-81 A.D. (*cf.* Magie, *op. cit.,* p. 1427 n. 9; Dio Chrysostom XXXI 112).

13. They are threatened with loss of freedom or an imperial *corrector,* which amounts to much the same.

14. Dorians.

15. *c.* 885 B.C.

16. The Pisistratid tyrants were expelled in 510 B.C. The crises alluded to were the Persian wars of 490 and 481-479 B.C.

17. In 404 B.C.; *cf.* XXIII 47-49.

18. In 403 B.C.; *cf.* XXIII 52.

19. *Cf.* § 45, and Thucydides VII 57, 6.

20. The history is obscure. The same affair is cited in I 261 and 371. I suspect that the bloody events of 370 B.C. are meant, when after the battle of Leuctra the upper classes of the Argives were accused apparently of siding with the Lacedaemonians; *cf.* the scholium to Aristides in vol. 3, p. 257, 7 ff. Ddf. 1200 or 1500 of them were butchered; *cf.* Diodorus XV 57. 3-58; Plutarch *Praecepta gerendae rei publicae* 814 B; and Isocrates V 52. Plutarch *loc. cit.,* at least, reports that when the Athenians heard of the slaughter, they decreed purificatory offerings to be made about the ecclesia. Aristides is the only source for the story of the embassy.

21. Apparently the dispute originated when the magistrates and priests, *i.e.* the wealthy class, borrowed money for the state and used as collateral the revenues and sacred vessels of the city; *cf.* § 40-41, where it is said that the rich demanded im-

munity. For such practices, *cf.* F. K. Dörner *Der Erlass des Statthalters von Asia* (1935), pp. 37 f., col VII = E. M. Smallwood *Documents Illustrating the Principates of Gaius, Claudius, and Nero,* no. 380: (from Ephesus, a decree of the proconsul Paullus Fabius Persicus *c.* 51 A.D.): "Equally it is ordered that no priest of Artemis nor any annual official borrow money on behalf of the public treasury, save as much as he can repay from the revenues of that year. But if ever someone pledges the revenue of the coming year, it is ordered that the lender be granted an action for recovery of the loan from him".

22. Aristides "improves" on Demosthenes XVIII 254. The public fund provided free seats for theater and other entertainments.

23. *Cf.* XXIII 20.

24. *Cf.* II 191 ff., XXVIII 123, 125 ff., XXXIV 53.

25. From the proverb: τῷ κακῷ τὸ κακὸν ἰᾶσθαι, "to cure evil with evil".

26. Ironic. The victory of a faction is compared to the victory of the Spartan king Cleomenes, a suicide in 491 B.C., over his rival Demaratus (*cf.* Herodotus VI 75, 3) because of which Cleomenes was said to have gone mad.

27. The Bacchants of Thebes.

28. After ridding the text of some glosses, I interpret τούτου to mean the end of faction. Reiske and Keil think that it signifies the attribution of blame to fortune.

29. *Cf.* XXIII 77, XXVII 35.

30. Also an allusion to Sarapis, *cf.* Behr, *Aelius Aristides,* p. 74 n. 48 a.

31. *Cf.* note 19.

32. The Heraclidae were both founders and kings, *cf.* Homer *Iliad* II 653 f. The Asclepiadae were only kings, *cf.* Aristides XXXVIII 13.

33. *Iliad* II 655-656.

34. "ordered".

35. *Iliad* II 668-669.

36. *Cf.* Strabo XIV 655.

37. *Cf.* XXV 29.

38. Odysseus' men killed the cattle of the Sun and were subsequently destroyed for the act; *cf. Odyssey* XII 260 ff.

39. Odysseus.

40. Prizes in poetic and musical contests.

41. In 142 A.D.; see oration XXV.

42. *Cf.* XXV 4.

43. They were notorious for the factious behavior immortalized in the poems of Alcaeus, *c.* 600 B.C.; *cf.* also II 336. However, a real current event may be alluded to.

44. As Terpander went to Sparta, see § 3, note 5.

45. With an allusion to γνωρίζειν as used in the reconciliation of faction in the sense of "acceptance of one another", *cf.* § 48 and III 693.

46. Doric; *cf.* Suetonius *Tiberius* 56.

47. On the high value of such honors at Rhodes, *cf.* Dio Chrysostom XXXI 110.

48. 'Εχεχειρία as if "holding back one's hands".

49. On the rights of foreigners in Rhodes, *cf.* IG XII 1, 383 (ξενωθέντος) and R.E. Suppl. 5 *s.v.* Rhodos 766-767.

50. One of the styles of Greek music, used for martial airs.

51. Georg Kaibel in Keil's edition has compared Pindar *Olympian* II 17-19; on similar thoughts, see the references in Turyn's edition *ad. loc.*

52. Homer in *Iliad* XIII 115; *cf.* also Wilamowitz, *Platon* II, p. 41.

53. *Cf.* Simonides 5, 17 Bergk (= 19 Edmonds); and the epigram quoted in Demosthenes XVIII 289.

54. *i.e. Iliad* XIII 115 spoken by Poseidon.
55. *Cf.* § 22 and notes 12 and 13.
56. *Cf.* XVIII 7, a play on the proverb "second things better".

NOTES TO XXV

1. In early 142 A.D. a great earthquake ravaged Lycia, Caria, Cos, and Rhodes. The dating of the earthquake to 142 A.D. depends on the Opramoas inscription = IGRR III 739. The earthquake is mentioned eight times in the inscription: chapters, 40, 42, 46, 47, 53, 55, 59, 63. The earliest datable document in this inscription concerning the earthquake is Pius' rescript (c. 40, dated from Rome *a.d. X Kal. Oct.,* in his *trib.pot.* 6 = September 22, 143 A.D.) in answer to a decree sent to him by the Lycian federation (evidently that described in c. 53 and dated only Gorpiaeus 7 = November 7, 142 A.D. (?), for the two documents are related by the fact that a certain Eupolemus is named as ambassador in both). The other documents of the decree are of the same or later date. More importantly none are earlier, and in the documents drawn up in 142 A.D. or before there is no mention of such a disaster. However, Magie, *Roman Rule in Asia Minor,* p. 1492, on the basis of c. 37 and c. 38 thought that the earthquake might have been as early as 139 A.D. Yet neither of these fragmentary rescripts of Pius mentions an earthquake. Further see Behr, *Aelius Aristides,* p. 15 n. 44.

Ambassadors from Rhodes were sent to Alexandria for help, and Aristides there delivered a speech of consolation, *cf.* XXIV 2-3. Oration XXV, however, was not this speech. The loose style, the preciosity in the use of words, the obvious puns, the tasteless and revolting detail, which has a grisly quality too reminiscent of Seneca's tragedies, could not be more unlike Aristides' manner. We may also note that this author looks with favor on "sophists", *cf.* § 18, and differs from Aristides in the more conventional account of the numbers involved in the seizure of Phyle, *cf.* § 65-66. Yet the oration is a contemporary work and was actually delivered in the ruined city, *cf.* § 53. Its place among Aristides' speeches can be due to nothing more than its similarity to oration XXIV and to some editor's desire to fill the gap of the lost speech of Aristides with a well-known version of another orator. But it may well have been found among Aristides' own papers. For it seems that Aristides was familiar with this speech and borrowed from it for his own later works, *e.g. cf.* § 8 with XXVI 29 and § 38 with XX 15 (and other parallels to be noted in the apparatus of my edition of the Greek text).

The speech is divided into the following sections:
A. § 1-8 Proem. Former greatness
B. § 9-10 All lost
C. § 11-16 Rhodians must endure
D. § 17-33 Description of the immensity of the destruction
E. § 34-49 Endure: the greatness of the disaster will show the greatness of Rhodes
F. § 50-56 Reconstruction of city compared to its founding
G. § 57-68 Examples of history
H. § 69 Peroration.

2. Semele, from Thebes, daughter of Cadmus and Harmonia, mother of Dionysus; Leda, from Lacedaemonia, mother of Castor and Pollux.

3. For the Etruscan spoils, *cf.* XXIV 53. For the Rhodian fleet's service with Alexander the Great, *cf.* Arrian *Anabasis* II 20, 2 (10 vessels); see also R.E. supp. 5 (1931) *s.v.* Rhodos (Hiller v. Gaertringen) 777.

4. *Cf.* Dio Chrysostom XXXI 146.

5. An allusion to the *pax Romana.*

6. The Greek has been emended. It means I think in their number and beauty; *cf. e.g.* § 29 for another of many such word plays. On the statues, *cf.* Dio Chrysostom XXXI 146. Pliny *Natural History* XXXIV 7, 36 reports that there were 3000 statues.
7. § 2.
8. *Cf.* Plato *Laws* 934 A.
9. *Cf.* Cicero *Ep. ad Quint.* I 2. 4, 13; Seneca *Ep.* 85, 33; O. Hense *Teletis Reliquiae*, pp. L ff., 62.
10. *Cf.* for this use of οἴκοθεν II 301 (with 313) and *Paroemiographi Graeci* 291 n. 29.
11. *Cf.* Sophocles *Oedipus Tyr.* 263.
12. *i.e.* at sea.
13. An allusion to Rhodes' hitherto perpetual good fortune.
14. *Cf.* Euripides *Telephus* frg. 720 N², parodied by Aristophanes *Acharnians* 8.
15. At funeral rites the dead were customarily called upon three times; *cf.* Homer *Odyssey* IX 65, Vergil *Aeneid* VI 506.
15a. This powerful description may be no more than a rhetorical commonplace, although ultimately derived from fact; *cf.* Aristotle *Meteorologica* 366a ff.; Seneca *NQ* VI 12. 2; Pliny *NH* II 192; Ammianus XVII 7, 11 ff.
16. The sun, Helios, had an especial cult at Rhodes.
17. When a cure for a diseased portion of the body was sought from some god and subsequently effected, little models of these members were often dedicated in gratitude.
18. *Cf.* § 19, the event took place at "noon" and § 46, it lasted "an hour".
19. *i.e.* the bodies were so mangled that in some cases a piece of another body would be found on an unrelated corpse.
20. A time when fires were not lit, *cf.* Philostratus the Elder *Imagines* II 27, 3 (381 K) and Pindar *Olymp.* VII 48 ff. Turyn.
21. *Cf.* Dio Chrysostom XXXI 122.
22. *Cf.* XXIV 50, Pindar *Olymp.* VII 54 ff. Turyn.
23. *Iliad* II 670.
24. Mythical king of Argos and founder of the three cities of Rhodes.
25. *Olymp.* VII 49 Turyn.
26. Islands south-west of Rhodes.
27. On the mainland. It also suffered in this earthquake.
28. Two of the original three cities of the island of Rhodes.
29. *Cf.* Athenaeus XIII 561 E.
30. Helius and Rhode.
31. Keil cites, not very appositely, Polybius IV 56, 3, who reports that the Rhodians sold "hair" for export. Reiske, without authority, refers to the famous siege of Demetrius Poliorcetes in 305 B.C.
32. The theater and council chamber were not themselves destroyed, *cf.* § 53; but they were "shorn" of their beauty.
33. More precisely 550 years. The city of Rhodes was founded in 408 B.C.; *cf.* § 50.
34. *i.e.* the dedication of statues and public buildings.
35. Literally "endure with closed eyes".
36 The author plays with the idea of "fate" and the notion that fate has gone beyond due measure.
37. *Theogony* 703-704.
38. *Cf. Odyssey* XIII 174. The conveyance of Odysseus to his home marked the end of such kind acts on the part of the Phaeacians.
39. *Cf.* XXIV 57.
40. § 38. The third quality is to endure their sufferings best.

41. Homer *Iliad* XXIV 527-533.
42. *Cf.* Seneca *Quaestiones Naturales* III 27. 2.
43. *Cf.* § 29.
44. *Cf.* § 33 Lysander was killed in 395 B.C.
45. *Iliad* II 656; *cf.* Aristides XXIV 46.
46. The Colossus.
47. The ecclesia or council chamber used as an auditorium where orators, such as the author, had lectured or performed.
48. Antoninus Pius, who in fact did generously contribute to the restoration of the city; *cf.* Pausanias VIII 43, 4; *SHA Antoninus Pius* IX. 1.
49. §§ 10, 38.
50. The Trojan war. Heracles captured Troy just one generation before.
51. In 86 B.C. by Fimbria; *cf.* Strabo XIII 594.
52. Once certainly by Alexander the Great in 335 B.C. To which other occasion the author alludes in unclear. He may refer either to the mythical sack by the Epigoni in the generation following the Seven against Thebes or, less likely, to the mythical expulsion of the Thebans by the Pelasgians during the Trojan war; *cf.* Diodorus XIX 53. 6-8.
53. One of the Seven against Thebes. On his return from the war, near Oropus on the border between Attica and Boeotia, the earth opened up and swallowed him down. The site became a famous oracle. Δύναται in the Greek seems to me to have the same force which the noun δύναμις sometimes has, a magical or supernatural power.
54. Just the opposite advice, in the same words, is given in § 34.
55. *Cf.* Alcaeus 35. 10 Diehl = 112 Lobel-Page; Aristides III 298; XXIII 68.
56. *Cf.* Xenophon *Hellenica* II 4, 2; Plutarch *Bellone an Pace* etc. 345 D. Aristides himself I 254 gives the number as "little more than fifty". In Pausanias I 29, 3 the number is sixty. The event occurred at the end of 404 B.C.
57. In 405 B.C.; *cf.* I 243, 252, 280.
58. He led the band which seized Phyle; *cf.* § 65.
59. In the Persian war, 480 B.C.; *cf.* I 154 ff.; III 247.

NOTES TO XXVI

1. In late 155 A.D., eleven years after his disastrous first journey, Aristides made a second trip to Rome (*cf.* LII 3). Here in the presence of the imperial court, he delivered the XXVIth oration. The only datable events in the speech are found in § 70, for which see note 77; on the dating, see Behr, *Aelius Aristides,* pp. 88-90 and *Studies on the Biography* § 8. Other commentators assume that the speech was given in 144 A.D. during Aristides' first trip to Rome. But his extreme ill health at that time (*cf.* Behr, *Aelius Aristides,* p. 24) and the irreconcilable historical problems which result from such a date render their assumption most improbable. The speech shows affinities to the other orations given at this time, I, XLIV, and XLVI. It should not be, as has been done, too closely pressed as a source of contemporary political information. It is primarily rhetorical, its enthusiasms either traditional, as we can see by comparison with Dionysius of Halicarnassus (see note 66 to § 59), Plutarch, and Dio Chrysostom or informed by Aristides' own circumstances (*e.g. cf.* §§ 32, 37) or that of his province (*e.g. cf.* §§ 36, 67, 95). It can even be occasionally rather misleading, as in Aristides' comments on the Roman army (§§ 75, 85, 88). Naturally this speech has attracted many commentators. The most comprehensive and fullest work is that of J. H. Oliver, *The Ruling Power,* TAPS 43, 1953, an excellent study, although Oliver is inclined to overwork his material and is occasionally in need of correction.

The speech divides into the following sections:

A. § 1-5 Proem. Difficulty of speech
B. § 6-13 Geography
C. § 14-57 Comparison with other empires
D. § 58-71 Civil policy and administration
E. § 72-89 Military policy
F. § 90-91 Constitution
G. § 92-106 The empire flourishes in peace
H. § 107 The emperor
I. § 108-109 Peroration.

2. Pindar frg. 267 Turyn (so scholium from Parisinus graecus 2995, see Keil, *Hermes* 48 (1913), pp. 319 ff.; but this scholiast surely made a wrong attribution at XXVII 15, *cf.* n. 24 to or. XXVII; in any case wrongly attributed to comedy as Aristophanes frg. 913 K and CAF III Anon. 784 K). A rich man is mocked for a stupid vow; *cf.* also n. 135 to XXVIII.

3. *Cf.* XXX 10, XXXV 2. On these disclaimers, which are not seriously meant, *cf.* Norden, *Antike Kunstprosa* (5th ed.) p. 595, n. 1.

4. *i.e.* they describe heaven in terms suitable to humans.

5. From the lost *Sthenoboea*, frg. 663 N.

6. The Persian king who led the expedition against Greece in 480 B.C.

7. Probably Janus, although Oliver, *The Ruling Power,* p. 909 suggests the emperor in the guise of Helius.

8. *Iliad* XII 282-284.

9. I suppose that the mountains in the interior, if anything, are meant.

10. "Rome" happens to be the Greek word for strength.

11. Thucydides I 10.

12. Aeschines Socraticus in the *Alcibiades; cf.* III 348, Pap. Oxy. 1608, also below § 16.

13. As they did the Persian empire according to the terms of the Peace of Callias in 448 B.C.; see *e.g.* I 274.

14. *Cf. e.g. Iliad* XVI 776.

15. It seems to me that in its traditional version the passage is corrupt. I presume that Aristides is speaking hyperbolically since the Mediterranean was effectively closed by storms to ancient sailors between October and March.

16. Both islands of the Cyclades group in the Aegean sea.

17. *Theogony* 736 ff.

18. *Cf.* Bergk LGF (4th edition) III p. 704, no. 55; Edmonds, *Lyra Graeca* III Anonymous no. 45 (p. 437).

19. *Cf.* § 10 and note 12. Aeschines Socraticus is speaking of Xerxes in 481-479 B.C.

20. *Cf.* § 10 and note 13.

21. On the children's game of *King, cf.* Herodotus I 144, Dio Chrysostom IV 47-48.

22. The Spartan king Agesilaus fought in Asia between 396-395 B.C. The Spartan Clearchus (famous from Xenophon's *Anabasis*) led the mercenary force of the Ten Thousand in 401 B.C.

23. A similar story is told of Alexander in Plutarch's *Life of Alexander* 65. 6. This version comes from Ctesias' *Persica* according to Oliver's suggestion, *The Ruling Power,* p. 912; from Aeschines Socraticus according to Keil in his edition of Aristides. This last is denied by Dittmar, *Aeschines von Sphettos,* p. 73 n. 25, who attributes it to Antisthenes.

24. § 19.

25. Δεσπότης, "master".

26. Alexandria; *cf.* XXI 4. The city was probably founded by Ptolemy.

27. Of course, this is only true of those generals, like Ptolemy and Seleucus, who ruled foreign kingdoms. Macedonians still held Macedonia.

28. The king of Persia. For the uprooting of people, *cf.* § 19.

29. Probably our Red Sea, but the designation could include the Persian Gulf as well as the Indian Ocean (*cf.* § 70; I 119; IX 34; XXXVI 87; Tacitus *Annales* II 61). Lake Maeotis is now the Sea of Azov.

30. *Iliad* IX 476.

31. *Cf.* Herodotus II 23 and IV 36 and Plutarch *Life of Caesar* 23. 2-3.

32. Britain, *cf.* § 82, XXXVI 91, and possibly XXVII 32.

33. Tribes of Asia in the Persian empire. Aristides came from Mysia.

34. Oliver, *The Ruling Power,* p. 916, compares Demosthenes XXI 60.

35. The impersonal use of ἄρχεται is surprising. Hence perhaps the addition of ὑπό, which I have removed from the corrupt Greek text. On the idea, *cf.* XLIII 30.

36. Far from being in revolt. For some reason the interpretation of this passage troubles Oliver, *The Ruling Power,* pp. 917-918.

37. The expression is vague, but in the province of Asia seems to allude to the administrative distinction between πόλις and δῆμος.

38. Aristides hints at his own legal problems just past, *cf.* Behr, *Aelius Aristides,* pp. 77-86; *Studies on the Biography* § 6, see also below § 37 and note 43.

39. By imperial "rescripts", which had the force of law.

40. Persian satraps from the end of the fifth century B.C.

41. Highly exaggerated, although some senatorial officers were nominally elected to their earlier prerequisite urban posts. On the annual succession of governors in Asia, *cf.* XXIII 62.

42. *Cf.* Aristotle *Respublica Atheniensium* 42. 1.

43. Aristides refers to his own experiences when he appealed against election to civil office to the governor of Asia and threatened (actually in one case he carried out the threat) to go over the governor's head in appealing to the emperor; *cf.* § 32 and the references cited in n. 38. The sense is badly misunderstood by Oliver, *The Ruling Power,* p. 920.

44. *Cf.* I 47, of Athens.

45. Badly corrupt, but *cf.* XXXV 19 and L 79.

46. *Works and Days* 5.

47. § 14.

48. Another name for Pylus, the site of Cleon's victory over the Lacedaemonians in 429 B.C.; *cf.* I 229.

49. The comparison is drawn from amatory enchantments, where the hair and nails of the person over whom the spell was cast play the principal role, *cf.* Jones, American Journal of Philology, 1964, p. 65.

50. Where the victor suffered as badly as the vanquished, as in the mutual slaughter of Oedipus' sons, Eteocles and Polynices.

51. Pausanias, of the royal family, victor over the Persians at Plataea in 479 B.C., afterwards a ruthless, greedy tyrant; *cf.* Thucydides I 94-96, 130.

52. In 404 B.C.

53. A rule of ten under a Lacedaemonian Harmost, for whom *cf.* § 49.

54. Conon at Cnidus in 394 B.C.; *cf.* I 243, 252, 280.

55. The Harmosts, *cf.* n. 53.

56. At Leuctra in 371 B.C.

57. The citadel of Thebes, seized by the Lacedaemonians in 383/2 B.C.; *cf.* I 293.

58. *The Three-Headed Monster* (referring to Athens, Sparta, and Thebes) was written by Anaximenes of Lampsacus, of the fourth century B.C., under the name of the great historian Theopompus; *cf.* Pausanias VI 18. 5; Jacoby *FGH* II A, frg. 21, p. 214.

59. A major part of Athens' philanthropy in Aristides' *Panathenaic Oration*. Hence a plausible restoration of the corrupt Greek text that speaks of "opposing their rulers", which makes little sense as a virtue.

60. *Cf.* Herodotus I 15-22. However, Oliver rejects the reference to Lydians and prefers to emend ἀναλῶσαι (expending wealth).

61. Another theme from the *Panathenaic Oration; cf.* I 313.

62. If the text is sound, the citizens (the inhabitants of the city) seem to be distinguished from the natives of the region.

63. And allusion to the stone of Sisyphus.

64. *Cf.* Plutarch *Moralia* 872 A; CAF II Xenarchus frg. 7. 2 K. Oliver *ad loc.* rightly suggests a game of draughts from Plutarch *Moralia* 1068 C.

65. Fable 162 Chambry, Babrius 72. In a beauty contest, in which the winner was to be king of the birds, the daw adorned himself with the plumage which had fallen from the other birds, but they detected the imposture and plucked him clean.

66. *Cf.* XXVII 32; on this theme, see also Dionysius of Halicarnassus *Antiq. Roman.* II 17, XIV 6; Dio Chrysostom XLI 9; Tacitus *Annales* XI 24. 4.

67. *i.e.* they kept the citizenship of their own people; *cf.* § 64; Behr, *Aelius Aristides*, p. 5.

68. Allusions to Sparta and Athens. The *Perioeci* were "settlers around" Sparta, who managed their own affairs but had no political rights in Sparta. Athens was divided into thirty demes or townships.

69. Hopelessly corrupt. The emendation is based on an imitation of this passage in Boissonade *Anecdota Graeca* II, p. 148; *cf.* also Aristides XXXVI 32 and on the idea Seneca *Quaestiones Naturales* III 4 and 8.

70. § 11 and *cf.* also § 59.

71. Hopelessly corrupt; *cf.* §§ 34 and 57; also Rutilius Namatianus I 69-70.

72. Μόρα, here used for "cohort", is properly a division of the Spartan army. The correct term would be σπεῖρα. Ἴλη, however, is the normal equivalent of *ala*, the Roman cavalry troop. *Cohors* and *ala*, to all intents and purposes, cover the divisions of the Roman army.

73. *Cf.* L 85, where a *legatus pro praetore* appears as an overseer of Smyrna's finances (see Behr, *Studies on the Biography* § 6), an official usually called a *curator rei publicae*. The following sentence alludes to the overspending of these cities which necessitated the *correctores*. The whole passage is badly misunderstood by Oliver, *The Ruling Power*, p. 923.

74. Homer *Odyssey* xxiv 6-8.

75. Plato *Republic* 614 B.

76. *Cf.* I 12.

77. *Cf.* § 105. See Behr, *Aelius Aristides*, pp. 88-89. The Getae of the Greek are the Dacians; *cf. SHA Pius* V 4. M. Statius Priscus is known to have obtained a victory over them at the time of this speech, *cf.* CIL III 1416 (see my remarks in *Studies on the Biography* §8). W. Hüttl, *Antoninus Pius* Bd. I, p. 284, has invented a Dacian war in 143 A.D. He is followed by most modern historians. The Libyans of the Greek are the Moors and refer to the protracted Moorish wars of the time, cf. *SHA Pius loc. cit.*, Pausanias VIII 43, 3 (Hüttl, *op. cit.*, pp. 311 ff.). This war was ended by 150 A.D., but troubles with robbers and guerrilla actions are still mentioned in 153/4 A.D., *cf.* Hüttl, *op. cit.*, p. 312 n. 457, who cites Fronto I 236 Haines. The reference to the troubles about "the Red Sea" (for the meaning of which, see n. 29 to § 28) is problematical. We know of unrest in Egypt in 154 A.D., *cf.* Hüttl, *op. cit.* p. 294 (citing p. 293 n. 356 BGU I 372). Certainly not meant is the event described by Malalas PG 97, p. 423 = XI, p. 280 Schenk, which Hüttl, *op. cit.*, pp. 290 ff. and D. Magie, *Roman Rule in Asia Minor*, p. 1528 (n. 1) connect with Pius. As Magie himself, *op. cit.*, p. 1529 n. 2, says, the event belongs to the reign of

Caracalla. If, as is alleged (see n. 1), this speech were given in 144 A.D., it is surprising that there is no mention of the British wars which had ended in 142 A.D., *cf.* Hüttl, *op. cit.*, p. 254.

78. On this doublet to § 77 οὐ γὰρ κτλ., see my comments in the introduction to the *editio maior* of *Aelii Aristidis Opera* edd. Lenz-Behr, vol. I, fasc. 1, pp. LXVIII ff.

79. *Cf.* § 59.

80. *Cf.* Herodotus II 144, 164-165; Diodorus I 73, 7-9; 94, 4; Plato *Timaeus* 24 AB; Aristotle *Politics* 1329 A 40.

81. In fact, unless given a medical discharge, a foreign recruit had to serve for twenty-five years (twenty-six in the fleet) before being granted citizenship. (The officer class was exclusively made up of Roman citizens). On the difficulty of recruitment at this time, *cf.* Hüttl, *Antoninus Pius* Bd. I, p. 229.

82. Foreign recruits generally served in other than their native provinces.

83. *Cf.* III 687, XXIX 18, IX 33.

84. *i.e.* segregated them, *cf.* § 73 ἀποκρῖναι. For the difficult construction, *cf.* II 327. Otherwise I would emend <κατὰ> τὸ κοινὸν τῶν ἀρχόντων, "in the common way of rulers"; *cf.* Justin Martyr *Dialogus* 54. 2; 88. 2; 119. 5.

85. § 75.

86. Semiramis; *cf.* Diodorus II 7-10.

87. There was a wall in Republican times, the so-called *agger Servii Tulii*. But the city had long grown beyond it. Rome's famous walls were built later, begun under Aurelian in 271 A.D.

88. The *limes,* the Roman system of fortifications against dangerous border tribes, mostly in Scotland, Germany, and the Danube, was perfected under Trajan and Hadrian, *e.g. cf.* Hüttl, *Antoninus Pius* Bd. I, p. 230.

89. A Persian measurement, often used by the Greeks, of about 35 miles.

90. The Phasis is a river in Colchis which empties into the Black Sea. The "great island" is England; *cf.* § 28.

91. *Iliad* XVI 212-213.

92. *Cf.* Behr, American Journal of Philology 95 (1974), p. 147 n. 25 on "Firminus" quoted in Anonymous Περὶ Πολιτικῆς Ἐπιστήμης, Script. Vet. Nov. Coll. ed. Mai, II (1827), p. 592, 20 ff.; also *cf.* Alcaeus 35 a 10 D.; Demosthenes XVIII 299; Vegetius *De Re Militari* I 20.

93. *Iliad* XVI 214 ff.

94. § 83.

95. *Cf.* Arrian *Tactica* 11. 6, who reports that the elevated shields of the *testudo,* a closely compacted formation of infantry, could sustain the weight of javelin throwers running on top of it.

96. *Phoenissae* 110-111.

97. *Cf.* § 88. For διέξοδοι meaning "tactical revolutions", see the references in Liddell-Scott-Jones, Plato *Laws* 813 C, Cassius Dio LXXV 5, 5. The "human" and the real, fixed wall are meant.

98. Eretria, 490 B.C.; *cf.* I 102, 119 (on the idea of preventing escape, I 164), III 181, and the probable source Plato *Laws* 698 CD.

99. For the rare dative of instrument, *cf.* XXIV 55, XXXII 25. For κοινοῖς = "partner", *cf.* § 76.

100. § 78.

101. If Aristides means that the highest offices were not limited to the "patricians", he is correct. But they were limited, with the exception of some equestrian posts, to members of the senatorial class. It is highly misleading to imply that a foreign recruit could rise to command. At this time such advancement was impossible. But after his discharge a citizen soldier could theoretically have a career in the equestrian order, which might lead to a military rank of centurion or tribune or prefect.

102. *Iliad* IX 379.
103. The passage is corrupt. Emended it means that if ten enemy met one Roman, the enemy would be annihilated (one less than one is none).
104. *Cf.* Diodorus I 46. Cambyses, the second king of Persia, conquered Egypt in 525 B.C.
105. Thucydides V 66. 4.
106. These remarks, which seem traditional in Greek writers of the time, have nothing to do with the Roman army. Arrian, a contemporary of Aristides, and a man who actually commanded a Roman army, borrowing from the much earlier treatise of Asclepiodotus, in writing of the Greek phalanx, describes an officer, ἐνωμοτάρχης, who was the commander of perhaps four men (*Tactica* 6. 2, 3). Among the non-commissioned officers in the Roman army, the *principales*, there are no formal ranks which would correspond with such a concept.
107. *Odyssey* IV 74, where "court", αὐλή, has been replaced by "empire".
108. *Cf.* the myth in Plato *Protagoras* 320 C ff.
109. *Cf.* I 383 ff.; Isocrates IX 46; Plato *Laws* 712 D; Aristotle *Politics* 1265 B 33.
110. The emperor.
111. *Cf.* I 11 and 30.
112. Presumably a version of the wheel of fortune; *cf.* Herodotus I 207. 2; Anonymous *Epitome De Caesaribus* 18. 3, who speaks of the *"fortunae....pila"*. Reiske and Oliver see here an allusion to a ball game. But one wonders at the number of teams and the point of the comparison.
113. *Cf.* I 335.
114. *Cf.* §§ 28 f.; 34, 66; 59 f.
115. *Cf.* I 11, XVII 14.
116. The district in which Smyrna, Aristides' home, was located is singled out for special mention.
117. *Cf.* XIX 1 and 4.
118. *Cf.* I 1, 332.
119. It is unclear whether client kingdoms, such as Armenia, or free states, such as Athens, are meant. Probably the latter.
120. A Platonic expression; *cf. e.g.* III 401 and Plato *Gorgias* 516 E.
121. *Cf.* Thucydides I 6. 1, 3.
122. The vainglorious competition of the leading cities of the province of Asia for precedence and titles is castigated in oration XXIII; see note 1 to that speech.
123. A mountain pass in southern Turkey, leading to Tarsus.
124. *Iliad* XV 193.
125. *Cf.* I 36 f. The Athenian Triptolemus was the foster child of Demeter. It was he who distributed ears of wheat and the technique of sowing throughout the world.
126. *Cf.* XX 23.
127. See § 104.
128. *i.e.* if two Roman citizens, who were citizens of two different Greek communities, married, the marriage had validity in either community. Previously such marriages were generally not legal in their respective communities and rights of inheritance and citizenship of the offspring were jeopardized.
129. *Cf.* Plato *Symposium* 197 B.
130. "Light," φῶς, has primarily a religious significance. Oliver well compares Tacitus *Agricola* 44. 5.
131. An allusion to Saturn's emasculation of his father Uranus, and to Saturn's eating his own sons.
132. Perhaps Aristides simply refers to the common enough expression καλὸν ἔργον, often used by Plato, *e.g. cf. Charmides* 165 D ὑγίειαν καλὸν ἡμῖν ἔργον. Oliver compares Dio Chrysostom XLVIII 14.

133. *i.e.* of beauty (Aphrodite, *cf.* XXX 18) or grace, if the text is sound.

134. Asclepius and the Egyptian gods, Sarapis and Isis, were the paramount healing gods of antiquity. Aristides was devoted to all three. One otherwise wonders at the presence of the Egyptian gods in the Greco-Roman pantheon.

135. Perithous, king of the Lapiths, invited to his wedding banquet the Centaurs and all the gods except Ares. Angered, Ares caused fighting to break out between the Lapiths and the Centaurs; *cf.* Servius on Vergil *Aeneid* VII 304.

136. *Cf.* n. 77 to § 70; on the image of dancing, *cf.* XXVIII 108, XXXVII 8.

137. *Iliad* XX 307-308.

138. *Works and Days* 181. In Hesiod, Aidos and Nemesis leave the earth. Here Aristides follows the myth in Plato *Protagoras* 320 C ff.; *cf.* § 89.

139. Antoninus Pius, 138-161 A.D.

140. The passage is corrupt, but this seems to be the sense. Aristides either means the whole imperial administration or the emperor's *Consilium; cf. SHA Pius* VI 11.

141. Like Pindar, a favorite poet of Aristides.

142. For the phrase, *cf.* II 454 from Plato *Republic* 391 D. These are men such as Aeneas, Theseus, and Achilles.

143. From the oath of the Phocaeans, who swore never to return to Phocaea, held by the Persians, until the anvils which they had sunk in the harbor rose to the surface; *cf.* Herodotus I 165; Horace *Epode* XVI 25. If the unemended πέσοιεν is accepted ("fall above"), *cf.* v. Arnim *Stoicorum Veterum Fragmenta* I 100.

144. From the epitaph of King Midas, *cf.* Plato *Phaedrus* 264 D, *Certamen Homeri et Hesiodi* 324 Goettling = vs. 266 in the OCT.

145. The Caesar Marcus Aurelius and Lucius Verus, both adopted.

NOTES TO XXVII

1. The temple of Hadrian at Cyzicus, which was regarded by some, *e.g. Anthologia Palatina* IX 656. 15 f., as one of the seven wonders of the world, was begun under Hadrian (*cf. Chronicon Paschale,* p. 475 Ddf. in 123 A.D.; Malalas XI, p. 279 ed. Bonn.; scholium to Lucian *Icaromenippus* 24, ed. Rabe p. 107, with the implication that it was a far older work) as a new site for the provincial worship of Rome and the emperors of the Κοινόν of Asia. Hadrian (see *Chronicon Paschale,* Malalas, and scholium to Lucian *loc. cit.*) and the whole province (*cf.* IGRR IV 140) contributed money to its construction. The work was either completed or very near completion in the reign of Antoninus Pius (a picture of the finished temple appears on a coin from his reign, *British Museum Cat. Mysia,* p. 47, no. 218). However, in 161 A.D. an earthquake severely damaged the temple (*cf.* Xiphilinus = Cassius Dio LXIX 15. 4, Aristides XXXI 13—I now feel that the temple had no connection with Persephone and that the reference to the χθονίων θεῶν in XXXI 13 is to Eteoneus' dying as an ἄωρος, see my comments *ad loc.; cf.* also Behr, *Aelius Aristides,* pp. 92 ff., 100 ff.; *Studies on the Biography* §8). Repairs were completed by 166 A.D. (*cf.* §§ 22, 40-41), and a festival for the temple was held around September (*cf.* LI 11 ff.), to coincide with the celebration of the Cyzicene Olympiad. Aristides was admonished by Asclepius in a dream to participate, and he delivered this oration (twice, *cf.* LI 16), which is not so much in praise of the temple, as the clearly false addition to the original title implies, but is directed toward a favorite theme, the harmony between the cities of Asia, which found fuller expression four months later in the XXIIIrd oration.

The speech falls into the following sections:
A. § 1-4 Proem. Asclepius' encouragement

B. § 5-15 Geography and description of Cyzicus
C. § 16-21 The temple
D. § 22-39 The harmony between the emperors
E. § 40-45 The cities should behave concordantly
F. § 46 Peroration.
   2. *Cf.* LI 11 ff.
   3. Frg. 117. 1 Turyn = 98 Schroeder; *cf.* XXXIII 1 (from about the same time).
   4. For this word, *cf.* Behr, *Aelius Aristides,* pp. 163-164.
   5. *Cf.* § 46. Aristides enjoyed a certain notoriety for an unwillingness or inability to extemporize, *cf.* Behr, *Aelius Aristides,* p. 46 n. 21.
   6. But *cf.* XLIV 10.
   7. Legendary dwellers in the extreme north, the equivalent of saying "someone at the ends of the earth".
   8. Apollo, founder of Cyzicus (*cf.* the oracle quoted in the scholium to Apollonius Rhodius I 955, 959, and Pfeiffer on Callimachus frg. 109), also interpreted oracles for other cities (*cf.* I 399, Plato *Republic* 427 C).
   9. "Fortunate".
   10. It is now and was for most of antiquity a peninsula; Strabo XII 575 also calls it an island.
   11. *Cf.* Dio Chrysostom XXXVII 13; Aristides XLVI 22.
   12. The seas are the Mediterranean and the Euxine.
   13. Gadira (Cadiz) and the Phasis, at the east end of the Euxine sea, were traditional termini in ancient geography.
   14. *Odyssey* XIX 172.
   15. Lake Maeotis (the sea of Azov), *cf. e.g.* Arrian *Periplus* 19. 1 ff.: the river Tanais rose from Lake Maeotis and emptied into the Euxine sea, which emptied into the Mediterranean and so on.
   16. The Hellespont.
   17. The Propontis.
   18. The city of Cyzicus lay on the east coast of the neck of the peninsula and extended toward the west. Harbors were built on both coasts of the peninsula. Between the area of the city and the mainland of Turkey lay a vast swampy region. In Aristides' day the city was joined to the mainland by two causeways (perhaps 1500 yards in length, as I conjecture from the map at the end of F. W. Hasluck's *Cyzicus.*). In § 11 these are apparently called σχέλη, "legs", in imitation of the walls which ran from Athens to the Peiraeus, but in § 12 χώματα, "embankments" (*cf.* also Dittenberger *Sylloge* ed. 3, 799 II = *Sylloge* ed. 2, 543), and in Strabo XII 575 γέφυραι, "bridges". These causeways were intersected by canals (διώρυγες, *Sylloge* ed. 3, 799 II or εὔρειποι, IGRR IV 146, 147, *cf.* Plutarch *Lucullus* IX. 3 in the singular), which joined the harbors on either coast and presumably were spanned by drawbridges (*cf.* § 12 γέφυραι).
   19. VI 1. 2. Twenty stades are about two miles.
   20. Apollo, *cf.* § 5 (n.8).
   21. A proverbial expression; *cf.* XXVIII 45; XXXVII 27; Liddell-Scott-Jones *s.v.* ἀγορά I.
   22. Cyzicus was a colony of Miletus and hence (mythologically) of Athens.
   23. A reference to its famous quarries on Proconnesus, the island north of Cyzicus (*cf.* § 17, IGRR IV 1464, 1465; D. Magie, *Roman Rule in Asia Minor,* p. 805 n. 32); a similar statement in regard to Athens is made in I 21, 364.
   24. TGF Anon. 162 N = Aeschylus frg. 272 Sidgwick. A scholium in Parisinus gr. 2995, which uncovered the Pindar fragment at XXVI 1 (see note 2 to or. XXVI) wrongly credits this verse to Dionysius Periegetes (*cf.* the vaguely similar lines at 874, 877-878).

25. *cf.* III 51, 301; Eupolis frg. 94 K.
26. The most difficult part of the speech. For the metaphor, *cf.* Behr, *Aelius Aristides,* p. 163 n. 4.
27. The quarry at Proconnesus, see n. 23 to § 14.
28. Homer, *e.g. Iliad* XII 17 ff.; Hesiod *Eoae* frg. 116 Rzach, 83 ed. Loeb.
29. For the temple, *cf.* n. 1. Nothing remains of the superstructure, but the temple is depicted on a contemporary coin (*British Museum, Cat. Mysia,* p. 47, no. 218), and before its total destruction was described in some detail by that indefatigable Renaissance traveler, Cyriac of Ancona, who visited the site twice in 1431 and 1444; *cf.* F.W. Hasluck, *Cyzicus,* pp. 10 ff. and B. Ashmole, *Cyriac of Ancona,* Journal of the Warburg and Courtland Institutes, vol. 19 (1956), pp. 179-191. The temple precinct seems to have measured some 1475 × 325 feet, once entirely paved in marble (*cf. Chronicon Paschale,* p. 475 ed. Dindorf, though some refer this paving to the market place of Cyzicus). The temple itself was octastyle, with Corinthian capitals, fifteen columns on a side, approximately 252 feet long and 133 feet wide. These dimensions do not equal the largest Greek temples, but the size of the columns, given as 70 feet long by Cyriac, are the tallest yet known. (Xiphilinus in Cassius Dio LXIX 15. 4, surely corrupt, gives the dimensions of the columns as 4 fathoms thick (!) and 50 cubits high, each cut from a single block of marble.)
30. For the comparison with "triremes", *cf.* C. Torr, *Ancient Ships,* p. 55 n. 126.
31. The great underground vaults of the temple are all that now remain.
32. The meaning of "hanging walks" is not entirely clear. I suspect that Aristides refers not to something like the *pensilem ambulationem* of Pliny *N. H.* XXXVI 83, but rather to walks built over the subterranean vaults of the temple, where would be found "the underground walks" also mentioned. Pliny *N. H.* XXXVI 94 and 104 remarked that Egyptian Thebes, built over the "Labyrinth", and Rome, over its sewer system, could be called *urbes pensiles.*
33. Hadrian. Less a compliment to him, more to the current regime. According to Malalas XI, p. 279 ed. Bonn, the inscription ran Θεῷ Ἁδριανῷ (*sic* Reinach: θείου Ἁδριανοῦ in the unemended text). D. Magie, *Roman Rule in Asia Minor,* p. 1472, would prefer a slightly more elaborate titulature. Cyriac (for whom see note 29), who is the source of IGRR IV 140, fancifully depicted an elegiac verse inscription honoring the architect Aristenetos as inscribed on the temple.
34. Presumably the restoration of the damage from the earthquake; see note 1.
35. Marcus Aurelius and Lucius Verus. Officially their line went back four generations without interruption to the Emperor Nerva.
36. For one of their teachers, Alexander of Cotiaeum, see oration XXXII.
37. *Iliad* XV 193; *cf.* Aristides XXVI 101.
38. *Cf.* Arrian *Anabasis* II 25; Plutarch *Life of Alexander* 29.
39. Famous deeds of Alexander the Great.
40. Traditional Greek names for messengers and spies of the Persian kings.
41. *Cf.* Homer *Odyssey* XI 263 (Aristides II 394, from Plato *Gorgias* 506 B and the lost play *Antiope* of Euripides). Zethus is meant, who quarreled with his brother over the latter's love of music.
42. Rome, *cf.* XXVI 59 ff.
43. The Romans.
44. *Cf.* XXVI 60, 100.
45. *Cf.* I 66.
46. Perhaps the mythical island of Plato, but very probably Aristides is thinking of England as in XXVI 28, 82.
47. In the past each year the Romans offered the names of a different pair of *consules ordinarii* for dating the year. Now mankind can more conveniently use the *tribuniciae potestates* of the unchanging names of a pair of emperors, the *Caesares Augusti* ("one patronymic and in concert").

48. *Iliad* II 196.
49. The doctrine of Empedocles; *cf.* XXIII 76.
50. "Ways" is intentionally ambiguous. For the phrase (= "customs"), *cf.* Plato *Symposium* 195 E; for the rest, *cf.* Aristides XLVI 36; Behr, *Aelius Aristides,* pp. 90, 155.
51. *Cf.* III 111, 355; Plato *Protagoras* 326 D.
52. An Egyptian king; *cf.* Herodotus II 103, but whom Herodotus had in mind is unclear. Senworset III of the 12th Dynasty and Rameses II of the 19th have been suggested.
53. An allusion to the vows of the Κοινόν of Asia (*cf.* Behr, *Aelius Aristides,* p. 104).
54. Asclepius and Sarapis, *cf.* Behr, *Aelius Aristides,* p. 149.
55. An allusion to the temple.
56. Refers to the construction of the temple.
57. *Cf.* Euripides *Medea* 222 ff., *Suppliants* 891 ff.; Plato *Laws* 949 E ff.
58. *Cf.* XXIII 71.
59. § 43.
60. Presumably so that their conduct, praised at this dedication ceremony, will continue to be harmonious. For the expression, *cf.* XLVII 31, concerning a contemporary event.

NOTES TO XXVIII

1. Between 145 and 147 A.D., during his incubation at the temple of Asclepius at Pergamum, Aristides delivered a speech to Athena (*cf.* L 25), now lost and not to be confused with the later oration XXXVII. In the course of this speech, Aristides made some remarks in passing on its excellence, which provoked the objections of an unnamed critic. The result was the present work, which in style and disposition is very close to the IInd oration. The reference to the "sacred tale" §§ 116-118 (= L 52) and to Aristides' life as an incubant §§ 88, 132-133 also fix the date to this period (*cf.* Behr, *Aelius Aristides,* p. 53). These literary feuds were not uncommon, as is attested by Lucian's *Adversus Indoctum* and *Pseudologista,* to name but two of his more vituperative performances. Aristides' work, however, maintains a more moderate and literary tone.
The speech is divided into the following sections:
A. § 1-2 Proem. The quarrel
B. § 3-17 Right to honest opinions about one's own writing
C. § 18-97 Just pride is a Greek characteristic. Examples from writers
D. § 98-134 The circumstance and cause of the remark must be considered
E. § 135-152 Supplementary examples
F. § 153-156 Peroration. The reasonableness of Aristides' act.
2. *Cf.* Plato *Apology* 18 D.
3. *i.e.* Athena, *cf.* L 25.
4. Ironic; *cf.* Plato *Timaeus* 17 AB.
5. Contemptuous; *cf.* §§ 6, 14; Catullus 93, 1.
6. When declaiming, he would present a speech imitative of the style and subject, *e.g.* of Demosthenes; *cf.* IV 3.
7. As payment for the speech, *cf.* § 155; Homer *Iliad* IX 577.
8. *Cf.* Thucydides I 15, 3.
9. *Cf.* Athenaeus 219 A; Parke and Wormell, *The Delphic Oracle,* vol. II, no. 46.
10. Egypt was divided into 42 nomes or administrative districts, *cf.* XLV 32.
11. *Oedipus Tyrannus* 462.

12. *Cf.* Isocrates II 25; Aristotle *Nicomachean Ethics* IV vii ff.
13. *Cf.* Plato *Republic* 397 E.
14. Ironic; *cf.* note 5 (to § 3).
15. A reputed saying of Thales, inscribed on the temple of Apollo at Delphi.
16. A reputed saying of Chilon, also inscribed on the temple of Apollo at Delphi.
17. The passage is corrupt. But a new punctuation seems to help; *cf.* § 33.
18. Homer *Iliad* II 231.
19. Homer *Iliad* IX 328-331.
20. In the ninth book of the *Iliad*. This event formed the subject of Aristides' XVIth oration.
21. *Homeric Hymn* III 166-178; *cf.* Aristides XXXIV 35; for the reference to tattletales, *cf.* § 131.
22. *Theogony* 22.
23. *Theogony* 11.
24. *Theogony* 18
25. In a dream, a frequent source of Aristides' inspiration, *cf.* §§ 75, 102; Behr, *Aelius Aristides,* p. 46 n. 21.
26. *Theogony* 30.
27. *Iliad* I 237-238.
28. *Theogony* 31; one might consult Wilamowitz's remarks in *Die Ilias und Homer,* p. 471 n. 1.
29. *Theogony* 31.
30. *Theogony* 32.
31. *Theogony* 32.
32. *Theogony* 38.
33. *i.e.* worth as much as the verses.
34. Actually Homer alone is now considered; for the plural, *cf.* § 44.
35. *Iliad* XVIII 104-105.
36. *Iliad* XIX 216-219.
37. *Iliad* XIX 217-218.
38. *Iliad* XIX 218-219.
39. *Iliad* XIII 355.
40. *e.g. Iliad* I 544.
41. *Iliad* II 707-708.
42. *Iliad* II 768-769.
43. § 25.
44. *Iliad* XVIII 106; *cf.* § 26.
45. *Iliad* I 250-252.
46. *Iliad* I 260 ff.
47. *Iliad* I 273.
48. *Iliad* I 269-270.
49. *Iliad* I 271.
50. *i.e.* heroes of old.
51. *Iliad* VII 133 slightly confused with 157.
52. *Iliad* VII 155-156.
53. *Iliad* VII 161.
54. *Iliad* XI 645 ff.
55. *Iliad* XI 761.
56. *Iliad* IV 317 ff.
57. *Cf. e.g.* Sophocles *Philoctetes* 1217.
58. *Iliad* XXIII 634-637.
59. *Iliad* XXIII 667-668, 672-675.

60. *Iliad* XXIII 694-695.
61. *Odyssey* VIII 170-173; *cf.* Aristides II 96, 389, 418.
62. *Odyssey* VIII 176.
63. *Iliad* IX 673.
64. *Odyssey* VIII 408.
65. *Odyssey* VIII 214-218.
66. *Odyssey* VIII 229.
67. *Odyssey* IX 19-20.
68. *Iliad* VIII 17.
69. *Iliad* VIII 18-24.
70. *Iliad* VIII 27.
71. *Cf.* Herodotus I 47 for a somewhat similar, but not identical version; also Parke and Wormell, *The Delphic Oracle,* vol. II, no. 52.
72. A fanciful etymology, which derives ἀλαζών, "humbug", from ἀλήτης, "beggar".
73. Lobel-Page frg. 193 = Lobel frg. 77; *cf.* Lobel-Page frg. 32 and 147 = Lobel frg. A 3 App. and 32 respectively.
74. Alcman frg. 30 Page = 7 Bergk = 10 Diehl.
75. Alcman frg. 148 Page = 118 Bergk.
76. Alcman frg. 148 Page = 118 Bergk; for the name, *cf.* also Aristophanes *Birds* 1553.
77. *i.e.* under god's influence.
78. Alcman frg. 106 Page = 47 Bergk.
79. Pindar *Olympian* II 95-97 Turyn = 86-88 OCT.
80. Pindar frg. 283 Turyn = 273 Schroeder.
81. Pindar frg. 231, 1-3 Turyn = 194 Schroeder.
82. Pindar frg. 231, 4-5 Turyn = 194 Schroeder.
83. Pindar *Paean* VI, frg. 46, 1-4 Turyn.
84. The Delphic Theoxenia, *vide* vs. 45 Turyn of this *Paean.*
85. *Cf.* Homer *Iliad* XXII 60.
86. Simonides frg. 146 Bergk = 175 Edmonds.
87. *ibid.*
88. Παράγραμμα plays on ἐπίγραμμα and παράφθεγμα.
89. Simonides frg. 90 Bergk = 117 Edmonds.
90. Simonides frg. 104 Bergk = 131 Edmonds.
91. Simonides frg. 142 Bergk = 171 Edmonds; *cf.* Aristides III 140, on the great victory at the Eurymedon in 468 B.C.
92. Simonides frg. 132 Bergk = 161 Edmonds; Herodotus V 77.
93. Simonides frg. 91 Bergk = 118 Edmonds; Herodotus VII 228.
94. Simonides frg. 97 Bergk = 124 Edmonds.
95. "Simonidean" = "in the style of Simonides". (Simonides) frg. 60 Bergk = Edmonds Testimony p. 258.
96. (Simonides) frg. 46 Bergk = vol. 3 Anonymous frg. 88 Edmonds.
97. *ibid.*
98. Herodotus I, 1.
99. Alluded to is the expression "most important war" in Thucydides I, 1.
100. Historians, traditionally, before the time of Thucydides.
101. *Cf.* Thucydides II 60-64; Aristides III 85.
102. *Cf.* § 45.
103. Thucydides VI 16, 1. Alcibiades is speaking.
104. Thucydides VI 77, 1; a slight error for it is from Hermocrates' speech at Camarina.
105. Thucydides VI 34, 4.

106. Thucydides II 62, 3 from Pericles' speech cited in §§ 71-72.
107. Homer *Odyssey* VIII 492; *cf.* Aristides XXXVI 64.
108. XVIII 221.
109. The gods had sent him by means of dreams certain expressions to use; *cf.* § 21.
110. XVIII 222.
111. XVIII 304-305.
112. *Cf.* [Plutarch] *Vitae Decem Oratorum* 847 A. The epigram ran: "If you had possessed strength equal to your spirit, Demosthenes, never would the war god of Macedon have ruled Greece".
113. *Cf.* II 428, IV 26.
114. Socrates, *cf.* Plato *Apology* 23 B.
115. Plato *Apology* 30 E.
116. Plato *Apology* 20 E.
117. Plato *Apology* 30 A.
118. This famous trial occurred in 355 B.C.
119. *Cf.* [Plutarch] *Vitae Decem Oratorum* 836 D, who accepts the speech as Lysias' and Dionysius of Halicarnassus *Lysias* 12, who points out that Lysias was dead at the time.
120. Lysias frg. 39 Sauppe.
121. Athenian national heroes, slayers in 514 B.C. of Hipparchus, brother of the tyrant Hippias; *cf.* XXXI 19.
122. Lysias frg. 40 Sauppe; *cf.* Aristotle *Ars Rhetorica* 1398 A 17.
123. Lysias frg. 41 Sauppe; *cf.* Aristotle *Ars Rhetorica* 1397 B 30.
124. Lysias frg. 42 Sauppe.
125. Lysias frg. 128 Sauppe; *cf.* Aristotle *Ars Rhetorica* 1398 A 5.
126. *Cf.* Plutarch *Regum et Imperatorum Apophthegmata* 187 A.
127. *Cf.* § 148. According to Nepos 15 *(Epaminondas)*, 8, having been put on trial with two fellow generals in 370 B.C. for exceeding the authority granted to him by the government of Thebes, he took full responsibility and dared his judges to condemn the architect of the great Theban victory at Leuctra.
128. At the temple of Asclepius in Pergamum. Just possibly Q. Tullius Maximus is meant, *cf.* Behr, *Aelius Aristides,* p. 48 n. 26.
129. Parrhasius, a painter born at Ephesus, flourished c. 400 B.C.; *cf.* Diehl vol. I, p. 95 = Edmonds *Elegy and Iambus* II, p. 20.
130. *Cf.* Plato *Gorgias* 450 C.
131. *Cf.* Diehl vol. I, p. 96 = Edmonds *Elegy and Iambus* II, p. 22.
132. A parody of Homer *Odyssey* IV 242, 271 from Plato *Symposium* 220 C.
133. *Iliad* III 156-157. The same story is told by Valerius Maximus III 7, ext. 3.
134. *Cf.* Plato *Symposium* 189 B.
135. A scholium in Parisinus gr. 3005 attributes the fragment to the *Maricas* of Eupolis, but Aristides obviously thought that it was by Cratinus (frg. 306 K). The lection αὐθημερινῶν given by the editors of Aristides, with the exception of Keil, from the Juntine edition may well have been the original reading of Q (for its relation with the Juntine edition, *cf.* Lenz-Behr, *Aelii Aristidis Opera* I, p. CI n. 25) and actually have some manuscript support against the obviously corrupt ἀπό θ' ἡμερινῶν of the archetype. Perhaps it came from the scholium which declared the play Eupolis'. These inferior manuscripts can have good scholia as is witnessed by that of Parisinus gr. 2995 on XXVI 1 (see note 2 to or. XXVI).
136. Cratinus frg. 237 K.
137. Aristophanes *Wasps* 1030.
138. Aristophanes *Wasps* 1043.
139. Aristophanes *Wasps* 1046-1047.

140. Isocrates *Panegyricus* IV 14.
141. Isocrates *Panegyricus* IV 188.
142. *i.e.* pantomimes and such. Reiske, Keil, and now D. Bain, *Classical Quarterly* 25 (1975), p. 14 n. 3, take ἀναγκαίοις as "a necessary evil". But why should this be said of tragic poets?
143. An allusion to the parabasis, whose alleged presence in tragedy may well be fictional, *cf.* Bain, *Classical Quarterly* 25 (1975), pp. 14-17.
144. If the emendation of "slave", οἰκέτου for οἰκείου of the manuscripts, is sound, the reference is to § 97 and the remarks in §§ 99-100. Keil suggested a lost speech, which in view of ἀρτίως is highly unlikely.
145. The Cynics; *cf.* II 157, 372; IV 38.
146. *i.e.* the dream, which inspired the speech; *cf.* note 25 (to § 21).
147. *Cyropaedia* VII, 1.
148. Similar, it would seem, to the μαντευτοί (see note 1 to or. XXXVII); also cited by Apsines in Spengel *Rhetores Graeci* I, p. 343, 8-10.
149. Homer *Iliad* V 185.
150. *Iliad* XV 605-607.
151. *i.e.* by assuming that the critic knows something.
152. Hector.
153. *Iliad* XIX 364-368.
154. *i.e.* professional or skilled soldiers, *cf.* XXVI 105; XXXVII 8. For the phrase, *cf.* Nonnus *Dionysiaca* XXVII 119 and XLIII 74.
155. Homer *Iliad* VI 143.
156. Homer *Iliad* VI 127.
157. A people known from Homer *Odyssey* IV 84; *cf.* the scholium *ad. loc.;* Strabo I 42; and Dionysius Periegetes 963 f. οἳ βίον ἐν πέτρῃσι κατωρυχέεσσιν ἔθεντο, γυμνοί. They were regarded as a wretched Ethiopian or Arabian tribe who, I assume, lowered their gaze because of the blazing sun, or because they were likened to their neighbors, the cave-dwelling Troglodytes, or because they were thought by some to be Pygmies.
158. Priests of Cybele, who performed noisy, armed dances for the goddess.
159. *Iliad* V 4.
160. Athena.
161. Unknown, but probably the Persian king, who figures in the Pseudo-Heraclitus-Darius I correspondence, given in Diogenes Laertius IX 12 ff. and Clement of Alexandria *Stromateis* I 65. The doctrine espoused is Heraclitean and similar to Heraclitus frg. XXII Bywater.
162. On this *topos, cf.* Callimachus *Hymn* II 108; Cicero *De Natura Deorum* II 20; Longinus *De Sublimitate* 35, 4.
163. *Cf.* XXXIX 11; Homer *Iliad* XVIII 376.
164. Homer *Iliad* I 46 ff.
165. On all of this, which is taken from Aristides' own experience, *cf.* Behr, *Aelius Aristides,* pp. 45 ff.; *Studies on the Biography* § 4.
166. On this theme, *cf.* § 135, and the contemporary XLI 2; Behr, *Aelius Aristides,* p. 45 n. 18, p. 107; *Studies on the Biography* § 4.
167. "The Chariot" was a region of Attica, *cf.* Strabo IX 404, where lightning was a rarity. Hence the expression came to mean something which never or rarely occurs.
168. *Cf.* XLV 13; Pindar *Isthmian* VIII 62; Plato *Phaedrus* 246 E; Lucian *Rhetorum Praeceptor* 26.
169. *Cf.* XLVIII 32.
170. Homer *Odyssey* XIV 466.
171. Asclepius.

172. A later version in L 52; *cf.* Behr, *Aelius Aristides,* pp. 53, 117.
173. Euripides *Andromeda* frg. 114 N.
174. *Odyssey* XIX 562 ff. True dreams passed through the gate of horn; *cf.* Behr, *Aelius Aristides,* pp. 174, 191 n. 64.
175. There follows this passage: "It is also clear what sort of deeds the lion will do when he roars out, not to mention when he is in your midst". I believe that these lines are interpolated since no comparison is implied. The use of the eagle and the lion, in a somewhat different sense, is found in Maximus of Tyre XXXI 3 ed. Dübner.
176. Homer *Iliad* VI 509-511.
177. *Cf.* § 123; II 191 ff; XXIV 35; XXXIV 53.
178. § 119.
179. Aristides despised people who taught for money; *cf.* II 431, III 98-99, XXXIII 19; Behr, *Aelius Aristides,* p. 8.
180. In the Greek, the metaphor seems taken from the tilling of a field; *cf.* XXXVI 23.
181. Ironically. Either hiding their heads in shame or deserving to die. Presumably a punishment is not meant; hence the middle voice in the Greek. On ἀξία, *cf.* §§ 13 ff., 145.
182. A play on a word which can mean protection (against cold) and an excuse.
183. *i.e.* jump from one side of the stage to the other; *cf.* Plato *Euthydemus* 276 D; E. Norden, *Antike Kunstprosa* 5th ed., p. 374 n. 2.
184. *Cf.* § 112.
185. *Cf.* XVII 18 and note 38.
186. Sophocles *Philoctetes* 263, 267; Philoctetes himself was bitten by a viper.
187. *Cf.* § 19, and Behr, *Studies on the Biography,* § 4.
188. Untrue. It was only after unsuccessful experiences with human doctors that Aristides turned to Asclepius; *cf.* Behr, *Aelius Aristides,* pp. 25, 169.
189. at Pergamum.
190. His fellow incubants, *cf.* Behr, *Aelius Aristides,* p. 42 n. 5.
191. Perhaps Alexander of Cotiaeum, *cf.* Behr, *Aelius Aristides,* p. 10 and oration XXXII.
192. *Iliad* IV 412.
193. *Iliad* VIII 523.
194. *Iliad* IX 190.
195. On the mysteries of rhetoric, *cf.* § 113 (note 166).
196. Frg. 23, 21-22 Diehl. The text of this poem and of the following poem is edited mostly in agreement with that in Aristotle *Athen. Pol.* 12, 3-4. Aristides' manuscripts offer in several places a corrupt version.
197. Frg. 24, 3-22 Diehl. On the circumstances of Solon's land and credit reforms, *cf.* Aristotle *Athen. Pol.* 12 and Plutarch *Solon* 14-16, who also uses this poem.
198. Xerxes in Thucydides I 129, 3.
199. Frg. 24, 22-27 Diehl.
200. A sign of decorum; we first note mention of it in Aeschines I 25; Demosthenes XIX 251.
201. Plato *Phaedrus* 247 C.
202. Plato *Phaedrus* 265 DE.
203. Plato *Phaedrus* 271 B.
204. Lysias.
205. Plato *Phaedrus* 257 C.
206. Plato *Phaedrus* 263 D.
207. Plato *Phaedrus* 264 CD.

208. For the four virtues of oratory, *cf.* II 235 f., 382.
209. Plato.
210. *Cf.* Plato *Laws* 858 DE.
211. The other incubants, *cf.* §§ 133, 154.
212. § 88.
213. *Cf.* Edmonds *Elegy and Iambus* II, p. 272. Pausanias IX 12, 6 and XV 6, who also gives this epigram, reports that it was to be found in Thebes. Perhaps there were two identical versions, the second being at Megalopolis, the center of the Arcadian federation which Epaminondas helped to found.
214. Athenian general. The battle took place in 376 B.C.; *cf.* Plutarch *Regum et Imperatorum Apophthegmata* 187 D.
215. III 32.
216. *Cf.* § 18.
217. For the expression, *cf.* XLVIII 33.
218. In both cases oratorical displays may be meant. The theater was a somewhat grander site, *cf.* LI 30, though the patron could be praised in a poem as well.
219. His fellow incubants, *cf.* §§ 133, 147.
220. The order of justice was that all have an equal share, *cf.* Xenophon *Cyropaedia* I 3, 18 and Polybius VI 45, 3.
221. For Asclepius, Aristides' patron in oratory, *cf.* Behr, *Aelius Aristides,* pp. 45-47, 49-51, 159.

NOTES TO XXIX

1. This oration was delivered in Smyrna, apparently between 157-165 A.D., to oppose the suggestion (real or fictitious) that there be permitted to be performed in the theater, during the celebration of the Dionysia (here the equivalent of the Anthesteria at Athens, *cf.* § 20 and note 16 to or. XVII 5), a kind of public satire or comedy, elaborated from the impromptu "jests from the wagons", τὰ ἐκ τῶν ἁμαξῶν, which were always a part of this feast. Aristides expands upon traditional criticism of the Old Comedy at Athens, a criticism which goes back to Plato and Aristotle and which inspired Hellenistic theorists to invent laws prohibiting comedy (on this *cf.* Behr, *Aelius Aristides,* pp. 95-96 and W. Schmid in Schmid-Stählin, *Griech. Literaturgeschichte* Teil 1, Bd. 4, pp. 447-450). The speech's concern over reputation is very close to the contemporary *Defense of the Four,* which also dilates on comedy, and to the outraged morality which can be descried in Libanius' reply to Aristides' lost speech *Against the Dancers* (*cf.* Behr, *op. cit.,* p. 88).
The argument falls into the following sections:
A. § 1-3 Proem. Use of advice
B. § 4-15 Malicious slander is inappropriate to a sacred occasion
C. § 16-32 Refutation of the alleged utility of satire and a consideration of its dangers
D. § 33 Peroration.
2. The gods.
3. Κακοήθεια from κακία.
4. κακηγορία.
5. As if they were part of the contest.
6. According to Pausanias IX 11, 7 a temple of the Κληδόνες (note the plural) stood outside the wall of the city.
7. *Cf.* Isocrates I 15.

8. *Cf.* the indignation expressed in XLVI 32 ff. over the murals of Palaemon and Leucothea.

9. Proverb. Corinth was famous for its luxury and vice, and only the rich could benefit from the trip; *cf.* Aristophanes frg. 902 a K.

10. At the Olympic games incompetent competitors were flogged; *cf.* III 687-688.

11. The text is corrupt. There may be a play on σπουδαιογελοῖα, a genre of literature practiced by the Cynics, whose freely expressed insults Aristides detested, *cf.* III 628 and XXXIV 57.

12. *Cf.* A. Pickard-Cambridge, *The Dramatic Festivals of Athens,* pp. 268 ff. (for Athens).

13. On the Sacred Marriage, in which at Athens during the second day of the three day Anthesteria (the Χόες), the wife of the King Archon was ceremonially married to the god Dionysus, *cf.* Pseudo-Demosthenes LIX 73-78 and A. Pickard-Cambridge, *The Dramatic Festivals of Athens,* p. 11.

14. On the night of the second day and into the third and final day (the Χύτροι) of the Anthesteria, this festival was held, originally to placate the dead; *cf.* A. Pickard-Cambridge, *The Dramatic Festivals of Athens,* pp. 12 ff.

15. *Cf.* Aristophanes *Frogs* 736 ff.

16. *Cf.* Polybius XXXIX 2, 3; it signifies a matter of no importance.

17. *Cf.* Libanius LXIV 93, who imitates this or a similar passage in the lost speech *Against the Dancers.*

18. *E.g. cf.* I 263.

NOTES TO XXX

1. In 147 A.D., towards the end of his nearly two year period of incubation at the temple of Asclepius in Pergamum, Aristides was commissioned by the powerful Pergamene family of the Quadrati to compose this oration in honor of the fourteenth(?) birthday of C. Julius Apellas, Aristides' pupil. The circumstances of the speech are somewhat puzzling, but it may be that Apellas, a minor, had just served as a judge during the games of the Provincial Assembly, *c.* February (*cf.* §§ 2-3, 21; Behr, *Aelius Aristides,* p. 57; *Studies on the Biography* § 7), and in summer of that year was going to preside over the Asclepieia (§ 27). The speech was condemned as spurious by Bruno Keil on alleged historical grounds, which are in fact only Keil's misapprehension concerning the family of the Quadrati (see on §§ 7, 10) and because of certain stylistic peculiarities such as μοι δοκῶ with the infinitive and accusative at § 15, the employment of δίχα and the use of ἄνευ in a postpositive position with a noun (both § 19). But in the first example καί μοι is easily emended to καίτοι, or δοκῶ may be corrupt for δοκεῖ, and the latter two stylistic anomalies may be poetic borrowings from some unknown author. This stylistic argument has not been accepted, particularly since the speech is replete with Aristides' mannerisms, and the subscription virtually guarantees its genuineness (*cf.* Boulanger, *Aelius Aristide,* p. 335). I myself find the style of the speech highly contorted and artificial, far beyond that of Aristides' other works. But I feel that the cause is to be found in the circumstances of its delivery, Aristides' search for effect and his desire to make a strong impression after a long retirement.

The speech falls into the following sections:
A. § 1-3 Proem. The public celebrations
B. § 4-5 Pergamum and Apellas
C. § 6-15 The family of Quadratus
D. § 16-22 Apellas' qualities

E. § 23-27 Apellas' future career
F. § 28 Peroration.

2. This introduction is pure scholium, and is written as such in the margin of *e.g.* Laurentianus gr. LX, 8. On the other hand, it appears at the head of the text of the oration in the oldest preserved manuscript, Laurentianus LX, 3. One notes the same variation in the introductory scholia to I and III in sundry manuscripts. This introduction contains no historical information which could not have been taken from the text of the speech (except possibly the notice that Apellas was a patrician and the guess at his age), but the very fact that it was preserved at all in a portion of the corpus, which has little scholia, makes it interesting.

3. § 17.

4. Asclepius.

5. An allusion to Pergamum's much sought official title of μητρόπολις........δὶς νεωκόρος πρώτη. On these titles, *cf.* note 1 to or. XXIII.

6. Perhaps an allusion to multiple citizenships, as well as to the presence of the cities of Asia at the games of the Provincial Assembly, just held (?); *cf.* § 21.

7. *Works and Days* 11-24; *cf.* XXIV 13.

8. Asclepius.

9. Instead of receiving "a bastard" education in another city. On the notion of legitimacy, *cf.* I 29 f.

10. The donation of money to various civic enterprises, games, charities *etc.*, for which his ancestor C. Antius A. Julius Quadratus was famous (see note 14).

11. The Pergamenes and Apellas; *cf.* §§ 4-5.

12. Apellas.

13. One branch of the family settled in Ancyra in Galatia (*cf.* Behr, *Aelius Aristides,* p. 80), another branch seems to have had connections in Rome (*cf.* Behr, *op. cit.,* pp. 84 ff.); see to also note 14.

14. This man seems to have come from Thermae Theseos, at least a family cult is attested there, IGRR IV 1377 (*cf.* Behr, *Aelius Aristides,* p. 58, where much of what I said about this family I now think was wrong). It is unclear by how many generations he preceded our Apellas (see also notes 18 and 23 to § 10 and note 28 to § 12). Part of the stemma of Apellas' family seems supplied by IGRR IV 1687, an inscription of Julia Polla, daughter of Aulus, the *regina sacrorum* ἐν Θεᾷ 'Ρώμῃ ("divine" Rome, a confusion with the cult of Θεὰ 'Ρώμη in Asia?), who, with her two sons the senators C. Julius Nabus and C. Julius Fronto honors her mother Julia Tyche after 114 A.D. (*cf.* Boulanger, *Aelius Aristide,* pp. 333 ff. Groag, R.E. *s.v.* Julius Apellas (73, 74), Julius Fronto (247, 250), Julia Polla (588), denies the attribution of this inscription to the father and grandmother of our Apellas. Also Groag wrongly, I believe, feels that Apellas' father and grandfather were direct descendants of Quadratus (so too Boulanger, *op. cit.,* p. 337), whereas I, with Ippel, Athenische Mitteilungen 37 (1912), pp. 299 ff., on the basis of IGRR IV 1687, see in the grandfather a son-in-law of A. Julius Quadratus. A Julius Fronto is known from a rescript of Trajan, *Digesta* XLVIII 19, 5, whom I would identify as the great-grandfather of our Apellas, but Groag regards as the Fronto of IGRR IV 1687. One more point: the office of *regina sacrorum* of Julia Polla is puzzling. It hardly seems likely that Apellas' grandfather was the *rex sacrorum* and so we must assume two marriages for Julia Polla (*cf.* CIL XIV 3604 *Cn. Pinarius Cn. f.....Severus, rex sacrorum,* and apparently [quaest. cand.] of Trajan, son of the consul ord. 90 A.D., the second husband?). Yet the *flaminica dialis* was permitted only one marriage. But it is possible that something is amiss in the inscription itself. Of C. Antius Aulus Julius Quadratus we are extremely well informed (*cf. e.g.* the series of inscriptions in IGRR IV 275, 336, 373-398, 499, 1686, and *Altertümer von Pergamon* VIII³, pp. 41 ff. for another inscription and further references). He was

one of Pergamum's great benefactors, one of the first Asians to reach the consulship, cos. suff. 94 A.D., cos. II ord. 105 A.D., and governor of Asia probably 109/110 A.D. His first consulship and his appearance as an Arval Brother in 72 A.D. (*cf.* M. McCrum and A. G. Woodhead, *Select Documents of the Principates of the Flavian Emperors,* p. 16 (no. 5)) point to a birth date *c.* 50 A.D. His father's name was also Aulus, and he had a sister....Polla, for whom his daughter was no doubt named (ILS 8819 A, between 105-109 A.D. I, along with some others, once thought that Polla and Julia Polla were synonymous and that A. Julius Quadratus and Julia Polla were brother and sister). The stemma would seem to be as follows:

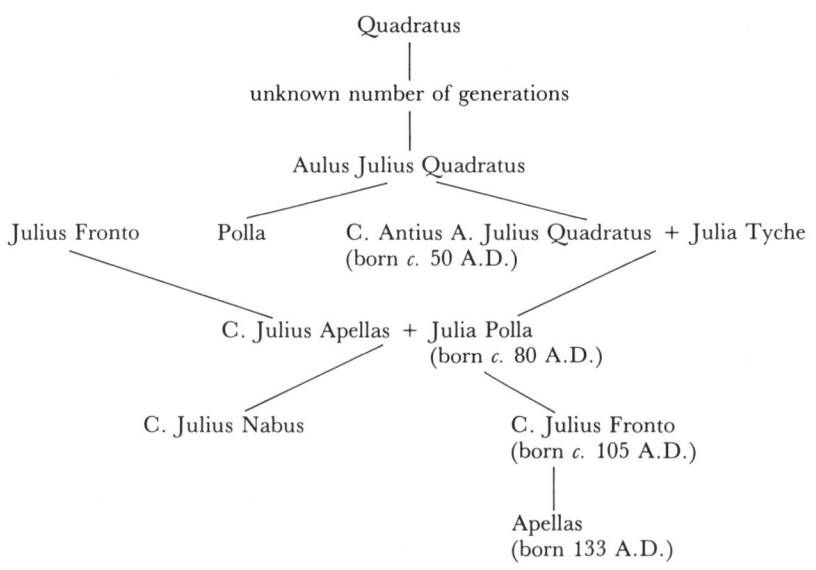

```
                              Quadratus
                                  |
                    unknown number of generations
                                  |
                         Aulus Julius Quadratus
                        /          |          \
Julius Fronto      Polla    C. Antius A. Julius Quadratus + Julia Tyche
                                (born c. 50 A.D.)
                    \           /
                  C. Julius Apellas + Julia Polla
                                (born c. 80 A.D.)
                    /                        \
          C. Julius Nabus                C. Julius Fronto
                                          (born c. 105 A.D.)
                                                |
                                             Apellas
                                          (born 133 A.D.)
```

15. *Cf.* Euripides *Heracles* 178.
16. Asclepius.
17. Euripides frg. 484 N; *cf.* II 132.
18. Many generations may be meant (*cf.* note 14). For the expression, *cf.* §§ 22 and 28.
19. *Cf* Iliad XX 308; the oracle in Herodotus V 92 ε 2; Plato *Republic* 363 D; also Aristides I 1.
20. Not, I think, received Roman citizenship; *cf.* Behr, *Aelius Aristides,* pp. 5, 58.
21. *Cf.* I 3.
22. *Cf.* XXVI 2.
23. Those between Quadratus, the founder, and Apellas' grandfather (see note 14 to § 7). The number of generations is unknown.
24. C. Julius Apellas, the son of Fronto (in its Greek form, at least).
25. *i.e.* "noble gentleman"; *cf.* XXXII 2.
26. *Odyssey* IV 611.
27. § 10.
28. From Quadratus, the founder, up to Apellas, the grandfather, the number of generations is unknown (*cf.* note 14 to § 7). If collateral ancestors, such as uncles are meant, as is possible, then the list would be far longer. The passage imitates Homer *Odyssey* II 276 ff.
29. Asclepius.

30. In § 1 or perhaps even before this speech.
31. Homer *Iliad* VIII 563; *cf.* Aristides XXXVII 26.
32. *i.e.* by prescribing a cautery.
33. This is a hieratic expression. The θεραπευταί, "worshippers", seem to have formed a special group at the temple; *cf.* XXXIX 5; XLVII 23; XLVIII 47; L 16, 19, 50, 104 (with my restoration; see *Studies on the Biography* § 6); Galen XIX 19 K (= vol. 2, p. 99, 9 ed. Teubner); *Altertümer von Pergamon* VIII³, p. 114; F. Sokolowski, *On the New Pergamene* Lex Sacra, Greek, Roman, and Byzantine Studies 14 (1973), pp. 411-413.
34. Apollo.
35. *Odyssey* VI 162-163.
36. *Cf.* Pindar *Olympian* IX 29 and Euripides *Hippolytus* 76-77.
37. Eupolis frg. 94 K.
38. Homer *Iliad* I 249.
39. *Cf.* Plato *Phaedrus* 276 B. The source of these two apparent quotations is unknown.
40. *Laws* 643 C.
41. The passage before emendation was lacunose and perhaps corrupt. The sense seems to be that Apellas did not excessively indulge his athletic interests, but limited them to training himself for his future needs.
42. Perhaps at the games of the Provincial Assembly; *cf.* §§ 2-3
43. *Cf.* Xenophon *Cyropaedia* I 3, 16 ff.; Herodotus I 114.
44. *Theaetetus* 194 E.
45. Zeus and Asclepius respectively.
46. *Cf.* XLII 5, XLIII 21; Plato *Symposium* 206 E, 208 B.
47. *Cf.* Plato *Menexenus* 247 B.
48. Play on ἀρχή, "commencement" and "office" of agonothete of the Asclepieia (see § 27).
49. Other members of the family presided over the games. Since there is no evidence that the games are older than the second century A.D. (*cf. Altertümer von Pergamon* VIII³, p. 85), perhaps among other acts of generosity, the family helped found these games.
50. Anticipating offices strictly limited to adults.
51. If as the *Introduction* theorized, doubtless from this passage, Apellas' fourteenth birthday was being celebrated (*cf.* n. 2), it would be two years before he would assume the *toga virilis*. The office of agonothete then was not forbidden to boys, but it was not customary for them to hold it (assuming the restoration of the passage, otherwise corrupt, is correct).
52. The emperor is Antoninus Pius. "The honors" no doubt refer to the *cursus honorum* of the politically active Roman aristocrat, whose career began about the 19th or 20th year.
53. *Iliad* V 122.
54. The games were held in summer, in June (?); *cf.* IGRR IV 494, *Altertümer von Pergamon* VIII³, p. 8 n. 21; or perhaps in the month of August, *cf.* Behr, *Aelius Aristides*, p. 32 n. 47.
55. Homer *Iliad* V 5.
56. *Cf.* XLII 4.
57. Antoninus Pius; *cf.* XLVI 42.
58. of Quadratus.
59. *Cf.* § 10.
60. On these subscriptions, *cf.* note 23 to XVIII.
61. Aristides' whimsical name, "time of inactivity", for the period of his incubation at the temple of Asclepius in Pergamum in 145-147 A.D.; *cf.* Behr, *Aelius Aristides,* p. 26 and n. 20.

62. Perhaps <καὶ μηνῶν β̄> = "and two months" should be added, if, indeed, the games of the Provincial Assembly are meant in §§ 2-3, 21.

NOTES TO XXXI

1. Shortly after the earthquake of 161 A.D., which devastated Cyzicus and partially destroyed the temple of Hadrian, Aristides, well again and at the peak of his career, delivered this oration to mourn the death of one of his pupils (cf. on § 13). The speech is stiff, formal, and even marred by Aristides' vanity (cf. § 7 f.), yet it closes with an affective consolation (§§ 15-18), which deserves attention. It also displays most fully Aristides' own attitudes on prudery and ambition. On the speech, cf. Behr, *Aelius Aristides*, pp. 92-94, where I now retract my comments on the temple, which, with Hasluck, I mistook for that of Persephone, shared with Hadrian.

The speech is divided as follows:
A. § 1-2 Proem. Mourning justified
B. § 3-10 Eteoneus' birth, character, and education
C. § 11-13 Lament
D. § 14-18 Consolation
E. § 19 Peroration.

2. This Antiochus was a prince of Thessaly; cf. Simonides frg. 34 Bergk, 24 Edmonds, *Lyra Graeca*.

3. *Iliad* II 204.

4. The teacher would speak on various themes and the student would learn by imitation.

5. Cf. XXXIX 3; Plato *Symposium* 214 B.

6. Homer *Iliad* XII 104.

7. Aristophanes *Clouds* 995 (cf. 992).

8. A cult term, applied to Apollo, the father of Asclepius.

9. Frg. 140 Turyn = 136ᵃ Schroeder.

10. So Keil ingeniously emends. For the earthquake which damaged the temple of Hadrian at Cyzicus in 161 A.D., cf. note 1 to oration XXVII. Eteoneus' death is likened to the calamity.

11. Cf. *Tragicorum Graecorum Fragmenta* Suppl. Adespot. 37 B.

12. The misfortune concerns the gods of oratory because a potentially good speaker has been lost. The gods beneath the earth are affected because Eteoneus died prematurely, an ἄωρος (cf. § 12, ἀωρία) and so could not go to Hades (for this concept, cf. e.g. R. Lattimore, *Themes in Greek and Latin Epitaphs*, pp. 184 ff.). See also §§ 15, 18; Behr, *Aristides and the Egyptian Gods* in Hommages à Vermaseren (Leiden, 1978), p. 20 n. 31. For the opposite idea, timely death, καθ' ὥραν, cf. XXXII 31.

13. Decrees, which other states, not knowing the misfortune, have offered in praise of Eteoneus; cf. LI 56.

14. *Deus ex machina*. The machine was a crane, which swung its occupant through the air and gave the illusion of flying; cf. A.W. Pickard-Cambridge, *Theatre of Dionysus*, pp. 127 f.

15. Rivers in Hades.

16. Sometimes an ἄωρος (see note 12 to § 13), who could not be received in Hades, was made a hero in compensation; cf. IGRR IV 1377 and F. Cumont, *After Life in Roman Paganism* (1959, Dover edition), pp. 136 ff.

17. He would share honors in the temple of the hero founder of the city.

18. Apollo was regarded as playing a part in the founding of Cyzicus; *cf.* XXVII 5 (note 8).

19. The addition of Amyclas, the father of Hyacinthus, to this list of favorites of Apollo may be an error of Aristides, as Wilamowitz, Hermes (1926), p. 295, points out.

20. *i.e.* to the grave.

21. Canter and Keil remove the period after ἄμεμπτον, which they understand as the subject of καταλῦσαι and make τοῦτο δὲ the apodosis or predicate of the sentence: "to close one's life unblamed by man or god, this does not...".

22. Famous long livers. Arganthonius was king of Tartessus in Spain, who was said to have lived 120 years, *cf.* Herodotus I 163, 2. Anacreon frg. 8 D. = Page *PMG* 361 gives 150 years. Tithonus, from mythology, the lover of Eos, was granted immortality, but not youth by her, so that he did not die but grew ever older. For Nestor, *cf.* Homer *Iliad* I 250, *Odyssey* III 245.

23. Corrupt, but this seems to be the sense. The praise of the dead is secure from envy; *cf.* Thucydides II 45, 1; Demosthenes XVIII 315; Plato *Hippias Maior* 282 A.

24. *Cf.* Edmonds, *Lyra Graeca,* vol. III, p. 566; see also Aristides XXVIII 85 (note 121).

25. As if, as in athletic contests, different standards were applied to an older person.

26. Probably public approval of a statue.

NOTES TO XXXII

1. Before he studied under professional orators, the penultimate stage of Aristides' education lay in the hands of the *grammaticus,* who lectured on and explicated the famous writers of the past. Aristides attended the school of one of the greatest of these, Alexander of Cotiaeum (a city approximately 200 miles to the east of Smyrna), whose high reputation later secured him a post in the training of the Caesar Marcus Aurelius (§ 13 f.; *cf.* Behr, *Aelius Aristides,* pp. 10 ff.). The present work, in the form of a letter, was sent from Smyrna to the people of Cotiaeum at the time of Alexander's death *c.* 150 A.D. (the date is established on internal grounds, *cf.* Behr, *op. cit.,* p. 76). The eulogy, for a man whom Aristides genuinely admired and to whom he owed his thorough knowledge of Plato and the lyric poets, especially Pindar, is not untainted, I think, by a latent jealousy (*cf.* §§ 8, 16). Most of our knowledge of Alexander comes from this work. The handful of authors who cite Alexander's writings are conveniently collected in R.E. *s.v.* Alexandros (95), pp. 1455-1456. Marcus Aurelius *Ad Te Ipsum* I 10 has left an indirect characterization of him, when he thanked him for the knowledge of how not to be censorious and hypercritical over ungrammatical speech or bad pronunciation, and how to correct the errant speaker in a tactful way. This completely agrees with Aristides' own picture of the man.

This work is divided into the following sections:
A. § 1-4 Proem. The propriety of sending the letter
B. § 5-13 Alexander's career
C. § 14-21 His kindness
D. § 22-27 His distinguished academic career deserves honor
E. § 28-36 Perfection of his life
F. § 37-38 Exhortation to honor Alexander's family
G. § 39-41 Peroration. Aristides' relations with Alexander.

2. *Cf.* § 14. For this term, which was particularly meaningful to Aristides, *cf.* Behr, *Aelius Aristides,* p. 9 n. 15.

3. For the antiquity of the Phrygians, cf. Herodotus II 2.
4. Cf. Plato *Gorgias* 497 C. The Lesser Mysteries (a preliminary to the Greater Mysteries of Eleusis in September, cf. XXII 12, note 30) were celebrated at Athens in the month of Anthesterion (February/March).
5. Of the Attic dialect, it would seem.
6. Sophist; cf. XLVII 46; Behr, *Aelius Aristides*, p. 106; *Studies on the Biography* § 4.
7. Grammaticus; cf. note 1; Marcus Aurelius *Ad Te Ipsum* I 10; *SHA Vita Marci* II 3.
8. Cf. §§ 20, 28. Almost a hieratic expression, cf. Behr, *Aelius Aristides*, p. 50.
9. By interpreting them.
10. Just as the founder of a colony extends the ambit and influence of the mother city, so he spread the knowledge of Greek culture, cf. § 21.
11. *Works and Days* 26.
12. The Roman nobility and high officials.
13. The Emperor Antoninus Pius and his two adoptive sons, the Caesar Marcus and Lucius Verus, are included in the term βασιλεῖς, cf. L 75. On Alexander's instruction of Marcus, cf. Marcus Aurelius *Ad Te Ipsum* I 10; *SHA Vita Marci* II 3.
14. Alexander would seem to have come to Rome c. 139 A.D., cf. Fronto vol. I, p. 18 (Loeb edition), where Marcus writes that he must practice Greek composition, "quod non didici"; cf. Behr, *Aelius Aristides*, p. 10.
15. Cf. note 2 to § 2.
16. In contrast to Aristides, who would not accept fees; cf. Behr, *Aelius Aristides*, p. 8 n. 12; p. 10 n. 26.
17. Cf. note 8 to § 9.
18. *i.e.* Plato, the son of Ariston, or Plato, the philosopher.
19. By perpetuating the works of her writers; cf. note 10 to § 10.
20. The Spartan general who died in 422 B.C. defending Amphipolis against the Athenians; cf. Thucydides V 11, 1.
21. *i.e.* his commentaries on them.
22. Cf. Anacreontea 32, 7 B. = 34 Edmonds; Xenophon *Anabasis* I 4, 10; *Cynegeticus* 5, 34; Plutarch *Moralia* 646c; Aristides XXVI 11, XLIV 16.
23. *Phaedrus* 277 E ff.
24. It was called Τὰ Ἐξηγητικά.
25. The nature of this work is unknown. Aside from the picaresque stories which grew up about Aesop and the proverbs which were attributed to him (one of which is used by Aristides, see XLVII 49), the prose version of the fables were undoubtedly composed (near this time) as a source book for orators (cf. Perry, *Aesopica*, pp. 295 ff.).
26. An allusion to the proverb "second attempts better", cf. XX 23. Some held (e.g. *The Suda* s.v. Αἴσωπος) that Aesop came from Cotiaeum.
27. Cf. note 8 to § 9.
28. Cf. e.g. III 369 ff. for Plato's unhappy relationship with Dionysius II, tyrant of Syracuse.
29. A proverb referring to the uncertainties of life. After he was overthrown in 344 B.C., Dionysius lived in exile at Corinth.
30. For the opposite, "untimely death", cf. XXXI 13, note 12.
31. Frg. 643 K.
32. "Helping man"; cf. similar word play in III 599, XVII 22, XXXVIII 7. Alexander died while writing. Keil, however, suggests that Aristides simply refers to "grammaticus".
33. Frg. 135 Turyn = 129/130 Schroeder.
34. Cf. *Apology* 40 E ff.

35. All of the authors upon whom Alexander commented.
36. *Cf.* Norden, *Vergilius Maro Aeneis Buch VI,* on verse 665.
37. *Cf.* Aristophanes *Frogs* 785.
38. *Cf.* Aristophanes *Frogs* 761 ff., 1515.
39. §§ 28-34.
40. § 2.
41. Spring to autumn 144 A.D.; *cf.* XLVIII 63 ff.
42. In the library of Cotiaeum.

NOTES TO XXXIII

1. In late September 166 A.D., in semi-retirement on his Laneion estate in Mysia, after two severe illnesses, smallpox in 165 A.D. and another debilitating disease in 166 A.D., to justify his lengthy absence from Smyrna and apparent inactivity, Aristides issued this apologetic work in the form of a letter to a friend (perhaps the Smyrnaean seer Corus, *cf.* § 14, where the allusions to prophecy are made in the second person singular, while the persons addressed in the main body of the work are otherwise referred to in the plural, and XLVII 54 from nearly the same time). The work was evidently intended as a speech to the Smyrnaeans, but Aristides' wish to recuperate on his estate and the opportune occasion of using it as a *propempticon* (*cf.* notes 2 and 3) forestalled its delivery. Aside from addition of the preface §§ 1-2 (see note 2), a change in the number to the second person singular at § 14 marks its hasty revision. On the circumstances, *cf.* Behr, *Aelius Aristides,* pp. 102-103; *Studies on the Biography* § 4.

The work is divided into the following sections:
A. § 1-2 Proem
B. § 3-6 Second introduction. The charge against him
C. § 7-15 The employment of the artist
D. § 16-23 Aristides' behavior
E. § 24-33 Audience's behavior
F. § 34 Peroration.

2. §§ 1-2 are a new preface addressed to a friend, perhaps the Smyrnaean seer Corus (see note 1). The two occasions referred to are this man's return from a journey and his intention to depart again on another trip. Aristides missed the opportunity of commemorating the return, but he has sent this letter as a *propempticon* for the planned departure.

3. *i.e.* the speech was finished when the news of the friend's impending departure arrived.

4. Frg. 117 Turyn = 108 Schroeder; *cf.* Aristides XXVII 2 (from about the same time).

5. *Cf.* Behr, *Aelius Aristides,* pp. 46-47.

6. For the conjunction of Asclepius and Zeus, *cf.* Behr, *Aelius Aristides,* p. 158.

7. For the proverb, *cf.* XX 23.

8. *Cf.* Euripides *Iphigenia in Taurus* 407.

9. *Cf.* frg. 46 Bergk = 18 Edmonds = 64 Page.

10. *Cf.* Aristophanes *Acharnians* 504. In Athens, Old Comedy, which allegedly had the right of "speaking freely" (*cf.* note 1 to oration XXIX), was presented at two festivals, the Lenaea and the Dionysia. The former took place in winter, when foreigners were less likely to be present.

11. Asclepius.

12. He refers to the smallpox in 165 A.D. (*cf.* Behr, *Aelius Aristides,* pp. 96 ff.,

166 ff.; *Studies on the Biography* § 3). The speech in question is lost; *cf.* Behr, *Aelius Aristides,* p. 102 n. 22 C.

13. *Cf.* § 16 (note 18).

14. *Cf.* XXXIV 16 and XLV 13 for the preferred form of the metaphor; also III 97, 184, 300 (after Demosthenes XIII 34).

15. Legendary seers. Perhaps Aristides' friend, the Smyrnaean seer Corus, is being addressed (*cf.* note 1).

16. *Cf.* the argument in II 362 ff.

17. *Cf.* XXXII 17; Plato *Epistle* VII 328 C; and especially Dionysius *Ars Rhetorica* VII 2.

18. *Cf.* § 7; Alexis frg. 146, 8 K.

19. Asclepius.

20. *Cf.* III 690, XXXII 6.

21. The story is in Book V of *The Odyssey; cf.* Aristides XLVIII 42.

22. *Cf.* XLVIII 11 for the phrase.

23. Asclepius.

24. *Cf.* II 429 ff. for a similar personal statement; Behr, *Aelius Aristides,* pp. 51-52.

25. *i.e.* his sexual pleasure is sublimated in oratory; *cf.* note 46 to § 34.

26. As if he were courting a girl.

27. Smyrna.

28. In part the audience learned by listening to an orator declaim.

29. Yet in Smyrna there were several market places, *cf.* XVII 10 (note 22).

30. *Iliad* XX 250; *cf.* Aristides III 42.

31. *Cf.* II 16 ff.

32. *Cf.* Behr, *Aelius Aristides,* p. 14. Keil, however, interprets these as a sign of victory.

33. Cos was settled by the Meropes; *cf.* XXXVIII 11. It lies near Smyrna, and with the word "this" we may picture Aristides gesturing in that direction (or at least intending to).

34. For this incident at the beginning of Aristides' career, *c.* 141 A.D., *cf.* Behr, *Aelius Aristides,* p. 14.

35. Homer *Odyssey* XII 184-185, from the song of the Sirens.

36. Because he carries a palm-leaf fan, *cf.* § 27 (note 32).

37. The river outside of Smyrna, *cf.* XVII 14-15.

38. Ironically instead of "to bathe there".

39. *Laws* 761 C.

40. *Cf.* Athenaeus 24 CD.

41. Canter understands this phrase differently: "quasi nusquam ei nisi..... corruptus ad infernos descenderet, futurus esset locus". But such a man, as most rational Greeks and Romans, would have no belief in an after life, *cf.* Behr, *Aelius Aristides,* p. 150.

42. In place of "such corruption", Keil understands "such things as are told in the fables about the underworld".

43. This is taken from the doctrine of the Eleusinian Mysteries, *cf.* XXII 10; Behr *Aelius Aristides,* p. 110.

44. Asclepius.

45. X 76.

46. Characters in mythology who rejected the advances of older married women and in retaliation were falsely accused by these same women of making sexual advances against them; *cf.* note 25 to § 20.

NOTES TO XXXIV

1. The circumstances of this oration, which was delivered in the Council Chamber of Smyrna in January 170 A.D. during the games of the Provincial Assembly, are described in LI 38-41. This speech again represents Aristides' conviction that oratory was pure and sacred like a mystery religion and that the orator was a *mystes*, an initiate into it. Hence the word in the oration's title, ἐξορχεῖσθαι, which means "to reveal a mystery or secret", especially by burlesquing it (*cf.* Behr, *Aelius Aristides*, pp. 45, 106-107; *Studies on the Biography*, § 4).

The speech is divided as follows:
A. § 1-18 It is a feeble excuse when corrupt orators lay the blame for the poor quality of their speeches upon the masses
B. § 19-37 The best style will prove most effective
C. § 38-47 The sophisticated and unlettered audience
D. § 48-62 Gratification of the audience shamefully debases oratory
E. § 63 Peroration. Need for good order.

2. *Cf.* Sophocles *Electra* 1415.
3. *Cf.* Aesop 185 Chambry = 233 Halm = 133 Perry.
4. Pindar frg. 270 Turyn = 226 Schroeder.
5. Pindar frg. 209 Turyn = 182 Schroeder.
6. *Cf.* Plato *Protagoras* 345 E.
7. § 5. Pindar *Pythian* III 83.
8. Odysseus.
9. *Cf.* Herodotus III 153 ff.
10. Homer *Odyssey* IV 244, 246, 249.
11. *Cf.* Behr, *Aelius Aristides*, p. 107 n. 44; *Studies on the Biography* § 4.
12. *Cf.* XXXIII 13 (note 14).
13. *Cf.* III 690 for the notion of purging drunkenness.
14. *Cf. e.g.* Homer *Iliad* XIII 159-168.
15. Contests where the prize was some sort of "floral" crown.
16. Plato *Symposium* 201 A.
17. *Cf.* Pindar *Olympian* I *passim*, from which the earlier examples of Ganymede and Pelops are taken.
18. *Cf.* Behr, *Aelius Aristides*, p. 38.
19. A striking example since some, including Galen, thought that Aristides himself was a consumptive; *cf.* Behr, *Aelius Aristides*, pp. 107, 165.
20. For the proverb, *cf.* Euripides *Supplices* 520-521; and in an abbreviated form Aristides XXXIII 9.
21. All works of Phidias, who flourished in the last half of the 5th century B.C., under Pericles. The Lemnian Athena was also cast in bronze.
22. He lived in the middle of the 4th century B.C. and was patronized by both Philip and Alexander the Great of Macedon.
23. A play on the word λόγος, which, among other things, means both "oratory" and "proportion".
24. The single word λογική embraces both concepts.
25. Or perhaps "oratory", as Canter translated it.
26. "Corrupt" and "uncorrupt".
27. Homer, as an interpolator explains.
28. *Homeric Hymn* III 169-172. These verses are alluded to by Aristides in XXVIII 19, which led to the strange theory concerning an alleged relationship between these two speeches. On the Homeric hymn, *cf.* Wilamowitz, *Ilias und Homer*, pp. 441, 454.
29. Demosthenes.

30. *Cf.* Homer *Odyssey* VIII 170 ff.; Hesiod *Theogony* 80 ff.; Aristides II 389, 391.

31. Aristides plays on the antithesis of παρρησία, free speech, and speaking πρὸς χάριν, to please one's audience, as in § 43; *cf.* Behr, *Aelius Aristides,* p. 55 n. 53.

32. *Cf.* XXXIII 19 ff.

33. *Cf.* § 61. On this reprehensible practice, *cf.* Lucian *Rhetorum Praeceptor* 15, 19, 20; *Demonax* 12 (of Favorinus); Philostratus *Vitae Sophistarum* I 8 (492 Olearius), 20 (513 Olearius); Dio Chrysostom XXXII 49 on modulations; Norden *Antike Kunstprosa* (5th ed.), pp. 294-295, 374 n. 2.

34. *Cf.* L 28 (nearly a quarter of a century earlier). Polemo may be meant; *cf.* Behr, *Aelius Aristides,* p. 12 n. 30, *Studies on the Biography* § 4.

35. Aristophanes *Clouds* 555; *cf.* also Norden *Antike Kunstprosa* (5th ed.), p. 310 n. 2.

36. *Cf.* Behr, *Aelius Aristides,* p. 154.

37. *Cf.* Euripides *Medea* 1078-1080.

38. Frg. 322 K.

39. *Cf.* Behr, *Aelius Aristides,* p. 169.

40. *Cf.* II 191 ff., XXIV 35, XXVIII 123, 125 ff.

41. Attacked in Aristides' lost oration *Against the Dancers,* to which Libanius replied in his LXIVth oration (ed. Foerster); *cf.* Behr, *Aelius Aristides,* p. 88.

42. *Cf.* Herodotus VII 114.

43. And allusion to the Cynic literary genre σπουδαιογέλοιον, *cf.* XXIX 18 (note 11).

44. When he was sold to Omphale, queen of Lydia.

45. His insanity ought not to be mentioned because he was a god; *cf.* XLVI 32-41 for a similar concept and Behr, *Aelius Aristides,* pp. 90, 155.

46. Aristides only objected to modern forms of dance, *cf.* Behr, *Aelius Aristides,* p. 88 n. 91 b.

47. Caenis, a girl, was loved by Poseidon, who, at her own request, changed her into a man.

48. *Cf.* § 47 (note 33).

49. *Cf.* § 16 (note 12).

50. The last Assyrian king, who through an apparent literary fiction was turned into a Greek stereotype of effeminacy; *cf.* Diodorus II 23 ff.

51. At this time Marcus Aurelius was the only living emperor; *cf.* LI 44 (note 69).

52. XX 167.

53. An allusion to the rejection of incompetent athletes from the games; *cf.* III 688 and XXVI 77 (note 83).

54. On the games, *cf.* Behr, *Studies on the Biography* § 4 and § 7.

55. *Cf.* LI 39-41.

NOTES TO XXXV

1. It has long been recognized that this clumsily written and bombastic speech could not be the work of Aristides (*cf.* especially B. Keil, *Eine Kaiserrede,* Nachrichten, Göttingen Gesellschaft der Wissenschaften, phil.-hist. Kl. (1905), pp. 381-428; E. Groag, *Die Kaiserrede des Pseudo-Aristides,* Wiener Studien 40 (1918), pp. 20-45; A. Boulanger, *Aelius Aristide* (1923), pp. 382-384; Behr, *Studies on the Biography,* § 10, where I have answered C.P. Jones, *Aelius Aristides* ΕΙΣ ΒΑΣΙΛΕΑ, Journal of Roman Studies 62 (1972), pp. 134-152, who believes that it is indeed a work of Aristides and that the recipient was Antoninus Pius. Recently in an interesting, if somewhat flawed, paper, Stephen A. Stertz, *Pseudo-Aristides,* ΕΙΣ

ΒΑΣΙΛΕΑ, Classical Quarterly (29) 1979, pp. 172-197, has re-examined Jones' arguments and rightly rejected his conclusions. Stertz himself believes that the speech is only a declamation and that no specific individual is meant). It is, however, clear that this hack writer was familiar enough with Aristides' works, particularly oration XXVI, to attempt some imitations (*cf.* §§ 2, 4, 19, 24, 25, 33, 35, 37-38). Perhaps it was this man, an orator himself, who inserted the speech into the corpus of Aristides' writings. On the other hand, the recipient of the speech has remained controversial. Over the years the following emperors have been suggested: Antoninus Pius, Marcus Aurelius, Pertinax, Macrinus, Philip the Arab, Decius, Gallienus, and it has even been proposed that the speech is nothing more than a Byzantine literary exercize of about the ninth century (*cf.* the recapitulation in Jones, *op. cit.*, p. 134). The reason for this uncertainty is the small amount of solid biographical material which this wretched panegyrist has provided us. We know the following: 1) the emperor was not related by birth or adoption to his predecessor (*cf.* § 5), although Jones, *op. cit.*, p. 140 disputes even this; 2) he had a son (§ 39); 3) he was not a soldier (*cf.* § 32 ff. as well as the *argumentum ex silentio*, here valid); 4) he had some involvement with the Parthians (*cf.* §§ 14, 32, 35); 5) he had some involvement with "the Celts", who are possibly "the Germans" (*cf.* § 35); 6) he annihilated some unknown people (*cf.* § 35), although Jones, *op. cit.*, p. 148 does not so understand the passage; and finally 7) he was not favorably disposed toward his predecessor (otherwise the innuendos, which presuppose a critical attitude toward the previous reign, would be impossible). The other so-called evidence is really ambiguous: *e.g.* mention of the alleged low state to which Greek culture had fallen under the emperor's predecessor (§ 20) may be no more than an oblique compliment to the incumbent ruler. Groag, *op. cit.*, saw in the recipient Philip the Arab—the speech being delivered *c.* 247 A.D.—and with some dissents, notably Jones', his view has maintained itself (*cf.* especially the additional remarks of L. J. Swift, *The Anonymous Encomium of Philip the Arab*, Greek, Roman, and Byzantine Studies 7 (1966), pp. 267-289, who also gives a translation. See too J. H. Oliver, *The Piety of Commodus and Caracalla and the* Εἰς Βασιλέα, Greek, Roman, and Byzantine Studies, 19, 1978, pp. 386-388, who supports the identification of Philip). Except for the ambiguity in the account of the accession (§§ 5, 8), a politically sensitive point, obscurely and incompetently handled in any case in this speech (*cf.* notes 8 and 12), Groag's identification still seems satisfactory enough to me, although I cannot approve of his suggestion that this speech is Nicagoras' *Embassy* (*cf.* Behr, *Aelius Aristides*, p. 89 n. 92). Accordingly I have so composed the notes and in one case supplemented the text.

The oration is divided as follows:
A. § 1-4 Proem. Greatness of the theme
B. § 5-15 Circumstances of his accession
C. § 16-20 His justice
D. § 21-26 His generosity
E. § 27-29 His self-control
F. § 30-37 His courage and good counsel
G. § 38-39 Peroration. Address to the Emperor and his son.

2. Perhaps the Eleusinia, *cf.* § 37.
3. *Cf.* XXVI 2; Isocrates IV 13; and Norden *Die Antike Kunstprosa* (5th ed.), p. 595 n. 1.
4. *Cf.* Plato *Republic* 374 E; Isocrates IX 11.
5. *Cf.* I 49.
6. *Cf.* Isocrates IX 35.
7. "As it were" since these successions were often preserved by adoption as in the series of emperors from Nerva to Marcus Aurelius (five emperors—including Lucius Verus—each adopted by his predecessor).

8. If Philip is the subject, this obscure remark is explained by the story put out by his administration that Gordian III died of disease on the campaign against the Parthians in 244 A.D. (*cf.* SHA *Vitae Gordianorum trium* 31. 2 and Zonaras I 19) and that Philip was elected emperor by the army (*cf.* SHA *op. cit.* 29. 5; Groag, Wiener Studien 40 (1918), pp. 31-32). However, it is difficult to see why the panegyrist expresses himself so obscurely and why he apparently contradicts himself in § 8 (see note 12), where an act of violence on the part of others is implied. Perhaps the story of Gordian III's death by disease was only promulgated at the time of his murder and not pressed by the new regime afterwards.

9. § 5, where it is affirmed that he did not offer himself as a candidate for emperor.

10. For the dative, *cf.* XXXII 25. Canter, however, translates: "ii, qui ante ipsum regnarunt, facile possunt animadvertere---".

11. Canter translates: "ex magistratu multis occisis", but *cf.* § 9 τῶν ἐν τέλει, which would have this meaning.

12. Apparently this refers to the mutiny which took place in 244 A.D. over the failure of the commissariat in the Parthian campaign (a failure which it was said Philip himself caused; cf. SHA *Vitae Gordianorum trium* 29-30, especially 30. 8). It seems to contradict the claim in § 5 (see note 8) that Philip did not receive the throne "through others", but the panegyrist probably did not intend to create this impression, but only to allude to the mutiny which all knew had occurred and which Philip had claimed took place through the incompetence of the previous administration. However, the panegyrist's ineptitude has let the truth slip out that there was indeed a close connection between the violence and Philip's accession; *cf.* Behr, *Studies on the Biography* § 10. Groag, Wiener Studien 40 (1918), p. 32 sees this as an act of candor: "...Philipp konnte nicht leugnen und hatte gar keinen Anlass, dies zu tun, dass dem Tode Gordians ein (zweifellos nicht unblutig verlaufener) Aufruhr des hungernden Heeres vorangegangen war". For as Groag adds in a note: "Er musste hohen Wert darauf legen, den nach den erfochtenen Siegen doppelt unrühmlichen Friedensschluss (with Parthia) vor der Öffentlichkeit zu rechtfertigen".

13. *Cf.* Isocrates IX 25.
14. *Cf.* Plato *Theaetetus* 144 A.
15. *Cf.* Isocrates IX 23.
16. Praetorian prefect.
17. *Cf.* Plato *Phaedrus* 254 A ff.
18. The Parthian war is presumably meant; see note 20.
19. Starting with Crassus' defeat at Carrhae in 53 B.C.
20. In 243 A.D. Timesitheus, the praetorian prefect and Gordian III's general, in a series of victories was in the course of winning this war which the Parthian king Sapor had started against the Romans. But then Timesitheus died and Philip was appointed in his place. After the army's mutiny and the death of Gordian III, Philip forbore to continue the campaign and made peace with Sapor (244 A.D.)
21. Judges of the dead.
22. As former practorian prefect.
23. *Cf.* § 35; *Cambridge Ancient History* vol. XII, p. 213; but see now Jones, Journal of Roman Studies 62 (1972), pp. 144-145.
24. A fulsome imitation of XXVI 38.
25. *Cf.* Xenophon *Agesilaos* 7. 4 and 7.
26. *Cf.* on the theme Isocrates IX 50.
27. Or possibly the *frumentarii*, the secret police, may be meant.
28. *sc.* in his administration. If this is not metaphor passing into hyperbole, it is a strong argument against the identification of Philip. Canter has *in tanta potentia*.

But aside from Greek usage, I would cite a phrase from the Arval acts of 213 A.D. (Pasoli no. 86, line 18) from an acclamation of Caracalla (aged 25 years): *iuvenis triumphis, senex imp(erio)!* Elsewhere in the speech the "youth" of the recipient is not stressed.

29. *Cf.* Xenophon *Agesilaos* 7. 3.
30. *Cf.* XXIII 79, XXVII 35.
31. *Cf.* XXVI 45 (and note 51 there).
32. *Cf.* Xenophon *Agesilaos* 5. 1.
33. § 15.
34. *Iliad* III 179.
35. *Iliad* I 350.
36. *Cf.* § 27.
37. *Cf.* Xenophon *Agesilaos* 8. 8.
38. *Cf. Cambridge Ancient History* vol. XII, p. 267.
39. Apparently an allusion to the peace made with Parthia in 244 A.D. (*cf.* note 20). "Good counsel" here and elsewhere seems to be the equivalent of "diplomacy".
40. Xerxes.
41. Themistocles; *cf.* I 139.
42. *Cf.* Xenophon *Agesilaos* 11. 9.
43. *Cf.* Isocrates IX 28.
44. *Cf.* Xenophon *Agesilaos* 6. 5.
45. If Philip is the recipient and Κελτοί means "Germans", their defeat in 246 A.D. is referred to, for which Philip took the title *Germanicus Maximus.*
46. *Cf.* I 143. The supplement ("and when the Carpi... no longer exist and") is made after Groag's suggestion in Wiener Studien 40 (1918), pp. 34-35. Unfortunately his explanation that the scribes could not understand how an emperor conquered τοὺς καρποὺς ("the fruits of the field"), while ingenious, does not explain the corruption. For the form of the passage should have been as I have given it in the Greek text. Philip styled himself as *Carpicus Maximus* in 247 A.D. The Carpi continued to cause trouble throughout the century.
47. *Cf.* V 10. For the campaign against Parthia, *cf.* note 20.
48. From this point through § 37 the panegyrist imitates XXVI 99-100.
49. *Cf.* § 1.
50. The orator plays on the titles Εὐσεβής and Εὐτυχής, "Pius" and "Felix"; *cf.* Oliver, Greek, Roman, and Byzantine Studies, 19 (1978), p. 387.
51. Philip the Younger was named Augustus in 247 A.D., apparently after this speech. Γενναῖε γενναίων may be the equivalent of "nobilissimus", *cf.* Groag, Wiener Studien 40 (1918), p. 22, but see now Jones, Journal of Roman Studies 62 (1972), p. 150 n. 148.
52. *Cf.* XLVI 32; XLVII 38.

NOTES TO XXXVI

1. This treatise on the rising of the Nile was composed in Smyrna sometime between 147-149 A.D. It is the result of Aristides' earlier sojourn in Egypt in 142 A.D. (*cf.* Behr, *Aelius Aristides,* pp. 15-21, 62-63). The search for an answer to the paradox that the Nile rises at a time when other known rivers sink to their lowest level aroused lively interest throughout antiquity. Innumerable theories were proposed and those current up to the end of the fourth century B.C. were collected in a treatise by Aristotle or his pupil Theophrastus. This work, in three books, is lost, although a faint trace of it may be preserved in a very brief, mutilated, and bar-

barous Latin version under the name *Liber Aristotelis de inundacione Nili* (frg. 248 Rose). Moreover, vestiges of this work are found in the similar collections of theories, all arranged in diverse order, made by a number of later writers: Diodorus I 38-41; Lucretius VI 711 ff.; Seneca *Naturales Quaestiones* IV a 2; The *Anonymus Florentinus* printed at the end of the second book of Athenaeus; the scholium on Apollonius Rhodius IV 269; Aetius IV 1. These collections and their relationship to Aristotle have been much studied, *cf.* especially H. Diels, *Doxographi Graeci* (1929), pp. 226-229; J. Partsch, Abhandlungen d. saechsisch. Akademie d. Wissenschaften, phil.-hist. Kl. 27 (1909), pp. 553-600, whose conclusions are approved by W. Jaeger, *Aristotle* Oxford (1948), p. 331 n. 2; W. Capelle, Neue Jahrbücher für das klassische Altertum 33 (1914), pp. 317-361; Pauly-Wissowa *s.v.* Nilschwelle (Rehm), pp. 571-590. Aristides' treatise belongs to this group. He too limits himself to the older theories contained in the putative book of Aristotle or Theophrastus, and he does not consider more recent speculation. Aristides' purpose is negative, limited to combating false theories. His work's originality lies in its artistic reworking of these scientific themes, much as when he treated anew a speech of Demosthenes (*cf.* IV 4), or some other rhetorical commonplace. The importance of the artistic side of this work can be seen from the fact that Aristides names only the authors of theories who were poets or historians, and suppresses the names of all the philosopher-scientists. Aristides also prided himself on the contributions of his own scientific observations (*cf.* § 103), which are contained in §§ 9, 18, 30, 34, 46-63, 70, 74, 113—some of which provide an interesting picture of life in Egypt, particularly on the Ethiopian frontier—as well as on his reports of the observations of other contemporaries (*cf.* §§ 15, 20, 31, 34, 81, 82, 115, 125). One of his scientific comments even passed into the tradition (*cf.* § 33 and the rebuttal of Proclus *In Platonis Timaeum* 37 D). In composing his refutations, Aristides seems to have used at least three sources: Herodotus (§ 3), Ephorus (§§ 77, 85), and a (peripatetic) work similar, although far from identical, to the doxographic collections enumerated above. This third work would seem to have arranged the arguments by cause, and Aristides chose to follow its system. Some traces of the book can be found in Aristides' treatise, particularly near the end §§ 104-113. For after Aristides, apparently in preparation for the conclusion of his study, had summarized most of the theories which he had discussed, §§ 100-103, he suddenly takes up Homer's allusions to the Nile, which we know were employed by the peripatetics (Aristotle) to support their arguments that rain was the cause (*cf.* scholium to Homer *Odyssey* IV 477). This work has also been translated into English, with a few original notes, by W. G. Waddell, *On Egypt, A Discourse by P. Aelius Aristides,* Bulletin of the Faculty of Arts 2 (1934), pp. 121-166, Faculté des Lettres, Université Fouad I, Cairo.

The treatise is divided into the following sections:
A. § 1-2 Proem. Refutations
B. § 3-12 (Thales)
C. § 13-18 (Anaxagoras), Aeschylus, and Euripides
D. § 19-40 (Democritus, Callisthenes, and Agatharcides)
E. § 41-63 Herodotus
F. § 64-84 Ephorus
G. § 85-96 Euthymenes
H. § 97-99 (Diogenes of Apollonia)
I. § 100-103 Summary of refutations
J. § 104-113 Homer
K. § 114-125 The inexplicable miracles of the Nile.

2. In fact he seems to have sailed only once to Ethiopia. "The four times" probably refers to trips from Alexandria through Lower Egypt and the northernmost parts of Upper Egypt; *cf.* Behr, *Aelius Aristides,* p. 15 n. 44.

3. The ruins of a building of Amenhemhet III at Crocodilopolis; *cf.* Herodotus II 148. 1.
4. A recurrent problem; *cf.* XLVIII 3.
5. If the reading is sound, he plays on the idea of paying back a debt as well as dealing with a question, which he does not solve.
6. II 20. The theory of Thales, beginning of the 6th century B.C.; *cf.* H. Diels, *Die Fragmente der Vorsokratiker* (6th ed.) I, pp. 71, 78 (frg. A 1, A 16). The Nile floods for the first 100 days after the summer solstice (*cf.* Herodotus II 19). The Etesian ("annual") winds blow from the north-west from the summer solstice to about "the Dog Days" = July 26 (*cf.* Seneca *Naturales Quaestiones* V 10).
7. Of the Mediterranean.
8. The Tanais is the Don; for the Phasis, *cf.* XXVI 82.
9. Perhaps corrupt, but this seems to be the sense.
10. II 17.
11. A friend of Aristides' at Pergamum; *cf.* Behr, *Aelius Aristides*, p. 17 n. 53.
12. *Cf.* XLV 29.
13. § 9.
14. Anaxagoras, middle of the fifth century B.C.; *cf.* H. Diels, *Die Fragmente der Vorsokratiker* (6th ed.) II, pp. 16, 27 (frg. A 42, A 91). This was actually partly the true cause.
15. Euripides *Helen* 1-3.
16. Ethiopia and Egypt.
17. A Thracian and a Macedonian tribe respectively.
18. *Cf.* Herodotus II 22. The sentence breaks off intentionally, I think, as if it were absurd to argue more.
19. Aeschylus frg. 300 N.; *cf.* Athenaeus II 87 B; also Aeschylus frg. 228, 2-4 N.
20. For the craze for snow as a coolant, *cf.* Seneca *Naturales Quaestiones* IV b. 13.
21. Frg. 381 N.
22. *Cf.* § 9.
23. This is similar to Democritus' theory, *c.* 440 B.C.; *cf.* H. Diels, *Die Fragmente der Vorsokratiker* (6th ed.) II, pp. 107-108 (frg. A 99). This theory was espoused by the Peripatetics, Aristotle, Callisthenes; also by Eudoxus, Eratosthenes, Agatharcides, Posidonius; *cf.* note 1 and § 104 on Homer.
24. The text is lacunose, but Upper Egypt seems to be meant; *cf.* § 66.
25. *Cf.* § 115.
26. The phrase in Greek is Homeric; *cf. Odyssey* IX 244.
27. *Cf.* §§ 6, 24. "The same phenomena" are the rivers' rising; "the indications" are the way in which they rise.
28. For the expression, *cf.* § 120 and Herodotus II 11. 4 and 20. 2. It has been hesitantly suggested that ultimately this notion may derive from Egyptian NWY (= flood) and NW'I (= tend).
29. In growth and recession.
30. For πλείονι, *cf.* § 54 and I 109. On the other hand, Keil understands the text to mean that the Nile, in summer and winter, would have an increase and decrease different from other rivers because of its size.
31. The western side.
32. *Cf.* § 81.
33. *Cf.* § 55. Meroe, thought to be a great island, lies near Khartoum, at the confluence of the Blue and White Nile and was the capital of the Ethiopian or Nubian kingdom. It was about as far south as the Greeks' knowledge of Africa extended.
34. *Cf.* Strabo XVII 786 and Aristotle frg. 248 (p. 197, 3 ed. Rose).
35. *Cf.* § 55.

36. *Cf.* XXVI 62.

37. Proclus *In Platonis Timaeum* 37 D specifically attacks Aristides' argument and quotes part of it.

38. "Pinnacle" was a standard term for the region of the first cataract (in Egyptian = TP-ŠM ⟨W⟩), *cf.* also §§ 46 and 66. Egypt is Upper Egypt as opposed to the Delta; *cf.* note 90 to § 65. For the trip, *cf.* Behr, *Aelius Aristides,* p. 15 n. 44.

39. *i.e.* the Thebaid, one of the three *epistrategiae* of Egypt.

40. Alexandria.

41. Perhaps by Euare(s)tus of Crete, *cf.* L 23; Behr, *Aelius Aristides,* p. 17. For the name Draucus (= a strong man), *cf.* A.E. Housman, Classical Review 44 (1930), pp. 114-116.

42. The main longitudinal street of Alexandria, running from the Canobic gate on the east to the gate of the Necropolis on the west.

43. *i.e.* the recession has not been complete.

44. § 35.

45. In describing a circle.

46. So I would translate "necessities".

47. The sun. Probably Helius Sarapis.

48. § 38.

49. II 24-27.

50. Herodotus is meant.

51. Homer *Iliad* XXI 361 ff.

52. *Cf.* Strabo XVII 818-819, and Plutarch's general attack on Herodotus in *De Herodoti Malignitate.*

53. II 8.

54. *Cf.* § 33, note 38.

55. An Egyptian measurement from 24, 000 to 36, 000 feet.

56. II 28.

57. II 29.

58. 4200 feet.

59. The location of the Altars must remain conjectural. But I suspect that Aristides may mean modern Qertassi, which lies on the west bank of the Nile between Philae (at that time the border between Egypt and Ethiopia) and Talmis, the famous site of the cult of Mandulis. In favor of this assumption, I would note that Qertassi seems to have been too insignificant to have received a name. Yet it possessed a fort (for the Ethiopian garrison?) and a shrine in a rock quarry with a Meroitic inscription and altars (*cf.* Bertha Porter and Rosalind Moss, *Topographical Bibliography of Ancient Egyptian Hieroglyphic Texts, Reliefs, and Paintings,* vol. VII Nubia, pp. 6-8, Oxford, 1951). The quarry seems not to have been exploited by the Romans before 204 A.D. (*cf.* IGRR I 1330), which may indicate that they did not recover this territory until this time. A cult of some sort is then indicated by a long series of προσκυνήματα incised in a chapel in the rock (*cf.* CIG 4980-5037). Three deities are mentioned: Isis, Srouptichis (feminine), and Poursepmounis (masculine). The borders between Roman Egypt and Ethiopia seem constantly to be shifting. Earlier they extended south even of Pselchis and later appear to have again included Talmis, *cf.* IGRR I 1356 (on a possible Roman withdrawal in the time of Antoninus, *cf.* W. Hüttl, *Antoninus Pius* I, p. 295 and n. 366, with whom I would disagree only in that *all* the inscriptions at Talmis need not imply that the Romans then occupied the territory). As is shown by § 55 relations between the Romans and Ethiopians were quite friendly at this time and intercourse between them easy. However, Canter understands Aristides' trip to the Altars as the beginning of the journey, "Cum ad aras ascendissem...." and he is followed by Waddell (see note 1), who translates, "When I approached the Tombs..." and who

describes these as rock tombs on the west bank, north of Elephantine. But first Aristides was on the east bank going south and second it is hardly likely that the Romans would tolerate an Ethiopian garrison in what was evidently their territory. On the road from Syene to Philae Strabo XVII 818 saw many stone pillars with other stones upon them, and these could be the Altars, but still not a suitable location for a garrison.

60. The road from Syene to Philae in fact does this.

61. *Cf.* § 91, XLV 34, and Behr, *Aelius Aristides,* p. 18.

62. Strabo XVII 817, 819, 820, reports that there were three cohorts stationed here in the time of Augustus; but now there were apparently only two, the I Flavia Cilicum Equitata and the II Ituraeorum Equitata (*cf.* CIL III 14147³, IGRR I 1348, and W. Hüttl, *Antoninus Pius* I, p. 298).

63. Abatos, present day Bigeh; *cf.* § 50 and Diodorus I 22. 3; Strabo XVII 817-818; Seneca *Naturales Quaestiones* IV a 2. 6; Lucan X 323.

64. Doubtless Aristides had a letter of commendation from the Prefect of Egypt, C. Avidius Heliodorus, with whom he was acquainted; *cf.* L 75.

65. The island Elephantine and Syene.

66. II 29; *cf.* Strabo XVII 818-819.

67. The quotation is fictitious, as if from II 28. Sais is in the Delta at the opposite end of Egypt.

68. The Greek, if the text is sound, appears to be negligently constructed with ὥστε, as if Aristides had meant to write either ὥστε μὴ χρήσασθαι ἄν or ἢ ἐχρήσατο ἄν.

69. II 28.

70. *Cf.* XXXIV 27.

71. Frg. 300 N. (*cf.* § 15) is referred to, but Keil is doubtless right in recognizing here a new fragment.

72. *Cf.* W.W. How and J. Wells, *A Commentary on Herodotus* I, p. 172 on II 28; also Seneca *Naturales Quaestiones* IV a 2. 7.

73. *Cf.* XXXIX 18; Strabo XVII 819; Tacitus *Annales* II 61.

74. Apparently at the Altars, *cf.* § 48 and note 59.

75. *Cf.* § 31.

76. Pselchis, presumably the headquarters of the prefect, is the modern Dakeh, 70 miles south of Syene. The geography is preposterous, for there are only six cataracts.

77. The White Nile and the Blue Nile. Aristides must be one of the earliest surviving writers to distinguish, as we do, the Astapus and the Astaboras by color.

78. *Cf* § 75.

79. As *e.g.* Plutarch, *cf.* note 52 to § 46.

80. *Cf.* XXVIII 1.

81. Essentially Egypt, outside of the Delta, is regarded only as the Nile valley. The eastern desert is Arabia, the western Libya (= our Africa), and south of the first cataract Ethiopia.

82. §§ 46-54.

83. *i.e.* at the summer solstice.

84. *Cf.* Strabo XVII 817; Arrian *Indica* 25. 7.

85. As against Ethiopia, *cf.* note 81 to § 58.

86. If the supplement, "no differently than all other rivers", is sound, *cf.* § 6.

87. Aristides apparently refers to the expression "goes to the Ethiopians", which is somewhat like Herodotus' (II 24) rather primitive ἔρχεται (the sun) τῆς Λιβύης τὰ ἄνω, although the thesis of II 25 is referred to. So *cf.* § 61, where Aristides censures this notion, and §§ 41, 45, 60 for similar criticism.

88. Homer *Odyssey* VIII 492; *cf.* Aristides II 89, XXVIII 75.

89. Actually a historian, died last quarter of the 4th century B.C.; *cf.* F. Jacoby, *Fragmente der griechischen Historiker* II A, F 65.

90. The Thebaid (*cf.* note 39 to § 33). Aristides seems to express what in Coptic is *Ma* (place) *res* (southern), and still in Arabic *maris*. Apparently the term was used even then for the ancient Egyptian TP-ŠM ʿW (*cf.* note 38 to §33).

91. *Cf.* § 115, where the figure given is 28 cubits.

92. *Cf.* § 33 and note 38.

93. *i.e.* from the Delta to the south.

94. Ephorus came from Cyme in Asia, where the people were said to be stupid.

95. Near Mons Claudianus, *cf.* IGRR I 1255.

96. There follows a comment of some reader, which has intruded itself into the text: "The land is so barren of water, and therefore has been made a desert".

97. Ephorus' alleged cause; *cf.* § 83.

98. *Cf.* § 107 and Thucydides I 104. 1.

99. *Cf.* Herodotus II 6. 1, III 5. 3; Diodorus I 30. 4. Strabo's (XVII 804) odd and inaccurate remarks on the two lakes "in the swamp, beyond Pelusium in Arabia" connected by a channel to the Nile probably in part refer to Serbonis.

100. *Cf.* Strabo XIII 621.

101. This is a direct quote from Ephorus.

102. §§ 74-75.

103. The usage is strange and is perhaps modeled after "the pinnacle" of Upper Egypt (*cf.* note 38 to § 33).

104. *Cf.* Herodotus II 2.

105. *Cf.* § 30.

106. Bethsean, 15 miles south of the sea of Galilee. Syria Palestina was the designation of the old province of Judaea after 135 A.D., but the term is as old as Herodotus.

107. *Cf.* Behr, *Aelius Aristides,* p. 17 n. 53. There is no such lake, and Aristides or his source appears to have meant the far distant Dead Sea (*cf.* § 88), which had according to an Arab legend a subterranean outlet. Strabo XVI 763 calls the Dead Sea "Lake Serbonis" and Aristides seems to have believed that the rise of Lake Serbonis was somehow similar to the rise of the Nile, *cf.* §§ 74-75. *Cf.* the story of the Inopus in Delos, Pliny *NH* II 229.

108. *Cf.* § 27.

109. *Cf.* Aristotle frg. 248 (pp. 191, 22; 192, 9 Rose).

110. *Cf.* Diodorus I 39. 7.

111. Euthymenes, one of the earliest Greek writers on geography (his account here preserved in Ephorus, *cf.* C. Müller, *Fragmenta Historicorum Graecorum* IV, pp. 408 ff.), lived *c.* 500 B.C. and came from Massalia (modern Marseilles). The reference to Sybaris (in Italy) is obscure in connection with Ephorus. There was a genre of fables called Sybaritic (*cf.* the scholia to Aristophanes *Vespae* 1259 and *Aves* 471).

112. For Thales, *cf.* Diogenes Laertius I 34 (*cf.* also R. Helm, *Lucian und Menipp,* p. 280 n. 2). Aristides plays on the proverb, "fleeing the smoke, he fell into the fire".

113. *Cf.* I 119.

114. *Cf.* Herodotus IV 45. 2, who preferred the Phasis. For the Tanais as the boundary (the modern view), *cf.* Arrian *Anabasis* III 30. 8 and *Periplus* 19. 1 ff.

115. A peninsula of Asia. On Arabia, *cf.* § 60. For the "Red Sea", *cf.* note 29 to XXVI 28.

116. The Mediterranean and the Red Sea. For the supplement, *cf.* XLVI 21.

117. Even in Aristides' day this theory was outmoded, *cf.* Behr, *Aelius Aristides,* p. 20 n. 70.

118. *Cf.* XLVIII 60. Proverbial, from the long story which Odysseus told to Alcinous' court in books IX to XII of *The Odyssey.*

119. § 88.

120. Antoninus Pius; cf. XXIV 31 and XXVI 100 ff.
121. Cf. § 49 and note 61.
122. Britain, cf. note 32 to XXVI 28.
123. Perhaps an allusion to the troops required to defeat the Brigantes in 142 A.D. At that time there seem to have been stationed there 3 legions, 10 alae, and 37 cohorts, a total of 43, 800 men; cf. W. Hüttl, *Antoninus Pius* I, pp. 254 ff.
124. The Archbishop Arethas (c. 900 A.D.) in his capacity as scholiast remarks that Aristides refers to the Carthaginian navigator Hanno (c. 500 B.C.), whose writings translated into Greek are still preserved.
125. Aristides plays on the proverb, "May you sail to Massalia" (cf. Athenaeus XII 523 C), which, like "Not every man may go to Corinth", refers to the city as a place of luxury and rich living.
126. Aristides means only Diogenes of Apollonia (cf. H. Diels, *Die Fragmente der Vorsokratiker* (6th ed.), vol. 2, p. 54, frg. A 18), second half of the 5th century B.C. Aristides often uses the plural in this way (e.g. cf. § 42), but he may have negligently cited his source which conjoined in one chapter Diogenes and the somewhat different view of Oenopides, as we once find them side by side in the doxographies cited in note 1 and twice find Oenopides with Euthymenes. Cf. also Timaeus in Pliny *NH* 55-56. For "the scientific theory", cf. XLIII 12.
127. Cf. XXXIII 14.
128. In summer than in winter.
129. Of the Danae.
130. Cf. II 464.
131. Cf. §§ 3-12.
132. Cf. §§ 19-40.
133. Cf. §§ 13-18.
134. Cf. §§ 41-63.
135. Cf. §§ 64-84.
136. Cf. IV 4.
137. *Odyssey* IV 581. Homer was used by Aristotle as a witness in support of the theory that rain caused the rise of the Nile; cf. the scholium on *Odyssey* IV 477 and for this addendum, note 1.
138. E.g. *Iliad* I 544.
139. Cf. XLIII 21, 28.
140. Also called the Scamander with the epithet "Zeus-nourished" in *Iliad* XXI 223.
141. § 104.
142. The first two rivers are in the Troad, the last in Mysia.
143. *Odyssey* IV 355-357.
144. Cf. § 113; III 577, 582, 586, 663; and XLV 1 ff.
145. *Odyssey* IV 357.
146. The mole, which connects the Pharus to the mainland, was called the Heptastadion (= seven stades = 4200 feet).
147. Cf. Strabo I 30, 37; scholium to *Odyssey* IV 356. In § 74, Aristides himself believes that there has been a change.
148. Hecataeus, first half of the 5th century B.C.; cf. F. Jacoby, *Die Fragmente der griechischen Historiker* I, p. 41 (F 308) and p. 369. On the tradition, cf. Pauly-Wissowa s.v. Kanobus 1869-1870.
149. Probably GW3T (= small piece of land) NBW (= of gold). On the other hand, v. Bissing, Zeitschrift für Ägyptische Sprache 72 (1936), p. 79, thinks that the phonogram for G was misread as the ideogram for "seat". On Aristides' knowledge of Egyptian, cf. Behr, *Aelius Aristides*, p. 17 n. 56.
150. Cf. note 175 to § 125.

151. 120 stades = 72, 000 feet; 1200 stades = 720, 000 feet. Herodotus IV 86. 1 computes a day's sailing at 130, 000 fathoms = 780, 000 feet.
152. Frg. 241 Turyn = 201 Schroeder.
153. Mountains in the neighborhood of Thebes in Greece.
154. *Cf.* note 144 to § 106.
155. § 85.
156. *Cf.* Herodotus II 19. 3.
157. **Cf.** §§ 13-18.
158. Thus the size of the harvest could be calculated; *cf.* § 20, Pliny *Natural History* V 9. 58. At Elephantine one such Nilometer is preserved, *cf.* IGRR I 1290.
159. *Cf.* XXXIX 9.
160. *Cf.* XVII 15.
161. *i.e.* in having more water added by rain.
162. *Cf.* § 41.
163. For this and the following, *cf.* Seneca *Naturales Quaestiones* IV a 2. 8-12.
164. As Keil notes, the absence of the article may mean that this is a nautical term; the same expression is found in III 591; *cf.* XXXVI 10.
165. On the law of nature, *cf.* I 390, XXIII 77, XXXVII 26; also Lucan X 238: "sic iussit natura parens discurrere Nilum".
166. *Cf.* § 23.
167. *Cf. e.g.* Arrian *Anabasis* VII 7. 5.
168. *Cf.* Behr, *Aelius Aristides,* p. 17 n. 53.
169. The Egyptian Sea, *cf.* § 16 and XLIX 3.
170. Sarapis; *cf.* XLV 32.
171. *Cf.* Seneca *Naturales Quaestiones* IV a 2. 1; also Aristides XLV 32.
172. Asclepius and Sarapis; *cf.* Behr, *Aelius Aristides,* pp. 19, 63, 73, 149; *Aristides and the Egyptian Gods,* p. 14 in Hommages à Vermaseren (Leiden, 1978).
173. Aristides confuses the Egyptian name of the Apis Bull (= Sarapis), ḤP, with that of the Nile, Ḥ'PY; *cf.* Behr, *Aelius Aristides,* p. 17 n. 56.
174. *Cf.* XLII 8-9; Behr, *Aelius Aristides,* pp. 36-40.
175. *Cf.* § 110; Aeschylus *Suppliants* 561; Herodotus II 77; Plato *Timaeus* 22 E; Isocrates XI 12 ff.; Seneca *Naturales Quaestiones* VI 26. 1 ff.
176. Perhaps Dion, § 10 or Draucus, § 33; cf. Behr, *Aelius Aristides,* p. 17 n. 53.

NOTES TO XXXVII

1. Μαντευτοί: This title, chosen either by Aristides or his first editor (*cf.* Lenz-Behr, *P. Aelii Aristidis... Opera Omnia* I, p. LXX) comes from the earliest edition (it was already known in the 3rd century A.D. to Menander Περὶ Ἐπιδεικτικῶν, vol. III, p. 344 Sp.). It comprehends the present orations XXXVII to XLI and LIII. For the influence, which dreams had on Aristides' literary career, *cf.* Behr, *Aelius Aristides,* pp. 45-46.

2. This oration was delivered *c.* January 153 A.D. at the small town of Baris (modern Gönen) on the east bank of the Aesepus where Aristides had an estate (*cf.* L 1-7, 71). The speech, in prose-hymn style, is cast in the form of an aretology—the concerned divinity being exalted as far as possible at the expense of other gods. However, Aristides does seem to have especially venerated this goddess, so that the stilted tone of the speech is no indication of the genuineness of his feelings. This work is quite separate from that which is mentioned in L 25 and which precipitated oration XXVIII; *cf.* Behr, *Aelius Aristides,* pp. 80-81, 153-154. F.W. Lenz has studied this work in *Der Athenahymnos des Aristeides,* Rivista di Cultura Classica e Medioevale 3 (1963), pp. 329-347, republished in *Opuscula*

Selecta (Amsterdam, 1972), pp. 355-373. His chronological observations are quite mistaken.

The speech is divided into the following sections:
A. § 1 Proem
B. § 2-7 Birth
C. § 8-17 Benefits conferred by the goddess
D. § 18-25 Her relationship with other gods
E. § 26-28 Her titles and powers
F. § 29 Peroration.

3. Zeus.
4. *Cf.* J. Amann, *Die Zeusrede des Aelios Aristeides,* Tübinger Beiträge zur Altertumswissenschaft 12 (1931), pp. 14-23; O. Weinreich, *Typisches und Individuelles in der Religiosität des Ailios Aristeides,* Neue Jahrbücher für das klassische Altertum, Geschichte, und deutsche Literatur 33 (1914), p. 602; Behr, *Aelius Aristides,* p. 154.
5. A protective goat skin, in general thought to be used only by Zeus and Athena.
6. *Cf.* Homer *Iliad* VIII 387 ff.
7. There is also an allusion here to Homer *Odyssey* IV 742, Ζηνὸς αὐλή ("the court of Zeus"); *cf.* XXVI 29.
8. Ares.
9. Homer *Iliad* XXI 401.
10. Frg. 154 Turyn = 146 Schroeder; *cf.* also Horace *Carmina* I 12. 19.
11. A pun on κατὰ κρατός = "from head to foot".
12. *Cf.* Homer *Iliad* XIX 93.
13. *Cf.* Plato *Timaeus* 40 D.
14. Almost used in the sense of "professionals"; *cf.* note 136 to XXVI 105 and XXVIII 108.
15. In Macedonia. A good account of this battle in Apollodorus I vi, 1 ff.
16. For a similar reluctance to discuss such matters, *cf.* XLVI 36 and Behr, *Aelius Aristides,* pp. 90, 155.
17. *Cf.* XLII 5; also I 330 and II 412.
18. "City Holder".
19. *Cf.* Plato *Timaeus* 24 B.
20. The Athenians; *cf.* I 43.
21. The Saite nome. Athena is equated with the Egyptian goddess Neit.
22. *Cf.* I 43, 354.
23. *Cf.* I 36, 199.
24. The passage is seriously corrupt, but can, I think, be simply cured by purging a gloss. ἕν τε, which answers πρός τε, has as its predicate τὸ αὐτό (*cf.* I 225). With ὁλκάδας *etc.* understand εἰς from εἰς ἄμφω.
25. *Cf.* I 43.
26. An Attic hero, who first yoked oxen to the plough; *cf.* scholia in Aristides 3, 473, 15 ff. Ddf.; Plutarch *Moralia* 144 B; U. v. Wilamowitz, *Der Glaube der Hellenen,* Bd. 2, p. 44; P. Foucart, *Les Mystères d' Éleusis* (1914), pp. 51 f., 166.
27. Homer *Odyssey* V 437.
28. *Cf.* I 48.
29. Delos; *cf.* XLIV 11.
30. *Cf.* I 13; Macrobius *Saturnalia* I 17. 55.
31. Apollo and Artemis.
32. The god of health, to whom Aristides was most especially devoted. The connection is through Apollo who was Asclepius' father.
33. *Odyssey* VIII 193 ff.
34. *Cf.* § 25.

35. Cf. I 41.
36. A crown of wild olive was the prize at the Olympic festival.
37. These are all scenes from Homer's *Odyssey*.
38. The bridle; cf. §§ 14, 20.
39. *i.e.* turned to stone by Medusa.
40. Polydectes and the people of Seriphos.
41. Theseus.
42. Cf. Homer *Iliad* V 392 ff.
43. Cf. § 22.
44. Cf. XXX 14 for the proverb "to save from fire".
45. Athena Nike; cf. § 17.
46. Cf. on XXXVI 120. She is Athena Sotira.
47. Cf. Teles, p. 54, 2 in the edition of Hense.
48. Cf. XXVI 44.
49. Cf. XXVII 14. He means that the gods are involved in all of mankind's activities.
50. Cf. § 2-7.
51. Wilamowitz compares the Homeric phrase Διὶ μῆτιν ἀτάλαντος (*e.g. Iliad* II 169).
52. Cf. I 152-153.
53. Frg. 388 N.
54. *i.e.* Imperator Antoninus Pius and Caesar Marcus Aurelius; cf. L 75, LI 44 (for the style); and Behr, *Studies on the Biography* § 1.
55. *i.e.* of the Greeks. As a title, cf. XXXIII 32 and L 78.
56. For these subscriptions, cf. note 23 to oration XVIII; Behr, *Studies on the Biography* § 1. For the site of Baris (present day Gönen) on the river Aesepus, cf. Behr, *Aelius Aristides,* pp. 6-7.
57. C. Julius Severus, cf. L 12, 71 ff.; Behr, *Aelius Aristides,* p. 80; *Studies on the Biography* § 1.

NOTES TO XXXVIII

1. This speech was delivered *c.* August 147 A.D. at the temple of Asclepius in Pergamum, perhaps just after Aristides had produced a choral spectacle in honor of Asclepius (cf. § 23 with L 43-47). Since the sons of Asclepius had no part in the Pergamene cult and Aristides otherwise shows no interest in them, the speech may have been intended to honor the hereditary priest of the temple, T. Flavius Asclepiades (cf. §§ 14-18 and *Die Inschriften des Asklepieions* (1969) no. 47); cf. also Behr, *Aelius Aristides,* pp. 59, 153. The speech has been translated by E. and L. Edelstein, *Asclepius* (1945) I, Testimony 282.
It is divided into the following sections:
A. § 1-4 Proem
B. § 5-7 Birth and education
C. § 8-13 Deeds in lifetime
D. § 14-18 Benefits of medical tradition
E. § 19-21 Deification and divine nature
F. § 22-24 Invocation.
2. Homer *Iliad* II 56.
3. Cf. Behr, *Aelius Aristides,* p. 192.
4. Cf. Behr, *Aelius Aristides,* p. 192 n. 67.
5. Cf. XXXIII 1.
5a. The construction would appear to be τὰ δοκοῦνθ' ὥστε εἰπεῖν (as in Thucydides VIII 79. 1) τὸν Ἀπόλλωνα .... καλοῦσιν (sc. εἰπεῖν).
6. Cf. XLII 1, XLVIII 4.

7. *Cf.* XLII 11, L 26.
8. For the same idea, *cf.* Plato *Symposium* 177 D.
9. The *Thesmothetai* were six of the nine members of the annual board of Archons at Athens. They were chosen by lot and their ancestry was examined through the two previous generations, father and his father and mother and her father (*cf.* Aristotle *Atheniensium Res publica* 55. 3), *i.e.* "four ancestors", not generations.
10. *Cf.* XLII 4. Aristides plays on the number four.
11. *Cf.* XXX 16.
12. The centaur who educated Achilles.
13. In Greek "Chiron" means "worse". On these puns, *cf.* XVII 22.
14. *Cf.* Homer *Iliad* II 729 ff.
15. Achilles.
16. Not in Homer.
17. As his former friend and companion, Philoctetes inherited Heracles' bow and arrows.
18. *Cf.* Sophocles *Philoctetes* 1333; Philostratus *Heroicus* V 1.
19. Pergamum.
20. *Cf.* XXXIII 27.
21. Podalirius. Traditionally Machaon is thought to have died in the Trojan war (*cf.* E. and L. Edelstein *Asclepius* II, p. 14 n. 48).
22. Corsica. Podalirius has some connection with Apulia in Italy, *cf.* Strabo VI 284. But perhaps there has been some confusion with Syrna in Caria, of which Podalirius was the traditional founder, *cf.* Stephanus Byzantinus *s.v.* Σύρνα.
23. *Cf.* I 36, 199.
24. The future.
25. *Cf.* XXVIII 78 (and Demosthenes XVIII 61) for the phrase. Hippocrates was traditionally regarded as the 17th in direct descent from the sons of Asclepius, *cf.* Tzetzes *Chiliades* VII 944 ff. (= E. and L. Edelstein *Asclepius* I, Testimony no. 213). However, Apollodorus placed him in the nineteenth generation, *cf.* F. Jacoby, *Apollodors Chronik* (1902), frg. 48.
26. § 15.
27. *i.e.* faction.
28. Homer *Odyssey* IV 564.
29. Hygieia means "health". On these sisters, *cf.* E. and L. Edelstein *Asclepius* I, Testimony nos. 278 ff.
30. Epione is derived from ἤπιος = "gentle".
31. Probably an allusion to Aristides' own choral productions, *cf.* note 1.
32. An office of this name in the cult of Asclepius is known at Euboea, *cf.* IG XII, 9, no. 194 (= E. and L. Edelstein *Asclepius* I, Testimony no. 787).
33. Castor and Pollux, who were also beneficent, particularly at sea. They were one generation earlier than the sons of Asclepius.
34. On the full significance of the expression for Aristides, *cf.* Behr, *Aelius Aristides,* p. 163.

NOTES TO XXXIX

1. This speech, if it was inspired by the dream reported in XLVII 42 (it is one of the μαντευτοί, for which see note 1 to XXXVII), would seem to have been delivered in Pergamum in January, 167 A.D., near the time of oration XXIII. Aristides often used this well in his therapy (*cf.* XLVIII 71, 74-75). Three wells have in fact been discovered in the courtyard of the temple complex, but, I believe, the one of Roman date, to the north of the temple of Asclepius, is meant; *cf.* Behr,

Aelius Aristides, pp. 29, 105, 156. The speech has also been translated by E. and L. Edelstein, *Asclepius* I (1945), Testimony no. 804.
It is divided into the following sections:
A. § 1-3 Proem. Difficulty of subject
B. § 4-6 Location
C. § 7-11 Quality of water
D. § 12-17 Benefits
E. § 18 Peroration. Superiority to other famous waters.
 2. *Cf.* XXXI 8 and Plato *Symposium* 214 B.
 3. Asclepius.
 4. *Cf.* XLVII 35; Behr, *Aelius Aristides,* p. 156; *Inschriften des Asklepieions,* p. 134.
 5. *i.e.* as a thematic beginning.
 6. Epidaurus was the parent temple from which Archias founded the temple at Pergamum *c.* 350 B.C.; *cf.* Pausanias II 26. 8-9; L. and E. Edelstein, *Asclepius* II, p. 249.
 7. *Cf.* XXX 15. Probably connected with the θεραπευταί, who formed an association at the temple, for which *cf.* XLVII 23, XLVIII 47, L 16, 50, and Behr, *Studies on the Biography* § 6.
 8. *Iliad* II 754; *cf.* Arrian *Periplus* 8. 2.
 9. The Titaresius; *cf.* Homer *Iliad* II 755.
 10. Of the Danae.
 11. *Iliad* XVIII 470 ff.
 12. *Cf.* especially XXXVI 120. For the idea of contrariety, on which the supplement, "again is it subject....as other waters, but", is formed, *cf.* I 330, XXX 9, XXXVI 6, XLIV 5.
 13. *Cf.* Homer *Iliad* II 469 ff.
 14. The word may also be translated "slaves".
 15. *Olympian* VII 7. But Pindar used the word χυτόν (= "flowing") and αὐτόχυτον (= "originating in itself") is found in the scholium on this passage. Remarks from this same scholium seem to be alluded to in § 7, "you would not want wine besides".
 16. *Cf.* Behr, *Aelius Aristides,* p. 32.
 17. *Cf.* Herodotus I 188.
 18. *Cf.* XXXVI 54; Herodotus II 28. All ancient authors refer to these springs as being two in number. Hence the supplement, "the Nile... by a separate".
 19. *Cf.* § 5. Here apparently a proverb.

NOTES TO XL

 1. Prompted by a dream (*cf.* § 22), Aristides delivered this praise of Heracles in Cyzicus in August 166 A.D., at about the same time as oration XXVII. Heracles is honored as in the traditional Stoic eulogies as the benefactor of mankind. Aside from the present speech Aristides seems not to have had any interest in this god. This fact and the rather rare concept of Heracles as a healer (§§ 12-13) induce me to think that the two great plagues just passed momentarily turned a desperate Aristides to the worship of Heracles; *cf.* Behr, *Aelius Aristides,* pp. 102, 155; also F. W. Lenz, *Der Herakleshymnos* in *Aristeidesstudien,* pp. 223-233.
The speech is divided into the following sections:
A. § 1 Proem
B. § 2-3 Birth
C. § 4-9 Benefits in lifetime
D. § 10-15 Divinity

E. § 16-17 Descendants
F. § 18-21 His power and relations with other gods
G. § 22 Aristides' dream.
   2. The exclamation "O Heracles"! *cf.* § 14.
   3. Zeus and Alcmene.
   4. The Nemean lion (labor 1), the Lernaean hydra (labor 2), the Cerynitian stag (labor 3), the Erymanthian boar (labor 4), the Stymphalian birds (labor 6), the Cretan bull (labor 7).
   5. *E.g.* Diomedes of Thrace, Busiris of Egypt, and Lycus of Thebes.
   6. *Cf.* XXXVII 9.
   7. The birds at Stymphalus (the 6th labor), as an interpolation notes.
   8. *Cf.* Solon frg. 24. 15 ff. Diehl.
   9. For the expression, *cf.* Plato *Symposium* 197 B.
   10. *Cf.* Herodotus II 43.
   11. Apparently Melkarth; *cf.* also O. Kern, *Die Religion der Griechen* (1938) vol. 3, p. 45.
   12. Apollo; *cf.* § 22; Arrian *Anabasis* IV 11. 7.
   13. He burned himself alive on Mt. Oeta. Aristides' distaste for these myths causes him to omit the specific circumstance; *cf.* Behr, *Aelius Aristides.* p. 155.
   14. In the Eleusinian Mysteries; *cf.* I 35, 50 ff.; also Libanius XIV 70 (Foerster).
   15. Or "more divine".
   16. But *cf.* Philochorus, cited in Plutarch *Theseus* 35, who excepts four Theseia. On this matter, *cf.* Lenz, *Herakleshymnos (Aristeidesstudien),* p. 227.
   17. Cadiz; *cf.* Diodorus V 20.
   18. There was a Laconian divinity called the Messanian Heracles; *cf.* Pausanias IV 32. 1. On Heracles as a healer, cf. Joannes Lydus *De Mensibus* IV 67 and Philostratus *Vita Apollonii* VIII 7. 9; also Behr, *Aelius Aristides,* p. 102 n. 22 B; Preller-Robert, *Griech. Myth.* (1921) II⁴ p. 645 n. 4.
   19. A municipal office building. That of Cyzicus is meant, I think; *cf.* Behr, *Aelius Aristides,* p. 102 n. 22 A. But Keil *ad loc.* in his edition and Lenz, *Herakleshymnos (Aristeidesstudien),* p. 229 place it (and the speech) in Smyrna.
   20. *Cf.* Nauck *Tragicorum Graecorum Fragmenta*² Adespct. 38 (p. 846).
   21. *Cf.* Libanius XVIII 186 (Foerster).
   22. *Philoctetes* 174.
   23. "He of fair victory".
   24. "Averter of evil". On these epithets, *cf.* Preller-Robert, *Griech, Myth.* (1921) II⁴, pp. 644 ff.
   25. For this trip to Cos in 141 A.D., *cf.* XXXIII 27; Behr, *Aelius Aristides,* p. 14.
   26. A good example of Aristides' exaltation of the divinity whom he happens to be praising; for a different view of the Heraclidae, *cf.* XXXVIII 17.
   27. *E.g.* Syracuse was founded by the Heraclid Archias from Corinth; *cf.* Thucydides VI 3.
   28. In the word διῴκησαν there is perhaps, as Keil suggests, an allusion to Homer *Iliad* II 655.
   29. *Cf.* Thucydides IV 36. 3.
   30. All Spartan kings.
   31. *Cf.* Plutarch *Lycurgus* 30.
   32. On these, *cf.* Behr, *Aelius Aristides,* p. 164 n. 7.
   33. Lenz, *Herakleshymnos (Aristeidesstudien),* p. 231 doubts whether paintings or statues are meant. But the ἀγάλματα in § 19 are definitely statues.
   34. Allegorically for love and drink.
   35. Which in Greek is "hebê", the name of Heracles' wife.

36. *Cf.* Preller-Robert, *Griech. Myth.* (1921) II⁴, p. 643 n. 5 and for the further pairings in § 20, p. 646 n. 8.

36a. Aristides would seem to have identified Heracles with the mysterious bearded figure discussed by M. J. Vermaseren, *Cybele and Attis* (1977), p. 79 (*cf.* p. 144).

37. *Cf.* L 42 from 146 A.D.; also Behr, *Aelius Aristides,* pp. 42 n. 5, 155.

38. Presumably that of the Dindymene Mater in Cyzicus, *cf.* F.W. Hasluck, *Cyzicus,* pp. 214-221. But Keil (on p. 328 vs. 5 of his edition) and Lenz, *Herakleshymnos (Aristeidesstudien),* p. 232, who place the speech in Smyrna (see note 19 above), assume that the Smyrnaean Metroon is meant, for which *cf.* note 22 to oration XVII.

39. A reference to the plague. For the phrasing, *cf.* XLVIII 42 from the same time; also Behr, *Aelius Aristides,* p. 102.

40. For Apollo, a major god of Cyzicus, *cf.* XXVII 5, XXXI 15; also Behr, *Aelius Aristides,* p. 102 n. 22 A.

41. For these subscriptions, *cf.* note 23 to oration XVIII.

NOTES TO XLI

1. This prose-hymn, inspired by a dream from Asclepius (*cf.* § 1 and L 25), was delivered in the early part of Aristides' incubation at the temple of Asclepius at Pergamum, 145-147 A.D. It is the first preserved example of Asclepius' effort to reembark Aristides on his oratorical career. The emotional strain of this period of Aristides' life seems to have aroused Aristides' interest in Dionysus, who otherwise was neglected. Themes in the speech closely copy those which Plato used in his praise of Eros in *The Symposium.* Indeed, the concluding two paragraphs (§§ 12-13) could refer to either divinity, a point which has considerable bearing on Aristides' emotional state at this time; *cf.* Behr, *Aelius Aristides,* pp. 52-53, 154-155; *Studies on the Biography* § 4; F.W. Lenz, *Der Dionysoshymnos,* Rivista di Cultura Classica e Medioevale (1961), pp. 153-166 = *Aristeidesstudien* (1964), pp. 211-222.

The speech is divided into the following sections:
A. § 1-2 Proem
B. § 3 Birth
C. § 4-5 Double nature
D. § 6-11 Power and relations with other gods
E. § 12-13 Dionysus and Eros (Love).

2. *Cf.* Plato *Symposium* 197 E.

3. *Cf.* Plato *Laws* 665 A ff.

4. On the concept of "the initiate into rhetoric", *cf.* Behr, *Aelius Aristides,* pp. 45 n. 18, 34 n. 57, 107 n. 42; *Studies on the Biography* § 4.

5. So too ἀρρενόθηλυς in Porphyrius in Eusebius *Praepar. Ev.* 109 D. I think that the redundancy here, which bothered Keil, is intentional and is not caused by an interpolation.

6. A Zeus Bacchus was worshipped at Pergamum, *cf.* IGRR IV 360; also Preller-Robert, *Griech, Myth.* I, p. 664 n. 2.

7. *Cf.* the Orphic hymn concerning Zeus in Pseudo-Aristotle *De Mundo* 401 B 2; also Plato *Symposium* 189 D ff.

8. A bearded manifestation of this god; *cf.* Macrobius *Saturnalia* I 18. 9.

9. Frg. 114 Turyn = 99 Schroeder.

10. *Cf.* Herodotus II 145. 1.

11. As Poseidon made Pegasus winged.

12. Alcman frg. 56 Page *Poetae Melici Graeci* = frg. 34 Bergk.

13. *Cf.* XL 7; Plato *Timaeus* 41 AB.

14. *Cf.* Plato *Laws* 666 B and 671 E.

15. For the idea, *cf.* Aristotle *Poetics* 1457 B 20.
16. § 8.
17. *Cf.* Plato *Symposium* 177 E.
18. *Cf.* Euripides *Bacchae* 302 ff.; Plato *Symposium* 196 D.
19. *Cf.* Plato *Protagoras* 321 CD, *Critias* 109 C, *Politicus* 274 D, *Symposium* 197 B.
20. *Cf.* note 11 to XXII 4.
21. *Cf.* Pindar *Isthmian* VII 3.
22. *Cf.* III 319; VI 52; XXII 6.
23. A ventriloquist; *cf.* Aristophanes *Wasps* 1019 ff.
24. *Cf.* XXVI 3; Euripides frg. 663 N. (Plato *Symposium* 196 E).
25. *Cf.* Plato *Laws* 653 E ff.
26. *Cf.* Euripides frg. 136 N.; Plato *Symposium* 197 E.
27. *Cf.* I 73; Plato *Symposium* 178 C, 196 A.
28. *Cf.* Euripides *Bacchae* 424 ff.
29. *Cf.* II 465.

NOTES TO XLII

1. This speech was delivered in the Temple of Zeus Asclepius at Pergamum, perhaps on January 6, 177 A.D., at the celebration of the Night Festival, when Aristides, at Asclepius' urging, was passing on his way from Smyrna to his Laneion estate. The speech is almost a summary of Asclepius' benefactions over the years in health and oratory, with emphasis on the latter. Orations XLII-XLVI seem to me to be joined by a tenuous connection in that they all involve "tempests" whether metaphorical (*cf.* §§ 1, 7) or actual, and as such may have belonged to a "tomus" quite separate from that of orations XXXVII-XLI and LIII. Menander (see note 1 to or. XXXVII) knows of an oration to Asclepius included in the Μαντευτοί. The speech has also been translated by E. and L. Edelstein, *Asclepius*, vol. I (1945), Testimony no. 317; *cf.* Behr, *Aelius Aristides*, pp. 32 n. 47, 111-112, and 157-159; *Studies on the Biography* § 9.

It is divided into the following sections:
A. § 1-3 Proem. Expression of gratitude through oratory
B. § 4-5 Asclepius' power and benefits
C. § 6-8 Medical aid
D. § 9-12 Oratorical aid
E. § 13-14 Fame. Friendship with Emperors
F. § 15 Peroration.

2. *Cf.* Behr, *Aelius Aristides*, p. 163.
3. *Cf.* Behr, *Aelius Aristides*, p. 34; *Studies on the Biography* § 4.
4. *Cf. The Aristides Prolegomena* 6 = vol. 3, p. 738, 10 ff. Ddf. and the scholium p. 432, 31 ff. Ddf.; also Lenz, *The Aristeides Prolegomena* (1959), pp. 57-58.
5. *Works and Days* 336, "to sacrifice according to one's means".
6. Recently built by L. Cuspius Pactumeius Rufinus, cos. 142 A.D.; *cf.* Behr, *Aelius Aristides*, pp. 27-28, 152.
7. Not in those extant. Apparently this point was discussed in the lost portion of the sixth *Sacred Tale*.
8. Anonymous frg. 39 N.; *cf.* also Aristides XXX 28 and Iamblichus *De Mysteriis* 7. 2.
9. Second generation: *cf.* XXXVIII 6. Combined names: Zeus Asclepius, *cf.* note 6 and Behr, *Aelius Aristides*, pp. 157 f. for the theology.
10. *Phaedrus* 246 D.
11. *Cf.* XXX 23; XLIII 21.
12. Aristophanes *Birds* 1334.

13. *Cf.* XXXVII 11.
14. *Cf.* XXIII 16.
15. *Cf.* XLVIII 18.
16. Both Canter and Edelstein understand this as an expression of caution: "tutissime" and "safe to say".
17. *Cf.* XLVII 3.
18. If the reading of the manuscripts is sound, *cf.* Behr, *Aelius Aristides*, p. 190 n. 64 for this type of dream. Keil, however, emended to ἰάμασι = "cures".
19. For these cures, *cf.* Behr, *Aelius Aristides*, pp. 36-39.
20. The word can also mean "performing the act of incubation".
21. A frequent site of public lectures.
22. On this concept, *cf.* Behr, *Aelius Aristides*, p. 163 n. 5.
23. The passage is corrupt, but this seems to me to be the sense; *cf.* § 14.
24. *Cf.* Philostratus *Heroicus*, p. 146, 24 ff. Kayser.
25. *Cf.* L 26.
26. *Cf.* III 111 and Plato *Protagoras* 326 D.
27. *Cf.* § 5 and II 412.
28. Frg. 110 Turyn = 95 Schroeder; *cf.* Aristides III 191.
29. Marcus Aurelius and his son Commodus, who visited Smyrna in 176 A.D. and heard Aristides lecture; *cf.* XIX 1; Philostratus *Vitae Sophistarum* 582-583 Olearius; Behr, *Aelius Aristides*, p. 111.
30. The daughters of Marcus Aurelius. The Empress Faustina had died shortly before.
31. *Cf.* XX 11.
32. *Cf.* Homer *Odyssey* VII-XII.
33. *i.e.* the circumstance of the speech.

NOTES TO XLIII

1. In early February 149 A.D. in an unsuccessful attempt to sail from Clazomenae to Phocaea (see XLVIII 12), Aristides nearly suffered shipwreck in a storm. Back at Smyrna, in payment of a vow made then, this oration was delivered. The picture of Zeus as a supreme deity who delegates his authority to the rest of the Hellenic pantheon owes much to Plato, the Stoics, and the Orphics; *cf.* Behr, *Aelius Aristides*, pp. 72-73 and 151-152. For a translation and commentary, *cf.* J. Amann, *Die Zeusrede des Aelios Aristeides*, Tübinger Beiträge zur Altertumswissenschaft, Heft 12, 1931.
The speech is divided into the following sections:
A. § 1-6 Proem. The difficulty of fulfilling the vow
B. § 7-13 The creation of the Universe
C. § 14-22 Creation and care of living things, gods and men
D. § 23-30 Zeus is the cause of all things, natural and divine
E. § 31 Peroration.
2. *Cf.* Lucian *Quomodo Historia Conscribenda Sit* 51.
3. Zeus.
4. For the mention of Olympus, Pieria, and Helicon, *cf.* Hesiod *Theogony* 37, 53, 1 ff. respectively; for the form, *cf.* Plato *Phaedrus* 237 A.
5. *Cf.* Homer *Iliad* II 485.
6. In contrast to the assertion *e.g.* of Aratus *Phaenomena* 33 ff.; *cf.* below § 26.
7. On the word αὐτοπάτωρ (Aristides uses the compound αὐτοκέλευστος at III 556), *cf.* Behr, *Aelius Aristides*, p. 73 *contra* O. Weinreich, *Typisches und Individuelles in der Religiosität des Aelios Aristeides*, Neue Jahrbücher für das klassische Altertum,

Geschichte, und deutsche Literatur (1914), Bd. 33, p. 602 and Amann, *op. cit.* (see note 1), p. 34. For the concept of the whole paragraph, *cf.* Aeschylus *Suppliants* 592, Cleanthes in StVF I 537, Orphic Hymn frg. 298 Kern (= frg. 39 Gesner) and frg. 21 Kern (= frg. 6 Gesner).

8. As against those who said that time existed from the beginning, *cf. e.g.* Macrobius *Commentarii in Somnium Scipionis* II 10. 8 and Augustine *De Civitate Dei* XI 4.

9. *Cf.* § 30.

10. The passage is hopelessly corrupt and its emendation and supplement, "with the very matter...solidified", is merely a suggestion. For "the roots of the world", *cf.* Hesiod *Works and Days* 19, *Theogony* 728; Orphic Hymn frg. 168 vs. 29 Kern (= frg. 6 vs. 39 Gesner); Aristotle *Meteorologica* B 1 353 a 35 f.

11. *Cf.* XXXVI 97 f.

12. *i.e.* mountains and plains.

13. *Cf.* Diogenes Laertius VII 137.

14. *Cf.* I 11 and XLIV 14.

15. *Cf.* A.D. Nock, *Sallustius,* pp. LXXXVII f. n. 202 on this concept.

16. For the emendation and supplement, "the ends....power", and general idea, *cf.* II 166 and XLV 22.

17. *Cf. Iliad* VIII 19 and Aristides XXVIII 45.

18. *Cf.* Plato *Symposium* 195 B (and 191 D).

19. Homer *Iliad* IV 299.

20. *Cf.* Plato *Protagoras* 322 B.

21. But *cf.* XXXVII 13.

22. *Cf.* § 16 (the first example) and Plato *Protagoras* 322 A.

23. *Cf.* Plato *Symposium* 196 C.

24. *Cf.* Plato *Protagoras* 322 C.

25. *Cf.* XXX 23; XLII 5.

26. *Iliad* VIII 1 ff.

27. The Greek preposition διά (= "because of" or "through") is equated with the accusative form of "Zeus", Δία. On this theme, *cf.* also Plato *Cratylus* 396 A; Diogenes Laertius VII 147; Cornutus c. 2.

28. The Greek forms Ζεύς and ζωή (= "life") are equated.

29. *Cf.* Plato *Timaeus* 40 C.

30. Homeric Hymn III (to Apollo) 132.

31. If the supplement, "assisting", is sound, there may be an allusion to the Pergamene temple of Zeus Asclepius, *cf.* XLII 4. Others prefer to emend the version of Laurentianus LIX, 15: "whom he cures are dearer to Zeus", which I regard as more of a scholium or at best a very clumsy attempt to fill an obvious lacuna.

32. *Cf.* Aratus *Phaenomena* 2; Aristides XLV 30.

33. *Cf.* § 30; II 166; Plutarch *Moralia* 1056 C.

34. Homer *Odyssey* IV 581; *cf.* Aristides XXXVI 104.

35. The phrase can be understood in two ways: either metaphorically as the chief Roman officer in Egypt who was the prefect; or as a deputy of Zeus himself, *cf.* § 18; XL 2.

36. *Cf.* XXXVI 13, 123; Euripides *Helen* 2.

37. *Cf.* § 27; XLV 22 (of Sarapis).

38. *Cf.* XXVI 30.

39. *i.e.* than other gods.

40. Frg. 21 Turyn = 145 Schroeder.

41. *Cf.* Homer *Iliad* IX 97; Theocritus XVII 1.

NOTES TO XLIV

1. This speech was delivered, apparently on Delos (*cf.* § 4), shortly after April 155 A.D., in the course of Aristides' journey to Greece and Rome. Mindful of the terrible storm, which he had suffered in 144 A.D. (*cf.* XLVIII 68), Aristides thought it wise to propitiate the divinity of the sea on this occasion. In his effort to forestall all sources of danger, momentarily he may have been prepared to see in the Aegean an operative force with a will of its own; *cf.* Behr, *Aelius Aristides,* pp. 87, 156.

The speech is divided into the following sections:
A. § 1-2 Proem. Paying back a debt
B. § 3-6 Geography. Climate
C. § 7-10 Magnitude and habitations
D. § 11-17 The islands: their security, charm, and utility
E. § 18 Peroration. Crossing for the celebrations.

2. *Iliad* XI 298.
3. *Iliad* XXIII 316.
4. *Iliad* XVI 391.
5. *Cf.* Euripides *Troades* 1.
6. *Cf.* Aristophanes *Clouds* 284; Bacchylides XVII 76 Snell.
7. For surviving the storm in the earlier crossing in 144 A.D., *cf.* XLVIII 68 and Behr, *Aelius Aristides,* p. 87.
8. As is done, *e.g.* in orations I, XVII, XXIII, and XXVII.
9. *Cf.* XXXIX 18.
10. *Cf.* I 19, XXIII 9; Herodotus I 142; Hippocrates *De Aere* 12. 16; Galen XVI, p. 393 K; Plato *Timaeus* 24 C.
11. *Cf.* *Odyssey* III 270, XII 351.
12. Euripides *Troades* 2-3.
13. *Cf.* I 10.
14. *Cf.* XXVII 4 and for the contrast of fearsome/gentle, XLV 26.
15. The Echinades, Cercyra, and Cos (*cf.* XXXVIII 12), as Callimachus IV 155 ff. reports.
16. *Cf.* I 11.
17. *Cf.* XXXII 25.
18. *Odyssey* XIX 113 ff.
19. The reference is obscure to me. Perhaps Aristides refers to the legend that after Lycurgus expelled Dionysus from Edonia, the god took refuge in the sea with Thetis (*cf.* Apollodorus *Bibliotheca* III v 1). Pausanias III 24. 3 knows a unique legend from Brasiai in Laconia that after Semele gave birth to Dionysus, his grandfather Cadmus locked him (and her) in a chest and threw him into the sea. But this version does not square with Aristides' standard account of the god's birth in XLI.
20. Pleasing to the Dioscuri because they too were concerned with the protection of sailors from storms; to the Nymphs because of the streams found on the islands in the Aegean.
21. *Cf.* Homer *Iliad* XVI 640, XXIII 169; Aristophanes *Plutus* 650.
22. *i.e.* the prose-hymn.

NOTES TO XLV

1. This speech, the earliest preserved work of Aristides, was delivered in Smyrna in 142 A.D., perhaps on April 25 at the festival of Zeus Sarapis. The speech antedates Aristides' use of the prose-hymn style, whose need was keenly felt (*cf.* §§

1-13; and see Menander Περὶ 'Ἐπιδεικτικῶν, vol. III, p. 343 (also p. 338) Sp.). Its primary purpose was the fulfillment of a vow which Aristides made during a storm on his return from Egypt (cf. §§ 13, 33). Although § 34 certainly contains an allusive plea for the complete restoration of Aristides' health, which was somewhat undermined during the trip to Egypt, in this speech Sarapis' function as a healing god does not have anything like the prominence which it acquired in Aristides' mind during the years after 144 A.D. Here he is chiefly venerated in his manifestation as Helius Sarapis, the sun god (cf. § 18 note 41). On the history of Aristides' worship of Sarapis, which ebbed and flowed in rivalry with that of Asclepius, cf. Behr, *Aelius Aristides,* pp. 21-22, 26, 73, 149; Hommages à Vermaseren (1978), pp. 13-24. The whole speech has been translated into German with a commentary by A. Höfler, *Der Sarapishymnus des Ailios Aristeides,* Tübinger Beiträge zur Altertumswissenschaft, Heft 27 (1935); §§ 1-13 in large part by A. Boulanger, *Aelius Aristide* (1923, reprinted 1968), pp. 304-307.

The speech is divided into the following sections:
A. § 1-14 Proem. Poetry versus prose. Aristides' vow
B. § 15-16 General discussion of Sarapis' nature
C. § 17-32 He controls all aspects of our lives. His pervasive, unlimited, terrifying and beneficent power
D. § 33-34 Peroration. The storm.

2. On the theme of §§ 1-13, cf. Isocrates IX 9-11; Plato *Laws* 669 D; Antiphanes frg. 191 *Comicorum Atticorum Fragmenta* Kock; Cleanthes I 486 *Stoicorum Veterum Fragmenta.* Pliny the Younger *Epistle* VII 9. 14 took the opposite view.

3. The *deus ex machina,* who often appeared at the end of a Greek tragedy, was a convenient means of solving the difficulties of the plot.

4. Homer *Odyssey* II 270 ff.
5. Homer *Odyssey* III 51 ff.
6. Homer *Odyssey* XIX 34.
7. *Iliad* VI 138.
8. Poet unknown; possibly Pindar.
9. *E.g.* Homer *Iliad* I 419.
10. Poet unknown; possibly Pindar.
11. Pindar *Olympian* III 11 ff.
12. Pindar *Olympian* VI 50.
13. Pindar *Isthmian* III 70.
14. Poets unknown; possibly Pindar in both cases. For the latter, cf. Pindar *Olympian* I 116.
15. Three rhetorical procedures are alluded to: invention, disposition, and elocution.
16. Homer *Odyssey* III 48.
17. On this, cf. E. Norden, *Antike Kunstprosa* (5th ed.), p. 33 n. 3; A. Boulanger, *Aelius Aristide,* p. 306 n. 1.
18. *Contra* Strabo I 2. 6; cf. Plutarch *De Pythiae Oraculis* 24 (406 B ff.); Isidore *Etymologiae* I xxxviii 2.
19. For the contrary sentiment, cf. II 1-12; Libanius LXIV 5 Foerster.
20. Or "meter".
21. On the "measures" or "meters" of logic, cf. Zeno I 48, 49 *Stoicorum Veterum Fragmenta.*
22. *i.e.* its "measure" or correct use.
23. § 10, *i.e.* the measure of the whole speech; cf. the beginning of § 12.
24. Cf. the end of § 12.
25. Cf. the end of § 9.
26. §§ 3-4.

27. Poet unknown; perhaps Pindar.
28. Pindar *Isthmian* VIII 62 with the word order reversed.
29. Poet unknown; perhaps Pindar. The reading of the mss., μυριοφόρον "250 tons", though accepted by Aristides' other editors and B. Snell frg. 355 in the 1964 Teubner edition of Pindar, is common in prose (Aristides used it himself in II 371); otherwise *cf.* C. Torr, *Ancient Ships*, p. 25 n. 67.
30. Poet unknown; perhaps Pindar. The restoration of the text is uncertain and the word νεφελόγρυπας is not found elsewhere, although νεφελοκένταυροι appears in Lucian *Vera Historia* I 16.
31. *Cf.* III 97 and note 14 to XXXIII 13.
32. From the storm at sea; see note 1.
33. *Cf.* XLIII 30 (of Zeus).
34. The first request was to be saved from the storm; the second refers to the composition of §§ 15 ff.
35. *Iliad* II 489 ff.; *cf.* Aristides XLVII 1; Apuleius *Metamorphoses* XI 25.
36. *Cf.* § 32.
37. *Cf.* Plato *Timaeus* 29 B, 48 B.
38. As opposed to mere existence; *cf.* Plato *Protagoras* 322 AB.
39. § 17.
40. *Cf.* Ariphron frg. 813 *Poetae Melici Graeci* Page.
41. In his manifestation as the sun, Ἥλιος Σάραπις; *cf.* §§ 25, 29, 33, XXXVI 38, and perhaps XXIV 42; Plutarch *De Iside et Osiride* 52 (372 D); Macrobius *Saturnalia* I 20. 13-18.
42. As being blind and not seeing the sun.
43. In his manifestation as Pluto; *cf.* Plutarch *De Iside et Osiride* 27 (316 E); Eusebius *Praeparatio Evangelica* IV 23.
44. An allusion to the famous *scolion* or "drinking song", frg. 890 (and 651) *Poetae Melici Graeci* Page.
45. *Cf.* Plato *Alcibiades* I 104 A.
46. *Cf.* XLIII 11.
47. *Cf.* XLIII 23 ff. (of Zeus).
48. Alexandria; *cf.* XXVI 26.
49. On this formula, *cf.* Behr, *Aelius Aristides*, p. 158; Julian, Or. IV 136 A.
50. *Cf.* XLIII 30 (of Zeus).
51. *Cf.* II 166; XLIII 15 (both of Zeus).
52. *Iliad* XV 187 ff.
53. *Iliad* XV 193.
54. *Cf.* Pindar *Pythian* VIII 3.
55. In his manifestation as Osiris, god of the dead.
56. In his manifestation as ψυχοπομπός, "guide of the dead".
57. *Cf.* XXX 10; Pindar *Olympian* VI 99, VII 4.
58. *i.e.* as both the sun (*cf.* §§ 18, 29, 33) and the god of the dead.
59. *Cf.* XLIV 10 (of the Aegean sea).
60. *Iliad* IX 497.
61. For the phrasing, *cf.* Plato *Timaeus* 17 A. The *cena Serapica* (*cf.* Tertullian *Apologeticus* 39. 14) is meant; *cf.* IG XI 1299 = J.U. Powell *Collectanea Alexandrina* p. 70, vs. 36.
62. *Cf.* XLIV 18.
63. *Odyssey* III 62.
64. *Cf.* XXXIV 60.
65. *i.e.* in answer to the dance, follows a religious banquet, the *cena Serapica*, *cf.* note 61.
66. For the tithes, *cf. e.g.* IG XI 1248 ἀπαρχὴν ἀπὸ τῆς ἐργασίας δεκάτην. Isis

(Sarapis' consort) was a particular patroness of sea traders. Her festival of the πλοιαφέσια ("launching of the ships") yearly inaugurated the opening of the sea lanes of the Mediterranean on March 5; cf. Joannes Lydus De Mensibus IV 45.; Apuleius Metamorphoses XI 17.

67. Homer Odyssey X 22.
68. Cf. XXXVI 10.
69. In his manifestation as the sun; cf. §§ 18, 25, 33.
70. Astrologers; cf. Strabo XVII 806, 816.
71. Cf. Aratus Phaenomena 2; Aristides XLIII 26.
72. A proverb; cf. I 103; Callimachus Epigram XXXI 5; Corpus Paroemiographorum Graecorum I 345.
73. § 16.
74. An apparent reference both to the κάτοχοι of the temple, lay persons who, in their devotion to the god, lived permanently within the temple precinct; and to the sacred animals worshipped by the Egyptians, especially the Apis bull.
75. Cf. XXXVI 123.
76. Egypt was divided into forty-two nomes and each had a temple of Osiris.
77. Smyrna. Again Sarapis is depicted as the sun (on the image, cf. XVIII 7) as in §§ 18, 25, 29.
78. Apparently on April 25; cf. (§§ 20, 27), XLIX 48; Behr, Aelius Aristides, pp. 21, 73.
79. A prayer, it would seem, for the complete restoration of his health, which was somewhat impaired during the preceding trip to Egypt; cf. XXXVI 49, 91. Cf. Macrobius Saturnalia I 20. 13 ff. on Sarapis' powers over past, present, and future.

NOTES TO XLVI

1. This oration was delivered in summer 156 A.D., at Corinth, for the Isthmian festival, after Aristides had returned to Greece from his trip to Rome. As Aristides admitted, he had no belief in Poseidon, and the work is purely an elaborate, formal production, much of it a panegyric of Corinth. However, Aristides was attracted to the mystery cult of Leucothea and Palaemon on the Isthmus, and he has devoted the final portion of this speech to them; cf. Behr, Aelius Aristides, pp. 90, 154.

The speech is divided into the following sections:
A. § 1-4 Proem. Circumstances of the address
B. § 5-6 The element of water
C. § 7-15 Poseidon's mythology and generosity
D. § 16-19 Places consecrated to him
E. § 20-31 Corinth, geography, benefits, charm, history, festival
F. § 32-41 Leucothea and Palaemon
G. § 42 Peroration.

2. In 153 A.D.; cf. Behr, Aelius Aristides, p. 86.
3. For the phrase, cf. XXXVII 6.
4. For this modesty, cf. XLII 13.
5. i.e. sacrifice.
6. i.e. the speech.
7. A proverb; cf. XLVII 2; Plato Theaetetus 173 D; Libanius XI 124 Foerster; Behr, Aelius Aristides, p. 163.
8. Cf. XXIII 17 (of Asclepius).
9. sc. εἴρηκασιν. Cf. I 388. In particular Thales is meant, cf. e.g. Aristotle De Caelo 294 a 28, Metaphysics 983 b 6.
10. Homer Iliad XIV 201; cf. Plato Cratylus 402 B.

11. *Cf.* Homer *Iliad* XV 37-38.
12. *Iliad* VII 99.
13. Hades; *cf.* Homer *Iliad* XV 187.
14. For the phrase, *cf.* XXXVI 85; R. Helm, *Lucian und Menipp* (1906), p. 280 n. 2.
15. *Cf.* Plato *Critias* 113 E, 114 E-115 B.
16. In Greek the word also means "oars".
17. Zeus.
18. Corinth.
19. His winged steed Pegasus, stung by a gadfly sent by Zeus, threw him and he was crippled by the fall.
20. In giving birth to Athena; *cf.* XXXVII 3.
21. *Cf.* Homer *Iliad* XV 166.
22. §§ 35 ff.
23. The plural is used by Apollonius Rhodius *Argonautica* I 3.
24. *Cf.* Homer *Odyssey* XII 55 ff.; Apollonius Rhodius *Argonautica* I 3 ff. This whole section is in a very confused state because of a number of interpolations.
25. In Asia.
26. *Cf.* Pliny *Naturalis Historia* V 149.
27. Leucas, as the interpolator remarks.
28. Drepane, which also means "sickle".
29. *i.e.* castration, as the interpolator remarks.
30. The Myrtoan sea.
31. Either in the lost cyclic poem, *The Nostoi,* or *Odyssey* III 103 ff. coupled with 177.
32. *Cf.* Euripides *Cyclops* 292; in 295 Geraestus (see just above) is also mentioned.
33. *Iliad* XIII 21 confused with VIII 203 and *Odyssey* I 22.
34. *Iliad* XIII 27-31.
35. *Iliad* XIII 6.
36. *Cf.* XXXVII 15 (of Athena).
37. *Iliad* VIII 48; *Odyssey* VIII 363.
38. *Cf.* § 27.
39. *Odyssey* IV 74; *cf.* Aristides XXVI 89.
40. *i.e.* each land, the Peloponnesus and the mainland of Greece, and each sea, the Aegean and the Gulf of Corinth-Ionian-Adriatic seas.
41. *Cf.* Homer *Iliad* II 570; Aristides XXVII 7; Thucydides I 13. 6.
42. The Isthmia; *cf.* § 31.
43. *Proxenos* ("public host").
44. *Cf.* XXVI 61 (of Rome).
45. Paraphrasing Homer *Iliad* XIV 216-217.
46. A charmed girdle, an attribute of Aphrodite, *cf.* Homer *Iliad* XIV 214.
47. *Cf. Homeric Hymn* VI 10 ff.
48. *Cf.* XX 21; Pindar frg. 91 vs. 15 Turyn = 75 Schroeder.
49. Zeus: *cf.* Homer *Iliad* V 749 ff., VIII 393 ff. Poseidon: *cf.* Pindar *Olympian* XIII 5.
50. There might just be an allusion to the notorious vice of the city.
51. *Cf.* I 361; Pindar *Olympian* XIII 6.
52. As the seat of the proconsul of Achaea; *cf.* § 20.
53. *i.e.* there is something to be learned from the very buildings; for the phrase, *cf.* Cicero *De Finibus* V ii. 5 (of Athens).
54. A proverb concerning those who incessantly repeat something; *cf.* scholium on Pindar *Nemean* VII 105 (155), scholium on Aristophanes *Frogs* 439 (443).

Sisyphus founded Ephyra, which later became Corinth. Bellerophon was his grandson.

55. Either Phidon (*cf.* Aristotle *Politics* 1265 b 12) or Periander.

56. *Cf.* Thucydides I 13. 2.

57. *i.e.* Jason did not start from Thessaly, as is said, but from Corinth since he left his ship here at the conclusion of his expedition. Therefore the Argo was built at Corinth.

58. Bellerophon; *cf.* § 13.

59. *Cf.* § 23. The other festivals are the Olympia, Pythia (both quadrennial) and the Nemea which was also biennial. But perhaps the emperor Hadrian effected some change in the Nemean cycle, for Pausanias VI 16. 4 (*cf.* II 15. 3) speaks of "winter Nemean games", to which that emperor made a contribution. There may now have been a single quadrennial summer and a single quadrennial winter Nemean game two years later. Otherwise Aristides indulges in a clumsy exaggeration.

60. *Cf.* Apollonius Rhodius *Argonautica* III 1240 ff.

61. *Cf.* the imitation in XXXV 39; for the rare placement of τίς, *cf.* Demosthenes I 14 (a *varia lectio*) and Plato *Republic* 337 E.

62. The myth is somewhat as follows. When Zeus gave birth to Dionysus, he entrusted the baby to Athamas, king of Boeotia, and his wife Ino to rear. In revenge Hera caused the couple to become insane. Ino boiled her son, Melicertes, alive and then ran off to the coast and threw herself and dead baby into the sea (from the Scironian rocks near Megara according to Lucian *Dialogi Marini* VIII 1). Both were deified: she under the name Leucothea and Melicertes as Palaemon, in whose honor the Isthmian games were founded.

63. For Ares, *cf.* Homer *Odyssey* VIII 266 ff.; for Apollo, *cf.* Euripides *Alcestis* 1 ff.; for Hephaestus, *cf.* Homer *Iliad* I 590.

64. *i.e.* a lunatic. Aristides totally rejected the myth that Leucothea was transformed from Ino.

65. Homer *Odyssey* V 334.

66. But these "loves" were respectively a seduction under false pretenses and a rape.

67. From Boeotia, or Cithaeron, or the Scironian rocks near Megara (*cf.* Lucian *Dialogi Marini* VIII 1, IX 1) to Corinth.

68. *i.e.* Athamas, Ino's husband.

69. For the mysteries of Palaemon, *cf.* § 40; Pausanias II 2. 1; U. v. Wilamowitz, *Der Glaube der Hellenen* (3rd ed.) II, p. 499.

70. *Cf.* XXVII 35; Behr, *Aelius Aristides,* pp. 90, 155.

71. *Cf.* Aristotle *Rhetoric* 1400 b 7; Plutarch *Moralia* 228 E.

72. In the standard version Odysseus only blinded Polyphemus.

73. Homer *Odyssey* V 351.

74. Homer *Odyssey* XIII 332.

75. *Cf.* Pausanias II 2. 1.

76. *Cf.* § 36 (note 69).

77. Apparently the shrine.

78. The supplement, "as he....dolphin", seems confirmed by the statue described by Pausanias II 1. 8.

79. For a statue of the Sea, *cf.* Pausanias II 1. 7, who also enumerates the statuary dedicated by Herodes Atticus (Aristides' contemporary, teacher (?), and rival); *cf.* also Philostratus *Vitae Sophistarum* 551 Olearius; P. Graindor, *Athènes sous Hadrian* (1934), p. 261 n. 5. If Herodes' dedications were earlier than this speech, it is worth noting how Aristides describes only paintings.

80. Depicting the deaths of Ino and Melicertes; *cf.* note 62.

81. *Cf.* Thucydides II 46. 2.

82. Antoninus Pius; *cf.* XXVI 109; XXX 28.

NOTES TO XLVII

1. *The Sacred Tales* were composed in retirement on the Laneion estate during the winter 170/171 A.D., the first somewhat before the succeeding five (*cf.* Behr, *Studies on the Biography* § 3). Most of the sixth tale has been lost. They should not be regarded as biography, but rather as a testimonial to the efficacy of Asclepius' help in the past and as a silent prayer for the future. Aristides' discovery of the Diary (XLVII 5-57), the surest form of evidence, among his papers, probably gave him the idea of composing a work which on a large scale is similar to the many epigraphic testimonies to Asclepius found in his temples (*cf.e.g.* E. and L. Edelstein, *Asclepius* vol. I, testimony 423 = IG IV², 1, nos. 121-122, with a fuller text, and R. Herzog, *Wunderheilungen: Die Wunderheilungen von Epidaurus,* Philologus, Suppl. Bd. XXII, 3, 1931). But the three stories of the first *Scacred Tale* were plainly insufficient to present a picture of the relationship between Asclepius and Aristides, and Aristides embarked on the more ambitious task of detailing in the five following *Sacred Tales* every occasion in his life which he could remember and in the order in which he remembered it when Asclepius had directly or indirectly aided his health, saved his life, or advanced his career. *The Sacred Tales* give the appearance of an exercize in free thought, and in a sense that is what they were. They are the mental processes of a deeply neurotic, deeply superstitious, vainglorious man, and by the act of dictation they were free to follow their own course. It should be noted how the first three *Sacred Tales* concentrate on matters pertaining to health and the last two on events concerning Aristides' hitherto successful career. From this development it becomes clear, if it was not before, for what Aristides was chiefly praying; *cf.* Behr, *Aelius Aristides,* pp. 109-110. The translation appended to that work has been thoroughly revised and I hope much improved through my continuing studies on this subject, careful comparison with Canter's version, and the not infrequently helpful criticisms published by A.-J. Festugière in Revue Des Études Grecques, LXXXII (1969), pp. 117-153.

The work is divided into the following sections:
A. § 1-4 Proem
B. § 5-60 Diary and related matters
C. § 61-68 The "dropsical tumor"
D. § 69-77 The death of Zosimus
E. § 78 The cure of Philumene.

2. *Odyssey* IV 241.
3. On this word from the schools of oratory, *cf.* Behr, *Aelius Aristides,* p. 47 n. 24.
4. Asclepius *par excellence.*
5. Homer *Iliad* II 489. *Cf.* Aristides XLV 16.
6. Aristides alludes to the proverb "to count the waves". For the psychological implications of the metaphor, *cf.* Behr, *Aelius Aristides,* p. 163.
7. *Cf.* XLVIII 56, L 20.
8. In dream oracles; *cf.* Behr, *Aelius Aristides,* p. 191.
9. For the phrase, *cf.* Plato *Republic* 383 A.
10. *Cf.* XLII 7.
11. *Cf.* Behr, *Aelius Aristides,* pp. 168 ff.
12. Here begin excerpts from Aritides' diary (§§ 5- 57), which cover January 4-February 15, 166 A.D. at the Laneion estate; *cf.* Behr, *Aelius Aristides,* pp. 97-100.
13. December 24-January 23.
14. From his indigestion.
15. *Cf.* XLVIII 78. On this interpretation, *cf.* also Michenaud-Dierkens, *Les Rêves dans Les "Discours Sacrés"* (1972), p. 107 against that of Festugière REG LXXXII (1969), p. 120.

16. *Cf.* Behr, *Aelius Aristides*, p. 32.
17. *Cf.* Behr, *Aelius Aristides*, p. 194.
18. *sc.* μοι φανθέντα (so § 17); *cf.* Behr, *Aelius Aristides*, p. 195.
19. The Propylaea or entrance built by A. Claudius Charax, cos. 147 A.D.; *cf.* Behr, *Aelius Aristides*, p. 27.
20. *Cf.* Behr *Aelius Aristides*, p. 29; *Altertümer von Pergamon VIII³, Die Inschriften des Asklepieions*, 1969, p. 177 n. 46.
21. *Cf.* Behr, *Aelius Aristides, p. 32; Altertümer von Pergamon VIII³*, p. 184.
22. There were two; *cf.* Behr, *Aelius Aristides*, p. 31.
23. A building, as it seems. Perhaps a bath; *cf.* IG IV², 1, 126; Behr, *Aelius Aristides*, p. 28 (also CIL III 986 *auribus Aesculapii;* Weinreich, Athenische Mitteilungen 1912, pp. 57 ff.); *contra* Marinus *Vita Procli* 32.
24. A Pergamene doctor, whom Aristides consulted during his incubation at Pergamum 145-147 A.D. Perhaps now dead; *cf.* Behr, *Aelius Aristides*, p. 44.
25. *Cf.* Behr, *Aelius Aristides*, pp. 167-168.
26. *Cf.* Behr, *Aelius Aristides*, p. 193; *contra* Festugière REG LXXXII (1969), p. 121.
27. *Cf.* IV 3 ff.; XXVIII 6.
28. *Cf.* Demosthenes VIII 23; XVIII 170.
29. *Comicorum Atticorum Fragmenta* I 529 Kock.
30. *Cf.* Behr, *Aelius Aristides*, pp. 26, 62; for the district of the Gymnasium, *cf.* Strabo XIV 956.
31. Unknown. Perhaps M. Antonius Zeno, cos. 148 A.D.; *cf.* Behr, *Aelius Aristides*, pp. 12, 138.
32. If not the god Apollo, Asclepius' father, unknown. Perhaps a slave.
33. *Cf.* XXXIII 29-31.
34. *Cf.* LI 51.
35. *Cf.* L 28. Perhaps C. Julius Bassus Claudianus, now apparently dead; *cf.* Behr, *Aelius Aristides*, pp. 48-49.
36. *Cf.* Pseudo-Lucian *Hippias* 5.
37. Outside Smyrna, where Aristides was first converted to the cult of Asclepius; *cf.* XLVIII 7 and note 10 there; Behr, *Aelius Aristides*, p. 25 n. 23.
38. *Cf.* LI 29, 31; Behr, *Aelius Aristides*, p. 307.
39. *Phoenissae* 3.
40. Statius Quadratus, proconsul of Asia 165/166 A.D.; *cf.* Behr, *Aelius Aristides*, pp. 98-100; *Studies on the Biography* § 1.
41. Long dead; *cf.* oration XXXII; Behr, *Aelius Aristides*, pp.10-11.
42. Possibly a cult designation; see or. XXX 15 and note 33 there; on kissing, *cf.* Fronto, Loeb edition vol. I, p. 220.
43. *Cf.* LI 19, 25. In Mysia. Perhaps the same as or near to Mt. Pelecas (in Polybius V 77. 9); *cf.* Boulanger, *Aelius Aristide*, p. 120 n. 1; Behr, *Aelius Aristides*, pp. 103-104.
44. Aristides visited Elephantine in 141/142 A.D.; *cf.* Behr, *Aelius Aristides*, p. 16; Hommages à Vermaseren, p. 22.
45. *Cf.* XLIX 49-50; Behr, Hommages à Vermaseren, p, 22.
46. Customarily offered to the sun, here Helius Sarapis; *cf.* Plutarch *De Iside et Osiride* 372 D, 383 E ff.; Behr, Hommages à Vermaseren, p. 22 and n. 40.
47. Died November 148 A.D.; *cf.* Behr, *Aelius Aristides*, p. 9; *Studies on the Biography* § 3.
48. *Cf.* Behr, *Aelius Aristides*, pp. 167-168.
49. January 24-February 20.
50. In Pergamum; *cf. Altertümer von Pergamon VIII³*, p. 10.
51. *Cf.* Bergk *Poetae Lyrici Graeci* III, pp. 684 ff. For the boys, *cf.* Behr, *Aelius Aristides*, p. 31.

52. Aristides was born on the fourth of Aydnaios (= November 26), but like many other ancients, celebrated his birthday on the fourth of each month (here Lenaeon 4 = January 27); cf. Behr, *Studies on the Biography* § 1.
53. Cf. Behr, *Aelius Aristides*, p. 33 n. 53.
54. Hadad and Atargatis; cf. Behr, *Studies on the Biography* § 1.
55. Unknown.
56. Apparently Sex. Julius Maior Antoninus Pythodorus, benefactor of the Asclepieion at Epidaurus (cf. Pausanias II 27. 6), a citizen of Nysa on the Maeander; cf. IG IV², pp. xxxiii-xxxv; *Altertümer von Pergamon VIII³*, p. 65.
57. Goddess of health and Asclepius' wife.
58. Marcus Aurelius. The scene is fictitious, but relates to the conclusion, nominally under Lucius Verus (the younger emperor), of the Parthian war in 165 A.D.
59. Cf. Plato *Euthydemus* 300 D and *Menexenus* 235 C.
60. Unknown.
61. Cf. XLIX 47; Behr, *Hommages à Vermaseren*, p. 19.
62. Presumably the current governor Statius Quadratus; cf. § 22 n. 40.
63. Unknown.
64. Cf. L 18.
65. Cf. XXXIX 13.
66. The temple of which Aristides' father was priest; cf. Behr, *Aelius Aristides*, pp. 5-6.
67. As if he had assisted the ham in performing an incubation in the temple; cf. Behr, *Aelius Aristides*, p. 34; *Altertümer von Pergamon VIII³*, p. 175 n. 27.
68. A servant, The man's name derives from the notion of "good fortune", and implies a good omen.
69. The temple had two wardens, who assisted the priest; cf. Behr, *Aelius Aristides*, p. 31 n. 42.
70. Philumene. Presumably long dead; cf. Behr, *Aelius Aristides*, p. 9.
71. Child of Philumene, wife of Alcimus, mother of another Philumene; cf. Behr, *Aelius Aristides*, p. 9.
72. Part of the Asclepieion at Pergamum; built by the consular Rufinus, c. 145 A.D.; cf. Behr, *Aelius Aristides*, pp. 27-28.
73. Marcus Aurelius and Lucius Verus.
74. Cf. XXXII 8. He means the sophists; cf. Behr, *Aelius Aristides*, p. 106; *Studies on the Biography* § 4.
75. On this ditch, which long antedated their reign, cf. Pliny the Younger *Epistles* VIII 17; ILS 207 (time of Claudius), 5797 a (time of Trajan).
76. Cf. II 392 and the references cited there in volume I of the Loeb edition of Aristides, to which add the *Proverbia Aesopi* no. 83, p. 277 in Perry's *Aesopica*.
77. Cf. Behr, *Aelius Aristides*, p. 193.
78. Unknown. Keil *ad. loc.* and Festugière REG LXXXII (1969), p. 123 take γνώριμος as "clarissimus" or "distinguished", but this need not be so; cf. L 23, 106.
79. He was forbidden to bathe; cf. § 45.
80. A major city in Mysia, 120 stades = c. 14 miles, it would seem, south of the Laneion estate, where the dream took place; cf. Behr, *Aelius Aristides*, p. 6.
81. "Nomen omen". "Menander" is understood as indicating the Greek verb *menein* = "to remain".
82. *i.e.* the dream about Menander, as Festugière REG LXXXII (1969), p. 124 has explained.
83. "Nomen omen". "Corus" in Greek means "satiety". For this man, cf. Behr, *Aelius Aristides*, p. 102.

84. *Cf.* § 13 n. 24.
85. Porphyrio, it would seem; *cf.* Behr, *Aelius Aristides,* p. 100.
86. Julius Asclepiacus. Now dead, it would seem; *cf.* Behr, *Aelius Aristides,* p. 42; *Altertümer von Pergamon VIII³*, p. 101.
87. Either Apollo and the plain of Apia, for which, *cf.* the inscription quoted in vol. I p. xvi n. a of the Loeb edition of Aristides (= Athenische Mitteilungen, 1904, p. 280); or less likely Asclepius and the Provincial Assembly of Asia now meeting in Pergamum; *cf.* Behr, *Aelius Aristides,* p. 103.
88. *Cf.* Plato *Symposium* 223 D.
89. *Cf.* Behr, *Aelius Aristides,* p. 62. The "tumor" may be no more than a swelling. Dr. R. Leclercq in Michenaud-Dierkens, *Les Rêves dans les "Discours Sacrés",* p. 109 diagnosed this as an omental hernia, later strangulated. Possibly true. For unlike most such ills, it apparently can cure itself.
90. *Cf.* Herodotus II 37. 3; Festugière, *Personal Religion Among The Greeks,* p. 169 n. 18; Behr, *Aelius Aristides,* pp. 30, 63.
91. Of Smyrna.
92. The skin left over from the tumor.
93. For a similar miraculous closing of a scar left from the disappearance of a tumorous growth, *cf.* William of Malmesbury *Gesta Regum Anglorum* II § 222 (edition of The English Historical Society, 1840).
94. *Cf.* Behr, *Aelius Aristides,* pp. 68 ff.
95. About 40 stades = *c.* 5 miles north of the Laneion estate; *cf.* § 75 and Behr, *Aelius Aristides,* p. 6.
96. *c.* 14 miles.
97. Apparently part of the incantation, which is echoed in § 77.
98. Wife of Apollo, mother of Asclepius. For these poems to Asclepius, *cf.* Behr, *Aelius Aristides,* pp. 32-33.
99. The same doctor, I think, as in XLIX 18.
100. *Cf.* § 69 and n. 95.
101. *Cf.* § 71 and n. 97.
102. *Cf.* Behr, *Aelius Aristides,* p. 67.
103. The letter was surely part of the dream; *cf.* Behr, *Aelius Aristides,* p. 194. *Contra* R. Crahay and J. Dierkens in Michenaud-Dierkens, *Les Rêves dans les "Discours Sacrés",* p. 18 n. 7.

NOTES TO XLVIII

1. For the purpose and time of composition, see note 1 to or. XLVII. The work is divided into the following sections:
A. § 1-4 Proem
B. § 5-10 Introduction to cult
C. § 11-23 The dream of the years
D. § 24-36 Dreams of protection
E. § 37-45 The plague
F. § 45-59 River baths
G. § 60-70 Trip to Rome
H. § 71-80 Baths in the Temple
I. § 81-82 Trip to Ephesus.
2. *Cf.* Behr, *Aelius Aristides,* pp. 109-110.
3. *Cf.* Behr, *Aelius Aristides,* pp. 25, 45, 116 ff.
4. Like our "touch wood!" *Cf.* Behr, *Aelius Aristides,* p. 156.

5. On these, cf. § 8; scholium vol. 3, p. 432, 31 ff. Ddf.; *Prolegomena* vol. 3, p. 738, 9 ff. Ddf. = § 6 Lenz; F. W. Lenz, Mnemosyne, Supp. 5 (1959), pp. 57-58; Behr, *Aelius Aristides,* pp. 33, 145.
6. Cf. XLII 1.
7. Cf. Behr, *Aelius Aristides,* p. 25.
8. Cf. § 69; II 67.
9. Literally "my tendons trembled"; cf. § 62. This symptom caught Philostratus' attention, *Vitae Sophistarum* 581 Olearius.
10. c. 5 miles southwest of Smyrna; cf. XLVII 22; Strabo XIV 645; Philostratus *Heroicus* 300; Behr, *Aelius Aristides,* p. 25.
11. Cf. Behr, *Aelius Aristides,* pp. 25-26.
12. Cf. Behr, *Aelius Aristides,* p. 192.
13. Cf. Behr, *Aelius Aristides,* pp. 26, 41 ff.
14. Cf. § 4.
15. Cf. § 3; Behr, *Aelius Aristides,* p. 116.
16. Because his help has been greater than one might expect.
17. Zosimus; cf. Behr, *Aelius Aristides,* p. 41; *Studies on the Biography* § 3.
18. L. Salvius Julianus, the famous jurist, consul ordinarius 148 A.D. The use of the *nomen* instead of the *cognomen* ("Salvius" instead of "Julianus") is unusual in Aristides, but is probably caused by the notion of "health" implicit in the name. If the emendation ("one of the consulars" for "the present consul") is correct, Aristides means that Salvius is now, 170/171 A.D., a consular; cf. the Loeb edition of *Aristides* vol. I, p. x note b; and *Studies on the Biography* § 3. If the reading of the manuscripts, "Salvius, the present consul", is preserved, then *Sacred Tales* II-VI would have to have been composed in 175 A.D., when another Salvius Julianus was consul ordinarius. In the above cited article, I have pointed out the difficulties which that interpretation entails.
19. As an incubant in the Temple; cf. § 48.
20. I prefer this rendering to my earlier "signified his approval of the project by calling them *etc.*"
21. A deity originally unrelated, but now regarded as Asclepius' son.
22. Cf. Behr, *Aelius Aristides,* pp. 69-70.
23. At the time Aristides was at the Temple of Asclepius in Pergamum. To reach the island of Chius, he traveled south, through Smyrna, and took ship at Clazomenae.
24. Cf. XXXIII 18; L 33.
25. Cf. §§ 13, 26; Behr, *Aelius Aristides,* p. 70. This is a circuitous route. Clazomenae is south of Phocaea, across the Gulf of Smyrna.
26. In his stomach.
27. Cf. Behr, *Aelius Aristides,* pp. 70-73.
28. Probably Flavius Rufus; cf. Behr, *Aelius Aristides,* p. 70.
29. January 27. Dystrus was the province's official name of the month which elsewhere is called Lenaeon, January 24-February 20; cf. XLVII 29. On the emendation of the text ("the fourth" for "the fourteenth") and the question of the monthly celebration of Aristides' birth date (a fourth), cf. *Studies on the Biography* § 1.
30. "He of the handsome child", *i.e.* Asclepius.
31. Cf. Behr, *Aelius Aristides,* p. 29.
32. The fingers on one hand signified fives, those on the other units. Depending on which hand signified which, the extension of three fingers on one hand and two on the other could indicate either $3 + 10$ or $15 + 2$. On the whole question, cf. Behr, *Aelius Aristides,* pp. 71-72; *Hommages à Vermaseren,* p. 20.
33. Cf. Homer *Odyssey* XIX 547.
34. It is unclear whether Aristides means the Meles, or some other unknown stream; cf. C. J. Cadoux, *Ancient Smyrna,* p. 174 n. 6.

35. A public distribution of grain, or a charitable distribution of food or money made by some wealthy individual.
36. Unknown.
37. He apparently means a muscle spasm, or perhaps a form of tetany where the head and neck are drawn backwards and locked in that position; *cf.* Behr, *Aelius Aristides,* p. 166.
38. *Cf.* § 7; *Altertümer von Pergamon VIII³* no. 34.
39. On these states, *cf.* Behr, *Aelius Aristides,* p. 164.
40. § 18.
41; In Pergamum; *cf.* Behr, *Aelius Aristides,* pp. 43-44.
42. *Cf.* § 51. The Selinus.
43. On these coins, used at Pergamum, *cf.* OGIS 484 = E.M. Smallwood, *Documents Illustrating the Principates of Nerva, Trajan, and Hadrian* no. 451.
44. *Cf.* Behr, *Aelius Aristides,* p. 33.
45. *i.e.* his fellow incubants; *cf.* Behr, *Aelius Aristides,* p. 42.
46. *Cf.* E.R. Dodds, *The Greeks and the Irrational,* p. 130. For the dedication of a ring, *cf. Altertümer von Pergamon VIII³* no. 72.
47. In Pergamum; *cf.* Behr, *Aelius Aristides,* pp. 43-44.
48. *Cf.* §4.
49. Otherwise unknown. His colleague was Asclepiacus, XLVII 58; *cf.* also XLVII 11.
50. Part of the temple complex. It could hold 3500 spectators; *cf.* Behr, *Aelius Aristides,* p. 28.
51. The wearing of white was common in the cult; *cf.* Behr, *Aelius Aritides,* p. 32.
52. By his statue.
53. *Cf.* XLVII 10 and note 19 there.
54. *Cf.* Behr, *Aelius Aristides,* p. 32; *Altertümer von Pergamon VIII³*, p. 181 n. 68.
55. *Cf.* XLIII 27 (of Zeus); Behr, *Aelius Aristides,* pp. 157-161.
56. *Cf.* Behr, *Aelius Aristides,* p. 160 n. 77.
57. *Cf.* XLVII 13 and note 24 there.
58. *Cf.* § 30 and note 49 there.
59. *Cf.* Behr, *Aelius Aristides,* pp. 30, 42.
60. The passage is corrupt. For the idea, *cf.* §§ 30, 31. The supplement ("many dangers....me") is borrowed from § 25. With τὰ τῶν μοιρῶν, understand ἐλέγετο. Festugière, REG LXXXII, p. 128 offers another interpretation in criticizing a suggestion which I later abandoned.
61; *i.e.* §§ 26-27 and §§ 31-32. With τοῖς .....γενομένοις, understand ὀνείρασι.
62. § 18 ff. At Smyrna; *cf.* Behr, *Aelius Aristides,* pp. 96-97, 166-167.
63. *Cf.* Behr, *Aelius Aristides,* p. 7.
64. Smallpox; *cf.* Behr, *Aelius Aristides,* pp. 96-97, 166-167; *Studies on the Biography* § 3; R. and M. Littman, American Journal of Philology 94 (1973), pp. 243-255.
65. *Iliad* XI 813.
66. *Cf.* Behr, *Aelius Aristides,* p. 192 n. 69. I assume that Aristides' bed was placed along the right wall of his room and that Aristides lay on his right side, which caused an untrue dream through pressure on the liver (for which *cf.* Tertullian *De Anima* 48. 2; Diocles frg. 141 Wellmann). When Aristides turned to the outside, the left side, the untrue dream ceased.
67. Aristides plays on the word, which can mean the end of the fever, of his life, or of the play.
68. *Cf.* Behr, *Aelius Aristides,* pp. 14, 153.
69. Callityche; *cf.* XLVII 45 and note 71 there.
70. *Cf.* XXXIII 18.

71. *Cf.* XL 22.
72. Since Athena aided Odysseus and Telemachus throughout *The Odyssey.*
73. As Keil noted, implicit in the adjective "long" is that Aristides traveled in a recumbant position.
74. Hermias; *cf.* LI 25; Behr, *Aelius Aristides,* pp. 9, 72, 97, 160-161.
75. In Pergamum; *cf.* Behr, *Aelius Aristides,* pp. 43-44, 47.
76. § 18. "In the beginning" is loosely employed, but true in relation to the time of composition. On bathing, *cf.* Behr, *Aelius Aristides,* p. 38 n. 73.
77. Metaphorically for "everything was swollen and inflamed".
78. *Cf.* XXX 15 and note 33 there.
79. *Cf.* Behr, *Aelius Aristides,* p. 31.
80. Unknown.
81. L. Sedatius Theophilus, a citizen of Nicaea on the Cayster and Laodiceia ad Lycum, of praetorian rank (possibly the following phrase "the best of men" may refer to his rank as a *vir clarissimus,* although Aristides' choice of words is strange; one would expect λαμπρότατος); *cf.* L 16; CIG 3937; Behr, *Aelius Aristides,* p. 47; *Studies on the Biography* § 3; contra *Altertümer von Pergamon VIII³,* p. 94; G. W. Bowersock, *Greek Sophists in the Roman Empire,* pp. 86-87.
82. A river just south of Pergamum.
83. *Cf.* § 58.
84. *Cf.* Behr, *Aelius Aristides,* p. 26.
85. *Cf.* § 7 and note 10 there.
86. *Cf.* Behr, *Aelius Aristides,* pp. 43-44.
87. The Selinus; *cf.* § 27.
88. Pergamum was the seat of the school of the Platonist Caius; *cf.* Behr, *Aelius Aristides,* p. 54.
89. A hymn of victory or praise.
90. *Cf.* § 51.
91. Elaea was the port of Pergamum; *cf.* Behr, *Aelius Aristides,* pp. 43-44.
92. *Cf.* XLII 6 ff.
93. *Cf.* § 59.
94. Homer *Odyssey* III 113-114.
95. *Cf.* Homer *Odyssey* III 115.
96. In Mysia; *cf.* Behr, *Aelius Aristides,* pp. 23-24.
97. *Cf.* XXXVI 88 and note 118 there. He means the length and complexity of the story.
98. At the warm springs. *Cf.* L 2; Behr, *Aelius Aristides,* pp. 6-7; A.J. Festugière, REG LXXXII, p. 131.
99. After crossing the Hellespont, Aristides traveled on the *via Egnatia.*
100. No doubt an allusion not only to the frequent defeats of the Persians by the Greeks, but also to the Romans' recent victory over the Parthians.
101. Formerly Aegae, it would seem, but this is not certain; *cf.* I 334. The *via Egnatia* passes here on the way to Dyrrachium. The cataract is that of the Axius river not far from Edessa.
102. The journey should have taken no more than a month.
103. *Cf.* Behr, *Aelius Aristides,* p. 24.
104. *Cf.* § 6. The literal translation of "I trembled with cold" would be "my tendons were chilled".
105. A purgative based on squirting cucumber.
106. *Cf.* Behr, *Aelius Aristides,* pp. 24-25.
107. Near Rhion; *cf.* III 325.
108. *Cf.* Behr, *Aelius Aristides,* pp. 24-25.
109. *Cf.* Behr, *Aelius Aristides,* p. 25.

110. *Cf.* Behr, *Aelius Aristides*, pp. 25-26.
111. On the role of gymnastic trainers in medicine, *cf.* also III 589 ff.
112. *Cf.* § 5.
113. *Cf.* § 7.
114. *Cf.* § 5 ff.
115. "Cathedra" means properly a period of inactivity. But it had a special significance for Aristides, who used the term exclusively for this time of his life, and it may well have been chosen wistfully with an eye on the sophistic chair; *cf.* the subscription to oration XXX; XLIX 44; similarly L 14; Behr, *Aelius Aristides*, p. 26.
116. In Pergamum; *cf.* Behr, *Aelius Aristides*, pp. 43-44.
117. *i.e.* performing an incubation to receive a cure or a dream containing a prescription.
118. Homer *Odyssey* X 46; *cf.* Behr, *Aelius Aristides*, p. 190.
119. *Cf.* Hesiod *Works and Days* 218.
120. *Cf.* Behr, *Aelius Aristides*, p. 31 n. 43.
121. In Pergamum; *cf.* Behr, *Aelius Aristides*, pp. 43-44.
122. *Cf.* Behr, *Aelius Aristides*, p. 32; E. and L. Edelstein, *Asclepius* II, pp. 184-185. Keil compared Plutarch *De Superstitione* 168 D, but here the practice is an act of penitence.
123. In Pergamum; *cf.* Behr, *Aelius Aristides*, pp. 43-44.
124. The site remains uncertain; *cf.* Behr, *Aelius Aristides*, p. 28; *Altertümer von Pergamon VIII*³, p. 84.
125. *Cf.* Homer *Iliad* XIX 258, *Odyssey* XIX 303.
126. Without the temple complex, it would seem; *cf.* Behr, *Aelius Aristides*, p. 30 n. 39.
127. *Cf.* Plato *Laws* 633 B.
128. Hygieia; *cf.* Behr, *Aelius Aristides*, p. 27.
129. *Cf.* Behr, *Aelius Aristides*, p. 108.
130. The great festival of the Temple of Asclepius in Pergamum was celebrated, it would seem, in the month of August; *cf.* Behr, *Aelius Aristides*, p. 32.
131. Perhaps the gymnasium built by P. Vedius Antoninus twenty years before; *cf.* SEG IV 533. Coressus was a hill and a suburb southwest of Ephesus.

NOTES TO XLIX

1. For the purpose and time of composition, see note 1 to oration XLVII. The work is divided into the following sections:
A. § 1-6 Trips to Aliani
B. § 7-14 Trip to Lebedus
C. § 15-20 An attack of *opisthotonus* and other terrible symptoms
D. § 21-37 Drugs and diet
E. § 38-43 The earthquake
F. § 44-46 Sacrifices
G. § 47-50 Zosimus' death and the Egyptian gods.

2. Events in Pergamum and Aliani. For the spelling of the latter, *cf.* Revue des Études Grecques III (1892), pp. 51-52 n. 1. Aliani lay about 15 miles west of Pergamum, it would appear, near Germe, modern Soma; *cf.* Behr, *Aelius Aristides*, pp. 43-44.
3. "The very edge" of the sea. I note this because of the confusion of Festugière, REG LXXXII (1969), p. 133.
4. *Cf.* Libanius V 1 (vol. 1, p. 305, 4 Foerster); Homer *Iliad* XV 290.

5. *Cf.* XLVIII 3.
6. *i.e.* even to leave the house to get on the horse.
7. In Pergamum and Aliani; *cf.* Behr, *Aelius Aristides,* p. 69.
8. *c.* 30 miles.
9. Pergamum and Lebedus; *cf.* Behr, *Aelius Aristides,* pp. 61-62. Lebedus, a major coastal city of the province of Asia, lay between Smyrna and Ephesus.
10. The Temple of Zeus Asclepius; *cf.* Behr, *Aelius Aristides,* p. 28.
11. Galen's teacher; *cf.* Behr, *Aelius Aristides,* pp. 61, 169. On the contempt implied by the term "sophist"—an iatrosophist is not meant—, *cf.* Behr, *Aelius Aristides,* p. 106; *Studies on the Biography* § 4.
12. A proverb: good did not come from it.
13. *Cf.* Behr, *Aelius Aristides,* p. 62.
14. Satyrus said "abdomen", *cf.* § 8.
15. *Cf.* Behr, *Aelius Aristides,* pp. 163, 165 n. 10.
16. On the meaning of κατετείνετο, *cf.* Festugière, REG LXXXII (1969), pp. 133-134.
17. Apollo.
18. 120 stades, *c.* 15 miles.
19. Pergamum.
20. In northern Mysia, near Hadriani; *cf.* Behr, *Aelius Aristides,* pp. 6-7.
21. § 11. Events in Pergamum; *cf.* Behr, *Aelius Aristides,* p. 67.
22. At the Ancestral estate; *cf.* Behr, *Aelius Aristides,* p. 67.
23. Particularly from "the tension" in his muscles; *cf.* § 16.
24. The same as at XLVII 73.
25. For the terminology, *cf.* Galen, *On the Natural Faculties* I xiii, p. 40 K. τὰ μὲν διαχωρήματα μηδὲν ὅλως ἐν αὐτοῖς ἔχοντα χολῆς.
26. 600 feet.
27. In Pergamum; *cf.* Behr, *Aelius Aristides,* pp. 68-69.
28. *Cf.* XLVIII 20 and note 37 there.
29. *Cf.* Behr, *Aelius Aristides,* p. 29 n. 34; *Altertümer von Pergamon VIII³,* pp. 131, 133, 174.
30. The wife of Asclepius; *cf.* the dream in § 21. On the temple, *cf.* Behr, *Aelius Aristides,* p. 29 n. 34; *Altertümer von Pergamon VIII³,* p. 155.
31. Probably Julia Tyche, of the stock of Julius Quadratus, the foremost family in Pergamum (for an ancestress(?) with the same name, *cf.* the stemma in note 14 to XXX 7). The word also means "chance" or "good fortune".
32. Malobathrum.
33. So too Canter "circum collum meum". However, Festugière, REG LXXXII (1969), p. 135 *s.v.* § 21 renders: "dansant de joie au sujet de mon cou", with a reference to § 21. But I should think that this would require τὰ περὶ κτλ.
34. Asclepiacus, one of the temple wardens of the Temple of Asclepius at Pergamum, was a doctor only in the dream; *cf.* Behr, *Aelius Aristides,* p. 69.
35. *Cf.* XLVIII 3, 8; XLIX 30; L 25; Behr, *Aelius Aristides,* p. 116.
36. Presumably breakfast, so that in accordance with medical praxis, as is stated just below, he might eat before taking the drug.
37. *Cf.* Behr, *Aelius Aristides,* p. 29 n. 35.
38. Invented by Philo; *cf.* Galen XVII 2, p. 332 Kühn.
39. Literally "stood out".
40. *Cf.* § 26 and note 35 there.
41. *Cf.* Athenaeus 479 AB, where also two "demiroyals" appear to equal a cup, contrary to the opinions of the glossators who are cited there. Evidently there was some dispute about the volume of the measure. Hence Aristides' explanation.
42. In Diogenes Laertius VI 18 the book is listed as *On the Use of Wine or Intoxication or On the Cyclops.*

43. The god of wine.

44. At the Laneion estate; cf. Behr, Aelius Aristides, p. 109 n. 52. If one translates as Canter, "hoc fere tempore quo..." and Festugière, REG LXXXII (1969), p. 137, "c'était environ le temps où....", then § 34 belongs to the time of the sections just preceding and the year 170/171 A.D. starts with § 35. However, considering Herodotus I 160. 5 and the use of τις as an adjective of extent as in III 385 (cf. οὐκ ὀλίγος in Herodotus loc.cit.), I feel that literally the expression means "it was some time this during which..."

45. Because he was so abstinent, even this limitation seemed excessive.

46. Cf. XLVII 59; Behr, Studies on the Biography § 3.

47. Cf. Galen XII, p. 855 ff. Kühn.

48. Cf. Galen X, p. 791 Kühn.

49. In Smyrna; cf. Behr, Aelius Aristides, p. 73.

50. Cf. XLVII 69 ff.

51. The end of a dactylic hexameter.

52. In Smyrna; cf. Behr, Aelius Aristides, pp. 74-76.

53. L. Antonius Albus, consul c. 132 A.D., proconsul of Asia 149/150 A.D.; cf. Behr, Aelius Aristides, pp. 74-75 and particularly Studies on the Biography § 8.

54. Of Apollo.

55. Cf. Behr, Aelius Aristides, pp. 72-73, 152 n. 21.

56. Both were forbidden in the dream of § 37. He was going to sacrifice an ox.

57. Near Aristides' Laneion estate, now called Asar Kale, as it seems; cf. L. Robert, Études Anatoliennes, pp. 217-220; Behr, Aelius Aristides, p. 6.

58. Outside Smyrna; cf. XLVIII 7 and note 10 there.

59. On the meaning of "Cathedra", cf. XLVIII 70 and note 115 there. On this incident, cf. Behr, Aelius Aristides, pp. 26, 119.

60. On the name "Milates", cf. Altertümer von Pergamon VIII³, p. 81; and on the Acropolis district, IGRR IV 330, 424.

61. In Smyrna; cf. Behr, Aelius Aristides, pp. 25-26, 149.

62. Cf. Behr, Aelius Aristides, p. 26 n. 17; Hommages à Vermaseren, pp. 14, 16.

63. Cf. § 37. In Smyrna; cf. Behr, Aelius Aristides, p. 73.

64. On the meaning of this supplement, cf. Hommages à Vermaseren, pp. 17-19, although I have slightly changed its form; also XLVII 40. The dream, I believe, disguises the wish to be circumcised (at this time permitted only to Jews and Egyptian priests), to which is joined self-hatred (mutilation of the mouth of an orator). The cause lies in the traumatic effects of Zosimus' death (particularly a momentary dissatisfaction with Asclepius and a compensatory turning to Sarapis).

65. Egyptian gods, apparitors of Osiris; cf. Behr, Aelius Aristides, p. 150 n. 11; Hommages à Vermaseren, pp. 19-20.

66. In Smyrna; cf. Behr, Aelius Aristides, p. 73.

67. "Gladly" because he was deemed worthy of receiving visions not granted to ordinary people.

68. i.e. into this religious secret (cf. note 67).

69. Perhaps April 25; cf. XLV 33; Behr, Aelius Aristides, p. 73 n. 48.

70. E.g. cf. the two snakes or ravens who guided Alexander the Great to the shrine of Ammon in Arrian Anabasis III 3, 5-6.

71. Sarapis; cf. Behr, Aelius Aristides, p. 149 n. 6.

72. Because of the different form of the noun (σύμβολοι where Aristides uses σύμβολα), Keil plausibly suggests that this is a quotation and he compares Xenophon Apology 13 and Memorabilia I 1, 3.

NOTES TO L

1. For the purpose and time of composition, see note 1 to oration XLVII. The work is divided into the following sections:
A. § 1-13 Trip to the Aesepus
B. § 14-30 Return to the study of oratory
C. § 31-47 Lyric poetry
D. § 48-70 Inspiring dreams
E. § 71-108 Legal victories.
2. In Mysia; cf. Behr, Aelius Aristides, pp. 80-81.
3. Near the Çatal Dag; cf. Behr, Aelius Aristides, p. 6.
4. The Aesepus is a river in Mysia. The warm springs of Artemis Thermaea lie at Baris, modern Gönen; cf. Behr, Aelius Aristides, pp. 6-7.
5. Cf. XLVIII 60 ff.
6. i.e. returned back to the Ancestral Estate. With ἀφ' ὦν, sc. πρὸς ταῦτα τὰ ἐμά. Festugière, REG LXXXII (1969), p. 131 s.v. § 60. 4, translates: "contrairement...à la saison et à la maladie dont je relevais...", which is impossible.
7. Better Poemanenon, a town in Mysia, now apparently Eski Manyas; cf. Behr, Aelius Aristides, pp. 5-6.
8. i.e. by Asclepius; cf. § 107; XLVIII 23.
9. Cf. LI 19; contra Festugière, REG LXXXII (1969), p. 138: "attend (sc. the god) quelques jours".
10. Cf. Behr, Aelius Aristides, p. 166.
11. Cf. Behr, Aelius Aristides, p. 34 n. 57.
12. Cf. Behr, Aelius Aristides, pp. 163-164.
13. Cf. XLVIII 58.
14. Cf. XLVIII 57, XLIX 1 for the supplement ("in my...tension"). As even Festugière, REG LXXXII (1969), p. 138 n. 5, in essence admits σφάκελοι and φλέβες do not cohere.
15. This is true. Aristides' career flourished for the next thirteen years.
16. The smallpox in Smyrna; cf. XLVIII 37 ff.; Behr, Aelius Aristides, pp. 96-97, 166-167.
17. A symptom of smallpox. On this word, cf. Hippocrates Aphorisms III 17; Behr, Aelius Aristides, p. 167. Therefore I cannot agree with Festugière, REG LXXXII (1969), p. 139, who feels that it should mean "desiccation" or "thinness".
18. Cf. § 73. At the Ancestral Estate; cf. Behr, Aelius Aristides, p. 81.
19. For her age and sickness, cf. XLVII 78.
20. Perhaps sodium carbonate from a neighboring mine; cf. Pliny Naturalis Historia XXXI 113 and 122; Behr Aelius Aristides, p. 6 n. 8 c.
21. C. Julius Severus, cos. c. 138 A.D., proconsul of Asia 152/153 A.D., from Galatia; cf. § 71 ff.; Behr, Aelius Aristides, p. 80; Studies on the Biography § 1 and § 5.
22. Cf. § 68. On this arrangement, cf. Behr, Aelius Aristides, p. 118. Festugière, REG LXXXII (1969), p. 140, would translate: "celles (marques d'honneur) qui concernent les exploits que le dieu a accomplis relativement aux charges" (= ἡγεμονίας, which I think very improbable).
23. Literally "the results of the past events take place" or "occur" in this work. I mention this since it troubled Festugière, REG LXXXII (1969), p. 141, who rejects my supplement ("past") and consequently arrives at a pointless version: "quand on en sera venu au moment qui résulte de la suite chronologique". In the final system, there is no *suite chronologique!*
24. In Smyrna and then Pergamum; cf. Behr, Aelius Aristides, pp. 43-49.
25. Performed an incubation; cf. XLVIII 70 and note 115 there.

26. *i.e.* to study and use them as models for his own writing.

27. *Cf.* Behr, *Aelius Aristides,* pp. 28-29.

28. Called a ταυροκάθαψις, "bullfight" in IGRR IV 460; *cf.* L. Robert, *Les Gladiateurs dans l'Orient grec,* pp. 318 ff.

29. *Cf.* XLVIII 48 and note 81 there.

30. If the emendation ("Maximus, the African") is sound, Q. Tullius Maximus, consul designate between 161-169 A.D. is meant; *cf.* IV 2; XXVIII 88 (?); Behr, *Aelius Aristides,* p. 48 n. 26.

31. The same argument is given by Syrianus in Walz *Rhetores Graeci* IV 747, 25 ff.

32. Otherwise unknown. Perhaps of the school of the Platonist Caius; *cf.* Behr, *Aelius Aristides,* p. 54 n. 50.

33. *Cf.* § 51.

34. Dreams at this time of night were regarded as the most prophetic; *cf.* Behr, *Aelius Aristides,* pp. 179-180.

35. *Cf.* § 15.

36. The name signifies "man strengthener".

37. The name signifies "god giver". Theodotus was Aristides' doctor at this time; *cf.* XLVII 13 and note 24 there.

38. Since both were healers, and the latter was "the god giver". So Asclepius was "the man strengthener" or "encourager"; *cf.* § 19.

39. Q. Aelius Egrilius Euare(s)tus, perhaps of the school of the Platonist Caius; *cf.* the Loeb edition of Aristides, vol. I, p. x n. b; Behr, Studies on the Biography § 3. He was the friend of Salvius Julianus of XLVIII 9.

40. In 141/142 A.D.; *cf.* Behr, *Aelius Aristides,* pp. 15 ff.

41. Unknown.

42. The models of § 15 among others.

43. This *Athena* is lost and is not to be confused with oration XXXVII, which was written some seven years later (*cf.* note 1 to oration XXXVII). *The Dionysus* is oration XLI; *cf.* Behr, *Aelius Aristides,* pp. 52-53; *Studies on the Biography* § 4.

44. *i.e.* oratorical themes or subjects.

45. *Cf.* XXVIII 21.

46. On Aristides' difficulty in *ex tempore* speaking, *cf.* Behr, *Aelius Aristides,* p. 46.

47. L. Claudius Pardalas of Pergamum; *cf.* § 87; IGRR IV 238; Behr, *Aelius Aristides,* p. 48; *Altertümer von Pergamon VIII³,* pp. 141-142.

48. *Cf.* § 32; Plato *Epistle* VII 323 E.

49. *Cf.* § 52, and for a similar claim XXIII 16; Behr, *Aelius Aristides,* p. 46 n. 20.

50. L. Cuspius Pactumeius Rufinus of Pergamum, consul ordinarius 142 A.D.; *cf.* Behr, *Aelius Aristides,* p. 48 n. 29; *Altertümer von Pergamon VIII³,* pp. 23 ff. (no. 2).

51. Or, if one wishes to keep the manuscript reading, "multiform".

52. For the phrase "for....expression", *cf.* Demosthenes *Proem.* 50, 3.

53. *Cf.* XXXIV 47 of a man who "sang" his speeches. Perhaps Antonius Polemo is meant; *cf.* Behr, *Aelius Aristides,* p. 12 n. 30.

54. *Cf.* XLVII 21 and note 35 there. That Keil's correction of the corrupt text is impossible is shown well enough by the muddled attempt in Festugière, REG LXXXII (1969), p. 143, to defend it.

55. The change in punctuation, so that there is a parenthesis, may help this otherwise perplexing (most think lacunose) passage. For the words translated "have so much ease", *cf.* XXVIII 129, LI 39.

56. At the Laneion estate, it would seem; *cf.* Behr, *Aelius Aristides,* pp. 108-109.

57. *The Third Sacred Tale,* as I think; *cf.* XLIX 36.

58. At Rome; *cf.* XLVIII 62 ff.; Behr, *Aelius Aristides,* p. 24.

59. *Cf.* Pindar *Olympian* II 1.

60. For some reason, in antiquity it was customary to express doubts about well-known, but slightly technical matters, when one did not wish to seem to be a professional.
61. The *Ludi Apollinares Circenses* on July 13.
62. In Delus; *cf.* XLVIII 68; Behr, *Aelius Aristides*, pp. 24-25.
63. Literally, "as it were plowed the sea".
64. There is a deeper implication in these words; *cf.* XLVIII 11.
65. The phrase imitates Demosthenes XX 73.
66. Homer *Odyssey* III 139.
67. § 31.
68. Frg. 510 Page, *Poetae Melici Graeci;* *cf.* Cicero *De Oratore* II 86.
69. A play on the word "paean", "healer", which also connotes the hymn which Aristides wrote.
70. Asclepius.
71. For the phrase, *cf.* I 151; Plato *Epistle* III 318 E. The scene is again Pergamum; *cf.* Behr, *Aelius Aristides*, pp. 43-44, 52.
72. On this, *cf.* Behr, *Aelius Aristides*, p. 31 n. 44; p. 33 n. 51.
73. *Cf.* XLVII 13 and note 24 there.
74. *Cf.* XLI 7; Plutarch *Moralia* 613 C. Of Asclepius, *cf.* LI 20.
75. The Nemeseis; *cf.* XX 20; Behr, *Aelius Aristides*, p. 156 n. 6.
76. Probably Zosimus; *cf.* XLVII 27 and note 47 there.
77. *i.e.* recollections of his dreams.
78. *Cf.* XL 21; Behr *Aelius Aristides*, p. 116.
79. In Pergamum; *cf.* Behr, *Aelius Aristides*, pp. 43-44, 59.
80. *Cf.* § 28 and note 50 there.
81. *Cf.* XLVIII 48 and note 81 there.
82. Literally, "with the greatest of care".
83. *i.e.* with no other end in view. Festugière, REG LXXXII (1969), p. 144, prefers Keil's interpretation, "as much as is enough for the author himself", since he feels that the subject must be Aristides.
84. There are magical implications in this word, *i.e.* to achieve power over it.
85. The priest was Flavius Asclepiades (?) (*cf. Altertümer von Pergamon VIII³*, pp. 7, 92 ff. (no. 45, where incidentally one might restore one fragmentary line of that inscription [ὁ κατὰ τὴν ἱερὰν φαρ]μακείαν). The temple wardens were C. Julius Asclepiacus and Philadelphus (*cf.* XLVII 58, XLVIII 30). For permission to dedicate such offerings, *cf. Altertümer von Pergamon VIII³*, p. 189 n. 113.
86. *i.e.* "Aristides, the son of Eudaemon, of Hadriani".
87. *Cf.* Behr, *Aelius Aristides*, p. 50 n. 35. Arrian *Anabasis* I 12. 5 makes the same sort of boast, but while awake.
88. *Cf.* Behr, *Aelius Aristides*, p. 158 n. 65.
89. Referring to the ritual exclamation, εἷς θεός, "God is one!", and to Aristides as the greatest orator; *cf.* Behr, *Aelius Aristides*, p. 50 n. 35, p. 158 n. 65.
90. Also in XXVIII 116; *cf.* Behr, *Aelius Aristides*, p. 41 n. 2, p. 117.
91. "God's gift". So far it is known on one inscription of Aristides, OGIS 709 = IGRR I 1070; *cf.* Behr, *Aelius Aristides*, p. 1 n. 1, p. 47 n. 73.
92. A title apparently synonymous with that of "the high priest of the provincial assembly of Asia", the highest provincial office; *cf.* § 101 ff.; J. Deininger, *Die Provinziallandtage*, pp. 41 ff.; Behr, *Studies on the Biography* § 7.
93. *Cf.* Behr, *Aelius Aristides*, p. 9 n. 19.
94. *Cf.* Behr, *Aelius Aristides*, p. 156. She had a famous temple in Smyrna, *cf.* XVII 10 and note 25 there.
95. *Cf.* Behr, *Aelius Aristides*, pp. 157-158 n. 63.
96. Unknown. Another philosopher from the school of the Platonist Caius; *cf.* Behr, *Aelius Aristides*, p. 54 n. 50.

97. *Cf.* Plato *Timaeus* 34 B.
98. *Cf.* XLVII 56.
99. In Smyrna; *cf.* Behr, *Aelius Aristides,* p. 65.
100. Which letter is not clear. Aristides most often cites the seventh and eighth epistles.
101. Caninius Celer, *ab epistulis Graecis* (certainly under Hadrian, and very probably still under Pius); *cf.* Behr, *Aelius Aristides,* p. 65 n. 16; *Studies on the Biography* § 6.
102. On this sense of μεμνῆσθαι Festugière, REG LXXXII (1969), p. 145, well compares Theocritus III 28 (to which could be added Apollonius Rhodius III 535). The verb may be used with an ellipse, as Gow on Theocritus *loc.cit.* thinks, "thought [and wondered] whether.....", or the verb itself may have the nuance of "to think over something" or of "to turn something over in one's mind". I doubt whether Festugière's "ask" is correct.
103. The genius of those born on the fourth day of any month; *cf.* Behr, *Aelius Aristides,* p. 1; *Studies on the Biography* § 1.
104. *Cf.* Behr, *Aelius Aristides,* pp. 43-44.
105. From this data and the fact that Aristides was born on the fourth day of a month is computed his birth date November 26, 117 A.D.; see my discussion in *Studies on the Biography* § 1. The horoscope needs interpretation. It should be noted that 1) the dream and the horoscope do not agree on the position of Jupiter. 2) the positions are (tacitly) given by the house system. The planets are in quartile aspect—which is horoscopically unfavorable—in the zodiac, but sextile in the houses. 3) while Leo lies in the tenth house, "Mid-heaven", Jupiter plainly does not. It is to be located in the eleventh house, "Good Fortune", and Mercury in the first house, "Horoscope", still beneath the horizon. In this latitude, the right ascension, the arc from the horizon to mid-heaven, is 81°. 4) the expression "both planets oriental" means that Jupiter and Mercury are to the west of the sun. 5) the positions are Mercury in Scorpio 14; Jupiter in Leo 23; and the sun in Sagittarius 4.
106. The name "Lysias" is derived from the verb *lyein,* "to end".
107. Perhaps Alexander of Cotiaeum; *cf.* oration XXXII; XLVII 23; Behr, *Aelius Aristides,* p. 10 n. 24.
108. In Mysia or Smyrna; *cf.* Behr, *Aelius Aristides,* pp. 84-86.
109. As I believe, C. Julius Quadratus Bassus, a Pergamene, consul suffectus 139 A.D., proconsul of Asia 153/154 A.D. An orator, *cf.* Philostratus *Vitae Sophistarum* p. 576 Olearius. He is to be distinguished from Statius Quadratus of XLVII 22; *cf.* Behr, *Aelius Aristides,* pp. 84-86; *Studies on the Biography* § 1 and § 5.
110. His problems in obtaining immunity from having to hold public office; *cf.* §§ 71-104.
111. One of the Flavii. The priesthood was hereditary; *cf.* § 46 and note 85 there.
112. For Asclepius' surgery, *cf.* Behr, *Aelius Aristides,* pp. 35-36.
113. A real compliment as compared to the qualified one in XXVII 22 (there a comparison of emperors).
114. *Cf.* the dream of C. Fannius in Pliny *Epistle* V 5. 5.
115. *Comicorum Atticorum Fragmenta* III Anonymous 235 Kock; *cf.* Athenaeus 337 B.
116. In Mysia; *cf.* Behr, *Aelius Aristides,* p. 109.
117. He had been dead for some 22 years; *cf.* XLVII 69 ff.
118. § 63.
119. In Mysia; *cf.* Behr, *Aelius Aristides,* pp. 79-82; *Studies on the Biography* § 6.
120. *Cf.* § 12 and note 21 there.

121. Apparently the orator (hence "comrade") Quadratus of § 63. "I think" is to be taken as rhetorical; *cf.* note 60 to § 31.
122. At Baris; *cf.* § 2; Behr, *Aelius Aristides,* p. 80.
123. The temple of Olympian and Ancestral Zeus; *cf.* § 1 and note 3 there.
124. The name of the office was εἰρηνάρχης, which Aristides avoids as not an Attic word (*cf.* note 163 to § 96). The function of the εἰρηνάρχης of Smyrna is vividly depicted in *Letter on the Martyrdom of Polycarp* 6-8; *cf.* Behr, *Aelius Aristides,* p. 81 n. 69.
125. Hadriani; *cf.* Behr, *Aelius Aristides,* pp. 4-5; *Studies on the Biography* § 2.
126. A legal quibble. Aristides was born in the district of Hadriani, but at the time of his birth Hadriani was not constituted as a πόλις (this happened in 123 A.D.) and so entitled to an εἰρηνάρχης. Therefore Aristides, being also a citizen of Smyrna, should only be liable to serve in Smyrna; *cf.* Behr, *Aelius Aristides,* p. 82 n. 72; *Studies on the Biography* § 6.
127. *i.e.* with what lawyer (ἀντίδικος), since there was none to represent the governor.
128. *Cf. Paroemiographorum Graecorum* I 403. The oracle was historical, being given in 278 B.C. during the incursion of the Galatian Brennus. Severus too came from Galatia. In the oracle "the white maidens" signified snow (*cf.* Valerius Maximus I Ext. 9; for other citations, *cf.* Parke and Wormell, *The Delphic Oracle* II, no. 329); in Aristides they mean letters.
129. In reply to an appeal filed in an earlier case; see § 96.
130. Antoninus Pius and Marcus Aurelius.
131. See the contemporary law in *Digesta* XXVII 1. 6. 2, which provided exemptions among other professions for practicing orators, 3 exemptions for small cities (as Hadriani), 4 for the sites of assizes, and 5 for the metropolises (as Smyrna). But this rigid prescription was somewhat undermined by another law (*ibid.* XXVII 1. 6. 10), which permitted exemptions above this number for an ill-defined category of οἱ ἄγαν ἐπιστήμονες, to which it would seem Aristides sought admission; *cf.* Behr, *Aelius Aristides,* p. 78 n. 58; *Studies on the Biography* § 6.
132. C. Avidius Heliodorus, prefect of Egypt 138-142 A.D., during Aristides' stay there; also a distinguished orator; *cf.* Behr, *Aelius Aristides,* p. 15 n. 44, p. 16 n. 46.
133. Perhaps an allusion to poor health (*cf.* Behr, *Studies on the Biography* § 6), or to Asclepius' providence (*cf.* Behr, *Aelius Aristides,* p. 82 n. 76).
134. *i.e.* previous governors, Festus (see § 104) and Pollio (see § 99).
135. It would seem that Severus held the *ius gladii,* which should have precluded an appeal to Rome, although later Aristides threatened one (§ 92); *cf.* Behr, *Aelius Aristides,* p. 82 n. 71; *Studies on the Biography* § 6.
136. In Mysia and Pergamum; *cf.* Behr, *Aelius Aristides,* p. 83.
137. Ephesus was the seat of government, although the governor also traveled throughout the province to hold court.
138. of Hadriani, who acted according to the legal fiction described at § 74; *cf.* Behr, *Aelius Aristides,* p. 83 n. 78.
139. *Cf.* § 28 and note 50 there.
140. *Cf.* § 78.
141. A typically neurotic remark; *i.e.* he was too sick to be bothered with these legal problems. If it were not for the appearance of the same phrase at § 106 and XLVIII 1, I would accept the interpretation of Festugière, REG LXXXII (1969), p. 146: "là était pour moi le corps du débat". Although to prevent confusion, I believe that one would have to assume a lacuna and restore *e.g.* τὸ σῶμα <τῆς γνώσεως> κτλ., "such for me was the substance of the judgment".

142. *i.e.* in Latin. The native tongue of both Rufinus and Severus was no doubt Greek, but this was official correspondence; *cf.* Behr, *Studies on the Biography* § 3.

143. In Smyrna; *cf.* Behr, *Aelius Aristides,* pp. 83-84.

144. March 3-5; *cf.* XVII 6; XXI 4; Behr, *Aelius Aristides,* p. 83 n. 80.

145. The governor had three legates.

146. I cannot agree with G.P. Burton, Journal of Roman Studies 65 (1975), p. 93 n. 15 and p. 95 n. 27, that this legate had charge of the assizes and Severus' presence in Smyrna was coincidental. At most the legate seems to have held court before and after the governor's stay; *cf.* §§ 96 and 98. In any case Aristides distinguishes between assize district and assizes; *cf.* §§ 78 and 106; Behr, *Studies on the Biography* § 6.

147. *Cf.* § 27 and note 46 there.

148. In other words, if Aristides wanted immunity, he should go to the Council of Smyrna, since he claimed Smyrna as his legal residence, and persuade them that he ought to be named as one of the immune orators; see note 131 to § 75.

149. At Smyrna; *cf.* Behr, *Aelius Aristides,* p. 84; *Studies on the Biography* § 6.

150. The prytaneis served as chairmen of the various boards of "generals", or standing committees of the Council. The election took place about July 1; *cf.* Behr, *Aelius Aristides,* p. 77 n. 55, p. 84 n. 82.

151. *Cf.* Behr, *Aelius Aristides,* p. 84; *Studies on the Biography* § 6.

152. Aeschylus *Seven Against Thebes* 1.

153. About an hour and a quarter.

154. An expression chosen from the great days of Athenian democracy.

155. Smyrna.

156. The εἰρηνάρχης; see § 72 ff.

157. of Hadriani.

158. *Cf.* § 81.

159. In Smyrna and Philadelphia; *cf.* Behr, *Aelius Aristides,* pp. 77-79; *Studies on the Biography* § 6.

160. T. Vitrasius Pollio, consul year unknown, proconsul of Asia 151/152 A.D.; *cf.* Behr, *Aelius Aristides,* p. 77 n. 56; *Studies on the Biography* § 1 and § 5.

161. *Cf.* § 14.

162. Literally, "whose business it was to be distressed".

163. Properly ἐκλογιστής, also avoided (*cf.* note 124 to § 72) as not Attic Greek. The tax collector would himself be responsible for any deficiencies in the taxes; *cf.* Behr, *Aelius Aristides,* p. 77 n. 54.

164. The answer is reported in § 75. Such an appeal may have been illegal without the governor's review; *cf.* Behr, *Aelius Aristides,* p. 78 n. 59; *Studies on the Biography* § 6.

165. Husband of Callityche, who was Aristides' foster sister; *cf.* Behr, *Aelius Aristides,* p. 9 n. 18.

166. M. ' Acilius Glabrio Cn. Cornelius Severus, who was consul ordinarius in this year—hence "famous". He was earlier himself a legate in Asia and seems to have been a native of the province; *cf.* Behr, *Aelius Aristides,* p. 78 n. 60; *Studies on the Biography* § 5.

167. For ὡς + genitive = infinitive in direct discourse (hence the emendation, "that....would lend a hand"), *cf.* XLVII 43; LI 23.

168. For Festus and the former decision, *cf.* § 100 ff. For the suplement ("and it was made... about us"), *cf.* Behr, *Studies on the Biography* § 6. On the importance of gaining "an opportunity" of catching the governor's attention, *cf.* §§ 106, 107.

169. Properly called, it would seem, the Boularch; *cf.* Behr, *Aelius Aristides,* p. 77 n. 55.

170. For this term, *cf.* LI 46 and *e.g.* L. Robert, *Études Anatoliennes,* p. 51; Revue de Philologie 41 (1967), p. 49.

171. In Smyrna; cf. Behr, *Aelius Aristides,* pp. 61-62; *Studies on the Biography* §§ 4 5, 6, 7.

172. On this man and the impossibility of retaining the reading of the manuscripts, "The sophist, whom I mentioned....", since "sophist" is an insulting term in Aristides, cf. Behr, *Aelius Aristides,* pp. 65-67, 106 n. 39; *Studies on the Biography* §§ 4 and 5. Whether he is P. Valerius Festus and identical with the honorand of CIL II 6084 is unimportant.

173. In the lacuna at § 98.

174. September 23; cf. OGIS 458 v. 50; Behr, *Aelius Aristides,* p. 61 n. 3.

175. To Smyrna.

176. An odd way of phrasing "the high priesthood of the Common (Provincial) Assembly of Asia". Aristides was only offered a nomination; cf. Behr, *Aelius Aristides,* p. 61 n. 4, p. 64 n. 15; *Studies on the Biography* § 7.

177. Cf. Pausanias VII 5, 9; Behr, *Aelius Aristides,* p. 62 n. 5; *Studies on the Biography* § 6. Presumably the temple named at XLVII 17 is different.

178. Cf. Plato *Gorgias* 469 D.

179. At Laodiceia ad Lycum; cf. Behr, *Aelius Aristides,* pp. 63-64; *Studies on the Biography* § 7.

180. There seem to have been three; cf. Behr, *Aelius Aristides,* p. 64 n. 14.

181. Laodiceia ad Lycum, the only city in Upper Phrygia where the Provincial Assembly met.

182. Cf. XLVII 27 and note 47 there.

183. I assume that this means that groups of three or four high priests were elected at a time to serve successively after one another and that Dio Chrysostom XXXV 10 also alludes to such a practice. The variation was intentional to give all the sites of the Provincial Assembly a chance to be the site of an election, because the Assembly regularly met three out of every four years at Ephesus, Pergamum, and Smyrna. On this and the cycle of electoral meetings, cf. Behr, *Aelius Aristides,* p. 64 n. 15; *Studies on the Biography* § 7. However, J. Deininger, *Die Provinziallandtage* (1965), pp. 39-40, feels that these high priests served concurrently at different sites.

184. At the Laneion estate. Later the scene is at Pergamum; cf. Behr, *Aelius Aristides,* pp. 64-68; *Studies on the Biography* § 6.

185. Cf. *Paroemiographorum Graecorum* II 686; Cicero *Epistulae ad Quintum* I 1. 45.

186. For the supplement ("I did not take... precinct"), cf. Behr, *Studies on the Biography* § 6. It is in part ironic (cf. note 187). The term θεραπευτής, "worshipper" in a cult association (cf. XXX 15 and note 33 there), is used as the titulature of other provincial offices would be; e.g. cf. IGRR IV 821, 822.

187. *i.e.* Asclepius. The remark is also ironic.

188. In Pergamum; cf. Behr, *Aelius Aristides,* pp. 56-57.

189. If he means Laneion, he only mentioned it by name at XLIX 42.

190. 141-142 A.D.; cf. Behr, *Aelius Aristides,* pp. 15-21.

191. I understand this to mean that Aristides does not intend to state his adversaries' legal claims on the property. Festugière, REG LXXXII (1969), p. 149, unreasonably puzzled, I think, offers a wildly improbable interpretation.

192. A statue of Hadrian stood in the library of the Temple; cf. Behr, *Aelius Aristides,* p. 29 n. 31; *Altertümer von Pergamon VIII³,* p. 29 (no. 6).

193. I think Q. Fabius Julianus Optatianus, perhaps consul 128 A.D., proconsul of Asia 145/146 A.D.; cf. Behr, *Aelius Aristides,* pp. 56-57; *Studies on the Biography* § 5.

194. Cf. § 28 and note 50 there.

NOTES TO LI

1. For the purpose and time of composition, see note 1 to oration XLVII. The work is divided into the following sections:
A. § 1-10 Trip to Temple of Zeus
B. § 11-17 First trip to Cyzicus
C. § 18-37 Trips to Pergamum, Smyrna, and Ephesus
D. § 38-41 The oratorical display at Smyrna
E. § 42-55 Second trip to Cyzicus and return
F. § 56-67 The great dream.
2. In Smyrna and Mysia, just after Aristides' recovery from smallpox; *cf.* Behr, *Aelius Aristides,* p. 97.
3. The Hermus.
4. Literally "to join work to work"; *cf.* the proverb "to join thread to thread" in III 98; Strattis *Comicorum Atticorum Fragmenta* I frg. 38 K.
5. A symptom of smallpox; *cf.* Behr, *Aelius Aristides,* pp. 166-167.
6. In Mysia and Cyzicus; *cf.* Behr, *Aelius Aristides,* pp. 100-102.
7. The name of a feast day. For the time of this celebration, *cf.* Behr, *Aelius Aristides,* p. 101 n. 20.
8. Unknown; *cf.* Behr, *Aelius Aristides,* p. 100.
9. *Cf.* Homer *Odyssey* VIII 11 ff.
10. Today called Ilica Köy; *cf.* Behr, *Aelius Aristides,* p. 6 n. 8 c.
11. About 5 miles.
12. Lake Aphnitis, today called Manyas.
13. About 15 miles.
14. About 40 miles.
15. Oration XXVII; *cf.* Behr, *Aelius Aristides,* p. 101.
16. In Cyzicus; *cf.* Behr, *Aelius Aristides,* p. 102.
17. *Cf.* XLIX 41 and note 57 there.
18. For the phrase, *cf.* XXXVI 36.
19. *Cf.* Behr, *Aelius Aristides,* p. 6 n. 8 c.
20. About 50 miles.
21. In Mysia; *cf.* Behr, *Aelius Aristides,* pp. 103-104.
22. The Mysian or Apian Plain; *cf.* XLVII 58 and the inscription in Athenische Mitteilungen 1904, p. 280 (as supplemented in the Loeb edition of Aristides I, p. xvi n. a).
23. A direct sign that there would be clouds and rain.
24. Philumene, the daughter of Callityche; *cf. e.g.* XLVII 45; Behr *Aelius Aristides,* p. 9 n. 18.
25. 1200 feet.
26. *Cf.* XLVII 24 and note 43 there.
27. In Mysia and the Temple of Apollo; *cf.* Behr, *Aelius Aristides,* p. 1 n. 2, p. 104; *Studies on the Biography* § 1.
28. I understand this to allude both to the practice of haruspicy and to astrology (the dream occurred on a fourth, the monthly celebration of Aristides' birth date). In haruspicy, "God" is a name of a part of the liver of the sacrificial animal, in astrology of the ninth house. Gods are named "Deliverers" from fate in Iamblichus *De Mysteriis* VIII 7. On this whole question, see Behr, *Studies on the Biography* § 1. Both Keil and Festugière, REG LXXXII (1969), pp. 150-151, understand "God" as Asclepius and consequently place a lacuna after θεόν.
29. Either of death or of a new disease.
30. *Cf.* L 58.
31. For this meaning of προεξελθεῖν, *cf.* § 18, which renders improbable the inter-

pretation of Festugière, REG LXXXII (1969), p. 150: "qu' elle fût morte avant mon arrivée (where ?)".
32. In Mysia, at the Temple of Apollo; *cf.* Behr, *Aelius Aristides*, p. 104.
33. Asclepius' son in the Pergamene tradition; *cf.* Behr, *Aelius Aristides*, p. 153 n. 28. His name means "bringing a conclusion or end" and in this dream may refer either to Philumene's death or to the effecting of the prophecy.
34. Where Philumene died. From the ancestral hearth apparently to Laneion.
35. Michenaud-Dierkens, *Les Rêves dans les "Discours Sacrés"*, p. 93 n. 18 wish to keep παρ' of the manuscripts and render "heard from Philumene". But the oracles were given to Alcimus, and surely not by Philumene.
36. The loops of the intestine.
37. This is ambiguous. It refers either to Aristides' way of life or to his stomach trouble.
38. "Safe-Abiding".
39. To Laneion, as it seems; *cf.* note 34.
40. *Cf.* § 12.
41. Athena; *cf.* XLVIII 41.
42. He died of smallpox; *cf.* XLVIII 44.
43. In Mysia, near the Temple of Apollo; *cf.* Behr, *Aelius Aristides*, p. 104.
44. In Pergamum; *cf.* Behr, *Aelius Aristides*, pp. 104-105. Probably the celebration of the *Nuncupatio votorum* on January 3, the vows for the new year, is meant. This was the main event of the New Year's festivities. For this reason I once conjectured <αἱ> ἐπευχαί (*cf.* Behr, *Aelius Aristides*, p. 104 n. 27), but I now think that Aristides intentionally chose the archaic and rare word ἐπίβδαι (generally used for the days following the Athenian feast of the Apaturia), and that we must understand ταύτης. The ἐπίβδαι, in any case, were not the first of the year.
45. *Cf.* Homer *Odyssey* IX 142.
46. *Cf.* the similar miracle told by Gregory of Tours *Historia Francorum* X 29, where rain clouds separate in two and leave a dry path between the two sections.
47. About 38 miles.
48. *Cf.* XLVII 11; Behr, *Aelius Aristides*, p. 32 n. 48.
49. In Smyrna; *cf.* Behr, *Aelius Aristides*, p. 105.
50. *Cf.* XLVII 22; Behr, *Aelius Aristides*, p. 307.
51. Of the oracle.
52. Obviously a rival. Perhaps Ptolemy of Naucratis; *cf.* Behr, *Aelius Aritides*, p. 105 n. 34.
53. *i.e.* donate grain or oil to the city or pay for some public building or temple.
54. The notice that Aristides was going to declaim.
55. In Ephesus; *cf.* Behr, *Aelius Aristides*, p. 105.
56. Of victory.
57. In Smyrna; *cf.* Behr, *Aelius Aristides*, pp. 106-107.
58. A sarcastic expression for one who "hogged" the stage for his own speeches.
59. Perhaps Heraclides of Lycia; *cf.* Behr, *Aelius Aristides*, p. 106 n. 40.
60. Oration XXXIV; *cf.* Behr, *Aelius Aristides*, p. 107 n. 41; *Studies on the Biography* § 4.
61. This audience was as attentive as the students of a lecturing orator would be. For the meaning of σχολῆς, *cf.* XXVIII 129, L 29. The Greek does not say "filled", but "acquired".
62. An allusion to the long periods which Aristides was accustomed to employ; *cf.* L 22.
63. In Cyzicus; *cf.* Behr, *Aelius Aristides*, p. 108.
64. Of Cyzicus; *cf.* Behr, *Aelius Aristides*, p. 101 n. 20.
65. For fasting, *cf.* § 11 (by implication). The poor quality of the water seems

implied by Aristides' thirst in § 15 and the praise of the water at Laneion in § 17. Festugière, REG LXXXII, p. 152, interprets the poor quality of the water as that of Aristides' urine, but Aristides nowhere mentions such an ailment.

66. The assizes may have been held in Cyzicus then; *cf.* Behr, *Aelius Aristides,* p. 108 n. 48.

67. Such is Keil's emendation; *cf.* L 98. The manuscript reading means "I began my prediction", which Festugière, REG LXXXII, p. 150 n. 1, prefers.

68. *Cf.* Homer *Iliad* IX 223 ff.

69. Actually Marcus Aurelius was then sole emperor. This is a dream. Verus had just died and perhaps Commodus is meant as Marcus' heir and an obvious candidate for Caesar; *cf.* XXXIV 61 and Behr, *Aelius Aristides,* p. 108 n. 48.

70. Festugière, REG LXXXII, p. 152, understands τούτοις τοῖς λόγοις as referring to the words, "For the good *etc."* But after πειρώμενος τῶν λόγων, I think that this is less likely.

71. Presumably in Aristides' record of his dreams; *cf.* XLVIII 2.

72. *Cf.* L 99 and note 170 there.

73. The following events in Mysia; *cf.* Behr, *Aelius Aristides,* p. 108.

74. *Cf.* Behr, *Aelius Aristides,* pp. 4-6, n. 3 and n. 6.

75. In Mysia; *cf.* Behr, *Aelius Aristides,* pp. 108-109.

76. About a mile and a quarter.

77. Cold baths seem to be mentioned only in Hippocrates Περὶ Διαίτης II 57. 10. There is, of course, no such specific advice in the Hippocratic corpus.

78. Aristides' formula for "a double dream", a dream within a dream, as this is; *cf.* Behr, *Aelius Aristides,* p. 195.

79. *Cf.* XLVII 20.

80. *Cf.* XLVII 34.

81. *i.e.* of bathing.

82. The river is the modern Kara Dere; *cf.* Behr, *Aelius Aristides,* p. 6 n. 8 b. Aristides was staying at Laneion.

83. For this practice, *cf.* Athenaeus 24 C-E; Behr, *Aelius Aristides,* p. 38 n. 75.

84. About 2 miles.

85. About 3/4 of a mile.

86. *Cf.* Hippocrates *De Insomniis* 89. 18.

87. In Mysia; *cf.* Behr, *Aelius Aristides,* pp. 108-110.

88. For these, *cf.* XXXI 14.

89. Aristides' Pergamene doctor during the time of his incubation, 145-147 A.D. (*cf.* XLVII 13 and note 24 there). The name may have arisen in this dream because of the contemporary Athenian sophist Theodotus (*cf.* Philostratus *Vitae Sophistarum,* p. 566 Olearius); *cf.* Behr, *Aelius Aristides,* p. 14 n. 34.

90. In reality this would not be possible since the chamber is on the west side.

91. Possibly Lucius of Macedonia, a Platonist; *cf.* Philostratus *Vitae Sophistarum,* p. 557 Olearius; Behr, *Aelius Aristides,* p. 13 n. 34.

92. *Cf.* L 62.

93. This seems to be the meaning; for ἐπισημαίνεσθαι, *cf.* XLVIII 9.

94. Where Aristotle taught. It lay just outside the city, to the northeast.

95. "The one hundred foot temple". Another name for the Parthenon (properly its cella), *cf.* Plutarch *Pericles* XIII. 4, *Cato Maior* V. 3.

96. For sale perhaps.

97. On the symbol of eggs, *cf.* Behr, *Aelius Aristides,* p. 200 n. 29.

98. I am reminded of the saying of the Stoic Zeno (*Stoicorum Veterum Fragmenta* vol. I 266) that cities should be adorned not with offerings, but by the virtues of their inhabitants.

99. His name is unknown.

100. An omen, signifying that the dreamer should remain at home, and so interpreted in § 67; cf. Artemidorus II 9 (p. 113, 11 Pack); Behr, *Aelius Aristides,* p. 197, for similar prognostications in this dream.
101. The man who examined the entrails of the sacrificial animals.
102. Presumably because they agreed with the omen of the lightning.
103. *Nomen omen!* "Eudoxus" means "glorious", cf. § 67.
104. See note 100 to § 64.

NOTES TO LII

1. For the purpose and time of composition, see note 1 to oration XLVII. The work, which is only a fragment, is not incomplete because Aristides died before finishing it, as the Byzantine scholar Nicephorus Gregoras has suggested (cf. Behr, *Aelius Aristides,* p. 91 n. 1). Rather it stood at the end of the archetype, whose concluding leaves were lost. The loss is a pity, since it is apparent from the opening dream that in this *Tale* Aristides would have given an account of his great oratorical triumphs between the years 155-165 A.D.
2. *Cf.* Behr, *Aelius Aristides,* pp. 86-90. For the departure from the Aesepus, cf. L 12.
3. The center of the worship of Asclepius and the parent temple of all those throughout the world. IG IV², 1, 577 seems to me to be a dedication, which Aristides made during his stay at Epidaurus.
4. Frg. 53 Hense. C. Musonius Rufus was a Stoic, who enjoyed the distinction of having been twice exiled from Rome, once under Nero and again under Titus. He was also the teacher of Epictetus.
5. This led to oration I, *The Panathenaicus* in 155 A.D.
6. This led to oration XXVI, *Regarding Rome* in 155 A.D.

NOTES TO LIII

1. This work seems to date from the last period of Aristides' life, after 177 A.D., when he was in retirement at Laneion and had become accustomed to send his speeches to their recipients. The reference to spring and Zeus Euangelios in § 3 may point to the month of May as the time of composition. The fragmentary state of the work is less likely to have been caused by Aristides' death than by the loss of the majority of the speech in the archetype itself, where its original position, I feel, was after oration XXXIX; cf. Behr, *Aelius Aristides,* p. 114 n. 78; Lenz-Behr, *P. Aelii Aristidis Opera* I fasc. 1, p. XCV. The speech has been translated by E. and L. Edelstein, *Asclepius* (1945), vol. 1, Testimony 805.
   It is divided into the following sections:
A. § 1-3 Proem. News of the event
B. § 4 Propriety of Aristides' composition
C. § 5 Mythological times.
2. *Iliad* IV 455.
3. An event unconnected with the preceding quotation; cf. *Iliad* IV 279.
4. Literally "I felt my body become lighter"; cf. XXX 26; L 6; Behr, *Aelius Aristides,* pp. 163-164.
5. For this temple, cf. IGRR IV 336.
6. In the *Hermologium Florentinum* there is a month Εὐαγγέλιος for April 24-May 23. Hence perhaps Aristides' preceding allusion to "a spring day".
7. *Cf.* L 73 (of Smyrna, and in an official sense). The Edelsteins (see note 1)

translate the passage: "although clearly that was less fitting for me than for anyone else in the city". For ἧττον οὐδενός, cf. Plato *Protagoras* 324 D οὐδενὸς βελτίους.

8. For Hermes and the Nymphs, cf. Fränkel, *Altertümer von Pergamon VIII²*, no. 183.

9. "He of the handsome child"; *i.e.* Asclepius; cf. XLVIII 18.

10. For the Cabiri in Pergamum, cf. IGRR IV 360, where it is said that in Pergamum the Cabiri, sons of Uranus, first beheld the new born Zeus; cf. also IGRR IV 294. These deities, whose precise functions vary, but are generally of a protective nature, are most normally associated with Samothrace, although they are located in other places as well.

Addendum

Add to note 107 (p. 407) to XXXVI 82: Josephus *BJ* 3.520 reports that some thought that the spring Capharnaum = Capernaum, near lake Gennesar(et), was an effluent of the Nile because it contained a species of fish found in Egypt. These waters are relatively near Scythopolis. The story shows that there existed a popular tradition in Aristides' day which connected at least one body of water in this region with the Nile.

APPENDIX

The following list contains those places where I differ from the Greek text of orations XVII-LIII published by Bruno Keil in his edition of 1898. The page and line numbers in the list refer to Keil's edition. I have not included corrections of misprints, changes in spelling, accentuation, and punctuation, except when the last radically affects the sense. Where names other than Keil's appear, it means that I translate the reading which is given there. The appearance of Keil's name (unless I note that I have taken a suggestion of his from the apparatus of his edition) always indicates the rejection of his text. I have not included the arguments for these alterations, palaeographical, testimonial, historical, or otherwise. These as well as changes in and augmentation of the apparatus will be found in volume II of the edition of Aristides to be published by Brill. In the list below the symbol O indicates a consensus, more or less, of the manuscripts. The letters ABCDQRSTUV refer to various manuscripts described in Keil's edition or in volume I of the edition of the Greek text published by Brill.

XVII

5 (p. 2, 9 K.) [ἀπὸ] τῆς brackets Behr; τῶν τῆς Keil.
5 (p. 2, 18 K.) ὥρᾳ πρώτῃ O; ὧραι πρῶται Keil.
6 (p. 2, 21 K.) κατὰ τὸν νεὼν Behr: κατὰ τῶν νεὼν T: κατὰ τῶν θεῶν AR: κάτα ἐκ τῶν θεῶν VDU.
7 (p. 3, 1 K.) ἆρα θρυλεῖται O; διαθρυλεῖται Keil.
7 (p. 3, 8 K.) καθαπερεὶ—ἔχοντα T: καθάπερ οἱ—ἔχοντες O, which words are bracketed by Keil.
8 (p. 3, 12 K.) τῇσδε O; τήνδε Wilamowitz, with Keil's approval.
8 (p. 3, 13 K.) πόλεως εἶναι O: πόλεως A, with Keil's approval.
9 (p. 3, 21 K.) μικρὸν O: μικρὰ A, with Keil's approval.
10 (p. 4, 2 K.) [ὥσπερ δι' ἀγαλμάτων] bracketed by Behr; [ὥσπερ] alone bracketed by Wilamowitz, with Keil's approval.
10 (p. 4, 9 K.) ἐκδέχεται, <καὶ στενωπός τε ἐπώνυμος ἱερῶν> supplemented by Behr; a lacuna is indicated by Keil.
10 (p. 4, 10 K.) αὖθις ὁ κάλλιστος Behr: ὁ κάλλιστος αὖθις O.
11 (p. 4, 18 K.) καὶ—ἀντ' ἀγορῶν were bracketed by Keil.

11 (p. 4, 18 K.) [καὶ στενωποὶ] omitted by VU, bracketed by Behr.
12 (p. 4, 24 K.) μιμήσασθαι bracketed by Keil.
14 (p. 5, 16 K.) after προιὼν a lacuna is indicated by Keil.
14 (p. 5, 18 K.) after ἐκβολαῖς Keil has marked a corruption.
15 (p. 5, 23 K.) before οὐκ Keil has marked a corruption.
16 (p. 6, 15 K.) ὅσον O; ὅλον Keil.
16 (p. 6, 17 K.) <ἀραίᾳ> χώρᾳ Behr: ὥραις O.
17 (p. 6, 18 K.) ταῦτα <τό> γε παντελές Behr: ταῦτά γε ἐν τέλει O; after τέλει a lacuna is indicated by Keil.
22 (p. 8, 2 K.) τῇ πόλει Behr: τῆς πόλεως O.

XVIII

title μονῳδία ἐπὶ σμύρνῃ TDU: ἐπὶ σμύρνῃ μονῳδία ARV.
2 (p. 9, 7 K.) after γοναὶ a lacuna is indicated by Keil.
2 (p. 9, 9 K.) after ἁπασῶν Behr punctuates as an aposiopesis.
3 (p. 9, 11 K.) στάσεις O: συστάσεις Keil.
5 (p. 9, 24 K.) ἀωρίαν [ἃ] <κινησάσῃ> Behr: ἀωρίαν ἃ archetype of O, as it seems; ἀωρίαν α....sic Keil.
5 (p. 10, 1 K.) παρέστης Behr: παρέσται O.
5 (p. 10, 2 K.) [ἐκφανὴς] is bracketed by Behr; after ἐκφανὴς a lacuna is indicated by Keil.
8 (p. 11, 7 K.) δόντων Behr: διδόντων O.
9 (p. 11, 15 K.) χορός, <οἵῳ δράματι νῦν ἐμέλλετε τοσοῦτον> is supplemented by Behr; a lacuna is indicated by Keil.

XIX

1 (p. 12, 5 K.) ὁ δαίμων ἑτέραν O: ἑτέραν ὁ δαίμων A, with Keil's approval.
6 (p. 14, 8 K.) τὸ πρᾶγμα διαλέγεσθαι Behr: διαλέγεσθαι τὸ πρᾶγμα O; after διαλέγεσθαι a lacuna is indicated by Keil.
14 (p. 16, 15 K.) μὲν TDU: μὲν οὖν AR, with Keil's approval.

XX

10 (p. 19, 14 K.) τῆς <τε> Kaibel, with Keil's approval.
11 (p. 19, 25 K.) <τῷ χορῷ> τῷ is supplemented by Behr after U; a lacuna is indicated by Keil.
12 (p. 20, 3 K.) πόλεων AR: πόλεως TDU.

14 (p. 20, 20 K.) [πόλεως] is bracketed by Behr; it was already suspected by Kaibel.
17 (p. 21, 8 K.) ἑαυτοῦ ἐποιήσατο TDU: ἐποιήσατο ἑαυτοῦ AR.

XXI

3 (p. 23, 18 K.) [Ταντάλου καὶ Πέλοπος] is bracketed by Behr.
5 (p. 24, 18 K.) καὶ is bracketed by Keil.
8 (p. 25, 10 K.) ὅ τε γὰρ [ἦν] καιρὸς Behr; after ὅτε γὰρ ἦν O a lacuna is indicated by Keil.
15 (p. 27, 15 K.) περὶ τὸν Μέλητα is bracketed by Keil.

XXII

2 (p. 28, 13 K.) μείζω O; μείζον' Keil.
3 (p. 28, 20 K.) [ποιῆσαι] is bracketed by Behr; <περι>ποιῆσαι Keil.
7 (p. 29, 28 K.) οὐ is bracketed by Keil and οὐ<δὲ> τὸν Keil.
8 (p. 30, 15 K.) ὅσα <ἂν> Behr (ὅσ' ἂν Kaibel).

XXIII

title [ταῖς πόλεσιν] is bracketed by Behr after Keil.
3 (p. 32, 16 K.) δεδρακότων Behr: δεδωκότων O.
8 (p. 34, 8 K.) ὡς εἰπεῖν is bracketed by Keil.
9 (p. 34, 12 K.) before ὡς a lacuna is indicated by Keil.
11 (p. 34, 27 K.) <μηδ' ἄχθεσθαι> τῷ is supplemented in part by Keil in his apparatus.
22 (p. 37, 11 K.) εἰκὸς <ἡμᾶς οἵτινες ἐν ταύτῃ τὰς τέχνας> is supplemented by Behr; a lacuna is indicated by Reiske and Keil.
24 (p. 37, 27 K.) <καὶ> αὐτὴν Keil, who later rejected the supplement.
27 (p. 38, 27 K.) τὸν τῆς παρακλήσεως is bracketed by Keil.
42 (p. 43, 7 K.) περὶ τῶν πραγμάτων is bracketed by Keil.
52 (p. 46, 16 K.) ᾤχετο <διὰ τὴν τότε στάσιν, ἐν τοῖς κακίστοις ἦσαν, ἀλλ' αὖθις> is supplemented by Behr; a lacuna is indicated by Keil.
52 (p. 46, 16 K.) κατελθόντος Behr: κατελθόντες O.
53 (p. 46, 23 K.) πάρεστι is bracketed by Keil.
59 (p. 48, 12 K.) [καὶ] is bracketed by Reiske; a lacuna is placed before καὶ by Keil.

64 (p. 49, 15 K.) [αὐτοὺς], omitted by T, is bracketed by Behr; it was already suspected by Keil.
64 (p. 49, 19 K.) κυρίους O; κυρίως Keil.
64 (p. 49, 21 K.) οὐκ <ἦν> ἄρξασθαι Behr; ἄρξασθαι οὐ Keil.
67 (p. 50, 19 K.) ῥήματα Behr: χρήματα O.
71 (p. 51, 26 K.) [ὃ καὶ—ἀλλήλοις] is bracketed by Behr; the whole is preserved, except that εἰ καὶ is read by Keil.
75 (p. 52, 28-29 K.) καὶ ταῖς—ὁμιλίαις is bracketed by Keil.
77 (p. 53, 9 K.) [ὡρῶν] is bracketed by Behr.
80 (p. 54, 12 K.) πρὸς ὑμᾶς is bracketed by Keil.

XXIV

6 (p. 56, 17-18 K.) [περὶ τῶν—ταῦτα] is bracketed by Behr; it was already suspected by Wilamowitz and Sieveking; ἀλλὰ—ταῦτα is omitted by S and by Canter, bracketed by Keil.
6 (p. 56, 18 K.) σαφῶς οὕτως Behr: σαφῶς αὐτῷ O; and εὖ <γὰρ> Behr. πείσεσθαι and σαφῶς αὐτῷ seem corrupt to Keil.
8 (p. 57, 14 K.) οὐδ' ἐννοεῖν Behr: οὐδ' εὑρεῖν O; οὐδὲ ζητεῖν Keil.
8 (p. 57, 16 K.) ταῖς ἰδίαις οἰκίαις Behr: τοῖς ἰδίοις οἴκοις O.
10 (p. 57, 25 K.) οὕτως D: omitted by O; deleted by Wilamowitz and Behr.
13 (p. 58, 24 K.) πάσας <διαιρεῖν εἰς δύο γένη καὶ παραινεῖν τὴν μὲν ἀγαθὴν φιλεῖν, τὴν δ' ἑτέραν> is supplemented by Behr; a lacuna is indicated by Keil.
20 (p. 60, 26 K.) καὶ τοῦτο <δείκνυται τῷ τοὺς παλαιοὺς πολλάκις ἑλέσθαι τυραννίδα, τῆς ἐλευθερίας παραχωρήσαντας, εἰς τὴν κατάλυσιν ὑπαρχούσης στάσεως.> is supplemented by Behr; a lacuna before καὶ τοῦτο is indicated by Keil.
23 (p. 61, 29 K.) ἦν is omitted by TU and deleted by Behr; it was already suspected by Keil.
31 (p. 63, 13 K.) συννοσεῖν Behr: συνοίσειν O; before συνοίσειν a lacuna is indicated by Reiske and Keil.
32 (p. 63, 20 K.) χαλεπώτατον O; χαλεπώτερον Keil, who later rejected this emendation.
32 (p. 63, 23 K.) ἑκόντες is omitted by A, with Keil's approval.
34 (p. 64, 13 K.) after κρείττους a lacuna is indicated by Keil.
38 (p. 65, 16 K.) νίκην O; δίκην Keil.
40 (p. 66, 2 K.) [αἰσχύνεσθαι] is bracketed by Behr; the word is saved and after it καὶ is added by Keil.

APPENDIX TO XXIV-XXV 451

40 (p. 66, 4-5 K.) [νομίσαντας λαμβάνειν] is bracketed by Behr.
58 (p. 71, 13-14 K.) [ὅς κε (τε AU, with Keil's approval)—ἐπιπείθηται] is bracketed by Wilamowitz.
58 (p. 71, 15 K.) after ἔχειν a lacuna is indicated by Keil.

XXV

4 (p. 73, 5 K.) <καὶ> [ἑτέρων] Behr, a comma placed before <καὶ>; before ἑτέρων a lacuna is indicated by Keil.
5 (p. 73, 14 K.) after ἱκανὴν Keil adds ἄν.
9 (p. 74, 12 K.) ἀμφοτέρως Behr: ἀμφοτέρων O.
9 (p. 74, 19 K.) σποδοῦ Behr: σκύλου TSD: σκοπέλου T in its margin, S in its margin, U; οἰκοπέδου Keil.
14 (p. 76, 4 K.) ἐπικαταβάλητε O; καταβάλητε Keil.
14 (p. 76, 5 K.) προκατέδυ TSD: κατέδυ U, with Keil's approval.
15 (p. 76, 10 K.) κἂν is bracketed by Keil.
15 (p. 76, 11 K.) [πολέμων] is bracketed by Behr; πολεμίων Keil.
17 (p. 76, 23 K.) before εἰ μὲν a lacuna is indicated by Keil.
20 (p. 77, 18 K.) <λιμέσι> [πύργοις] Wilamowitz.
20 (p. 77, 23 K.) [κατ' οἰκίας] is bracketed by Behr.
20 (p. 77, 24 K.) ἐξ οἰκιῶν is bracketed by Keil.
23 (p. 78, 9 K.) after προσεδόκων a lacuna is indicated by Keil.
25 (p. 79, 2 K.) σωμάτων O: σώματα Keil.
25 (p. 79, 2 K.) τάφων Behr: τάφοι O.
28 (p. 79, 21 K.) διωρυχῆς TSU; διώρυχος Keil.
29 (p. 80, 6 K.) μυθολογήματα is bracketed by Keil.
32 (p. 80, 29 K.) παριστᾶν [καὶ δεικνύναι] O with brackets by Behr; παριστάναι [δεικνύναι] Keil.
32 (p. 81, 1 K.) βουλευτήριον <ἔχοντα> Behr; before θέατρον a lacuna is indicated by Keil at the suggestion of Reiske.
33 (p. 81, 7 K.) <ἔστ'> ἐπιμαρτύρασθαι Keil.
33 (p. 81, 15 K.) after προσήκοντες a lacuna is indicated by Keil.
43 (p. 83, 29 K.) οὐδὲν <ἄν> Keil.
43 (p. 84, 3 K.) ἐπαγγέλλειν is bracketed by Keil.
46 (p. 84, 26-27 K.) ἡμέρας, οὐχ ὅλης, μιᾶς Behr: μιᾶς ἡμέρας, οὐχ ὅλης O; the passage is marked as corrupt by Keil.
49 (p. 85, 25 K.) τότε ἔχειν O; τὸ τελεῖν Kaibel, with Keil's approval.
51 (p. 86, 23 K.) ποῦ O; ὅπου Keil.
55 (p. 87, 19 K.) [ἐξέσται] <θαρροῦντες ἐλπίσαιτ' ἄν> Behr; ἕξετε Dindorf, with Keil's approval.

55 (p. 87, 20 K.) συνεπιλήψεσθαι <τῆς ἀναλήψεως> Behr; συνεπιλήψεσθαι is bracketed and after it a lacuna is indicated by Keil.
56 (p. 87, 25 K.) ὑμῖν Behr: ἀνθρώπων O; [ἀνθρώπων] <ἡ παρὰ τοῦ> Keil.
56 (p. 88, 1 K.) [εἶναι] is bracketed by Behr.
60 (p. 88, 30 K.) τῆς om U; bracketed by Reiske, with Keil's approval.
60 (p. 89, 1 K.) δύναται O; ἀνεῖται Keil.
66 (p. 90, 13 K.) δ' ἂν O; δὴ Keil.

XXVI

1 (p. 91, 10 K.) οὖν S, with Keil's approval; omitted by O and deleted by Behr.
2 (p. 92, 2 K.) οὖν is bracketed by Wilamowitz, with Keil's approval.
4 (p. 92, 19 K.) ἀλλ' ἢ O: ἀλλὰ Keil.
4 (p. 92, 19 K.) δεικνύειν <γε> Wilamowitz, with Keil's approval.
8 (p. 93, 22 K.) τῇδε O; τῇσδε Keil.
9 (p. 93, 28 K.) ὡς εἰπεῖν Behr: εἰπεῖν ὡς O; εἰπεῖν ἔστιν Wilamowitz, with Keil's approval.
10 (p. 94, 12 K.) δὴ O; μὴ Reiske, with Keil's approval.
11 (p. 95, 4 K.) <ἡμέραν> [<μέχρι> φθινοπώρου περιτροπῆς] Behr: φθινοπώρου περιτροπήν O.
13 (p. 95, 14 K.) [ὅτι περ—ὁλκάσιν] is bracketed by Behr; the words already seemed corrupt to Keil.
13 (p. 95, 21 K.) εἰς is bracketed by Keil.
14 (p. 95, 24 K.) μὴ ἔχοντος τοῦ λόγου seem corrupt to Keil.
18 (p. 97, 17 K.) ὅπως ἀεὶ κατέχειν εἰδότες, ἀλλ' οὐδὲ Behr: ὅπως ἂν ἀεὶ κατέχειν εἰδότες οὐδὲ O.
24 (p. 98, 26 K.) μεγάλην O; μεγίστην Kaibel, with Keil's approval.
27 (p. 99, 24 K.) ἢ O; ἂν Keil.
27 (p. 99, 28-29 K.) ἐοικότες σατράπαις ἐρήμοις TB: σατράπας ἔρημοι DU, with Keil's approval.
29 (p. 100, 16 K.) ἡ and γῆ are bracketed by Keil.
29 (p. 100, 21 K.) ἐκκεκαθαρμένος <πάσης ταραχῆς, κύκλος περιέχει τὴν ὑμετέραν ἀρχήν.> is supplemented by Behr; a lacuna is indicated by Keil.
29 (p. 100, 23 K.) ἡγεμόνος is bracketed by Keil.
30 (p. 100, 24 K.) [ὑπὸ] is bracketed by Behr; ὑπὸ—ἄρχεται seems corrupt to Keil.

38 (p. 102, 17-18 K.) <παρ' ὑμῖν δὲ νῦν ἔξεστι φεύγοντα ἁλόντα μὴ στέργειν τῇ γνώσει> μηδὲ τῷ νενικῆσθαι παρὰ τὴν ἀξίαν—κρατήσαντα Behr: παρὰ τὴν ἀξίαν—κρατήσαντα μηδὲ τῷ νενικῆσθαι O; a lacuna before παρὰ is indicated by Keil.
40 (p. 103, 7 K.) after χρῆσθαι a lacuna is indicated by Keil.
43 (p. 103, 26 K.) τρίχα Behr: ἄκρα O.
45 (p. 104, 4 K.) [ἑκόντας] μόνους Behr; ἑκόντας ἀσμένους Keil.
45 (p. 104, 7 K.) αὐτοῖς Reiske: αὐτοῖς TS, bracketed by Keil.
47 (p. 104, 19 K.) [τὸν αὐτὸν τρόπον ἀπ' ἐκείνων] is bracketed by Behr; [τὸν αὐτὸν τρόπον] ὑπ' (Reiske) ἐκείνων Keil after Dindorf.
50 (p. 105, 16 K.) Λακεδαιμονίων <Θηβαίους> Keil.
51 (p. 106, 1 K.) ἀδικοῦσινBehr: ἄρχουσιν O.
51 (p. 106, 1 K.) πλοῦτον <οὐ θαυμάσαι> Behr: πλοῦς τε Keil.
54 (p. 106, 30 K.) ἐν οἷς O: ὅποι Wilamowitz, with Keil's approval.
59 (p. 108, 6 K.) εἰ Behr: ἢ O.
62 (p.108, 21 K.) τούτους ἐν αὐτοῖς εἰσροῦν Behr: τούτου σὺν αὐτοῖς εἰς ῥοῦν O; the passage is marked as corrupt by Keil.
62 (p. 108, 22 K.) <οὔτε> is added before τῇδε by Keil.
65 (p. 109, 24 K.) <ἣν παρέχει καὶ> ἡ is supplemented by Behr; a lacuna is indicated by Keil.
66 (p. 109, 30 K.) μέγα γε καὶ οὐ κενόν· <καὶ ὑμεῖς γεγόνατε μόνοι τῶν ἐλθόντων εἰς τὸ> ἄρχειν Behr: μεγάλης γε καὶ οὐκ ἐνὸν (οὐ κενὸν Baroc. 136) ἄρχειν O; the passage is marked as corrupt by Keil.
69 (p. 111, 6 K.) ἄρ' ἰδόντες Behr: παριδόντες O.
71 (p. 111, 14 K.) κἂν—πολεμεῖν is marked as corrupt by Keil.
71 (p. 111, 14-20 K.) [οὐ γὰρ—ὑμᾶς]. Ἀλλὰ bracketed and punctuated by Behr; before οὐ γὰρ and after ὑμᾶς ἀλλὰ a lacuna is indicated by Keil.
78 (p. 113, 23 K.) [τῶν ἀρχόντων] is bracketed by Behr; τὸ κοινὸν τῶν ἀρχόντων is bracketed by Keil.
80 (p. 114, 14 K.) ὁρατέα Behr: ὁρατὰ O.
84 (p. 115, 5 K.) νομίσαντες O; νομίζοντες Keil.
84 (p. 115, 14-15 K.) [ἀπαντῆσαι—μέσου] is bracketed by Behr.
84 (p. 115, 17 K.) [τειχῶν τε] is bracketed by Behr.
84 (p. 115, 17 K.) ἐφόριος Behr:ἔφορος O; the passage is marked as corrupt by Keil.
85 (p. 115, 20-21 K.) κοινοῖς αὐτῆς [πολίταις] O, with brackets by Behr; κοινῇ [αὐτῆς] πολίταις Keil.
86 (p. 116, 10 K.) δεκάκις Sieveking: δέκα O.

86 (p. 116, 11 K.) περιτραπέντας <παρ'> ἄνδρα [παρὰ ἕνα] Behr: περιστραφέντας ἄνδρα παρὰ ἕνα O; the passage is marked as corrupt by Keil.
92 (p. 119, 3 K.) <τε καὶ> ἐγκρατείᾳ Behr; ἐγκρατείᾳ is bracketed by Keil.
92 (p. 119, 7 K.) ἦρξαν, <ὑμεῖς δὲ τὴν ὅλην ἀρχὴν ἐποιήσατε πεπολισμένην τε καὶ κεκοσμημένην.> is supplemented by Behr; a lacuna is indicated by Reiske and Keil.
99 (p 120, 17 K.) ἐκκεκόσμηται Behr: ἐγκεκόσμηται O; συγκεκόσμηται Wilamowitz, with Keil's approval.
101 (p. 121, 15 K.) <εἰ δὲ μὴ παντελῶς οὕτως>, ἀλλ' is supplemented by Behr; a lacuna is indicated by Keil.
105 (p. 122, 22 K.) καὶ χαρίτων· πότε O; ....καὶ Χαρίτων πότε Keil.
105 (p. 123, 2 K.) αἵματος <ἐμφυλίου> Keil.
106 (p. 123, 9-10 K.) ἀρξάμενος γενεαλογεῖν TU: ἄρξασθαι (SD) γενεαλογῶν Keil.
106 (p. 123, 10 K.) οὐδ' ἡνίκα Oliver: οὐδ' ἂν SD: ἡνίκα TU; οὐδ' <εἰ> δὴ Keil.
107 (p. 123, 17 K.) <μένει> τά γε Behr; after βεβαιούμενα (lines 18-19) a lacuna is indicated by Keil.
107 (p. 123, 18 K.) καὶ ἑξῆς ἀεὶ U: καὶ ἀεὶ—ἑξῆς ἀεὶ T: καὶ ἑξῆς ἀεὶ. καὶ ἀεὶ D: καὶ ἀεὶ S, with Keil's approval.
107 (p. 124, 1 K.) after ὑπεραίρει a lacuna is indicated by Keil.
107 (p. 124, 3-4 K.) καὶ τοῦτο πρὸ τῶν ἄλλων εἶναι· τί δέ; σαφῶς ὅτι τοὺς τῆς ἀρχῆς κοινωνούς, οὓς οἰκείους ἔχει [παῖδας], ὁμοίους ἑαυτῷ <κατέστησεν καὶ> Behr: τί δὲ καὶ τοῦτο πρὸ τῶν ἄλλων εἴη (marked as corrupt by Keil) σαφῶς ὅτι τοὺς τῆς ἀρχῆς κοινωνούς, οὓς οἰκείους (οἰκειοῦται conjectured by Keil) ἔχει παῖδας (παιδείᾳ conjectured by Keil) ὁμοίους ἑαυτῷ O.
109 (p. 124, 13 K.) στῶσιν Behr: πέσοιεν O; πέσωσιν the Aldine editions, Keil.

XXVII

title [περὶ τοῦ ναοῦ] is bracketed by Keil in an appendix.
5 (p. 126, 7 K.) τὸν is bracketed by Keil.
7 (p. 126, 20 K.) [τῆς Πελοποννήσου] is bracketed by Behr; it was already suspected by Keil.
8 (p. 127, 6 K.) [ὃ δὴ Προποντίδα κληθῆναι] is bracketed by Behr; it is kept and a lacuna after κληθῆναι is indicated by Keil.

APPENDIX TO XXVII-XXVIII 455

8 (p. 127, 6 K.) <τὸ> πᾶν Behr.
12 (p. 128, 5 K.) [ἐξεῖναι] is bracketed by Behr.
12 (p. 128, 7 K.) νήσων is bracketed by Keil.
14 (p. 128, 20 K.) οὖ Behr: οὐ O.
14 (p. 128, 20 K.) [τῆς Ἀθηναίων πόλεως] is bracketed by Behr; it is preserved and after πόλεως a lacuna is indicated by Keil.
15 (p. 129, 10 K.) [καὶ τὸ δὴ νεανικώτατον] is bracketed by Behr.
23 (p. 131, 11 K.) ἐλλογίμων Behr: ἐν λόγῳ O; ἑνὶ λόγῳ Keil.
25 (p. 132, 5 K.) κοινωνὸν ἑαυτῷ TD: ἑαυτῷ AR, with Keil's approval.
31 (p. 133, 28 K.) ἂν <εἰ> Behr.
31 (p. 133, 29 K.) ἐκεῖνοι—κατ' ᾠδὴν Behr: ἐκείνων—κατ' εὐχὴν O; the passage is marked as corrupt by Keil.
32 (p. 134, 9 K.) <ἂν> before εἴποι is added by DU: it is omitted by TAR, with Keil's approval.
33 (p. 134, 15 K.) [ὀνομάζειν] <τοῖς οἴκοι καὶ> Behr.
41 (p. 136, 22 K.) ὑπὲρ ἔργων [οὐδὲ] Behr: ὑπηρετῶν οὐδὲ TAU; after ὑπηρετῶν a lacuna is indicated by Keil.

XXVIII

1 (p. 142, 2 K.) δὲ T: omitted by O, with Keil's approval.
6 (p. 143, 22 K.) [λόγους] is bracketed by Behr; λόγων Keil.
8 (p. 144, 5 K.) εἰ is bracketed by Keil.
11 (p. 145, 7 K.) τὴν ἀξίαν is bracketed by Keil.
15 (p. 146, 11-12 K.) σκέψῃ δ' ὅπως; <δι'> ἁπάντων—οὐ διάξεις Behr: σκέψῃ δ' ὅπως—οὐ δείξεις TASU; the passage is marked as corrupt by Keil.
16 (p. 146, 17-18 K.) τῶν Ἀχαιῶν is bracketed by Keil.
17 (p. 147, 1 K.) ἀλλ' οὐ O; ἀλλὰ and the sentence made into a question Keil.
19 (p. 147, 12 K.) κλάειν Behr: καλεῖν O; the passage is marked as corrupt and after κελεύων a lacuna is indicated by Keil.
21 (p. 148, 19 K.) before Ἡσιόδου Keil adds τοῦ.
23 (p 149, 7 K.) before δρέψασθαι Keil adds δάφνης ἐριθηλέος ὄζον.
24 (p.149, 20 K.) after ἐπῶν a lacuna is indicated by Keil.
29 (p. 151, 10 K.) προσῆκον Wilamowitz: προσήκειν O.
29 (p. 151, 16 K.) [ἐν πολέμῳ] is bracketed by Behr.
34 (p. 152, 20 K.) αὐτὸς O; αὐτῶν Keil.
36 (p. 153, 16 K.) ἀλλ' is deleted by a late hand of U; it is bracketed by Keil.

37 (p. 153, 26 K.) ἦν is bracketed by Keil.
39 (p. 154, 19 K.) παρακολουθῶν (U: παρακολουθεῖν O; παρακολου-θοῦντ' Keil) αὐτῷ Behr (αὐτῷ O).
40 (p. 155, 2 K.) ἐν—Φαιάκων is bracketed by Keil.
40 (p. 155, 3 K.) <τοῦ> ἐν σώματι [καὶ] Behr; the passage is marked as corrupt by Keil.
40 (p. 155, 4 K.) ἀντάξιον O; ἀντάξιοι, <ὧν> Keil.
40 (p. 155, 11 K.) τοῦ ἐναντίου is bracketed by Keil.
40 (p. 155, 13 K.) [τὸ λοιπόν] is bracketed by Behr; it was already suspected by Keil.
53 (p. 158, 24 K.) <ὁ> χορὸς Wilamowitz.
53 (p. 158, 24-25 K.) [ἀντὶ τῆς Μούσης] is bracketed by Behr.
57 (p. 159, 28 K.) [τοῖς ῥήμασιν] is bracketed by Behr.
58 (p. 160, 16-17 K.) εἰπὼν εἰς αὐτὸν is bracketed by Wilamowitz, with Keil's approval.
70 (p. 164, 14 K.) ἐξειλοχὼς U: ἐξειλεχὼς O, with Keil's approval.
70 (p. 164, 15 K.) περὶ τούτων is bracketed by Wilamowitz, with Keil's approval.
73 (p. 165, 14-15 K.) μοι <μᾶλλον ἑτέρων> Keil.
78 (p. 167, 5-7 K.) οὐδ' ἀμφισβήτησις αὐτῷ πρωτείων οὐδὲ πρὸς οὓς <διελέγετο σεμνυνόμενος ἐφ' ἑαυτῷ. τί οὖν ἄνευ φρονήματός τινος>.....; Behr: οὐδ' ἀμφισβητήσαις αὐτῷ πρωτείων οὐδὲ πρὸς οὓς O; after οὐδ' Keil adds ἂν, he reads <τῶν> πρωτείων, and after ἀποχρῆν he indicates a lacuna.
82 (p. 168, 8 K.) Σωκράτης is bracketed by Keil.
83 (p. 168, 17 K.) λείπεται ἢ περὶ <τῶν ἄλλων διανοηθῆναι> Behr: ἢ περιλείπεται O; the passage is marked as corrupt by Keil.
88 (p. 170, 1 K) κάθηται ASQ; καθήκει Keil.
92 (p. 171, 17-18 K.) αὐθημερινῶν Juntine: ἀπό θ' ἡμερινῶν O; ἀπό θ' .... ἡμερινῶν Keil.
93 (p. 172, 8 K.) σφετέρων Behr: ἑτέρων O.
97 (p. 173, 1 K.) <τοῖς> ἀγωνισταῖς Behr.
101 (p. 173, 22 K.) ἄνδρας O; ἄνδρα Keil.
101 (p. 174, 1 K.) οἰκέτου Behr: οἰκείου O.
103 (p. 174, 21 K.) ἐξετάζεις U: ἐξετάσῃς O; ἐξετάσεις Keil.
110 (p. 177, 4 K.) εἰς O; ὑπὲρ Keil.
115 (p. 178, 7-8 K.) ναῦν τὸν λόγον TSQU: ναῦν // τὸν λόγον A; ναῦν αὐτὸν [τὸν λόγον] Keil.
119 (p. 179, 9 K.) ποιητῶν <κράτιστον> Behr.
121 (p. 180, 6 K.) perhaps φασί Keil in his apparatus: φησί O.

APPENDIX TO XXVIII-XXX 457

122 (p. 180, 10 K.) before διδάσκει a lacuna is indicated by Keil.
124 (p. 180, 20-21 K.) [δῆλος—μεσῶν (μέσων TSQU: μασῶν A) is bracketed by Behr; the passage is marked as corrupt by Keil.
129 (p. 182, 11-12 K.)after ἱματίοις Behr punctuates with a question mark and after αὐτοῖς with a period.
129 (p. 182, 12 K.) ἐτιμήσαντο Behr: τιμήσαντες O; τιμησάμενοι Keil.
130 (p. 183, 2 K.) σιωπῇ is bracketed by Keil.
138 (p. 185, 15 K.) χρειοῦς φυγόντας Aristotle: χρησμὸν λέγοντας O, with Keil's approval.
138 (p. 185, 17 K.) δουλείην Plutarch: δουλείης O, with Keils's approval.
140 (p. 186, 20 K.) ἀλκὴν—ποιεύμενος Diehl from Aristotle: ἀρχὴν —κυκεύμενος O, with Keil's approval.
143 (p. 187, 18 K.) ὡς τὸν Φαῖδρον is bracketed by Keil.
146 (p. 188, 10 K.) οὔκουν Behr: οὐκοῦν O.
146 (p. 188, 12-13 K.) φάσκων εἶναι is bracketed by Keil.
147 (p. 188, 17 K.) εἶναι <βούλου> Behr after Reiske; before εἶναι a lacuna is indicated by Keil.
147 (p. 188, 21 K.) ἐμοὶ TQU: ἐμοῦ AS, with Keil's approval.

XXIX

12 (p. 195, 12 K.) μὴ οὐ T: μὴ O, with Keil's approval.
18 (p. 196, 23 K.) [τῶν] σπουδασμάτων Behr: τῶν σπουδαιοτάτων O; after σπουδαιοτάτων a lacuna is indicated by Keil.
22 (p. 197, 22 K.) after χρῶνται a lacuna is indicated by Keil.
27 (p. 198, 28 K.) <εἰπεῖν> is added by AR: omitted by TDU; bracketed by Keil.
29 (p. 199, 13 K.) ἀλλ' ὥς τι Behr: ἄλλως τε O; the words are marked as corrupt by Keil.
30 (p. 199, 15 K.) ἀλλ' <ὡς> Behr.

XXX

2 (p. 202, 9 K.) [τοῦτον] is bracketed by Behr after Keil.
2 (p. 202, 10 K.) δὲ αὐτὰς οὐκ T(DU): δὲ οὐδ' αὐτὰς οὐκ A, which Keil prints, but marks as corrupt.
13 (p. 206, 8 K.) ἀρχομένου Behr: ἀρχόμενος O; Keil marks this as corrupt.
13 (p. 206, 9 K.) προσὸν Behr: πρόσω O.

15 (p. 206, 21 K.) καίτοι Reiske: καί μοι O.
20 (p. 208, 19 K.) ἂν is bracketed by Keil.
20 (p. 208, 19 K.) ἄλης T: ἄλλης O; ἀγέλης Keil.
20 (p. 209, 3 K.) λέγω (A after erasure: λόγων TDU: λέγων A before erasure, with Keil's approval) δ' <ἀγωνίσμασιν· ἦσαν γὰρ> Behr; after λέγων a lacuna is indicated by Keil.
22 (p. 209, 14 K.) αὐτῶν O; αὐτὸς Keil.
25 (p. 210, 7 K.) οὔ τι Behr: ἔτι O; ἔτι παίδων is bracketed and after παίδων a lacuna is indicated by Keil.
27 (p. 211, 6 K.) [καὶ] is bracketed by Behr.
27 (p. 211, 7 K.) <καὶ> δηλοῦν Reiske; before δηλοῦν a lacuna is indicated by Keil.

XXXI

11 (p. 214, 18-19 K.) φανεὶς καὶ πρεσβύτερος TB: καὶ πρεσβύτερος φανείς SDU, with Keil's approval.
12 (p. 214, 24 K.) after κεκλειμένοι a lacuna is indicated by Keil.
12 (p. 215, 1 K.) ἢ θρηνεῖν is bracketed by Keil.
16 (p. 216, 7 K.) after ἄμεμπτον Behr punctuates with a period.
18 (p. 216, 25 K.) τῶν ἐπαίνων [ἀπ]όντων [δὲ] ἐν ἀσφαλεῖ Behr: ἀπόντων δὲ ἐν ἀσφαλεῖ τῶν ἐπαίνων O; Keil marks ἀπόντων as corrupt, and before it indicates a lacuna.

XXXII

4 (p. 218, 9 K.) μνήμῃ TB: γνώμῃ SDU, with Keil's approval.
5 (p. 218, 20 K.) κατέστησε(ν) O; παρέστησεν Keil.
15 (p. 221, 8 K.) <διὰ> πάντων Behr: <εἰς> πάντων Keil.
25 (p. 223, 8 K.) τοσοῦτον καὶ Wilamowitz: καὶ τοσοῦτον O.
32 (p. 225, 4 K.) οὐκ<ἔτ'> Keil.
37 (p. 226, 15 K.) <δ' ἂν> ὀρθότατα Behr; ὀρθοτατ' ἄ<ν> Keil.
39 (p. 227, 1 K.) φιλοῦντος Behr: ἐφίλουν O; Keil marks the passage as corrupt.

XXXIII

4 (p. 228, 20 K.) βουληθῇ ποτε. O; βουληθῇ, πότε; Keil.
13 (p. 230, 27 K.) <ἐν>τυχόντας Behr: τυχόντας O.
14 (p. 231, 1 K.) κατὰ λόγον ὄντων Behr after Keil in his apparatus: λόγον καταλιπόντων O; Keil marks the passage as corrupt.

16 (p. 231, 24 K.) <ἐλ>λελοιπότα Reiske, Kaibel, with Keil's approval.
17 (p. 232, 8 K.) <τοῖς ἀρίστοις> καὶ Keil in his apparatus.
18 (p. 232, 15 K.) τοὺς <ἀκάτους> Behr; a lacuna is indicated by Keil.
24 (p., 233, 19 K.) οἳ Canter: οὐ O; Keil marks the passage as corrupt.
24 (p. 233, 19 K.) μέν <με> Behr.
24 (p. 233, 25 K.) <τὸ> ἅπαν Behr; <εἰς> ἅπαν Keil.
34 (p. 236, 14-15 K.) ἀπολογίαν—ἐπιτίμησιν O; ἀπολογία—ἐπιτίμησις Keil.

XXXIV

5 (p. 238, 7 K.) <ἄλλοι δέ τινες ἴσως τούτοις συμφήσουσιν>, ἀλλ' οὐ Behr; after οὐ a lacuna is indicated by Keil.
14 (p. 240, 11 K.) τὸ καὶ TR: καὶ τὸ O, with Keil's approval.
16 (p. 241, 4 K.) πορνείας O: παροινίας R, with Keil's approval.
22 (p. 242, 27 K.) καλόν O: κάλλον A; κάλλιον Keil.
35 (p. 245, 18 K.) [Ὅμηρος] is bracketed by Behr.
40 (p. 247, 1 K.) <τὴν> οὖσαν Behr; the passage is marked as corrupt by Keil.
51 (p. 249, 17 K.) [εἶναι] is bracketed by Luppe.
63 (p. 252, 20 K.) <τῶν> λόγων Behr.

XXXV

2 (p. 253, 19-20 K.) ἐπαγγέλλονται καὶ O; καὶ ἐπαγγελλόμενοι Keil.
26 (p. 260, 6 K.) διατεθῆναι O; διαθεῖναι Keil.
28 (p. 260, 17 K.) <αὐτὸς> οὗτος Keil.
28 (p. 260, 28 K.) ταῦτα δὲ TSU: ταῦτα C, with Keil's approval.
28 (p. 261, 3 K.) after ἐλεῶν a lacuna is indicated by Keil.
30 (p. 261, 16 K.) [—αὐτοῖς] <γιγνομένων τῶν στρατιωτῶν> is supplemented by Keil in his apparatus.
35 (p. 263, 7 K.) πολεμεῖν, <Καρποὶ δ', οἳ φοβερώτατοι καὶ ἐπικινδυνότατοι πρότερον ἦσαν τοῖς προσοικοῦσιν, ὑπ' αὐτοῦ πανσυδὶ διεφθαρμένοι, νῦν εἰσιν οὐδαμοῦ καὶ> is supplemented by Behr; a lacuna is indicated by Keil.

XXXVI

1 (p. 265, 3 K.) ἀπολῦσαι O; ἐπιλῦσαι Reiske, with Keil's approval.
7 (p. 266, 29 K.) [καὶ λίμναι] is bracketed by Behr.
7 (p. 266, 29 K.) ἐπεγχεῖται Behr: ἐπέγχεται T after a correction: ἐπέχεται A; ἐπέχει Keil.
7 (p. 266, 30 K.) οὔ τι, ὅσον φάναι Behr, partly after Keil in his apparatus: οὐ πόσον φῶ O; the passage is marked as corrupt by Keil.
8 (p.267, 10 K.) ῥεύματι <ὑπερέχει> Reiske; a lacuna is indicated by Keil.
12 (p. 268, 13 K.) [καὶ ἀντίσχυρον] is bracketed by Behr; before ἀντίσχυρον a lacuna is indicated by Reiske, with Keil's approval.
13 (p. 268, 27 K.) <οὖσαν> [Αἴγυπτον] Behr; the passage is marked as corrupt by Keil.
14 (p. 269, 8 K.) ὥσπερ <ἂν εἰ λέγοιμεν ὅτι σύνισμεν> Behr, with a question mark after ἀντίσχειν in verse 10; lacunas before ὥσπερ and after ἀντίσχειν are indicated by Keil, who has a question mark after γίγνεται in verse 8.
18 (p. 270, 10 K.) ἄγειν O; αἴρειν Keil.
18 (p. 270, 14 K.) [ἄνω] is bracketed by Behr; the passage is marked as corrupt by Keil.
20 (p. 270, 21 K.) <ἐκ τῶν περὶ> τὰ ὑψηλά is supplemented by Behr; a lacuna is indicated by Reiske and Keil.
26 (p. 272, 1 K.) ἐπὶ προσθήκην is bracketed by Keil.
33 (p. 274, 4 K.) [εἰς Αἴγυπτον] is bracketed by Behr.
33 (p. 274, 5 K.) εἰς <Αἰγύπτου> κορυφὴν Behr.
36 (p. 275, 7 K.) τῆς ἐπιρροῆς is bracketed by Keil.
37 (p. 275, 16 K.) μετ' ἰσημερίαν is bracketed by Wilamowitz, with Keil's approval.
42 (p. 277, 10 K.) [οὐρανοῦ] is bracketed by Behr.
43 (p. 277, 15 K.) τὰ is bracketed by Keil.
51 (p. 280, 1 K.) after πρῶτον μὲν Behr has transposed περὶ τῶν ἀρχαίων πηγῶν τοῦ Νείλου ζητῶν, which were originally after ὥστε [πρῶτον μὲν] in verse 2; Reiske has supplied the brackets.
51 (p. 280, 3 K.) [καὶ] is bracketed by Behr.
51 (p. 280, 6 K.) <ἢ> ἄλλοις Keil.
54 (p. 280, 28 K.) αἱ is bracketed by Keil.
56 (p. 281, 24 K.) μεθ' O; ἐφ' Kaibel, with Keil's approval.

APPENDIX TO XXXVI-XXXVII 461

60 (p. 282, 30 K.) αὐτόν Keil in his apparatus: αὐτοῦ O.
62 (p. 283, 10 K.) <οὐ διαφέροντα παρὰ πάντας> οὓς Behr; the passage is marked as corrupt by Keil.
63 (p. 283, 13 K.) <ἐν τούτῳ> τῷ Behr; a lacuna is indicated by Keil.
74 (p. 287, 11 K.) ἀσπόρου Reiske: ἀσπάρου O; ἀνύδρου Kaibel, with Keil's approval.
75 (p. 287, 20 K.) ὁρῶν O; ὄρων Keil.
83 (p. 289, 25 K.) ὁρῶν O; ὄρων Keil.
85 (p. 290, 15 K.) <ἢ> ὥσπερ Keil.
86 (p. 291, 3 K.) after λοιπόν Keil punctuates with a question mark.
87 (p. 291, 13-14 K.) ποιεῖ, <ἀναπεπταννυμένην> Behr; a lacuna is indicated by Keil.
89 (p. 292, 7 K.) [γῆς] is bracketed by Behr; the passage is marked as corrupt by Keil.
91 (p. 292, 23 K.) [ἑκάστοτε] is bracketed by Behr.
91 (p. 292, 25 K.) after ἑκάστοτε a lacuna is indicated by Keil.
93 (p. 293, 6 K.) after ἐξεπίτηδες Behr punctuates with a comma.
97 (p. 294, 4 K.) ἑτέρων O; ἑτέρου Keil.
99 (p. 294, 26 K.) <αὐτόν, τίν'> ἔχει Behr; <τίν'> was already added by the Juntine edition; a lacuna is indicated by Keil.
99 (p. 294, 31 K.) γε O; τε Keil (printer's error?).
104 (p.296, 18 K.) πατὴρ αὐτῶν πάντων O; πάντων πατὴρ αὐτῶν Aᶜ with the approval of Dindorf and Keil.
105 (p. 296, 23 K.) παντὶ <πάντων> Keil.
107 (p. 297, 12 K.) <καὶ> ὑπὲρ Keil.
115 (p. 299, 27 K.) τεχνωμένου Behr: χῶν μὲν οὐ O; μαχομένου Keil.
122 (pp. 301, 24-302, 1 K.) προσκείμενον [τὸ Αἰγύπτιον] πέλαγος κρίνομεν· Behr ([τὸ Αἰγύπτιον] was already deleted by Wilamowitz): προχείμενον κρίνομεν τὸ Αἰγύπτιον πέλαγος O; the passage is marked as corrupt by Keil.
123 (p. 302, 5 K.) [ἐπὶ τοῦ ξηροῦ] is bracketed by Behr.

XXXVII

2 (p. 304, 7 K.) μὲν οὖν TDU: μὲν AS, with Keil's approval.
7 (p. 306, 1 K.) κατὰ κράτος O; κατ' ἄκρας Wilamowitz, with Keil's approval.
9 (p. 306, 17 K.) συμφύτους is bracketed by Kaibel, with Keil's approval.

13 (p. 307, 18 K.) ἑκάστους O; ἕκαστα Keil.
14 (p. 307, 27 K.) ζεῦξαι ἵππων O; ζεῦξαι A, with Keil's approval.
15 (p. 308, 6 K.) [εἰ καὶ—ἤπειρον] is bracketed by Behr; the passage is marked as corrupt by Keil.
18 (p. 309, 11 K.) καὶ τὸν τῶν Behr: κατὰ τὸν TA; κατὰ is bracketed by Keil.
27 (p. 312, 8 K.) θεῶν is bracketed by Keil.
27 (p. 312, 13 K.) ἐν is bracketed by Keil.

XXXVIII

2 (p. 313, 8 K.) παραλιπεῖν O: παραλείπειν A, with Keil's approval.
3 (p. 313, 15 K.) συμβαῖνον ἐκ O: σύμπαν ἐπὶ TVA, which words are kept by Keil and bracketed.
7 (p. 314, 20 K.) <τοὺς> ἔχοντας Keil.
10 (p. 315, 17 K.) <τὰ> τοῦ Keil.
12 (p. 316, 5 K.) εἶναι κυρίαν O; κυρίαν A, with Keil's approval.
14 (p. 316, 15 K.) ἐπιλίπῃ O: ἐπιλείπῃ A, with Keil's approval.
18 (p. 317, 14 K.) after πᾶσιν Behr has transposed τοῖς ἀνθρώποις (O: omitted by A, with Keil's approval); the words were originally after σωτηρία.
21 (p. 318, 14 K.) αὐταὶ Behr, with a comma after ἀνεῖνται: αὐτοῖς O, which is bracketed by Keil.
24 (p. 319, 9 K.) διαθέντες (O: θέντες AV, with Keil's approval) [αὐτὸν] εἰς καλλίους <ἐλπίδας> Behr; before θέντες a lacuna is indicated by Keil.

XXXIX

4 (p. 320, 19 K.) ἀθρόον <πᾶν ἐκπίνομεν ὅσον> supplemented by Keil in his apparatus.
6 (p. 321, 11-12 K.) ἢ—ῥέον is bracketed by Keil.
7 (p. 321, 15 K.) αὐτόχυτον is bracketed by Keil.
12 (p. 322, 24 K.) οὐδ' <αὖ πάσχεται τὰ αὐτὰ ἅπερ τὰ ἄλλα ὕδατα, ἀλλ'> is supplemented by Behr; a lacuna is indicated by Keil.
15 (p. 323, 20 K.) ἀνέλαβον Behr: ἀπέλαβον O.
18 (p. 324, 12 K.) οὔτε <Πηνειὸν> and on verse 13 [Πηνειόν] is bracketed by Behr.
18 (p. 324, 13 K.) οὔτε <Νεῖλον οὗ ῥεύματος τῷ ἥμισυ ἑκατέρῳ φασίν τινες ἐπιβοηθεῖν ἑκατέρωθεν καθ' αὐτὴν> is supplemented by Behr; a lacuna is indicated by Keil.

XL

3 (p. 325, 15 K.) τὰ σπάργανα O; τοῖς σπαργάνοις Keil.
5 (p. 326, 4 K.) [τὰ περὶ Στύμφαλον] T, bracketed by Behr: τὰς [περὶ Στύμφαλον] SU, bracketed by Keil.
7 (p. 326, 19 K.) ἀνέπαυσε O: ἀπέπαυσεν A, with Dindorf's and Keil's approval.
14 (p. 328, 14 K.) after Σοφοκλέους Behr punctuates with a question mark.
20 (p. 329, 28 K.) ποταμίων U: ποταμῶν O; ποτίμων Kaibel, with Keil's approval.
22 (p. 330, 7 K.) ἐστι πρὸς αὐτόν TVDU: πρὸς αὐτόν ἐστιν AS, with Keil's approval.

XLI

1 (p. 330, 14 K.) αὐτὸς is bracketed by Keil.
4 (p. 331, 11-12 K.) εἰς αὐτόν is bracketed by Keil.
7 (p. 332, 1 K.) ἀλλὰ <ὁ νοσῶν ῥᾴων τε ἔσται> is supplemented by Behr; before πίεται on verse 2 a lacuna is indicated by Keil.
11 (p. 333, 7 K.) καὶ TFU: τε καὶ AS, with Keil's approval.
13 (p. 333, 16 K.) αὐτὸς is bracketed by Keil.

XLII

4 (p. 335, 12 K.) αὖθις <δ'> Keil, with a lacuna indicated after ὀνόμασιν.
8 (p. 336, 19 K.) ὁράμασι O; ἰάμασι Keil.
8 (p. 336, 21 K.) οὐχ ὅλως Behr: οὐδόλως O; the passage is marked as corrupt by Keil.
9 (p. 337, 3 K.) Εὐρώπης, καὶ <τὴν εὔνοιαν πάντων ἐπαινούντων> is supplemented by Behr; after Εὐρώπης a lacuna is indicated by Reiske, with Keil's approval.
9 (p. 337, 8-9 K.) εἴπερ <ἥδιον> εἴη μεμνῆσθαι O, with <ἥδιον> supplemented by Behr; εἴπερ εἴη μεμνημένος Keil.
12 (p. 337, 23 K.) ὑγιώτατον TCS: οἰκειότατον DU, with Keil's approval.
12 (p. 338, 2 K.) ὧν <σὺ ἐποίησας, φημὶ> Reiske; a lacuna is indicated by Keil.
14 (p. 338, 11-12 K.) οἰκειῶσαι—ἐπὶ—ἀποδεῖξαι O; οἰκειοῦσθαι—διὰ (Wilamowitz with Keil's approval) — ἐπιδείξασθαι Keil.
15 (p. 338, 20 K.) οὔ τε <ἐπιλῆσμον> Behr: οὔτε O; after οὔτε a lacuna is indicated by Keil.

XLIII

1 (p. 339, 7 K.) ὡς πλεῖστον is bracketed by Wilamowitz, with Keil's approval.//
7 (p. 340, 16 K.) <καὶ ὅσα> ἄνω Amann; ἄνω is bracketed by Keil.
7 (p. 340, 16 K.) ὑπὸ O; ὑπὲρ Keil.
11 (p. 341, 9 K.) τῇ δ' ὕλῃ <δήπουθεν> ἢ Behr: τηδαλη O; the passage is marked as corrupt by Keil.
11 (p. 341, 9 K.) πυκνῶσθαι TSD: πυκνῶσαι C, with the approval of the editors.
11 (p. 341, 11 K.) [ὅτι περ δύναμιν] is bracketed by Behr; after ὅτι περ a lacuna is indicated by Keil.
14 (p. 342, 9 K.) [λαμπρότερον] is bracketed by Behr; λαμπρότατον Canter, with the approval of the editors.
14 (p. 342, 10 K.) <καὶ> ἁγνότατον Reiske and Keil.
14 (p. 342, 17 K.) ἐπιτεταγμένον TC: ἐπιτεταμένον SDU, with Keil's approval.
15 (p. 342, 21 K.) ἀλλήλοις <εἶναι> Canter; a lacuna is indicated by Keil.
15 (p. 342, 22 K.) <τὰς> τοῦ Keil, with a comma after οἰκιστής.
15 (p. 343, 1 K.) δυνάμεως <τὸ τέλος> Behr, with a comma after παντός on p. 342, 22 K.: δυνάμεις U², with Keil's approval.
21 (p. 344, 16 K.) τὸ θνητὸν O: θνητὸν U², with Keil's approval.
23 (p. 345, 11 K.) after ἐποιήσαμεν Keil punctuates with a comma.
25 (p. 345, 24 K.) ἰᾶται <συλλαμβάνων Διί·> Behr: ἰᾶται οὓς ἰᾶται Διὶ φίλτεροι C: omitted by O with the exception of the first ἰᾶται; ἰᾶται οὓς ἰᾶσθαι Διὶ φίλτερον Keil.
28 (p. 346, 15-16 K.) [Νεῖλος ἦν] bracketed by Amann; [Νεῖλος] already bracketed by Wilamowitz, with Keil's approval.
29 (p. 346, 18 K.) καὶ ποταμῶν bracketed by Keil.
29 (p. 346, 21 K.) ἔφορος καὶ προστάτης O: προστάτης καὶ ἔφορος C, with Keil's approval.
30 (p. 347, 1 K.) κλήρους O: καιροὺς S, with Keil's approval.
31 (p. 347, 6 K.) after εἰκός Amman punctuates with a comma.

XLIV

10 (p. 349, 22 K.) after θεῖον C adds μᾶλλον δὴ, with Keil's approval.
14 (p. 350, 18 K.) οὕτως [περ] Behr: ὥσπερ S: οἷσπερ TCDU; καὶ Keil.

14 (p. 350, 20 K.) ἄλλο <ἂν> Wilamowitz.
14 (p. 350, 24 K.) [κεκόσμηται] is bracketed by Behr.
16 (p. 351, 7 K.) εὔοινος, εὔφορος <δὲ> Kaibel; after φύουσιν on verse 8 εὔφορος is transposed by Wilamowitz, with Keil's approval.
18 (p. 352, 5 K.) <ἐμὲ> αὐτόν Behr.

XLV

3 (p. 353, 6 K.) δὴ O: γε δὴ C, with Keil's approval.
3 (p. 353, 7 K.) [ἀφ' οὗ πᾶς ὅδε (O: ὅδε ὁ C)—εὐδαίμονες] is bracketed by Behr; <καὶ> ἀφ' οὗ πᾶς ὅδε ὁ—[ὥς εἰσιν] εὐδαίμονές τε καὶ (C: τε καὶ are omitted by O) Keil.
4 (p. 353, 20 K.) καὶ οὗ δὲ Behr: καὶ οὐδὲ TSDU: οὐδὲ καὶ C; ᾧ δὲ καὶ Keil.
8 (p. 354, 24 K.) τὰ O: καὶ τὰ C, with Keil's approval.
11 (p. 355, 29 K.) παρ' O; πρὸς Keil.
13 (p. 356, 11 K.) μυροφόρον Behr: μυριοφόρον O.
13 (p. 356, 11 K.) νεφελόγρυπας Behr νεφέλας οὐ γρῦπας O; after νεφέλας a lacuna is indicated by Keil.
19 (p. 358, 11-12 K.) [μεθ' ὧν—νοεῖν] is bracketed by Behr; it is a gloss on πάνθ' and perhaps originally read μεθ' ὧν ἄνθρωπον <βιοῦν> δεῖ νοεῖν; νοεῖν is marked as corrupt by Keil.
19 (p. 358, 13 K.) εὐεργεσίαν O: ἐργασίαν Keil.
22 (p. 358, 29 K.) [τοῦτον καλεῖν] is bracketed by Behr; τοῦτ' ἐπιτελεῖν Keil.
23 (p. 359, 8 K.) [τριῶν] is bracketed by Wilamowitz; the passage is marked as corrupt by Keil.
23 (p. 359, 12-13 K.) [ἐκείνῳ—αἱρεῖ] is bracketed, with a period after νεφέλαις and <κατ'> ἀνάγκην (TS: ἀνάγκης DU, with the approval of the editors) Behr; before ἐκείνῳ a lacuna is indicated by Keil.
28 (p. 360, 22 K.) ὁμοτίμου Behr: ὁμότιμος οὐ O; ὁμοτίμων Keil.
32 (p. 361, 22 K.) ζῶσιν Wilamowitz: σῴζειν O; <νῦν> σῶς εἶναι Keil.

XLVI

2 (p. 363, 1 K.) ταῦτα οἱ Behr: τούτων οἱ O; τούτων οἵ Keil.
3 (p. 363, 15 K.) μήτε [αὐτοῦ] Wilamowitz; αὐτοῦ μήτε Keil.
3 (p. 363, 20 K.) the first καὶ is bracketed by Wilamowitz, with Keil's approval.

5 (p. 364, 1 K.) <ὡς> πᾶν Behr, with a comma after λόγους on p. 363, 30 and the comma removed after παντὶ on p. 364, 1; a lacuna is indicated by Reiske and Keil.
7 (p. 364, 20 K.) ταῦτα O; αὐτὰ Keil.
8 (p. 364, 21-22 K.) τῆς—αὐτῶν is bracketed by Keil.
12 (p. 365, 27 K.) ὄντα O: ἐνόντα Keil.
12 (p. 365, 28 K.) ἀνῆκε <ὅπου μὲν> Behr.
12 (p. 365, 28 K.) δὲ O; γε Keil.
16 (p. 366, 26 K.) διέξημεν Behr: διέξιμεν O.
17 (p. 367, 3 K.) [καὶ] is bracketed and a comma placed before it by Behr.
17 (p. 367, 7 K.) [τὴν ἐνταυθοῖ Λευκάδα] is bracketed by Behr; τὴν ἐνταυθοῖ <Λευκάταν ἄκραν, ὥσπερ ἡ περὶ> Λευκάδα by Keil) καὶ ἡ καταίρουσα O.
17 (p. 367, 6 K.) <ἡ> θάλαττα, Λευκάτης Behr: θάλαττα Λευκάτα τε O.
17 (p. 367, 7 K.) [τὴν ἐνταυθοῖ Λευκάδα] is bracketed by Behr; τὴν ἐνταυθοῖ <Λευκάταν ἄκραν, ὥσπερ ἡ περὶ> Λευκάδα <κατὰ> τὴν Keil.
19 (p. 368, 4 K.) after ὃν τρόπον Behr has transposed [ὃν τρόπον] καὶ εἰς γαλακτοφάγους τὸν ἀδελφὸν αὐτοῦ and added the brackets; [ὃν τρόπον]—αὐτοῦ were after ἔφη on verse 6. After these words in their original place a lacuna is indicated by Reiske, with Keil's approval.
21 (p. 368, 16 K.) ἀναπετάσας O; προπετάσας Keil.
22 (p. 369, 3 K.) [τὴν] Behr; τοῦ Keil.
22 (p. 369, 3 K.) <ὥσθ'—ὃ> θεαμάτων Behr; <ὃ> θεαμάτων Keil.
22 (p. 369, 5 K.) ἑκατέρους Behr: ἑκάστους O.
22 (p. 369, 8 K) εἶναι O; ἔστιν Keil.
25 (p. 369, 25 K.) after πλῆθος Behr transposes αὐτῆς; it was after κάλλους on verse 24.
27 (p. 370, 18 K.) πόλις <ἦν πάλαι καὶ> is supplemented by Behr; a lacuna is indicated by Reiske and Keil.
27 (p. 370, 19 K.) ἀγαθῶν <ἴδοις ἂν αὐτὴν οὖσαν> ἐν κύκλῳ μεστήν [τῶν ἀγαθῶν], is supplemented and transposed by Behr, with a comma placed after εἰκός on p. 370, 20; ἐν κύκλῳ—τῶν ἀγαθῶν were after ὁλκάδα on p. 371, 1.
29 (p. 371, 7 K.) [ἢ τῆς—συνέσεως] is bracketed by Behr; it was already suspected by Keil.

31 (p. 372, 1 K.) διὰ δυοῖν <ἐτοῖν>[δὶς] Behr; διὰ....[δυοῖν] δὶς Keil.
31 (p. 372, 2 K.) προσιούσῃ O; παριούσῃ Keil.
32 (p. 372, 13 K.) βραχυτάτῳ, τὶς <ἄν> (added by the Juntine edition) as punctuated by Behr; Keil marks the words as corrupt.
35 (p. 373, 12 K.) γε is bracketed by Keil.
37 (p. 374, 6 K.) ἔχοντα O; ἔχοντας Keil.
39 (p. 374, 27 K.) ὁπόσοι σοφίας ἐρῶσιν Behr: ὁπόσοις σοφίας ἔρως ἦν O; ἦν is bracketed by Wilamowitz, with Keil's approval.
40 (p. 375, 5 K.) γράμματι, <ὅπου μὲν ἐπὶ δελφῖνος φερόμενον> Juntine edition; after γράμματι a lacuna is indicated by Keil.

XLVII

3 (p. 377, 4 K.) παρὼν O; παρ' ἕν Keil.
5 (p. 377, 15 K.) <οὐκ ἔστη> Behr.
16 (p. 380, 1 K.) Δημοσθένη O; Δημοσθένους Keil.
18 (p. 380, 22 K.) ἤδη O; ἥδε Keil.
21 (p. 381, 18 K.) ψυχροῦ τοῦ ἔξω A: ψυχροῦ O, with the approval of Keil.
41 (p. 386, 2 K.) καταχεάσαι Behr: καταχέασθαι O.
42 (p. 386, 8 K.) ὅπως καὶ ἐπισχὼν ὀλίγα is transposed by Behr: ἐπισχὼν ὀλίγα, ὅπως καὶ O; before ἐπισχὼν a lacuna is indicated by Keil.
48 (p. 387, 23 K.) πῶς O; πως Keil.
49 (p. 388, 1 K.) λυσιτελεῖν O; λυσιτελεῖ Keil.
54 (p. 389, 12 K.) σύκων O; σιτίων Keil.
60 (p. 390, 16 K.) after σχεδόν Behr places a comma; after τούτῳ Keil places a comma.
60 (p. 390, 17 K.) παρετείναμεν O; παρατείναντες Keil.
78 (p. 394, 15, K.) <ἐν> τοῦ Διὸς Behr.

XLVIII

2 (p. 395, 11 K.) ὑπαγορεύων <γε> Keil.
3 (p. 395, 19 K.) after θεόν· a lacuna is indicated by Keil.
9 (p. 396, 25 K.) τοῦ τῶν ὑπάτων Behr: τοῦ νῦν ὑπάτου O.
10 (p. 397, 2 K.) χρῆσθαι TD: χρεῖσθαι A; χρίεσθαι Keil.
12 (p. 397, 23 K.) ἀποτραπέντες Behr: ἀνατραπέντες O.
16 (p.398, 13-14 K.) τετρὰς προτέρα Behr: τετρὰς ἐπὶ δέκα O.

22 (p. 399, 30 K.) χρόνου O; χρωτός Haury, with the approval of Keil.
28 (p. 401, 3 K.) <οὐκ> ἔξεστιν Behr.
31 (p. 401, 24 K.) <περὶ> τὸ ἱερὸν Behr; τὸ [ἱερὸν] Keil.
31 (p. 401, 25, K.) πρέποντα O; πρέποντι Keil.
36 (p. 402, 21 K.) κατέστησε τὰ ἐμὰ πρὸς <πολλοὺς τοὺς ἐφεστηκότας κινδύνους> is supplemented as a parenthesis by Behr: κατεστήσατό μοι πρὸς O; after πρὸς a lacuna is indicated by Keil.
36 (p. 402, 22 K.) λόγια <τοῖς> Behr.
41 (p. 404, 1 K.) σύντροφος Behr: τροφός O.
42 (p. 404, 12 K.) ἐλλείποντος O; ἐλλείποντα Kaibel, with Keil's approval.
47 (p. 405, 8 K.) παράδοξον O; παραδοξότατον Keil.
48 (p. 405, 14 K.) Σηδάτιος Behr: Σηδᾶτος O.
51 (p. 405, 30 K.) ταυτὶ O; τοιαυτὶ Keil, who removes the period after κατεκείμην on p. 406, 2 and indicates a lacuna before τοιαυτί.
81 (p. 413, 5 K.) εἰσὶν γὰρ οἳ Behr: εἰσὶν γὰρ οἱ O; ἦσαν γὰρ οἳ Keil.

XLIX

1 (p. 413, 16 K.) συνίστατο O; προσίστατο Keil.
3 (p. 414, 14 K.) [τῆς σχεδίας] ἐπ' ἀκροτάτῳ Behr: τῆς σχεδίας ἐπ' ἄκρῳ τε καὶ τῷ O; τε καὶ are marked as corrupt by Keil, who in his apparatus conjectures ἀκροτάτῳ τῷ καί.
6 (p. 415, 9 K.) after σύμπαν a lacuna is indicated by Keil.
7 (p. 415, 11 K.) Σωτήρων O; Σωτῆρος Keil.
15 (p. 417, 13 K.) after ἔχοντι a lacuna is indicated by Keil.
22 (p. 419, 2 K.) αὐτῆς Keil in his apparatus: ταύτης O.
24 (p. 419, 15 K.) ἔδει τὸ Behr: ἐδεῖτο O.
24 (p. 419, 16 K.) χρίματι, <καὶ μάλ' ὤνησεν>. is supplemented by Behr; a lacuna is indicated by Keil.
27 (p. 420, 1 K.) ἅπαξ D: ἅπας TAS; ἄπαστος Keil.
27 (p. 420, 2 K.) ἐσθίων <ἢ> Keil.
36 (p. 421, 28 K.) διακλύζειν O; διακλύζεσθαι Keil.
40 (p. 423, 5 K.) <ὃ δ'> οὐχ Canter; the passage is marked as corrupt by Keil.
47 (p. 424, 23 K.) <ἐν> ᾧπερ Behr: ὥσπερ O.
47 (p. 424, 24 K.) ὑπ' αὐτό πως τὸ οὖλον <ἐν τῇ τῶν χειλῶν> ῥίζῃ Behr: ὑπ' αὐτό πως τὸ ὀρίζηλον O; the passage is marked as corrupt by Keil.
49 (p. 425, 13 K.) [γενόμενον] is bracketed by Behr.

L

5 (p. 427, 6 K.) [οὐ] καθάπαξ Behr: οὐκ εἰσάπαξ O; the passage is marked as corrupt by Keil.
8 (p. 427, 29 K.) σφάκελοι <εἰς τὴν κεφαλὴν καὶ τάσις> Behr.
13 (p. 428, 26 K.) τῶν <ἄνω> Behr.
16 (p. 429, 14 K.) Behr punctuates with a comma after Νικαεύς; Keil after ἀνήρ.
16 (p. 429, 15 K.) Σηδάτιος Behr: Σηδᾶτος O.
18 (p. 430, 3 K.) <Μάξιμος ὁ> Λίβυς Behr: Βύβλος ASD: βίβλος T.
20 (p. 430, 26 K.) ἢ <τὸ ὄναρ περὶ αὐτὸν> is supplemented by Keil in his apparatus.
23 (p. 431, 20 K.) προσήκοντος O; προσήκοντας Keil.
28 (p. 432, 30 K.) πολυεδής Hepding: πολυειδής O.
28 (p. 433, 4 K.) πρὸς Βάσσον· 'τουτογί· Behr: πρὸς τουτονὶ Βάσσον O; πρὸς τουτονί· Βάσσε Keil.
29 (p. 433, 10 K.) ποῦ—τοσοῦτον; is punctuated as a parenthesis by Behr; before ποῦ a lacuna is indicated by Dindorf and Keil.
37 (p. 435, 3 K.) ὁπότερά O; ὁποτέρως Keil.
43 (p. 436, 27 K.) Σηδάτιον Behr: Σηδᾶτον O.
61 (p. 441, 11 K.) σοφιστής <τις> Keil.
73 (p. 443, 24 K.) προσῆκον Wilamowitz: προσήκει O.
91 (p. 448, 10 K.) συνέδρων <τάξεως εὗρον> is supplemented by Keil in his apparatus.
94 (p. 448, 30 K.) ὅμοιον Keil in his apparatus: οἷον O.
97 (p. 449, 14 K.) συγκαταστήσοντος Behr: συγκαταστήσαντος O.
98 (p. 449, 21 K.) γενομένου <καὶ δηλωθέντος ὅ ποτ' ἔγνω Φῆστος ὁ ἡγεμὼν γενόμενος> Behr.
100 (p. 450, 6 K.) Φῆστος Behr: σοφιστὴς O.
102 (p. 450, 26-27 K.) οὔ τι—ἔχειν is punctuated as a parenthesis by Behr; the passage is marked as corrupt by Keil.
104 (p. 451, 6 K.) ἐν περιόδῳ <μὲν ἀρχιερεὺς τῆς 'Ασίας οὐκ ἐγενόμην, οὔποτε δὲ πέπαυμαι θεραπευτὴς ὢν ἐν περιβόλῳ> Behr, with a semicolon before ἐν περιόδῳ; before ἐν περιόδῳ a lacuna is indicated by Keil.
106 (p. 451, 22 K.) χρήσωμαι TS: χρήσομαι AD, with Keil's approval.

LI

5 (p. 453, 15 K.) οὐ κεχλεισόμενον Behr: οὐκ εἰσόμενον O; the passage is marked as corrupt by Keil.
7 (p. 454, 1 K.) χρίσεσθαί A꜀D: χρήσεσθαί O, with Keil's approval.
16 (p. 455, 31 K.) ἥδιστον O; ἥδιον Valckenaer, with Keil's approval.
20 (p. 456, 26 K.) after θεόν a lacuna is indicated by Keil.
20 (p. 456, 30 K.) after ἡγουμένῳ a lacuna is indicated by Keil.
22 (p. 457, 10 K.) περὶ Behr: παρ' O.
26 (p. 458, 2-3 K.) ὡς <ὁ θεὸς> Keil.
26 (p. 458, 4 K.) <αἱ> ἐπίβδαι Behr.
48 (p. 462, 12 K.) ἔκαμον Juntine edition: ἔκαμεν O.
50 (p. 462, 33 K.) μετέβαλον Canter: μετέλαβον O.
50 (p. 462, 33 K.) δηλοῦντι τὴν κατάβασιν Behr: δηλοῦν τὴν κατὰ φύσιν O; the passage is marked as corrupt by Keil.
54 (p. 463, 29 K.) τὸ <ἱμάτιον> Wyttenbach.
58 (p. 464, 29 K.) τινα. <καὶ τὸν> Λούκιον Behr, with the period after νέους removed, following Sohlberg; τινα [Λούκιον] Keil.
61 (p. 465, 19 K.) <ἔνιοι> ἔνθεν is supplemented by Behr; a lacuna is indicated by Keil.

INDEX

TO ORATIONS XVII-LIII

(References are to oration and section).

Abatos XXXVI 49, 50.
Ab epistulis = secretary of the emperor L 57.
Achaea, proconsul of XLVI 20, 27.
Achaeans XXVIII 16, 17, 22, 25, 34, 35, 37, 41, 90, 107; XXXV 27, 28; XXXVIII 8, 10; XLV 16; XLVI 18.
Achaean Strait XLVIII 67.
Achelous, The XXVIII 144; L 39.
Acheron, The XXXI 15.
Achilles XXIII 19; XXIV 58; XXVIII 16, 25, 26, 28, 29, 33, 36, 37, 107; XXXV 28; XXXVIII 6; LI 44.
Actium XLVI 17.
Adrasteia XXI 12; XLVIII 2.
Adriatic, The XLVIII 66.
Aeacus XXXV 17; XXXVIII 6.
Aegae XLVI 19.
Aegean, The XLIV *passim;* XLIV 2, 5, 6, 8, 11, 13, 14, 15, 16, 18; XLVI 18; XLVIII 68.
Aegle XXXVIII 22.
Aegospotami XXV 65.
Aegyptus = The Nile XXXVI 104.
Aeolians XXVI 16, 17; XXVII 15.
Aeolian poets XXVI 14.
Aeolis XLIV 4.
Aeolus XLV 29.
Aeschines XXVIII 76; Aeschines Or. I 25 XXVIII 141.
Aeschines Socraticus XXVI 10, 16.
Aeschylus XXII 11; XXXII 32; XXXIV 36; XXXVI 15, 18, 53; XXXVII 29; L 61; Aeschylus *Septem* 1 L 89; frg. 300 N. XXXVI 15; frg. 388 N. XXXVII 29; frg. incert. XXXVI 53.
Aesepus, The L 2, 4, 6, 9, 12, 71; LII 1.
Aesepus, warm springs at the (Gönen, *cf.* Baris) L 2, 4, 6.
Aesop XXXII 27; Aesop 24 Chambry XVII 15; 162 Chambry XXVI 57; 185 Chambry XXXIV 3.
Aetolia XXXVIII 21.
Africa (see also *s.v.* Libya) XXVI 10, 12; XXVII 32.
African(s) (see also *s.v.* Libyans) XXVI 70; L 18.
African wind = southwest wind XXXVI 3; XLVII 65; XLVIII 65.
Agamemnon XXI 3; XXVIII 16, 37; XXXV 27, 28.
Ἀγαθὴ Τύχη = Good Fortune XLVII 11.
Agathion XLVII 44.
Agesilaus XXVI 17; XL 17.
Agis XL 17.
Ἀγῶνες στεφανῖται = crown contests XXXIV 23.

Aidos = Reverence XXVI 106; XXXI 10; XLIII 20.
Ajax, son of Telamon XXVIII 28.
Albus, L. Antonius XLIX 38.
Alcaeus XXIII 68; XXXII 24; XXXV 10; Alcaeus 35. 10 D. XXV 64.
Alcimus L 97; LI 22, 24.
Alcinous XXXVI 88; XLII 14; XLVIII 60.
Alcman XXVIII 51; Alcman frg. 7 B XXVIII 51; frg. 34 B XLI 7; frg. 47 B XXVIII 54; frg. 118 B XXVIII 54.
Alcmene XL 2.
Alexander of Cotiaeum XXXII *passim;* XXXII 3, 15, 21, 26, 27, 33, 34, 38, 40; XLVII 23; L 62. Students of (especially Aristides) XXXII 1, 2, 3, 6, 12, 39, 40, 41. As teacher of Aristides XXVIII 133; XXXIII 17. *Aesopica* XXXII 26; *Treatise on Homer* = Ὁμηρικὴ συγγραφή XXXII 26. Sons XXXII 37, 38. Wife XXXII 37.
Alexander the Great XIX 4; XX 5, 7, 20; XXI 4; XXII 8; XXIII 51, 61; XXV 4; XXVI 24-26, 95; XXVII 26; XXXII 29; XXXVI 18, 74; L 18, 49.
Alexandria XXI 4; XXVI 26, 95; XXXVI 18, 33, 74; XLV 21; XLIX 4, 48.
The great avenue by the porticoes = μέγας δρόμος κατὰ τὰς στόας XXXVI 34. The sacred days of Zeus Sarapis at XLIX 48.
Alexandrians XLIX 48.
Alexis frg. 146, 8 K. XXXIII 16.
Aliani XLIX 1, 3. Warm springs at XLIX 2, 6.
Alpheius, The XXII 7.
Altars, The (of the Ethiopian garrison) XXXVI 48, 55.
Amalthia's horn = Cornucopia XLIX 9.
Amazons XVII 5.
Amphiaraus XXV 60; XXXVIII 21.
Amphilochus XXXVIII 21.
Amphion XXVII 31.
Amphipolitans XXXII 23.
Amphitrite XLVI 31, 42.
Amyclas XXXI 15.
Amymone XLVI 35.
Ἀνάγκη = Necessity XLIII 16.
Anaxagoras' theory of the Nile XXXVI 13-18, 102, 114.
Anaximenes (*qua* Theopompus) *Tricaranos* XXVI 51.
Ancaeus XXVIII 37.
Antaeus XLV 3.
Antiochus XIX 11.
Antiochus of Thessaly XXXI 2.
Antipater XXII 8; XXIII 51.
Antisthenes XLIX 33; Antisthenes Περὶ οἴου χρήσεως XLIX 33.
Antonines, The XXIII 62.
Antoninus Pius XXIII 73 (if not Hadrian); XXIV 31; XXV 56; XXVI 29, 31, 32, 38, 39, 60, 84, 88, 89, 90, 107, 109; XXVII 31; XXX 25, 28; XXXII 12, 13, 28, 29, 30; XXXVI 91; XLVI 42; XLIX 21; L 92.
Antoninus Pius and Marcus Aurelius XXXVII 29; L 75.
Antoninus, son of Pythodorus XLVII 35.
Ἀπαρκτίας = north wind XLVIII 54.
Ἀπηλιώτης = east wind XXXVI 6.
Apellas, C. Julius (I) XXX 10, 12, 13, 14, 15.
Apellas, C. Julius (II) XXX *passim;* Protheoria, XXX 10, 12, 13. Aristides teacher of XXX Protheoria; XXX 27.

Apelles XXXIV 29.
Ἀφνῖτις λίμνη = Lake Manyas LI 14.
Aphrodite XXVI 105; XXVIII 58, 136; XXIX 4; XXX Protheoria; XXX 18; XXXIII 20; XXXVII 18; XXXVIII 13; XL 19; XLI 10; XLVI 14, 25. Aphrodite Pandemus XXXVII 18. Cnidus sacred to XXXVIII 13.
Apia XXI 3.
Apollo XVII 14; XXIII 43; XXVI 105; XXVII 5, 6, 14, 18, 31; XXVIII 15, 48, 81, 111, 114; XXX 12, 15, 26; XXXVII 18, 19, 21, 22, 25; XXXVIII 4, 6, 7, 11, 12; XL 10, 11, 22; XLI 1; XLII 4; XLIII 6, 25; XLIV 11; XLVI 14, 33; XLVII 24, 58; XLVIII 18; XLIX 12; L 31, 32, 34, 36, 37, 41; LI 7, 8, 19; LII 4. Apollo Callitecnus XLVIII 18; LIII 4. Apollo at Clarus XLVIII 18; XLIX 38; oracle of, XLIX 12, 38. Apollo at Colophon XLIX 12. Apollo Cynegesius (the Hunter) XXXVII 19. Apollo, Delian L 32. Apollo, Delus sacred to L 32. Apollo at Delphi, oracle of, XXXVII 22; L 75. Apollo, Miletus sacred to L 32. Apollo Musegetes (Leader of the Muses) XXXVIII 4; XLI 1; XLIII 6. Apollo Paean (The Healer) XXX 12; XXXVII 18; XL 21; L 31, 37; Paeon XXXVII 18; LIII 4. Apollo Patrius (= Ancestral) of Cyzicus XXXI 15. Apollo, Portico of at Cyzicus XL 22. Apollo, Propylaeus (of the Entrance) XXXVII 25. Apollo, Priest of at temple of Mt. Milyas XLVII 25, 26, 40. Apollo, Sacred Night of at Colophon XLIX 12. Apollo, Temple of at Delus L 34; at Gryneion LI 7; at Mt. Milyas XLVII 24, 58; LI 19; at Pergamum XLVIII 18.
Apollonia (feast of Apollo) at Rome L 31
Appeal = ἔφεσις XXVI 32, 37, 38; L 74, 79, 88, 96, 103.
Arab XXVI 100; XXXVI 30, 64, 67, 69, 115.
Arabia XXXVI 60, 82, 87.
Arabia Felix XXVI 12; XXXVI 87.
Arabia land, ἄσπορος XXXVI 67, 74.
Arabian Mountain XXXVI 64, 66, 67, 69, 72, 74, 75, 78, 80, 83.
Aratus *Phaenomena* 2 XLIII 26; XLV 30; *Phaenomena* 33 XLIIII 8.
Arcadia XXIII 15; XXVIII 77; XL 5.
Arcadians XXIII 26, 60.
Ἀρχαί = officials of Smyrna L 101.
Archidamus XL 17.
Ἀρχιερεὺς τοῦ κοινοῦ τῆς Ἀσίας = High priest of the Provincial Assembly of Asia L 101, 103, 104.
Archilochus XXXII 24.
Ἄρχων (= President of the Council) of Smyrna L 99.
Ἄρχοντες (= officials) of Hadriani L 73, 74, 93.
Ares XXVI 105; XXVIII 64, 106; XXXVII 22; XLI 10; XLVI 33; XLVII 33.
Arganthonius XXXI 17.
Argives XXII 7; XXIV 27.
Argive dirge XXII 11.
Argo XLVI 29.
Argos XX 13; XXXVII 17.
Argus XXVI 6.
Ariadne's Crown XVII 8.
Aristides, P. Aelius: Aelius Aristides XIX 1; LI 24: Aristides XXVIII 6; XXXII 1; XLVII 41; XLVIII 48; XLIX 45; L 5, 23, 45, 78; LI 31: Theodorus L 53, 54, 70: Theodotes L 21: Sosimenes LI 24. Aristides, birth day of XLVII 31; XLVIII 16; LI 20. Horoscope of L 58. Genius Hermes of L 57. Parents of XXXIII 20. Father of XLVIII 40. Mother of XLIX 16. Children of XXXIII 20. Ἀκόλουθοι = attendants of LI 14, 28. Γνώριμοι = acquaintances of

XLVII 49; L 23, 106. Elsewhere = distinguished man L 12, 16, 27; LI 29. Εἰωθότες = acquaintances of XLIX 2. Ἐπιτήδειοι = friends of XLVII 10, 15, 66; XLVIII 1, 12; LI 6, 30, 60; LIII 3. Ἑπόμενοι = attendants of LI 4. Ἑταῖροι = comrades of XLVII 49; XLVIII 20, 72, 76; L 24, 55, 71, 87; LI 57. Ξένοι = hosts of XXXVI 82; XLVIII 15; LI 6. But ξένος = stranger in XL 21. Οἰκέται = servants of XLVII 31, 75, 76; XLVIII 38, 56, 61; L 5, 34, 94, 105; LI 5, 8, 13, 38. Παῖδες = slaves of L 34; cf. παιδάριον LI 61. But παῖδες = boys in XLVII 30; XLIX 4; L 10, 38, 43; LI 58, 59. Σύμπλους = sailing companions XLIV 18. Συνήθης = companion of L 23, 42. Σύντροφος = foster brother LI 64. See also s.v. Callityche (foster sister), s.v. Epagathus (foster father), s.v. Philumene (nurse), s.v. τροφεῖς = foster fathers, s.v. Zosimus (foster father). Ὑπηρέτης = servant of LI 28. Φίλοι = friends of XLVII 2, 29, 55, 56, 63, 64; XLVIII 20, 41, 51, 52; XLIX 2, 49, 50; L 30, 36; LI 32, 43. Teacher of Eteoneus XXXI 1, 7, 8, 9. Ancestral Estate of (see also Temple of Olympian Zeus) XLVII 43 (μέγας οἶκος = main house); XLIX 13 (πατρῴα ἑστία = ancestral hearth), 16, 20, 41; L 28, 48, 49; LI 10. Hearth of foster fathers XLIX 20. Statue of Zeus at ancestral Estate XLIX 20. Temple of Olympian Zeus at Ancestral Estate XLVII 41; XLIX 41; L 1, 2, 21, 48, 49, 71, 105; LI 10, 47. Asclepius' garden at Temple of Olympian Zeus L 49. Estate and farm house near the Aesepus L 2. Farm XLVII 69, 75; LI 17. House in Cyzicus LI 46. Possessions in Hadriani L 72. Laneion Estate of XIX 6; XLIX 42; L 55, 103, 105, 108; LI 17, 50, 53, 54. Estate in suburbs of Smyrna XLVIII 38; XLIX 39; LI 2, 4. Smyrnaean citizenship L 73. Writings of Poem on the marriage of Coronis and birth of Asclepius XLVII 73. Verses XLIX 4; L 4. Poems to Apollo L 31, 36, 37, 41; to Asclepius L 39, 41; to Pan, Hecate, the Achelous L 39; to Athena L 39; to Dionysus L 39, 40; to Zeus L 50; to Hermes L 40; to the Nemeseis L 41; to Heracles Asclepius L 42; chorus in honor of Asclepius L 43-46; dedicatory verse L 45-47. Prose: Speech to Athena (now lost) XXVIII 18, 21, 52, 53, 75, 93, 94, 105; L 25; *In Defense of Running* L 25; *Dionysus* L 25; Third speech to Asclepius L 30; *The Sacred Tales* XLII 4, 10; *Against the Sophists* LI 39; *Monody* XX 3; *Prooemia (Introductory Hymns)* XXVIII 105, cf. XXXIV 35; a speech during the plague XXXIII 6; a commentary on his dreams XLVIII 2, 3, 8; XLIX 30; L 25.

Aristides the Just XXVIII 6.
Aristonicus XIX 11.
Aristophanes XXVIII 93; XXXII 32; XLVII 16; LI 18. Aristophanes *Acharnians* 504 XXXIII 5; *Acharnians* 1131 XXVIII 19; *Aves* 1334 XLII 5; *Equites* 1321 XX 19; *Nubes (Clouds)* LI 18; *Nubes* 284 XLIV 1; *Nubes* 555 XXXIV 47; *Nubes* 995 XXXI 10; *Plutus* 650 XLIV 17; *Ranae* 736 XXIX 28; *Ranae* 785 XXXII 34; *Ranae* 1515 XXXII 34; *Telemessians* XLVII 16; *Vespae* 1019 ff. XLI 11; *Vespae* 1030 XXVIII 93; *Vespae* 1043 XXVIII 93; *Vespae* 1046-1047 XXVIII 94; frg. 529 K XLVII 16; frg. 643 K XXXII 32.
Aristophon XXVIII 86.
Aristotle XXXII 29. Aristotle *Ars Rhetorica* 1397 A 15 XXVIII 85; 1397 B 30 XXVIII 85; 1398 A 5 XXVIII 86; *Res Publica Atheniensium* 42. 1 XXVI 37.
Army, disposition of troops XLIII 17, 26; draft XXVI 75-78, 85-86; Roman legions XXXVI 91; Roman soldiers, discipline of XXXV 30, 31; the service of military couriers = *cursus publicus* XLVIII 61.
Artaphernes XXVI 85
Artemis XXIII 25; XXVI 105; XXXVII 18, 19, 25; XLIII 25; XLIV 11; XLVI 14; XLIX 21; L 4; LI 66. Artemis Cynegetis (Huntress) XXXVII 19; XLIII 25. Artemis Lochia (of lying in) XXXVII 18; XLIII 25. Artemis Thermaea (of the warm springs) L 4. Artemis, Temple of in Ephesus XXIII 25.

INDEX

Asclepiacus, Julius XLVII 58, 76; XLVIII 35, 46, 47, 48, 49, 52; XLIX 14, 22, 23, 25; L 46.
Asclepiadae (The sons of Asclepius) XXIV 45; XXXVIII *passim;* XXXVIII 9, 13, 14, 15, 16, 17, 18, 19.
Asclepius XIX 6; XX 2; XXI 2; XXIII 14, 15, 16, 17, 18; XXIV 1; XXVI 105; XXVII 2, 3, 39; XXVIII 102 (if not Athena), 105, 116, 117, 132, 133, 156; XXX Protheoria, 1, 4, 9, 12 (if not Apollo), 14, 15, 16, 22, 25, 26, 27, 28; XXXIII 2, 6, 17, 18, 33; XXXIV 42(?); XXXVI 124; XXXVII 20; XXXVIII 3, 4, 5, 6, 7, 11, 18, 20, 21, 23; XXXIX 3, 4, 5, 6, 11, 12, 14, 18; XL 21; XLI 1; XLII *passim;* XLII 1, 4, 12; XLIII 25; XLV 7; XLVII 1, 2, 3, 4, 6, 10, 13, 17, 19, 23, 30, 38, 42, 43, 44, 45, 52, 55, 57, 58, 60, 61, 63, 66, 67, 69, 71, 72, 73, 74, 77, 78; XLVIII 1, 2, 3, 4, 7, 8, 9, 11, 12, 13, 14, 15, 16, 17, 18, 21, 23, 24, 25, 27, 28, 30, 31, 35, 40, 44, 47, 52, 54, 55, 59, 71, 72, 73, 74, 82; XLIX 1, 4, 7, 9, 10, 11, 12, 13, 14, 15, 29, 31, 33, 39, 40, 44, 46, 47; L 1, 3, 4, 5, 8, 9, 11, 12, 13, 14, 16, 17, 18, 19, 20, 21, 23, 24, 26, 27, 28, 32, 36, 37, 38, 39, 41, 42, 43, 45, 46, 47, 49, 50, 51, 52, 53, 54, 56, 58, 63, 64, 67, 68, 69, 75, 76, 80, 83, 86, 87, 94, 95, 97, 102, 103, 104, 106, 107, 108; LI 1, 22, 26, 29, 34, 36, 38, 40, 41, 43, 45, 48, 56; LII 1, 2; LIII 2, 3. Asclepius μοιρονόμος (arbiter of fate) XLVIII 31. Asclepius Paean L 37, 42; Paeon LIII 4 (if not Apollo). Heracles Asclepius XL 21; L 42. Zeus Asclepius XLII 4; XLVII 45, 78; XLIX 7; L 46. Asclepius, Epidaurus sacred to LII 1. Asclepius in Pergamum L 56. Asclepius in Teuthrania = Pergamum XXXVIII 11. Asclepius, Temple of in Pergamum XXIII 14-18; XXVIII 132, 133; XXXIX 4, 5, 6, 17; XLII 1, 9; XLVII 10, 11, 12, 30, 31, 32, 42, 43, 55; XLVIII 7, 9, 11, 27, 31, 71, 79, 80; XLIX 22; L 15, 16, 55, 66, 90, 106, 107; LI 27, 28. The three temples (τρεῖς νεώς) in Pergamum (of Apollo Callitecnus, Telesphorus, and Hygieia) XLVIII 18, 75; LI 28. Precinct of the temple XLVIII 71; L 104. Statues in the temple. Good fortune and good god ('Αγαθὴ Τύχη, 'Αγαθὸς Δαίμων) XLVII 11; cult statue (ἄγαλμα or ἕδος) XLVII 11, 12; L 50. Temple of Zeus Asclepius XLII 4; XLVII 45, 78; XLIX 7; L 28, 43, 46; cult statue of temple of Zeus Asclepius L 46. Temple of Hygieia XLVIII 18, 80; XLIX 22; L 16; statue in Temple of Hygieia XLIX 21, 22; L 16. Temple of Telesphorus XLVIII 18; XLIX 21, 22(?); statues in the temple of Telesphorus, of Telesphorus XLIX 21, 22, of Artemis XLIX 21, of Hygieia XLIX 22. Temple precinct in Pergamum: Bath (*cf.* Ears) = βαλανεῖον XLVIII 76; Court = αὐλή L 106; The doors and lattice windows of the Temple of Asclepius XLVIII 71. The Ears (ἀκοαί) of the god XLVII 13; Sacred Gymnasium XLVIII 77; Hadrianeion XLVII 29; Sacred Ladder or Stairway = κλίμαξ XLVIII 30; Sacred Lamps = λύχνος XLVII 11; LI 28; Sacred Lamp of Hygieia = λαμπάς XLVIII 80; Bringing in of the Lamps = λύχνων εἰσφορά XLVII 32, *cf.* λαμπαδοφορία XLVII 22. Propylaea XLVII 10; XLVIII 31. Road of the Temple XLVIII 80. Stoa of the Temple L 15, 17. Sacred Theater XLVIII 30; L 15. Sacred Tripod XLIX 28. The Well XXXIX *passim;* XXXIX 1, 2, 15, 17; XLVII 42, 59; XLVIII 59, 71, 74, 76. Temple of in Pergamum Door Keeper = θυρωρός XLVII 32. Priest XLVII, 11, 12, 15, 40, 41; L 46, 64. Servant = ὑπηρέτης XLVII 11. Temple Warden = νεωκόρος XLVII 11, 44, 58, 76; XLVIII 30, 35, 46, 47, 48, 49, 52; XLIX 14, 22, 23; L 46. Worshippers = οἱ θεραπευταὶ καὶ τάξεις ἔχοντες XXX 15; XXXIX 5; XLVII 23; XLVIII 47; L 16, 18, 19, 50. Garden of at the temple of Olympian Zeus L 49. Statue of Asclepius there L 50. Temple of at Poimanenos L 3. Sacred precinct of in the gymnasium at Smyrna XLVII 17, 19. Temple (νεώς) there XLVII 17. Temple at the harbor at Smyrna L 102. Priesthood of the temple at the harbor L 102. Choruses for XXXVIII 23;

L 43-48. Crowns (large-sized) XLVII 44. Festivals = θεωρίαι XXX 27; XLVIII 81; L 2, 16(?). Festival (with mud) at vernal equinox XLVIII 74. Night festival = παννυχίς XLVII 6. Games = 'Ασκληπιεῖα XXX Protheoria; XXX 24, 25, 27. President of games = ἀγωνοθέτης XXX 27. Incubation at temple of Pergamum (see also s.v. Cathedra) XLII 8; XLVII 43, 55; XLVIII 57, 71, 80; XLIX 7. Incubants XXIII 16; XXVIII 88, 133; XLVIII 9, 27, 48; L 42, 43. (In Greek ἑταῖροι, συμφοιτηταί, cf. προσεδρεύων). Temple of at Pergamum Paeans L 50. Purificatory ceremony = καθάρσιον XXXIX 17; XLVIII 31. Sacrifices XXXVIII 23. Sacrifices (full = τέλεια) XLVIII 27. Incense XLII 2. Sacred Portions = μοῖραι ἱεραί XLVIII 27. Votive offerings XLVII 31; XLVIII 27; XLIX 13; L 45-47. Votive tablets XLII 7. Wearing of white = λευχειμονία XLVIII 30, 31; XLIX 21. Wine bowls (sacred) = κρατῆρες ἱεροί XLVIII 27.

Asclepius (Ship) XLVIII 54.

Asia XVIII 7, 9; XIX 1, 3, 12, 13; XX 15, 18; XXI 7, 13; XXIII 10, 15, 46; XXV 58; XXVI 10, 60; XXVII 6, 26, 32; XXVIII 64; XXXI 1, 3; XXXVI 79; XXXVII 14; XXXVIII 11; XL 16; XLII 9; XLIV 3; XLVI 17; XLVIII 16; XLIX 38; L 12, 63, 71, 94, 101; LIII 3.

Asia, Province of (see also s.v. Asia) XXIII 8-11, 27, 32, 79; XXXI 1; Administration, see s.v. Governors, Roman and s.v. Legates, and s.v. Assizes. High priest of the Provincial Assembly L 101, 103, 104. Official year begins September 23 L 100.

Asiarches L 53.

Assizes = *Conventus iuridicus* XVII 23; XXI 16; L 78, 88, 89-93, 96-98, 106, 108; LI 43.

Assyrians (Syrians) XXVI 91.

Ate = Folly XXXVII 7.

'Ατέλεια = Immunity or Exemption L 75, 76 (ἄφεσις), 78, 79, 83, 84 (ἄφεσις), 93, 99 (ἄφεσις), 99, 104 (ἄφεσις).

Athamas XLVI 33, 41.

Athena XXVI 105; XXVIII 2, 7, 21, 53, 75, 94, 102 (if not Asclepius), 105, 110, 111, 114, 137; XXX 26; XXXIV 28; XXXVII *passim*; XXXVII 1, 2, 3, 5, 6, 7, 8, 10, 13, 14, 15, 16, 17, 18, 19, 20, 24, 25, 27, 28; XL 19; XLI 10; XLII 14; XLIII 9, 25; XLIV 11; XLV 27; XLVI 34; XLVIII 41, 42, 44; L 9, 25, 39; LI 12, 25, 57. Athena Alexicacus (= Warder off of evil) XXXVII 26. Athena Enagonios (= of contests) XXXVII 21. Athena Ergane (= Worker) XXXVII 26; XLIII 25. Athena Hygieia (= of health) XXXVII 20. Athena Katharsius (= of purifications) XXXVII 26. Athena Lochia (= in charge of lying in) XXXVII 18. Athena Nike (= of victory) XXXVII 17, 26. Athena, πάρεδρος (= assessor) of Zeus XXXVII 5. Athena Poliouchus (= City holder) XXXVII 13. Athena Pronoia (= of providence) XXXVII 18, 22, 25, 26. Athena Propylaea (= of the entrance) XXXVII 25. Athena, dancers of XXXVII 8. Temple of at Athens = Parthenon ὀπισθοδόμος = back chamber LI 57. Hecatompedos LI 61. Statue of Phidias XLVIII 41; cf. XXXIV 28. Athena and the olive XXXVII 22.

Athena, Nome in Egypt XXXVII 14.

Athenians XVIII 7; XXII 4, 6; XXIII 26, 42, 45, 47, 52, 59, 61; XXIV 25, 27, 29; XXV 65; XXVI 9, 17, 43, 45, 47, 48, 51, 101; XXVII 14; XXVIII 63, 64, 71, 72, 73, 74, 76, 81, 85; XXIX 27; XXXII 23; XXXVII 14, 20; XL 11; XLVII 16; LII 3.

Athens XVII 5; XX 12; XXI 11; XXII 4, 5, 12, 13; XXIII 26, 46; XXVI 12, 45, 48, 61; XXVIII 138; XXXII 24; XXXIV 28; XXXVII 17; XLVIII 41; LI 57, 64; LII 3. The Acropolis of LI 57, 64. Those who live on the Acropolis = οἱ ἐξ 'Ακροπόλεως XXXVII 16.

Atlantic Ocean XXVI 16, 28; XXVII 27; see also *s.v.* Ocean.
Atlantis = Britain(?) XXVII 32.
Atlas XL 7.
Atreus, sons of = Atreidae XXXVIII 10.
Attica XXII 4; XLIV 6.
Attic XXVIII 65, 138.
Attic honey XLVIII 43.
Attic race XXI 4.
Atys XLIX 41, 42.
Aurelius, Marcus = Antoninus XIX 1; XLVII 23, 33, 36, 38, 47, 48, 49; LI 44, 45.
Aurelius, Marcus and Commodus XIX 1, 4; XX 1, 5, 9, 15, 23; XXI 2, 8, 9, 12; XLII 14; LI 44(?).
Aurelius, Marcus and Lucius Verus XXIII 3, 78, 79; XXVI 109; XXVII 23, 24, 25, 26, 27, 28, 30, 31, 32, 33, 34, 35, 36, 37, 38, 39, 40, 43, 45, XXX 28; XXXII 12(?), 13, 14, 15, 28, 29, 30; XLVII 46, 47, 49, 50; LI 44 (if not Commodus).
Aurelius, Marcus Imperial court of XLII 14.
Αὐτοκράτωρ (= Emperor) XIX 9; XLVII 23, 33, 36, 46, 49, 50; L 75, 106. αὐτοκράτορες of poets XLV 13.

Babylon XXVI 18, 79; XXXIV 15.
Babylonian(s) XXIII 69; XXVI 12; XXVIII 10.
Bacchae XLI 9.
Bacchant XXVIII 114.
Bacchic rites XVII 6; XXI 4.
Barbarian XVIII 1, 10; XXII 2, 4; XXIII 2, 3, 25, 47, 52, 61; XXIV 4, 37; XXV 12, 27, 39, 67; XXVI 11, 12, 14, 41, 63, 96, 100; XXVII 32; XXVIII 69, 106; XXXV 25, 32, 34, 36; XXXVI 88; XXXVIII 12, 15; XL 4; XLVII 9; XLVIII 61.
βαρβαρίζειν = "to know no Greek" XXXVI 15.
Baris Subscription XXXVII; L 1-7, 71.
Bassus, C. Julius Bassus Claudianus XLVII 21; L 28.
Bellerophon XXXIII 34; XXXVII 14, 24; XLVI 13, 29.
Bisalti XXXVI 14.
Blessed, Isles of XLVII 38; *cf.* XXVII 9.
Boedromion XXII 12.
Boeotia XXXVIII 21; XLVI 35.
Boeotian(s) XXII 7; XXVIII 64; XXXII 24; XLIII 6.
Boreas = north wind XXXVI 6, 8, 101; XLVIII 19, 50, 74, 75, 76; LI 9, 27, 49, 54.
Borysthenes XVIII 10.
Bosporus XVIII 10; XLVI 17.
Brasidas XXXII 23.
Briseis XXXV 28.
Britain XXVI 28, 82; XXVII 32; XXXVI 91.
Buzyges XXXVII 16.
Byblos (corrupt) see *s.v.* Maximus, Q. Tullius.
Byzantium XXVIII 63.

Cabiri LIII 5
Cadmea XXII 7; XXVI 50.
Cadmean victory XXVI 44; XXXVII 27.

Cadmus L 89.
Caeneus XXXIV 61.
Caicus, The XLVIII 48; XLIX 12.
Calchas XXXIII 14.
Callias, Peace of XXVI 10, 17.
Callisthenes, see s.v. Democritus.
Callitecnus (Apollo) XLVIII 18; LIII 4. (Athena) XXXVII 18. (Eteoneus' mother) XXXI 11.
Callityche XLVII 45; XLVIII 41; LI 19, 24, 25.
Cambyses XXVI 86.
Camirus XXIV 46; XXV 31.
Canobus (city) XXXVI 109, 111.
Canobus (helmsman) XXXVI 108, 111.
Caria XXV 3, 31; XXVI 36.
Carian region XXXVIII 13.
Carpathus XXV 31.
Carpi XXXV 35.
Carthaginians XXXVI 93, 94.
Carthaginian temple XXXVI 93.
Carystian XXXIV 23.
Casius, Mt. XXXVI 78.
Caspian Gates XXVII 27; XXXVI 87.
Caspian Sea XXXVI 87.
Casus XXV 31.
Catadoupa = Cataracts XXXVI 48, 64, 65.
Cataploi = The Landings XXI 4.
Cataracts XVIII 10; XXV 25; XXVI 28; XXXVI 30, 46, 47, 48, 49, 50, 53, 55, 59, 64, 65, 66, 81.
Cataract at Edessa XLVIII 62.
Cathedra = time of idleness Subscription XXX; XLVIII 70; XLIX 44; cf. L 14.
Caucasus XX 6; XXVII 27.
Ceans XXXII 24.
Celadon, The XXVIII 34.
Celer, Caninius L 57.
Celeus XXII 4.
Celts XXII 8. = Germans XXXV 35.
Cephalus XXVIII 144.
Cephallenia XLVIII 66.
Cephallenian XXIV 51; XXXIV 15.
Ceramicus XXVIII 79.
Cerberus XXXVII 25; XL 7.
Certamen Homeri et Hesiodi 324 XXVI 109.
Chabrias XXVIII 149.
Chalcidians XXVIII 9, 64.
Chancellery = ἀρχεῖα (of the Proconsul of Achaea) XLVI 20. (of the Proconsul of Asia) = ταμιεῖον XXIII 24. (metaphorically) XXXII 7.
Charidemus XLVII 34.
Charioteer (sign in zodiac) XLVIII 26.
Charites = Graces XVIII 8; XXIII 22; XXVIII 58; XXX 16; XXXVII 22.
Chelidonean Isles XXVI 10.
Chians XVII 6; XIX 12; XXI 4.
Chimaera XXXVII 24.
Chiron XXXVIII 7.

Chius XXXIV 35; XLVIII 11, 17.
Choaspes, The XXXIX 18.
Chronos = Time personified XLIII 9.
Chryseis XXXV 28.
Cilician XXVII 15.
Cilician Gates XXVI 100.
Cithaeron XXXVI 113.
Clarus XLIX 38. Oracle of Apollo XLIX 12, 38.
Clarian XLVIII 18.
Claudianus, Mt. XXXVI 67.
Clazomenae XLVIII 12.
Clearchus XXVI 17.
Cledon = Omen, Altar of in Smyrna XXIX 12.
Cleombrotus XXXV 25.
Cleomenes XXIV 38.
Cluvius, P. Cluvius Maximus Paullinus (?) XVII 23. Son of the same name(?) XXI 1, 7, 16.
Clytomedes XXVIII 37.
Cnidus XXXIII 27; XXXVIII 13.
Coans XXXVIII 11, 15; XL 15.
Cocytus XXXI 15.
Cohortes, turmae = μόραι, ἶλαι XXVI 67, *cf.* XXVI 88.
Colophon XLIX 12.
Colossus of Rhodes XXV 53.
Comedy, present artificial kind XXIX 28. Parabasis in XXVIII 97; XXIX 28.
Comic actors XXVIII 97; XXIX 4; XXXIV 7.
Comicorum Atticorum Fragmenta Anon. frg. 235 K. L 65.
Commodus, L. Aurelius (see also *s.v.* Aurelius) XIX 1.
Conon XXV 65, 66; XXVI 49.
Consules ordinarii XXVII 33; *consularis* XLVIII 9.
Coptus XXXVI 115.
Core XXII 3, 11.
Coressus XLVIII 82.
Corinth XXVIII 9, 66; XXIX 17; XXXII 30; XLVI 13, 20-31, 32.
Corinthians XXII 7; XXVI 49; XXVII 7.
Corinthian Gulf XLVI 21, 26, 33.
Corinthus (hero) XLVI 29.
Coronis XLVII 73.
Cornucopia = Amalthia's horn XLIX 9.
Corus XXXIII 1-2(?), 14(?); XLVII 54; *cf.* LI 20, 65.
Corybants XXVIII 109.
Coryphaesium XXVI 43.
Κορυφή = Pinnacle of Egypt XXXVI 33, 46, 66.
Cos XXXIII 27; XXXVIII 11.
Cotiaeum, Council and People of XXXII 1, 5, 15, 17, 18, 19, 20, 21, 23, 24, 27, 31, 35, 36, 37, 40.
Council Chamber = βουλευτήριον, βουλή see *s.v.* Cotiaeum, Cyzicus, Pergamum, Rhodes, Smyrna.
Cratinus *Chirones* XXVIII 92; frg. 237 K. XXVIII 92; frg. 306 K. (error ?, *cf. s.v.* Eupolis *Maricas*) XXVIII 92; frg. 322 K. XXXIV 51.
Cretan L 23.
Crete XXVII 8, 12; XLIII 8.
Cronus XXVIII 20; XLIII 8; XLVI 8, 17; XLVIII 27.

Crown Contests = ἀγῶνες στεφανίται XXXIV 23.
Cumae XXXVI 76. People of XXXVI 66.
Curator civitatum XXVI 67, 96.
Curator rei publicae or *corrector totius Italiae* XIX 10.
Curetes XVII 3; XVIII 2; XXI 3.
Cursus honorum XXI 16.
Cursus publicus = military couriers XLVIII 61.
Cyanean Isles XXVI 10, 17.
Cyclades XXVI 43; XLVI 18.
Cyclops XLVI 38.
Cydnus, The XXXIX 18.
Cyme LI 4.
Cyprus XXIII 47; XXV 3.
Cyrnus XXXVIII 13.
Cyrus (King of Persia) XXVI 18; XXVIII 104; XXX 21.
Cyrus (Satrap) XXIII 52.
Cythnus XXVI 12.
Cyzicus XXVII *passim;* XXVII 5, 17; XXXI 1, 3, 11, 13, 19; LI 14, 18, 42, 43, 45, 46, 48. Council chamber LI 16. Metroon XL 22. Panegyris (Hieromenia, sacred month) XXVII 1, 46; LI 11, 16. Olympic games LI 42. Portico of Apollo XL 22. Praetorium XL 13. Temple of Hadrian XXVII *passim*; XXVII 16-21, 46; XXXI 13; LI 11. Theater LI 12.
Cyzicus, people of LI 11, 12, 16.
Cyzicus, village near LI 14.
Cyzicus (hero) XXXI 15.

Dacians = Γέται XXVI 70.
Δαίμων = god of fortune XIX 1, 13; XX 5, 18; XXII 11; XXV 16, 28, 30, 38; XXVIII 109; XXXII 33; XXXVII 6. XXXII 37 (ἀγαθός); XLVII 11 (ἀγαθός). XXXI 13 (tragic). Δαίμονες XXV 33; XXXVII 25; XLV 32; LIII 5 (= Cabiri). XLVI 42 (θαλάττιοι).
Δαιμόνιον XXXII 28; LI 21.
Danae's Jar XXXVI 99; XXXIX 10.
Dancers (of Athena) XXXVII 8; (of Dionysus) XLI 1, 8, 11; (of Enyo and Enyalius) XXVIII 108, *cf.* XXVI 105; (of Hermes and the Muses) XXVIII 109, *cf.* XXVIII 114; (of Sarapis) XLV 27.
Danube = Ἴστρος XXXVI 115; XLV 3.
Darius XXVI 85; XXVII 26.
Darius (philosopher or king) XXVIII 110.
Datis XXVI 85.
Dea Roma, Temple of (in Pergamum) XXIII 13; *cf.* XXIII 65, 66; (in Smyrna) XIX 3.
Dead Sea XXXVI 82, 88, 89.
Decelian War XXIII 49.
Decree LI 30.
Decrees, honorary XXXI 14; LI 56.
Delatores = informers XXXV 21.
Delian XXXIV 35; L 32, 34.
Delian tree XXX 15.
Delus XLIV 11; XXXVIII 12; XXXIX 17; XLV 3 (Dalos); L 32, 33, 35. Sacred to Apollo L 32.
Delphi XXIII 43, 46; XXVIII 81; XXXVII 22; XLV 7; L 75. Prophetess in Delphi XLV 7.

Delta XXXVI 79. Pinnacle = κορυφή of Delta XXXVI 79. Marsh in Delta XXXVI 115.
Demeter XXI 10; XXII 3, 11; XXVI 105; XXXV 37; XXXVII 14, 22.
Democritus' and Callisthenes' theory of the Nile XXXVI 19-40, 102, 114, 116, 117.
Demosthenes XXVIII 6, 75, 78, 79, 150; XXXIII 34; XXXIV 62; XXXVI 10; XLVII 16; L 18, 19, 97; LI 63; Demosthenes *II 17* XXXVI 10; *III 32* XXVIII 150; *VIII 23* XLVII 16; *X 76* XXXIII 34; *XVIII* XXVIII 75; L 97; *XVIII 170* XLVII 16; *XVIII 221* XXVIII 75; *XVIII 222* XXVIII 76; *XVIII 304-305* XXVIII 77; *XVIII 315* XXXI 19; *XIX 251* XXVIII 141; *XX 167* XXXIV 62; *XXIII 50* XXVIII 50; *Epist. III 45* XXIII 71.
Diadochi = Successors of Alexander the Great XXVI 27.
Dike = Justice XXVI 106; XLIII 20.
Diogenes of Apollonia, theory of the Nile XXXVI 97-99.
Diomedes XXVIII 110; XXX 26.
Dion XXXVI 10; *cf.* XXXVI 33, 125.
Dionysia XVII 6; XXI 4; XXIX 4, 7, 12, 14, 20; XLI 10; L 85.
Dionysiac XLI 9.
Dionysius XXXII 30; L 57.
Dionysus XVII 6; XXIV 52; XXVI 105; XXVIII 94; XXIX 4, 29; XL 19; XLI *passim;* XLI 1, 2, 3, 4, 7, 8, 9, 12; XLIV 16; XLIX 33; L 25, 39, 40. Dionysus Briseus XLI 5. Lysius = Deliverer L 39. πάρεδρος of Eleusinian goddesses XLI 10. Temple of at Rhodes XXIV 52.
Dionysus, dancers of XLI 1, 8, 11.
Diophanes XLVII 49.
Dioscuri XXII 4; XXXVII 22; XXXVIII 24; XL 20; XLIII 25; XLIV 16; L 36.
Diospolis XXXVI 109.
Doctors (see *s.v.* Asclepiacus, Heracleon, Porphyrio, Satyrus, Theodotus) XLVII 62, 63, 67; XLVIII 5, 20, 38, 39, 69; XLIX 27; LI 9, 49, 50, 51, 52.
Doctors, Egyptian XXXVIII 15. Mysian XLVII 73; XLIX 18, 19; *cf. s.v.* Porphyrio. Roman XLVIII 63.
Dodona XLV 7.
Domitian XIX 9.
Dorians XXII 5; XXIV 45, 57; XXV 42; XL 16.
Doric XXVIII 65.
Dorieus XXXIV 23.
Draucus XXXVI 33.
Dreams, Interpreters of XLVIII 13, 72, 73.
Dreams Technical terminology in Greek ἀκούειν λέγοντος XLIX 14; *cf.* φωνὴ λέγοντος L 52. ἀφυπνίζεσθαι XXVI 69; XLVII 56; L 40, 46, 56; LI 8, 31, 35. δηλοῦν XLVII 45, 51, 55; XLVIII 31, 47; XLIX 48; LI 67. ἐδόκουν XXXVIII 1; XL 22; XLVII 7, 10, 15, 16, 17, 19, 22, 23, 26, 27, 29, 30, 33, 35, 36, 38, 41, 42, 44, 46, 49, 51, 54; XLVIII 7, 31; XLIX 2, 3, 4, 13, 25, 37; L 21, 25, 28, 46, 48, 55, 56, 57, 62, 66, 69, 81, 97; LI 18, 20, 31, 44, 45, 49, 50, 57, 60, 66. ἐδόκει XLVII 7, 17, 18, 20, 24, 35, 37, 42, 47, 76; XLVIII 30, 31; XLIX 33, 47; L 1, 5, 19, 42, 54, 64; LI 12, 22, 23, 24, 59, 65, 66. δοκεῖν XLVII 36, 50; XLVIII 32; LI 61. ἔδοξα XLVII 9, 11, 18, 40, 45, 52, 55, 56; XLVIII 17, 40; XLIX 30, 39; L 41, 49, 53, 60, 69; LI 12, 51. ἔδοξε XLVII 21; XLIX 15; LI 12. δόξα XL 21, 22; XLIX 25; ἐγρήγορσις XLVIII 32. μέσους ἐγρηγορότων καὶ καθευδόντων XXVIII 109. ἐγκαθεύδειν XLII 11. ἐνύπνιον XXXVIII 1, 24; XLVII 3; XLVIII 35, 72; XLIX 5, 43; L 25, 31, 38, 54, 55, 86; LI 8, 16, 34, 40, 46, 50. ἐνυπνίου δόξα XL 22. ἐπικαταδαρθεῖν XLVII 49, 55; *cf.* κατέδαρθον XLIX 20. ἐπιστάν L 89. ἐπιφάνεια XLVIII 18, 20, 45. θεάσασθαι L 59.

καθεύδειν XXX 14; LI 11. ἴαμα XXXVI 124; XLII 8 (as emended by Keil for ὅραμα). λόγια XLVIII 36. ὄναρ/ὀνείρατος XVIII 6; XXVI 69; XXXVII 1, 8; XXXVIII 1, 2; XLI 1, 2; XLV 7; XLVII 7, 8, 9, 12, 16, 17, 21, 22, 28, 39, 43, 51, 57, 63, 69, 76; XLVIII 2, 7, 8, 15, 18, 30, 32, 34, 35, 40, 71; XLIX 2, 3, 13, 20, 21, 26; L 5, 6, 15, 17, 20, 23, 25, 28, 39, 41, 42, 44, 45, 46, 54, 58, 62, 68, 69, 80, 82, 86, 89, 101, 106, 107; LI 12, 18, 19, 30, 31, 32, 47, 49, 53, 56, 66; LIII 2. ὀνειροπολήσαντες XXVI 43. ὄνειρος XXXVIII 1. ὀνειρώττομεν XXIII 63. ὅραμα XLII 8 (emended to ἴαμα by Keil). ὁρᾶν κτλ. XLVII 55, 56; XLVIII 34, 41; L 40, 50, 56, 57, 59, 61, 62, 69. 107; LI 22, 23, 50. ὄψις XLI 13; XLVII 38, 69; XLVIII 21, 29, 35; XLIX 13, 22, 47; L 5, 55, 106. ὄψις ὀνείρατος XLVII 8, 76; XLVIII 2, 30, 71; LI 56; LIII 2. πρόσοψις L 60. προφαίνειν XXXVII 29. σημαίνειν XLVII 55, 66; XLVIII 13, 15, 74; XLIX 11, 29, 44; L 37, 39, 71, 97; LI 1, 22, 43; LII 1. ἐπισημαίνειν XLVIII 9, 25, 35, 48; XLIX 14, 48. σημεῖα L 101; LI 20. σημεῖα φαίνειν XLVIII 72; XLIX 39. ὕπαρ XXXVII 1; XXXVIII 1; XLVIII 7, 18, 32; L 20; LI 31. ὕπνος (of Alexander and the foundation of Smyrna) XX 7; (ὕπνου μεστός) XXVIII 69; XXX 17; XXXVI 96; (ὕπνου φάρμακα) XXXVI 96; XXXVIII 24; XLIII 27; XLVII 3; XLVIII 32; L 39, 46; LI 11, 12. φαίνεσθαι XXXVII 1 (φανθέντα); XL 21 (πεφηνός); XLI 1; XLVII 14 (φανθέντα), 17 (φανθέντα), 24, 32, 33, 39 (φανθέντα), 50, 57, 69, 77 (φανθέντα); XLVIII 9, 18, 41, 42, 47, 72, 81 (φανθέντα); XLIX 13, 21, 23, 36, (φανθέντα), 46, 48, 48 (φανθέντα); L 61, 98 (φανθέντα); LI 25, 49. φαντάζομαι L 48. φαντάσματα LII 1. φάσματα XXVIII 102; XLVIII 8; L 1. φήμη ὀνείρατος L 46. φήμη ἐνυπνίου LI 16, 46; cf. φήμη solum LI 29. φράζειν XLVIII 13; L 31, 40, 89. φωνὴ λέγοντός του XLIX 5, 20; L 6; LII 3. φωνὴ ἐνυπνίου L 86. χρηματίζειν XLVIII 7; L 5, 70. χρησμός XLIX 37; L 54, 76, 97; LI 21, 23. χρῆζειν XLVIII 71; L 1, 46, 98; LI 22. χρησμῳδία XLVIII 8, 24, 37.
Δρώμενα = Rites XXII 2; XXIII 22; XXXVIII 1; XLVI 36; (cf. XLVI 40); L 7.
Drymussa XLVIII 12.
Dystrus XLVIII 16.
Dyseris XXXI 2.

Earth (personified) XXVIII 138; XXXI 18.
Earthquakes in Asia XIX 12. In Cyzicus XXXI 13. In Mysia XLIX 38-44. In Rhodes XXIV 3, 53, 59; XXV *passim.*
East wind = ἀπηλιώτης XXXVI 6.
Ecbatana XXVI 18.
Edessa XLVIII 62.
Eion XXIII 47.
Εἰρηνάρχης = Police Commissioner L 72, 73 (φύλαξ εἰρήνης), 79 (ἀρχή), 93 (ἀρχή).
Εἷς (of Sarapis) XLV 21, 23, 24.
Εἷς ἀνήρ XXXII 9, 10, 28.
Εἷς θεός (of Asclepius) L 50.
Egypt XXIV 3; XXV 3, 25; XXVI 12, 26, 36, 86, 95, 100, 105; XXVII 15; XXVIII 10, 87; XXXVI 1, 7, 10, 13, 16, 18, 30, 32, 33, 34, 42, 43, 46, 47, 48, 54, 57, 58, 59, 60, 64, 65, 66, 69, 72, 73, 78, 79, 80, 87, 106, 107, 108, 116, 122, 123; XXXVII 14; XXXVIII 15; XLI 6; XLIII 28; XLV 21, 32; XLVII 24; XLIX 4; L 23, 75, 105.
Egypt, Lower XXXVI 32, 33, 54.
Egypt, Upper XXXVI 32, 34, 42, 53, 79, 120, 125.
Egyptian(s) XXII 11; XXVI 73, 86; XXXVI 11, 15, 23, 54, 107, 109, 112, 113, 116, 122, 125; XXXVII 14; XL 10; XLV 15; XLVII 61; XLIX 3; LI 30.
Egyptian, doctors XXXVIII 15. Drug XLVII 26 (*Kouphi*). Festivals XXXVI

125. Interpreters XXXVI 15. Lakes XXXVI 70, 72, 73, 74, 75, 78, 83, 84. Language XXXVI 23, 65, 109, 120, 124. Nomes, see *s.v.* Prefect XLIII 28 (= the Nile); L 75 (= Heliodorus). Priests XXXVI 1, 109, 122; XLI 6; XLV 15, 29; XLVII 61. Priests' slippers XLVII 61. Sacred Animals XLV 32. Sea XXXVI 9, 10, 11, 16, 32, 33, 53, 66, 99, 122; XLIX 3. Temples XLV 32.
Ἐκλογεύς of Smyrna = Tax Collector L 96.
Elaea XLVIII 54, 78, 80; LI 8.
Elephantine XXXVI 46, 47, 49, 50, 51, 52, 53, 54, 59, 60, 65, 109, 115; XLVII 24.
Eleusinia XXII 7.
Eleusinian Title XXII; XXII 11.
Eleusinian goddesses XXXVII 22; XLI 10.
Eleusinium (temple) XXII 9.
Eleusis XXII 1, 2, 3, 4, 5, 6, 7, 8, 11.
Eleusis, Eumolpidae XXII 4; XLI 10. Heralds (κήρυκες) XXII 4; XLI 10. Mysteries (δρώμενα, ὁρώμενα, ἀκοαί) XXII 2. πρόρρησις of Mysteries XXII 12.
Elysium XXXVIII 20.
Emmelia XXXIV 60.
Empedocles XXVII 35.
Emperors XXIII 3, 8, 11, 51, 54, 73, 78, 79; XXV 39; XXX 12; XXXIV 61; XXXVII 13; XLV 18; XLIII 29 (of Zeus). Before Antoninus Pius XXVI 107. Ancestors of Antoninus XXX 28. Ancestors of Marcus and Verus XXVII 23, 31, 32. Ancestors of Marcus and Commodus XX 5. Before Julius Philippus XXXV 5, 7, 9, 14, 22, 38.
Emperor's Affairs XXXII 15. *Ab epistulis* = secretary L 57. Judges L 77. Ointment XLIX 21; L 57. Ornament XXXII 13. Palace XXXII 12, 13; XXXVII 29; XLVII 46; XLIX 21. Rescripts XXVI 33; L 75.
Empresses (Lucilla *etc.*) XIX 4; XLII 14.
Enceladus XXXVII 9.
Enyo and Enyalius, dancers of XXVIII 108.
Epagathus L 54.
Epaminondas XXVIII 88, 148. Epaminondas' *Apology* XXVIII 88, 148. *Epigram* XXVIII 148.
Epeus XXVIII 38, 39.
Ephesian XLIX 38.
Ephesus XXIII 23-25, 24, 26; XLVII 20; XLVIII 81, 82; L 78, 88; LI 35. Gymnasium (of Vedius) XLVIII 82. Temple of Artemis XXIII 25.
Ephorus XXXVI 64, 65, 66, 70, 71, 72, 73, 74, 82, 85. Theory of the Nile XXXVI 64-84, 102. Quoted XXXVI 70, 72, 77, 78, 83.
Epidaurus XXXVIII 21; XXXIX 5; LII 1.
Epione XXXVIII 22.
Equinox XXXVI 37. Equinox, vernal XXXVI 70; XLVIII 74.
Erechthids XVII 5; XL 7.
Erembi XXVIII 109.
Eretria XXVI 85.
Eretrians XXVIII 9.
Erichthonius XXXVII 14.
Ἠριδανός = Po XXXVI 6.
Eriphyle XXXIV 5.
Eros XLI 12; XLIII 16; LI 57, 65.
Erythraeans XIX 12.
Eteoneus XXXI *passim;* XXXI 1, 14. Aristides his teacher XXXI 1, 7, 8, 9. Brother XXXI 6, 9. Father XXXI 3. Mother XXXI 2, 3, 4, 6, 8, 9, 11, 18.

Etesian winds XXXVI 3, 4, 5, 6, 8, 9, 10, 11, 19, 34, 40, 85, 101.
Ethiopia XXVI 82; XXXVI 13, 42, 47, 48, 55, 58, 59, 60, 80; XLI 3.
Ethiopian XXXVI 1, 31, 48, 55, 56, 57, 63. Language, interpreters of XXXVI 55. Prefect at the Altars XXXVI 55. Prefect's Deputy XXXVI 55. Palace of XXXVI 55.
Etna XXXVI 14.
Etruscans = Τυρρηνοί XXIV 53; XXV 4; XLI 8.
Euare(s)tus, Q. Aelius Egrilius L 23.
Euboea XLVI 18.
Eudoxus LI 66.
Eumenides XXXVII 17.
Eumolpidae XXII 4; XLI 10.
Euphrates, The XXVI 17, 82; XXXV 35; XXXVI 122.
Eupolis frg. 94 K. XXVII 15 and XXX 18; *Maricas* XXVIII 92.
Euripides XXXIV 36; XXXVI 13, 15, 18. Euripides *Helen* 1-3 XXXVI 13; *Heracles* 178 XXX 7; *Hippolytus* 76-77 XXX 16; *Iphigenia in Taurus* 407 XXXIII 2; *Medea* 1078-1080 XXXIV 50; *Phoenissae* 3 XLVII 22; *Phoenissae* 110-111 XXVI 84; *Troades* 1 XLIV 1; *Troades* 2-3 XLIV 9; *Antiope* XXVII 31; frg. 114 N. XXVIII 117; frg. 381 N. XXXVI 18; frg. 663 N. XXVI 3 and XLI 11; frg. 882 N. (*sic* mistake for *Iliad* XVI 391) XLIV 1.
Euripidean (of Euripides) XLVII 22.
Europa (Zeus' beloved) XLVI 15.
Europe XXVI 10, 60; XXVII 32; XXVIII 64; XXXVII 14; XLII 9; XLIV 3.
Eurus = east wind XLVIII 12.
Euryalus (boxer) XXVIII 39.
Euryalus (Phaeacian) XXVIII 40.
Eurycles XLI 11.
Eurymedon, The XXIII 47; XXXIX 18.
Euthymenes XXXVI 85, 94, 95. Theory of the Nile XXXVI 85-96.
Euxine Sea XXVII 6; XLVI 17.

Fasti Consulares XXVII 33.
Fate = Μοῖρα XLIII 27.
Festus L 98, 100.
Fimbria XXV 58.
Flavius, T. Flavius Asclepiades (?) L 64; see also *s.v.* Asclepius, Temple of, priest.
The Flood XXIV 39.
Foster Father see *s.v.* τροφεύς.
Fronto, C. Julius XXX 11, 12, 25.

Gadira XVIII 7; XXVII 7; XXXVI 85, 87, 90, 91, 93; XL 12.
Γαλακτοφάγοι = Milk-eaters XLVI 19.
Galatia = Phrygia Superior L 12.
Galene XLVI 40.
Game, Children's XXVI 17, 54; XXX 20.
Ganymede XXXIV 25.
Garrison Commander (= φρούραρχος) at Syene XXXVI 49.
Gennais XLVIII 17. Warm springs at XLVIII 17.
Geraestus XLVI 18.
Germans = Κελτοί XXXV 35.
Γέται = Dacians XXVI 70.
Giants XXXVII 9; XL 7.
Glabrio, M.' Acilius Glabrio Cn. Cornelius Severus L 97.

INDEX 485

Glaucus XXXIV 23.
God and Deliverer (ὁ θεὸς καὶ λυτήρ) LI 20.
Gods, Ancestral (θεοὶ πατρῷοι) XXX 1. Beneath and above the earth XXII 13 (cf. gods of the Underworld). Of birth (θεοὶ γενέθλιοι) XXX 1. Of emperors and Greeks XX 23. Of oratory XXXI 13; XXXIV 47; XXXVII 21. Who hold Syria XLVII 33. Of Underworld (θεοὶ χθόνιοι) XXXI 13; XLV 23, 25; XLVI 8; XLIX 47.
Good fortune = 'Αγαθὴ Τύχη XLVII 11.
Gordian III XXXV 8.
Gorgons XVIII 9; XXXVII 24. Gorgon's head XXVIII 101.
Governor (kind not specified) XXXIV 61; XXXVII 13; cf. XLIII 29 (of Zeus).
Governor, Roman (in general) XXVI 31, 32, 36, 65.
Governor, Roman, of Asia (ἡγεμών or ἄρχων) XVII 23; XXI 1, 7, 16; XXIII 62, 64, 79; XLVII 22, 41; XLIX 38; L 12, 13, 63, 67, 68, 71, 72, 75, 76, 81, 83, 86, 88, 94, 98, 100, 103, 104, 106, 107. With *ius gladii* (βασιλικοὶ δικασταί) L 77. Assessors of L 91. Clerk of L 81, 85, 86. Legates of see *s.v.* Legates. Lictors of L 90. Staff of (οἱ ἡγεμόνες) L 99; LI 46.
Governors, Roman, of Britain XXXVI 91.
Graces = χάριτες XVIII 8; XXIII 22; XXVIII 58; XXX 16; XXXVII 22.
Γραμματικός = school teacher XXXII 8. = grammarian L 31.
Γραμματιστής = elementary teacher XXVIII 26, 54; XXXVI 47, 51, 52.
Granicus, The XXXVI 106.
Greece XVIII 8, 10; XIX 1; XX 19; XXII 6, 7, 8, 11; XXIII 15, 42, 43, 46, 51; XXIV 25; XXV 5, 17, 43, 54, 66; XXVI 16; XXVIII 65, 78, 87; XXXII 1, 21; XL 4, 16; XLIV 4, 18; XLVI 33; L 32.
Greek XXIII 26; XXIV 2; XXV 10; XXVI 14, 40, 41, 63; XXVIII 18, 152; XXXII 13, 30; XXXV 20; XXXVI 109; XLVI 23.
Greek, Ancient authors XXXII 10; L 18, 24.
Greek cities XXIV 29, 45; XXV 27; XXVI 47, 94; XXVII 1; XXVIII 77; XL 11; XLVI 30.
Greek, to speak = ἑλληνίζειν XLVII 36.
Greeks XVII 5, 15; XVIII 1, 7, 8, 10; XX 1, 4, 5, 12, 16, 23; XXI 1, 7; XXII 2, 4, 6, 7, 8, 13; XXIII 1, 10, 28, 42, 43, 44, 45, 46, 47, 48, 49, 50, 51, 59; XXIV 2, 4, 23, 24, 26, 29, 31, 37, 45, 47, 55; XXV 1, 12, 33, 39, 42, 43, 44, 55, 58, 65, 67; XXVI 11, 15, 41, 44, 45, 47, 48, 50, 51, 63, 73, 95, 100; XXVIII 43, 63, 69, 77, 147, 150, 152; XXXI 12; XXXII 1, 3, 5, 7, 10, 20, 23, 29, 33, 34, 38; XXXIII 2, 19, 24, 32; XXXV 20, 25, 28, 33, 36; XXXVI 65, 88, 95, 109, 115, 125; XXXVII 18; XXXVIII 5, 8, 9, 11, 12, 14, 15; XL 9, 10, 17; XLI 10; XLII 1; XLIV 4, 5; XLVI 2, 23, 24, 27, 39, 42; XLVII 64; L 27, 45, 87; LII 3.
Gryneion LI 7, 8.
Gymnastic trainers XLVIII 69.

Hades XXXII 34; XXXVII 25; XL 7; XLVI 8 (name surpressed); XLIX 4.
Hadrian XXIII 73 (?, if not Antoninus Pius); XXVII 22; L 106.
Hadrianeion XLVII 29.
Hadriani L 72, 73. City attorneys of L 78, 79. Officials of (ἄρχοντες) L 73, 74, 93. Police Commissioner of L 72, 73, 79, 93.
Hadrianutherae XLVII 51, 52.
Halicarnassians XIX 12.
Halicarnassus XXVIII 69.
Halieia (contest at Rhodes) XXV 32.
Harma XXVIII 114.

Harmodius XXXI 19; and Aristogeiton XXVIII 85.
Harmonia XXV 2.
Haruspicium LI 20, 23.
Hebe XL 19.
Hebrus, The XLVIII 61.
Hecataeus XXVIII 70; XXXVI 108, 110. Hecataeus frg. 308 F Jacoby XXXVI 108.
Hecate L 39.
Hecatompedos (Parthenon) LI 61.
Hector XXVIII 34; XXXV 28.
Helen XX 3; XXVIII 90; XXXVI 108; XLVII 1.
Heliadae = Daughters of the Sun XVIII 10.
Helice XLVI 19.
Helicon XXXVI 113; XLIII 6.
Heliodorus, C. Avidius L 75.
Heliopolis XXXVI 46, 109.
Helius see *s.v.* Sun.
Hellanicus XXVIII 70.
Hellespont, The XXVI 43; XXVII 6, 8; XXXV 25; XLIV 3, 17; XLVI 18; XLVIII 60; LI 47. Of the Hellespont XXVIII 74; XLIV 17.
Hephaestus XXIII 19; XXVI 105; XXVIII 111; XXXVI 45; XXXVII 22; XXXIX 11; XLI 6, 10; XLVI 33.
Hera XXVI 105; XXVIII 45; XXXVI 104; XL 7, 19; XLI 6; XLIII 25. Hera Gamelia (= of marriage) XLIII 25.
Heraclea XXVIII 89.
Heraclean XL 13, 20.
Heracleion (= temple of Heracles) XL 13; Heracleia (= shrines of Heracles) XL 11.
Heracleon XLVIII 20.
Heracles XX 6; XXII 4; XXIII 36; XXV 58; XXVIII 57, 93; XXXIV 59, 60; XXXVII 25; XXXVIII 10, 11, 17; XL *passim;* XL 1, 2, 7, 8, 10, 11, 12, 13, 15, 17, 18, 19, 20, 21, 22; XLV 3. Heracles Alexikakos (= warder off of evil) XL 15. Heracles Alexis (= warder off of evil) XL 15. Heracles Callinikos (= of fair victory) XL 15, 21.
Heracles Asclepius XL 21; L 42.
Heraclidae (= sons of Heracles) XXII 5; XXIV 45; XXXVIII 13, 17; XL 16.
Heraclides the Lycian (?) LI 38.
Heralds (Κήρυκες) at Eleusis XXII 4; XLI 10.
Hermes XXII 4; XXVI 105; XXVIII 109, 144; XXXVII 21; XLVI 34; L 40, 57, 58; LIII 4. Hermes Agoraios (= of merchandise) XXXVII 21. Hermes Empolaios (= of sale) XXXVII 21. Hermes Enagonios (= of contests) XXXVII 21. Hermes Logios (= of oratory) XXXVII 21, see also *s.v.* gods of oratory.
Hermes (and the Muses), dancers of XXVIII 109; *cf.* XXVIII 114.
Herms (Hermes with Heracles) XL 19.
Hermes, name of a part of Egypt = *RSY* XXXVI 65.
Hermias XLVIII 44; LI 25.
Hermius, Sinus = Gulf of Smyrna XVII 22.
Hermocrates of Rhodes L 23.
Hermocrates of Syracuse XXVIII 74.
Hermounthi XXXVI 33.
Hermus, The XXXVI 76, 77; LI 2.
Herodotus XXVIII 69, 70; XXXVI 3, 41, 45, 46, 48, 51, 57, 63. Theory of the

INDEX

Nile XXXVI 41-63, 102. Herodotus *I 1* XXVIII 69; *I 47* XXVIII 48; *I 114* XXX 21; *I 141* XVII 15; *I 165* XXVI 109; *I 188* XXXIX 18; *I 191* XXIII 69; *II 8* XXXVI 46; *II 19* XXXVI 114; *II 20* XXXVI 3; *II 28* XXXVI 47, 52, 53; *II 29* XXXVI 47, 51; *II 43* XL 10; *II 103* XXVII 38; *II 145* XLI 6; *III 153 ff.* XXXIV 15; *IV 36* XXVI 28; *V 77* XXVIII 64; *VII 114* XXXIV 56; *VII 228* XXVIII 65; *VIII 3* XXIV 19.

Hesiod XXVI 106; XXVII 18; XXVIII 19, 20, 21, 22, 23, 24; XXX 3; XXXII 11, 24; XLII 2. *Theogony* XXVIII 20; *Theogony* 11 XXVIII 20; *Theogony* 22 XXVIII 20; *Theogony* 30 XXVIII 22; *Theogony* 30-31 XXVIII 23; *Theogony* 31 XXVIII 23; *Theogony* 32 XXVIII 24; *Theogony* 38 XXVIII 24; *Theogony* 80 ff. XX 8 and XXXIV 42; *Theogony* 703-704 XXV 39; *Theogony* 736 ff. XXVI 13; *Works and Days* 5 XXVI 39; *W.D.* 11-14 XXIV 13; *W.D.* 17-24 XXX 3; *W.D.* 26 XXXII 11; *W.D.* 181 XXVI 106; *W.D.* 218 XLVIII 72; *W.D.* 336 XLII 2.

Ἱερομηνία of Cyzicus XXVII 1; LI 11; *cf.* panegyris XXVII 46; LI 16 (LI 42). of Rhodes XXV 28. Ἱερομηνία(ι) XXVI 46; XXIX 7; XXXV 1 (Eleusis ?), *cf.* XXXV 37.

Ἱερὸς Γάμος = Sacred Marriage XXIX 20.

Ἱερὸς Λόγος see *s.v.* Sacred Tale.

High Priest of Asia = ἀρχιερεὺς τοῦ Κοινοῦ τῆς Ἀσίας L 101, 104; *cf.* L 103.

Himeraeans XXXII 24.

Hippocrates XXXVIII 16; LI 49, 50.

Hippolytus XXXIII 34.

Hippon XLVIII 52.

Homer XVII 8, 15, 21; XVIII 2; XXI 5, 8; XXIII 36; XXIV 7, 47; XXVI 106; XXVII 18; XXVIII 19, 22, 25, 28, 35, 39, 45, 48, 90, 106, 110, 119; XXX 15, 26; XXXII 24, 34; XXXIII 26, 29; XXXIV 21, 22, 35; XXXV 27; XXXVI 104, 106, 107, 110; XXXVII 6, 21; XXXIX 2, 7, 11; XLIII 15, 22; XLIV 1, 9, 16; XLV 3, 16, 23, 24, 26, 27, 29; XLVI 6, 18, 19, 20, 33, 34, 38; XLVII 1; XVLIII 39; LI 27, 63; LIII 1. Homer a Smyrnaean XVII 8; XXIII 21. Homer's theory of the Nile XXXVI 104-113. *Iliad passim* XXIII 58; *Iliad* XXVIII 42; *Iliad I 46* ff. XXVIII 111; *I 218* XXIV 58; *I 237-238* XXVIII 22; *I 249* XXX 19; *I 250-252* XXVIII 30; *I 260* ff. XXVIII 31; *I 269-270* XXVIII 32; *I 271* XXVIII 33; *I 273* XXVIII 31; *I 316* XLIV 16; *I 350* XXXV 28; *I 419* XLV 3; *I 544* XXVIII 28, XXXVI 104, 105; *II 56* XXXVIII 1; *II 196* XXVII 34; *II 204* XXXI 7; *II 231* XXVIII 16; *II 243* XXXV 22; *II 330* XXI 8; *II 457* XVII 20; *II 469* ff. XXXIX 13; *II 489* XLV 16 and XLVII 1; *II 570* XLVI 22; *II 655-656* XXIV 46; *II 656* XXV 50; *II 668-669* XXIV 46; *II 670* XXV 30; *II 707-708* XXVIII 28; *II 754* XXXIX 7; *II 768-769* XXVIII 28; *III 156-157* XXVIII 90; *III 179* XXXV 27, 29; *IV 279* LIII 1; *IV 299* XLIII 17; *IV 317* ff. XXVIII 37; *IV 412* XXVIII 134; *IV 442-443* XXIII 58; *IV 455* LIII 1; *V 4* XXVIII 110; *V 5* XXX 27; *V 117* XIX 5; *V 122* XXX 26; *V 185* XXVIII 105; *VI 127* XXVIII 108; *VI 138* XLV 3; *VI 143* XXVIII 108; *VI 509-511* XXVIII 124; *VII 99* XLVI 6; *VII 133* (confused with *VII 157*) XXVIII 34; *VII 155-156* XXVIII 34; *VII 161* XXVIII 35; *VII 203* XIX 5; *VIII 1* ff. XLIII 22; *VIII 17* XXVIII 45; *VIII 18-24* XXVIII 45; *VIII 19* XLIII 15; *VIII 27* XXVIII 45; *VIII 48* XLVI 19; *VIII 203* XLVI 19; *VIII 387* ff. XXXVII 5; *VIII 523* XXVIII 134; *VIII 563* XXX 14; *IX 63* XXIII 21; *IX 97* XLIII 31; *IX 190* XXVIII 134; *IX 223* ff. LI 44; *IX 328-331* XXVIII 16; *IX 379* XXVI 86; *IX 476* XXVI 28 (*cf.* XXVI 29); *IX 497* XLV 26; *IX 577* XXVIII 9; *IX 673* XXVIII 41; *XI 298* XLIV 1; *XI 645* ff. XXVIII 36; *XI 761* XXVIII 36; *XI 813* XLVIII 39; *XII 104* XXXI 9; *XII 282-284* XXVI 7; *XIII 6* XLVI 19; *XIII 21* (confused

with *VIII 203, Odyss. I 22*) XLVI 19; *XIII 27-31* XLVI 19; *XIII 115* XXIV 58; *XIII 159-168* XXXIV 21; *XIII 355* XXVIII 28; *XIV 201* XLVI 5; *XIV 216-217* XLVI 25; *XV 37-38* XLVI 6; *XV 166* XLVI 14; *XV 187* ff. XLV 23; *XV 193* XXVI 101, XXVII 24, and XLV 24; *XV 605-607* XXVIII 106; *XVI 212-213* XXVI 83; *XVI 214* ff. XXVI 84; *XVI 391* XLIV 1; *XVI 640* XLIV 17; *XVI 776* XXVI 11; *XVIII 104-105* XXVIII 25; *XVIII 106* XXVIII 29; *XVIII 376* XXVIII 111; *XVIII 470* ff. XXXIX 11; *XVIII 478* XXIII 19; *XIX 93* XXXVII 7; *XIX 216-219* XXVIII 26; *XIX 217-218* XXVIII 27; *XIX 218-219* XXVIII 27; *XIX 364-368* XXVIII 107; *XX 250* XXXIII 26; *XXI 361* ff. XXXVI 45; *XXI 401* XXXVII 6; *XXII 60* XXVIII 60;*XXIII 148* XVII 15; *XXIII 316* XLIV 1; *XXIII 634-637* XXVIII 37; *XXIII 667-668* XXVIII 38; *XXIII 672-675* XXVIII 38; *XXIII 694-695* XXVIII 39; *XXIV 527-535* XXV 45; *XXIV 615* XVII 3. *Odyssey* XLVIII 42, 65; *Odyssey I 22* XLVI 19; *II 270* ff. XLV 2; *III 48* XLV 5; *III 51* ff. XLV 2; *III 62* XLV 27; *III 113* XLVIII 58; *III 177* XLVI 18; *III 270* XLIV 9; *IV 74* XXVI 89 and XLVI 20; *IV 241* XLVII 1; *IV 246* XXXIV 15; *IV 271* XXVIII 90; *IV 355-357* XXVIII 106; *IV 357* XXXVI 106, 107, 111; *IV 564* XXXVIII 20; *IV 581* XXXVI 104 and XLIII 28; *IV 611* XXX 11; *V 334* XLVI 34; *V 351* XLVI 38; *V 382* ff. XXXVII 23; *V 437* XXXVII 16 *VI passim* XXV 40;*VI 162-163* XXX 15; *VI 182-184* XXIV 7; *VIII 11* ff. LI 12; *VIII 170-173* XXVIII 40 and XXXIV 42; *VIII 176* XXVIII 40; *VIII 193* ff. XXXVII 21; *VIII 214-218* XXVIII 42; *VIII 229* XXVIII 42; *VIII 408* XXVIII 41; *VIII 492* XXVIII 75 and XXXVI 64; *IX 19-20* XXVIII 43; *IX 94* XXXIX 2; *IX 142* LI 27; *X 22* XLV 29; *X 46* XLVIII 72; *XII 55* ff.XLVI 17; *XII 184-185* XXXIII 27; *XII 351* XLIV 9; *XIII 332* XLVI 39; *XIII 429* ff. XXXVII 23; *XIV 466* XXVIII 115; *XIX 34* XLV 2; *XIX 113* ff. XLIV 16; *XIX 172* XXVII 8; *XIX 547* XLVIII 18; *XIX 562* ff. XXVIII 117; *XXII* ff. XXXVII 23; *XXIV 6-8* XXVI 68.
Homer *Hymn III 132* XLIII 25;*III 166-178* XXVIII 19; *III 169-172* XXXIV 35. *Cypria* frg. 4 (Oxford) XXXII 25; XLIV 16. *Nostoi* (if not *Odyssey III 103* ff. and *117*) XLVI 18.
Homer, interpreters of XXXVI 107.
Homeric **XX**VIII 71; XXX 11; XXXI 7; XXXII 26; XXXVII 5; LI 44.
Horae = Seasons XLVI 25.
Hyacinthus XXXI 15.
Hygieia XXXVIII 7, 22; XLVII 35; XLIX 21, 22; L 46. Temple of Hygieia in Pergamum XLVIII 18, 80; XLIX 22; L 16.
Hyperborea XXVII 5.
Hyperboreans XLV 3.
Hyrcania = Caspian Sea XXXVI 87.

Iacchus XXII 6; XXXVII 22; XLI 13.
Ialysus XXV 31.
Ielysus XXIV 46.
Iamus XLV 3.
Iapetus XXVIII 20.
Iaso XXXVIII 22.
Ida XLVI 14.
Ilica Köy, Warm Springs at LI 13, 42.
Ilium XVIII 7; XXV 58; XLVI 18.
Immunity = ἀτέλεια L 75, 76, 78, 79, 83, 84, 93, 99, 104.
Inachus XLVI 15.
Indian XXXVI 115; XLIX 36.
Indians XXVI 12; XXVII 27; XLI 8; L 18.

Informers = Delatores XXXV 21.
Ino XLVI 33, 34.
Interpreters of dreams XLVIII 13, 72, 73
Interpreters of Egyptian XXXVI 15. Of Ethiopian XXXVI 55.
Io XLVI 15.
Ion XXII 12.
Ionia XXI 13; XXII 5; XXV 3; XXVI 16, 95; XLIV 4, 6.
Ionian Sea XXVI 8; XXXVI 6; XLVI 18, 21, 26.
Ionians XXI 4; XXIII 60; XXVI 16, 17; XXVII 15; XXVIII 74.
Iphiclus XXVIII 37.
Iphicrates XXVIII 84, 85, 86, 87, 88. Iphicrates *Apologia* XXVIII 84, 86.
Ischuron XLVIII 47.
Isis XLVII 25; XLIX 45, 46, 49; L 97. Sacred geese of XLIX 49, 50. Temple of in Smyrna XLIX 45, 49, 50. Temple of, priest of XLVII 25, 26, 40(?), 61.
Isocrates *IV 14* XXVIII 95; *IV 15* XXIII 2; *IV 188* XXVIII 95.
Isthimian XLVI title.
Isthmian festival XXII 7; XLVI 23, 31.
Isthmus (of Corinth) XXVII 7; XLVI 3, 20, 21, 22, 33, 34, 35.
Ἴστρος = Danube XXXVI 115; XLV 3.
Italy XIX 10; XXVI 8; XXVII 15; XXXVI 116; XL 16; XLVIII 5; L 2, 75; LII 3.

Janus XXVI 6.
Jason XLVI 29.
Julianus, Q. Fabius Julianus Optatianus(?) L 107.
Jupiter (planet) L 58.
Justice (personified) = Dike XXVI 106; XLIII 20.

Kara dere (river near Laneion) LI 50, 53, 55.
Κατοχή or κατέχεσθαι (possession) XXVIII 109, 114, 127; XXXIV 47; in XVII 18 deleted.
Κήρυκες = Heralds at Eleusis XXII 4; XLI 10.
Κληδών (= Omen), Altar of at Smyrna XXIX 12.
Κοινόν, τὸ Κοινὸν τῆς Ἀσίας see *s.v.* Provincial Assembly of Asia.
Κοινά, τά see *s.v.* Provincial Assembly, Games of.

Labyrinth XXXVI 1.
Lacedaemon XXV 65; XXVIII 85.
Lacedaemonians XXII 7; XXIII 42, 45, 47, 50, 59, 61; XXIV 24; XXV 61, 65, 66; XXVI 9, 17, 43, 45, 47, 50, 79, 88; XXVIII 63; XXIX 30; XXXV 25; XL 17. ἄλη of see *s.v.* Spartan Band.
Laconian XXIV 38; XXVIII 65, 155; XXXIV 60. Laconian poet = Alcman XXVIII 51; XLI 7.
Laneion XIX 6; XLIX 42; L 55, 103, 105, 108; LI 17, 53, 54.
Laodiceia ad Lycum = Phrygia Superior L 103.
Lapiths XXVI 105.
Larissa XXXVI 77; LI 4.
Latin language L 84.
Law, eldest of the gods XXIV 42.
Lebedus XLIX 7, 10, 12, 13. Warm springs at XLIX 10.
Leda XXV 2.
Legate of the governor of Asia XXI 3 (P. Cluvius ?); L 85 (in charge of assizes at Smyrna); L 96, 98, 99 (in charge of assizes at Philadelphia).

Legates XXVI 89.
Lemnian XXXIV 28.
Lemnus XXXVIII 10.
Lenaeon month XLVII 29.
Lenaeum XXXIII 5.
Leo constellation L 58.
Leonidas XL 17.
Leoprepes XXVIII 60.
Leotychidas XL 17.
Lesbian XXIV 3, 54, 55.
Leto XXVIII 20; XXXVII 18; XLIV 11; XLVI 14, 15.
Leucas XLVI 17.
Leucates XLVI 17.
Leucothea XLVI 15, 31, 32, 34, 35, 36, 37, 38, 39, 40, 42.
Leuctra XXVI 50.
Libya (see also *s.v.* Africa) XXXVI 30, 41, 42, 58, 60, 61, 82, 85, 87, 90, 93, 107 (Libyans).
Libyan Mountain XXXVI 64, 66, 67, 69, 72, 74, 75, 80, 83.
Libyans (see also *s.v.* Africans) XXXVI 64, 67, 69, 107 (Libya in translation).
Licinius, P. Licinius Crassus Mucianus XIX 11.
Lictors of governor of Asia L 90.
Lindus XXIV 46.
Lous (month) Subscription XXII.
Lucilla, *etc.* (Empresses) XIX 4; XLII 14.
Lucius LI 57, 58, 59.
Lyceum XLVII 60; LI 61.
Lycurgus XXIV 24; XL 17.
Lydians XXVI 17, 51; XXXIV 59, 60.
Lysander XXV 50.
Lysias XXVIII 84, 143, 144; L 59. Author of the *Apologia* of Iphicrates XXVIII 84; frg. 39 S. XXVIII 85; frg. 40 S. XXVIII 85; frg. 41 S. XXVIII 85; frg. 42 S. XXVIII 85; frg. 128 S. XXVIII 86.
Lysimachus XIX 4.

Macedonia XXVI 27; XLVIII 5.
Macedonian(s) XXVI 27, 91; XL 21; L 42.
Machaon XXXVIII 1, 8, 16, 17.
Macrinus, M. Nonius Subscription XXII.
Maeotis XXVI 28; XXVII 8, 32; XXXVI 87.
Magnet XVII 17.
Μαντευτοί = Speeches prescribed by oracle Title XXXVII.
Manyas, Lake LI 14.
Marathon XXVIII 63.
Mareia (see also *s.v.* Egyptian Lakes) XXXVI 74.
Massalia = Marseilles XVIII 10; XXXVI 95.
Massalian XXXVI 85.
Massaliotes = people of Massalia XXXVI 95.
Maximus, Q. Tullius XXVIII 88 (?); L 18.
Meander, The XXI 7.
Medea XXXVIII 15.
Mede(s) XXII 6; XXVI 91; XXVIII 63, 64; XLVII 37. Tent of XVII 12.
Μηδικός = Persian XXII 6; XLI 10.

Mediterranean Sea XXVI 16, 17; XXXVI 87, 90, 91, 92; XL 9; XLIV 3; XLV 29.
Medusa XVIII 9.
Meles, The XVII 14, 15, 16, 19, 21; XVIII 9; XX 21; XXI 8, 14, 15; XXXIII 29; XXXVI 117; XLVIII 18, 21, 24, 45, 50(?).
Memphis XXXVI 20, 115.
Menander XLVII 51.
Mendes XXXVI 112. Nome of XXXVI 113.
Menelaus XXXVI 108, 109, 111; XXXVIII 20; XLVII 1.
Mercury (planet) L 58.
Meroe XXXVI 31, 55, 56, 66.
Meropes XXXVIII 11.
Meropis XXXIII 27; XXXVIII 11, 12,
Messene XXVIII 148; XL 12.
Metaneira XXII 4.
Metrodorus XLVII 42.
Metroon of the Mother of the gods in Smyrna XVII 10. In Cyzicus XL 22; see also s.v. Mother of the gods.
Midas XXVIII 144.
Milates XLIX 44.
Miletus XXXVI 110; XLVIII 68; L 32. Sacred to Apollo L 32.
Milk-eaters = Γαλακτοφάγοι XLVI 19.
Milo XXXIV 23.
Miltiades XXVIII 6.
Milyas, Mount XLVII 24, 58; LI 22, 26.
Minos XXXVIII 6; XLV 3.
Mithradatic War XIX 11.
Moeris (see also s.v. Egyptian Lakes) XXXVI 74. Canals at XXXVI 1, 11, 73, 74.
Μοῖρα = Fate XLIII 27.
Momus XXVIII 136.
Moorish War XXVI 70.
Mopsus XXXIII 14.
Morning Star = ἑωσφόρος L 55; LI 7.
Mother of the gods (see also s.v. Metroon and Rhea). XL 20; L 54.
Musaeus XXII 1; XLI 2.
Muses XVII 13; XX 21; XXIII 22; XXVI 105; XXVII 31; XXVIII 20, 21, 22, 24, 51, 52, 53, 58, 67, 97, 109, 114; XXXIV 56; XXXV 2; XXXVII 21; XXXVIII 4; XLIII 6, 25; XLV 3, 16; LIII 4.
Muses, Dancers of XXVIII 109; cf. XXVIII 114 (and XLIII 6 Muses dance for Zeus).
Musonius Rufus LII 2, 3.
Myrina LI 2, 5.
Myrmidons XXVI 84.
Myrtoan Sea XLVI 18, 21, 26.
Mysia XLVII 69; L 3, 72.
Mysian Plain XLVII 58; LI 18.
Mysian(s) XXVI 29; XLVII 58; L 105; LI 18.
Mysteries XVII 18; XXII 4, 6, 7, 8, 9, 10, 12, 13; XXIII 16; XXVIII 110, 113, 116, 135; title XXXIV; XXXIV 56, 60; XXXV 37; XL 11; XLI 2, 13; XLII 1; XLIV 18; XLVI 36, 40; XLVIII 28, 32; XLIX 47, 48; L 4, 7; LIII 5.
Mytilenaeans XXIV 54; XXXII 24.
Mytilene XLIX 38.

Naiads XLVI 25.
Narcissus XXXI 15.
Nasamones XIX 9.
Nauplius XXII 11.
Nausicaa XXIV 7.
Naxus XXVI 12. Battle of XXVIII 149.
Necessity = 'Ανάγκη XLIII 16.
Neit = Athena in Egypt XXXVII 14.
Nemeseis of Smyrna XX 20, 23; L 41.
Nereids XVII 14; XLIV 9; XLVI 42.
Nereus XVII 14.
Neritus XLIX 15.
Nestor XXVIII 30, 36, 42; XXX 19; XXXI 17.
Nicaean L 16.
Nicias XXVIII 73.
Nike = Victory XXXVII 17.
Nile, The XXI 4; XXIII 10; XXVI 28, 86; XXVIII 111; XXXVI 1, 2, 3, 4, 5, 6, 7, 8, 9, 10, 13, 14, 18, 19, 20, 21, 26, 27, 28, 30, 32, 34, 35, 37, 39, 41, 43, 44, 45, 46, 47, 48, 49, 51, 52, 53, 56, 57, 62, 63, 64, 70, 74, 77, 79, 82, 97, 98, 99, 101, 104, 105, 114, 115, 122, 123, 124, 125; XLIII 28; XLV 29, 32. Nile Zeusfallen = διιπετής XXXVI 104; XLIII 28.
Nile, Blue XXXVI 56. White XXXVI 56. Springs of XXXVI 47, 51, 52, 54, 56, 57, 97, 98, 99; XXXIX 18.
Nilometer at Memphis XXXVI 115.
Nomes of Egypt XXVIII 10; XXXVI 33 (Hermounthis); XXXVI 113 (Mendes); XXXVII 14 (Sais); XXXVI 51 (Sais). Cf. 42 temples XLV 32.
North wind = άπαρκτίας XLVIII 54.
Notaries of governor of Asia L 77, 94.
Νότος = south wind XXXVI 3, 6; LI 60.
Nymphs XVII 14; XVIII 8; XX 21; XXI 15; XXVIII 144; XL 20; XLI 3, 11; XLIII 25; XLIV 16; XLVI 25; XLVII 35; L 4; LIII 4. Nymphs who hold the Sacred Well at the temple of Asclepius in Pergamum XXXIX 3. Those maddened by = νυμφόληπτοι XXI 15.
Nysa XLI 3.

Ocean = ἡ ἔξω θάλαττα XXVI 13, 28; XXXVI 6, 85, 86, 87, 88, 89, 91, 92; XL 9; XLIII 24; XLVI 5. Four gulfs of Caspian, Mediterranean, Persian, and Red Sea XXXVI 87, 88, 89.
Odrysians XXXVI 14.
Odysseus XXIV 7, 51; XXVIII 17, 26, 29, 33, 40, 43; XXXIII 18; XXXIV 15, 17; XXXVII 23; XXXVIII 10; XLII 14; XLVI 38, 39; XLVII 1; XLVIII 42; LI 44.
Oebaras XXVI 18.
Oenops XXVIII 37.
Olympian XXXVII 27.
Olympian gods XXVIII 138; XXXVII 9.
Olympic games XXVI 25; XXXIV 23; XLVI 1.
Olympic games at Cyzicus = Olympia Hadriana LI 11, 16, 42.
Olympus XXXVII 7; XLI 3; XLIII 6; XLV 24.
Omen (= Κληδών), Altar of at Smyrna XXIX 12.
Omphale XXXIV 60.
Opisthodomos of the Parthenon LI 57.

Oracles XXVIII 9, 14, 15, 48, 103; XXXVII 22; XXXVIII 21; XXXIX 15; XL 10, 15; XLIII 25; XLV 7; XLIX 12, 38; L 75.
Orchomenians XL 3.
Orestes XXXVII 17.
Orpheus XXII 1; XXIV 55; XXXIV 45; XLI 2.
Ostracine XXXVI 74.

Paean XL 21; L 31, 37, 42.
Paeon XXX 12; XXXVII 18; LIII 4.
Palace XXXII 12, 13; XXXVII 29; XLVII 46. Servant of XLIX 21.
Palaemon XLVI 15, 31, 32, 35, 36, 40, 42.
Palestine, Syrian XXXVI 82.
Pamphylian XXVI 69.
Pan XXVIII 144; XLI 6; XLII 12; L 39.
Pans XLIII 25; XLIV 11.
Panacea XXXVIII 22.
Pannonian War XXIII 3.
Pannychides = Night festival or Vigil of Smyrna XXIX 4, 20. Pannychis of Asclepius XLVII 6.
Pantomimes XXVIII 97; XXXIV 7, 55, 57.
Pardalas, L. Claudius L 27, 87.
Πάρεδρος XXXI 15, 19 (Eteoneus to Cyzicus); XXXVII 5 (Athena to Zeus); XLI 10 (Dionysus to Eleusinae).
Parians XXXII 24.
Parrhasius, Epigram of XXVIII 88.
Parthenon (Hecatompedos) LI 61; cf. Opisthodomos LI 57.
Parthian War XXIII 3 (of Verus); XXXV 14, 35 (of Gordian III).
Patrae XLVIII 67.
Patroclus XXVIII 36, 37, 134.
Pausanias XXVI 45; XXXV 25.
Pax Romana XXIII 3, 53-57; XXIV 30, 31; XXV 8, 15, 55; XXVI 70, 71, 100, 104, 105; XXVII 45; XXXV 36, 37; XXXVI 91; XLVI 31.
Pegasus XXXVII 24; XLVI 29.
Pele XLVIII 12.
Peleus XXVIII 26; XXXV 28; XXXVIII 6.
Pella L 49.
Peloponnesians XVII 5; XXII 7; XXIII 52.
Peloponnesus XVIII 2; XXI 3; XXII 5; XXIV 45; XXVII 7; XXVIII 65, 85, 148; XL 16; XLVI 33.
Pelops (contemporary of Aristides) XLVII 39.
Pelops (mythological) XVIII 2; XXI 3, 10; XXXIV 25.
Peloric Promontory XLVIII 66.
Pelusium XXXVI 74.
Peneus, The XVII 16; XXI 10; XXXIX 7, 18.
Pentheus XXIV 39.
Pergamene XLVIII 10.
Pergamum XXIII 13-18, 26; XXX 1-7, 9, subscription; XXXVIII 11 (Teuthrania); XXXIX 4, 5, 6; XLII 9; XLVII 42 43, 51, 55, 69, 78; XLVIII 7, 18, 27, 46, 51, 52, 70, 78, 81; XLIX 3, 6, 8, 12, 44; L 14, 16, 39, 49, 56, 58, 83, 89, 90, 103, 106; LI 1, 8, 26; LIII 1, 2, 3, 5. Acropolis district of XXIII 13; XLIX 44. Asclepius' temple see *s.v.* Bouleuterion = Council Chamber XXIII 13. Bull hunt in L 16. Temple of Dea Roma XXIII 13, 65, 66.
Periclean XXVIII 77.

Pericles XXVIII 71, 72.
Perseus XXXVII 24; XLVI 13.
Persia XXXVI 87.
Persian(s) XX 9; XXI 12; XXII 6; XXIII 25, 46; XXVI 15-23, 26, 28, 41, 51, 91; XXVIII 63, 66, 155; XXXIV 56.
Persian = μηδικός XXII 6 XLI 10.
Persian Gulf XXXVI 87.
Persians, King of (Great King) XXVI 15, 27, 29; XXVII 29; XXXIX 18. Eye and ear of King XXVII 29.
Phaeacians XXV 40; XXVIII 40, 43; XLII 14; LI 12.
Phaedrus XXVIII 143.
Pharnabazus XXVI 36.
Pharsalus XX 13.
Pharus, The XXXVI 74, 106, 107, 111.
Phasis, The XXIII 10, 24; XXVI 82; XXVII 7; XXXVI 3, 87, 115; XLV 3.
Phician Peak XXXVI 113.
Phidias XLVIII 41. Phidias' statues: Athena, ivory, bronze, Lemnian, Olympian Zeus XXXIV 28.
Philadelphia L 96, 98.
Philadelphus XLVIII 30, 31, 35, 47; L 46.
Philae XXXVI 48, 59.
Philhellene XXXV 20.
Philip of Macedon XXII 8; XXIII 51, 61; XXVIII 76; XXXII 29; L 49.
Philippus C. Julius XXXV *passim;* as emperor XXXV 1-8, 12-16, 20, 22, 24, 26, 27, 29, 31, 34, 36, 38. As praetorian prefect XXXV 13, 17, 18.
Philippus, C. Julius Severus XXXV 39.
Philo XLIX 29.
Philoctetes XXVIII 130; XXXVIII 10.
Philumene (nurse) XLVII 45, 78; XLIX 16; L 10.
Philumene (daughter of Callityche) LI 19, 21, 22, 23, 24, 25.
Phlegra XXXVII 9.
Phocaea XLVIII 12, 15, 17.
Phocaean, XLVIII 15.
Phocian(s) XXIII 51; XXVIII 38.
Phoebus XLVII 18.
Phoenicia XXV 3; XLVII 34. Syrian Phoenicia XXXVI 88.
Phoenicians XXVIII 64.
Phoenix XVII 2; XVIII 9; XX 19.
Φρούραρχος = Garrison Commander XXXVI 49.
Phrygia XXVI 17, 36.
Phrygia Superior = Galatia L 12; = Laodiceia ad Lycum L 103.
Phrygians XXII 11; XXXII 5, 20.
Phyle XXV 65. Seventy who seized XXV 65, 66.
Phyleus XXVIII 37.
Pieria XLIII 6.
Pierians XXVIII 58.
Pillars of Hercules XX 6; XXIII 24; XXXVI 85, 90, 91; XL 9.
Pindar XXVIII 55, 56, 61; XXXI 2, 12; XXXII 24, 34; XXXIII 1; XXXIV 5, 8; XXXVI 112; XXXVII 6; XXXIX 16; XLI 6; XLII 12; XLIII 30. Pindar *Olympian* I *passim* XXXIV 25; *Ol.* I 26-27 XX 19, XXI 10; *Ol.* I 37 XVII 3; *Ol.* I 116 XLV 3; *Ol.* II 17-19 XXIV 58; *Ol.* II 95-97 XXVIII 55; *Ol.* III 17 ff. XLV 3; *Ol.* VI 50 XLV 3; scholia to *Ol.* VII 7 XXXIX 16; *Ol.* VII 49 XXV 30; *Ol.* IX 29 XXX 16; *Pythian* III 43 XVII 4; *Pyth.* III 83 XXXIV 8; *Pyth.*

VI 11 XLV 13; *Pyth.* IX 98 XXIII 36; *Isthmian* III 70 XLV 3; *Isth.* VIII 62 XLV 13; frg. 21 T. XLIII 30; frg. 46, 1-4 T. XXVIII 58; frg. 91 T. XX 21; frg. 92 T. XX 13; frg. 110 T. XLII 12; frg. 114 T. XLI 6; frg. 117, 1 T. XXVII 2; frg. 117 T. XXXIII 1; frg. 135 T. XXXII 34; frg. 140 T. XXXI 12; frg. 154 T. XXXVII 6; frg. 209 T. XXXIV 5; frg. 219-220 T. XVII 5; frg. 231 T. XXVIII 57; frg. 241 T. XXXVI 112; frg. 267 T. XXVI 1; frg. 270 T. XXXIV 5; frg. 283 T. XXVIII 56; frgg. (?) XLV 3 and 13 (three apiece; *cf.* ed. Snell frg. 355).

Pinnacle of Egypt = κορυφή XXXVI 33, 46, 68.
Piraeus XXV 65.
Pisidians XXVI 29.
Plague = smallpox XXXIII 6; XLVIII 38-45; L 9; LI 25.
Plato XXVIII 142, 143; XXX 20, 22; XXXII 25, 26, 30, 34; XXXIII 29; XXXIV 5; XLII 4; L 19, 55, 56, 57; LI 58, 62, 63. Statue of in dream LI 62. Temple of in dream LI 61-63. Plato's works L 15. *Apology of Socrates* XXVIII 82; *Apol.* 20 E XXVIII 81; *Apol.* 30 A XXVIII 81; *Apol.* 30 E XXVIII 81; *Apol.* 40 E ff. XXXII 34. *Epistle* (III) to *Dionysius* L 57; *Ep.* III 318 E L 38; *Ep.* VII 328 C XXXII 17 and XXXIII 16. *Euthydemus* 300 D XLVII 38. *Gorgias* 450 C XXVIII 88; *Gor.* 497 C XXXII 7; *Gor.* 516 A XXVI 96. *Laws* XXVIII 146; *Laws* 643 C XXX 20; *Laws* 665 A ff. XLI 2; *Laws* 666 B XLI 7; *Laws* 698 CD XXVI 85; *Laws* 710 DE XXIV 20; *Laws* 761 C XXXIII 29; *Laws* 858 DE XXVIII 146. *Menexenus* 235 C XLVII 38; *Menex.* 247 B XXX 23. *Phaedo* 69 C XXII 10. *Phaedrus* 246 D XLII 4; *Phaedr.* 246 E XXVIII 114; *Phaedr.* 247 C XXVIII 142; *Phaedr.* 257 C XXVIII 143; *Phaedr.* 263 D XXVIII 144; *Phaedr.* 264 CD XXVIII 144; *Phaedr.* 264 D XXVI 109; *Phaedr.* 265 DE XXVIII 143; *Phaedr.* 271 B XXVIII 143; *Phaedr.* 277 E XXXII 26. *Politicus* 286 A XVII 4. *Protagoras* 326 D XXVII 37; *Prot.* 345 E XXXIV 5. *Republic* 363 D XXX 10; *Rep.* 397 E XXVIII 13; *Rep.* 614 B XXVI 69. *Symposium* 178 C XLI 13; *Sym.* 196 A XLI 13; *Sym.* 201 A XXXIV 25; *Sym.* 214 B XXXI 8 and XXXIX 3; *Sym.* 217 E XVII 18; *Sym.* 220 C XXVIII 90; *Sym.* 223 D XLVII 60. *Theaetetus* 173 D XLVI 3; *Theaet.* 194 E XXX 22. *Timaeus* 17 AB XXVIII 2; *Tim.* 22 E XXXVI 110, 125; *Tim.* 24 B XXXVII 14; *Tim.* 34 B L 56; *Tim.* 40 D XXXVII 8; *Tim.* 48 B XLV 16.
Platonists XXXII 25. At Pergamum XLVIII 52; L 19, 23, 55, 56; LI 57-59.
Pleuron, of XXVIII 37.
Plutarch *De Herodoti Malignitate* XXXVI 57. *Vitae Decem Oratorum* 836 D XXVIII 84; *Vitae Decem etc.* 847 A XXVIII 79.
Pluto XL 7; XLV 23.
Po, The = Ἠριδανός XXXVI 6.
Podalirius XXXVIII 1, 8, 16, 17.
Poeas XXVIII 130.
Poemanenos L 3, 5.
Poets Unknown (if not Pindar) XLV 3, 13, 24. PLG, p. 684 B. XLVII 30.
Polemo, Antonius XXXIV 47; L 28; but both references doubtful.
Police Commissioner = εἰρηνάρχης L 72, 73, 79, 93.
Pollio, T. Vitrasius L 94, 96, 98.
Polydorus XXVIII 37.
Pontus, The XXXVI 42; XLIV 3.
Porphyrio XLVII 57; LI 12, 19, 24.
Poseideon month XLVII 5.
Poseidon XVII 16; XX 23; XXI 10; XXII 4; XXVI 105; XXVII 18; XXVIII 28; XXXVI 105; XXXVII 20, 22; XXXVIII 6; XL 12; XLIII 25; XLV 23; XLV *passim;* XLVI 1, 8, 11, 16, 20, 25, 29, 31, 32, 34, 35, 38, 40, 42; XLVII

6. Poseidon Asphalios = The Securer XLVI 1. Poseidon Hippios = of horses XXXVII 20. Poseidon Pontios = of the sea XXXVII 20. Poseidon, holiday of XLVII 6.
Possession see *s.v.* Κατοχή
Poulydamas XXXIV 23.
Praetorian rank L 16.
Praetorium at Cyzicus XL 13.
Princesses, daughters of Marcus Aurelius XLII 14.
Προβουλεύειν = chief voice in the Provincial Assembly of the leading cities of Asia XXIII 34.
Proconnesus XXVII 17.
Proconsul of Achaea XLVI 20, 27.
Prometheus XL 7; XLII 7.
Propontis, The XXVII 8; XLIV 3; XLVI 18.
Πρόρρησις XXII 12 (of Eleusis); XXXVIII 1; XLII 6; XLVIII 37, 45; XLIX 39; 48; L 9, 94; LI 18, 41, 51; LII 3.
Προστάτης = leader XXX 2. προστάται of Smyrna XIX 8; XX 1; *cf.* XXI 8 (of emperors).
Protesilaus XXVIII 28.
Proverbs XVII 3, 12; XVIII 7; XX 18, 23; XXI 6, 13; XXII 7; XXIII 36, 57, 65; XXIV 42, 59; XXV 11, 13, 33, 34, 54; XXVI 44, 68, 73, 100, 101, 105; XXVII 14, 24, 42, 44; XXVIII 1, 2, 3, 4, 14, 15, 37, 60, 80, 114, 121, 130, 136, 141, 144, 149; XXIX 17, 28, 29; XXX 14; XXXII 7, 17, 25, 27; XXXIII 2, 7, 9, 16; XXXIV 2, 27, 31; XXXVI 47, 52, 57, 66, 85, 88, 100; XXXVII 26, 27; XXXIX 3, 18; XL 1, 14; XLI 11, 13; XLII 5; XLIII 3, 6; XLIV 16, 17; XLV 25, 30, 31; XLVI 3, 29; XLVII 2, 5, 49; XLVIII 11, 38, 60; XLIX 9; L 33, 44, 65, 82, 102, 104; LI 7; LIII 3.
Provincial Assembly of Asia = τὸ Κοινὸν τῆς Ἀσίας XX 15; XXIII 40, 65, 66; XXXIV 62; L 103 (συνέδριον). Delegates of Smyrna of (σύνεδροι) L 103. προβουλεύειν of the leading cities XXIII 34. Games of (τὰ κοινά) XXX 2, 3, 21(?); subscription XXXIV. High priest of L 53, 101, 103, 104.
Prytanis, election of at Smyrna L 88.
Pselchis XXXVI 55, 81.
Ptolemy of Naucratis (?) LI 30, 34.
Πύλαι or Πυλαία = Thermopyle XXIII 51; XXVIII 77.
Pylian XXXI 17.
Pylus XXVIII 32.
Pyrallianus L 55.
Pyramids XXXVI 1, 122.
Pythian XXVIII 103.
Pythian Festival XXII 7.
Pytho XXVIII 58.
Pythodorus, Sex. Julius Maior Antoninus XLVII 35.

Quadratus, Julius Protheoria XXX; XXX 7, 8, 9. Family of (see also *s.v.* Apellas and Fronto) XXX 6, 7, 8, 9, 10, 12, 16, 22, 23, 24, 25, 27, 28.
Quadratus, C. Julius Quadratus Bassus L 63, 64, 65, 67, 71.
Quadratus, Statius XLVII 22, 41.

Red sea = Ἐρυθρὰ θάλαττα XXVI 28, 70; XXXVI 87. People of XXVI 70.
Rescripta of the emperor XXVI 33; L 75.
Retrogression of planets XXXVI 120.
Reverence = Αἰδώς XXVI 106; XXXI 10; XLIII 20.

Rhadamanthys XXXV 17; XXXVIII 6, 20; XLV 3.
Rhea (see also s.v. Mother of the gods) XVII 3; XLVI 8.
Rhine XXXVI 6.
Rhode XXV 32.
Rhodes XVIII 7; XXIV 46, 59; XXV 1, 7, 8, 17, 25, 29, 31, 32, 33, 38, 39, 41, 43, 49, 50, 53, 56, 59, 69. Council chamber XXV 53. Foundation of 600 years ago XXV 33. Halieia contest at XXV 32. Hieromeniae = festival at XXV 28. Temple of Dionysus XXIV 52.
Rhodian(s) XXIV title, 1, 4, 28, 30, 37, 52, 54, 58; XXV 1, 12, 13, 42, 43, 49, 50, 51, 59; XXXIV 23; XXXVIII 13; L 23. = 'Ροδιακός XXV title.
Rhosander L 19, 21.
Roman(s) XVII 7; XXVI 63, 100; XXXII 30; XLVIII 48; L 16, 31; LI 26.
Roman citizenship XXVI 59, 60, 63-66, 74, 75, 78, 85; XXVII 32; XXX 10 (but here probably public office is meant). Empire XXIII 9, 62; XXVI passim. Law (on age of manhood) XXX 25.
Romans as ruling class XVIII 2; XIX 12; XXIV 22; XXVI 3, 10, 11, 14, 26, 28, 30, 34, 36, 51, 58, 64, 65, 66, 71, 75, 78, 86, 88, 91, 93, 94, 95, 96, 98, 99, 100, 101, 102, 103, 105, 106, 107; XXXII 12, 30; XLII 13; L 99; LI 46.
Rome XXIII 62; XXVI passim; XXVI 8; XXXII 39; XLVIII 60, 62; L 31, 78, 96. Drainage ditch in XLVII 46, 50. Horse racing during the festival of Apollo at L 31.
Rufinus, L. Cuspius Pactumeius L 28, 43, 83, 84, 107.
Rufus, Flavius XLVIII 15, 16.

Sacae XXVI 29.
Sacred Marriage = ἱερὸς γάμος XXIX 20.
Sacred Tale (of Asclepius) = ἱερὸς λόγος XXVIII 116; XLII 4; title orations XLVII-LII; XLVIII 9. (On the castration of Cronus) XLVI 17. (On Palaemon and Leucothea) XLVI 32, 39. (= Iliad XV 166) XLVI 14.
Sacrifice at the trench = ἐπιβόθρια XLVIII 27.
Saite Clerk XXXVI 47, 51, 52. Nome XXXVI 51; XXXVII 14.
Salamis XXII 6; XXV 67; XXVIII 66; XLI 10.
Salmoneus XLVI 35.
Salvius, L. Salvius Julianus XLVIII 9.
Sappho XXVIII 51; XXXII 24. Sappho frg. 193 Lobel-Page XXVIII 51; frg. 196 Lobel-Page XVIII 4.
Sarapis XXIV 42; XXVI 105 (with Isis); XXVII 39; XXXVI 38, 123, 124; XLV passim; XLV 7, 14, 16, 18, 20, 25, 26, 32; XLVII 38; XLVIII 18; XLIX 46, 47, 48, 49; L 97. Dancers of XLV 27. Dinner of XLV 27. Festivals of XLV 20, 33. κάτοχοι = those possessed by XLV 32. Statue of XLIX 47. Zeus Sarapis XLV 21; XLIX 48. Sacred days of at Alexandria XLIX 48.
Sardanapallus XXXIV 61.
Saronic Gulf XLVI 21, 26, 33.
Satraps XXVI 27, 29, 95; XLIII 18.
Satyrus XLIX 8, 9, 10.
Satyrs XLIV 11.
Scamander, The XXXVI 106.
Σχοῖνοι (Egyptian measure) XXXVI 46; LI 54.
Scolion vol. 3, p. 566 Edmonds XXXI 19.
Scythia XXXVI 13.
Scythian(s) XXVI 18; XXXVI 42, 82.
Scythopolis XXXVI 82.
Sea, The (personified) = ἡ θάλαττα XLVI 40.

Seasons = Horae XLVI 25.
Sedatius, L. Sedatius Theophilus XLVIII 48; L 16, 43.
Selinus, The XLVIII 27, 51.
Semele XXV 2; XLI 3.
Semiramis XXVI 79.
Senate, Roman XIX 1; XX 10, 11; XXVI 90; protheoria XXX; XLVIII 48.
Senatorial and Equestrian Class (?) XXVI 60.
Serbonis (see also *s.v.* Egyptian Lakes) XXXVI 74, 75.
Seriphus XXV 38.
Sesostris XXVII 38.
Sestus XXIII 47.
Severus, C. Julius Subscription XXXVII; L 12, 71, 77, 78, 79, 83, 85, 90, 92.
Shadow-feet = Σκιάποδες XXVIII 54.
Sicilian Strait XLVIII 66.
Sicily XVIII 7; XXIII 52; XXVI 12; XXVII 12; XXVIII 74; XL 12, 16; XLVIII 66.
Sicyon XXVIII 9.
Sileni XLI 8.
Simonidean XXVIII 67.
Simonides XXVIII 59, 60, 61; XXXI 2; XXXII 24; L 36. Simonides frg. 34 B. XXXI 2; frg. 46 B. XXVIII 67; frg. 60 B. XXVIII 67; frg. 90 B. XXVIII 63; frg. 91 B. XXVIII 65; frg. 97 B. XXVIII 66; frg. 104 B. XXVIII 63; frg. 132 B. XXVIII 64; frg. 142 B. XXVIII 64; frg. 146 B. XXVIII 60.
Simous The XXXVI 106.
Sipylus, Mt. XVII 3, 4; XVIII 2, 8; XXI 3.
Siren XXVIII 51, 52.
Sisyphus XXVI 53; XLVI 29.
Smallpox XXXIII 6; XLVIII 38-45; L 9; LI 25.
Smyrna XVII-XXI *passim;* XVIII 1, 8, 10; XIX 1, 3, 9, 10, 13; XX 6, 11, 22; XXI 4, 12, 16; subscription XXII; XXIII 19-22, 21, 26; subscription XXXIV; XXXVI 110; XLV 33; XLVII 12, 17, 22, 25, 42, 54; XLVIII 7, 11, 12, 17, 18, 38, 43, 50, 68, 69, 80; XLIX 39, 43, 45, 49; L 41, 53, 58, 73, 85, 92; LI 1, 10, 18, 29, 30, 34, 38, 56. Acropolis (or ὁ Πάγος) at XVII 10, 19; XVIII 3; XXIII 20. Altar of Omen (= Κληδών) at XXIX 12. Assembly = ἐκκλησία of L 100, 101. Council = βουλή of L 87, 88, 92, 95, 96, 98, 99. Decree of Council of LI 30, 56. Council Chamber = βουλευτήριον of XVIII 8; subscription XXII; LI 31, 32, 34, 38. Ephesian Gates XLVII 20. Foundation of (1st city by Tantalus or Pelops) XVII 3; XXI 3. (2nd city by Theseus) XVII 4; XX 20; XXI 4. (3rd city by Alexander) XVII 4; XX 20; XXI 4. Golden Way XVII 10. Golden and Sacred Way XVIII 6. Gymnasium(s) XVII 11; XVIII 6; XIX 3; XLVII 17. Harbor(s) XVII 11, 19, 22; XVIII 3, 6; XIX 3; XX 21; XXI 5; XXIII 20; XLVII 65; L 102; LI 30. Market place(s) XVII 6, 11; XVIII 6; XIX 3; XXI 5; XXXIII 24; XLVII 22; LI 31. Metroon XVII 10. Nemeseis of XX 20, 23; L 41. Odeum of LI 30, 34. Sacred Trireme XVIII 6; XXI 4. Sacred Way of XVII 10. Suburbs of XVII 10, 17; XVIII 5; XIX 8; XXIII 21; XLVIII 38; LI 2. Swimming pools = κολύμβηθραι of XXXIII 25. Temples XVIII 6; XIX 3, 10; XXI 5; XXIII 20. Temple of Asclepius (at gymnasium) XLVII 17, 19; (at harbor) L 102. Temple of Dionysus Briseus XVII 6. Temple of Isis XLIX 45, 49, 50. Priest of that temple XLVII 25, 26, 40, 61. Temple of Mother of the gods XVII 10. Temple of Nemeseis XVII 10. Temple of Tiberius, Livia, Roman Senate XIX 13. Temple of Zeus Acraeus XVII 10. Theater XVII 11, 13; XVIII 6; LI 30. Warm springs near XLVIII 7, 50, 69; XLIX 43, 45. Officials of: City

attorneys = σύνδικοι L 92. Councilors = βουλευταί LI 30. Delegates to the Provincial Assembly = σύνεδροι L 103. Προστάται = leaders XIX 8; XX 1; XXI 8. Officials = ἀρχαί L 101. People = δῆμος L 100, 101, 102. President = ἄρχων L 99. Prytanis, election of L 88. Tax collector L 96. Contest of poets at XLVII 42; Night festivals at XXIX 4, 20.
Smyrna, Gulf of XVII 14, 19, 22.
Smyrnaean(s) XVII 5; XXI 4; XXIX 1, 2, 27, 33; XXXII 24; XLVII 22; XLIX 38; L 103.
Socrates XXVIII 81, 82, 83, 84; XLVII 60; L 15.
Solon XIX 7; XXVIII 137, 139, 140, 142, 146. Solon *Elegies* frg. 5 D. XXIV 14. *Iambi* XXVIII 138. *Tetrameters* XXVIII 138; frg. 23. 21-22 D. XXVIII 137; frg. 24. 3-22 D. XXVIII 138; frg. 24. 22-27 D. XXVIII 140.
Solstice, summer XXXVI 58, 63. Winter L 1.
Σόφισμα = trick or contrivance XXXVI 115; XLII 11; XLVIII 14; L 29.
Sophist XXIII 2; XXV 18; XXVIII 24, 81, 128, 131; XXXII 8; XXXIII 29; XXXIV 47; XXXVI 9, 32, 115; XLVII 46; XLIX 8; L 61, 95, 100 (corrupt for Festus); LI 39.
Sophocles XXXIV 36; XL 14; L 60. Sophocles *Ajax* 1353 XXIII 71. *Oedipus Tyrannus* 257 XXV 16. *Oedipus Tyrannus* 462 XXVIII 11. *Philoctetes* 174 XL 14. *Philoctetes* 263 XXVIII 130. *Philoctetes* 1217 XXVIII 37. frg. 402 N. XXII 11.
Sosimenes (dream name of Aristides) LI 24.
South Wind = Νότος XXXVI 3, 6; LI 60.
Spain XXXVI 91.
Sparta XXVI 48, 61; XXVIII 148.
Spartan XXIII 48; XXXV 25; XL 17. Spartan Band = ἄλη XXX 20.
Sperchius, The XVII 15.
Sphodrias XXII 7.
Stesichorus XX 3; XXXII 24; XXXIII 2. Stesichorus frg. 46 B. XXXIII 2.
Strymon, The XXXVI 115.
Stymphalus XL 5.
Styx, The XXXIX 8; XLVI 6.
Sun = Ἥλιος XVIII 7; XXIV 50, 51; XXV 19, 29, 31; XXVI 105; XXXVI 38, 109; XLVII 22.
Σύνδικοι = City attorneys L 78, 79, 92.
Susa XXVI 18.
Sybaris, of XXXVI 85.
Syene XXXVI 47, 49, 50, 53, 54, 59, 65, 115. Sacred well of XXXVI 59.
Syme XXV' 38.
Syracusans XXVIII 74.
Syracuse XXVIII 74.
Syria XXXVI 82, 88, 89; XLVII 33.
Syrians XXVII 15. = Assyrians XXVI 91.

Taenarus XLVI 18.
Tanais, The XXVII 32; XXXVI 3, 87.
Tantalus XXI 3.
Tartessus XVIII 10.
Tax Collector of Smyrna = ἐκλογεύς L 96.
Teans XIX 12.
Telemachus XLVII 1; XLVIII 42.
Telephus XXIII 15; XLIX 12.
Telesphorus XLVIII 10, 18, 27; XLIX 15, 21, 22, 23; L 16, 46; LI 22, 24. Temple

of at Pergamum XLVIII 18; XLIX 21. Statue of in the temple of Hygieia L 16.
Tempe XXI 10.
Terpander XXIV 3.
Teuthrania XXXVIII 11.
Θάλαττα (personified) = The Sea XLVI 40.
Thales XXXVI 85. Doctrine of XLVI 5-6. Theory of the Nile XXXVI 3-12, 101-102.
Thamyris XXII 1.
Thasian or Macedonian stranger (ξένος) XL 21; cf. L 42.
Theban Wall XXI 5.
Thebans XXIII 50, 51, 59; XXVI 49, 50; XXVIII 57, 63, 88, 148; XXXII 24; XL 3.
Thebes XVIII 7; XX 13; XXV 58; XXVII 31; XXVIII 57.
Thebes (Egyptian) XXVI 86. Region of XXXVI 33.
Themis XXIV 42.
Themistocles XX 9; XXVIII 6; XXXV 33.
Theodorus (name assumed by Aristides) L 53, 54, 70.
Theodotes (dream name of Aristides) L 21.
Theodotus XLVII 13, 55, 56; XLVIII 34; L 21, 38, 42; LI 57.
Theopompus' *Tricaranos* (see *s.v.* Anaximenes) XXVI 51.
ὁ θεὸς καὶ λυτήρ = The god and deliverer (terms from haruspicy and astrology) LI 20.
Theoxenia XIX 2.
Thermopyle (Πυλαία) XXIII 51; XXVI 43; (Πύλαι) XXVIII 77.
Thersites XXVIII 16.
Theseus XVIII 2; XIX 4; XX 5, 20; XXI 4; XXXVII 25; XXXVIII 6; XL 7, 11. Shrines of XL 11.
Thesmothetae XXXVIII 5.
Thespiae XXII 7.
Thessalian(s) XXXI 2; XXXIV 61; XXXVIII 15.
Thessaly XVII 16; XXI 10; XXVIII 77; XXXVIII 8, 15; XLVI 29.
Thetis XXXV 28.
Thmouis XXXVI 113.
Thrace XXVI 43; XLVIII 5.
Thracian XXXVI 85.
Thrasybulus XXV 66.
Thucydides XXVIII 70, 71, 72; L 15, 58. Thucydides I. 1 XXVIII 70; I 6 XVII 5 and XXVI 97; I . 10 XXVI 9; I 15 XXVIII 9; I. 129 XXVIII 139; II. 12 XXIII 48; II. 45 XXXI 19; II. 60-64 XXVIII 71; II. 62 XXVIII 74; III. 82 XXIII 48; IV. 36 XL 17; V. 11 XXXII 23; V 66 XXVI 88; VI. 1 XXVII 12; VI. 16 XXVIII 73; VI. 34 XXVIII 74; VI. 77 XXVIII 74.
Tiber, The XLVII 46.
Tigris, The XXXV 35.
Tissaphernes XXVI 36.
Titans XXVI 103; XXXVII 9.
Titaresius, The XXXIX 7, 8.
Tithonus XXXI 17.
Tlepolemus XXV 30.
Tragic actors XXVIII 97; XXXIV 7; XLVIII 40.
Tragicorum Graecorum Fragmenta Anon. 39 N. XLII 4; 40 N. XXIII 71; 162 N. XXVII 15.
Tribute, reduction of by Julius Philippus XXXV 16.

Triptolemus XXII 4; XXVI 101; XXXVII 14; XXXVIII 15.
Trojan Ida XLVI 14.
Trojan Wall XXVII 18.
Trojan War XXV 58.
Trojan Xanthus, The XXXVI 105.
Trojans XXVIII 90, 107, 134; XXXIV 15; XXXV 28; XXXVIII 9.
Τροφεύς = Foster father XVII 15 (Homer for the Greeks); XXVI 95 (Greeks for the Romans); XXXII 2, 14 (Alexander for Aristides and for Marcus and Verus); XLIV 16 (Aegean for Dionysus); XLVII 27, 66; XLVIII 9; XLIX 3, 15, 20; L 41, 54, 103.
Trophonius XXXVIII 21; XLV 7.
Troy XXVIII 16; XXXIV 15; XXXVI 106; XXXVIII 10, 11.
Tyche, Julia XLIX 22.
Tyrants, The Thirty XXV 65.
Tyre XXVII 11.
Tyrians XL 10.
Tyro XLVI 35.
Tyrrhenian Sea XXVII 15; XLVIII 65.
Τυρρηνοί = Etruscans XXIV 53; XXV 4; XLI 8.

Venus (planet) L 55; LI 7.
Verus, Lucius XLVII 47, 48, 49.
Victory = Νίκη XXXVII 17.
Vologases XLVII 36, 37.

Warm Springs XLVIII 7, 17, 50, 69; XLIX 2, 6, 10, 43, 45; L 2, 4; LI 13, 42.
West Wind = ζέφυρος XIX 3; XXI 1; XXXVI 5, 6, 8; XLIV 13.
White Maidens = λευκαὶ κόραι from Delphi L 75, 76.

Xanthus, The XXXVI 45, 105.
Xenophon XXVIII 104. Xenophon *Anabasis* 1. 4. 10 XXXII 25; XLIV 16. *Cynegeticus* 5. 34 XXXII 25; XLIV 16. *Cyropaedia* 1. 3 XXX 21. *Cyropaedia* 7. 1 XXVIII 105.
Xerxes XXII 6; XXIII 46; XXVI 5; XXVIII 139. Xerxes' abandonment of Athens XXV 67. Xerxes' invasion XXIII 43; XXVI 16; XXXV 33.

Zeno, M. Antonius (?) XLVII 17.
Ζέφυρος see *s.v.* West Wind.
Zethus XXVII 31.
Zeus XVII 3; XVIII 1; XXI 3; XXII 1, 7; XXIII 46, 57, 58, 61; XXIV 17, 42, 46; XXV 28, 30, 31, 69; XXVI 84, 89, 103, 105; XXVIII 6, 20, 26, 28, 36, 45, 46, 48, 65, 68, 71, 72, 82, 88, 90, 98,102, 106, 109, 110; XXIX 4, 31, 32; XXX 22, 28; XXXIII 2, 9, 20, 27; XXXIV 12, 24, 38, 59; XXXV 24, 28; XXXVI 76, 104, 105, 109, 114; XXXVII 2, 3, 4, 5, 6, 7, 18, 25, 27, 28; XXXVIII 5, 6, 7; XL 2, 7, 19, 22; XLI 3, 4; XLII 4; XLIII *passim*, 1, 2, 5, 6, 7, 8, 9, 15, 19, 20, 21, 22, 23, 24, 25, 26, 27, 28, 29, 30; XLIV 11; XLV 3, 7, 21, 23; XLVI 1, 2, 8, 13, 14, 15, 19, 20, 25, 29, 32; XLVII 30, 33, 43, 45, 78; XLVIII 27, 53, 61, 77; XLIX 20, 39, 40, 41, 48; L 1, 21, 40, 46, 48, 49, 58, 71, 105; LI 10, 47, 52, 66; LIII 3. Zeus Agoraios (= of the Assembly) XLIII 30. Zeus Basileus (= the King) XLIII 30. Zeus Eleutherios (= of freedom) XXIII 46 and XLIII 30. Zeus Euangelios (= of good tidings) LIII 3. Zeus Hyetios (= of rain) XLIII 30. Zeus Kataibates (= descender) XLIII 30. Zeus Koryphaios (= of the summit) XLIII 30. Zeus Meilichios (= of

502 INDEX

gentleness) XLIII 10, 30. Zeus, Olympian XXVI 89; XXVIII 58; XXXIV 23, 28; XLVII 43; XLIX 41; L 1, 21, 46, 48; LI 10, 47. Zeus Ouranios (= of heaven) XLIII 30. Zeus Polieus (= of the city or city protector) XX 23; XLIII 30. Zeus Philios (= of friendship) LIII 2. Zeus Soter (= savior) XLIII 1, 21, 30; XLVI 1; XLIX 39, *etc.* Zeus Tropaios (= of the rout) XLIII 30. Temple of Olympian Zeus in Mysia XLVII 43; XLIX 41; L 1, 2, 21, 48, 49, 71, 105; LI 10. National sacrifice of Olympian Zeus LI 47. Priest of the temple of Olympian Zeus (?) XLVII 41. Sacred Herald L 48. Statue of Zeus XLIX 20; L 48, 49. Temple of Zeus Philios in Pergamum LIII 2.
Zeus Asclepius XLII 4; XLVII 45, 78; XLIX 7; L 46.
Zeus Sarapis XLV 21; XLIX 48.
Zeuxis XXVIII 89. Zeuxis *Epigram* XXVIII 89.
Zopyrus XXXIV 15, 17.
Zosimus XLVII 27, 40, 66, 69, 71, 72, 74, 76; XLVIII 9; XLIX 3, 12, 16, 37, 47; L 41, 69, 103.